# THE
# SERIOUS
# JOKE
# BOOK

## George Coote

HERRON PUBLICATIONS

THE SERIOUS JOKE BOOK
© G. COOTE 1994

Published by
HERRON PUBLICATIONS PTY LIMITED
91 Main St
Kangaroo Point
Queensland 4169 Australia

Printed in Australia by
Australian Print Group
Maryborough, Victoria

ISBN 0 947163 89 1

# DEDICATION

*To Bonny, my first wife.*

# ACKNOWLEDGEMENTS

WHO told the first joke? Who makes them up?

Are there really any new ones, or are they the same old yarns adapted and re-cycled through generations with only the names changed, not to defend the innocent, but to ensure we dob in the guilty.

I make no claim to the yarns in this book, indeed, I have heard most of them over the years in so many forms and versions it would be impossible to source their origin.

Most have been gathered from fellow travel writers during delays at airports, long flights and longer train rides. Swapping yarns is an affliction of the profession. (I was destined to be a travel writer. My first job was a proof reader for a sky-writing firm. And I hope that didn't go over your head).

I pay tribute to those fellow journos who could always see the funny side of lost luggage, or missing the last flight out of Mozambique, and to those who could still swap eye-watering belly laughs when broke and far from home in dire straits.

# Contents

# INTRODUCTION

EVEN a baby smiles at its father, which is proof that human beings are quick to recognise a joke. From then on, throughout life, any gathering of good folk is better off if it raises a laugh.

A life of journalism and travelling has meant listening to hundreds of speeches, most of them dull. But the speakers remembered were those who had a sense of humour and those who included a few gags. I always remembered the wisecracks and usually forgot the earth-shattering theme of the speech, and if the gags were good I wrote them down. Be it parliament, a municipal council meeting, a court case, a dinner party, a family reunion, a wedding, or even a funeral, these events are all the more memorable, if someone cracks a joke and creates a smile.

The purpose of this book is to make sure there is plenty of ammunition for those who find themselves having to "say a few words" at the rostrum, standing beside the wedding cake, bidding farewell to a retiring colleague at the office, or leaning on the bar holding court at the local.

Given a free choice most people would rather be amused than be on the receiving end of a lecture, and no matter how informative the speech may be it can be improved if peppered with a few gags. It will keep the audience alert, waiting for the next one.

The aim of this book is not to turn speeches into an entire comedy routine. Too many jokes will detract from the purpose of the address, and there are important things to be said at weddings, 21st birthdays or an election speech for local council. The art of public speaking is to select a few anecdotes central to the theme and select a few gags that can be tailored to the topic.

# KEEPING THEM CLEAN

JOKES are known by the company they keep and their tendency to slip below the belt doesn't necessarily rule them out of order. Rude need not be crude, and some of the roughest can be salvaged with different wording to retain the same punchline in an acceptable form. What we are saying here is best illustrated by the limerick, those compact rhymes so often concerned with the bawdy;

The limerick packs laughs anatomical
Into space that is quite economical
But the good ones we've seen
So rarely are clean
And the clean ones so seldom are comical.

In this volume we give readers the option;

If you are ultra-fastidious by far
And never tell yarns to your Ma
Here are jokes by the mile
That will sustain a wide smile
But don't read any marked (R).

# NOTES ARE ESSENTIAL

PUBLIC speaking is a comparatively simple business if you are properly prepared, but notes are essential. Unless you are an orator of the calibre of Winston Churchill, or have a phenomenal memory, don't try to deliver a speech without notes. Prime ministers don't.

One of the funniest speeches delivered recently was Michael Palin's tribute to George Harrison at a dinner to honour Harrison's financial backing of Handmade Films. Palin, of Monty Python fame, made sure he didn't miss one point of his hilarious monologue by shuffling a sheaf of foolscap notes, held at arm's length because of his long-sightedness. His note-reading was central to his delivery.

Most talks are delivered from completely written speeches, delivered word for word with few, if any, ad-lib departures. With a little practice it can appear to be friendlier and be appreciated as more spontaneous with note cards in one hand and several wisecracks up your sleeve.

The art is delivery and timing. If you have the advantages of a rostrum where your notes can be laid out on the lectern, then it is a comparatively simple matter to prepare well in advance and control the presentation with confidence, especially with a microphone.

Everybody tests a microphone, so turn yours to advantage to gain composure:

"Can you hear me over in that far side? Last time I asked if anybody could hear me in that far corner a bloke stood up and said indeed he could. And he offered to change places with somebody who couldn't!"

Standing before your contemporaries at a less formal office farewell, with no microphone, is a little more difficult but there is usually a semblance of order at these functions and there is at least the expectation of an address. Small prompt cards that can be shuffled in your hand is the most practical way to tackle this gathering.

The third, and most difficult arena for "public speaking" is the club, the pub, or around the dinner table where there is no order, and where contributing rather than dominating the conversation is a fine art. It takes a certain amount of confidence to embark on a lengthy yarn and expect to hold attention while you construct the plot to the punchline. Interjections, distractions and the waiter bringing the soup can cripple a good story unless the teller can cope with the interruption, anticipate the waiter's arrival, or suddenly stop the yarn at a high point of the teller's choosing. When the waiter leaves he shouldn't have to say, "Now where was I?" It is much more satisfying to have his listeners chase him for the rest of the yarn with someone eagerly asking "C'mon, what happened next?"

One-liners are the ideal tin-openers to tap the conversation with strangers around the table. Just raise your glass and say: "You can tell the happy motorcyclists by the insects on their teeth." And just leave it at that. Listen for the appropriate break in the conversation and say: "Oh I heartily agree. I was only saying the same thing to my wife in the bath last night." These are throw-away lines to test the water, and there are two pages of these profound statements in this volume. Your kind of humour will either be quickly embraced, or totally ignored.

A trick to hold attention in the rough and tumble of the bar or dinner table is to introduce your story with an off-beat opening line that will grab their attention.

"Did you hear about the one-armed Irish publican called Jock McTavish who took his first holiday abroad after pulling right-handed beers for 30 years?"

This story about the publican's trip to the Canary Islands is a top yarn and appears in the Travel section of this book. The "one-armed publican called Jock" has nothing to do with the thrust of the yarn but the introduction enables the construction of the story to continue. The listeners wait for the relevance of an Irishman called Jock and are led down a different trail to the punchline.

## SALTING THE TALE

THE art of making an implausible story believable is to salt it along the way.

For example, did you hear about the woman who complained that passing trains rocked her bed so much she couldn't sleep?

4

"Unbelievable," is what the estate agent said, too, but the woman, who had just taken a lease on the flat near the railway line, insisted it was true and demanded the estate agent come around.

As he was shown in he noticed a mouse trap with a fish in it. "What's that?" he enquired.

"Oh, I'll talk to you about the rising damp later. Right now there is a train due and I want you to experience the vibrations."

They entered the bedroom. It was quiet. "I can't believe passing trains rock the bed," he said.

"Shakes the living daylights out of it," she persisted, looking at her watch. She heard a distant train whistle.

"Here's the five-thirty-five. Quick, lie down on the bed yourself," she said, and she climbed on to the other side.

That's when her husband came in. "What do you think you are doing?" he roared, glaring at the estate agent stretched out on the eiderdown.

"Would you believe, waiting for a train?" he ventured.

Remember, this book provides the raw material presented here in cold type. A little acting, timing and delivery will greatly enhance their reception to your audience. Delivering the appropriate gag at the right time is what it is all about, and when one joke follows another on the same topic, then it's a double-whammy. A series of yarns on the same theme raises those belly laughs that are good for the soul.

So if these cold pages make you smile, then imagine the effect when they are delivered as repartee.

The categories are designed to cover every occasion from births to funerals, including bonking (which actually comes before births).

If it is your responsibility to farewell a retiring office colleague, toast the happy couple, propose the toast at the coming of age party or make a presentation, there are anecdotes in this book suitable for adapting to your guest of honour... or the victim of your address.

Select some, tinker with them and enjoy them yourself, and before taking centre stage remember the ABC and the XYZ of public speaking. ABC is Always Be Cheerful, and XYZ is Examine Your Zipper.

## A WEDDING

LET'S take a wedding anniversary as an example. It depends on how formal the function is, and how well everybody knows each other, but if you have drawn the short straw to "say a few words" then do some serious research on the couple for the proper tribute which needs to be said, and cobble in as many of these one-liners you judge the gathering will appreciate.

Ladies and gentlemen, in-laws and outlaws, friends and foe ... it has befallen my lot to say a few words on behalf of you all and to toast Bill and Mabel who have been married 30 years today.

Mabel tells me that includes ten years of wedded bliss. And Bill reminds us all that the sentence for manslaughter is only 25 years. But they both agree, that the reason they have stuck together so long is that neither will take custody of the kids. I can well remember the day they had to get ... sorry, the day they got married. Bill has always remembered it too. Unlike most husbands who forget these anniversaries, their wedding day never slipped Bill's memory. It was the day Arsenal thrashed Liverpool.

And of course Mabel was not the street-wise matron she is today. Bill says she was so naive when he married her she thought intercourse was a ticket to the races.

Although it was a big wedding with family and friends from both sides, I am reliably informed that Bill and Mabel still sat up all night waiting for their sexual relations to arrive. It was also the night Bill exploded the myth about oysters. He tells me he had a dozen on his wedding night but only eleven of them worked.

Marriage is a marvellous institution. No family should be without it. (Or, marriage is a marvellous institution, but who wants to live in an institution?) Bill tells me that marriage is a matter of give and take, and that he gives and Mabel takes. And Mabel says they have stopped giving each other anniversary presents long ago, now they shake hands each year and call it quits.

Those who miss out on marriage miss a great deal in life. It reminds me of a bishop I know, right in this very town, who was touched with compassion when he saw an elderly couple standing together in the queue at the Op Shop sale. He thought to himself, "They have shared a lifetime together, through thick and thin, and now here they are, fallen upon hard times, in their twilight years." He went up to them and asked if they would like to spend a week's holiday at Bishop's Retreat in the mountains and packed them off in his chauffeured limousine before they could express their thanks. It was a month later when the bishop saw the old man in the Op Shop again, standing alone this time.

"Did you enjoy the holiday? Did you enjoy the food?" he asked.

"Oh, everything was tops," said the old-timer. "But tell me yer grace, who was that old-boiler I had to share the room with?"

And so, ladies and gentlemen, back to the topic in hand. Could we have two minutes silence ... oops, sorry. Could we all raise our glasses and drink to the long and happy health of our dear friends, Bill and Mabel.

## THE ANNUAL MEETING

ANOTHER example is the reunion, the annual general meeting, the yearly bunfight or social gathering. Whether it is pompously formal or loosely ad hoc, somebody has to say a few words:

Gentlemen. Excellent to see such a roll-up tonight. It has befallen my lot to give you a short address. Here it is: 29 Bay Street.

Since last we met we've passed a lot of water under the bridge. We have an apology. Smithers can't get bail.

New members will be delighted to know that our president is a man of substance, a pillar of society who needs no introduction. So he won't get one.

We have the treasurer's report from Sticky Fingers Smithers who has cooked the books to show we have a healthy bank balance. As already stated, Sticky can't be here tonight. He is helping the police with some enquiries.

We should move a vote of thanks to our honorary president who slaves all day over a hot secretary on behalf of us all. And it should be said that his dedication to the club is such that in pursuit of its well-being he never leaves a turn unstoned.

And let's pay tribute to our committee. As you all know, half the members of most committees are hopeless lay-abouts while the other half do all the work, but with our committee it is completely the reverse.

## GET THE PUNCHLINE STRAIGHT

MANY people who enjoy a good joke lament that they cannot remember them. Those that can remember them, vaguely, lose the plot and lack the confidence to relate them.

The key to it all is to remember the punchline, get it straight, and store it in your mind with a recall word.

A stock of jokes, as this book sets out to supply, will provide the flexibility to match the repartee around the table, especially when you are halfway into the yarn and the resident smart alec (every function has one) interjects with: "Don't tell me its the white horse joke!"

"Wrong, again," you lie, and change direction for horse joke number two, three or four. Style is important.

## HOW TO USE THIS BOOK

MOST jokes can be reconstructed and adapted to suit all occasions.

Take this bland example of three politicians who died on the same day and arrived at the Devil's reception centre simultaneously.

"Ah, a Tory MP," said the Devil. "We've been waiting for you," and he took him to a dungeon where a terrible witch was the only occupant. The MP was pushed into the dingy cell and as the door clanged behind him the Devil's voice over the PA system boomed: "Tory MP, this is your punishment!"

Next was a Labor MP. "We've been waiting for you, too," and taking him to another dungeon which contained yet another horrible witch, he was given a push and, as the door clanged behind him, the Devil's voice over the PA system boomed: "Labor MP, this is your punishment!"

The third polly was the prime minister. "Ah, we have certainly been waiting for you," said the Devil and he was led to another dungeon. Inside, through soft lights, the PM could see Miss Lottzabazooma reclining naked on a satin couch. He was given a shove and, as the door clanged shut behind him, the Devil's voice over the PA system boomed: "Miss Lottzabazooma, this is your punishment!"

Consider how much better that story would be if you used the names of well-known politicians who fitted the bill.

Better still, personalise the same story by including

those around your table; Tom, Dick and Harry. And set up the guest of honour (Harry in this case) by saving him for the last dungeon.

First, Tom gets berated by the Devil over the sins for which he is notorious: "being late for your own wedding, never arriving at a golf match on time, and for collecting parking tickets."

Dick gets thrown into his cell for "telling those boring jokes, ad nauseum and for giving worthless racing tips to close friends" and Harry gets a similar drubbing listing his "in-house" personality traits that your listeners readily recognise. Involving your friends in the joke makes it far more humourous.

So run an astute eye over the "raw material" listed here and consider their modification to different professions and new situations.

# A

IN a Serious Joke Book the funniest jokes are not necessarily upfront. In alphabetical order we are obliged to start, like we all began, with accidents.

## ACCIDENTS
See CARS, MOTORING, DRIVERS.

THE young woman was giving details of the accident to the police and denied she was speeding.

"What gear were you in?" asked the cop.

"An apricot yellow two-piece with chartreuse picture hat," she said.

      ★    ★    ★

TEN per cent of all accidents are caused by drivers affected by alcohol. Which is another way of saying that 90 per cent of accidents are caused by non-drinkers.

      ★    ★    ★

THERE was a knock on the door and Fred found himself being asked to become a Jehovah's Witness.

"I didn't even see the bloomin' accident," he said.

      ★    ★    ★

THE woman at the cocktail party was intent on making the acquaintance of the young medical officer.

"Do you deal with many accidents?" she asked.

"I really don't know," he replied.

"But you are a doctor, what do you mean you don't know?"

"How could I," he said, "My field is obstetrics."

* * *

WHEN Harry arrived at the pub his mates noticed he was on crutches, his face was bruised and there was plaster over his eye. "I must have had one too many when I left here last night," he explained.

His mates said they thought he had been quite sober. "As maybe," said Harry, "but after I left the pub, I turned up High Street, did the roundabout on the corner three times, came back on the wrong side of the road, crossed the median strip and crashed right into the front door of this pub.

"Lucky I wasn't in my bloomin' car!"

* * *

"HOW did this accident happen, sir?"

"My wife fell asleep in the back seat."

* * *

"HOW did this accident happen, sir?"

"Well, the sign said, STOP, LOOK AND LISTEN, and while I was doing that a bloody train ran over me."

* * *

SAID the cop: "Have you ever had an accident, Missus?"

"Well, I met my husband at a service station."

* * *

THE wife told the police that although she had broken the umbrella over her husband's head it was an accident. "If I had known the umbrella would break I would have used a golf club," she said.

* * *

FRED had just parked his old car when a cop came and asked him if he had reported the accident.

* * *

FIVE Hells Angels walked into the bar, ordered their drinks and suggested the lone drinker at the end of the bar should pay. When he refused they punched him up and threw him out of the pub.

"He wasn't much of a fighter," said one of the bikies to the barman.

"He is not much of a driver either," said the barman, "He has just had an accident and driven his truck over five motorbikes."

\* \* \*

AFTER a terrible accident at the factory, where Fred fell into the upholstery machine, he is now fully recovered.

\* \* \*

THE cop pushed through the crowd at the scene of the accident to see a blonde and a young man having passionate sex on the nature strip.

He quickly put a stop to it and demanded to know what was going on.

"It's all my fault," she said. "He was thrown from his car in the accident and I was giving him mouth to mouth resuscitation, and, well, we both got carried away."

\* \* \*

HE was sitting at the bar knocking back double Scotches. As fast as the barman could place them in front of him he scoffed them down in one gulp.

"It's the only way I've been able to drink them since my accident," he explained to a friendly enquirer.

"What sort of accident?" asked his new friend.

"Shocking," he replied. "I knocked one over with my elbow."

## ACCOUNTANTS
See FINANCE

MY old Dad said I'd never make an accountant.

"There are three kinds of people in this world, son," he said. "Those who can count, and those who can't!"

A CHARTERED accountant is an undertaker who has had a charisma bypass.

*     *     *

THE chartered accountant went into the pub after work and ordered a pot of beer. As the publican pushed it across the bar the accountant said: "Do you think you could get a nip of whisky in that?"

"Certainly, sir," said the publican.

"In that case," said the accountant, "perhaps you'd just top it up with beer!"

*     *     *

THEY say Adam was the first accountant, after he turned a leaf and made an entry.

*     *     *

HE thought the new office girl was as beautiful as an Income Tax Refund.

*     *     *

HE told his wife he was changing their accountant.

"He's too shy and retiring," he explained.

"Is that a reason to sack him?" she asked

"Yes. He's $200,000 shy and that's why he's retiring."

*     *     *

ON his retirement after 35 years as Chief Accountant the company presented him with a silver-bound ledger book, framed and mounted on a little pedestal.

He looked at the trophy and said, "Well at least it has finally settled a concern of mine. I almost chose a career as a gynaecologist."

*     *     *

THE executive director visited the company's accountant who was sick in hospital. "John," he said, "the board decided to send you a Get Well Card and I would like you to know it was a majority decision."

*     *     *

THE partners in the accountancy firm crossed the road to their local bar for their usual afterwork drink.

"Oh, I forgot to lock the safe," said one.

"It's okay," said his partner. "We're both here aren't we?"

# ADVERTISEMENTS

PLACED in the personal column: "Fred, please do not come home. All is forgiven."

\* \* \*

GIRL wanted for petrol pump attendant.

\* \* \*

MAN wanted to wash dishes, and two waitresses.

\* \* \*

ACCOMMODATION, suit two girls willing to share room or young man.

\* \* \*

ACCOMMODATION: Honeymoon suite, sleeps three.

\* \* \*

STRADIVARIUS violin for sale. Almost new.

\* \* \*

"PHOTOGRAPHER setting up own business needs model, as sleeping or active partner."

\* \* \*

LOST dog. Has three legs, blind in left eye, right ear missing, broken tail, no teeth, recently castrated. Answers to Lucky.

\* \* \*

A SALESMAN was staying overnight in a country town where the only excitement was watching the spin-dry in the laundromat. Out of sheer boredom he opened the Gideon Bible provided in all motel rooms. On the fly-leaf was a message: If thou art bored and lonely and desireth some warm comfort, ring Susie, 58-6683.

\* \* \*

WONDERFUL opportunity for woman to join fishing partners. Must have own boat. Must be able to cook, wash and gut fish. Please send photo of boat.

# ALCOHOLICS

ALCOHOLICS Anonymous is a place where you drink in secret.

* * *

THERE is a new organisation called AAAA.
 It is for people being driven to drink.

* * *

THE vicar was invited to address the Alcoholics Anonymous meeting. "I have lived in this town all my life," he said sternly. "There are 95 hotels and I can honestly say I have never been in one of them."
 "Which one is that?" said a voice from the rear.

* * *

HE bought one of those audio tapes that help you to stop drinking while you're sleeping. It worked. He hasn't had a drink in his sleep since.

* * *

"ALCOHOL is your trouble," said the judge. "Alcohol alone is responsible for your present predicament."
 "Thank you, judge," said the drunk. "Everyone else says it's my fault."

* * *

THE wife sought some advice from the doctor about her alcoholic husband.
 "Has he tried Alcoholics Anonymous?" asked the Doc.
 "I expect so. He'll drink anything," she replied.

* * *

CHAP was walking home when an alcoholic stepped in front of him with a gun in one hand and a bottle in the other. Pointing the gun at his victim the drunk thrust the bottle forward and said, "Take a drink of this."
 The unfortunate man took a swig then spat it out. "It's awful," he gasped.
 "I know," said the drunk. "Now you hold the gun on me while I take a swallow."

THEY were in the Mexican army on curfew duty. "You patrol this side of the street, and I will patrol the other," said Pedro to his mate.

They hadn't gone very far when a shot rang out and Pedro ran across the street to discover his mate with a smoking gun and a dead man on the footpath.

"Why did you shoot him?" demanded Pedro. "The curfew is not in force for another half hour?"

"I know that," said his mate. "But I know where this hombre lives and there is no way he would have got home in time."

\* \* \*

THE difference between being a drunk and being an alcoholic is that the drunk doesn't have to bother attending all those boring meetings.

\* \* \*

AN alcoholic is somebody you don't like, but drinks as much as you.

\* \* \*

AN alcoholic believes a teetotaller is someone who practices moderation to excess, and abstinence is okay provided you do it in moderation.

\* \* \*

FRED joined Alcoholics Unanimous. "There are no arguments," he explained.

\* \* \*

THE drunk asked a passer-by if he knew the way to Alcoholics Anonymous.

"Why," he said, "do you want to join?"

"No, I want to resign."

\* \* \*

FRED stumbled into the AA meeting and knocked over a few chairs.

The secretary frowned: "Oh, we were so happy last night when you turned up sober."

"Well, tonight it's my turn to be happy," said Fred.

THE doctor noticed that the chronic alcoholic could not hold his hands out straight. They shook violently.

"How much have you been drinking lately?" he asked.

"Hardly any," said the drunk. "I spill most of it!"

* * *

SHE answered a knock on the door. "I am collecting for the Home for Alcoholics," said the caller.

"Well come back around nine o'clock," she said. "My husband will be home then, and you can have him."

* * *

HE preached moderation in all things. "First, I never drink whisky without water. Second. I never drink water without whisky."

## ANIMALS

THERE is a big difference between buffaloes and bisons.

For a start, you can't wash your hands in a buffalo.

* * *

WHERE would you find a turtle with no legs?

Exactly where you left him.

* * *

THE bi-sexual donkey had a hee in the morning and a haw at night.

* * *

THE suicidal seal flip-flopped into the pub and asked for a Canadian Club on the rocks.

* * *

A BLOKE went to the pub with a giraffe. They drank all afternoon. By six o'clock the giraffe collapsed in an ungainly heap on the floor and his drinking partner staggered towards the door.

"Hey," said the barman, "Don't go and leave that lyin' on the floor."

The man turned and said, "It's not a lion. It's a giraffe!"

LEO the Lion was swaggering down the jungle path confronting each animal in turn: "Who's the king of the jungle?" he asked Gerald the giraffe.

"You are, of course," said Gerald.

"Who's the king of the jungle?" he asked Harold the hyena.

"You are, of course."

The answers were the same until he confronted Jumbo the elephant. "Who's the king of the jungle?" he asked, blocking Jumbo's path.

With a blast from his trumpet the elephant picked the lion up in his trunk, threw him in the air, caught him, dashed him against a tree then flung him over his shoulder.

"Alright," said Leo dusting himself off. "You don't have to get nasty just because you don't know the answer!"

\*     \*     \*

LEO the lion was drinking from a stream with his bottom in the air, just as a big chimp was passing. From the chimp's viewpoint it looked like Lily the lion so he crept up for a quiet slap and tickle.

The lion let out a mighty roar and the chimp, realising his mistake, took off like greased lightning. He sped through the jungle with the lion in hot pursuit.

The chimp dashed into a hunter's camp, quickly donned a safari suit, slapped on a pith helmet, dived into a chair, grabbed a copy of The Times and hid behind it as if was reading. The lion screeched into the clearing and as soon as the dust settled asked the "hunter", "Have you seen a chimp dash past here?"

"Not the chimp that dated the lion down by the stream?"

"Hell," said the lion, "don't tell me it's in the papers already."

\*     \*     \*

THE visitor was admiring the family's pet pig.

"Yes, he's an amazing animal," said the farmer. "Once

he raised the alarm and saved the house from burning down. Another time he saved young Johnny from drowning and pulled him out of the dam ..."

"That's incredible," said the visitor, "but tell me, why does he have one leg missing?"

"Well," said the proud farmer, "you don't eat a pig like that all at once!"

* * *

ONE zebra got to thinking. "Hey, Zeke," he said to his mate, "are we white with black stripes, or black with white stripes?"

Zeke didn't know and they pondered this problem for a week before asking the king of the jungle.

"Hey Leo, are we white with black stripes, or black with white stripes?"

Leo didn't know but he directed them up to the top of a mountain. "Ask God," he said.

They spent a day sitting on top of the mountain shouting: "Hey God. Are we white with black stripes or black with white stripes?"

It wasn't until sunset that the booming voice of God bellowed out: "You are what you are."

Next day Leo asked them the result. "You are what you are. That's what God said. What the heck does that mean?"

Leo thought this over for a while and then gave his verdict: "It means you are white with black stripes. Otherwise he would have said 'Yo is what yo is'."

# ANNIVERSARIES

ON their golden anniversary he said there was nothing he wouldn't do for his wife and there was nothing she wouldn't do for him.

"And that's how it's been for the past 50 years," he added. "We've done nothing for each other."

* * *

"I'M afraid I can't make the darts match tomorrow night,

Fred. I promised to take Thingummy out for our silver anniversary."

* * *

FOR 22 years Harry and his wife were deliriously happy. Then they met each other.

* * *

HE asked how they should celebrate their 25th anniversary.

She suggested two minutes' silence.

* * *

HE was telling his mate how he and his wife spent their 25th anniversary. "We left town on the same train, went to the same hotel, managed to get the same room. But this time it was me who went to the bathroom and cried!"

* * *

ON quiet nights, when he is alone, Fred runs their wedding video backwards, just to watch himself walk out of the church a free man.

* * *

IT was their 40th wedding anniversary and Rachael took Izzi to an upmarket part of town and proudly showed him a block of flats. "It's ours, Izzi, we own it," she said.

"But how?" he asked.

"You remember all these years how I charged you $10 each time we made love?" said Rachael. "Well, I saved all that money and bought this block of flats."

"Oh, Rachael, if only I had known, I would have given you all my business."

* * *

THERE'S not much difference between a toilet seat and an anniversary. Men usually miss them both.

## ARMY

THE old diggers were renewing old acquaintances at the Anzac reunion. "Was it you or your brother who got killed in New Guinea?"

A SIGNAL from HQ circulated along the front line declared that there was a $10 bounty for anyone who shot one of the enemy.

Next day at a forward observation post Paddy whispered to Mick, "Psst. There's two hunnerd t'ousand dollars creeping up my side of the hill!"

*       *       *

THE new rookie looked a trifle uncomfortable when the brigadier stopped in front of him.

"Aren't you happy, man?" asked the officer.

The rookie nervously agreed he was happy.

"And what were you in civvy street?"

"A bloody sight happier," said the rooky.

*       *       *

CALLED up for national service the young man was being examined by an army doctor.

"Just give me a gun, I'll show 'em," said the lad. "If they shoot off my hands I'll work the trigger with my arms. If they shoot off my arms then I'll do it with my legs. If they shoot off my legs, then b'jeezus I'll pull the trigger with my teeth."

"Good show, that's the spirit," said the doctor.

"Hang on," said the lad. "Don't you think I'm a little crazy?"

*       *       *

A TOUGH drill sergeant ordered his men to hold up their left legs. One recruit mistakenly held up his right leg, thus placing it beside his neighbour's left.

"Alright, alright," roared the sergeant. "Who's the wise guy holding up both legs?"

*       *       *

THE sergeant major had been lecturing the new recruits on their duties for the past two hours and suddenly noticed that Private Murphy was dozing.

"Now then, Murphy!" he roared. "Why should a soldier be ready to die for his country?"

Paddy scratched his head for a moment. "You're damned right sir. Why should he?"

\* \* \*

THE court martial decreed that the deserter be taken to Boot Hill where he would be shot. It was a grim and rainy day and at dawn the firing squad arrived to escort the condemned man a mile or more to his execution.

He grumbled all the way. "Fancy having to march all this way in this terrible weather just to be shot," he lamented.

"Yeah, but think of us," said one of his guards. "We've got to march back again."

\* \* \*

THE tough sergeant major knew that he was unpopular with the ranks and while carpeting a soldier who was due for discharge said: "I've heard it said that when I die some of you blokes are coming back to piddle on my grave. I suppose you will be among them?"

"Not me, sarge," said the soldier. "Once I get out of this army I've promised myself I will never stand in long queues again."

\* \* \*

AS the sergeant major approached the camp he was challenged by the new recruit on sentry duty.

"That's not bad Private Smithers," said the officer, "but the expression is 'Friend or Foe' not 'Goodies or Baddies'!"

\* \* \*

A PARTICULARLY unpopular sergeant major popped his head up above the trench and a sniper's bullet whizzed within one centimetre of his ear.

"Paddy! Get out and get that sniper," he roared to private Kelly.

Kelly was the regiment's best scout and within ten minutes he was back, the enemy sniper, with raised hands, walking before him.

Then Paddy began to punch hell out of his prisoner.

"Hey go easy," said his mates. "What's that for?"

"It's for missing the bloody sar'major," said Paddy.

*　　*　　*

THE navy recruiting officer looked the applicant up and down. "Can you swim?" he said.

"Why," said the prospective sailor, "don't you have any boats?"

*　　*　　*

THE visitor breasted the Returned Servicemen's Bar and asked for a double Scotch.

"That'll be eight-dollars-fifty," said the bartender.

"Hell," said the visitor. "If you had have charged like that at Gallipoli we would have won."

*　　*　　*

THERE was once a discreet brigadier
Fond of his ten thousand a year
But when he heard the guns rattle
Said: "Sounds like a battle!"
And quietly slipped to the rear.

*　　*　　*

THE C.O. had just welcomed the young army officer, shown him around the camp and was outlining the recreational facilities.

"On Mondays we have a snooker tournament, a jolly good show with the winner taking the jackpot."

"I'm afraid I don't play snooker sir," said the officer.

"Well, on Tuesdays we have a darts match," continued the C.O., "and first to make 301 wins the drinks."

"I'm afraid I don't like gambling or playing darts, sir."

"Really?" said the C.O. "Well, on Wednesday nights a few girls come up from the village for a dance and a bit of hanky panky and..."

"Sorry sir," said the officer. "I have no time for women."

"Good God, man," said the C.O. "You're not gay are you?"

"Certainly not sir," said the officer.

"Oh dear," said the C.O., "then you are not going to like Thursday and Friday nights much either."

# ARTS

FRED is a bit of an artist. He doesn't understand women, but he knows what he likes.

*　　*　　*

SALVADOR Dali took Picasso aside and said, "Excuse me friend, could I have a word in your eyeball?"

*　　*　　*

AN artist's model is a girl who shows the painter where to draw the line.

*　　*　　*

THE model got off the couch and came to inspect the painting. She blushed and said, "Oh Mr Renaldo. You've been looking."

*　　*　　*

AN artist and his model were smooching on the sofa when they heard a car arrive. "Quick, it's my wife," cried the artist. "Get your clothes off and pretend we're working."

*　　*　　*

THE mayor had officially opened the one-man art show and was browsing along the paintings when he stopped with a start in front of a picture of a woman reclining nude on a couch.

"That's my wife," he cried. "You scoundrel. You have had my wife up here posing nude in your studio."

The artist, a little terrified, said it wasn't the case at all. "I painted it from memory," he said.

*　　*　　*

A SOCIALITE approached a prominent portrait artist and asked if he would paint her in the nude.

"Sure," he said, "but I'll have to keep my socks on otherwise I'll have nowhere to stick my brushes."

*　　*　　*

THE artist said: "I only paint what I see."

The critic said: "Then you should never paint in that condition."

FRED's Dad was an artist. He was always drawing corks.

\* \* \*

"MY art is becoming internationally acclaimed. One of these days I will be immoral."

"Don't you mean immortal?"

"I know what I mean."

\* \* \*

"DID you sell any of your paintings at the art show?"

"No, but I am encouraged," he replied. "Somebody stole one."

\* \* \*

"MUM, what is pop-art?"

"Why do you ask, son?"

"Well, it's what Dad says when he's going to pop-art for a quickie down the pub."

\* \* \*

A BLOKE cleaning out his attic discovered an old violin and an oil painting. Thinking they might be valuable he took them to an art dealer.

"Well, that's a Stradivarius," mused the dealer, "and this here is a Rembrandt."

"Then, are they valuable?" he asked hopefully.

"Not really," said the dealer. "Stradivarius was a hopeless painter, and look at Rembrandt's violin. You'd never get a tune out of it."

\* \* \*

SALVADOR Dali was robbed while on a visit to New York, but he managed to get a good look at the offender and was able to provide the police with a rough sketch of the felon.

For the next two weeks New York police searched for a man with a head like a horse, a fried egg on his forehead and a sword in his mouth.

## ASTROLOGY

A FAMOUS astrologer was quite entranced by the baby in the pram. "Beautiful," she said, "absolutely beautiful," and beaming at the proud mother she said, "Do you happen to know what sign she was conceived under?"

"Yes," blushed the young mum. "It said 'Keep off the Grass'!"

*　　*　　*

IT has got to the stage where people who introduce themselves now add their birthsigns.

"Hi, I'm Bill Moloney, Sagittarius."

"Hi, I'm John Spriggs, Cancer."

"Hi, I'm Joe Bloggs, bladder infection."

*　　*　　*

"WHAT sign were you born under?"

"I think it was a red and green flashing Neon.

## ATHEISTS

AN atheist is a man with no invisible means of support.

*　　*　　*

FRED was an atheist, but he gave it up. He said there were no holidays.

*　　*　　*

GRAFFITI. "Thank God I'm an Atheist."

*　　*　　*

IF God is good
　Why do his peoples
　Put lightning rods
　On top of steeples?

*　　*　　*

ROSES are red
　Violets are bluish
　If it wasn't for Jesus
　We'd all be Jewish

# B

## BACHELORS

A BACHELOR is a man who comes to work every morning, from a different direction.

*     *     *

AFTER his check-up the doctor told Barry the bachelor he was getting on in years and his lifestyle of wine, women and song would have to change.

"In fact, you will have to give up the first two," said the doc, "but you can sing as much as you like."

*     *     *

THE bachelor finished his meal and placed his tip on the table. The waiter took one look at the 15 cents and said: "Thank you for your generosity. You can always tell the character of a diner by the way he tips."

"Oh, really," he said. "What do these five-cent coins tell you about me?"

"Well, you put the three coins in a row," said the waiter. "That tells me you are tidy for starters. The first coin tells me you are frugal and the second coin tells me you are a bachelor."

"That's true," said the diner, impressed. "And what does the third coin tell you?"

"That tells me your father was a bachelor too."

FRED is safe now that he has joined Bachelors Anonymous.

Each time he feels like getting married the club sends round a woman in hair-curlers to nag him for a while.

* * *

MANY a poor husband was once a rich bachelor.

* * *

HE had so much fun at the bachelor party he postponed the wedding.

## BARBERS

THE sign on the barber shop read: Haircuts, while you wait!

* * *

HIS hair was neatly departed in the middle.

* * *

HE asked the barber if he had something to stop falling hair. The barber sold him a net.

* * *

WHEN one barber cuts another's hair, which one does the talking?

* * *

"HOW do you like your hair cut, sir?"
  "Off."

* * *

"JUST a shave please, I haven't time to listen to a haircut."

* * *

"DO you shave yourself all the time?"
  "No. I often stop for food."

* * *

THE barber was late for work. While shaving that morning he talked himself into a shampoo and hair tint.

* * *

EVERY time the nation's economic recession gets worse,

the local barber puts up his prices. He says longer faces take more time to shave.

*　　*　　*

THE customer noticed the barber's dirty hands and complained about it.

"Can't help it if nobody has been in for a shampoo yet," he replied.

*　　*　　*

THE boss demanded to know where he had been.

"I've been for a haircut."

"You can't have your hair cut in office time?"

"Why not? It grows in office time."

"Not all of it," said the boss.

"So I didn't get it all cut off," he replied.

*　　*　　*

THE sign said: "Beatles' Style Cut Here."

So he went in and was aghast to be shorn almost bald.

"That's not how the Beatles have their hair cut," he protested.

"It will be if they come here," said the barber.

*　　*　　*

TWO business acquaintances were seated side by side in the hairdresser's. One barber asked his client if he would like some French toilet water on his hair.

The man declined. "No way, the wife would think I'd been in a French brothel."

The second barber asked the same question to his client who responded: "Sure, I'll have some. My wife has never been in a French brothel."

*　　*　　*

FRED had just retired and was about to go on a world trip. He popped in to Bob the Barber's for a short back and sides on the eve of his departure.

"Be sure to come and tell me all about it when you come home," said Bob after he had finished the cut.

Two months later Fred was back in the chair again

relating the highlights. "I even went to see the Pope at St Peter's" he said.

"Wow," said Bob.

"And what's more, the Pope came over and spoke to me."

"That's unbelievable," said Bob, still clipping away. "What did the Pope say?"

"He said, 'Where the hell did you get a haircut like that'!"

\* \* \*

FLIRTY Fred popped into the hotel's barber shop for a haircut and while waiting for the barber to strop his razor he was enjoying a manicure from the very shapely blonde assistant and took the chance to chat her up.

"What time do you knock off," he leered out the side of his mouth.

"About six," she said.

"What about coming up for a drink?"

"I'm married," she said. "What would I say to my husband?"

"Just tell him straight. Tell him you are going out tonight," said Fred.

"You tell him," she said. "That's him stropping the razor."

\* \* \*

A MAN entered the barber's saloon and asked, "How long will you be?"

"About an hour," replied the barber.

"Okay, I'll come back," said the man who then left.

He didn't return until the next day when he entered the doorway again and asked, "How long will you be?"

The barber had six customers waiting and said, about an hour or more.

"Okay, I'll come back."

When the prospective customer did this every day of the week and never returned as he always promised the barber became intrigued and asked his apprentice to follow him.

"Tell me where he goes," he said.

The apprentice was back in five minutes. "He goes straight round to your place," he told the barber.

\* \* \*

THE bald man was astounded to be charged $15 for a cut and trim.

"That's more than you charge for people with a full head of hair," he complained.

"Yeah," said the barber. "A treasure hunt costs more."

\* \* \*

IF barristers can be de-barred, and ministers be de-frocked, can a barber be dis-tressed?

\* \* \*

HARRY Cox was looking for his brother Bob. He couldn't find him in his usual haunts or in the pub. Thinking he might be having a haircut Harry went to the barber's shop.

"Bob Cox in here?" he asked.

"Sorry sir," said the barber. "We only do shaves and haircuts."

\* \* \*

(R) THE barber broke his leg in a skiing accident.

Now he can only cut hair on crutches.

## BEAUTY

HIS wife used to have a nice firm chin. But now the firm has taken on a couple of partners.

\* \* \*

SHE said: "Will you love me when I'm old and grey?"

"Why not," he said. "I've loved you when you were blonde, henna, brunette and blue."

\* \* \*

IT'S no use making your mind up to stay in if your wife has made her face up to go out.

\* \* \*

SHE was wearing a faint perfume. One sniff and you fainted.

WHEN she came down tl
you look lovely. That must l

* *

BEAUTY comes from within
tubes, phials, compacts...

* *

"DOES your sister still make uj
"Yes, she still works at the bea

* *

SHE approached the hairdresser.
"What do you have for grey hai
"The greatest respect, madam."

* * *

THE better a woman looks, the longer a man does.

# BEDS

MORE than one-third of our lives are spent in bed. Most
of us were begotten in a bed, and born in a bed and
we will probably die in a bed. In between these important
events the bed is an essential accessory for play and
rest; and no joke book should be without a bed section,
and no bed should be without a joke section.

* * *

A BED is where one good turn can get all the blankets.

* * *

BEDS cause hangovers. Statistics prove that drunks will
go to bed happy, and wake up feeling terrible.

* * *

WHEN he was in bed he was terrified that somebody
might be underneath it. When he got underneath it he
was terrified that somebody might be on top of the
bed.

The psychiatrist told him he had bed phobia and was
treating him at $100 a visit.

After a year of treatment, and the loss of a small

...e psychiatrist he wasn't coming back

...alk to the barman and he solved my problem,"

...h, and what did he do?" enquired the psychiatrist.
"He came round and sawed the legs off my bed!"

## BETS

"REMEMBER I bet a tenner I'd beat my drink problem?"
"Yeah."
"Well now I've got a gambling problem."

* * *

CARRYING his bat nervously he walked on to the ground
for his first match with the seniors. A spectator called
to him: "I've got a bet on you."
"That's nice of you," he said modestly, "I'll probably
get a duck."
"That's what I bet."

* * *

THE argument at the bar was on religion.
"And I betcha a tenner you don't know the Lord's Prayer."
"You're on."
"Okay, say it"
"Now I lay me down to sleep..."
"Gawd. Here's the money. I didn't think you knew it."

* * *

THE Elderly Citizens' Club now has a community bus
and each Sunday they go off on a mystery tour. To make
it interesting the oldies dob in 50 cents in a sweep to
guess the mystery destination. Bert the driver has won
it three times in a row.

* * *

A PUNTER would bank $500 every Monday morning
so regularly that finally the bank manager's curiosity
got the better of him. Where did he get the money?

34

"I am a punter," explained the customer, "but I only bet on sure things."

Intrigued, the banker pressed him for an example of a sure thing.

"No worries," said the punter. "I'll bet you $500 that you've got red jocks. That's a sure bet for a start."

The banker could hardly believe his ears, and slapping the money on the counter he said "You're on."

"Okay, drop your trousers so I can check," said the punter.

"Not here," said the banker, "come into my office."

Once inside the banker said, "There you are, they are definitely not red."

"Not good enough," said the punter, "they look red to me, but I'm colour-blind. D'yer mind if your accountant checks the colour?"

The accountant was called in and immediately fainted.

"What's up with him?" asked the manager.

"Oh, I bet him $1000 I'd get you to drop your dacks before 10 this morning."

## BIRDS

MY wife does bird imitations. She watches me like a hawk.

*     *     *

A BIRD in the hand is better than two in a photograph.

*     *     *

A BIRD in the hand is useless when you have to blow your nose.

*     *     *

HE was responsible for feeding the pelicans at the zoo. It wasn't much of a job but it filled the bill.

*     *     *

AT the Stork Club. "Do any deliveries today?"

"No, but I frightened hell out of a few secretaries."

*     *     *

"NEXT!" roared the theatrical agent, and when Bert

shuffled in self-consciously before him he muttered, "Well, what do you do?"

"I do bird impressions," said Bert.

"Not another one," said the agent without raising his eyes from documents on his desk. "Get on with it then."

So Bert flapped his arms, dropped a deposit on the window ledge and flew off into the blue sky yonder.

## BIRTHS and BIRTHDAYS

SHE'S just turned 32, but the way she's turned it, makes her 23.

&ast; &ast; &ast;

A husband who forgets his wife's birthday will get something to remember her by.

&ast; &ast; &ast;

WHEN a man has a birthday he takes a day off. When a woman has a birthday she takes a year off.

&ast; &ast; &ast;

SHE was born in the year of our lord only knows.

&ast; &ast; &ast;

I WAS so surprised by my birth, I was speechless for a year and a half.

&ast; &ast; &ast;

IN what State were you born?
In the nude.

&ast; &ast; &ast;

SHE was looking forward to her 30th birthday. But she was looking in the wrong direction.

&ast; &ast; &ast;

"HAVE you known your wife long?"
"Yes. Ever since we were the same age."

&ast; &ast; &ast;

LIFE is full of complications. Even when you are born there is a string attached.

"MY mother was disappointed when I was born."
"Why, did she want a girl?"
"No. She wanted a divorce."

* * *

"THE stork brought a little peach,"
The nurse said with an air.
"I'm bloomin' glad," the father said,
"He didn't bring a pear!"

* * *

ANOTHER candle on the cake
Well that's no cause to pout
Be glad you still have wind enough
To blow the damn thing out

* * *

THE best way to remember your wife's birthday is to forget it once.

* * *

SHE: "I hate to think about my 30th birthday."
He: "Why? What happened?"

* * *

IT'S terrible to grow old alone. My wife hasn't had a birthday for three years.

* * *

SHE'S celebrating the second anniversary of her 16th birthday.

* * *

YOU'RE getting old when the only thing you don't want for your birthday is to be reminded of it.

* * *

IT was a brave husband who whispered to his mate, "I'm so glad she was born in winter. The birthday candles heat up the house. If it was in summer she'd need a fire permit."

* * *

IT was one of those cruises so well patronised by the elderly when a sprightly old geezer approached a spinster reclining on a deck chair.

"Guess how old I am," he said.

She looked him up and down for a moment, then put her hand up the leg of his shorts. She grabbed his crown jewels, felt their weight, moved them gently from side to side and then declared with authority: "You are 83 and seven months."

"That's amazing," said the old codger, "how do you know?"

"Because you told me yesterday you silly old fool," she replied.

## BOASTERS

WHEN the sliding door opened in the confessional box he started: "Father, I had sex with a pair of lovely 18-year-old nymphomaniac twins five times last week."

"What kind of Catholic are you?" demanded the priest.

"I am not a Catholic," he replied.

"Then why are you telling me this?"

"I am telling everyone!"

★　　★　　★

"DO you think I am conceited?" he asked his girlfriend.

"No. What makes you ask, darling?" she said.

"Well, most blokes as handsome as me usually are."

★　　★　　★

HE had told her how he won the best and fairest award in his football club, all the details of his life, his training and the goals he scored and his philosophy on life.

Finally he said, "But that's enough about me. Let's talk about you. Tell me, what did you think of my performance in Saturday's game?"

★　　★　　★

THE old gent was getting sick and tired of Young Turk boasting of his sexual conquests.

"Listen," he said. "I am 87 and I make love nearly every night of the week."

The young bloke said he didn't believe him.

"True," said the old geezer. "I nearly made it Monday, I nearly made it Tuesday, ... "

★　　★　　★

YOUNG Father Murphy phoned the bishop to say he was ill and couldn't celebrate mass. As soon as he heard the bishop say he could get a replacement the young priest grabbed his golf clubs and was one of the first on the course.

St Peter saw this and nudged God. "Look at Father Murphy. Lied to say he was ill, and look at him down there. He has got to be punished."

"Okay," said God, and they watched as the priest pulled out a number one wood, swung a mighty stroke and belted the ball straight up the fairway, narrowly between two bunkers onto the green to roll slowly in for one.

St Peter was aghast. "I thought you were going to punish him."

"I have," said God. "Who can he boast to?"

# BONKS
(R)...

LET's face it, there is a lot of bonking going on. It is the reason we all got here, so we can hardly avoid it as a classification for jokes, especially when most jokes are about pre-bonking, trying to get a bonk, actual bonking and post bonking.

★　　★　　★

HE'S bi-sexual, which means if he can't get it, he buys it.

★　　★　　★

CHARLIE said he once went without sex for 12 years. "Wasn't even bothered by it," he said. "Then I had my 13th birthday."

★　　★　　★

FRED said he gave up sex and booze at the same time once. "It was the worst half hour of my life!" he said.

WHEN Paddy walked into the pub it caused a snigger among his mates at the bar. "Boy, the joke was on you last night, Paddy," they said. "You left your bedroom light on and the blind was up. You put on a great show with your missus."

"Well, the joke's on you lot," countered Paddy. "I wasn't home last night."

\* \* \*

A HOUSEWIFE was asked by her neighbour how she happened to have so many home appliances around the house.

"Bonking," she replied. "I charge my husband $10 for a bonk. In fact, I have a scale of charges. It costs him 50 cents for a fondle."

Her neighbour thought this was a wonderful proposition and said she would introduce the same scale of fees.

A month later they met again. "By the way, are you making any money," asked the first housewife.

"Afraid not," said the neighbour. "I charge him 50 cents for a fondle and pretty soon I have to get out of bed to lend him another 50 cents, and by then I don't mind paying him ten."

\* \* \*

FRED was complaining to his doctor that his wife had lost interest in sex. The doc explained that it was a matter of preparation. "Next time you come home from work, bring a bunch of flowers, give her a big kiss, then sweep her off her feet and carry her to the bedroom. You will be surprised."

On Fred's next visit he asked if it worked. "Yes, she was indeed surprised. And so were all the members of her bridge club."

\* \* \*

FRED was leaning on the bar recounting the most recent tragedy in the neighbourhood. "Ernie came home and found his wife in bed with the bloke next door. He got his gun and shot them both."

"Well, it could of been worse," said his listener.

"What d'yer mean," said Fred, "what could be worse than that?"

"Well, if Ernie had come home early the night before I'd be dead by now."

*    *    *

THE pretty fraulein approached the Aussie tourist in the Munich beer hall and invited him home. She gave him a nice meal and took him to bed.

In the morning, after a hearty breakfast, he was about to leave and made a little speech about the outstanding hospitality he had received.

"Ja, the speech is nice, but what about marks," she said.

"Bloody oath, nine out of ten I reckon," he said.

*    *    *

IT was their 50th wedding anniversary and Rachael took Izzi to the city and proudly showed him a block of flats. "It's ours, Izzi, we own it," she said.

"But how did you?" he said.

"You remember all these years I used to charge you $10 for a tumble in bed," said Rachael. "Well I saved all that money and bought that block of flats."

"Oh Rachael. If only I had known, I would have given you all my business!"

*    *    *

DAVE and Mable checked over their meagre finances and realised times were tough. "I've got an idea," said Dave. "Every time we have a bit of nookie in bed I will pay you a dollar. It will be a means of saving with pleasure."

Two months later they needed some extra funds and busted open the cash box. Dave was amazed to see the bundle of notes which included fives, tens and twenties.

"Mabel, where did you get all this money. Each time we did it I only gave you a dollar."

*41*

"Listen Dave," she said, "not everyone is as stingy as you."

* * *

OLD Dad and Mum overheard the above episode with Dave and Mabel. Convinced there was money to be made he suggested Mum should try her luck on the street.

Mum returned that evening, emptied her handbag on the kitchen table and out tumbled the cash which included fives, tens and twenties. It added up to $75 and 50 cents.

"What lousy cheapskate gave you the 50 cents?" demanded Dad.

"They all did," said Mum.

* * *

"MRS Smith," queried the doctor. "Do you smoke after intercourse?"

"I've never looked," she replied.

* * *

THE couple were laying on the bed naked, smoking a post coital cigarette.

After a while she said, "Mother always told me to be good. Was I?"

* * *

MRS Murphy, the young mother of triplets, was being congratulated by her neighbour, Mrs Kelly.

"Yes, 'tis a wonderful thing indade," said the proud Mum, "and you know the doctor says it only happens once in a hundred t'ousand times."

"Heavens," said Mrs Kelly in astonishment, "whinever did yer foind time to do yer housework?"

* * *

CHAP suffering from laringitis could hardly talk with his sore throat, so he went to the clinic after hours.

The door was opened by the doctor's pretty young wife.

"Is the doctor in," he whispered.

"No," she whispered. "Come on in."

42

CHAP walking along the beach one evening in the dark stepped on a bloke's bottom. And a girl's voice said "Thank you!"

* * *

HE was telling his mate that he and his wife had discovered a new way of making love; back to back.

"That would be nigh impossible wouldn't it?"

"Oh we have another couple in to help us," he explained.

* * *

BOB, Jane, Mary and Bill had been friends for years. The two couples went on a camping trip and pitched their tents close together. While sitting around the camp fire they got to talking about the current trend of swinging couples and ventured far enough to suggest they try it.

"Haven't had so much fun for years," said Bob later. "Do you think the girls are having as much fun as we are?"

* * *

ONE night the husband came home early from afternoon shift and found the lodger in bed with his wife.

"What's the meaning of this?" he cried. "It's a fine way to repay our hospitality. After all we've done for you ... and stop doing that while I'm talking to you!"

* * *

HE came home from the pub fairly late and his wife met him at the front door. "We've had a burglar," she sobbed.

"Did he get anything?" he said in alarm.

"He sure did," she said. "I thought it was you!"

* * *

IT was Friday night and Barbie had just finished preparing the evening meal for her husband John when there was a knock on the door. She opened it and was surprised to see her husband's best mate, Freddie.

"John's scored some overtime," said Fred. "He told me to tell you he won't be home until eleven-thirty."

43

A long chat on the doorstep resulted in Barbie inviting Freddie inside. "In fact, you might as well eat some of this food I have prepared."

Freddie was in like Flynn. And after the food, and half a bottle of good red, began chatting up Barbie about the good old days when they used to go together, before she was married. In fact, he soon got to the point. "Give us a kiss for old time's sake?" he said.

"No, I'm an honest married woman," she said.

"Okay," said Fred. "Give us a kiss for old time's sake... and twenty dollars," and with that he slammed the note on the table.

Barbie looked at the money. Well, she used to kiss him for nothing once. No harm in a kiss. So she gave him a quick peck and scooped up the cash.

Freddie had another drink and began praising Barbie's figure. "You're still in great shape," he said looking at her blouse. "Give us a quick look ... for fifty dollars."

And with that he dropped fifty on the table.

He used to do more than looking once, for nothing, thought Barbie. A quick flash shouldn't hurt anybody. So a quick flash it was, and again she scooped up the money.

To cut a long story short there was a bit more chit-chat and $200 dropped on the table, followed by a quick adjournment to the bedroom.

Indeed it was eleven-thirty when John arrived home that night and Barbie got out of bed to make him a cup of tea.

"Did Freddie call round?" he asked.

Barbie nodded.

"Did he bring my pay?"

*　　*　　*

A PLUMBER one night feeling free
Was plumbing his girl by the sea

*44*

Said the maid, "Quick, stop plumbing,
I fear someone's coming."
Said the plumber, still plumbing, "It's me."

## BOOBS

THE old man was the only other occupant of the train compartment and he looked like a kindly grandfather so the young mother had no qualms about breast-feeding her baby.

"What a lovely child," said the old man. "What do you feed him on?"

"Just milk and orange juice," she said.

The old man thought about this for a moment. "Which one is the orange juice?" he said.

\* \* \*

AFTER three years in a seminary three priests were assigned to parishes in Tottenham. At the railway station the clerk in the ticket box proved to be a buxom young woman with a deep cleavage. It brought the three of them out in a sweat.

"Three tickets to Titterton," stammered the first before retiring in embarrassment.

"Here, I'll have a go," said the second, and approaching the window stuttered: "Three titties to Tockerton."

"You are making a shocking mess of it," said the third, snatching the money and getting a grip on himself. He sternly approached the buxom wench and said: "Three tickets to Tottenham, Miss, and unless you dress more demurely St Finger will point his Peter at you."

\* \* \*

THE two gossips noticed young Mrs Lottzabazooma in the park.

"Is that hussy breast-feeding again, right out in public?"

"It's her right enough," said the other sticky-nose. "And look, the boy's at least 16, and not even her son.

WORRIED about her daughter's cough her mother took her to the doctor who proceeded to examine her chest.

"Big breaths," he said.

"Yeath," she replied. "And I'm only thixteen."

* * *

THE long legged blonde arrived at the wedding in a topless frock.

"You can't come in," declared the verger.

"I've got a divine right," she said.

"Your left's not bad either, but you can't come in this church without a hat."

* * *

A MOUSE dashed up a girl's leg, under her frock and came to rest in the crevice of two ample bosoms.

"You are obviously a Titmouse," she said.

"No I'm not," he replied. "I'm a Mickey Mouse, but I overshot the mark."

* * *

A BUXOM young Miss from Valetta
Loved to parade in a sweater
Three reasons she had
To keep warm was not bad
But the other two reasons were better.

* * *

ON a maiden a man once begat
Fine triplets named Mat, Pat and Tat
It was fun in the breeding
But when came time for feeding
She found she had no tit for Tat.

## BOOKS

"EXCUSE me Miss," he said. "I'm writing a phone book. Could I have your number?"

* * *

THERE'S a new dictionary published for the showbiz

world listing all the actors and actesses. It's called "Who's Whose."

*     *     *

A BLOKE lent me a book on memory training last week. I want to return it, but I can't remember his name.

*     *     *

BY the time a man learns to read women like a book, he's too old to start a library.

*     *     *

HE said to the librarian, "I'd like a book. Something very deep."
   "What about 20,000 Leagues Under the Sea?"

*     *     *

MY wife's preference is chequebooks. Once she starts one she can't put it down until its finished.

*     *     *

"I READ your new book," said the snobbish critic to the author. "Who wrote it for you?"
   "Who read it for you?" he replied.

*     *     *

CRITIC: "What do you consider your best work of fiction?"
   Author: "My last Income Tax Return."

*     *     *

DOOR to door salesman was selling leather bound dictionaries for a mere $5.
   "What's the catch?" asked the householder.
   "Oh, it's got all the words alright, but they are not in alphabetical order."

*     *     *

A BLOKE who was run over by the mobile library began to groan and moan. The librarian jumped out of the vehicle, bent down and said, "SSShhhhh!"

*     *     *

HAVE you noticed how every prominent politician, even former prime ministers, decide to write books when they retire? It would have been better for the country if they had read one.

## BROTHELS

(R)…

"IT'S a business doing pleasure with you," said the hooker accepting her fee.

\* \* \*

THE old chap toddled into the house of ill repute and the madam told him it would cost $100. He was quite surprised. "You're putting me on," he said.

"That will be an extra $10," said the madam.

\* \* \*

THE old bloke made it shakily into the Blue Light Brothel. The receptionist looked him over and noting his age said, "Just a moment, Pops, I had better call the Madam."

After a whispered conference the Madam nodded agreement and said to the old gent, "Sorry love, we think you've had it."

"Oh, then how much do I owe you?" he said reaching for his wallet.

\* \* \*

WHILE playing in the street two young boys noticed that only men were calling at the house with the red light and that after a short conversation which appeared to consist of "$30 for a short time," these men would disappear inside, only to emerge later looking satisfied and contented.

The boys decided to give it a go and pooling their resources they knocked on the door.

"We've only got $3," they said to the madam, "so can we just have a short time?"

The madam took them in, took their money, knocked their heads together, kicked them in the backside and threw them back on to the street.

As the lads got to their feet one said, "Gee, I'm glad we only had three dollars. I couldn't stand thirty dollars' worth of that!"

*　　*　　*

IZZY Cohen had just taken his trousers off and was about to get into bed with Tiger Lil when there was a hell of a commotion downstairs. The cops had raided the house.

He just managed to grab his clothes, climb through the window, slide down the drain pipe and dash into the bar next door where he met his friend Sam.

He related his narrow escape, which had effectively dampened his ardour. "But listen Sam," he said. "As soon as the cops disappear, whip up to the first floor and give Tiger Lil a bang. It's paid for."

## BUSES

CONDUCTOR: "Full fare for the kid, he's five."

Mother: "How could he be five, I've only been married three years!"

Conductor: "Look lady, I take fares, not confessions."

*　　*　　*

A WOMAN rushed into the hardware store and said: "A mousetrap please, and hurry because I have a bus to catch."

"Sorry, lady," said the shop-keeper. "None of the mousetraps we've got are big enough."

*　　*　　*

THE bus was so crowded even the young men couldn't get seats.

*　　*　　*

THE busline has a timetable, but it is against the rules to leave on time. It would upset the entire schedule.

*　　*　　*

THE arrogant bus driver was always telling people where to get off.

THE drunk on the bus told the ticket inspector that he had bought a ticket, but couldn't find it.

"It's okay," said the inspector, "I'm sure you have paid."

"It's not okay at all," insisted the drunk, still searching his pockets. "Without my ticket I don't know where I'm going."

\* \* \*

A COPPER arrested a bloke for smoking on a bus.

"Can't you see that sign which says No Smoking?" said the cop.

"No, and I can't read anyway," said the bloke, who appeared to have three too many.

"What's your name?" demanded the cop, but all he got was a mumbled reply.

"Write it down," said the cop handing him his notebook.

The drunk scribbled something illegible.

"What's that?" said the cop.

"I don't know," said the bloke, "I told you I can't read!"

\* \* \*

PADDY, his wife and their seven kids were waiting at the bus-stop when they were joined by a blind man. When the bus arrived it was almost full and the conductor said only eight could board.

"Okay Teresa," said Paddy to his wife, "you take the kids on board and me and the blind man will walk."

Without giving the blind man an option in the matter Paddy helped his family scramble aboard and the bus took off.

He and the blind man then set off walking down the road and all went well until the constant tap-tap-tap of the blind man's cane began to irritate Paddy.

"Tap-tap-tap, that damned tapping is driving me crazy. Can't you put a bit of rubber on the end of it," he complained irritably.

The blindman was quick to respond. "If you had've

stuck a bit of rubber on your own stick we would be on that bloomin' bus."

# BUSINESS

"HOW'S business?"

"Looking up."

"You mean it's flat on its back."

\* \* \*

"PRICES subject to change, according to customer's attitude."

\* \* \*

AT the board meeting: "All those in favour say Aye. All those against, resign."

\* \* \*

YOUNG Moishe was learning economics and asked his father about the ethics of business.

"Ethics?" repeated his father. "You ask me about ethics? Well, my lovely boy, let me put it this way. A lady comes in and buys a garment for $95 and she pays with a $100 note. She is very excited about the garment and as she leaves with the parcel under her arm I notice she has left her $5 change on the counter.

"Now here my son comes in the big question of ethics. Do I tell my partner or not?"

\* \* \*

AN art critic interviewing the famous contemporary artist asked why he tolerated the sexual escapades of his young wife.

"I would rather a 20% interest in a going concern, than 100% in a bankruptcy," he said.

\* \* \*

PLOTKIN met Rozenbloom on the street and said, "Tell me, Mr Rozenbloom, we bump into each other often on this street, we meet at the synagogue and we meet at the market. So why is it you never ask me how's business?"

"Okay Plotkin. How's business?"

"Oi voi, don't ask!"

* * *

IN a small school in Dublin the teacher told the class she would give 50 pence to whoever could name the holiest man in history.

One hand went up like a shot, that of little Izzie Cohen. "That would be St Patrick, Miss."

Teacher handed over the money and said, "Izzy, how come the only boy to know the answer is Jewish?"

To which Izzy replied, "In my heart of hearts I know it was Moses, but business is business."

* * *

THE landlord of a pub in Carlton was a fanatical Blues supporter and even had a large sign in the bar which read: "No Collingwood supporters served in this pub."

One day a bloke wearing a black and white scarf breasted the bar. "I know you don't serve Collingwood supporters, but I'm desperate for a drink and I'll pay $5 for a pot."

The publican thought this over, then decided to serve the beer.

It was gulped down in one draught.

"Same again," said the Magpie fan, "in fact I'll have two," and he slapped a tenner on the bar.

When he asked for a third the barman said tentatively, "That's another fiver?"

"That's okay," he said, pushing $20 across the bar, "I'll have a couple for the road." When the drinker had gone the publican put up a new sign: "Only Collingwood fans served here."

(N.B. Use your own local football teams and colours.)

* * *

WHEN the wife went on a dirty week-end and her rich lover bought her a fur coat worth $10,000, the problem was, how to bring it home.

After lengthy thought she pawned it. She then told

her husband that while driving to the airport, on the trip to see her mother, a woman had hailed her cab and begged a ride. She said the young woman only had minutes to catch a plane that would take her to a betrothed wedding in Istanbul which would make her rich. She had no money, except a pawn ticket which she insisted should be payment for the ride.

With this tale the wife urged her husband to redeem the ticket for her.

He did so and presented his wife with a pair of binoculars, which were ideal for viewing the new fur coat her husband's secretary was wearing at the races next day.

★　　★　　★

MOISHE had started in the second-hand trade but was now one of the richest businessmen in the city. As his Rolls Royce stopped in front of the Ritz one night an old school mate who had fallen on hard times was waiting for him.

"Hey Moishe, remember me?"

"Eddie Rozenbloom, of course I do. Haven't seen you in years. How's business?"

"Moishe," says Eddie. "I've hit a bad patch. In fact I was wondering if you could let me have five dollars for a bed."

"Sure Eddie. Bring it around in the morning!"

★　　★　　★

TWO Jewish gentlemen were seated together on a plane. They had been in the air for 30 minutes when the younger man asked the other if he had the time.

There was no answer. "Can you tell me the time please?"

Again there was no answer and the younger man detected some kind of deliberate resistance.

The aircraft was on its descent path when the older man quickly looked at his watch and said it was ten past three.

There was silence for a while before the young man said. "Why didn't you tell me the time earlier?"

"Well, you know what it is like on flights. People get talking to each other. We could become friendly, especially when we are both Jewish. I would be obliged to invite you home. I have a lovely daughter and you are a young man, quite handsome. Romance could blossom and before long you could be asking for her hand in marriage. And to put it bluntly, I don't want no son-in-law who hasn't got a watch."

\*     \*     \*

WHEN Abe met Isaac he said: "I hear your store was robbed last night. Lose much?"

Isaac replied: "A little, but it could have been much worse. Yesterday I just marked down the entire stock by 20 per cent."

\*     \*     \*

"SO your opening sale has just closed, what now?"

"So now we open the closing sale."

\*     ☆     \*

HE walked into the pawnbroker's shop in Russell St, Melbourne and asked for the loan of $20. "Where's your collateral?" asked the pawnbroker.

He indicated the Rolls Royce parked out front. "Right there," he said, "and here are the keys and ownership documents."

He got his $20 and was off. Three days later he returned to claim the car with a crisp $20 in his hand. He received the keys and was charged $5 interest.

He was about to leave when curiosity got the better of the pawnbroker. "Pardon me, but why should a man like you need the loan of $20?"

The businessman replied, "Oh I don't really. I'm down from *Sydney* to do some business, and where else can you park a car for a few days for $5?"

(N.B. You can replace 'Melbourne' and 'Sydney' with cities relevant to your situation.)

IT was three in the morning and the worried husband was pacing up and down the bedroom floor to the consternation of his wife who found it very difficult to sleep.

"What's wrong?" she asked.

"I'm sick to death with worry," he said. "We owe a thousand dollars on the mortgage tomorrow and we haven't got a cent," he said.

The wife got out of bed, looked up the phone book and dialed a number. When the bank manager answered, obviously still dazed from a deep sleep she said. "There is no way my husband can pay, so you will be a thousand dollars short tomorrow."

She hung up and said, "Now come to bed and let him worry about it."

* * *

IT was three in the morning when a busker began playing his banjo outside the bedroom window of a wealthy tycoon.

Eventually the window was opened. "What do you think you are doing waking me up in the middle of the night?"

"Listen, mate," said the busker. "I don't tell you how to run your business, so don't tell me how to run mine!"

# C

## CAMELS

ANGUS was delighted to find himself a girl at the pub who appeared to be no drain on the pocket. When he asked could he get her a glass of wine she said no, she didn't drink.

When he asked if she would like a cigarette she said no, she didn't smoke.

"What about a packet of crisps?"

"No, I'm not hungry," she said.

"A game of pool?"

"No, I don't play," she said.

"Then can I take you home?" asked Angus, who was delighted when she said yes.

When they arrived at her house she opened the front door, and there, lying in the hallway was a dead camel.

"Well," said the young woman, "I didn't say I was tidy, did I?"


## CARS
See ACCIDENTS, MOTORING, DRIVERS

WHEN it comes to used cars, it's hard to drive a bargain.

★   ★   ★

USED cars are alright, as far as they go.

SHE was trying to get a new car for her husband, but nobody would swap.

       ★      ★      ★

HE had a stereo system in his car for years. His wife in the front and her mother in the back.

       ★      ★      ★

FRED got behind in his car payments and, in an effort to shame him into paying the hire-purchase company wrote: "What would your neighbours think if we came and repossessed your car?"

He wrote back: "Dear Sirs. I took the matter up with my neighbours and they all reckon it would be a lousy trick."

       ★      ★      ★

"THIS car," said the salesman, "runs so smoothly you can't feel it, so quietly you can't hear it, so perfectly you can't smell it and so fast you can't see it."

Fred considered this for a moment. "Then how the hell do we know it's there?"

       ★      ★      ★

FRED listened to all the motoring advertisements and is now having a terrible time with his car. He bought a carburettor which saved 30% on petrol, an exhaust system which saved 50% on fuel and a set of spark plugs which saved 25%. Now every time he goes for a drive his fuel tank overflows.

       ★      ★      ★

WHEN it comes to petrol consumption some cars perform better than others. "But Fred's car is the best I've ever heard of," said Barney.

He explained: "Fred told me he met a blonde at the pub on Friday night and drove her home, hours and hours away. And he said he went all that way for nothing!"

       ★      ★      ★

FRED phoned the car yard and asked for the dealer who had sold him the car just two days before.

"You said this car had only one owner, a little old lady who drove it to church each Sunday?"

"That's right," said the salesman.

"Well, can I have her address," said Fred. "I have just cleaned out the glove box and there is a bottle of whisky, a packet of condoms and a bikini top she might be looking for."

# CATS

THEIR cat was called Ben Hur.

It had originally been called Ben, until it had kittens.

\* \* \*

THE music professor entered the spinster's home to hear the strains of classical music delicately performed on the piano, but he got the shock of his life when he entered the drawing room and saw that it was a large black tom cat at the keyboard.

"Taught himself," said Miss Haversham proudly.

"That's amazing," said the professor.

"Wrote that particular piece himself, too," she said.

"Astounding," marvelled the prof listening to the chords and nuances of the minuette.

"Marvellous," he said. "Have you had it orchestrated?"

The cat dived out the window and hasn't been seen since.

\* \* \*

WHEN he saw a lovely gold watch as the centrepiece of a window display, set on a velvet cushion with gold chain around it, he decided immediately it was to be the ideal present for his wife's 50th birthday.

"I'd like to buy that watch in the window," he told the shopkeeper.

"It's not for sale," was the reply.

And against the man's pleading to sell him the watch the shopkeeper said, "Look mate, I don't sell watches. I de-sex tomcats."

"Well, what are the watches in the window for?"

"What would you want me to put in the window?" replied the shopkeeper.

* * *

THE youngster ran to his mum crying. "Dad just drowned our cat," he blubbered.

"Maybe he had to do it," she said.

"No he didn't. He promised me I could."

* * *

"STOP pulling the cat's tail, Johnny."

"I'm not. "I'm just holding it. It's the cat that's doing the pulling."

* * *

THE elderly spinster had called the vet because her cat seemed to be off her food. He made a quick examination and pronounced that the cat was pregnant.

"Impossible," said the spinster. "Moggie never goes out. I feed her in here. She has had no contact with stray cats of any kind."

Just then a battered old Ginger Tom wandered out from behind the couch.

"There's the culprit," said the vet.

"Preposterous," said the spinster, "That's Moggie's brother."

* * *

HER tom cat was out every night ranting, wailing and impregnating all the other cats in the neighbourhood. It never spent a night at home.

So she took him to the vet and had him fixed.

Now he is still out every night, acting as a consultant.

* * *

WHEN Paddy's cat died he asked the priest to say requiem mass. "No way. What d'yer think the church is coming to?" said the priest.

Paddy asked the Anglican vicar to bury his cat and got the same response.

The priest met Paddy next day. "Are you still fussing about that cat?" he said.

"Yes," said Paddy. "I even asked the Jewish Rabbi if he would bury him for $500, but he refused too."

The priest's face lit up. "Why didn't you say he was a Catholic cat?" he said.

## CENSUS

A COW-COCKY was filling in the census form. In answer to the question, "Length of residence in Australia," he wrote: "Thirty feet, ten inches, with a verandah front and two sides."

★ ★ ★

THE census taker told the mayor of the little bush town that he was puzzled about the town's population. For the past five years he had been on the job the population was the same, 1,503. "Must be something wrong."

"No," said the mayor. "It's always been 1,503."

"But don't you have babies?"

"Yep," said the mayor, "and everytime we do some bloke has to leave town."

★ ★ ★

A CENSUS official was assisting a farmer's wife to fill in her forms. "How many children have you got?" he asked.

"Six," she replied. "Three sets of twins."

"How very extraordinary," said the census man. "Twins every time."

"Oh no," she said with a blush. "Not every time. Hundreds of times, nothing."

★ ★ ★

SHE told the census taker she had five children, and he was astounded to learn that they were all born two years apart, and all on August 12.

"What's your husband's profession?" he asked.

"Precision grinder," she replied.

YOUNG woman answered the door for the census taker and told him her husband had died five years ago.

The official noted this down, then asked if she had any children.

"Yes, three," she said. "Aged one, two and five."

The official queried this. "Didn't you say your husband was dead?"

"Yes. He is but I'm not!"

*     *     *

CENSUS taker went next door where the woman told him she had four children. "But I am definitely not having any more."

"Why?" said the official.

"Because I read in a magazine that every fifth child born in the world is Chinese."

# CHOOKS

CHOOKS are the only things you can eat before they are born and after they are dead.

*     *     *

WAITER: "Those are the best eggs we've had for years."

Diner: "Well, bring me some you haven't had for so long."

*     *     *

PADDY crept around the back of the country parish presbytery and stole one of the priest's chooks, then promptly went to confession.

"I stole a chook, father," he began. "I know it was wrong and I am sorry. Can I give it to you for penance?"

"Certainly not," said the priest. "Return it to the person you stole it from."

"I've offered it to him, but he says he doesn't want it," said Paddy.

"In that case you might as well keep it and say ten Hail Marys," said the priest.

THE young wife wanted to impress her husband that she was a good cook, so she rang him to ask if he could bring home a live chicken.

He bought the chook at the market and then realised his car was being serviced and would not be available for another two hours.

He decided to pass the time by going to a movie, and hid the chook by stuffing it down the front of his trousers.

Once in the theatre he became absorbed in the movie and was oblivious to the fact that the chook had stuck its head out of his fly.

Two women were sitting next to him and one nudged the other. "You should see what's sticking out of this bloke's pants."

Her friend was blase, "Seen one, seen 'em all", she said, not bothering to take her eyes off the screen.

"Yeah, but this one is eating my pop corn!"

\* \* \*

FEELING guilty about running over what appeared to be a prize rooster, the travelling salesman stopped his car and approached the nearby farmhouse and knocked on the door.

He told the farmer's wife he would like to replace it.

"Please yourself, luv," she said. "The chooks are around the back!"

\* \* \*

"TWO of our chooks have stopped layin'," said the farmer to his wife.

"How do yer know?"

"Cos I just run over them with the tractor."

\* \* \*

SHE was stocking up for her hobby farm and ordered a dozen chooks, and a dozen roosters.

"Madam, you only need one rooster," he pointed out.

She gave him a stern look. "Evidently you don't know what it is like to be overlooked."

A FARMER was having his lunch on the front porch when a squawking chicken dashed around the corner with a rooster in hot pursuit. As the chooks dashed down the porch a few crumbs of bread fell from the farmer's sandwich and the rooster stopped to gobble them up while the hen got away.

"Strewth!" exclaimed the farmer, "I hope I never get that hungry."

* * *

WHEN the shire president arrived at the country town all the neighbouring chooks gathered in the main street. They heard he was to lay a foundation stone and they didn't want to miss it.

* * *

THE local vet was in the middle of a complicated operation when the phone rang. It was Farmer Brown's wife who wanted to know how long she should leave a rooster with her chooks.

"Just a minute," said the vet turning back to his operation. The woman thanked him and hung up.

* * *

THE old rooster had been king of the chook house for years and he intended to keep it that way, so when yet another young cock was tossed into the yard by Farmer Brown it was time for some quick negotiation.

"There are 40 hens here, buster, and I am not going to fight you for them. We will need all our strength. So let's decide it with a race. Three times around the perimeter of the yard gets the lot."

The young rooster looked at the stringy old geezer. "I don't think you could make it twice around, Pops."

"Then give me a start," said the old rooster and he was off and running with a three metre break. The old farmer was sitting on his porch when the roosters came in sight; the old one in front desperately hanging on to his lead, the young one flat-out and gaining slowly.

The farmer reached for his shotgun, took aim and shot the young rooster dead.

"Y'know, Martha," he said to his wife, "it's funny, but that's the third queer rooster I have had to shoot this month!"

## CHRISTMAS

GO to church this Sunday and avoid the Christmas rush.

      ★    ★    ★

A COUPLE of fattened turkeys were chatting in the chook house.

"Tell me, Cyril," said one, "do you believe in Santa Claus?"

      ★    ★    ★

ONLY 25 shoplifting days to Christmas!

      ★    ★    ★

WHY wasn't Christ born in Australia?

Well, where would you find three wise men, or a virgin?

      ★    ★    ★

ACTUALLY there were four wise men. On the way to Bethlehem one of them said he knew a short cut.

      ★    ★    ★

THE rich kid kept pestering his father that he wanted a Mickey Mouse outfit for Christmas.

So his old man bought him the NSW State Cabinet.

(N.B. Change 'NSW State Cabinet' to any political institution in the news.)

      ★    ★    ★

DON'T give me a watch for Christmas. I've already got one. And I can assure you a man with one watch knows what time it is, while a man with two watches would never be sure.

      ★    ★    ★

IN the department store at Christmas the little boy had been waiting patiently in the queue to meet Santa. When his turn came Santa picked him up, sat him on his knee and said: "Ho, ho, ho, little boy. And what would you like for Christmas?"

The little tyke jumped down and kicked Santa fair in the shins. "I just told you yesterday you silly old goat."

\* \* \*

THE kid said: "What's Christmas, Dad?"

So Dad took him to a department store where he met Santa Claus and saw the toy department. "That's Christmas, son!"

Little Isaac said to his father, Moishe, "What's Christmas, Dad?"

Moishe took the lad to a vast and empty warehouse. "That's Christmas, son!"

# CLAIRVOYANTS
## (AND THINGS SUPERNATURAL)

THE annual general meeting of the Clairvoyants' Society is postponed, due to unforeseen circumstances?

\* \* \*

DURING World War Two, Adolph Hitler consulted his clairvoyant to find out how long he would live and on what day he would die.

The clairvoyant looked into the crystal ball and said "Mein Fuhrer, I have a vision that you will die on a Jewish holiday."

Hitler flew into a rage. "Which Jewish holiday?" he screamed.

"Mein Fuhrer, any day you die will be a Jewish holiday."

\* \* \*

A MAN visited the fortune teller at the circus and sat down in front of her crystal ball. He was a sceptic.

"I see you are the father of two children," she began.

"Ha! That's what you think," replied the man, "I'm the father of three children."

"That's what you think," smiled the fortune teller.

FRED sat silently while she looked into the crystal ball. Suddenly she threw her head back and began roaring with laughter. She shook with mirth until Fred leaned across and punched her in the nose.

It was the first time he had struck a happy medium.

\* \* \*

"WHY do you call your father-in-law the Exorcist?"

"Because every visit he rids our house of spirits."

\* \* \*

THE two drunks at the bar were having a philosophical discussion on reincarnation.

"And how long have you believed in reincarnation?" said one.

"Ever since I was a frog," said the other.

\* \* \*

THE Olde English Pub was called the Black Cat. Legend had it that it was named after the favourite moggy of the first innkeeper on that site. The cat had met its death when a runaway stage coach had run over it, cutting off its tail.

And for the past two hundred years its ghost appeared each time the pub changed hands.

Thus it was that the new licencee, up late cooking the books, was confronted by the ghostly apparition of the cat, carrying its tail in its paw.

"My soul won't rest until my tail is restored," moaned the ghost. "Can you help me?"

The publican put down his pen. "I'm afraid it can't be done," he said, "I am not allowed to retail spirits after ten-thirty."

## CLUBS

IT was Groucho Marx who declared: "Any club which would admit me as a member isn't worth joining."

\* \* \*

THE club president was delivering his annual report and

66

was praising the committee. "Unlike other clubs where half the committee does all the work and the other half are hopeless, here, it is completely the reverse!"

\* \* \*

HE heard the club was looking for a treasurer.

"But didn't they take on a new treasurer just a month ago?"

"Yes. That's the one they are looking for!"

\* \* \*

"I SAY, old chap, who is Fonsonby talking to?"

"He is talking to himself."

"Then why is he shouting?"

"He's deaf!"

\* \* \*

THE oldtimers were lamenting that the club had gone to the pack. "Noisy lot, all on the make," said one. "All corduroy trousers, thin moustaches and crew-cut hair. And the women are just as bad."

\* \* \*

THE doorman to the swank club saw a limousine stop at the kerb. In his haste to get out and open the door he tripped on the step and went head-first into the gutter.

The manager rushed out and picked him up. "That's enough of that, James. People will think you're a member."

\* \* \*

WHEN Sam walked into his poker club it caused a snigger among his mates at the bar. "Boy, the joke was on you last night, Sam," they said. "You left your bedroom light on and the blind was up. You put on a great show with your missus."

"Well, the joke happens to be on you lot," Sam retorted. "I wasn't home last night!"

## CONMEN

HE took a young lady home to his flat, offered her a Scotch and sofa, and she reclined.

THE judge fixed him with a beady eye: "How could you take money from people who trusted you?"

"Because it just doesn't work with people who don't trust you," the conman replied.

\* \* \*

"GOOD Evening," said the barman. "What's your pleasure?"

"A Scotch and a box of matches," said Con.

He sinks the drink and puts ten cents on the counter, explaining that the money is for the matches. "I didn't really want a drink, but when you invited me so nicely, well..."

The barman said he was only being polite and when Con refuses to pay he is ordered out and barred from the pub.

A week later Con returns and the barman shouts: "Hey you. I told you last week you were barred from this hotel."

"I've never been here before," said Con. "You must have me mixed up with somebody else."

"Then you must have a double," said the barman.

"Thanks," said Con, "and a box of matches."

\* \* \*

AS Con walked into the pub he asked his friend: "What's your great ambition in life?"

"To own a pub," said his mate. "What's yours?"

"A double brandy, thanks," said Con.

\* \* \*

TWO conmen in an English pub called the publican over and asked him to settle an argument. "Are there two pints in a quart, or four?" asked one.

"There are two pints in a quart," confirmed the publican.

They moved back along the bar to where they had been drinking and soon the barmaid asked for their order.

"Two pints please Miss, and they are on the house."

When the barmaid appeared to doubt her boss would dispense free beer, one of the lads called out to the publican at the other end of the bar: "You did say two pints, didn't you?"

"That's right," shouted the publican. "Two pints."

★   ★   ★

THE blind man had his hand out. "Can you spare a dollar?"

She looked at him suspiciously. "Why, I'm sure you can see out of one eye."

"Well, fifty cents then?"

★   ★   ★

SHE stopped at the next blind man and dropped all her small change into his cup with a clunk.

"God bless you lady," he said. "I knew you was kind hearted the moment I saw you turn the corner."

★   ★   ★

SHE intended the 50-cent piece to drop into his hat, but she missed and it clinked on to the pavement. In a swift movement the blindman scooped it up.

"How did you see that?" she said. "I thought you were blind."

"No, I'm not blind," he said. "It's my mate that's blind, and I am filling in for him while he's at the movies."

★   ★   ★

HE was propped up against *Young & Jacksons* on crutches with his head bandaged and one arm in a sling. In the other hand he held his hat outstretched.

"You poor man," she said, dropping a fiver in the hat. "But think how much worse it would be if you were blind."

"You're dead right, lady" he said. "When I was blind I kept getting foreign coins."

★   ★   ★

WHILE leaning on the bar, Ron the Con said, "D'yer want to buy a watch, Fred?"

"Let's see it," said Fred.

"Shh," said Ron, "the bloke next to you is wearing it."

\* \* \*

THE gangling lad from the bush was amazed to learn that his new friend, Larry the Lounge Lizard was 100 years old.

"I'm surprised. You look very healthy," said the lad.

Old Larry gritted his teeth bravely, "Trouble is," he said, pushing his glass forward, "thirst doesn't show on the outside."

\* \* \*

BACK on the farm from his first visit to the city, Dave proudly showed the family a large, sparkling diamond ring.

"Is it the real thing?" they gasped in amazement.

"It had better be," mumbled Dave, "otherwise I've been done out of a tenner."

\* \* \*

RON the Con walked into the pub and ordered a pie and sauce. As it was served to him he told the barman he had changed his mind. He pushed the pie back and said he would have a beer instead.

When it came to payment Ron said he owed nothing. He had swapped the pie for the beer.

"But you didn't pay for the pie," argued the barman.

"And I didn't eat the pie. You've still got it," said Ron.

A little bamboozled, the barman said, "Here is a dollar. Go over the road to the pub opposite and pull the same stunt."

Ron pocketed the money. As he reached the door he said, "I might as well tell you. The publican over the road gave me $2 to pull the same stunt here."

\* \* \*

THEY had dined well and after the wine Con reminded Ron it was his turn to take care of the bill. Ron called the manager and asked for an interview in his office.

"We have been doing a survey on the prevalence of those people who order large meals and then declare they have no money. What do you do?"

The manager said there was nothing much that could be done. "It only means notoriety, bad publicity and costly litigation if we prosecute. We usually bring them into this office and give them a good kick in the backside."

Ron bent over and said: "In that case can you take for two?"

*     *     *

AS the train left the station the conman sized up the old prospector sitting opposite. When they got to talking the conman proposed they play a game to pass the time.

"What kind of game?"

"General knowledge quiz. You look like a man of the world," said the conman. "We each ask the other a question, and if one can't answer he pays the other a dollar."

The old geezer thought this over for a minute. "Yeah, I like a quiz. But I don't like the even money bit."

"What do you mean?"

"Well, I've spent most of my life in the bush. I'm just a simple man, whereas you look like a city-slicker to me. So I suggest that if you can't answer my questions, then it costs you a dollar, but if I can't answer yours, then you should let me off with 50 cents."

The conman was sure he was on a winner. "Okay, I pay 50 cents to your dollar."

"Then here's the first question," said the old geezer. "What's got five legs and flies backwards?"

"Don't know," said the conman slapping down a dollar.

"My question now, and I'm interested to know exactly what does have five legs and flies backwards?"

"Blowed if I know. Here's your 50 cents," said the old man.

# CONUNDRUMS

IF you weigh a whale at a weigh-weigh station, where do you weigh a pie? Somewhere over the rainbow, weigh up pie!

\* \* \*

FRED was a keen one for conundrums, so when the barman presented one he listened intently.

The barman said: "My mother had a child. It wasn't my brother and it wasn't my sister. Who was it?"

Fred scratched his head and admitted he was beat.

"It was me," declared the barman triumphantly.

Fred thought it was a good one and couldn't wait to relate it to his wife. In fact he woke her up to tell it.

"My mother had a child. It wasn't my brother and it wasn't my sister. Who was it?"

His sleepy wife said she didn't have a clue.

"Easy," said Fred. "It was Harry the barman down at the pub."

\* \* \*

"WHAT'S the difference between a tram and a taxi?" he said.

"I give in, I don't know," she said.

"Good, then we'll take the tram."

\* \* \*

WHAT did Mrs Quasimodo give Quasi for Christmas?

A Wok! She thought it would help her iron his shirts.

# COURTING
## See ENGAGEMENTS

"I DON'T believe we've met. I'm Mr Right."

\* \* \*

"I AM writing a phone book. Could I have your number Miss?"

"LET'S get married, or something."

"Let's get married, or nothing."

* * *

OUT on her first date her mother's words were ringing in her ears: "Say no to everything he suggests."

So after dinner and a couple of drinks he said: "Do you mind if we fool around in bed?"

* * *

IT was their second date and after a few drinks in the cocktail lounge he thought the time was right. He leaned over and whispered in her ear, "How about coming away with me for the week-end to a little cabin I have in the snow?"

She replied: "I suspect my anticipation of your proclivities in the esoteric aspects of sexual behaviour preclude such an erotic confrontation."

He scratched his head, "I don't get it."

"Exactly," she replied.

* * *

"I WILL go to the end of the world for you," he said.

"Yes, but will you stay there," she yawned.

* * *

HE said it was love at first sight.

Then why didn't he marry her?

Because he took a second look.

* * *

FRED'S been turned down so many times he is like the hot page in a naughty novel.

* * *

"I'VE heard plenty about your love-making."

* * *

"AM I the first man you've ever made love to, dearest?" he asked.

She studied him for a moment. "You could be," she said, "there is something familiar about your face."

* * *

THE ardent suitor was urging his girlfriend to live with

him. "It will be exactly like the real thing only we won't have the expense of getting married. And then if we find later that we have made a mistake, then we won't have the cost of the divorce."

"Yes," she said. "But what do we do with the mistake?"

*     *     *

HE had been watching the blonde at the other end of the bar for some time before he got sufficient courage to approach her.

"Would you like a Harvey Wallbanger?" he asked.

"Love one," she said. "But let's have a drink first."

*     *     *

HE snuggled up to her and said: "I'm yours for the asking."

She snuggled back and said: "I'm asking fifty bucks!"

*     *     *

IT was love at first sight and they had taken the big step and slept together for the first time. They were still in bed when the phone rang next morning.

He reached out and picked up the receiver, listened for a moment, then gave her a shake.

"It's for a Miss Sheila Kelly," he said. "Is that you?"

*     *     *

THE stern father took the lad aside when he had brought his daughter home. "I'd like a word," he said.

"If you are going to see our Ethel regularly I hope you know the difference between right and wrong."

The young man gulped. "But surely you yourself have brought her up to know what's right?"

"Indeed we have," said the father.

"Well, I've taken care of the other side, so everything's fine."

*     *     *

WHEN Myrtle finally brought a bloke home her parents were relieved that this might be the Mr Right that would take her off their hands. But when they took a closer look they took Myrtle aside.

"He's not exactly a young man," whispered Mum to her daughter. "He's fat, he's bald and he's pretty old isn't he?"

"There's no need to whisper, Mum," said Myrtle, "he's stone deaf too."

## CROCODILES

PADDY O'Reilly was walking up High St with a crocodile on a lead when a concerned policeman stopped him.

"Where are you going with that beast?" asked the cop.

"I am taking him to the zoo," replied Paddy, which satisfied the cop.

Next day the same cop saw the same Paddy with the same crocodile on the same lead.

"I thought you were taking that thing to the zoo?" said the cop.

"Aye, I did, and he liked it. Today I'm taking him to the pictures."

★ ★ ★

PADDY took his crocodile into a pub and said: "Do you serve Catholics?"

The barman said he did.

"Well, Oi'l be having a pot of stout, and two catholics for my crocodile!"

★ ★ ★

TARZAN was coming home after a hard day's work and turned the bend in the river just in time to see a crocodile taking one of his kids.

He rushed in and told Jane, but she was more intent on taking Tarzan to bed. "Don't worry about it," she said. "We've got plenty of kids. Let's go to bed and make another one."

The following evening after a hard day's work Tarzan staggered home just in time to see a crocodile taking another kid.

"Oh, don't worry," said Jane. "Come to bed and we'll make another one."

"Listen," said an angry Tarzan, "I'm not working all day and making love all night just to feed the damned crocodiles!"

## CRICKET

IT was the club's social dance and the young debutante had trouble dancing with her awkward partner.

"Sorry," he said, "I'm a little stiff from bowling."

"I don't care where you come from," she said, "just keep off my feet."

⋆     ⋆     ⋆

FRED'S wife rang the cricket club.

"Sorry, he has just walked to the crease. He is about to bat. Shall I ask him to ring you back?"

"No. I'll hang on," she said.

⋆     ⋆     ⋆

THE club's best batsman was on the phone to his captain trying to explain why he couldn't play next day.

"No, I can't let you off the game," said the captain who was made of stern stuff. "If I did, then I would have to do the same for any other player whose wife dies."

⋆     ⋆     ⋆

THE famous test player began his career with the Werribbee Wanderers so the social committee sent him a telegram asking if he would make a guest appearance for $100.

The cricketer sent back a telegram: "Will accept, but double the offer or count me out."

The committee's immediate reply was: "1, 2, 3, 4, 5, 6, 7, 8, 9, 10."

⋆     ⋆     ⋆

EVENTUALLY they got Allan Border as guest player at the Werribbee Wanderers testimonial fund raiser and indeed there was a large crowd at the ground.

Ned, the club's fast bowler, had never faced a test cricketer before and he felt the tension as he hurled down his first ball.

To Ned's surprise the off stump went flying. Clean bowled. "No ball," roared the umpire, and then took Ned aside. "Slow down you idiot. They've come to see Border bat, not you bowl."

* * *

TWO fans settled down at the MCG when one realised he had left his wallet in his mate's Mercedes. He returned from the car park 15 minutes later, pale and shaken.

"I've got bad news, Bob. A truck has crashed into your car and the impact set it on fire. It's totally destroyed."

"And have I got some bad news for you," said Bob to his mate. "Border is out for a duck."

* * *

FRED's wife snuggled up beside him in bed and whispered: "Remember the Saturday you proposed to me. My word you were bold then."

"No way," said Fred. "I was caught."

* * *

"SO, you had a hard time trying to explain the test match to your wife?"

"Yes, especially when she found out I wasn't there."

* * *

THE cricketer was getting a medical. "I dunno, Doc," he said. "My fielding is very bad lately. I can't bowl like I used to and everytime I go in to bat I get a duck lately."

"Why don't you try some other sport?" said the doctor.

"I can't," he said. "I'm captain of the Australian Eleven."

* * *

THE cricket fan was trying to interest his girlfriend in the game and took her to the Saturday match.

Pointing out a promising batsman he said, "It won't be long before that bloke will be our best man."

"Oh Frederick," she gushed, "this is so sudden."

77

THE visiting church team was surprised to see no scoring facilities at the sports ground. "Don't worry about that," said the bush captain, a well-muscled shearer, "we keep the scores in our heads, and if there is any dispute we settle the argument behind the shearing shed after the game."

* * *

"THAT was very sporting of you to cheer our team for winning the match," said the church captain to the Patchywollock host. "By the way, where's the umpire?"

"He's in the dam," was the reply.

* * *

THE Devil challenged St Peter to a cricket match. "Remember," said St Peter, "we have all the good cricketers up here." "Yes," said the Devil, "but we've got all the umpires down here."

* * *

THEY take their cricket seriously in the bush. A stranger at the Patchywollock v. Wonga Creek game was cheering the batsman's play and at the same time applauding the bowler and fieldsmen.

This bothered one local shearer.

"Do you come from Patchywollock?"

"No," said the stranger.

"From Wonga Creek then?"

"No," said the stranger.

"Well in that case mind you own bloody business and keep your trap shut."

* * *

THE batsman was describing his big hit.

"I gave it everything I had. The ball went into the sky and hit a passing duck."

"Hit a duck? Was it wild?"

"It was ruddy-well livid."

* * *

THE boys were playing cricket in the backyard with a shiny new ball. It attracted the interest of their father.

"Where did you get the ball?" he asked.

"We found it," chorused the kids.

"Are you sure it was lost?"

"Of course it was lost. We watched them looking for it."

*　　*　　*

THE bush town's cricket match was stopped when the ball was hit clear over the fence. While players from both sides searched in the long grass they were watched by an idle lad sitting against the fence.

"Did you see a cricket ball come over?" one of the cricketers asked him.

"No I didn't," said the lad, "but I have brought this fairly new one from home that I could sell you."

*　　*　　*

FRED was always bragging. "I walked out of the Gabba last Saturday," he said, "and a crowd of 30 or more clamoured around me for my autograph."

"Come off it, Fred."

"Fair dinkum. If you don't believe me, ask Allan Border. He was standing right beside me."

*　　*　　*

FRED was trying to join the local team.

"Have you had any experience?" asked the captain.

"Well, I think I once played with Don Bradman."

"Really?"

"Yes," said Fred, "he told me after the game who he was. He said if I was a batsman, he was Don Bradman."

*　　*　　*

THERE is a man in Wycheproof who has devised a game that in some aspects is similar to cricket.

What he doesn't know, is that the Australian Eleven has been playing it for years.

*　　*　　*

TWO old boys were bragging in the bar at Lords.

"What was your highest score," said one.

"One hundred and fifty," said the other.

"Well, mine was one hundred and fifty-five," said the first smuggly. "And what was the highest number of wickets you got?" he continued.

"Oh no. You go first this time."

\* \* \*

NED was building up record averages as the club's fast bowler, but he was a little worried when he learned that his father-in-law was to umpire the day's match.

Ned hurled the first ball down at terrific pace and caught the batsman LBW.

"Owzat!" he yelled.

"Not out," said the umpire.

The second ball came down like a missile, snicked the bat and was caught by the wicket-keeper.

"Owzat!" roared Ned.

"Not out," said the umpire.

With the wildest fury he could muster the third ball screamed down the wicket, hit the middle stump and snapped it in half, sending wickets and bails in the air.

"Ruddy-well nearly got him that time," said Ned.

\* \* \*

AFTER a series of bad decisions from the umpire, Ned approached him and said: "If I called you a stupid old goat who didn't know the first thing about cricket what would you do?"

"I would report you and you would be fined," said the umpire.

"What if I didn't say it, and just thought it?"

"Well, nothing could be done about it."

"Okay," said Ned, "then we'll just leave it at that, then, eh?"

\* \* \*

ON the train Fred couldn't keep his eyes off the old codger sitting in the opposite corner with one of his boots glued to his ear. He was listening with intense concentration.

Fred's curiosity finally got the better of him. He leaned across and said: "What's going on?"

The old man motioned him to be silent and continued listening until Fred pulled the boot away and asked again.

"If you must know," grunted the old man, "I'm listening to the test match."

"Here, give me a go," said Fred snatching the boot and putting it to his ear.

He listened for a while. "I can't hear a thing," he said.

"No, and you won't either," grinned the old man. "They just stopped for tea."

*　　*　　*

THE big shearer's cook was batting in the annual bush grudge match and had survived three appeals for obvious LBW.

The next delivery hit the middle stump and sent the bails flying.

"Owzat?" they roared.

"Not out," said the umpire.

"What kind of a damned decision is that?" cried the bowler. "He's been out four times already."

The umpire was adamant. "I say he stays. We've only got a nine-gallon keg and he's the best guzzler in the whole district"

*　　*　　*

AN expectant father rang the hospital to see how his wife was progressing. By mistake he was connected to the cricket ground.

"How's it going?" he asked.

"Going well," came the answer. "We've got three out and hope to get the rest out before lunch. The last one was a duck!"

## CRICKET INSULTS

"WHY are you looking so down-hearted?"

"The doctor says I can't play cricket."

"When did he see you play?"

* * *

CAPTAIN: "It's a pity you didn't take up the game sooner."

"You mean I'd be better now?"

"No, you would have given the game up long ago."

* * *

OUT for a duck the angry batsman marched into the pavilion and said, "I've never played so badly before."

The captain appeared surprised: "You mean, you've played before?"

* * *

"THAT was the best innings I've ever played."

"Well, you mustn't let that discourage you."

* * *

"ARE your team members good losers?"

"Good? They're perfect!"

## CRIMINALS

THE prisoner said to the social worker: "Women have been my downfall."

"What kind of women?"

"Those who carry handbags."

* * *

HE said his Dad gave him three words of advice on being financially solvent.

"What were they?"

"Stick 'em up!"

* * *

A TRAVELLER was walking down a dark street one night when he was stopped by a tramp who said: "Excuse me, Guv. Would you be so kind as to help a poor unfortunate who is hungry and out of work, with no money and no worldly possessions, except for this sawn off shot gun...!"

\* \* \*

THEY were walking arm in arm down High St when she saw a diamond ring in the showcase window. "Oh, it's lovely," she said.

So he heaved a brick through the glass and grabbed it.

A little further on she saw a fur coat on display and implored him to get it for her.

He heaved another brick through the window and snatched it.

Around the corner she stopped at the show window which featured a beautiful Jaguar sports car. "Oh, I'd love that," she said.

"Enough, Myrtle," he said. "Do you think I'm made of bricks?"

## CUSTOMS AGENTS

CUSTOMS officer was inspecting a sweet young thing's suitcase and discovered six pair of French knickers. "What are these for?" he asked.

"Sunday, Monday, Tuesday, Wednesday, Thursday and Friday," she replied.

"And what about Saturday?" he asked.

She replied with a smile and a wink and minced by.

Next was a big German frau who flung her suitcase onto the counter.

"And what are these for?" said the customs officer discovering 12 pair of thick flannel bloomers.

She replied: "January, February, March, April.........."

\* \* \*

CUSTOMS officer at the airport asked Paddy if he had anything to declare.

"No, only this bottle of holy water from Lourdes."

The officer was interested and asked to see it. When

Paddy produced it the officer removed the cork and put his nose to the bottle.

"That's not water," he said grimly. "That's whisky."

"Mother of God!" exclaimed Paddy, "It's another bloomin' miracle!"

* ⋆ ⋆

A MARRIED couple, Freda and Fred, had been successfully smuggling native birds out of Australia to the United States for years.

Freda suggested they could double their earnings by smuggling some American wildlife on the return trips.

"For example," she said. "I've got a squirrel here and I am going to hide it by stuffing it down the front of my pants."

"And this is for you, Fred," she said, handing him a skunk. "That will bring big money in Australia. Stuff it down the front of your trousers."

Fred protested: "What about the smell?"

Freda shrugged her shoulders. "If it dies ... it dies."

# D

## DANCING

DANCING is the perpendicular expression of horizontal desire.

*     *     *

"I DON'T dance, but I'd love to hold you while you do."

*     *     *

DANCING is a physical contact sport.

*     *     *

DON'T miss our next show. Six dancing girls and five beautiful costumes.

*     *     *

"COULD I have the last dance?"
  "You've just had it."

*     *     *

HE: "Doesn't this dance make you long for another?"
  She: "Yes, but he couldn't come tonight."

*     *     *

A GIRL is something you look damned silly dancing without.

*     *     *

THE clergyman had delivered a fiery sermon against the evils of dancing and made it clear that he was opposed to any kind of dancing. After the congregation had filed out he was approached by a young dancing enthusiast. "Just what's wrong with dancing?" he asked.

"Well, for one thing," said the minister, "it's the close touching of the bodies."

"Not so," protested the parishioner, "it is all in the mind of those who look at it with the wrong attitude."

"Then let's suppose," argued the minister, "that you came home from work and found me holding your wife in that manner. What would you think?"

"I'd think that you'd better be dancing," was the reply.

\* \* \*

AT a country dance a young couple were pressed together, dancing cheek to cheek. She whispered in his ear, "Come out to the car."

He declined, saying the tune being played was one of his favourite numbers, but she persisted and pleaded for him to come out to the car.

He finally agreed. When they left the hall it was pitch black outside so he produced a torch from his pocket to light the way to the car.

She said: "Did you have that torch in your pocket all night?"

"Yes," he said.

"Well let's go back to the dance," she said.

\* \* \*

FRED was asked how he got his black eye.

"I was teaching my girlfriend the tango when her father came in. How was I to know he was stone deaf?"

\* \* \*

THE debutante at the country ball
  Knows that pride goes before a fall
  So when she trips the light fantastic
  She always wears good strong elastic.

# DEATH
## See FUNERALS

DEATH is nature's way of telling you to slow down.

"SO Old Smithy is dead. Did he leave his wife much?"
   "Nearly every night."

* * *

"WHAT's the death rate around here?"
   "Same as any place. One death per person."

* * *

AS Woody Allen said: "It is not that I'm afraid to die. I just don't want to be around when it happens."

* * *

WHILE on holiday, Fred bought the local paper, and browsing through the death notices he was intrigued to see that everyone had died in alphabetical order.

* * *

HE died a natural death. He was hit by a car.

* * *

"DOC, I'm afraid I'm going to die."
   "Nonsense! That's the last thing you'll do."

* * *

THE clock and watchmaker millionaire died recently. They reckon it will take years to wind up his estate.

* * *

"HEY Mum, how did Dad know the exact date he was going to die?"
   "The judge told him."

* * *

THE relatives gathered around to hear the solicitor read Fred's short will:
   "Being of sound mind I spent the lot before I carked it."

* * *

SHE was complaining to her neighbour. She had made constant trips to the city, three times to the insurance office, twice to the probate office, hundreds of papers and documents to sort through. "I sometimes wish Fred hadn't died," she said.

SHE was ebbing fast and she raised herself on one elbow and beckoned her John to come closer. "On the day of the funeral," she gasped, "it would please me if you would ride in the same coach as mother."

"Okay" he said grudgingly, "but you know it will completely spoil my day."

*     *     *

OLD Jake was on his death bed. He raised himself on one elbow and beckoned his wife closer.

"Emily," he gasped. "You were with me through the Great Depression."

She nodded.

"Emily, you were with me through the worst droughts in the fifties."

She nodded.

"And you were with me when we lost the farm in the bush fires. Now here you are again, by my side when I'm about to cark it."

She nodded.

"You know Emily," he said, "I'm beginning to think you've been bringing me bad luck."

*     *     *

DYING at sea can have its complications. The captain informed the first mate that the passenger in Cabin 25 had died and ordered him to arrange for a burial at sea.

An hour later the mate came onto the bridge and reported that the matter relating to Cabin 27 had been attended to.

"What," said the captain aghast. "I said Cabin 25. Didn't the man tell you he wasn't dead?"

"Yes, Cap'n," said the mate, "but he was a Pommie and you know what lying bastards they are."

*     *     *

HERE snug in her grave
    My wife do lie

Now she's at rest
And so am I.

*    *    *

UNDERNEATH this pile of stones
Lies the remains of Harry Jones
His name was Smith
It was not Jones
But Jones was put
To rhyme with stones.

# DEFINITIONS

AUTOMATIC SHIFT: When the driver moves closer to his girlfriend.

AUTOBIOGRAPHY: The car's logbook.

APEX: The female of the gorilla species.

ADVERTISEMENT: Something that makes you think you've longed for it for years, but never heard of it before.

ALIMONY: A mistake by two people paid for by one.

ABSENTEE: A missing golfing accessory.

ANTI-FREEZE: When you don't talk to your uncle's wife.

ADAMANT: The very first insect.

ADIEU: Hymie Finklestein.

ADORN: What comes after the darkest hour.

AROMATIC: An automatic longbow.

ARTFUL: A painting exhibition.

AWE-STRUCK: Being hit with a paddle.

AVAIL: Helpful for ugly women.

ALPHABET: Not quite the complete wager.

ABUNDANCE: A local hop usually staged in a barn.

ACME: Pimples on the face running towards the top.

BURLESQUE SHOW: Where attendance falls off if nothing else does.

BADMINTON: The reason the lamb tasted off.

BORN EXECUTIVE: A bloke whose father owns the company.

BRAZIER: Something to warm your hands on.

BALANCE: Something you lose if the bank pushes you.

BARBARIAN: The man who cuts your hair.

BOOKCASE: Litigation about a novel which ensures wide sales.

BRUSSELS SPROUTS: A world famous statue found in that city.

BOXER: A bloke who stands up for the other fellow's rights.

CLIMATE: The best thing to do with a ladder.

CONDESCENDING: A Greek parachutist.

CONSCIENCE: The thing that aches when everything else feels good.

COWARD: A man who thinks with his legs.

CABBAGE: The fare you pay a taxi driver.

DETEST: The West Indies playing India (cricket).

ELECTRICIAN: A switch doctor.

FASTIDIOUS: A girl who is fast and hideous.

FAUCET: What you have to do if the tap won't turn.

FETE: A boring picnic worse than death.

FLOOSIE: A sweet girl with the gift of the grab.

GRANARY: A home for senior female citizens.

GALLERY: A hostel for young women.

HUMBUG: A singing cockroach.

HYACINTH: A yank greeting a gal called Cynthia.

IDOLISE: Eyes that refuse to look at anything.

INCOME: What you have to make first, because you can't make it last.

JEALOUSY: The friendship one woman shares with another.

LACTIC: A grandfather clock which doesn't work.

MONOLOGUE: A discussion between man and wife.

MARCONI: The first man to send a message through a length of spaghetti without it touching the sides.

NONDESCRIPT: A television play.

ODIOUS: Not very good poetry.

PARENTS: Couples who practise the Rhythm Method.

PEDESTRIAN: A motorist with teenage sons.

RACIAL DISPUTE: When the course judge calls for a photo.

REFLECTION: What a girl looks at, but is not given to.

SAGE: A bloke who knows his onions.

STALEMATE: A husband who has lost his ardour.

SNUFF: Sufficient unto the day.

SONATA: A song sung by Frank.

# DENTISTS

A MAN and his wife rushed into the dentist's surgery and offered double the going rate if he would pull a tooth immediately.

"We are in a hurry to get to the airport," explained the husband. "We are running late and there is not time for that anaesthetic stuff. Just rip it out."

The dentist said it would be painful.

"To hell with the pain. Just rip it out," he insisted.

"Very well," said the dentist. "You certainly have courage. Now which tooth is it?"

The man turned to his wife. "Hop up into the chair, Myrtle and show him."

\* \* \*

"GOOD grief, you've got the biggest cavity I've ever seen," said the dentist. "You've got the biggest cavity I've ever seen."

"Okay," said the patient, "you don't have to repeat it."

"I didn't" said the dentist, "that was the echo!"

\* \* \*

SHE thought the Tooth Fairy was a Gay Dentist.

\* \* \*

"I DON'T know which is worse," said the sweet young thing settling into the dentist's chair, "having a tooth pulled, or having a baby."

"Well make up your mind," said the dentist, "so that I can fix the chair in the appropriate position!"

&ast; &ast; &ast;

"SATISFACTION Guaranteed, or your teeth refunded."

&ast; &ast; &ast;

THE wharfie was built like the proverbial outhouse and as he settled in the chair he gripped the dentist by his short and curlies.

"We're not going to hurt each other, are we?" he said.

&ast; &ast; &ast;

"WHY are you screaming?" said the dentist. "I haven't started drilling yet."

"I know, but you're standing on my feet," said the patient.

&ast; &ast; &ast;

A DESPERATE looking gangster settled into the chair after telling the dentist he needed a tooth pulled out.

"Which one is it?"

"That's for you to find out," growled the tough guy. "I ain't no stool pigeon."

&ast; &ast; &ast;

A FARMER who had an abiding fear of dentists asked his neighbour what the new bloke was like. "Did that new dentist stop the pain in your tooth?" he asked.

"Well put it this way," said his mate. "You remember last week when I stepped on that rake, got cracked on the head by the handle, fell backwards, and sat on that rabbit trap?"

"Yeah."

"Well that was the first time since I visited that new dentist that the pain in my jaw didn't bother me."

&ast; &ast; &ast;

NERVOUS patient: "This will be the first tooth I've lost."

Nervous Dentist: "That's a co-incidence. This will be the first tooth I've pulled."

"WHAT was it like having all your teeth out?"

"Terrible. I'll never do it again."

## DESERT ISLANDS

"THE most important thing we have in common," he said as they staggered ashore on the desert island, "is that I'm a man and you're a woman."

\*     \*     \*

A FOOTBALL star fell overboard from a cruise ship and finally drifted ashore on a tropical island. He was eventually revived by a beautiful native girl.

She took him to her hut where she supplied him with food.

Then she produced a bottle of Scotch from a crate which had also drifted onto the beach.

Then she said: "Would you like to play with me?"

The footballer was frankly astonished. "Don't tell me you've got a football too?"

\*     \*     \*

AN Englishman, an Australian and an Irishman had been marooned on a desert island for 15 years. One day the Aussie saw a bottle floating past and waded in to the sea to retrieve it. When he pulled the cork a Geni appeared.

"Oh what a relief to get out," he said. "I've been stuck in there for a thousand years, and the rules say you three blokes have got one wish each."

The three mates could not believe their eyes, but the genie insisted he was real, and so were the wishes. "But remember, it's just one each."

The Englishman was sceptical, but said he would give it a try. "I wish I was back on the Old Kent Road in London town," he laughed. In a blinding flash he disappeared.

"I wish I was back in the Members' Stand at Flemington Races," said the Aussie quickly. Another flash and he was gone.

The Irishman thought hard, screwed his face in thought but couldn't make up his mind. "Oh, I wish my mates were back here to help me!"

# DIPLOMACY

DIPLOMACY is when you make your in-laws feel at home, when you wish they were.

\* \* \*

YOUNG bloke had just become engaged and met his fiancee's mother for the first time. "How old do you think I am?" she asked the lad.

"Well," he said after a moment's thought, "I am wondering whether to make you ten years younger to fit with your looks and figure, or ten years older on account of your wise intelligence."

\* \* \*

"LOOK at that ugly old bag over there," said one drinker to his mate, "got a face like the back of a bus."

"That's my wife," replied the other cooly.

"Got great legs," said the first.

\* \* \*

THE white missionary had lived with the Bullabukanki tribe for 18 months when the chief took him aside and said the reverend was in big heaps of trouble.

"Yesterday a white baby was born to my sister, and you are the only white man in this village," said the chief sharpening his axe.

The missionary broke out in a sweat. "Look, old man, I know it looks bad, but see your flock of sheep down by the river?"

"Yeah, I see them," said the chief.

"Well can you see the black sheep in the flock. There is only one and ... "

"Okay, okay," said the chief, "I'll keep quiet if you'll keep quiet."

# DIVORCE

SHE told the lawyer: "I want a divorce."

"On what grounds?" he said.

"Bigamy," she replied. "He can't have his Kate and Edith too."

\* \* \*

HARRY mumbled a few words in church and found himself married. A few years later he mumbled a few words in his sleep and found himself divorced.

\* \* \*

SHE was given a divorce because the judge found her husband had flat feet. They were always in the wrong flat.

\* \* \*

SHE says maintenance is the best policy. That's a man's cash surrender value.

\* \* \*

THEY had to admit she was a great housekeeper. Divorced three husbands and kept the house each time.

\* \* \*

SHE was suing for divorce. She told the judge that every time she and her husband drove past one of his girl-friends, he made her duck her head.

\* \* \*

HE left his wife because of another woman. Her mother.

\* \* \*

JUDGE: "I have taken all factors into account and decided to award your wife $150 a week."

Defendant: "That's real decent of you, yer honour. Why, I might throw in a few dollars myself."

\* \* \*

FRED was leaning on the bar and confided in Bill that he was going to get a divorce.

"The wife hasn't spoken to me in five months. Not a word," he said.

Bill pondered this and said "Don't be too hasty, Fred. Wives like that are damned hard to find."

&#8902; &#8902; &#8902;

HE said his father was very disappointed when he was born.

"Why, did he want a girl?"

"No, he wanted a divorce."

&#8902; &#8902; &#8902;

THE pretty young wife was suing for divorce.

"On what grounds?" asked her solicitor. "You've got to have grounds".

"But we do," she assured him. "Yes, we have large grounds, a 20 hectare block."

"No, no," he said. "Do you have a grudge?"

"Yes, we have a double garage because we have two cars."

"No, no," said the solicitor, near exasperation. "Does he beat you up?"

"Never," she said. "I'm always up at six, and he sleeps in till ten sometimes."

The solicitor finally grabbed her by the shoulders. "Reasons!" he shouted. "What are your reasons?"

"Oh, we don't seem to be able to communicate," she said.

&#8902; &#8902; &#8902;

FREE at last, ain't life grand
 I've just divorced my old man.
 I laughed til I cried at the judge's decision
 He gave him the kids
 And none were his'n.

## DOCTORS
See HOSPITAL

THE doctor felt the patient's thin purse and admitted there was nothing he could do.

MOST doctors can decide on the treatment you need just by feeling your wallet, but throughout history the medical profession has never ceased to produce an endless supply of doctor jokes. Here are but a few:

\* \* \*

DOCTOR to new patient: "First I need to study your medical history. Do you pay your medical bills promptly?"

\* \* \*

"I WILL examine you for twenty dollars."
"Go ahead, Doc. If you find it you can have it."

\* \* \*

WHAT'S the use of consulting a doctor about a cold when he gives you a heart attack with the bill?

\* \* \*

"I THINK I've got amnesia, Doc."
"Okay, then I will ask for my fee in advance."

\* \* \*

THE doctor finally discovered a cure for amnesia, but forgot what it was.

\* \* \*

"DOCTOR, I have a small, embarrassing wart."
"Divorce him."

\* \* \*

PATIENT: "Aren't these pills habit-forming?"
Doctor: "Rubbish, I've been taking them for years."

\* \* \*

"DOCTOR, I've got Parkinson's disease, and I think he's got mine."

\* \* \*

"ARE you taking the medicine regularly?"
"No, Doc. I tasted it and decided I'd rather keep coughing."

\* \* \*

"WELL Doc, how do I stand?"
"I don't know. It's a damned miracle."

PATIENT: "I'm having trouble breathing, Doc."
Doctor: "Well I'll soon put a stop to that."

* * *

THE woman marched into the doctor's surgery dragging her young son along by the ear. "Doc. I just want to ask you one question. Can a a boy of twelve take out his own appendix?"

"Most certainly not madam," said the surgeon.

She belted her son across the head. "Hear that, Nigel. Now put it back at once."

* * *

AFTER a lengthy examination the doctor came out of the surgery and said to the patient's wife, "I don't like the look of your husband."

"Neither do I, but he's nice to the kids," she said.

* * *

THE doctor told his patient he had better sit down. He had two items of bad news. "First, I am sorry to say you have a sexually transmitted disease," said the doc.

"Oh, that's terrible," said his patient. "How will I explain it to the family?"

"And you also have Alzheimer's Disease," added the doc. "Oh, no! A double calamity, what a shock," lamented the patient. "Er, what was that first thing you said I had?"

* * *

HE parked his sportscar outside the clinic and bounced in without an appointment. "I just want to thank the doctor for his treatment," he said.

"But, you're not a patient of mine are you?" said the Doc.

"No, but my late Uncle Harry was."

* * *

"THE doctor told me to take these pills for the rest of my life."

"So, what's the problem?"

"He only gave me half a dozen."

98

"THE doctor gave me two weeks to live."

"Goodness, what did you say?"

"I told him I'd take the first two weeks in December."

*   *   *

MURPHY was given two weeks to live. He decided to take one week in January and the other in March.

*   *   *

O'REILLY was given six months to live. But when he said he couldn't pay his bill the doctor gave him another six months.

*   *   *

A BUSINESSMAN went for his annual medical. The grim-faced doctor said he had better sit down because he had some bad news. "To put it bluntly, you've got ten hours to live," he said.

"No, I can't believe it," said the businessman, "I want a second opinion."

"Well, you've got a nasty disposition, too," said the Doc (no, that's not the joke).

The businessman hurried to another clinic and was given the same distressing diagnosis. "You have nine hours to live."

Finally accepting the inevitable he got into his car and drove home. "Edna my darling," he said looking at his watch, "I have about eight hours to live."

As soon as his wife grasped the gravity of the situation she said, "Ralph, your slightest wish is my command. What would you like?"

He thought for a moment and said: "To bed!"

They were at it for an hour, and after a short rest she said, "What now, Ralph?"

He thought for a second. "Let's do it again!"

She compliantly agreed and after another hour she asked if he would like anything else.

Ralph said he was ready for a third.

"Oh for goodness sake," she cried. "It's okay for you, but I've got to get up in the morning!"

*      *      *

THE doctor had given Fred the dreadful news that he had contracted cancer and only had six months to live, so why was Fred telling everyone he was dying from AIDS.

"It's like this Doc," he explained. "I don't want anyone fooling around with my wife after I'm gone."

*      *      *

THE doctor told him he had good news and bad news. Which did he want first. The patient opted for the bad news first and the doc told him he had three weeks to live. "Hell, what's the good news then?" he asked.

The doctor leaned close and whispered, "See that blonde nurse there. I'm taking her out tonight!"

*      *      *

THE Doc told his patient he had some bad news, and some very bad news.

"What's the bad news?"

"You've only got two weeks to live."

"What news can be worse than that?" cried the patient.

"I should have told you a fortnight ago."

*      *      *

THE doctor had finished his examination and with a smile on his face said: "Mrs Jones, I have some very good news for you."

"Miss Jones," she corrected.

The doctor wiped the smile off his face. "Miss Jones, I have some very bad news for you!"

*      *      *

"IT'S my nerves," she said. "Please doctor you have to give me something for my nerves."

The doctor reached for a packet of pills. "Take these, they are $10 a packet."

She said: "I'll give you $7 for them."

Doctor: "There's nothing wrong with your nerve, lady."

THE farmer's wife, the mother of ten kids, called in to tell the doctor cheerfully that she won't be coming back as an expectant mother any more now that she had her birth control appliance.

The doctor was puzzled because she indicated that her "appliance" was an ordinary hearing aid.

"Before I had it," she explained, "we would get into bed at night and my husband would say "Will we put out the light and go to sleep, or what?"

"And I would say 'What'?"

* * *

OLD Fred was having his annual check-up.

"Well, old man," said the doctor tactfully, "you are getting on in years and I suggest you play it safe and give up half your sex life."

Fred thought this over for a moment, then asked which half he was supposed to give up. "Talking about it? Or thinking about it?"

* * *

THE doctor checked his patient over and with a puzzled frown said: "I can't really tell what the trouble is. I think it must be due to drinking."

"I understand Doc. I'll come back when you're sober!"

* * *

THE doctor was explaining to Paddy O'Leary how nature adjusted some physical disabilities. "For example, if a man is blind he develops a keen sense of hearing and touch. If he is stone deaf, then he develops his other senses..."

"Oi know what you mean," said Paddy. "Oi've noticed that if a bloke has one short leg, then the other one is always a bit longer."

* * *

THE doctor answered the phone to hear an excited voice say: "Quick, send an ambulance. My wife Bridget is about to have a baby!"

"Calm down," said the Doc. "Is this her first baby?"

"No, this is her husband, Pat speaking!"

* * *

THE doctor examined the young woman and said with a smile: "You can go home and tell your husband he is going to become a Daddy."

"But doctor, I'm not married."

"Well, you can tell your boyfriend."

"But doctor," she said. "I haven't got a boyfriend. I have never been out with a man."

The doctor walked over to the window and looked into the night sky. "Last time this happened there was a big star in the east," he said.

* * *

FRED complained to his doctor that his wife had lost interest in sex. The doc counselled him that it was a matter of preparation.

"Next time you come home from the office, bring a bunch of flowers, greet her with a big kiss, sweep her off her feet and carry her upstairs to the bedroom. You will be surprised."

On Fred's next visit he asked if it had worked. "Yes, indeed she was surprised," said Fred, "and so were all the members of her bridge club."

* * *

PADDY went to the doctor. He had two burnt ears.

"The phone rang when I was ironing, didn't it," said Paddy explaining.

"But what about the other ear?" asked the doctor.

"Well I had to phone you for an appointment, didn't I!"

* * *

A MARRIED couple visited the doctor who specialised in sex therapy. Romance had gone out of their lives, they said. Sex wasn't interesting anymore.

The doc listened to their nightly routine of evening meal, television and the same old missionary position.

"No wonder it's dull," he said. "You have made it monotonous, even the same time every night. What you have got to do is make it spontaneous. Do it when the mood takes you." And he gave them a pep talk on spontaneity.

A week later they came back, all smiles.

"We did what you suggested," said the husband. "Half way through a candle-lit dinner I felt randy. Ethel said she did too, so I leant over and ripped off her blouse, then pulled her down to the floor and we made love under the table. It was ecstatic spontaneity," he said.

And Ethel added, "But they said we could never go back to that restaurant again!"

\* \* \*

"MY brother swallowed a box of fire crackers."

"Is he alright?"

"Don't know. We haven't heard the last report."

\* \* \*

THE aging playboy was having his annual medical check.

"Sex?" asked the doctor.

"Infrequently," came the reply.

"Hmmm," said the doctor, "is that one word or two?"

\* \* \*

FEELING run-down and listless, Fred visited the doctor for advice. The medic examined him and solemnly announced: "The remedy is simple. Whatever it is you are doing, stop it!"

\* \* \*

THE notorious casanova went to the doctor to complain of impotence.

The medic was astonished. "You of all people," he said. "Why, you have a reputation as long as my arm."

The patient replied, "What's the good of a reputation if it won't stand up?"

\* \* \*

PENSIONER couple wanted the doctor to check the way

103

they make love. He watched and said it is the way most people did it. They came back next day and asked him to check again. Doc approved.

When they arrived the third day the doctor asked what the heck was going on.

The old man finally explained: "I can't take her to the old men's home. We can't go to her place. We can't afford a motel room on the pension. So we do it here and get a 75% rebate on Medicare."

       ★     ★     ★

PADDY was angry, and his wife was obviously pregnant, when the doctor finally called.

"Look at this," said Paddy indicating his wife's condition. "I've been away at sea for a year and look at this. How do yer explain it?"

"Simple," said the doctor. "That's a vindictive pregnancy. Somebody has had it in for you while you have been away!"

## DO-GOODERS

THE social welfare officer was making an annual inspection of the asylum when he noticed a chap out in the garden who seemed to enjoy a contented composure.

"Oh no, I'm not like that lot in there," said the gardener. "They have all lost their marbles."

Indeed the official couldn't help notice the garden neatly divided into rows of vegetables and flowers and in further conversation learned that the gardener had not only built his own shed but the aerial on the roof was part of his short-wave radio system he had also built. "I write books on that computer, and I paint in oils in my spare time," he told the inspector.

The official was amazed. "You shouldn't be here in this institution," he said, "it's a crime."

"That's what I've been telling them for years," said

the gardener. "My papers were lost in a complicated change of solicitors and I have been unable to get a proper legal clearance," he said.

"Well I am going to do something about this first thing tomorrow morning," said the official turning to leave.

He had taken three steps when the gardener stooped, picked up a red brick, threw it and hit the official square on the back of his head knocking him to the ground.

"You won't forget, will you?" he asked.

## DOGS

THE dog entered the bar, sat up on a stool and ordered a gin and tonic. The barman served him, the dog swallowed the drink, left some money on the bar and left.

"That's extraordinary," said a drinker who had watched the whole thing.

"Yes," said the barman. "He usually has a brandy."

\*   \*   \*

"LOST Dog," said the newspaper notice, "Has three legs, blind in left eye, large scar on throat, right ear missing, tail broken in two places, no teeth, recently castrated, answers to Lucky."

\*   \*   \*

FRED said his dog Deefer could read.

He said he proved it the other day when the dog walked up to a "Wet Paint" sign, inspected it carefully, then followed the instructions.

\*   \*   \*

MY dog's so obedient
  He does as he's bid
  The park bench said "Wet Paint"
  And that's what he did!

\*   \*   \*

FRED put some Spot remover on his dog. Now he's gone.

"IS that an obedient dog, Fred?"

"Too right. I only have to say 'attack', and he has one."

* * *

SID the Spiv said his greyhound could run like greased lightning. "He is so fast on the track that on every third lap he has to jump over himself."

* * *

ONE drover was surprised to see his mate playing poker with his sheepdog. "I know kelpies are intelligent," he said, "but that one's a ripper."

"Ar, he's not that good," drawled his mate, throwing down another card. "Every time he gets a good hand he wags his tail!"

* * *

LEANING on the bar the drover said: "I am a man of simple tastes. I'm happy with a bottle of whisky, a tin of biscuits and a dog."

"Why the dog?" asked a listener.

"Hell, somebody has got to eat the biscuits!"

* * *

WHEN the publican spotted the little dog being brought into the pub he loudly declared it was not allowed.

"But you don't understand," said the drinker, "I'm blind and that's my guide dog."

"What?" roared the publican. "That's a Chihuahua."

"Well I'll be blowed," said the drinker, "they told me it was a Labrador."

* * *

MERV took his mongrel dog to a flea circus and the clever mutt stole the show.

* * *

WHEN drover Bill retired he set about fulfilling his dream of riding with the gentry at the hunt club. He was told that his scruffy horse barely met the equestrian standards, and not to come back until he had his own hound.

Not to be deterred, Bill fronted up for the Saturday

hunt with his trusty mount and his faithful greyhound. He was grudgingly accepted, but he failed to tell the officials that his greyhound bitch was on heat. Ten minutes after the chase started the Master of Foxhounds turned to his companion and said: "Which way are they headed?"

"West," was the reply.

"And where's the fox?"

"At the moment he's running seventh but gaining ground rapidly!"

* * *

"DID you say your dog's bark was worse than his bite?"

"Yes."

"Well for goodness sake don't let him bark. He's just bitten me."

* * *

THE salesman was bailed up by a ferocious dog. Finally its mistress came out and said: "It's okay. You know the old saying, a barking dog never bites."

The worried salesman replied: "I know it, you know it, but does that bloomin' dog know it?"

* * *

WHEN Mrs Moloney met Mrs Murphy at the market she noticed that her friend had a puppy under her arm.

"That's a nice pup," said Mrs Moloney.

"Yes, I got it for Murphy," said her friend.

"Lucky you. I wish I could swap Moloney for one!"

* * *

A MAN was sitting on the bank of the river having his lunch when a lady of 'the blue rinse set' came along the path with her pet poodle.

The yapping dog showed a lot of interest in the man's sandwich.

"Shall I throw him a bit?"

She nodded her approval.

So the man picked up the dog and threw it in the river.

IT was during the Great Depression and the drover had hit on hard times. Not to put too fine a point on it, he was starving. He looked at his faithful kelpie, Rufus, and with a tear in his eye said, "Sorry old-timer, it's you or me." And with that painful decision, Rufus ended up in the camp pot.

It was the first meal the drover had had for three weeks. And as he leant back against a stringybark, licking his lips after the satisfying meal he looked at the bones piled up on his plate.

"Pity Rufus is not here," he mused. "He would have loved those scraps!"

\* \* \*

"SORRY, Sir, dogs are not allowed in this restaurant," said the waiter.

"But this is a talking dog," said its owner.

"If that dog can talk I will give you both a free meal," said the sceptical waiter.

"Right then Rover," said the owner to his pooch, "what's on the top of this building?"

Rover growled: "R-r-r-roof!"

"Now I'll ask one," said the waiter."Who is the greatest footballer in the league?"

"R-r-r-roof," repeated Rover.

The waiter kicked them both out on the footpath, and as they walked away Rover said: "Who should I have said?"

\* \* \*

WORD had got around, and at the next pub the barman said, "Is it true that your dog can talk?"

"No," said the old man, "and if he tells you he can, he's a bloomin' liar."

\* \* \*

THE old-timer wandered into the pub with his dog and a tame goanna which he placed on top of the piano. The dog climbed up on the seat and began to play the piano while the goanna sang a number of popular songs.

The drinkers were amazed and the publican rewarded the old-timer with a beer and said, "That's a great act. You are wasting your time travelling around the Outback pubs."

"They are not as good as you think," confessed the old-timer. "The goanna is tone deaf and can't sing a note. The dog is a ventriloquist."

*　　*　　*

"I THINK your dog likes me Gladys. He hasn't taken his eyes off me all night."

"That's because you are eating off his plate!"

*　　*　　*

WE have a fine watch dog. So far he has watched somebody steal our car, watched the garage burn down and watched a bloke pinch the lawn mower.

*　　*　　*

THE Buddhist knocked on the vicar's door with the sad news: "My carma has just run over your dogma."

*　　*　　*

"I DON'T want you to bring your dog into the house. It's full of fleas," she said.

"Fido, stay out of the house. It's full of fleas."

*　　*　　*

I HAD a dog called Carpenter. He used to do little jobs around the house.

I had a dog called Mechanic. Give him a kick in the nuts and he would make a bolt for the door.

But I rue the day I called my third dog Sex. It got me into a lot of trouble. When I went to the town hall to register him I said to the clerk, "I would like a licence for Sex."

He said, "I wouldn't mind one myself."

When I got married I asked the vicar if we could have Sex at the wedding. He said okay as long as it didn't interrupt the ceremony.

When I booked into the hotel for our honeymoon I asked the receptionist if he had a room for Sex. "They all are," he said.

My wife and I were always fighting over Sex. Finally it caused our divorce. I told the judge I had Sex before marriage. "Didn't we all," he said. One night he slipped his lead and ran off. I was in the park when a cop asked me what I was doing. "I am looking for Sex," I said. My case comes up next Monday.

\*    \*    \*

"I HAD to shoot my dog yesterday."

"Was he mad?"

"Well, he wasn't too pleased about it."

\*    \*    \*

IT was winter and the regulars in the country pub were gathered around the fireplace when Pete the Punter entered the bar with a mongrel dog called Ralph.

He loudly announced to one and all that this dog understood every command he could give it. "Never gets it wrong," he said.

There were drovers who owned top dogs around the bar and they looked askance at the mangy dog which was supposed to be so obedient.

Pete said he wasn't talking about simple commands like "sit," "stay," and "all that rubbish."

"I'm talking about a five-word sentence, and instant obedience," said Pete.

This was too much for the sceptics and they soon collected $100 to prove him wrong. Pete matched it, put the money on the bar, picked up the dog, threw it on the blazing fire and roared: "Ralph, get off that fire!"

\*    \*    \*

A COUPLE of dogs met on the street. "What's your name?" said one.

"I'm not sure. I think it's Down Boy."

"HOW much did that terrier set you back, Fred?"

"Six hundred dollars … he's half bull and half foxie."

"Which half is bull?"

"The part about the six hundred dollars."

\*   \*   \*

THE grocer was alarmed to learn that Mrs Jones' weekly order of a dozen cans of pet food was being fed to her husband. "Oh he doesn't know the difference," she said. "He even likes it."

"But it could kill him," protested the grocer.

Mrs Jones took no heed, but a month later she entered the shop wearing a black armband.

"I told you so," said the grocer. "I told you that dog food would kill him."

"Oh no, it wasn't the dog food," she said. "We were going home the other evening when he sat on the tramline to scratch himself and got bowled over!"

\*   \*   \*

A FLEA had spent the evening in the pub. At closing time he hopped out and landed flat on his face.

"Who the hell moved my dog," he said.

\*   \*   \*

THE spectators at the local cricket match were surprised to see that the next batsman was a fox terrier. The dog shaped up at the crease and began hitting balls for sixers.

"That's amazing," said one of the spectators.

"Yes, he's good, but he is still a disappointment to his parents. They wanted him to play football."

\*   \*   \*

THE movie buff settled into his seat and was surprised to see a man in front with his arm around a large dog which seemed to be enjoying the movie. The dog was growling at the villain and giving excited yelps each time the hero escaped.

The movie buff was fascinated. "Excuse me," he said,

tapping the chap on the shoulder. "Your dog is amazing. I just can't get over it."

"Frankly, he has surprised me too," said the owner. "He hated the book."

\* \* \*

"DOES your dog bite?" enquired the friendly chap of the bulldog sitting beside Paddy.

"No," said Paddy.

The friendly chap extended a hand to pat the dog and nearly had it bitten off.

"I thought you said your dog didn't bite," the man said in alarm.

"That's not my dog," said Paddy.

\* \* \*

AN expensive poodle fell into a river and was having difficulty staying afloat. In fact it was drowning. Isaac Goldstein dived in, brought the dog to shore, gave it mouth to mouth resuscitation and revived it.

"'That was wonderful," said the grateful owner. "Are you a vet?"

"Of course I'm a vet," replied Goldstein. "I'm a bloody soaking."

# DRIVERS
See ACCIDENTS, MOTORING, CARS

THE model driver, of course, is the one who has just seen the car in front pulled up by the police.

\* \* \*

IF your wife insists on learning to drive, don't stand in her way.

\* \* \*

"HAS your wife learned to drive yet, Fred?"

"Only in an advisory capacity."

\* \* \*

"HOW's the wife's driving lessons going, Fred?"

"Improving. The roads are starting to turn when she does."

*    *    *

REMEMBER when the police didn't hide behind trees on the side of busy roads with radar guns, but took their chances out in the traffic like everybody else?

*    *    *

WHEN she drove the car up to the toll gate the keeper said: "That will be $5 for the car and $2.50 for the passenger."

Martha replied: "The car's yours for a fiver, but I won't take less than three dollars for my old man."

*    *    *

TWO men struggled into the pub dragging their mate between them. When they reached the bar they let him go and he collapsed in a heap on the floor.

"Two beers please," said one of those still on their feet.

The barman looked down at the crumpled heap on the floor. "What about him?"

"Oh, no more for him. He's driving."

*    *    *

FOLLOWING the sound advice to take a rest when sleepy, a motorist pulled over, stopped the car on the side of the road, settled down and closed his eyes.

He was just drifting off when a jogger rapped on the window and asked for the time. Bleary-eyed he reached for his watch and announced that it was 6 am.

Sleeping at last he was soon awakened by another jogger rapping on the window asking if he had the time.

"It's six-fifteen," he said grumpily. At this rate he wasn't to get any sleep so he wrote a note and stuck it on the window for all passing joggers to see. It read "I do not have the time."

Again he settled down for his badly needed nap, but only for a few minutes before there was another rap on the window.

"Hey mate," said yet another jogger, "it's seven o'clock!"

*113*

# DROVERS

DROVERS are the strong silent type and don't usually waste words. One night at the camp fire beside the river, Frank said: "There's a bloke down near the river bank."

"Getting fish is he?" said his mate.

"No."

"Gettin' rabbits then?"

"No."

"Well what's he gettin?"

"He's gettin' drowned," said Frank.

★　★　★

IT was the time of the great drought thoughout Australia and Dan the drover decided to move his mob south. He had them grazing in the Derwent Valley when a Tasmanian farmer asked where he had come from.

"Three thousand kilometres from the back o' Bourke," drawled Dan. "We were on the road for three months."

"Crikey," said the local. "How did you get that mob across Bass Strait?"

"Ah, we didn't come that way," Dan explained.

# DRINKERS

DRINKERS' Motto: Conserve water, always dilute it.

★　★　★

HE drinks to forget, but he has forgotten why.

★　★　★

HE believed the best way to pull himself out of trouble was with a corkscrew.

★　★　★

SHE said one glass was enough
　Or two at the most
　"Three and you're under the table
　Four and you're under the host."

114

# DRUNKS
See ALCOHOLICS

ABSTINENCE is a good thing, but it should always be practised in moderation.

* * *

THE difference between an Australian wedding and an Australian funeral, is one less drunk.

* * *

"AFTER three whiskies my husband turns into a most disgusting beast, but after the fourth I pass out altogether."

* * *

DRUNK, to barman: "Has Paddy been in tonight?"
   "Yes, he popped in about an hour ago."
   Drunk: "Was I with him?"

* * *

"TELL me, why do you swig your drinks so fast?"
   "Because I once had one stolen."

* * *

"THE doctor told me I would have to limit my drinking to one each day. I'm now up to April 10, 2005."

* * *

"TERRIBLE beer they serve in this pub."
   "Yes, I'll be glad when I've had enough."

* * *

BRUCE the Boozer has finally given up drink, for the sake of his wife and kidneys.

* * *

"I'VE got no sympathy for a man who spends every night drinking," she said sternly.
   "If I could spend every night drinking I wouldn't need your sympathy," he replied.

* * *

"I JUST got twenty bucks off Merv."
   "Off Merv? I always thought he was tight."
   "He was."

THE barman looked up to see a green rat, a pink elephant and a yellow snake wander into the pub together.

"You're too early fellas. He hasn't had his third pot yet."

*　　*　　*

HE suffers from alcoholic constipation. He can't pass a pub!

*　　*　　*

HE suffers from alcholic rheumatism.

He gets stiff in most joints.

*　　*　　*

A LARGE woman at a social function was startled to find herself seized and embraced by a man who was slightly under the weather. But the man quickly released her and apologised.

"Excuse me. I'm so sorry," he mumbled, "I thought for a moment you were my wife." The woman quickly recovered from her surprise and snarled: "Fancy having a drunken slob like you for a husband, you clumsy, gross disgusting beast."

"Crickey," he slurred, "you not only look like her, you sound like her too!"

*　　*　　*

DENIS went to the doctor because his hands kept shaking.

The doctor checked him over and said, "Do you drink much?"

"No," said Denis, "I spill most of it."

*　　*　　*

THE town drunk received an inheritance and was able to fulfill his dream and build a houseboat and retire. He named his boat Cirrhosis of the River.

*　　*　　*

"I THOUGHT you said you get drunk after one whisky."

"Yes, and I do. Usually it's the fifteenth."

"THEN what will we drink to?"

"What about three in the morning?"

* * *

HE said the reason he likes whisky is because it makes you see double and feel single. "But I always know when I've had enough. That's when I fall over."

* * *

"THERE is indeed an evil worsht than drink."

"Whatsh that then?"

"Thirsht, that's what."

* * *

THE drunk approached the policeman.

"Offisher, can you tell me where I am?"

"You are on the corner of Main St and Chester Avenue."

"Forget the details. What town is it?"

* * *

PASSING a cemetery late at night a drunk saw a sign: "Ring the bell for caretaker."

He did, and a sleepy voice growled: "What do yer want?"

"I want ter know why you can't ring the bloomin' bell yerself?"

* * *

"DRINKING makes you look beautiful, darling."

"But I haven't been drinking."

"No, but I have."

* * *

WOMAN looking under the table in a hotel saw Fred lying there. "Oh, I'm sorry," she said. "I was looking for a lady's husband."

"Well I'm one, luv," said Fred. "Crawl under."

* * *

IF your friend has had too much to drink, never fill him with coffee or you will have a wide-awake drunk on your hands.

PAT and Mick staggered out of the pub together but soon lost each other. Pat approached a policeman.

"Offisher," he said, "have you seen a fella wandering about without me?"

&#9733;   &#9733;   &#9733;

BRUCE went to the doctor for a check-up.

"It's quite obvious to me," said the Doc, "that alcohol is entirely responsible for your poor physical shape."

"Well I'm glad to hear that," said Bruce. "The wife keeps insisting it's my fault."

&#9733;   &#9733;   &#9733;

"WHY do you keep coming home three parts sloshed?" demanded his wife.

"Because I keep running out of money!"

&#9733;   &#9733;   &#9733;

FRED had been celebrating for most of the night before he staggered to the bar and loudly proclaimed: "Drinks for everybody, and have one yourself, barman."

There was a rush to the bar and after everybody was served the barman said to Fred, "That will be $57.80."

"But I haven't any money," said Fred quietly.

With that the barman grabbed him by the shirtfront, punched him several times and threw him out on the street.

A few minutes later Fred returned through the swinging doors, staggered up to the bar and loudly proclaimed: "Drinks for everybody, except you, barman, you get bloomin' nasty when you drink!"

&#9733;   &#9733;   &#9733;

THEY were leaning on the bar in a deep philosophical discussion. "Do you know that ten per cent of all road accidents are caused by drinking drivers?"

"Which means," said his mate, "that the other 90 per cent are caused by teetotallers."

&#9733;   &#9733;   &#9733;

AN old Scot on his death bed called his best friend, Jock,

to his side. "I bin saving a bottle of whisky, and when I'm gone I want you to sprinkle it on my grave. Will you do that, Jock?"

"Och Aye, but would ye mind if I pass it through my kidneys first?"

* * *

THE pub had just closed and Paddy was taking a short cut through the cemetery when he fell into a newly-dug hole which the grave-diggers had left uncovered. Paddy made a valiant attempt to get out but couldn't make it. He gave up, pulled a bottle from his hip pocket and decided to settle in the corner until morning.

Half an hour later another drunk fell into the hole.

"You'll never get out, lad," said Paddy.

But he did, in one mighty leap.

* * *

WHISKY kills more people than bullets.

That's because bullets don't drink.

* * *

FRED was having trouble with a drinking problem and swore that he would correct it with willpower. He had decided to walk straight past the pub without going in.

As he approached it he kept repeating to himself, "You can do it. You can do it."

The pressure was tough, but Fred persevered, right past he went.

Fifty metres past and he congratulated himself, "I knew you could do it. You were great. Let's go back and I'll buy you a drink."

* * *

PADDY entered the pub at lunchtime. "Was I in here last night?" he asked the barman.

"Yes," was the reply.

"Was I drunk?"

"Yes, very drunk."

"And did I spend much money," pressed Paddy.

"Yes, about twenty dollars," said the barman.

"Thank goodness. I thought I lost it!"

\* \* \*

IRISH publican: "I'm sorry gents, but the bar won't be open for another hour. But would you loike a drink while you are waiting?"

\* \* \*

TWO drunks were about to board the train when they saw the sign: "Dogs must be carried."

"Hold it," said one. "Where are we gonna get a dog at this time of night?"

\* \* \*

WIFE: "Why do you drink liquor?"

Husband: "What do you suggest I do with it?"

\* \* \*

THE sergeant answered the phone in the police station. The voice at the other end was slow and slurred.

"I wanna report a theft, offisher. I've been robbed. Shum dirty crook has shtolen things from my car."

"What kind of things?" asked the sergeant.

"My shteering wheel, brakes, dashboard, accellerator... the bloody lot's gone."

The sergeant humored him for a moment, and said he would investigate. "Bloody drunks," he said when he hung up.

Five minutes later the phone rang again.

"Cancel that report. It's all right. Yers can stop lookin," said the same voice. "My mishtake. I got inter the back seat!"

\* \* \*

THE cops had been instructed to clean up the neighbourhood so it was dead easy when one drunk staggered towards a constable and said: "Excuse me offisher, what time is it?"

The cop replied, "One o'clock," and hit him once over the head with his baton.

"Crikey," said the drunk, "I'm glad I didn't ask you an hour ago."

★　　★　　★

THE drinker was sobbing into his beer. "What's up, mate?" asked the barman.

"I can't remember the name of the girl I am trying to forget."

★　　★　　★

SAID the drunk as he staggered into the kitchen. "Am I home darling?"

## DUMB

SHE thought an aperitif was a set of dentures.

HE thought alter ego was a conceited priest.

SHE thought intercourse was a ticket to the races.

HE thought VAT 69 was the Pope's phone number.

SHE thought a bigamist was a thick Italian fog.

HE thought fidelity was unadulterated boredom.

SHE thought Good Friday did Robinson Crusoe's housework.

HE thought Robinson Crusoe was a world famous tenor.

SHE thought a Norwegian fjord was a Scandinavian car.

HE thought manual labour was a Spanish waiter.

SHE thought Chou En-lai was Chinese for breakfast in bed.

HE thought a brassiere was something you warm your hands on.

SHE thought Au Pair was a living bra.

HE thought polyunsaturated was a parrot in a raincoat.

SHE thought awe-struck was being hit by a paddle.

HE thought a bulletin was a can of pressed beef.

SHE thought climate was the only thing you could do with a ladder.

HE thought hyacinth was a greeting for anybody called Cynthia.

SHE thought an optimist was a hope addict.

HE thought odious was not very good poetry.

SHE thought an operetta was a girl who works at the telephone exchange.

HE thought Yoko Ono was Japanese for one egg please.

SHE thought a transistor was a nun in men's clothes.

HE thought grammar was the woman who married grandpa.

SHE thought Joan of Arc was Noah's wife.

HE thought a lieutenant commander was the lieutenant's wife.

SHE thought pregnant was the past tense of virgin.

HE thought a polygon was a dead parrot.

SHE thought the tooth fairy was a gay dentist.

HE thought the landed gentry were tricked into marriage.

SHE thought blue serge was a sad Russian.

HE thought a cross section of the public were taxpayers.

SHE thought a crowbar was where the girls hung out for a drink.

HE thought Badminton was why the lamb tasted awful.

SHE thought good housekeeping was the name of a magazine.

SHE thought a penal colony was an all-male nudist camp.

HE thought Karl Marx was the brother of Chico and Harpo.

SHE thought Columbine is the wife of the guy who discovered America.

HE thought that where there is life there's opium.

SHE thought Kosher is Jewish bacon.

HE thought myxomatosis was wiping out Rabbis.

SHE thought a meadow lark was a party in a paddock.

HE thought the Union Jack was something you got at the Trades Hall.

SHE thought hypocrisy was a Greek philosopher.

HE thought vice-versa was a rude poem.

SHE thought a teetotaller was the scorekeeper at golf.

\* \* \*

DUMB Doris said she was thin, and her friend Wendy was thin, but there was a girl in the office who was as thin as the two of them, put together.

\* \* \*

SOME blokes are three bricks short of a load, not the full two-bob, or two sandwiches short of a picnic.

\* \* \*

THE small outback community was getting a lecture on first aid and how to stop bleeding.

"Of course you all know what a corpuscle is," said the instructor.

"Most of us do," said the chairman, "but you'd better explain it for the sake of those who have never been in one."

## ECONOMY

IT is a recession when your friend loses his job. It is a depression when you lose yours. And it is a recovery when Paul Keating loses his. (Or substitute the politician of your choice).

&ast; &ast; &ast;

THERE are two types of people. Those with swimming pools and those who can't keep their heads above water.

&ast; &ast; &ast;

THE owner of a small business was telling his bank manager that the recession was tough: "Things are so bad that even people who don't pay have stopped buying."


## EDUCATION
See SCHOOLS, TEACHERS

EDUCATION is what you get from reading the fine print. Experience is what you get from not reading it.

&ast; &ast; &ast;

"EDUCATION has failed the younger generation," said the businessman. "Our survey shows that as many as 40 per cent can't read, another 40 per cent can't write and the other 30 per cent can't add up."

THE teacher pointed to little Solly Cohen and said, "Solly, what's three per cent?"

"You're right, teacher," said Solly shrugging his shoulders, "what is three per cent!"

* * *

LITTLE Nigel's mother had been away for a week and asked her son about events during her absence.

"There was a big thunderstorm on Wednesday and I was so scared me and Daddy snuggled up in the same bed."

"Nigel," said the boy's pretty nurse, "you mean Daddy and I."

"No," said the kid. "That was last night. I'm talking about Wednesday."

* * *

TWO Australians in London down on their luck saw an advertisement for two footmen. "References essential," it said. "That's okay," said Bruce, "I'll write yours and you can write one for me." Thus they arrived on the estate and offered the duchess two glowing references. "First things first," she said. "Formal wear here means wearing kilts, so drop your trousers while I check your knees."

The lads were a little surprised but they did so. The duchess gave the knees the nod of approval and said, "Okay, now let me see those testimonials."

After they were thrown off the property Bruce said: "With a little more education we would have got that job."

## EGO

THE human body is an interesting phenomenon. A pat on the back can result in a swollen head.

* * *

HIS ego was bigger than the Outback.

125

MOST actors are all ham and ego.

*　　　*　　　*

HE was the kind of chap who had plenty to be modest about.

*　　　*　　　*

HE makes so many enemies, he really needs an enemy agent.

*　　　*　　　*

THERE were so many famous egos at the theatrical awards, I was the only person in the room I'd never heard of.

## ELEPHANTS

WHY have Elephants got Big Ears?
 Because Noddy won't pay the ransom.

*　　　*　　　*

ONE reason elephants drink so much water is that nobody ever offers them anything else.

*　　　*　　　*

AN elephant was drinking from the Zambesi when he noticed a turtle asleep on a log. He ambled over and kicked it clear across the river.
 "What did you do that for?" asked a passing giraffe.
 "Because I recognised it as the same turtle which took a nip out of my trunk 53 years ago."
 "What a memory," exclaimed the giraffe.
 "Yes," said the elephant, "turtle recall."

*　　　*　　　*

"WHO'S the king of the jungle?" called the lion swaggering down the bush trail.
 "Oh, you are," replied the tiger with its tail between its legs.
 "Who's the king of the jungle?" said the lion to the leopard.
 "Oh you are," said the leopard cowering in the grass.

"Who's the king of the jungle?" said the lion to a huge elephant which blocked the jungle path.

Without answering the elephant gathered the lion in his trunk, hurled him in the air, caught him and smashed him against a tree.

"Look," said the lion. "Don't get mad just because you don't know the answer!"

*   *   *

AN elephant escaped from a circus and no trace had been found until a lady who had never seen an elephant before rang the police. She was panic-stricken.

"There is a weird monster in my back yard," she said. "It is pulling up the cabbages with its tail. But what is worse... I cannot describe what it is doing with them!"

## ENGAGEMENTS
See WEDDINGS, NEWLY-WEDS, MARRIAGE
and MARRIEDS

THE suitor had been shown into the lounge room to wait for his date while she got ready, when her little brother came in.

"Is Jean your oldest sister?" he said to make small talk.

"Yep," said the kid.

"And who comes after her?"

"You and two other blokes."

*   *   *

THE lad has just asked Paddy O'Leary for his daughter's hand in marriage. "Can you support our Teresa in the manner to which she is accustomed?"

"Indeed, sir I can."

"Have you ever seen her eat?" said Paddy.

"Indeed sir, I have."

"But have you ever seen her eat when there's nobody looking?"

127

I HAVE come to ask for your daughter's hand."

"Okay, take the one that's always in my pocket."

*     *     *

"SIR, I would like to marry your daughter."

"Okay, leave your name and address and if nothing better turns up we will contact you."

*     *     *

"SIR, I wish to marry your daughter."

"Do you drink alcohol young man?"

"Thanks all the same, but let's settle this business first."

*     *     *

"SIR, I wish to marry your daughter."

"Can you support a family?" enquired the prospective father-in-law.

"Yes sir, I can."

"There are eight of us."

*     *     *

"SIR, I want your daughter for my wife."

"Well I'm not swapping until I've seen your wife."

*     *     *

THE young man was so nervous when he approached his highly formal prospective father-in-law that he blurted out the words: "I am asking for your daughter's hole in handy matrimony!"

*     *     *

"IF we did become engaged," she said, "would you give me a ring?"

"Certainly, what's your number?"

*     *     *

WHEN he proposed she got so excited she insisted on showing the ring to her workmates in the office. She soon returned and threw it at him. Three of her girl-friends had recognised it.

*     *     *

"YOU have broken it off with Milicent?"

"Yes. She was just a passing fiancée."

"I HAVE been asked to get married hundreds of times," she pouted.

"By whom?"

"My mum and dad," she said.

* * *

"I WONDER if my fiancée loves me?"

"Of course she does. Why should she make you an exception?"

* * *

"NO," she said. "I don't love you, so I won't marry you. But I will be a sister to you."

"That's okay," he said. "How much do you think our father will leave us?"

* * *

"DO you believe in free love, Jack?" she asked.

"Well, I've never sent you an invoice, have I?"

* * *

"FRED," she said, "when we are married I want to share all your worries and troubles and help lighten your burden."

"Forget it, Madge, I've got no worries or troubles."

"But we're not married yet, darling."

## ESTATE AGENTS

A YOUNG Swedish woman was thinking of buying the house. The estate agent was showing her the property. They inspected the lower floor then he said "Now we'll go upstairs and I will show you the bedroom and den."

She looked at him sideways: "And den what?"

* * *

AN auctioneer has no friends. Only nodding acquaintances.

* * *

AFTER I got married I said to my mother-in-law, "My house is your house."

"Three days later she sold it."

SIGN outside a big home: COSTA PLENTI.

*     *     *

HE said Swindle & Wrun had the best salesmen in the business. "They sold me a block of land and when I went to see it I discovered it was five metres under water."

"Well, didn't you go back and complain?"

"Yes, that's the trouble. They then sold me a boat."

*     *     *

HE breasted the bar and announced: "The drinks are on me. I've just sold the house for $100,000."

And as they all placed their orders he added: "Mind you, the council might go bananas when they find out."

*     *     *

TWO country land agents were leaning on the pub's verandah rail looking at the dust storm going by.

"All that country changing hands, and we're not getting a cent commission," grumbled one.

*     *     *

A WOMAN who had just taken a lease on a unit near the railway line rang the estate agent to complain that passing trains rocked her bed so much she was in fear of falling out of it.

The agent came around. "But it's so quiet," he said, "I can't believe that passing trains rock the bed."

"Shakes the living daylights out of it," she persisted, looking at her watch.

She heard a distant train whistle. "Here's the five thirty-five. Lie down on the bed yourself," and she climbed on to the other side.

That's when her husband came in.

"What do you think you are doing?" he roared, glaring at the estate agent.

"Would you believe waiting for a train?" he ventured.

## FAIRYTALES

TWO young women were walking along a country lane when a large green frog jumped out before them and said: "Please dear maidens. One of you kiss me and I will turn into a handsome prince."

One girl quickly scooped up the frog and put it in her handbag.

"Aren't you going to restore him to a prince?" asked her friend.

"No. Princes are a dime a dozen. But a talking frog, now there is potential for making a dollar."

## FAMILIES

FRED can trace his family tree right back to the time when it was his ancestor's address.

*     *     *

I AM not saying my brothers were fast eaters, but ours was the only house with racing colours on our knives and forks.

*     *     *

CECIL got in after midnight and his mother wanted to know where he had been.

"I've been out with a boy I know."

"You mean a girl, don't you?" she said.

"Boy or girl, what's the difference?" he said.

"If you don't know the difference, then I guess it's alright," said his relieved mother.

* * *

THE teenage girl got home very late and explained to her mother: "You know how it is, Mum ... "

"Yes, I certainly do. And what is his name?"

* * *

BERT got interested in his ancestors. He looked up his family tree and found most of them still swinging in the branches.

* * *

THE family had gathered around because old Grandpa was dying.

"Is there anything I can do for you?" said his wife.

The old man raised himself on one elbow and peered at a jug of beer on the table.

"I wouldn't mind a swig of that," he gasped.

"Well you can't," snapped his wife. "That's for the wake."

* * *

"MUM, how do lions make love?"

"Don't know, son. All your father's friends are Rotarians."

* * *

"MUM, Dad's going out again.

"Well pour some more petrol on him."

* * *

JUST when your children get old enough, so that you can stand them, they can't stand you.

* * *

CHILDREN should be seen and not had.

* * *

EVERY family should have at least three children. Then if one is a genius the other two can support him.

THEY say children brighten the home. That's because they never turn off the bloody lights.

*　　*　　*

SHE took after the mother, who took after the father, who took after the maid.

*　　*　　*

ANY one of your friends can become an enemy, given time. But a relative is one from the start.

*　　*　　*

SUCCESS is relative. The more success the more relatives.

## FARMS

AT the National Agricultural Conference it was easy to pick the dairy milking champion. He was the bloke who shook hands with everybody, one finger at a time.

*　　*　　*

BATTLING Bill had brought his family down from the farm to attend the Royal Show. A prize winning bull was the major exhibit, with an entrance fee of one dollar. Bill asked the attendant if he could get a concession for his family; himself, his wife and 13 kids.

"Hang on a minute," said the attendant, "I'll bring the bloomin' bull out and give him a gawk at you."

*　　*　　*

IT was the night of the school concert and all the kids had their poems, songs and recitations at the ready; except little Charlie who had just come down from the country and had started school that day.

"C'mon Charlie," said the teacher. "Surely you can do something for the concert."

It took much cajolling, but finally Charlie agreed to do some farmyard impressions.

The instant applause gave Charlie a boost of confidence and he strode to centre stage. "Farmyard noises," he announced.

Then cupping his hands to his face like a megaphone he yelled at the top of his voice: "Get off that blasted tractor. Shut that blasted gate. Get that blankety bull out of that yard ...!"

\*    \*    \*

YOUNG Johnny was late for school again. "And what kept you this time, Johnny?" asked the young mistress in despair for yet another yarn.

"It's the breeding season, Miss, and I had to put the bull to the cows," he said.

"Couldn't your father do that?" she said.

"No," said Johnny, "it's gotta be a bull!"

\*    \*    \*

FARMER Murphy met Farmer O'Leary in town. "What did you give to your ailing bull when it had colic?" asked Murphy.

"A good dose of phenyl," said Murphy.

A week later they met in the pub. "What did you say you gave your sick bull?" said O'Leary.

"Phenyl," said Murphy.

"Well I gave phenyl to my bull and it died," said O'Leary.

"So did mine," said Murphy.

\*    \*    \*

THE farmer's sons were sent home from the bush school with a note from the teacher complaining that they swore too much. Their father gave them a lecture, a thump in the ear and sent them to bed without dinner.

Next morning when they sat at the table they were asked what they wanted for breakfast.

"I'll have some of those bloody cornflakes," said one, and immediately received a thrashing from his father.

"And what would you like," said the angry father to his second son.

"I don't know. But it won't be those bloody cornflakes, that's for sure."

TWO city slickers attended the Royal Agricultural Show and were impressed with the fine examples of life on the farm. They got absorbed in watching Paddy grooming a large fearsome bull, until he sat quietly on a stool beside it.

"Gee it must be late, what's the time?" said one of the city slickers. Paddy put two hands under the testicles of the bull and lifted them gently. "It's ten past six," he said.

The men were about to leave when the significance of Paddy's uncanny country skill sunk through.

"Did you see that?" said one.

"Amazing," said the other.

They couldn't believe it, and talked it over for awhile before gingerly approaching Paddy again.

"Er, can you tell us the time again, please?"

Paddy, still seated on his stool, gently lifted the bull's balls once more. "It's a quarter-past six," he said.

The city slickers could contain themselves no longer.

"How do you do that?" they asked.

Paddy told them to climb through the rail and bend down near him. "Look, when I lift the bull's balls you can see the town hall clock from here!"

*　　*　　*

FARMER and his son were on a train headed for their first visit to the city when a priest hobbled into their compartment on crutches, with his foot in plaster.

"Slipped in the bathtub," he explained.

When the priest got out at the next station the son said: "What's a bathtub, Dad?"

"I dunno son, I'm not a Catholic."

*　　*　　*

DAVE had come down from the farm for his first visit to the city and was enjoying a beer in a pub when a character sidled up to him and whispered: "How would you like to buy some pornographic material?"

"No use to me, mate," replied Dave. "We haven't got a pornograph."

* * *

A CENSUS official was assisting a farmer's wife to fill in her forms.

"How many children have you got?" he asked.

"Six," she replied. "Three sets of twins."

"How very extraordinary," said the census man. "Twins every time."

"Oh no," said the farmer's wife. "Not every time. Hundreds of times, nothing!"

* * *

THE union rep was checking on the farmer who was suspected of underpaying his employees and was being introduced to the farmhands.

"This is Harry," said the farmer, "he milks the cows, and looks after the dairy and gets $200 a week with room and board."

"And this is Mary. She cooks and does the housework and gets $130 a week with room and board."

"Fair enough so far," said the union rep. "Is there anyone else?"

"Yes," said the farmer. "There's the half-wit. He works fifty hours a week and gets around $15 a week with room and board."

"Ah," said the rep. "I'd like to speak to him."

"You're talking to him right now," said the farmer.

# FARTS

NO less a literary giant than Chaucer gave recognition to the humble fart in his 13th century writing of "The Miller's Tale." Then Jonathan Swift, author of "Gulliver's Travels," wrote in 1731 that the odd fart was notorious for its stifling effect on romance.

Farts are an undeniable part of life. They are often

tried to be denied with euphemisms like flatulence or breaking wind but it never disguises the reality that a fart is a fart.

Rich men, poor men, beggars and thieves, even politicians and bishops pay homage to the old adage: Better to have an empty house than a grumbling tenant.

It can be said that the sign of a consolidated marriage is when either partner can fart without the need to say "excuse me."

\* \* \*

IT's a sign of wedded security
A marriage that's reached its maturity
When neither accuses
Nor offers excuses
For farts that fly with impunity.

\* \* \*

THE Queen was showing the Archbishop of Canterbury around the Royal Stables when one of the stallions close by broke wind in such a loud and gusty manner it couldn't be ignored.

"Oh dear," said the Queen blushing, "how embarassing. I'm frightfully sorry about that."

"It's quite understandable," said the archbishop, and after a moment added, "as a matter of fact, I thought it was the horse."

\* \* \*

THE chubby matron was consulting her doctor and explaining her problem in a timid manner. "What can you do for me, doctor, I have a lot of wind."

The doctor gave her a kite.

\* \* \*

A BUSINESSWOMAN explained to her doctor that she had an unusual complaint. She was always breaking wind, at board meetings, during interviews, in lifts, on the tram. It was impossible to control.

"But at least I am fortunate in two respects," she told

the doctor, "they neither smell nor make a noise. In fact you will be surprised to know it's happened twice since I've been talking to you Doctor."

The doctor reached for his notebook, scribbled a prescription and handed it to her.

She read it. "What? Nasal drops?" she queried.

"Yes," said the Doc. "We'll fix your nose first then we'll have a go at your hearing."

*       *       *

SECOND businesswoman tells the doctor she is suffering from the same problem. The Doc listens to a few extraordinary blow-offs that register 6.2 on the Richter scale then asks her to lower her bloomers and hop up on the couch.

She is alarmed when he reaches for a long pole with a hook on the end of it.

"Goodness, what are you going to do with that," she said.

"First it's necessary to open some of these skylights," he replied.

*       *       *

THE feuding neighbours had decided to patch up their differences over a few drinks. All was going well until one of the blokes broke wind.

"How dare you fart in front of my wife," roared the husband.

"How was I to know it was her turn," replied the other.

*       *       *

LADY Fotheringham suffered from flatulence a great deal and was prone to make certain noises when she got excited while entertaining friends at the manor. She was fortunate in having in her employ a very loyal and discreet butler called James.

Upon hearing these subdued explosions James would instantly say "Excuse me," and promptly leave the room taking the blame with him and saving her ladyship great embarrassment.

But one day James fell ill and was replaced by a butler from the employment service to help out on an important tea party.

In the middle of a conversation with the vicar Lady Fotheringham suffered one of her attacks accompanied by the usual sound effects.

She turned to the new butler and said: "James, stop that!"

"Certainly madam," said the new James, "which way did it go?"

*　*　*

THERE was a young girl from Jakarta
　Who was widely renowned as a farta
　Her deafening reports
　At athletics and sports
　Made her much in demand as a starta.

*　*　*

OVER the years Fred had never attempted to control his bad habit of breaking wind. It sounded like a gale ripping a spinnaker to shreds and often registered 7.3 on the Richter scale. Constant pleas from his wife, Myrtle, to control these thunder claps failed to have effect until one day she threatened to leave him.

"Okay, I'll do my best," he said.

"Not good enough," said Myrtle. "Prove it by refraining from that terrible practice for one whole month," she insisted.

Fred promised. And despite times when he gripped the armchair until his knuckles went white, crossed his legs and grimaced in pain, he never let one go for weeks.

One night he arrived home from the office to find the dining table set with flowers and candles. "What's all this?" he asked.

"It's a month tonight and you've been so good I have cooked one of your favourite dishes as a reward." She then placed a blindfold over his eyes. "I want it to be a surprise," she said.

Fred sat there in silence, and while listening to Myrtle rattling pots in the kitchen he felt a king-sized fart gathering force. He crossed his legs, clenched his fists and the sweat gathered on his brow.

"What the hell," he thought, "the month is up, I've gone the distance and I'm sitting here like a fool with a blindfold on while I can still hear her out in the kitchen. It would be safe to let one rip."

With that he leant to one side, lifted one rump off the chair and with a grin of great relief let it rumble free.

It was just in time for he heard Myrtle's footsteps coming and felt her fumble with the blindfold before ripping it off.

That was the signal for a chorus of "Happy Birthday" from Fred's family all seated around him at the birthday table.

## FASHION

FASHION is something that goes in one era and out the other.

*   *   *

MY ol' Dad was dedicated to fashion. When we were kids he would say: "If you must polish your boots while you are still wearing them, take your socks off. Then if you get some black nugget on your ankles you simply put your socks back on and nobody knows."

*   *   *

AND if it is a formal occasion, do your best to get two matching thongs.

*   *   *

THE tall blonde told the attendant in the fashion store that she wanted a pair of low heels.

"To wear with what, madam?"
"A short, plump, rich stock-broker," she replied.

* * *

"HOW do you like the fit, madam?"
"Fit? It's a convulsion."

* * *

IT'S not the cost of a strapless gown, it's the upkeep.

* * *

THE bride wore a beautiful gownless evening strap.

* * *

HER dress looked pretty good considering the shape it was on.

* * *

WHEN he criticised the scantiness of her swim suit, she laughed it off.
OR... When he complained that her strapless dress was too daring, she laughed it off.

* * *

THE outfit made her look like a million dollars; all wrinkled and green.

* * *

"I WANT the dress in the window."
"Well it's in the window."

* * *

A TIGHT skirt has never yet stopped a girl's circulation.

* * *

"I'D like to see something cheap in a straw hat."
"Here, try this. And the mirror is over there."

* * *

"I'D like to buy that hat in the window."
"It's not necessary. We can sell it here over the counter."

* * *

SHE said she was a physical education instructor and she wanted a pair of bloomers to wear around her gymnasium.
"How big is your gymnasium," enquired the attendant.

SHOPPER: "I'd like to see something in silk stockings."
 Attendant: "You men are all alike."

*    *    *

WHEN he heard that Parisian women would not be wearing dresses much longer this season he decided to go there for his holidays.

*    *    *

HE chooses his own suits, but his wife picks his pockets.

*    *    *

THE latest thing in men's clothing is women.

*    *    *

FATHER: "Why are you wearing my raincoat?"
 Son: "Well you don't want your best suit to get wet, do you?"

*    *    *

SHE was ecstatic over the bargain. "Look at this dress," she said, "I bought it for a ridiculous figure."
 "Yeah, I know," said her husband, "but how much did you pay for it?"

*    *    *

"HOW many shirts does your husband wear a week?" she asked.
 "You mean how many weeks does he wear his shirts," she replied.

*    *    *

ACCORDING to the latest fashion magazine, women will be wearing their legs longer this summer.

*    *    *

HE asked what Mabel's new evening dress looked like.
 He was told: "In a lot of places it looks like Mabel."

*    *    *

"WHENEVER I am down in the dumps, I treat myself to a new hat."
 "We wondered where you got them."

*    *    *

"NO one knows," complained Miss Cox

142

"The pain that it engenders
"Keeping up my bobby-sox
"With ord'nary suspenders."

* * *

HE was a bit old-fashioned and it upset him to see the outrageous dress of some young people in the street.

"Just look at that one?" he barked at a bystander. "Is it a boy or a girl?"

"It's a girl, and she's my daughter," came the reply.

"Oh, I'm sorry," apologised the grump, "I didn't know you were her mother."

"I'm not," snapped the bystander, "I'm her father!"

* * *

MODERN fashions are crazy. Fish-net stockings and forcing feet into those high heel shoes is ridiculous. I've told my father to stop wearing them.

* * *

SOME dresses worn by women
   Are like fences at the zoo
   They safeguard lovely bodies
   But don't obstruct the view.

## FATHERS-IN-LAW
See MOTHERS-IN-LAW

THE old codger was hogging the fireplace, monopolising the telly and stinking the lounge room with his pipe. Finally, it got too much for the young couple and she whispered to her husband, "Look dear, fair's fair. He's been here ever since we were married. It's time your father went home."

"My father. My father," he gasped. "I thought he was yours!"

* * *

"WHEN I see your father coming up the front path," she said to her husband, "I sometimes wish I had loved and lost."

WHEN he arrived home his wife had a smug look. "There was a door-knock collection today," she said. "People were collecting for the Old People's Home. So I gave them your father."

*     *     *

MADGE: "I've just got a bottle of whisky for my father-in-law."

MARY: "That's a good bargain!"

*     *     *

MADGE: "I stuck up for Pops the other night."

MARY: "Yeah?"

MADGE: "They said he wasn't fit to eat with pigs. I said he was."

*     *     *

IT took time, but Madge eventually developed an attachment for her father-in-law. It fitted over his mouth.

*     *     *

HER father-in-law once got a job on a farm. He left it after a few weeks. He got tired of standing out in a wheat field with his arms outstretched scaring the crows away. He not only chased the birds off, they even brought back the grain they stole the previous year.

# FATHERS AND SONS

HE was a young father, wheeling the pram through the gardens while the baby was screaming its head off. "Take it easy Jason," he said calmly, "there's nothing to fuss about."

A middle-aged woman noticed his soothing manner and marvelled at the new breed of young husbands.

When the baby screamed even louder she heard him say: "Cool it, Jason, don't get excited, lad, cool it son."

Touched by his gentle manner the woman leaned into the pram and cooed: "There, there Jason, what's bothering you?"

"Excuse me, lady," said the father, "that's Jeremy, I'm Jason."

*　　*　　*

FATHER and son were posing for a picture to mark the son's graduation from university. "Stand closer," said the photographer to the father, "and put your hand on his shoulder."

"Wouldn't it be more appropriate," replied the father, "if he put his hand in my pocket?"

*　　*　　*

TWO fathers were at the bar of their club sharing their problems. "My son is at college and is always writing home for money. I don't know what he does with it," lamented one.

"My daughter is at college and never asks for money. I wonder where she is getting it," lamented the other.

*　　*　　*

HE came home from the office to find his lay-about son asleep in the garden hammock once more. It was time he had a lesson about life.

He shook him awake and said: "You've been out of school for three years, you haven't tried looking for a job. Isn't it time you smartened yourself and studied for a profession?"

"Why?" said the son sleepily.

"So that you can become a businessman like me."

"Why?" persisted the son.

"So you can make a lot of money."

"Why?"

"So you can have enough in the bank."

"Why?"

"So that you can retire and not go to work."

"But I don't go to work now," said the son.

*　　*　　*

"WHAT'S a monologue, Dad?"

"That's a conversation with your mother, son."

"WHEN I was your age," said the father to his teenage son, "I would be up at dawn, run ten miles across frosty ground, dive into the sea, run another mile along the beach and sprint all the way home. I would do all that before breakfast and think nothing of it."

The son yawned and said, "I don't think much of it myself."

★　　★　　★

IN many fields of endeavour the cleverness or fame of the father often proves the stumbling block for the son.

"Well thank goodness," said Mum, "our Johnny has nothing to fall over."

★　　★　　★

TWO fathers were discussing the trials and tribulations of bringing up teenage sons. "I insist on discipline," said one. "I have always insisted on discipline from the day he started to walk."

Just then the boy under discussion entered the room waving a set of car keys in his hand. "Hi Dad. I'm taking the car. I've pulled a bird and I have just raided one of your bottles of Scotch to make sure I'm on a winner. I won't be back tonight."

The visiting father's jaw dropped. "I thought you said you had disciplined him?"

"Of course I have," said the first. "He didn't have to come and tell me, did he?"

★　　★　　★

HIS father was sternly insisting that he continue his education to ensure he gained a profession. "Digging holes is the only job you can get where you start at the top," he said.

★　　★　　★

TWO old boys met at the club after years apart. "How's your son making out in life?" asked one.

"Oh he's the top car salesman of a nation-wide franchise. Going so well he topped the sales chart and they gave him a brand new Mercedes," said the proud father. "But he gave it away. Can you imagine that, gave it away."

"That's amazing," said the other old chap. "My son's in real estate and development. Clinched the biggest deal this year and they gave him a penthouse, but he gave it away. Can you imagine that?"

Right then a third old boy came in. "How's your son?" they asked him.

"Bit disappointing really," he said. "He's turned out to be a raving homosexual. But still, he's managing quite well. One of his best friends gave him a Mercedes last week, and another gave him a penthouse."

## FEMINISTS

MARRIAGE: It begins as you sink in his arms, and ends with your arms in the sink.

\* \* \*

EQUALITY is a myth; women are superior.

\* \* \*

WHAT do you call a man who has lost 90 per cent of his brain?

A widower!

\* \* \*

IF a woman does household chores for $200 a week, that's domestic science. If she does it for nothing, that's marriage.

\* \* \*

COMMON sense would save a significant number of marriages. If women used it, there wouldn't be any.

\* \* \*

THE feminists are hailing a miracle birth.

The baby has a dick AND a brain.

\* \* \*

SHE said she wouldn't mind having a baby, but unfortunately you have to marry one to get one.

THERE are three kinds of men; the handsome, the caring, and the majority.

* * *

A WOMAN who strives to be like a man lacks ambition.

* * *

THE only problem with women, is men. And the worst thing about men is that all the nice ones are gay.

* * *

SHE said we all have to live with our disappointments. "But why do I have to live with mine?"

* * *

WHEN the boss put the hard word on the lively new girl she had the answer: "No way, bozzo, you've got the words 'liberated' and 'free' mixed up."

* * *

LOVE is the delusion that one man is different from the rest.

* * *

WHEN a woman makes a fool of a man it's usually an improvement.

* * *

IT is said that the wisest of men can become foolish over women; and the most foolish of women is wise to men.

* * *

THE only difference between men and pigs is that when pigs drink they don't make men of themselves.

* * *

MEN are like pigeons. They should never be looked up to.

* * *

THE only thing wives have in common with their husbands is that they were married on the same day.

* * *

SHE wanted a husband and put an advertisement in the personal column. She got a hundred replies saying: "You can have mine!"

WOMEN are called birds because of all the worms they pick up.

\* \* \*

FRED was a window cleaner and he couldn't believe his eyes when he saw a young woman get out of the bath and start drying off, right in front of him.

She was a feminist, and instead of screaming she stared straight back at him in an effort to shame him.

Their eyes locked in confrontation for an interminable minute. Neither would budge.

Finally Fred roared: "What are ya staring at? Haven't ya ever seen a window cleaner before?"

\* \* \*

TWO unattached office girls decided it would make economic sense if they teamed up to take advantage of the twin-share prices on their next holiday. After they booked in to their first hotel room one turned to the other and rested her hand on her shoulder. "There's something I haven't told you about myself," she said. "I'll be frank..."

"Oh no you won't," interrupted her friend, "I'll be Frank."

\* \* \*

THE young couple had a knee-trembler against a paling fence and got so excited they knocked it down.

The commotion aroused the house-holder who grabbed the young man and collected $100 on the spot for repairs to the fence.

Later the young bloke said: "Listen Mabel. You are a feminist and you are always shouting about equal rights. Here's your chance. You owe me $50 for half cost of the fence."

"No way," she said. "It was you who did all the pushing."

## FINANCE
See ACCOUNTANTS

"I WOULD go through anything for you."

"Good. Let's start with your bank account."

149

THE ship's purser asked the sailor how he had spent his month's pay on shore leave.

"Some went on drink, some on women. And I guess I squandered the rest," was the reply.

*　　*　　*

EVERY day a ragged old man with a tray of shoe laces would take up a position at the entrance to a city skyscrapper, and every morning and executive entering the building would drop a dollar in his tray, without taking any laces.

One day the executive dropped his usual dollar and was about to walk away when the old man tapped him on the shoulder. "Excuse me, sir. I don't like to complain, but laces are now $1.50."

*　　*　　*

THRIFT is the most admirable virtue of any ancestor.

*　　*　　*

COP to bank manager: "Can you describe the missing teller?"

"Yes, he's six foot tall and $100,000 short."

*　　*　　*

A YOUNG Jewish lad was learning arithmetic. "What's two-and-two, Father?"

Dad: "Are we buying or selling?"

*　　*　　*

WITH the new world order, the USA will, from now on, be known as the IOUSA.

*　　*　　*

ALWAYS borrow money from a pessimist. He doesn't expect to get it back.

*　　*　　*

MONEY, money, money.

If a man is always chasing it, he's mercenary.

If he doesn't chase it, he lacks ambition.

If he hoards it, he's stingy.

If he spends it, he's a spendthrift.
If he gets it without working, he's a parasite.
If he scrimps and saves, he is wasting his life.

* * *

TREASURER'S report: "Last year we were poised on the edge of a precipice. This year we have made a great leap forward!"

* * *

I HAVE always tried to pay my bills with a smile. But invariably they want money.

* * *

REMEMBER, the darkest hour is just before the pawn.

* * *

"WHAT is your major worry?"
"Money."
"I didn't know you had any."
"I haven't."

* * *

"HEY Fred, lend us twenty bucks until pay day to buy a round of drinks."
"Okay, but when's pay day."
"How should I know. You're the one who's working!"

* * *

"HEY Fred, remember last time when I was broke and you helped me out with twenty bucks and I said I'd never forget you?"
"Yes."
"Well, I'm broke again!"

* * *

MONEY won't help you make friends. But you'll have a better class of enemy.

* * *

THE wealthy financier took a tumble for a blonde and lost his balance at the bank.

* * *

SHE told her banker: "I haven't got much collateral, but will you take one of those promiscuity notes?"

THE manager told the new clerk to count a package of one thousand single dollar notes. He noticed the clerk laboriously counting and heard him reach, "502, 503, 504, 505." Then the clerk threw the package into the drawer and remarked: "If it's right that far, it's probably right all the way."

\* \* \*

THE Prime Minister was on the dais as the parade of military might passed by. First squadrons of jets flew overhead, then lines of tanks, heavy artillery and columns of infantry armed to the teeth. Finally, a group of men in pin-striped suits, awkwardly marching out of step brought up the rear of the parade.

"Is that your Secret Service Mr Minister?" asked a foreign diplomat.

"Hell no. They are our economists. They can cause more damage than the rest put together!"

\* \* \*

THE Chinese businessman pressed the teller to explain why his interest rate had increased two points from the previous day.

"Fluctuations," said the teller.

"And the same to you, ya bloomin' ocker," said the Chinaman.

\* \* \*

A YOUNG accountant was overjoyed to learn that he had won a million dollars in Lotto. He lived with his Mum and Dad and they were equally excited when he broke the news.

"Naturally I want to share my good fortune so I am going to make you a present of $100 each," he told his parents.

There was silence for a moment before the old man spoke.

"Well son, we've done a lot for you," he began. "It was a struggle during the depression, and we never had much money. In fact, we didn't have enough to get legally married."

"What," said the shocked son, "you mean ... I am..."

"Yes, son, and a damned miserable one at that."

* * *

THEY had been down-and-outers all their life, but Bill and Jacko had always managed to share a Lotto ticket, and of course, one day their dream came true. They celebrated with a beer in their local pub and agreed that a million dollars would not change their nature, except for the flash car they had always wanted.

Bill paid for the beers and off they went to the car sales showroom where they shocked the salesman by buying a Rolls Royce each.

Bill produced his cheque book with a flourish and reached for his pen when Jacko said: "No, no, Bill. Fair go. You paid for the beers."

* * *

THE man who writes the bank's advertising is not the same man who makes the loans.

* * *

WHEN Jock McTavish received a letter from the electricity board threatening to cut off the electricity if he didn't pay his long-overdue account he stormed down to the office.

"Look here," he told the manager. "Each month I put all the bills in my hat, give them a good stir, then pull one out and pay it. But if you don't stop hounding me with threatening letters your bill won't even go in the hat next month."

* * *

"DEAR Bank Manager. Stop sending me letters, just because my account is in the red. I didn't pester you with letters when my account was in the black."

* * *

THE owner of the corner shop was adamant. She told Paddy: "I'm sorry, but you can have no more credit. Your bill's already bigger than it should be."

"I know that," retorted Paddy. "As soon as you cut it to the proper amount I'll pay it!"

## FIREFIGHTERS

THERE was a fire at the nurses home. It took the firemen 15 minutes to put it out. It took the nurses three hours to put the firemen out.

\* \* \*

THE phone rang at the fire station and a frantic voice said: "I have just had the front yard landscaped, and there is a new rock-garden which cost me heaps and a flower bed down the side..."

"What's this got to do with the fire station?" yelled the officer.

"Plenty," continued the caller. "The house next door is on fire and I don't want you blokes trampling all over my new garden."

\* \* \*

STATION officer Jones took the call. "There's a house on fire in Centre Rd," said the frantic voice.

"We're right in the middle of a poker game at the moment and I've got a winning hand. Can you throw a bucket of petrol on it and keep it going till we get there?"

\* \* \*

THE Mexican fireman was the proud father of twin boys. He called one Jose and the other Hose B.

\* \* \*

THERE's a bloke who sells Immitation Fire Insurance to people with imitation fireplaces.

\* \* \*

AND we all know why firemen have bigger balls than policemen. They sell more tickets.

\* \* \*

THE firefighter answered the phone to hear Paddy in a panic.

"Quick, there's a fire! There's a fire!"
"Where is it?"
"At my place of course."
"I mean what's the location?"
"It's in the kitchen."
"But how do we get there?"
"Crikey. Haven't you got a fire engine?"

## FISHERMEN

PADDY said that he once cleaned 500 fish in one day.
"Now that takes guts."

\* \* \*

"I WISH I could afford the time to go fishing."
"But you are always fishing."
"Yes, but I wish I could afford it!"

\* \* \*

HE went off for a week's fishing and didn't catch anything until he got home.

\* \* \*

AGAINST his wife's wishes he set off for another weekend. "What's that Dad's carrying?" said their young son.
"It is called a fishing rod, dear, and it has a worm at both ends."

\* \* \*

ONE dedicated fisherman told his fellow angler that he had a marvellous dream the previous night. "I dreamt I was alone in a boat with Raquel Welch and we were both nude."
"Well what was good about it," asked his mate.
"We caught 50 bream and a record sized salmon," he said.

\* \* \*

THE angler from the city settled down on the banks of the river with all his sophisticated gear and tried to make conversation with an old local seated on a nearby log with a line in his hand.

"Do you fish with flies here?"

"Fish with them? I've fished with them, camped with them, and tried to sleep with them," said the old timer.

* * *

TWO fishermen were out in their boat one Sunday morning when they heard the church bells ring in the distance. One said contritely, "You know, we really ought to be in church."

Baiting his hook the second chap replied: "I couldn't have gone today anyway. I've got the wife sick in bed."

* * *

TWO lads from went fishing and got caught in a terrible storm. Night fell and things began to look bad as they were blown to sea at the mercy of the wind. One began to sob and pray: "Oh Lord. I have not been very good in my life. I have drunk to excess, gambled my wages, cheated on my wife. But if you spare my life now I promise faithfully I will ..."

"Hang on a minute, Bert," interrupted his friend. "Don't go too far, I think I see a light."

* * *

AN angler's wife asked him for some money. He gave her two fifties, two twenties, three tenners and a fiver. She threw the small one back.

* * *

IT was the worst trout season New Zealand had experienced for years and the disgruntled American tourist held up his single fish.

"I've come half way round the world to catch this one darn fish so I reckon it has cost me at least $10,000."

"Bloomin' lucky you only caught one then," said his guide.

* * *

AT the waterside bar the young fisherman was describing

the crayfish he had pulled to the surface. "It was at least a metre long," he said.

His listeners were amazed. "Well, where is it?" they asked.

"Oh, it busted the top of the pot and got away," he said.

An old salt who had been leaning on the bar during this revelation said "I was fishing and my line hooked onto an old ship's lantern on Shipwreck Reef. When I hauled it up the lantern was still burning."

The young man eyed the old salt with suspicion. "Fair go mate, you don't expect us to believe that."

"Well," said the old man, "if you chop half a metre off your crayfish, I will blow the bloomin' candle out!"

*　　*　　*

OH give me the luck to catch a fish
　So big that even I
　When talking of it afterwards
　May have no need to lie.

## FLASHERS

THREE old maids were sitting on a seat in the park when a member of the raincoat brigade flashed at them. Two of the old ladies had a stroke. The third was too slow.

*　　*　　*

IT was so cold the other day that the local flasher was seen describing himself to a woman.

*　　*　　*

FRED the Flasher had been working the riverbank for 30 years and Pete the Perv asked him when he was retiring.

"I have been thinking about it seriously," said Fred. "But I think I will stick it out for another year."

# FLOOSIES

SHE has an impediment in her speech. She can't say no.

\* \* \*

SHE had always been a gold-digger, so when her husband's partner died she was quick off the mark to arrange a replacement she had groomed for the job.

"Darling," she said, "I have just the right candidate to replace your partner who died yesterday."

"That's alright with me," he replied, "provided you can arrange it with the undertaker."

\* \* \*

THE sugar daddy presented his floosy with a beautiful skunk coat. "Amazing," she said, "that such a beautiful coat could come from such a smelly little beast."

"Look," he said, "I don't expect gratitude, but there's no need to get personal."

\* \* \*

LIL went out with many men
   And accepted all they gave her
But she married a man with a will of his own
   Made out in her favour.

\* \* \*

FLOOSIE'S toast:
   Here's to the men I've loved
   And here's to the men I've kissed.
   And here's my profound apologies
   To all the men I've missed.

# FOOD AND WINE

EAT, drink and be merry, for tomorrow we diet.

\* \* \*

HERE'S a toast to Mum's cooking. And may my wife never know how bad it was.

PEOPLE who like home cooking should stay home.

* * *

WINE improves with age. I like it more the older I get.

* * *

HOW do you make Liviewitz wine?
  Leave without paying.

## FOOTBALL
See FOOTBALL FANS

THE team was facing defeat. At the final change the coach roared some fight into them. "And you Murphy, it's about time you got ferocious."
  "What's his number?" said Murph.

* * *

THE woman reporter asked him: "Are all the champion football players conceited?"
  "I don't really know, but I'm not."

* * *

"WHERE does your football team play, Grandpa?"
  "What football team? What are you talking about?"
  "Oh, Dad says that when you kick off we can get a new house!"

* * *

THE game was so close that the two football fans would not leave the stand, despite their hunger. "Send that kid for some pies," suggested one. They were $2 each so they gave the kid $6 and told him to get one for himself.
  The kid came back five minutes later and handed back $4. "They only had one pie left," he said.

* * *

THE star recruit who had just been transferred for an enormous sum was being interviewed on telly.
  "You appear to be earning more money than the prime minister," said the interviewer.

"Only fair," said the football star, "I play a lot better than he does."

*   *   *

YOUNG man looking for a job travelled to the country and approached the general store in a small town. The man behind the counter was also the president of the country football league and offered the lad a job immediately. "We need a centre-half forward with courage and a strong set of hands," he said.

"Sorry sir," said the lad. "I don't know a thing about football."

"No worries. We need umpires too."

*   *   *

THE player was dashing through with the ball when he was brought down with a blatant trip.

"Free kick," roared the umpire.

"Who to?" shouted one of the players.

"Us," said the Ump.

*   *   *

A PSYCHIATRIST has a thriving practice, particularly in the football season. He tried an idea-association test on a patient one day and asked him what came to mind when he thought of something brown, firm and had smooth curves.

"A football," said the patiently immediately.

"Good. And what do you think of when two arms slide around your waist?"

"An illegal tackle," was the instant reply.

"Now picture a pair of firm thighs..."

"A fullback."

"Top marks," said the psychiatrist. "Your reactions are quite normal. You would be surprised at some of the stupid answers I get."

*   *   *

IT was the jungle's soccer classic of the year, the annual grudge match between the animals and the insects, and by half time the elephants, zebras and cheetahs had proved too much for the grasshoppers, beetles and ants with a convincing score of 58 goals to nil.

However, when the match resumed the animals noted a substitute player run onto the field with the insects. It was a shiny black centipede.

From then on the centipede became the star of the game peppering the goals from all angles. Indeed, the animals failed to score another goal and the insects ran out winners, 59 goals to 58.

At the bar after the game the animals' captain, a tough looking elephant, said to the insects' skipper, a wily grasshopper, "Great game, but you were damned lucky that centipede arrived at half time."

"You're wrong," said the grasshopper. "He was here for the start of the game, but it took him until half time to put his boots on!"

*     *     *

THE champ from the bush was not all he was cracked up to be so the runner was sent out with a message.

"The coach says he will pull you off at half time."

"Great," said the country lad, "we only get oranges at Snake Gully."

## FOOTBALL FANS
See FOOTBALL

FOOTBALL fans are quite a different species from the rest of the human race. The average footy fan buys his final series tickets three months in advance, and waits until December 24 to do the Christmas shopping.

*     *     *

"I HEAR you had a difficult time explaining the grand final to your wife."

"Yes. She found out I didn't go."

AT the turnstiles it was being explained to McTavish that there were seats at $20, $15 and $10 and that programs were 50 cents.

"Okay," said McTavish, "I'll sit on a program."

\* \* \*

CLASSIFIED Ad: "Young football supporter of good appearance and sound health offers hand in marriage to any young lady with two tickets to the grand final next Saturday. Please send photograph of the tickets."

\* \* \*

THE two mates were down at the front fence for the rugby league match when the beer cans started to fly. One was so concerned about being hit he kept looking over his shoulder and couldn't concentrate on the game.

"Don't worry," said his mate, "as they say in the war, if there's one with your name on it ..."

"That's just it. My name is Foster!"

\* \* \*

ON a crowded train going to the football game the fan resplendent in black and white colours had a large duck tucked under his arm.

Sitting directly opposite, at face level with the duck, was an old codger flaunting a scarf in the opposing team's colours. "They won't let you take a pig into the ground ya know," he said loudly.

"It's not a pig, it's a duck ya burk," said the fan in the black and white scarf.

"I wasn't talking to you," said the old codger.

\* \* \*

"I BELIEVE you are a member of the school's football team," said the proud grandfather to his 13-year-old grandson. "What position do you play?"

"I'm not sure Gramps," said the lad, "but I heard the sports teacher say that I was the team's main drawback."

ONE-eyed supporter arrived at the ground. "How much to get in," he said.

"Sixteen dollars," said the ticket-seller.

"Well here's eight," said the fan, "I only watch one side."

* * *

IT was the day of the grand final when the officials took a call from the gatekeeper. "There are two life-members here. They are close friends of the umpire and they have lost their tickets."

"Throw them out," said the executive. "They are liars. Whoever heard of an umpire having two friends!"

* * *

WE all know that soccer is taken seriously in the United Kingdom, so when Ireland and Scotland clashed at Wembly a fan wearing the colours of neither side and cheering the goals of both teams was a thorn in the side of a Scot and an Irishman standing either side of him.

"Are ye from Scotland?" enquired the Scot.

"Or are ya from Ireland?" joined the Irishman.

"I'm neither. I'm English really," came the answer.

"Well then," said the Scot and Irishman together as they thumped him, "mind your own flaming business."

* * *

IT was a mid-winter Saturday. The two footy fans were huddled together in the wind and rain. Their team was being thrashed, their feet were soaked and they were both beginning to shiver. Fred turned to his mate and said: "Harry, tell me how much fun we are having here today. I keep forgetting."

* * *

A BLOKE took his black and white fox terrier in to the pub and was enjoying a few drinks until the footy scores appeared on telly. When it was announced that his team had lost the dog went mad, knocking over tables and snapping at customers.

"What's got into your dog?" asked the barman.

"He just can't take it when our team is beaten," explained the owner.

"Heck. What does he do when they win?"

"Don't know. I've only had him two years!"

\* \* \*

A BLOKE went into the pub with his dog. Both were supporters of the local team and they watched the match on TV with great interest. Every time their team kicked a goal the dog yelped with delight.

The barman was impressed. "What does he do when the other side scores?" he asked.

"Somersaults" said the owner.

"How many?" asked the barman.

"Depends on how hard I kick him!"

## FUNERALS
See DEATH

IF you don't go to your friends' funerals... they won't come to yours.

\* \* \*

THE difference between an Australian wedding and an Australian funeral is one less drunk.

\* \* \*

AN Irish funeral is merrier than an English holiday.

\* \* \*

A LARGE crowd had gathered at a funeral. A passer-by asked who had died.

"Dunno," he replied. "I'm only here for the beer."

\* \* \*

IT was an overcast and threatening sky the day Fred buried his mother-in-law. In fact, just as the funeral party left the cemetery there was a loud clap of thunder and flash of lightning.

"Crikey," said Fred. "She's there already."

AFTER the funeral she took her husband's suits to the Op Shop. The manager noted the thin material and the holes in the trousers. "My goodness," she said, "your old man died just in time."

* * *

BRIDGET took one look at her late husband, lying in his coffin with a smile on his face.

"Look at him now," she said.

"He's smiling because he died in his sleep and he doesn't know he's dead yet. He is dreaming he is still alive, so when he wakes up and finds that he is dead, begorrah, the shock will kill him."

* * *

HE had died a very rich man, and at the funeral service Paddy was beating his breast and wailing louder than any of the other mourners.

One of the relatives comforted him. "We didn't know you knew him."

"That's the trouble. I didn't," wailed Paddy.

* * *

LOUIE had been a big time gambler and all his race-track friends had assembled in the small church for his funeral.

With heads bowed they heard the priest solemnly intone: "Our friend Louie is not dead. He merely sleeps," when a voice from the back of the church said, "I've got a hundred to say he won't wake up."

* * *

AFTER three weeks during which her husband had been slowly dying in bed the doctor came downstairs and told Mrs Murphy he had good news. He said her husband had made a remarkable recovery.

Mrs Murphy burst out crying. "What am I going to do now? I've sold all his clothes to pay for the funeral."

A LAWYER was merely fulfilling a duty by being present at the funeral service of a millionaire when a colleague arrived, a little late, and stood in the pew beside him.

"How far has he got?" said the newcomer referring to the vicar's eulogy.

"He's just opened the defence," replied the lawyer.

* * *

DID you know there is a law which prohibits anybody living south of the river being buried in the cemetery? It's on account of them being not dead yet.

* * *

HARRY had been a workaholic journo all his life and his friends at the office took up a collection for a headstone, which read: "Erected in memory of Harry Bloggs, drowned in the river, by his relatives and friends."

The headstone had been installed hastily before the ground over the grave had settled. On inspecting the work next day the cemetery attendant found that it was tilting sideways. As a temporary measure he looped a wire around it and tied it to a nearby tree.

Harry's mates took the opportunity that afternoon to visit the grave for the first time. "Gawd, that's our Harry," said one, noting the wire. "He's still working. Now he's got the phone on!"

* * *

AT the funeral service the vicar and the undertaker had never seen a husband so grieved. Fred was sobbing his heart out and beating his breast. He was so distraught that the vicar took him aside in a bid to comfort him.

"It's tough, I know," said the vicar, "but believe me you will eventually get over it. And dare I say it," he paused, "in three or six months you might well meet another woman and ..."

"Yeah!" wailed Fred, "but what am I gonna do tonight?"

# G

## GAMBLERS

"DO you play cards for money?"

"No. But the blokes I play with do."

* * *

WHEN the little old lady fronted up to the bookie for yet another payout he was perplexed.

"You must study the form," he said.

"Oh, no," she said, "I just stick a pin in the paper."

"But how have you managed to pick four winners in one afternoon?"

"Oh, today I used a fork," she explained.

* * *

SLICK Sam was always winning at cards, and always losing at the races. "Why is that?" asked his mate Pete.

"Simple. They won't let me shuffle the horses."

* * *

DID you hear how Slick Sam lost $100 on the Melbourne Cup, and another $100 on the replay?

* * *

"WHAT'S the meaning of the three balls over the pawnshop?"

"It's two-to-one you won't get it back."

* * *

AFTER the last race a bloke who stuttered slightly approached a bookmaker who had a winning day.

"Excuse me, I b-b-backed a five-tt..."

The bookie was sharp. "There was no five-to-one winners, mate, nick off."

The bloke persisted. "I b-b-backed a five-tt."

"Look," said the bookie, "I've had a good day. Here's a fifty-note. Now nick off."

The punter shrugged his shoulders with resignation, accepted the note, walked over to his mate and said. "That bookie's a nice bloke. I tried to tell him I backed a five-ton truck into his Rolls Royce, and he gave me fifty dollars."

\* \* \*

THE lads had arranged to go fishing on Sunday morning. All turned up on time except Fred. He finally arrived ten minutes late. "What kept you?" they asked.

"It was a toss-up if I went to church or joined you blokes fishing."

"Well, that shouldn't have taken you long."

"I had to toss up 23 times."

\* \* \*

WHEN he got to the tote window a little voice in his ear said: "Put it all on number six."

He did, and it came in at 100 to one.

When he fronted the window for the second race a little voice in his ear said: "Put the lot on number 13."

He did and it romped home by a street.

When he pushed ten thousand over the counter at the tote window for the third race a little voice said: "Put it all on number nine."

He did and it ran stone motherless last, and the little voice in his ear said: "Oh well. Win some, lose some."

\* \* \*

THE gambler who had just won the $100,000 jackpot on the Melbourne Cup was asked by reporters how he would spend the money.

"Oh, I've got it all figured out," he said. "First I'll spend

$25,000 on whisky and beer, $25,000 on horses, dogs and cards, and $25,000 on women and wild living."

"Wow, and what of the other $25,000?"

"I will probably just squander that," he said.

*   *   *

ONCE again he had to explain his bad luck to his wife. "As I walked into the racecourse a sudden gust of wind blew my hat off. It was a sure sign," he said. "So I put it all on a horse called Gone with the Wind."

"And it didn't win?"

"No. Some foreign horse called Mon Chapeau won by a mile."

*   *   *

PETE the Punter was at the pub early and got a few under his belt before he noticed a large sign on the wall: Lunch 12 to 1.

"Bloody good odds," he said to himself. He called the barman over and said he wanted to put down a hundred for a win.

"No gambling here," said the barman, and ordered him out. Pete wandered down to the next pub where he saw another sign: Lunch 11 to 2.

"The odds are down already," he muttered. "It must be a good thing." He went straight in to the bar and said he wanted to place a bet.

He was immediately thrown out for a second time.

Pete wandered around the corner where a third pub displayed the sign: Lunch 1 to 2.

"That's blown it. It's odds on now." But he decided to go in and listen to the result. As he entered the pub the chef delivered a plate on the bar and called "Sausages one!"

Pete the Punter breathed a sigh of relief. "Just as well I didn't back that bloody Lunch!"

*   *   *

WHEN the well-dressed gambler left the club he was

accosted by a down-and-outer who asked him for a few dollars for a meal.

The gambler took pity. "Come inside and I'll buy you a beer."

"No, I don't drink," said the man.

"Well, how about a cigar?"

"No, I don't smoke."

"Well, I know a certainty tomorrow. I'll put a $100 on it for you."

"No. Just a few dollars for food," insisted the man.

"Then come home with me for a meal. I want my wife to see what happens to a man who doesn't drink, smoke or gamble."

\* \* \*

"HOW come you always come back from the races with a small fortune?"

"Cos I always go there with a bigger one."

\* \* \*

AFTER six months at Gamblers Anonymous, Fred believed he was cured. "I'd like to thank you all for helping me kick the habit," he said.

"I'll never gamble again. I'll wager a fortune on it."

\* \* \*

THEY had been gambling mates for years and finally it came to Fred's attention that his poker playing mate was having an affair with his wife.

"Let's settle this in a civilised way," said Fred. "We will play a hand of poker for her. And just to make it interesting how about a $50 wager on the side?"

\* \* \*

TWO London gamblers were on holiday in Italy and visited the Vatican. They were the last to leave the Cistene Chapel and happened to see a white robed figure fall down some stairs. They recognised him as the Pope and he was stone dead.

The first Vatican authorities on the scene begged them

not to say anything for 24 hours. There were world-wide implications. The two gamblers agreed. After all, they were flying home that night.

On the plane one of them had a brilliant idea. "As soon as we land I am going straight to Ladbrokes and getting great odds on the life of the Pope."

"Sounds like a great idea," said Paddy, his mate.

It was two days before the Pope's death was announced and the first gambler made a clean up.

"And what about you, Paddy?" he asked.

"Nothing at all," admitted Paddy. "I took the Pope in a double with the Archbishop of Canterbury."

## GARDENERS

A GARDENER is a bloke who calls a spade a spade; until he falls over one.

\* \* \*

NOW is the time of the year when the bulbs you forgot to plant last autumn will fail to bloom.

\* \* \*

FRED'S specialty was growing vegetables and he eventually won the Nobel Peas Prize, for being outstanding in his field.

\* \* \*

WE know a bonsai tree grower who has been so successful he is now looking for a house with a smaller garden.

\* \* \*

SHE talked to the trees. That's why they took her away.

\* \* \*

"DO you really think talking to plants makes them grow?" confided one keen gardener to the other.

"Nah," said Fred. "My Missus hasn't stopped talking to me for the last 25 years, and I haven't grown one iota."

171

MY wife talks to the rhododendrons for hours on end. One day I asked them how the heck they could stand it.

"Who listens?" they replied.

* * *

"I CAN'T find anything to say to my plants," she said while laying newspaper on the garden beds, "so I'm giving them something to read instead."

* * *

IT was such a serious drought the government placed a ban on sprinkler hoses. Then suddenly the drought broke and the heavens opened up with a downpour that flooded everybody's garden. "If this rain keeps up," said Fred, "we will be able to use our hoses again."

* * *

PHIL, the philsophical gardener, was asked how he remained so tranquil in such a frustrating hobby. "I learned long ago," he said, "that when it wants to rain the best thing to do is just sit back and let it."

* * *

"WHAT causes rain?" asked the horticultural student.

"Weekends," was the unanimous answer.

* * *

"MY husband is an invertebrate gardener," she said.

"Don't you mean inveterate?"

"No. Invertebrate. He's got no backbone for it."

* * *

THE customer in the nursery was spending such a long time looking at two wheelbarrows an attendant eventually asked if he wanted assistance.

"Yes," he replied. "I can't decide between the red one or the green wheelbarrow. It is a present for my wife's birthday."

"Will it be a surprise?" asked the attendant.

"I predict it will. She is expecting a diamond ring."

* * *

THE nurseryman was running a special on ferns this

week and filled his shop with fronds of every species. But the customer insisted he wanted an anemone.

"With fronds like these who needs anemones?" said the nurseryman.

\* \* \*

THE vicar was delighted to see Fred working up a sweat in his front garden. He leaned over the fence and gushed: "Your garden is looking lovely. Isn't it wonderful what man and God can do when they work in harmony?"

"Maybe," said Fred wiping his brow. "But you should have seen this yard when God had it on his own."

\* \* \*

WOULD you believe it? Forty-three years ago, while sunbathing in her garden, Mrs Gladys Nurkle, of 7 Paradise St, Moonee Ponds, lost her gold wedding ring.

Yesterday, while digging the garden in the very same spot, her son Clarence ruptured himself.

\* \* \*

GRANDPA was proud of his garden, and when it was admired by visitors he would say the key to his fine crop was "manure, manure, manure."

It embarrassed his daughter. "Can't you make Dad call it fertilizer?" she asked her mother.

"It took us years to make him say manure," she replied.

\* \* \*

OLD Jake from the Outback said his pumpkins grew so fast he kept a pack of greyhounds to round them up. And when they did it only took five to make a dozen.

\* \* \*

"WHEN are you going to prepare the garden beds?" she asked.

"I'm thinking about it."

"You mean you're turning it over in your mind?"

\* \* \*

THE local handyman letter-boxed his neighbours with

a handbill which read: "Don't kill yourself in the garden this spring. I will do it for you!"

* * *

HARRY Henpecked had been ordered by his wife to buy only organic vegetables from the market garden.

"These vegetables are for my wife," he said. "Have they been sprayed with any poisonous chemicals?"

"No," said the gardener, "you will have to do that yourself."

## GOLF

FUNNY how man blames fate for all accidents, yet claims full responsibility for a hole in one.

* * *

QUESTION on golf etiquette: What do you do when your opponent claims to have found his ball in the rough, and you know he is a liar because you've got it in your pocket?

* * *

THEY called it golf because all the other four-letter words were already taken.

* * *

HER golf is improving. Yesterday she hit a ball in one.

* * *

NOW she has improved so much she misses the ball much closer than she used to.

* * *

A BELOW par golfer always takes two or three lumps with his tee.

* * *

"I GOT a set of clubs for my husband."

"Lucky you, what a swap!"

* * *

FRED seemed off his game. He was morose and sulky. By the fifth tee his partner said, "What the hell's the matter with you, Fred?"

"It's Madge, my wife. Ever since she has taken up golf she has cut my sex down to only twice a week."

"Think yourself bloomin' lucky," said his partner. "She's cut me out altogether!"

\* \* \*

IN Africa native tribes beat the ground with clubs and utter blood-curdling screams. Anthropologisits call it the release of primative expression. Here we call it golf.

\* \* \*

FRED had swum through heavy seas to rescue a millionaire who fell from his yacht. The rich man was insisting that he accept some token of gratitude for saving his life. Fred said it wasn't necessary, but the millionaire persisted. "Okay," said Fred. "I'm a keen golfer. Maybe you might like to buy me a club?"

The millionaire, as good as his word, went out and bought two; Royal Melbourne and Huntingdale.

\* \* \*

IT was a tight game in the Scottish Highlands.

"How many strokes was that?" said McTavish when they finished the fifth.

"Six," said McSporran.

"Well, I had five, so that makes it my hole."

When they finished the sixth McTavish said. "Well, how many strokes was that then?"

"Hang on," said McSporran. "It's my turn to ask."

\* \* \*

A TOURING golf professional was having a drink at the club's bar when he was approached by a chap with a white cane and dark glasses who introduced himself as a golf champion.

"I am champion of the Blind Golfers' Association and as one champion to another, I would like to challenge you to a match which could be a fund-raiser for the blind." He said he didn't want any favors and told the pro he was keen to play for $50 a hole.

The embarrassed pro tried to avoid the challenge, but the blind man was so insistent he finally agreed.

"Okay, when will we play?" he asked.

"Any night. Any night at all."

* * *

THIS middle-aged couple had played golf together for most of their married life. One night over the evening meal she mused: "If I die before you, will you get married again?"

Although he was absorbed in the evening newspaper he muttered, "I guess so."

"Would you play golf with her?"

"I guess so," he mumbled.

"Would you take her to our club?"

"I guess so," he said.

"Surely you wouldn't let her use my clubs?"

"No, of course not. Anyway, she's left-handed!"

* * *

"I AM not playing my best game today,"

"Really, what other games do you play?"

* * *

ONE golfer was taking so much care before driving from the fifth tee that his partner asked: "Why the concentration?"

"I'm very anxious to make this shot a good one," said his partner. "My mother-in-law is down there in the club-house watching me."

"Impossible," said his mate. "You could never hit her from this distance!"

* * *

TWO businessmen took time from the office to play a round of golf during their lunch break but were hampered by two women playing ahead and slowing their game.

Finally one said, "Listen Jack, I'll go and ask if they mind if we play through."

He had only gone a hundred metres before he turned and hurried back. He was visibly shaken. "Jack, you won't believe this," he said, "but those two women… one is my wife and the other is my mistress."

Jack was a cool hand. "Listen Reg," he said. "Keep your head down while I approach them and we'll sneak past."

Jack had only gone a hundred metres when he turned back. "Listen Reg, you won't believe this …" he began.

*　　*　　*

HIS drive from the third tee sliced to the left of the fairway and the ball ended in an impossible lie in front of the greenkeeper's tractor shed.

His wife summed up the situation. "No need to take a penalty shot darling," she said. "Just open the doors of the garage, push the tractor out, open the rear doors, and with a number three wood you could hit straight through the shed."

"Brilliant, darling," he said. He took a mighty whack but the ball hit the rear of the building, cannoned back and struck his wife, stone dead.

The following day he was playing the same hole and by sheer coincidence landed at the same place in front of the shed.

"No need to take a penalty shot," said the caddie, "we can push the tractor out and open both sets of doors. You can hit straight through the shed."

"No way," he said. "I tried that yesterday and ended up with a double bogey."

*　　*　　*

THERE were no caddies left when Fonsenby arrived at the clubhouse, but the manager said old George, sitting in the corner could do the job. "He has amazing vision. Has eyes like an eagle," said the manager.

Fonsenby had his misgivings but he gave the old bloke

the benefit of the doubt and hit his first drive a magnificent 500 metres down the fairway.

"Did you see where that went?" he asked.

"Of course I did," said the old bloke.

"Good," said Fonsenby, "Where is it?"

"I can't remember," said George.

* * *

THEY were leaning on the bar at the 19th when Fred produced a golf ball from his pocket and proudly set it on the bar. "Have a look at this," he said to his mate Charlie. "It's a digital golf ball."

Indeed, the ball was a bright irridescent orange. It had a small antennae. "It sends out beeps," explained Fred. Charlie was impressed. "Where did you buy it?"

"I didn't," said Fred. "I found it."

* * *

THEY were watching the golf classic on television when Fred entered the room and was immediately interested.

"Turn it up a bit," he called.

"Sshh. Not while Norman's putting!"

* * *

WHEN the club secretary explained to Fred that he couldn't play because the course was fully booked out, Fred was more than upset. He had been a member for 20 years too.

"Look," said Fred, "If the President of the United States lobbed here for a game today I bet you would make room for him."

The secretary admitted that he would have to.

"Well I just happen to know that he's in Washington today, so I'll take his place!"

* * *

FRED said during his last game of golf he stepped on a rake. "They were the best two balls I hit all day!"

* * *

ABE and Louie had made a pile in the rag trade and decided to take things easy and join a prestige golf club.

On the first day they went into the club bar for a pre-game drink.

"How much?" said Abe when the two whiskies were placed in front of them.

"First day at the club? New members? Well it's on the house," said the barman.

They went into the dining room and ordered lunch. "How much?" asked Louie.

"It's complimentary to new members, sir," said the waiter.

Then they wandered over to the pro shop and ordered half a dozen balls each. The pro obliged. "How much?" asked Abe.

"First day in the club?" asked the pro.

"Yes," chorused Abe and Lou.

"Well, that will be fifty-five dollars and seven cents each," said the pro.

When they finally got onto the green Abe muttered to Louie: "It sure aint by the throat that they've got you in this club."

★   ★   ★

KEVIN had made his money as a car salesman and had done so well he thought it was time to move up in society and join the golf club.

On his first day he slashed and bashed his way around the course cutting divots from fairway and the greens alike. He left a trail of disaster.

He was in the club dining room half way through dinner when he was tapped on the shoulder.

"Excuse me," said the stern official. "I am chairman of the green committee ..."

"Just the bloke I want to see," said the new member. "These brussels sprouts are hardly fresh."

# GORILLAS

A GORILLA swaggered into a waterside pub, slapped a five dollar note on the bar and asked for a beer.

It quite took the barman by surprise for a moment, but ever ready to make a quid he capitalised on this unusual situation, pulling the beer, scooping up the fiver and giving the gorilla 60 cents in small change.

But as the primate sipped his beer, the phenomena of a talking gorilla aroused the barman's curiosity to the point where it could be contained no longer.

"Out for a walk, are you?" he ventured.

"Yeah," mumbled the gorilla.

"We don't get many gorillas in here," pressed the barman trying to make conversation.

"No wonder, at $4.40 a glass."

\* \* \*

THE advertisement in "Showbiz" read: "Non-speaking part, but athletic agility a must." Paddy applied for the job and found himself being directed to Taronga Park Zoo. It was explained to him that one of the zoo's major attractions, the gorilla, had died and they needed a substitute until the real thing could be imported.

"All you have to do is don this suit for a few weeks and swing around the branches," said the zoo's director.

The few weeks turned into a month and although it was hot in the suit the pay was good. Paddy had even worked out quite a routine leaping and tumbling about.

Indeed, the crowd's applause drove him to greater heights and more daring feats until one day, while attempting a somersault he lost his grip and fell out of the tree on the wrong side of the adjacent lion's enclosure.

When he recovered his senses he saw the lion approaching and his first reaction was to let out a shriek for help.

"Shut up, you fool," said the lion.

"Do you want to get us both the sack?"

IT was a month after World War 3 had devasted the earth. Not a human being survived. Indeed a battered and dazed chimpanzee had wandered for weeks through what was left of the smouldering jungle without seeing another living thing.

One day the chimp saw something move behind the rubble. He was delighted to find it was another gorilla, and a female at that.

He rushed up and embraced her, but she pushed him away. "No. Don't let's start all that over again," she said.

# H

## HEALTH

WHEN you feel like you need more exercise, lie down until the feeling wears off.

* * *

THERE are probably better cures for a cold than three whiskies, but who cares?

* * *

FRED thought he had a club foot for forty-two years. When he died they discovered he had his boots on the wrong feet.

* * *

HE used to be an all-round athlete. Now he's just all-round.

* * *

FRED took up exercising. Now he has the energy of a man twice his age.

* * *

THE Irish are great believers in health. They are always drinking to other people's.

* * *

DOC: "Do you suffer from stress?"
  "No, but I think I'm a carrier."

* * *

DON'T tell your friends
  About your indigestion

*182*

"How are You?" is a greeting
Not a bloody question.

\*     \*     \*

IT was the healthiest town in the region. They had to shoot a bloke to start a cemetery.

The only bloke to die over the last ten years was the undertaker. And he died of starvation.

\*     \*     \*

PEOPLE who say they are going on a diet are just wishful shrinkers.

## HISTORY

THE Magna Carta ensured that no free man could be hanged twice for the same offence.

\*     \*     \*

SIR Francis Drake circumcised the world.
And did it with a 100 foot clipper.

\*     \*     \*

HISTORY'S mysteries are those of the past
   Present intrigues seem worse, and are vast
   But before you condemn
   This generation, pro tem
Remember, you're also one of the cast.

\*     \*     \*

NAPOLEON came home tired and weary, wet and wounded, and went straight round to Josephine's flat. He was shocked to find a pair of large gumboots on her front doorstep.

"Josephine! Josephine!" he called out. "What are those rubber boots doing out here?"

"They're not rubber boots," said Josie. "They're Wellington's."

\*     \*     \*

HISTORY records how the first union and the first time-piece occured at the same time. It was when the soldiers in Alexander the Great's army got cheesed off swinging their swords against the foe from dawn to dusk. The troops appointed the first shop steward to parly with Alexander about shorter hours. The problem was the watch had yet to be invented.

By mutual agreement it was decided that the soldiers would tie a piece of rag around the wrist of their sword arm. When it got well and truly soaked with sweat, then it was time to call it a day. They called this timing device Alexander's rag time band.

\* \* \*

WHEN Noah was sailing his Ark there was a great accumulation of bulldust in the bull's pen and the crew wanted to know what to do with it.

"Push it over the side," said Noah.

Then in 1492 Christopher Columbus discovered it.

## HORSES

THERE is nothing like horse riding, to make you feel better off.

\* \* \*

WHAT has four legs and flies?

A dead horse!

\* \* \*

HE named his horse Radish because he got a kick out of introducing the beast when he took it out to social functions. "This is my horse, Radish," he would say.

\* \* \*

THE American tourist was leaning on the bar telling all and sundry about the size of things back in Texas.

"Why, I would hop on a horse and it would take three days to ride to the other side of the ranch."

"Yeah," yawned a local, "I've got a horse like that, too."

\* \* \*

MURPHY the horse trader sold a nag to a bloke and

it dropped dead on the way home. The bloke went back to complain.

"That's funny," said Murphy, "I've had that nag for years and it's never done that before."

* * *

TRAVELLER's car broke down ten kilometres from a remote town and had the driver puzzled as he tinkered under the bonnet looking for the trouble.

"I think it's the carburettor," came a voice from behind him. The startled driver looked around. There was nobody there but a horse in a nearby paddock. "Undo the petrol lead to the carby and clean it through," insisted the horse.

Almost panic-stricken the driver did as the horse insisted. Put the carburettor together again. Pressed the starter button and the engine burst into life.

He raced to town as fast as possible and stopped at the first service station. "You won't believe it," he gasped to the attendant, "I had carburettor trouble about ten kilometres out of town and a horse told me how to fix it."

"Was it a white horse?" asked the proprietor.

"Yes," answered the amazed driver.

"Well it must be your lucky day," he said. "There is usually a black horse in that paddock and he knows bugger-all about carburettors."

* * *

A WHITE horse leant against the bar and pondered the array of drinks on the top shelf. "I feel like something different tonight," he told the barman.

The barman said: "Why not have the whisky named after you."

"Really? Okay, I'll have a double Trevor."

* * *

THE travelling parson had decided to retire from his circuit in the bush and wanted to sell his horse. Old Jack was down from the high country and recognising a strong horse when he saw one soon struck a bargain with the parson.

But when Jack swung up in the saddle, the horse refused to move.

"Oh, I forgot to tell you he is a very religious horse," said the parson. "I have trained him reverently and he will only go when you say the words Jesus Christ, and he will only stop when you say Amen."

Old Jack thanked the parson, said "Jesus Christ" and the horse took off at a fast rate. They were travelling back to the high country when thunder clouds darkened the sky, and a bolt of lightning cracked to the ground.

The horse bolted in fright and a low branch struck Old Jack in the face momentarily blinding him. As the horse galloped madly through the bush he tried to think of the word to make it stop, finally yelling "Amen."

The horse skidded to a halt and when Old Jack opened his eyes he saw that his mount had stopped right on the edge of a frightening mountain precipice.

"Jesus Christ," he said.

★ ★ ★

A CITY girl arrived at the bush riding school. She said she had never been on a horse, so naturally, she wanted a horse that had never been ridden before.

## HORSE RACING

DURING racing trials a trainer took the jockey aside just before the start. "I've got an option to buy this horse, but I don't know its form," he whispered. "Try him out for me, and hold it to about fourth place."

The jockey had a strong pair of arms and held him back to finish fourth as instructed.

"He's a good horse," summed up the jockey.

"Do you think he could have beaten the first three?" asked the trainer.

"Easy," said the jockey, "but I don't know about the other 12 who finished behind him."

\* \* \*

A LEADING trainer was given an eye test and presented with a pair of glasses. The optician said they would cost $300.

"Too much," cried the trainer.

"They're bi-focal," said the optician.

"I don't care if they're by Phar Lap. It's too much."

\* \* \*

THE secretary of the bush racing club was worried about falling attendances. On the morning of the Boxing Day Cup race meeting he got a phone call. "I'm bringing a coach-load of people," said the voice. "What time is the first race?"

"What time can you get here," replied the secretary.

\* \* \*

THE drover looked over the field at the Oodnadatta Races and reckoned his nag could beat anything in the mounting yard, so he entered him for the main race.

"But what's his pedigree?" asked the steward.

"What d'yer mean, his pedigree?"

"What is he by, and what is he out of?" insisted the steward.

"He's by that bloody gum tree and out in that bloody paddock."

\* \* \*

AN old hack jockey had been killed in a car crash and a leading trainer had been called to the morgue to identify him.

The trainer lifted the sheet off one body and shook his head. It wasn't his jockey. He lifted the second sheet and shook his head again. He lifted the third sheet and sadly announced: "Again, he hasn't run a place."

\* \* \*

THE trainer was giving last minute instructions to the

jockey and appeared to slip something in the horse's mouth just as a steward passed by.

"What was that?" inquired the steward.

"Oh, nothing," said the trainer, "just a Mintie. He offered one to the steward. "Here, have one. And I'll have one myself."

After the suspicious steward left the scene the trainer continued with his riding instructions. "Just keep the horse on the rails. You are on a certainty. The only thing that could possibly pass you down the straight is either the steward or me."

\* \* \*

IT was the Grand National Steeplechase and there was a terrible pile up at the third fence. Horses and jockies everywhere.

Despite two broken ribs one jockey managed to remount and with agonising pain and great applause from the crowd he was the only one to finish the course.

The trainer greeted him with a kick in the bum. "You re-mounted the wrong horse, you dopey drongo!"

\* \* \*

THREE horses were in the pub talking about their racing days; about the times they were pipped at the post.

"Just missed the Melbourne Cup by a nose," said one.

"Same thing happened to me at Randwick," said another.

A greyhound sipping whisky at the bar moved over to their table.

"I couldn't help overhearing," he said, "but the same thing happened to me at Sandown."

The horses looked at each other. "Crikey Moses," said one, "that's amazing... a talking dog!"

\* \* \*

A HORSE was looking over the fence watching a game of cricket.

"Any chance of a game?" he asked the captain.

At first the cricketer was taken aback by the talking

horse, but when it insisted it was keen to play the skipper thought it might be a bit of a lark if he sent the horse in as opening bat.

The horse shaped up to the first ball and slammed it over the boundary for a six. He did the same with the second and third, indeed every ball he hit for six until the over ended.

He had been partnered by the captain, and when the bowler ran in from the other end and the captain managed his first hit for a meagre single he called for the horse to run.

But the horse stood there. Frantic calls by the captain to run were ignored and in the confusion the skipper was stumped out.

"Why didn't you run?" roared the angry captain.

"Listen mate," said the horse, "if I could run I would be at the racetrack today, not messing around with this cricket game."

\* \* \*

IT had started as an odds-on favourite, but by the home turn it had run out of puff and was going through the field backwards.

The irate trainer approached the jockey: "What the hell was going on?"

"The horse simply wasn't good enough," explained the jockey.

"Rubbish," roared the trainer. "You could have done much better."

"Maybe I could," said the jockey, "but you know as well as I do the rules state I must stay on the horse's back."

\* \* \*

THE tipster said this horse would walk it in. It did, but all the others galloped.

\* \* \*

IN the old days when tick-tackers were the stars of race

track relaying the prices and trends with hand signals one of the best, Paddy O'Reily, died.

"I can't believe Paddy's dead," said his mate at the funeral service, just as the priest blessed the coffin.

"He's dead alright," said Moloney, "He's just drifted out to 33s."

\* \* \*

CATHOLIC priests are often at the races, but Pete the Punter was surprised to see the priest sprinkle holy water over one nag which duly went out and won by half a street.

Pete followed him closely and witnessed another holy water sprinkle and another win, at ten-to-one.

Next time he had the money ready and as soon as the priest annointed yet a third horse, albeit a skinny nag, Pete was off to the bookies.

After the horse had dropped dead on the home turn Pete tackled the priest for an explanation.

"If you were a Catholic," said the priest, "you would have known the difference between a blessing and the last rites."

\* \* \*

PADDY the Punter cleaned out the bookies and his friends were soon pressing him to divulge his system.

"I'm superstitious, and I watch for omens," said Paddy. "On my way to the races I took a Number 5 tram. It made five stops on the way and it cost me $5 to get into the track.

"It was three fives telling me something. So I added them up, three fives are 16 so I backed Number 16 and it won by a street."

## HOSPITALS
See DOCTORS

A MINOR operation is one performed on somebody else.

A HOSPITAL is a place where people who are run down generally wind up.

* * *

A HOSPITAL is a place where they wake you at five o'clock in the morning to give you a sleeping pill.

* * *

FRED was in hospital. At the end of his bed was a chart with lots of complaints listed on it. All the nurses had written something.

* * *

FRED was in hospital for a complicated operation. In fact, while he was in there the surgeon took his wife out.

* * *

RECOVERING from an operation in a bush hospital Farmer Brown asked why the blinds were drawn.

"Well," explained the doc. "There's a bushfire outside, and I didn't want you to wake up and think the operation was a failure."

* * *

A GIRL from the country called at the hospital. "I'd like to see an out-turn, please," she said.

"You mean an intern," said the nurse.

"Whatever you call him, I want a contamination," she insisted.

"You mean an examination," said the nurse.

"Yes, I need to see the fraternity ward."

"You mean the maternity ward."

"Call it what you will," said the girl with annoyance, "but I certainly know I haven't demonstrated for two months and I think I'm stagnant."

* * *

THE indignant patient complained: "Why did you put me in a ward with this bloke?"

"Why, is he giving you trouble?"

"He's a lunatic," said the patient. "He keeps raving on about getting rid of the monkeys in this ward and look, the ruddy room is full of them."

MATRON at a large hospital answered a phone call in her office.

"Could you tell me how Paddy Murphy is getting on in ward three?" asked the caller.

"Paddy Murphy," repeated the matron consulting her list. "Oh yes. He had his operation last night. It was a complete success and he will probably go home in two days. Who is this speaking?"

"It's Paddy Murphy in ward three. They tell you nothing in here."

*　　*　　*

SURGEON to his assistant as he begins an operation: "How's that for openers?"

*　　*　　*

OLD Jock was sitting up in bed when the matron approached him. "I want you to pass a urine specimen in that bottle on the trolley at the foot of your bed."

"What, from here?" said Jock.

*　　*　　*

TWO Indian doctors were having an animated discussion. "I say it's spelt W-H-O-O-M," said one. "No, it is W-H-O-M-B," said the other. A nurse passing by said "Excuse me, you are both wrong. It is spelt W-O-M-B."

"Thanks nurse," said one, "but we prefer to settle this argument ourselves, besides, we don't think you are in a position to describe the sound of an elephant passing wind under water."

*　　*　　*

TWO nurses were climbing back into the dormitory window, trying to sneak in as quietly as possible when one said, "This makes me feel like a burglar."

"Me too," said the other, "but where would we find two burglars at this time of night?"

## HOTELS
See PUBS

"DO you want the porter to call you in the morning, sir?"

"No. I always wake promptly at seven."

"In that case, would you mind waking the porter?"

* * *

AN American business tycoon had just arrived at his Australian hotel. "I am a man of few words," he said to the porter. "If I beckon with my finger that means come."

"I'm a man of few words myself," said the porter. "If I shakes me head that means I aint coming."

* * *

THEY spent their honeymoon in two hotels. He didn't like the manager in the first place, and in the second place the first place was too expensive.

* * *

THE drunk in the lobby declared he could fight anybody in the entire hotel.

The elevator man took him up.

* * *

LIKE most travel writers he headed for the bar first before checking in at the hotel's reception desk. After his second drink he got the eye from a blonde drinking alone. Quick off the mark he bought her a drink and started to chat. By the third whisky he suggested going up to his room. "Look, I haven't booked in yet, so why don't I register us as man and wife?"

The blonde saw the logic in this and they had a wonderful night together.

Next morning when the writer was checking out he was presented with a bill for $1500. "Hey, I was only here one night," he protested.

"Yes," said the clerk, "but your wife has been here for a week!"

* * *

ON his first holiday to the Gold Coast the oldtimer from the bush settled at the bar and ordered a beer. The barman served him and asked for $5.

"Blimey, a fiver for one beer?"

The barman explained that the charge included the piped music, the lush drapes on the wall and the magnificent view... etc.

Next day the oldtimer fronted the bar for his usual beer and once again protested at the exorbitant price.

The barman began to repeat his routine about the carpets, the music, the view ...

"Hang on," said the oldtimer. "I paid for them yesterday."

*　　*　　*

WHEN Fred was given the bill for an overnight stay in a French hotel he thought the $500 charge was a tad excessive and raised it with the manager.

"If you remember Sir," said the manager, "you and your wife had a room with a bath."

"But we didn't take a bath," complained Fred.

"I can't help zat," said the manager. "Eet was there if you wanted it."

Fred thought about this for a moment then scribbled some words on a piece of paper and slapped it down on the counter with a $100 note.

"What eez this?" asked the manager.

Fred explained that the $100 was fair tarif for the room and that the piece of paper was an account for $400 to the manager for sleeping with Fred's wife.

"But I didn't sleep with your wife," protested the manager.

"I can't help that," said Fred, "She was there if you wanted her."

*　　*　　*

"DID you sleep well, sir?"

"No. There was a gorgeous blonde banging on my door for most of the night. I finally had to get up and let her out."

*　　*　　*

THE guest approached the hotel porter. "I know it is four in the morning, but could you let me have a glass of whisky?"

"What on earth would you be wanting with whisky at this hour?" said the porter.

"Soda?"

* * *

IN a very respectable hotel the old bloke in charge of the cloak room had been in the job for years and never bothered to give a ticket when coats were handed over to him.

A reporter got interested in him and asked the manager how the old geezer kept track of so many coats without dockets.

"Oh, don't worry about old Ted. He's been doing the job for years. Never had a complaint," said the manager.

The reporter decided to put him to the test on the next busy Saturday night. When leaving he asked for his coat and when he received one said, "How do you know if this is my coat?"

"I don't," replied Ted.

"Then why did you give it to me?" said the reporter with a hint of triumph.

"Because that's the coat you gave to me, sir," said Ted.

* * *

THE hotel manager told the elderly couple that the only room available was the bridal suite.

"But we've been married for forty years," grumbled the husband. "What the heck do I want with the bridal suite."

The manager smiled and answered, "Well, if I gave you the ballroom you wouldn't have to dance all night, would you?"

* * *

AT a party a man introduced himself, "Hello, my name is John Smith."

The other replied: "Please don't talk shop. I'm the night clerk at the motel."

* * *

THE manager of a large chain of hotels liked to travel incognito to check on the staff. After he booked in he seated himself in the dining room and when the waiter handed him the menu he tossed it aside. "Just bring me a good dinner," he ordered.

He did this at every meal during his stay and at the end of the week revealed his identity to the waiter and expressed himself highly satisfied with the food and service.

"That's alright mate," said the waiter. Then leaning over the table he added quietly, "When you or any of your mates who can't read come to town, tell 'em to stay here and ask for 'Arry."

\*　　\*　　\*

FRED booked into a small country hotel and the proprietor's pretty daughter showed him to his room. He asked what the rates were.

"Fifty dollars," she said.

"That's great. I'll pay fifty dollars with pleasure."

"With pleasure it will be another twenty-five," she said.

\*　　\*　　\*

"YOU won't find a single flea in this hotel, madam."

"That's what I'm afraid of," she replied. "Probably all married with children."

\*　　\*　　\*

OVER dinner one evening Fred turned to a fellow diner and said, "They call this the Palms Hotel. I've been here three days and haven't seen a palm within miles."

"Wait until you are leaving, when the staff line up at the door," said his new friend.

\*　　\*　　\*

THE rodeo at the Outback Hotel had put a strain on accommodation, but the American tourist was at least glad to know they had reserved his room.

"But we're short of staff," said the proprietor. "Do you mind making your own bed?"

"Not at all," said the Yank.

And he was given a hammer, a saw and some timber.

# HUSBANDS
See WIVES

WOMEN's faults are many
  Men have only two
  Everything they say
  And everything they do!

\* \* \*

SOME husbands come in handy round the house. Others come in unexpectedly.

\* \* \*

THE smart husband thinks twice before saying nothing.

\* \* \*

EVERY married man knows that the most perfect husband in the world belongs to the woman next door.

\* \* \*

"A HUSBAND like yours is hard to find."
  "He still is."

\* \* \*

"IF you were my husband I would give you poison."
  "If I was your husband I'd take it."

\* \* \*

THE first time Ethel saw her husband he was outside a junk shop picking his teeth. Then he went in and bought them.

\* \* \*

HUSBANDS regard themselves as the head of the household, and pedestrians know they have right of way. Both are safe until they try to prove it.

\* \* \*

FRED described the bump on his head as a glancing blow.
  "The wife caught me glancing at a blonde," he said.

\* \* \*

IT was tough luck for Ernie. He missed two maintenance payments last month and his wife repossessed him.

THE couple were on their way to a cocktail party.

"Now listen," she said, "if it's a dull party, then leave it that way."

\* \* \*

"I DON'T think I look 35, do you?" she asked her husband.

"No, I don't," he said, "but you used to."

\* \* \*

FRED told his mate at the bar, "I can't stay long. My wife thinks I'm in the bath."

\* \* \*

THE drinker turned to Fred and said: "You are a typical hen-pecked weak-spined husband."

Fred replied, "You wouldn't have the guts to say that if my missus was here."

\* \* \*

MEN have two reasons for staying at the pub all night. Either they've got no wives to go home to; or they have.

\* \* \*

"ARE you married, Albert?"

"No, I was hit by a car."

\* \* \*

"I WILL say this for Madge," said the henpecked husband. "Spending money is her only extravagance."

\* \* \*

THE two women met in the supermarket. "I thought I'd lost 560 kgms of ugly fat. Then Fred came home again."

\* \* \*

"HOW long have you been wearing that corset, Fred?"

"Ever since the wife found it in the car," he replied.

\* \* \*

FRED was hammering away at some woodwork in his back yard when his mate Charlie looked over the fence. "Aren't you coming to work today?" he asked.

Fred said no. He had to stay home and mind his wife who was sick with a sore throat and the flu.

Hearing a strange gurgling noise coming from the house Charlie asked: "Is that her coughing?"

"Don't be stupid," said Fred, "she'd never fit into this. She's 17 stone. This is a cage for the cocky!"

*     *     *

TWO husbands leaning on the bar. "Did you give your wife a lecture on economy like I told you?"

"Yes, I certainly did."

"And what was the result?"

"I've got to give up smoking."

*     *     *

THE henpecked husband reached the end of his tether. "Money, Money, Money. Those are the only three things you are interested in."

*     *     *

ANOTHER henpecked husband decided to revolt. "I'm fed up. I'm leaving you and going to join the Foreign Legion."

"Well, don't come back traipsing sand through the house," she said.

*     *     *

GIVE a husband enough rope, and he'll skip.

*     *     *

FUNNY how a wife can spot a blonde hair on a chap's coat, yet miss the garage doors.

*     *     *

"TODAY is the wife's birthday."

"What are your getting for her?"

"What are you offering?"

*     *     *

HE said he hasn't spoken to his missus for a month. "I've been unable to interrupt her," he said.

*     *     *

"MY Missus always has her own way. Why, she even writes her diary a month ahead."

HE had a problem about the future. He was getting married in a month and he still had not found her a job.

*   *   *

THEY were leaning on the bar. "I can't understand it," said one. "The wife asks for twenty dollars every Monday, says she needs another twenty by Tuesday. Has her hand out for another twenty on Wednesday. Every week it is the same."

"What does she do with all that money," said his mate.

"I don't know. I never give her any."

*   *   *

HE used to sit on the front door step and whistle at every young woman that went by. "Why do you let him get away with that?" asked the woman next door.

"It's no problem," said his wife. "I've seen dogs chase cars, but they can't drive."

*   *   *

ALBERT had a long session at the pub. He arrived home late and was ready for trouble.

"Is that you, Albert?" called his wife as he stumbled up the stairs.

"It had flamin' well better be," replied Albert.

*   *   *

A RATHER demanding wife returning home after a long trip abroad was met at the airport by her husband. Her first question was: "How's the cat?"

"Dead," replied the husband.

His wife erupted angrily. "What a way to break the news," she said. "Why couldn't you tell me something like, well, the cat was playing on the roof, say, and it slipped off and injured itself, and although you took it to the vet it eventually passed away quietly. Why not break the news that way and not be so brutal about it. Mother always said you were brutal. By the way, how is mother?"

"Well," said her husband slowly. "She was playing on the roof ..."

200

# HYPOCHONDRIACS

THE hypochondriac had only four words on his tomb stone: "See, I told you!"

* * *

SHE visited the doctor for the fifth time that week: "It's awful," she said. "The pain comes every 20 minutes and lasts for an hour."

* * *

THEY were the perfect pair. She was a hypochondriac, and he was a pill.

* * *

MRS Kelly rang the doctor. "Will you come round please. My husband says he is ill."

But the doctor replies, "Mrs Kelly, I'm not coming round again. He only things he is ill."

Next day Mrs Kelly rings again. "What is it this time," says the doctor tersely. "Does your husband think he is ill again?"

"Worse," she said. "He thinks he's dead."

# I

## INDIANS

GENERAL Custer's last words: "I can't make these Indians out. Just a minute ago they were singing and dancing!"

* * *

THE Lone Ranger and Tonto had been inseparable. Suddenly their path was blocked by a Navajo war party. To the left was a hundred Apache. To the right an equal number of Souix. And behind them they heard the blood-curdling cry of the dreaded Blackfeet.

"Looks like we're done for, Tonto."

"What d'yer mean, 'we', paleface?"

* * *

AN Australian travel writer touring Canada was checking out of the Spokane Hilton and as he paid his bill said to the manager, "By the way, what's with the Indian chief sitting in the lobby. He has been there ever since I arrived?"

"Oh that's Big Chief Forget-me-Not," said the manager. "The hotel is built on an Indian reservation and part of the agreement is to allow the chief free use of the premises for the rest of his life. He is known as Big Chief Forget-me-Not because of his phenomenal memory. He is 92 and can remember the slightest detail of his life."

The travel writer took this in and as he was waiting for his cab decided to put the chief's memory to the test.

"What did you have for breakfast on your 21st birthday?" said the Aussie.

"Eggs," was the instant reply, and indeed the Aussie was impressed.

He went off on his travel writing itinerary, right across to the east coast and on his return to the Spokane Hilton six months later was surprised to see the Indian chief still sitting in the lobby whittling away on a stick.

"How", said the Aussie.

"Scrambled," said the chief.

★　　★　　★

A RED Indian wishing to convert to Judaism was told by the rabbi that he would have to be circumcised.

"How much?" he asked.

"$100," replied the rabbi.

"Too much," said the Indian and he began to shop around.

Another rabbi offered $90.

"Too much," said the Indian.

Finally the medicine man said he would do it for nothing and wielded his tomahawk with one swift stroke.

The Indian looked at the result. "Too much," he said.

## INFIDELITY
See WARDROBES

THERE was an almighty row when Fred discovered his best friend, Bert, had been having an affair with his wife.

"But you mustn't blame her," said Bert. "It is all my fault. I was the one who answered her advert in the Truth."

★　　★　　★

OF course high fidelity is a drunk who always goes home to his wife.

A LAWYER and his wife were out walking when a blonde on the other side of the street waved and blew him a kiss. The wife demanded to know who she was.

"Oh, I just met her recently. Professionally of course," he said.

"Whose profession, yours or hers?" said the wife.

*　　*　　*

WITH good reason she was always suspicious of her husband's philanderings and each night there would be a row when she would discover a blonde or a brunette hair on his lapel.

One night she was really puzzled as she studied his coat for ten minutes.

"Okay, who's this bald-headed tart you are flirting with now," she said.

*　　*　　*

THE parish priest made his way to the front door of the farmhouse through a swarm of fighting kids. He knocked on the door repeatedly but there was no answer. He moved along to the bedroom window, looked in and was shocked to see them in a passionate embrace on the bed.

The priest made a discreet retreat through the fighting kids and went to the next property where the farmer met him at the gate.

The priest said: "Your neighbour sure likes making babies."

"He sure does," said the farmer. "His wife is in hospital having her tenth, and my wife is over there helping him out."

*　　*　　*

THE lovers were entwined in a passionate embrace on the loungeroom floor when suddenly a car was heard coming up the driveway. "Quick!" the woman shrieked. "That will be my husband. He's a policeman and he's twice as big as you."

Her companion hopped about frantically and said, "Where's the back door?"

"We haven't got one," she replied.

"Well, tell me quickly," he said, "where would you like one?"

\* \* \*

A RATHER fat woman was puffing away in the aerobics class with a worried look on her face.

"What's up?" said the instructor.

"I work out here every night because my husband says he wants to make love to a woman with a trim figure," she said, "and I'm just beginning to figure out what he means."

\* \* \*

SHE had her suspicions about her husband, Fred, so when they had an invitation to a fancy dress party at the Smithson's she conceived a plan to catch him.

When Fred was dressed in his gorilla suit ready to leave she feigned a headache, said she would stay home, but insisted Fred should go on without her.

Later she donned her own disguise and arrived at the party to see him flirting with every floosie at the party.

In her own masked outfit she approached him, whispered a seductive phrase in his ear and was surprised at the immediate response. He rushed her outside and made passionate love to her. She resisted declaring who she was in an effort to get all the evidence possible.

Just before the unmasking at midnight she left the party and drove home, and next morning was all set to confront Fred with his infidelity.

"How was it at the Smithson's?" she asked at breakfast.

"Dullsville. Boring without you, darling," he said. "When I arrived I saw Ben and the Murphy brothers without partners so we went upstairs and played poker. I lent my gorilla suit to Harry Forbes, and he said he had a wow of a time."

## INSECTS

THE fly walked almost to the top of the window pane, then had to go back. He left his specs behind.

*    *    *

THE last thing to go through a grasshopper's mind, as it slams into a sports car's radiator grill at 100-kmh, is its bum.

*    *    *

"NO! no!" cried the lady centipede, crossing her legs, "A thousand times no!"

*    *    *

LITTLE Johnny was watching two lanky-legged spiders.

"Hey, Dad," he said. "Is there such a thing as a Mummy Long-legs?"

"No, Son."

"I thought so," said the boy slamming his fist on the spiders. "Bloody queers."

*    *    *

A SINGLE gnat lays per day
  A hundred thousand eggs, they say
  It makes one gasp
  And wonder, too
  Just what a married one would do.

## INSURANCE

THIS policy guarantees absolute security in the event of any fatal accident.

*    *    *

WHEN Fred's house burned down he went off to the insurance company and demanded his compensation money. But he was soon to learn that the company didn't operate that way.

"It is our policy to replace your house and anything else you lost exactly in the same style and condition," said the manager.

"Hell," said Fred. "In that case I would like to cancel the policy I took out on my mother-in-law."

\* \* \*

SITTING beside her old husband in his hospital bed she had to crane forward to listen to him.

"I am worried about the cost of this treatment," he wheezed. His voice was hardly a whisper: "How will we ever pay the bills for the specialists, the hospital, the operations," he wheezed.

"Don't worry about it," said his wife. "It's all taken care of. I have had a talk with the hospital and they say I can pay as soon as I've collected your insurance!"

\* \* \*

THE pub was sending him bankrupt so Fred decided to burn it down and collect the insurance. But not without a master plan.

After he set it ablaze he called the police and told them a gorilla had done it.

"Would you be able to recognise him again?" asked the cop.

"It would be difficult," said Fred. "He was wearing a mask!"

\* \* \*

THE insurance company noted with suspicion that Fred's premises were burnt down the very day he took out the insurance policy. Suspecting fraud the company sent him the following message: "Sir. You took out a policy with us at 11-am, and the fire didn't break out until five the same evening. Will you please explain the delay?"

\* \* \*

ROZENBROCK and Solzberg met on a cruise ship, got to talking and found that they were both retired from the rag trade.

"Yes," said Rozenbrock, "when I got the settlement from the insurance company after the fire, me and Rachel decided to retire."

207

"Same here," said Solzberg. "The floods wiped us out, but the insurance company settled quickly."

Rozenbrock looked puzzled. "Tell me, Solzberg," he whispered, "how do you start a flood?"

*　　*　　*

HE left the court in his wheelchair, and a compensation payment for half a million dollars. But the insurance detectives followed him down the street. "You won't get away with this fraud," said one. "We will be watching you for the rest of your life," said another.

"No worries," he replied. "You can watch all you like. You can watch me go on my world trip and you can watch me go to Lourdes and you can watch, with your own eyes, one hell of a miracle."

## INVENTIONS

ONE of the greatest inventors was Pat Pending. He sure came up with a lot of gadgets, but the man who invented the convertible sofa should have been one of the richest men in the world. Millions have been made on it.

*　　*　　*

DID you know Alexander Graham Bell invented TWO telephones?

*　　*　　*

HE discovered a cure for amnesia, but forgot what it was.

*　　*　　*

AN Israeli chemist invented a new laxative and patented the brand name: 'Let My People Go.'

*　　*　　*

IT was the Irish who invented the helicopter ejection seat and the solar-powered torch while the Irish medical team developed the appendix transplant.

*　　*　　*

MY Old Dad was an inventor and among his accomplishments were:

Water-proof tea bags. Peddle wheelchairs. Parachutes which open on impact. L-shaped mobile homes.

The one-piece jigsaw puzzle.

An inflatable dartboard for campers.

An index for a dictionary.

Beer glasses with square bases that don't leave rings on the bar or tables.

*   *   *

HE invented a marvellous appliance for speeding up production in factories. He called it a whip.

## IRISH

THE reason there are so many Irish jokes is because the Irish have a quaint way with words. Like the Irish patient who hobbled into the surgery's waiting room: "I hope to God the doctor finds something wrong with me because I'd hate to feel like this if I was well."

*   *   *

ANOTHER example of Irish logic: "Hey Paddy, here's the five dollars I borrowed last week."

"Thanks, Mick, I had forgotten all about it."

"Then why the bloody hell didn't yer say so?"

*   *   *

THE O'Flaherty family were small. They were all small. Even the smallest was no bigger than the rest, and what's more they never went anywhere alone unless they were together.

*   *   *

MURPHY dropped dead the day he arrived back from a vacation in the tropics. He was laid out in the coffin for friends and neighbours to pay their last respects.

"He's got a great tan," mused Mrs Doolan from next door. "The holiday did him the world of good."

"And he looks so calm and serene," said Mrs McGinty.

"That's because he died in his sleep," explained Mrs

209

Murphy, "and he doesn't know he's dead yet. But when he wakes up and finds out, the shock will kill him."

* * *

THERE was a power failure in a Dublin department store. Thousands of shoppers were stranded on the escalators for hours.

* * *

"YOUR glass is empty O'Flaherty, will you be having another?"

"And why would I be wanting two empty glasses?" replied O'Flaherty.

* * *

THEY were two of the IRA's top men and the lay in ambush for the Chief Provost of the Ulster Brigade. "Okay," says Paddy, "let's go through the schedule once more.

"At 4.45 he leaves his office. At 4.50 his car leaves police headquarters with an escort through peak hour traffic. At 5 pm the first of his bodyguard turn this corner and we keep low and let them pass. At 5.10 the provost himself comes by in his disguised car and we let him have it. Is that all clear?"

"Clear as a bell," says Shaun looking at his watch. "But it is 5.15 now. I hope nothing terrible has happened to him."

* * *

MURPHY arrived home late from the pub, well oiled and ready for trouble. As he stumbled up the stairs his wife called out: "Is that you, Murphy?"

"Be Crikey it darned well better be!"

* * *

McTAVISH knew he was in an Irish pub, but nevertheless, when he had a few under his belt it always made him feel boisterous.

"Down with the Pope," he roared for his fifth toast. And Paddy O'Reilly stepped forward and flattened him.

When he came to his friends asked McTavish, "Didn't ya know O'Reilly was a Catholic?"

"Of course I did," he said. "But why didn't somebody tell me the Pope was?"

\* \* \*

TWO tough union men were working on a building site when Murphy fell from the second floor scaffolding.

"Are ya dead?" cried Gallagher calling from above.

"To be sure I am," replied Murphy.

"You are such a liar Murphy that I don't know whether to believe you or not," called Gallagher.

"That proves I'm dead," said Murphy's voice from the rubble below, "because if I was alive you wouldn't be game to call me a liar!"

\* \* \*

PADDY was coming through customs at the airport carrying a large bottle.

"What have you there?" asked the suspicious officer.

"Tis Lourdes holy water. I am bringing it home with me," said Paddy.

The officer took the bottle and tried some. "Why, it's Irish whisky," he spluttered.

"Lord bless me," said Paddy. "Another bloomin' miracle."

\* \* \*

PADDY had just become the proud father of twins and he was asked if they were identical.

"The boy is but the girl's not," he said.

\* \* \*

YOUNG Teresa came home and related the awesome news to her parents. She was pregnant.

"How do you know it's yours?" asked her dad.

\* \* \*

"TERESA has just had twins," roared Murphy angrily. "Wait till I get my hands on the other fellow."

\* \* \*

PADDY: "Hey Shaun, what's Mick's surname?"

Shaun: "Mick who?"

ON his way home one night Paddy dropped in to the pub. The barman poured him a beer and asked if he wanted to be in a raffle.

"What's it for?" asked Paddy.

"It's for a poor widow with 13 kids," said the barman.

Paddy shook his head. "No good to me. I'd never be able to keep them."

\* \* \*

DUBLIN'S contestant in the international quiz was waiting for his first question.

"First, what's your name and occupation?" the compere asked.

"Pass," came the reply.

\* \* \*

PADDY had been stranded on the deserted island for two years. Then one afternoon a lifeboat drifted close enough for him to swim to it and drag it to the beach, where he knocked it to bits and made himself a raft.

\* \* \*

SHAMUS asked Paddy how he got his black eye.

"You'd never believe it," said Paddy, "but I got it in church."

He said he had been sitting behind a fat lady and when they all stood for a hymn he noticed her dress was creased into the cheeks of her bum.

"All I did was lean forward and pull it out and she turned round an hit me," said Paddy.

It was a week later and Shamus was surprised to see Paddy had another black eye. "I got it in church," he began to explain.

He said he found himself behind the same fat woman and when they stood for the hymn her dress was once again creased into the cheeks of her bum.

"My little nephew reached forward and pulled it out. But I knew she didn't like that, so I leaned over and tucked it back!"

PADDY and Shamus were hitch-hiking.

"It's best if we split up," said Paddy. "I will meet you in the next city under the town hall clock."

Later that night Shamus was waiting at the appointed place when Paddy drove up in a swank car.

"Where the hell did you get that?"

Paddy explained that he had just walked a little way when a beautiful woman picked him up. She drove to the wood, got out and took all her clothes off.

"She said I could have anything I wanted, so I took the car," said Paddy.

"Good choice too," said Shamus. "You'd look ridiculous in her clothes."

\* \* \*

PADDY: "If you can guess how many chooks I have in this bag you can have both of them."

"Three?" suggested Shaun.

\* \* \*

PADDY was intent on saving the man on the edge of the cliff. "Don't jump," he said. "Think of your wife and kids."

"I have no wife and I have no kids," replied the man.

"Then think of your family."

"I have no family."

"Then think of St Patrick."

"Who is St Patrick?" said the man.

"Jump ya bastard," said Paddy.

## INSULTS

"CAN I have this dance?"

"Sure, if you can find someone to dance with."

\* \* \*

IF there is ever a price on your head, take it.

HE told her he was a self-made man.

She said she would accept that as an apology.

★　★　★

YOU are the kind of person Dr Spooner would have called a shining wit.

★　★　★

"I WROTE that song myself," he announced.

"It's nice of you to take the blame," they replied.

★　★　★

SHE said their neighbour must have taken offence at something as she hadn't been over for days.

"Be sure to find out what it was," he said, "and we'll try it on her again."

★　★　★

THE barmaid complained that it was only an hour to closing time and two improper suggestions had been made to her. She was quite upset about it. Normally she has nine or ten.

★　★　★

ONE night Fred took his mother-in-law to the pub and a stranger, a little the worse for wear, leaned over and offered her a double gin and tonic. Fred said she was affronted, but she managed to swallow the insult.

★　★　★

"I WOULD like to buy my girlfriend a ring but I don't know what she'd like."

"Does she like you?"

"Of course."

"Then she'd like anything."

★　★　★

"THAT'S a nice suit you are wearing. I wonder if the style will ever come back?"

★　★　★

"I WENT by your place yesterday."

"Thanks!"

AN Englishman boarded a train with a large shaggy dog and sat opposite an Irishman. Paddy looked at the dog awhile then said, "And what type of dog would that be?"

The surly Englishman replied: "It's a cross between an ape and an Irishman."

Paddy was quick with his reply: "You mean its related to both of us!"

*　　*　　*

BERT had just been fired and told his boss: "You are nothing but a miserable rogue and blackguard, and I've got a darned mind to tell you so."

*　　*　　*

IT was in the outer at the cricket match when Fred returned with two beers only to find his mate, Bert, laying flat on his back. Worse, he was dismayed to find Bert's face swollen with bruises, a cut lip and a black eye.

"Which rotten so-and-so did it?" asked Fred, all fired up. "Can you describe him?"

"That's exactly what I was doing when the whacker hit me," said Bert.

*　　*　　*

HE: "I've got an idea"

She: "Beginner's luck."

He: "Are you trying to make a monkey out of me?"

She: "No. Why should I take the credit?"

He: "So this is a battle of wits between us?"

She: "No. I never pick on a man that's unarmed."

He: "I manage to keep my head above water."

She: "That's because wood floats."

He: "I won't stand these insults. I've gots lots of backbone."

She: "Yes, but the bone is all at the top."

He: "Intelligence reigns supreme in our family."

She: "Well, you must have been born during a dry spell."

He: "I'm nobody's fool."
She: "Perhaps you can get someone to adopt you."
He: "My mother thinks I'm a great wit."
She: "She's half right."
He: "You are going to drive me out of my mind."
She: "That's not a drive, it's a putt."

# J

## JAIL

THE prisoner was banging on the bars making a heck of the racket. "What do yer want?" said the warder.

"I want to know the time," said the prisoner.

"It's 1992," said the warder.

\*     \*     \*

JOE was in for the term of his natural. He was given the job of organising the social events, because he was usually the lifer of the party.

\*     \*     \*

IN prisoner of war camps it is tougher. One day the commandant marshalled all the inmates together and announced he had good news.

"For the first time in five years we are changing the sheets," he said. "Those in Hut A will change them with those in Hut B."

\*     \*     \*

AFTER years in a high security jail Pat devised a way of communicating with his mate Mick. It was an ingenious ploy using a secret code to tap out messages on pipes.

However the scheme was eventually thwarted when they were transferred to separate cells.

# JEEVES

JEEVES said as a hostess, Lady Entwhistle was hopeless. She couldn't even entertain a doubt.

*       *       *

THE lady of the manor was becoming increasingly alarmed at Jeeves' practice of walking in to her bedroom without knocking. Finally she took him to task.

"It could be very embarrassing if I was in a state of undress," she admonished.

"No need to worry about that, m'lady," said Jeeves. "I always take a peek through the keyhole first!"

*       *       *

SHE called Jeeves into her bedroom. "Jeeves, please unzip my dress." With a great deal of embarrassment he did so.

"Now Jeeves," she said. "Take off my stockings."

Jeeves was now in a sweat.

"And now take off my underwear … and if I ever catch you wearing them again you will be instantly dismissed."

*       *       *

JEEVES was interviewing a prospective maid for the household and asked the girl for her references.

She began rumaging around in her handbag. "I am afraid I've lost my reference from the Dorchester," she said, "but I've got these two spoons with the Dorchester crest to prove I worked there."

*       *       *

WHEN the squire announced that he was to get married Jeeves was alarmed about his future at the manor. And although the squire assured him that his position was safe, Jeeves still worried while they were away on their honeymoon.

"Jeeves, how many times do I have to tell you it's business as usual," said the squire on his return.

Sure enough, next morning, the squire was up at dawn for his breakfast, promptly at 6-30 his horse was ready, and at seven Jeeves went into the bedroom slapped the bride on the bottom and said: "Okay, back to the village my lass!"

*   *   *

JEEVES was called by Lord Ponsonby. "Jeeves, could you ride down to the village and fetch a bottle of whisky, a box of cigars and a few ounces of snuff. That free-loading bishop will be calling in this afternoon."

Jeeves mounted his trusty bicycle and was off on his errand. It was not until the return trip and he had pedalled up the long hill to the manor gates that he realised he had forgotten the snuff.

What to do? It was too hot and too far to ride back down to the village. By chance the problem was solved, right there on the nature strip was a barker's nest with three of those white eggs dogs leave in neat little clumps. When dried in the sun and ground back to powder it looks for all the world like snuff.

Did he dare take the chance?

Jeeves quickly bent down, snatched up three portions and put them in his pocket.

"Did you get the whisky, Jeeves?"

"Yes, M'lord."

"And the cigars, and the snuff?"

"Yes M'lord," said Jeeves as he prepared to leave the room.

"I say, Jeeves," said Lord Ponsonby sniffing the air. "You didn't by any chance stand in something down in the village?"

"No M'lord."

The bishop arrived soon after and headed for the Scotch. "You don't mind if I have a drink, Ponsonby old boy?"

"Not at all, Bishop, go for your life," but Ponsonby was pre-occupied with the pervading odour.

"I say bishop, can you smell dog's doings in here?"

"Can't say as I can dear boy," said the bishop. "I happen to have a heavy head cold."

"In that case, take a pinch of snuff," said Ponsonby.

The bishop responded by taking two pinches and sniffing it up both nostrils.

"Gracious me," he said. "You always get the best snuff. That's cleared my head completely and I can smell that dog's stuff now!"

*    *    *

THE lady of the manor decided to dismiss the parlour maid and dressed her down with some sarcastic remarks about her unsatisfactory service as a cook and general housekeeper.

But the fiery parlour maid took the opportunity for a parting shot. "Your husband happens to think I am a better cook and a better housekeeper than you are," she retorted. "And what's more I am a damn sight better in bed than you are."

"Oh, and my husband told you that too?"

"No, Jeeves told me that!"

*    *    *

LADY Fontigue-Smythe took more than the usual care of her staff. So when her butler was hurt in an accident she was quick to attend the hospital.

"Sorry," said the nurse. "No visitors except family. Are you his wife?"

"Indeed not," said her ladyship. "I'm his mistress."

*    *    *

HIGH society couple were making love.

She: "Darling, do poor people do this?"

He: "I believe so, my sweet."

She: "It's much too good for them, don't you think?"

*    *    *

THE squire of the manor awoke with a raging erection one morning and immediately called his valet.

"Congratulations sir," said Jeeves. "Shall I awaken madam?"

"No, Jeeves. Get me my baggy shorts and we'll smuggle this one down to the village."

# JEWISH

PREP school son was studying his arithmetic and asked for help from his dad. "What's two and two, Dad?"

"Depends, son. Are we buying or selling?"

*　　*　　*

"PAPPA," said the lad. "What's Yiddish for a hundred per cent?"

"Izzy, my son, a hundred per cent is Yiddish."

*　　*　　*

OLD Abraham Cohen is knocked down by a tram and is laid gently on the median strip. A lady gets a pillow from her car and places it under his head.

"Are you comfortable?" she asks.

"Ah well," he says, "I make a living."

*　　*　　*

A JEWISH mother gave her son two ties for his birthday, a striped one and a spotted one. Next day she saw him wearing the striped one.

"So what's the matter with the spotted one? You don't like it?"

*　　*　　*

THE reporter was interviewing the socialite who had organised the charity ball and couldn't take his eyes off a massive diamond on her left hand.

"Oh, that," she said. "It's the famous Guggenheimer diamond."

The reporter was dazzled by it.

"Unfortunately it has a curse attached to it," said the socialite.

"A curse?" gasped the reporter. "What curse?"

"Mr Guggenheimer," she said.

* * *

ABRAHAM wandered into Sam's pawnshop and placed a leather coat on the counter. "How much will you give me for this jacket?"

Sam checked it over. "$20, and that's the best."

"But that jacket is worth $100."

Sam was adamant. "$20 or nothing."

"Are you sure that's all it's worth?" pressed Abe.

"Positive."

"Okay," said Abe. "Here's your $20. The jacket was hanging in your doorway and I was wondering how much it was worth."

* * *

IN a small school in Dublin the teacher told the class she would give 50 pence to whoever could name the holiest man in history.

Only one hand went up, that of little Izzy O'Cohen. "That would be St Patrick, Miss," he said.

Teacher handed over the money and said to Izzy, "How come the only boy to know the answer was Jewish?"

To which Izzy replied: "In my heart of hearts I know it was Moses, but business is business."

* * *

THE aircraft was flying into Honolulu when the man in the window seat spoke to his fellow passenger for the first time.

"How do you pronounce it, Hawaii or HaVaii?"

"HaVaii." said the passenger.

"Thanks."

"You're Velcome."

* * *

MRS Goldberg was heartbroken when young Moishe told her he was getting married to Rosie McEvoy.

"Oh, why are you not marrying a lovely Jewish girl? Why are you marrying a shikseh?"

"Jewish girls are terrible, Momma," said Moishe, "they grow fat and get varicose veins."

"So do all the shiksehs," cried his mother.

"Yes, but who cares about shiksehs?" said Moishe.

*　　*　　*

MRS Plotkin was waiting for an appointment with Dr Goldstein and the only other person in the waiting room was a young businessman reading the Financial Review.

"Excuse me young man," she said. "Are you Jewish?"

"No I'm not," he replied.

A little later she repeated the question: "Are you sure you are not Jewish?"

"Definitely not," he said without looking up from his newspaper.

But she kept her eyes on him, and a little later: "Are you really certain you are not Jewish?"

The young man threw his paper aside. "Okay," he said in utter exasperation, "I am Jewish."

Another five minutes went by. "That's funny," she said. "You don't look Jewish."

*　　*　　*

A JEWISH man went into Izzy's corner shop and asked for some ice-cream.

"We don't sell ice-cream to Jews," said Izzy.

"But you are Jewish yourself. This is disgraceful."

"Have you tasted our ice-cream?" said Izzy.

*　　*　　*

IZZY entered the room all agitated.

"There is a new Nazi party and their manifesto states they intend to kill a million Jews and five postmen."

"Why five postmen?" somebody asked.

"That's typical," cried Izzy in despair. "Nobody ever cares about the Jews."

*　　*　　*

IZZY and Rachel went to Switzerland for a holiday and

223

while in the mountains Izzy decided to try his hand at skiing. Down the slope he went and disappeared with a scream over a crevasse. When he didn't return that night a Red Cross rescue team was despatched to the area.

They searched all night and most of the next day until they discovered some tracks.

"Mr Guggenheim, Mr Guggenheim," they kept shouting. "It's the Red Cross."

And finally a feeble voice was heard in reply. "I've given already."

* * *

IT was interval at the opera when Mrs Sternberg rose from her seat and called: "Is there a doctor in the house. Is there a doctor in the house?"

A man in a tuxedo pushed his way towards her. "I'm a doctor," he said.

"Oh doctor," she said, "Have I got just the loveliest daughter for you!"

* * *

THE rabbi was hit by a bus and first on the spot was his old friend the Catholic priest who thought it was an excellent opportunity for conversion.

"Do you believe in the Father, Son and the Holy Ghost?" whispered the priest.

The rabbi opened his eyes. "I'm dying and he asks me riddles!"

* * *

MOISHE was on his death bed and raised his head gently. "Moira, are you there?"

"Yes, Moishe, I am here."

A moment later Moishe said, "Izzi, are you there?"

His son, Izzi assured him he was by his side.

"Joshua," said the ailing Moishe, "Are you there?"

"I'm here poppa," said Joshua taking his hand.

Moishe raised himself on his elbow, "Then who the hell is minding the shop?"

GOLDSTEIN and Plotkin had spent a lifetime in competition climbing the social ladder, but Izzi Goldstein's barmitzvah was to be the calendar event of the year. It began at the London Ritz where guests were delivered in white Rolls Royces. The cabaret featured Liza Minelli and Barbara Striezand accompanied by the London Philharmonic Orchestra. The food was flown in from Vienna. Then the 100 guests were flown first class to Kenya where they set out on safari riding a team of elephants.

Two hours out from the village there was an elephant jam and the safari came to a halt.

"What's the hold-up?" demanded Mr Goldstein of the lead elephant boy.

A runner came back with the message: "There appears to be another barmizvah up ahead, by the name of Plotkin," he said.

\* \* \*

IT was with much wringing of the hands that Rachael discovered her husband, Hymie, had a mistress. Rachael, however, was not the sort to kill the goose that lays golden eggs, rather, she decided to find out what the mistress had that she didn't.

After long interrogation Hymie finally relented. "Well to tell you the truth, Rachael, you are too cold. When we make love you don't do anything. You just lay there, whereas she moans and groans with feeling."

"Is that all," thought Rachael. "Is that all there is to it?"

That night she dressed in her most alluring lingerie, slipped Hymie a shot of his favourite cognac and got him into bed.

Half way through the business she decided to give her most passionate moans and groans.

"Oh Hymie, darling," she began. "I've had the most terrible day. Our shares have dropped two points. The washing machine broke down. You don't give me enough housekeeping money..."

A TOURIST asked a Jewish gent where Plotkin's jewellery store was located.

The Jew was loaded with parcels and began handing them over until the tourist was holding them all.

When his arms were completely free he shrugged his shoulders: "How should I know?" he said.

\* \* \*

MOISHE is on his death-bed and and finally realises that he is about to cash in his worldly chips.

He calls for his wife, Beckie and says, "I want to leave the business to Izzi."

"No, not Izzi, he's too much of a gambler. Leave it to Abie," said his wife.

"Okay, the Rolls I will leave to Michael."

"Na, not Michael. He has smashed up three cars this year," said Beckie.

"Okay," said Moishe, "Then the summer house I will leave to Rachael and her husband."

"Na, don't let that schmuck get his hands on that property, leave it to Rachael herself."

Moishe raised himself on his elbow. "Listen Beckie. Tell me who's dying here?"

\* \* \*

MR GOLDBERG ran a clothing factory and had the reputation of wringing a full day's work from his employees. Abe had worked there for 30 years and had never been late... until today.

He limped in an hour late on crutches with his head bandaged. Mr Goldberg pointed to the clock and asked him to explain.

Abe said he was on his way to work when he stepped on his son's skate and crashed down seven flights of stairs. He tumbled out into a laneway only to be hit by a truck.

Goldberg listened to the story and then said: "And this takes an hour?"

THE eldest son took his father aside and said he had a problem. "I have had a bit of a fling Dad and unless I come up with a thousand dollars she will sue me."

Dad reluctantly wrote a cheque to save the family name.

A week later his second son approached him. "Father I have had a bit of a fling and unless I pay a thousand dollars she will sue me."

Dad coughed up another cheque to save the family name.

A week later his daughter approached him. "Father, I am ashamed to say that I have had a bit of a fling and...

Her father interrupted, and rubbing his hands said, "At last. We make a collection this time."

\* \* \*

A JEWISH man boarded an overnight train and found himself sharing a sleeping compartment. As they were preparing for bed the Jew said: "Excuse me, I wonder if I could borrow a towel." The man lent him a towel.

"Excuse me," said the Jew again, "I appear to have left my pyjamas at home." The man lent him a tracksuit.

"Excuse me," said the Jew yet again, "Will you lend me your tooth brush?"

This time the man refused.

When he was met by his son at Central Station he was asked if he enjoyed the journey.

"No, I had to share with an anti-semite," he replied.

\* \* \*

WHILE Abe Rosenberg waited at the Pearly Gates, St Peter thumbed through his lengthy personal file with an ever darkening frown. Finally, he said, "I am afraid you can't come in Mr Rosenberg."

"Look at this file," said St Peter, "it's nothing but good deeds, practically every day. The problem is Abe, we've got popes, archbishops and rabbis up here and if we let you in with this impecable record it would cause great embarrassment to the social order, not to mention putting a few pontifical noses out of joint. We can't have a mere tailor coming up here with a clean slate."

Old Rosenberg didn't protest. He was that type of bloke.

"Tell you what," said St Peter leaning forward on the counter in a confiding manner. "I'll zap you back to earth for the afternoon. You've got six hours to blot your copy book with a little sin. Do you think you could commit just one minor infringement? Then we could let you in without disturbing the heirarchy up here."

Rosenberg said he would do his best, and in a flash he found himself sitting in his lounge chair by the fireplace in his flat.

The mantelpiece clock chimed 12 noon and he began thinking. "What sin could I commit?"

He didn't smoke. He didn't like strong drink and no way would he risk a dollar on a horse.

He spent the first three hours racking his brain before he remembered the middle-aged spinster in the flat above, Miss Leonski. Yes, it was definitely a sin to make love to a woman to whom you were not married. And hadn't Miss Leonski gone out of her way at the last Body Corporate social function by deliberately sitting beside him and offering him tea and biscuits?

"That's what I'll do," he thought, and putting on his hat and coat he made his way up to her flat and knocked on the door.

"Oh, Mr Rosenberg," she said, "This is a surprise. Last thing I am hearing of you is that you are very sick, maybe dying. Will you come in for a glass of tea?"

Rosenberg sat there sipping tea, checking his watch and mentally noting that his life was fast ticking away while he was wasting time with small talk. By five o'clock he was beginning to panic as he realised there was no tactful way to dive into sin.

So suddenly he jumped up, grabbed Miss Leonski,

pushed her into the bedroom, ripped off her clothes and threw her onto the bed.

Then he sinned.

And while he was at it, he thought that if this was to be the only sin in his life he might as well give it all he had.

About five-to-six he began to feel life slipping away and he got out of bed to reach for his clothes. He turned to smile down at Miss Leonski and said: "Miss Leonski, I want to thank you. This afternoon you have shown me the way to heaven."

Miss Leonski looked up with a tired little smile. "Mr Rosenberg," she said. "You shouldn't mention it. Only me and the good Lord will know what a good deed you have done for me today!"

# JOBS

MOST young blokes stop looking for work the moment they get a job.

*     *     *

MY father works as a blacksmith in a butcher shop. He shoos flies.

*     *     *

MY uncle works as an espionage agent at the Mint.

He's a Mint Spy.

*     *     *

I ONCE worked at factory that made fire hydrants, but there was nowhere to park.

*     *     *

"ARE you looking for work, my man?"

"No. But I wouldn't mind a job."

*     *     *

BOSS: "How many times have I reprimanded you about being late?"

"I don't know. I thought you were keeping score."

BOSS: "You should have been here at nine o'clock."

"Why, what happened?"

* * *

BOSS: "It distinctly says on the notice out front that we have no vacancies."

"Yes, I saw that. But take a chance. The bit of work I do would make no difference."

* * *

THE boss told the applicant there was a vacancy for a responsible worker. "Are you responsible?"

"I'm the right bloke alright," said Fred. "Every job I've had, when anything happened, everybody said I was responsible!"

* * *

HE started as an office boy on January 1. By February he was a salesman. Two months later he was regional manager. By mid year he was assistant general manager, and by November he was general manager.

On the first anniversary of his start with the firm he took over as chairman of the board. As he met the outgoing chairman at the office door he shook his hand and said, "Thanks Dad."

* * *

THE teenager was complaining that his job was menial and boring. His father reminded him that digging holes was the only job you can get where you start at the top.

* * *

HE saw the sign "Handyman Wanted" outside the convent and immediately applied. Mother Superior gave him a quick approval and asked if he could mend the fuse.

"Oh, I'm no good at electical matters," he said.

"Well, the front fence needs painting," said the nun.

"Oh, I'm no good at painting," he said.

"Well, we need a new door on the kitchen," she said.

"Oh, I'm no good at carpentry, sister," he said.

"Well tell me," she said. "What makes you think you are a handyman?"

"Oh, I just live around the next corner," he said.

\* \* \*

HIS new job is touting for a doctor. He goes around making people sick.

\* \* \*

FRED said if the foreman didn't take back what he said that morning he was leaving the job.

"What did he say?"

"He gave me a week's notice," said Fred.

\* \* \*

"WHAT are you working at now?"

"Nothing, but it's steady."

\* \* \*

THE young man was having a very loud argument with his girlfriend. "That's it. I am going to end it all," he cried and climbed on the the parapet of the bridge.

"I'm going to jump and I don't want anybody to save me," he said as he leapt into the water.

A young bloke who had witnessed this dived in after him.

"I told you I don't want to be saved," cried the young man.

"That's okay," said the other bloke, "I don't want to save you. Just tell me where you work."

\* \* \*

THE manager was giving the applicant the job.

"I think you will be very happy with us," he said. "We have a bonus scheme, a non-contributory pension scheme, special medical and hospital insurance schemes, free training and recreational facilities and a profit-sharing plan."

"Sounds wonderful," said the applicant, "and what are the wages?"

"Wages?" said the manager. "Hell, with all that we can't afford wages!"

THE man at the employment centre said there was indeed a job.

"What does it involve?" asked Fred.

"It is a photographer's assistant. Seems he wants a bikini-line shaver to ensure there are no pubic hairs showing when he photographs models in the latest swim gear."

"I'll take it," said Fred.

"Then you will have to go to Bachus Marsh."

"Why Bachus Marsh?"

"Because that's the end of the queue!"

*　　*　　*

THEY were arguing about which was the oldest profession.

The surgeon rose to his feet and said: "When God created Eve he took a rib from Adam in the first surgical operation."

The architect made his claim: "In order to restore order from chaos, God must have needed the services of an architect."

The civil servant came in with the clincher: "Ah, but who created the chaos?"

## JOGGERS

FRED joined Joggers Anonymous. Whenever he feels like a run they send someone round with a dozen bottles to talk him out of it.

*　　*　　*

FATHER: "Why don't you go for a run around the block?"

Son: "Why? I'm already here."

*　　*　　*

FRED was told that he should exercise and that jogging would add years to his life.

"How do you feel?" asked his wife when he staggered once around the block.

"They're right. I feel ten years older," he said.

WHEN the husband came home unexpectedly, Larry the lover had to leap from the bedroom window. Spotting some joggers running by he quickly joined them.

"Do you usually jog in the nude?" asked one of the runners after a while.

"Oh yes," said Larry. "It's very stimulating."

"And do you usually jog with a condom on?"

Larry kept his cool. "Well, to tell you the truth, it was raining when I set out."

*    *    *

HAVING trouble with his sex life, Fred was advised by the doctor to take up jogging.

"Take it easy to start with, just two miles a day," said the Doctor, "and give me a call this time next week."

Fred did so. "And how is your sex life now?" asked the Doc.

"Worse," said Fred. "I'm 14 miles from home."

*    *    *

AFTER a very heavy night he left the nightclub at dawn and being in no condition to drive he stopped the car in the first recreation reserve and tried to sleep it off.

He had just settled down when a jogger tapped on the window and asked for the time.

"It's 5.30," he grumbled.

He snuggled down again, but only a few minutes passed before another jogger rapped on the window and asked the time. "It's 5.35," he roared.

In desperation he scribbled a note in large letters and stuck it against the window. It read: "I haven't a watch and I don't know the time."

Five minutes later a jogger stopped to rap on the window and told him it was 5.40.

# JOKES

THE only catch in telling a good story, is that it usually reminds the other bloke of a bad one.

*     *     *

"I'VE got a million jokes," he said.
  "Then why did you tell us that one," they said.

*     *     *

HE always wanted to be a comedian, but he was afraid people might laugh at him.

*     *     *

A MAN who says his wife can't take a joke forgets himself.

*     *     *

HE who laughs last doesn't get the joke.

*     *     *

"DID you hear my last joke?"
  "I hope so."

*     *     *

THE comedian's first professional engagement was at the Oodnadatta Social Club and his first performance was greeted with stony silence.

He was sitting in his dressing room drowning his sorrows while the bingo session was in full swing and he heard the MC trying to call the crowd to order.

"Now then," said the MC. "If you don't shut the noise while we're running the bingo I'll get that comedian on again!"

*     *     *

THE travelling salesman's car broke down and he wandered across the paddock to the farmhouse and asked if he could sleep the night.

"You're most welcome," said the farmer, "but I must warn you that I don't have daughters, I am a bachelor and you will have to share the only bed with me."

"Oh hell," said the salesman, "I'm in the wrong bloomin' joke."

234

THE Taxation Department is putting jokes and cartoons on the back of the income tax form now, so that taxpayers can see the funny side.

\* \* \*

FRED was often the butt of office jokes. "Have you heard the story of the dirty window, Fred?" they said.

When he said no, they said: "It's no use telling you. You wouldn't see through it."

Fred could hardly wait until he got home. "Darling," he said. "Have you heard the story of the window you couldn't see through?"

"No," she said.

"Well I can't tell you. It's too dirty."

\* \* \*

"THE trouble with you, Mabel, is that you have no sense of humour," he said.

She thought about it for a moment. "Well, I don't think that's funny."

\* \* \*

WHEN the little man came home, his rather formidable wife gave him such a wallop on the head with a rolling pin that his knees buckled and he fell to the floor.

Shaking his head groggily he said: "Was that a joke, or did you mean it?"

"I bloody-well meant it," she said.

"That's okay then. Because I don't appreciate jokes like that."

\* \* \*

DON'T worry if your life's a joke
And your successes are but few
Remember that the mighty oak
Was once a nut like you.

\* \* \*

WE editors may dig and toil
Till our fingertips are sore

235

But still a few are bound to say
"I've heard that joke before."

★　　★　　★

EVERYBODY'S idea of a joke is different. Like the fellow who hit his mate on the head with a dead chicken.

"Hey," said the victim, "are you having a go at me, or was that a joke?"

"I'm having a go at you," was the reply.

"Well that's okay then. 'Cos I don't like that kind of joke."

★　　★　　★

A WISE man never laughs at his wife's old clothes.

★　　★　　★

HE is convinced women don't have a sense of humour. He asked one to his room and she said: "Don't make me laugh."

★　　★　　★

HE who laughs last usually has a tooth missing.

★　　★　　★

HISTORY records that when Churchill met Stalin at the famous Yalta conference they discussed their hobbies.

Churchill said he collected jokes people told about him.

Stalin said he collected people who told jokes about him.

# K

## KIDS

CHILDREN, what a comfort in old age. And how soon they bring it on.

* * *

PRIDE is something you feel when your kids run a garage sale and raise a few hundred dollars.

Panic is when you go to get your car, and find it gone.

* * *

YOUNG Billy brought a note home from school. His Dad read it and announced to his wife: "They want a written excuse for his presence."

* * *

THE little boy in the crowded showgrounds was obviously distressed. "I've lost my Dad," he sobbed when the policeman approached him.

"What's your Dad like?" said the cop.

"Beer, women and the odd bet," said the lad.

* * *

LITTLE Mary stuck her head around the kitchen door, "Hey Mum. Can an eight-year-old girl get pregnant?"

"Of course not," said her mother.

Mary turned round. "It's okay fellas, we can keep playing the game."

237

THE RSPCA inspector stopped three kids in a billy-cart. It was being pulled by a big mongrel dog they had harnessed to the cart. He accused the kids of cruelty.

"Rubbish," chorused the kids. "Bonzo loves it, he has been doing it for years. He doesn't look unhappy does he?"

The officer had to admit that the big dog seemed to be enjoying himself.

"Okay," he conceded, "but that piece of string hanging from his testicles will have to come off. That could hurt him."

"Arr hell," said one of the kids. "There goes our brakes!"

\* \* \*

"ARE you a gardening expert?" asked the small girl when the visiting neighbour was seated in the lounge.

"No Mary I'm not. What makes you think that?"

"Mum says if there is any dirt about you'll dig it up!"

\* \* \*

LITTLE Johnny was having a lot of trouble with his arithmetic and when teacher asked him what two plus two was he counted on his fingers and said, "four."

"And how much is three and three?"

Again Johnny counted on his fingers and came up with "six."

"Johnny," stormed the teacher, "it is cheating to use your fingers. Now put your hands in your pockets and tell me what is five and five."

There was a fumble and a pause before the answer came up. "Eleven," he said.

\* \* \*

WHEN young Billie returned from his first time at church they asked him how he liked it. He said the music and singing was good, but he didn't think much of the news.

\* \* \*

HIS dad asked what he had learned in Sunday school that morning.

"I learned about a cross-eyed bear whose name was Gladly," replied the youngster.

Dad was puzzled and had to press the point further to finally discover it was a hymn: "Gladly, the Cross I'd Bear."

* * *

A COP saw a little boy standing in the pub smoking a cigarette and drinking a pot of beer.

"Why aren't you in school?" he asked.

"Because I'm only four years old," replied the kid.

* * *

"MUM," said the little boy, "where did I come from?"

"The stork brought you, dear," was the reply.

"And where did you come from, Mum?"

"The stork brought me too."

"And what about grandma?"

"The stork brought her too."

"Gee," said the little lad, "Doesn't it ever worry you to think that there have been no natural births in our family for three generations?"

* * *

"HEY Mum, where do babies come from?"

"From the stork of course."

"But who gets the stork pregnant?"

* * *

SMALL boy watching his Mum do the washing. "Mum, where did you work before you got this job here with us?"

* * *

LITTLE Tommy, aged eight, marched into the living room with an important announcement for his father. "Dad," he said with great seriousness, "I'm gonna get married."

His Dad grinned indulgently, "Who to, son?"

"My girlfriend, Mary, next door."

Mary was also eight and his Dad decided to carry the joke along. "Found a place to live yet?" he asked.

"Well, she gets 50 cents pocket money and you give me a dollar. So if she moves in with me, we can manage," said Tommy seriously.

His Dad nodded. "Well, $1-50 a week is okay for now, but what will you do when the kids start to arrive?"

"Don't worry," said Tommy confidently. "We've been lucky so far."

\* \* \*

GRANDMA was spending a few days with the family, and on the fourth morning when everybody was seated around the breakfast table little Freddy said: "When are you going to do your trick, Dad?"

"What trick is that, son?"

"You know. You said if Grandma stayed more than three days you would climb the wall."

\* \* \*

YOUNG Basil had moved to town from the country and had settled in at the suburban primary school fairly well; except for his constant swearing. It was "bloody" this and "bloody" that until he was sent home with a note: "If this boy won't stop swearing he will not be allowed to school anymore."

His father gave him a bloody hiding and sent him back next day with a note to say he wouldn't bloody-well swear again.

The teacher was impressed and sent home another note. "Basil has been so good he can come to the school picnic on Saturday week."

When the big day came, little Basil set off for the picnic, with a caution and yet another note. "If he swears again, please send the little blighter straight home."

In less than an hour Basil was back, weeping his eyes out, and copped another hiding from his father for swearing.

"I didn't swear," he protested. "You sent me off on the wrong bloody Saturday. The bloody picnic is not until next bloody week!"

240

TWO young brothers were sent home from their country school with a note to say they had been suspended for the afternoon for swearing.

Their father gave them a hiding, a lecture and sent them to bed without dinner.

Next morning as they sat down for breakfast their father, in a more conciliatory mood, asked what they would like for breakfast.

The first one said: "I'll have some of those bloody cornflakes." He received an immediate thrashing from his father and was sent back to bed for the day.

The father then asked the second boy what he would like for breakfast. "I don't know," he said. "But it won't be bloody cornflakes, that's for sure."

\* \* \*

BECAUSE he had been heard swearing, young Billie had been put across his father's knee and given a few good whacks. "Now son," said his Dad, "tell me why I punished you."

The kid threw up his hands in despair. "That does it. First you belt hell out of me and now you don't know why you bloody-well did it!"

\* \* \*

"DAD, all the kids at school hit me and call me Pansy."

"That's all right son," said his father. "Next time they do that, whack them over the head with your handbag."

\* \* \*

LITTLE Johnny had just met the new kid at playgroup.

"How old are you?"

"I don't know," said the new kid.

"Do women bother you?"

"No."

"Then you are five."

\* \* \*

A YOUNG boy was approached by the young housewife who had just moved into the flat next door. "Sonny, I need some bread at the corner store. Do you think you could go for me?"

"No," said the lad, "but I've heard Dad say he could."

* * *

DAD had just settled down with a book when young Johnny came home from school and asked the question he had dreaded to hear: "Where did I come from, Dad?"

Wiping the sweat from his collar Dad began the lengthy explanation beginning with the birds and the bees right through to sexual intercourse, and after an agonising half hour summed it all up with, "Now, do you understand, son?"

"Not really, Dad," said the lad. "Luigi says he comes from Italy and Ng VanDong says he comes from Vietnam. Where do I come from?"

* * *

WHEN his wife said she was going to change the baby, he said: "Well get a quieter one!"

* * *

SHE married a sailor because she wanted to have children and rear admirals.

* * *

"I HEAR you have finally cured little Tommy of biting his nails?"

"Yeah, we pulled his teeth out!"

* * *

LITTLE Agatha was crying bitterly because her father drowned the three new kittens. He had promised her she could do it.

* * *

"MUMMY, you know the vase you were always worried I would break?"

"Yes."

"Well, your worries are over."

# KIWIS

A BLOKE went into the fish shop and asked for some "Fush 'n chups."

"Ar! You're a Kiwi, eh?" said the proprietor.

The Enzedder got sick and tired of this so he spent the next three months at an elocution class.

He finally returned to the shop and asked, in perfect English for some "Fish and Chips."

"Ar, you're a Kiwi, eh?"

"How the hell did you know that?"

"Because this has been a hardware shop for the last two weeks."

\* \* \*

THE potato farmer had recently arrived from Rotorua and had taken up a farm in Gembrook. "You look worried," said his mates in the pub, "what's bothering you?"

"Sex!" he replied.

They gathered around for more information.

"Well," explained the Kiwi, "as you know this is my first harvest here. I've got a wonderful crop of spuds, but not enough sex to put them in."

\* \* \*

THREE couples went into a restaurant in Auckland and asked for a table for sex.

"And three pillows," they added.

# L

## LAW
See POLICE

IT'S illegal to make liquor privately, and to make water publicly.

\* \* \*

THE lag in the dock said: "As God is my judge I am not guilty."

The magistrate replied: "He's not. I am. You are. Three years."

\* \* \*

THE judge called the court to order to make a serious announcement. He said he had been bribed $2000 by the defendant and $3000 by the plaintiff.

"This is a serious matter and I have given it earnest consideration," he said. "I've decided to return $1000 to the plaintiff, and judge the case on its merits!"

\* \* \*

THE judge, he populates
  The city jails
  By grave decisions
  Heads or tails

\* \* \*

DAN Murphy was a popular bloke in the one-horse town, but he was charged with stealing cattle. After the bush jury of his peers heard the evidence the foreman stood up and said: "Not guilty. So long as he returns the cattle."

The circuit magistrate was infuriated with the finding and demanded they go back and reconsider their verdict.

After a short wrangle among themselves the foreman stood once more. "Okay, not guilty, and he can keep the bloomin' cattle."

\* \* \*

"YOU seem to have more than an average share of intelligence for a man of your background," sneered the lawyer at the witness stand.

"Thank you," said the witness. "If I wasn't under oath I'd return the compliment."

\* \* \*

FRED knew that a former partner owed him $500 but he was unable to legally prove it. He asked his solicitor what to do about it.

"Easy," replied the legal eagle. "We will send him a letter demanding payment of the $1000 within seven days and ..."

"But it is only $500," said Fred.

"And that's exactly what he will reply in his letter, and then we have the proof."

\* \* \*

THE clerk turned to the little bloke in the dock. "Prisoner at the bar," he said, "do you wish to challenge the jury?"

Fred eyed the jury. "Not all of them at once," he said, "but I think I could go a few rounds with the little fat geezer in the middle."

\* \* \*

A BLOKE due to appear in court was talking about the case in the bar and was advised by his drinking mate: "If you want to get off, just send the judge a case of whisky."

The defendant discussed this with his solicitor next morning. "On no account do anything like that," said the legal man. "We've got a thin argument already without complicating it with a bribe."

To the solicitor's astonishment our bloke won his case. "We would have lost if you sent that case of whisky."

"Oh, but I did," said our bloke, "but I put the other party's name on the card."

*     *     *

JUDGE: "Can't you settle this out of court?"

"That's what we were doing when the police interferred."

*     *     *

"THIS pen leaks," said the prisoner as the rain came through the roof.

*     *     *

THE Melbourne lawyer received a fax from his partner representing a client in Sydney. It read "Justice has prevailed."

The Melbourne man faxed back a message; "Appeal at once!"

*     *     *

McTAVISH was as shrewd as they come and when he sat down with the lawyer he said: "I'm not into throwing money about, but I will certainly pay if you can give me an undertaking that you can win my case."

The lawyer said that was fair enough and told McTavish to outline the story.

McTavish launched into a terrible tale of breach of contract, lying, cheating and fraudulent business practices.

"That's an open and shut case," said the lawyer. "I will cheerfully accept such a brief."

"Oh that's bad news," said McTavish.

"Why?" asked the lawyer.

"That was my opponent's side of the story."

*     *     *

THE defendant had just been convicted and fined and was asked by the judge if he could pay anything at all towards the penalty and costs.

246

"Not a brass razoo," he replied. "All the money I had has gone to my lawyer and five of the jurors."

\* \* \*

CHARGED with stealing a barrel of beer from the back of the pub the old defendant was not familiar with legal jargon. So when the judge said he would have to dismiss the case due to insufficient evidence the old lag scratched his head and said "What d'yer mean?"

The clerk explained: "It means you are let off."

"And does it mean I can keep the grog?" he asked.

\* \* \*

DAD is very popular in prison. He's the lifer of the party.

\* \* \*

"YOUNG man, you are accused of stealing a petticoat."

"It was my first slip."

\* \* \*

"HAVE you ever been cross-examined before?"

"Yes, your honour, I'm a married man."

\* \* \*

"DO you plead guilty or not guilty?"

"What else have you got?"

\* \* \*

"DO you plead guilty or not guilty?"

"How do I know. I haven't heard the evidence yet."

\* \* \*

"HAVE you anything to offer before judgement is passed?"

"No, judge, my lawyer has left me skint."

\* \* \*

"GUILTY. Ten days or two hundred dollars."

"I'll take the two hundred thanks, judge."

\* \* \*

"ORDER, order in the court."

"Whisky, on the rocks for me thanks."

\* \* \*

JUDGE: you are charged with habitual drunkeness, what is your excuse?"

"Habitual thirst, yer worship!"

BOSS to pretty secretary: "Just because I made love to you last night, who said you could come in late?"

Secretary: "My solicitor."

\* \* \*

JUDGE, to jury: "What possible reason could you have for acquitting this man?"

"Insanity," said the foreman.

"What, all of you?"

\* \* \*

FRED consulted his lawyer. "I've been receiving threatening letters," he said.

"That's terrible," said the legal eagle. "We'll put a stop to that. Who are they from?"

"The Taxation Department," said Fred.

\* \* \*

TWO tramps were hauled before the court and charged with vagrancy.

"And where do you live?" asked the judge.

"Nowhere," said the first tramp.

"And where do you live," he asked the second tramp.

Indicating his mate he replied, "Next door to him!"

\* \* \*

SHE was seeking maintenance for her baby.

"Do you know who the father is?" asked the solicitor.

"Yes," she sobbed. "It was Tommy."

"But we can't sue Tommy. Don't you know his surname?"

"No. You see I didn't know him personally."

\* \* \*

TWO magistrates were rolling home from a reunion, arms around each other, singing Sweet Adeline.

"Hey," said one. "I think we're drunk."

"You're right. And according to law I will have to charge you with being drunk and disorderly," said his mate.

"And you will have to appear before me at 10 tomorrow," said the first.

Next morning in court the first pleaded guilty to the charge and was fined $10. They then changed places.

"Drunk and disorderly, eh, fined $20."

"Hey," protested the first. "When I was in the chair I only fined you $10."

"Yes," said the second magistrate. "But the offence is getting too prevalent. You are the second drunk to appear before this court this morning!"

\* \* \*

JUDGE to habitual defendant: "Is this the first time you have been up before me?"

"I dunno yer honour. What time do you get up?"

\* \* \*

THE solicitor told Paddy that if he wanted to be defended in court tomorrow he would need money, but Paddy was broke.

"All I've got is an antique gold watch," he said.

Solicitor: "Well that's okay, you can raise cash on that. Now what are you accused of stealing?"

Paddy: "An antique gold watch!"

\* \* \*

"HAVE you got anything to say for yourself?" said the judge sternly after hearing the case.

"Stuff all," muttered the defendant.

"What did he say?" asked the judge learning forward to the clerk.

The clerk stood up, turned, and whispered quietly to the judge: "He said 'stuff all' your worship."

"That's funny," said the judge, "I'm sure I saw his lips move."

\* \* \*

WHEN the stranger entered the bar the publican said, "Good evening, Sir, would you like a drink?"

"Yes," he replied, "I will have a double Scotch."

It was plonked in front of him and the publican said, "That'll be five dollars, thanks."

"No," said the stranger, "It's your treat. I clearly heard you invite me to have a drink."

Another gent at the bar who heard the argument said to the publican. "He's right you know. I am a solicitor and I distinctly heard you invite him to have a drink."

The angry publican told the stranger to drink his whisky and leave and never come back.

Ten minutes later the stranger returned. "I thought I told you never to come back," roared the publican."

The stranger protested. "I've never been here before in my life."

The publican grudgingly conceded, "Well you must have a double."

"Thanks very much," said the stranger, "and one for my solicitor friend."

\* \* \*

TWO workers entered the same pub, pulled their stools up to the bar and opened their cut lunches.

"Hey," said the barman, "You can't eat your own sandwiches here."

So they swapped.

## LAZINESS

HE was so lazy he married a pregnant woman.

\* \* \*

HE was so lazy he had his window box concreted over.

\* \* \*

HE was so lazy he used to ride the underground in peak hours just to press his clothes.

\* \* \*

THE only thing he ever took up at school was space.

\* \* \*

HE called her Baseball because she would never play without a diamond.

\* \* \*

THE lazy German lived by the sweat of his frau.

# LETTERS

HE got a letter from his wife: "Fred, I missed you yesterday. Come home and let me have another shot. — Beatrice."

* * *

SMOOTH Sam was confiding to Fred over a beer that he had a problem. "I'm worried, Fred," he said. "This letter came the other day and it said if I didn't stop making love to this bloke's wife he was going to kill me."

"So what's the problem?" said Fred.

"It wasn't signed," said Sam.

* * *

FRED was always coming home from the pub in the early hours of the morning, and eventually found this note from his missus:

"The day before yesterday you came home yesterday morning. Yesterday you came home this morning. So if today you come home tomorrow morning you will find that I left you yesterday."

* * *

"DEAR Sir. Please find enclosed $10.50 for one of your razors as advertised. — Billy Bong. PS: I forgot to enclose the money, but no doubt a firm of your reputable standing will send the razor anyway.

Dear Mr Bong. Thank you for your order and we have pleasure enclosing the razor as requested.

PS: We forgot to enclose the razor, but no doubt a man with your cheek doesn't need one."

* * *

"DEAR John. I have been unable to sleep since I broke off our engagement. Won't you forget and forgive? Your absence is breaking my heart. I was a fool, nobody can take your place. I love you. I love you. — Marsha.

PS: Congratulations on winning the lottery."

* * *

THE university chancellor discovered that one of his

professors had been messing about with his wife. So he sent **him** a letter demanding his presence in the office on **Tues**day morning.

The offending professor sent the following reply: "I received your circular letter. I regret that I cannot attend, but rest assured that I will accept the majority vote."

\* \* \*

LETTER from a travel agent: "Dear Sir, in reference to your proposed trip to London, the flight you requested is completely full, but we will keep in contact and inform you immediately somebody falls out, as is often the case."

\* \* \*

## LETTER FROM AN IRISH MOTHER

DEAR SON. Just a few lines to let you know I'm still alive. I'm writing this letter slowly because I know you can't read fast. You won't know the house when you get home because we have moved.

About your father. He has a lovely new job. He has 500 men under him; he cuts grass at the cemetery. There was a washing machine in the new house when we moved in but it hasn't been working too good. Last week I put Dad's shirt in, pulled the chain and haven't seen it since.

Your sister Mary had a baby this morning but I haven't found out if it is a boy or a girl yet, so I don't know if you are an auntie or an uncle.

Your Uncle Patrick drowned last week in a vat of whisky at the Dublin Brewery. Some of his workmates tried to save him but he fought them off bravely. They cremated him and it took five days to put out the fire.

I went to the doctor last Thursday and your father came with me. The doctor put a small glass tube in my mouth and told me not to talk for ten minutes. Your father offered to buy it off him.

It only rained twice this week, first for three days and then for four.

We had a letter from the undertaker. He said if the last payment on your grandfather's plot isn't paid within seven days, up he comes.

— Your loving mother.

PS: I was going to send you $10 but I had already sealed up the envelope.

*　　*　　*

## WHY I FIRED MY SECRETARY

TWO weeks ago it was my 45th birthday. I didn't feel too well that morning, but I knew that when I went to breakfast my wife would be pleasant and say "Happy Birthday". But she didn't even say "Good Morning".

I thought, that's wives for you. At least the children will remember. But the kids came in for breakfast and didn't say a word, so when I started for the office I was feeling pretty low and despondent.

As I walked into the office, Janet said "Good Morning, boss. Happy Birthday." I immediately felt better because somebody remembered.

About noon she knocked on my door and said that it was such a lovely day we should go out to lunch. It was the best news I had all day.

We went to lunch. We didn't go where we normally go. Janet said she knew a little private place out in the country. We had two martinis and enjoyed lunch tremendously.

On the way back to the office she said, "You know, it's such a beautiful day it would be a shame to go back to the office." When I agreed she said: "Let's go to my apartment and I will fix you another martini."

We did just that, in fact she fixed two martinis which put me in a very pleasant mood. Then she said, "Boss, if you don't mind, I think I will go into the bedroom and slip into something more comfortable." I assured her I didn't mind at all.

She went into the bedroom and in about six minutes

253

she came out carrying a big birthday cake followed by my wife and children, all singing Happy Birthday, and there I sat with nothing on except my socks!

*　　*　　*

## AUSTRALIAN EXPORT

MEIN Tear Herren.

Der last two pecketches ve got from you off coffee vas mitt rattschidtten mixt. Ve did not see any rattschidtten in der samples vich you sent us. It takes much valuable time to pick de ratten durden from der coffee. Ve order der coffee clean but you schipt schidt mixt mit it.

Ve like you schip us der coffee in vun sek, und der rattenschidtten in an udder sek. Und zen ve can mix it to suit der customer. Write please if we should schip der schidt bek und keep der coffee, or should ve chip bek der coffee und keep der shidt, or should ve schip bek der whole schidtten vurks?

We remain at your conwenience...

# LIARS

THE lie is an abomination to the Lord; but damned helpful in getting out of trouble.

*　　*　　*

SHE said she can tell by looking at your husband's face if he is lying.

"Yes," she said. "If his lips are moving, he's lying."

*　　*　　*

DOES your husband lie awake at night?

Yes, and he lies in his sleep, too.

*　　*　　*

THEY say the first lie detector was made out of the rib of a man. And they have been unable to improve on that model ever since.

*　　*　　*

THE vicar from the pulpit announced that his sermon

that day would be on the sin of perjury. "How many of you have read the 25th chapter?"

All in the congregation raised their hands.

"That's good," said the vicar. "There is no 25th chapter so you are exactly the people I want to talk to."

\* \* \*

THERE are two kinds of people who live in Sydney. Those who admit they have cockroaches and the others who lie about it.

\* \* \*

THERE is only one thing that stops him from being a bare-faced liar.

What's that?

His moustache.

\* \* \*

MADGE fixed her eye on her husband Fred and said: "So, where are you going today?"

"I'm going to the pub."

"Ha, when you tell me you are going to the pub I know that you think that I'll think you are going to the races, but this time I know you are really going to the pub, so why are you lying?"

\* \* \*

HE described his wife as having a keen sense of rumour.

\* \* \*

HE's not really a liar. He just arranges the truth in his favour.

## LIFE

THE best way to face life is with a stiff upper lip, a firm chin, your feet planted firmly on the ground your head high in the air, your nose to the grindstone, an ear to the ground and a shoulder to the wheel... and you'll find it's damned uncomfortable.

IF I had my life to live over again, I'd start making the same mistakes earlier.

* * *

NEVER let life get you down. Remember, when one door closes, another slams in your face.

* * *

ABOUT the time you are financial enough to eat, drink and be merry, the doctor limits you to a glass of milk.

* * *

THE only certain way to reduce the cost of living is to drop dead.

* * *

LIFE is to be enjoyed. We will never get out of it alive.

* * *

LIFE. The first half is ruined by your parents. The second half is ruined by your kids.

* * *

IF you want to remember, tie a short string around your finger.

If you want to forget, tie a long rope around your neck.

* * *

LIFE begins at 40, but you could miss a lot if you wait till then.

* * *

LIFE is like a shower. One wrong turn and you are in hot water.

* * *

WHAT is the reason women live longer than men?

Because they have no wives.

(And of course the reverse applies.)

* * *

HE was asked if he ever realised any of his childhood dreams.

"Yes. When I was young and my mother kept insisting on combing my hair I often wished I didn't have any."

LIFE can be hard, but some hearts can be harder as the tramp found out when he knocked on the back door of the inn looking for a hand-out.

The landlady fixed him with a steely glare. "Would you eat yesterday's stew?"

"Yes," he said eagerly.

"Well, come back tomorrow," she said.

## LITERATURE

SHE went to Stratford-on-Avon to see her first play, A Midsummer Night's Dream, and was so moved by it that on the final curtain she stood and called: "Author! Author!"

\* \* \*

A CRITIC, said Kenneth Tynan, is a man who knows the way but can't drive a car.

\* \* \*

A CRITIC is a legless man who teaches running.

\* \* \*

AND the critic's response. "I can't lay an egg either, but I am a better judge of an omelette than any hen."

\* \* \*

"WHAT do you think of Kipling?"

"Don't know. I've never tried it."

\* \* \*

THE English teacher looked dejected. "I have just given that class a lecture on Keats, and I doubt if any of them know what a keat is."

## LOCAL GOVERNMENT

A TEDDY Bear got a job on a council road gang. Monday went well, Tuesday likewise, but on Wednesday when he returned from his lunch break he discovered his pick had been stolen.

He complained to the foreman who was undismayed and had the obvious answer.

"It's Wednesday," he said. "That's the day the Teddy Bears have their picks nicked!"

*　　*　　*

SOCIETY matron was crowing over her husband's re-election on the municipal council. "Yes. My John got elected for his third time and got in unexposed!"

*　　*　　*

WHEN the municipal council decided to build a fountain outside the town hall they put the project to tender and got three quotes, from contractors in Brisbane, Sydney and Melbourne.

The town clerk interviewed the Brisbane builder and asked his price. "$3000," was the reply.

"And how do you break that down?" asked the clerk.

"That's $1000 for the material, $1000 for the workers and $1000 for me."

The town clerk called in the Sydney contractor who quoted a price of $6000. "And how do you break that down?" asked the clerk.

"That's $2000 for materials, $2000 for the workers and $2000 for me."

The clerk called in the Melbourne bloke, whose price was $9000.

"And how do you break that down?" asked the clerk.

The bloke from Melbourne said, "$3000 for you, $3000 for me, and we give the job to the bloke from Brisbane."

*　　*　　*

THEY had never had a woman on the town council before and newly elected Cr Flossie Firebrand intended to make her mark.

The first item on the engineer's agenda was the cost of constructing a urinal.

"What's a urinal?" she asked.

258

When it was fully explained to her she immediately demanded that the funds be doubled.

"If we are gonna have a urinal I insist that we have an arsenal too."

*　　*　　*

PAYING his parking fine at the town hall the commercial traveller complained to the clerk that the town didn't have enough parking spaces.

"We're a small country town with lots of expenses," said the clerk. "If we can't catch you blokes for speeding, then we rip a little bit off for standing still."

*　　*　　*

HE was mayor of the town, and a justice of the peace which meant he sat on the bench on court days. He glared over his glasses at the tramp charged with vagrancy.

"Have you ever earned a dollar in your life?" he sneered.

"Yes, yer honour," answered the defendant. "It was a tenner remember, for voting for you at the last election."

## LOGIC

TWO Catholic women were enjoying a cup of coffee opposite a house owned by a notorious call girl when they saw a protestant minister go in.

"Disgraceful," whispered one to the other.

Later they saw the local rabbi emerge from the same door and they shook their heads in despair.

"What's the world coming to?"

They were on their second cup of coffee when they saw Father O'Kelly knock on the door and enter.

"Dear, the poor woman must be awfully sick," they agreed.

*　　*　　*

TWO travellers, one with years of experience, found themselves in a strange town without lodgings. It was a warm night so they decided to sleep out in what appeared to be a quiet lane.

The older of the two elected to lay in the middle of the road. His younger companion, declaring his mate a fool, settled down on the side of the road.

As they were sleeping a truck came down the road and the driver, seeing the old bloke in his path, swerved to avoid him and ran over the young man on the pavement.

\* \* \*

SOCIETY Sally said to the good-looking stranger: "Gee you look like my fifth husband."

The stranger was taken aback. "How many times have you been married?" he asked.

"Four," she replied.

\* \* \*

THE club's fund-raiser approached the born loser.

"Will you buy a raffle ticket for a keg of beer?"

"I don't like beer," he said.

"Not to worry," she said. "There are too many in it already. You haven't a chance of winning."

"Good," he said. "I'll take two."

\* \* \*

AFTER catching a stranger in bed with his wife the irate husband reaches for his gun.

"Wait!" cries his wife. "Remember the world cruise we went on after I told you I won the lottery. Well, Lionel paid for it. Remember the strange circumstances which caused our mortgage to be paid off. Well, Lionel actually paid it. Remember the diamond ring I found. Well, again, Lionel paid for it..."

The husband lowers his gun.

"For goodness sake, woman. Cover him up he'll catch a chill."

# M

## MAGIC

AN old magician was working the Titanic on its last fateful voyage. He used to put a rabbit in his top hat and pull a hair out of his bum. (No, that's not the joke).

The old-timer had been down on his luck and couldn't afford one of those attractive leggy blonde assistants. On the Titanic he had to make do with a parrot, but to give it credit, the parrot had developed repartee and would squawk to the audience: "It's up his sleeve", or "It's under his cloak, folks."

They were half way through their act when the Titanic hit the iceberg and sank.

The magician swam all night while the parrot fluttered overhead. He swam all next day and the parrot still fluttered overhead. It was evening of the second day when the parrot finally alighted on the magician's head.

"Okay, I give up. What have you done with the bloomin' ship?"

*    *    *

AFTER the leggy blonde had flagged him down on the country road he asked her what she did for a living.

"I'm a magician," she said.

"Get away, prove it then."

And with that she touched him on the knee and turned him into a motel.

THE party had been very entertaining and now it was Paddy's turn to do a magic trick. He stretches his arms forward, thumbs up, and says to the person opposite: "Pick a thumb, any thumb at all will do."

The volunteer makes his choice and Paddy quickly whips his arms behind himself and fumbles for a moment. Then, holding his clenched fists forward he says: "Okay, okay. Which hand is it in?"

# MARRIAGE
## See WEDDINGS, NEWLY-WEDS

REMEMBER, Socrates died from an overdose of wedlock.

★    ★    ★

MOST marriages are happy. It is trying to live together afterwards that causes the tension.

★    ★    ★

MARRIAGES are made uneven.

★    ★    ★

MARRIAGE is the price men pay for sex and sex is the price women pay for marriage.

★    ★    ★

MARRIAGE has its good side. It teaches you loyalty, forebearance, self-restraint, and many other qualities you wouldn't need if you stayed single.

★    ★    ★

MARRIAGE is not a word, it is a sentence.

★    ★    ★

MARRIAGE is not a lottery. In a lottery you have a chance.

★    ★    ★

MARRIAGE is like a three ring circus. First the engagement ring, second the wedding ring and third the suffer-ring.

★    ★    ★

THERE'S a lot to be said about marriage. But try not to say it in front of the children.

STATISTICS prove that at least 50% of all people who get married at Easter are women.

* * *

IF a woman does household chores for $250 a week, that's domestic science. If she does it for nothing, that's marriage.

* * *

LAUGH, and the world laughs with you. Quarrel with your wife and you sleep alone.

## MARRIAGE COUNSELLING

COUNSELLOR: "Are your relations pleasant?"
  "Mine are, his are horrible."

* * *

THE marriage counsellor asked the wife: "Did you shrink from love-making?"
  "No," she replied, "I've always been tiny like this."

* * *

"OF course we are incompatible," she said, "but he's far more incompatible than I am."

## MARRIEDS

DARLING is the wife's maiden name.

* * *

THEY got off to a bad start at the altar.
  When he said "I do," she replied, "Oh no you don't," and they have been arguing ever since.

* * *

ONE month after the wedding Arthur began to wonder if he has made the right decision. Every evening meal had consisted of wedding cake and chips.

* * *

"I SHOULD never have got married, Fred."
  "Why not, Harry?"

"Because the wife hates me when I'm drunk and I can't stand the sight of her when I'm sober."

* * *

"MONEY, money, money, they are the only three words you know!"

* * *

HE said his wife doesn't understand him, but it is his own fault. He shouldn't have married a Chinese girl.

* * *

"I'VE been married five years, and believe me, when it comes to making money you've just got to hand it to Madge."

* * *

"TELL me dear, before we were married did you say you were oversexed, or over sex?"

* * *

"DOES your wife pick your clothes?"

"No, only the pockets."

* * *

"I HAVE a clever wife."

"Mine always finds out, too."

* * *

"TELL me Charles," she said. "If I died before you, would you still go to our golf club on week-ends?"

"Oh, I suppose so, dear."

"I guess, after a time, you would take up with another partner?"

"Oh, I suppose so, dear."

"Tell me Charles, would you let her use my clubs?"

"No dear, she's left-handed."

* * *

SHE nudged her husband awake when she thought she heard a burglar, but he refused to get out and investigate.

"What's happened?" she whispered. "You were brave when you married me."

"Yes, that's what all my mates said," he replied.

SHE arrived at the breakfast table in an old chenille dressing gown and her hair in rollers.

"Why can't you look like you did when I married you?" he grumbled.

"Because I'm not pregnant now," she said.

\* \* \*

IT was another domestic that had reached the stage where they were not talking to each other. Notes were in vogue.

She found a note pinned to her pillow: "I have to be at the office early. Wake me at seven."

When he woke at 9-30, there was a note pinned to his pillow which said: "It's seven o'clock, wake up!"

\* \* \*

THE old couple sat on the porch, as they had for many years. "I was just thinking," said the old lady, "we've had such a grand life together, but sooner or later one of us will pass on."

"Yes, but don't worry about that now," he said.

"Well I was just thinking," she said, "when it does happen, I'd like to go and live in Queensland."

\* \* \*

REMEMBER that your wife is a romantic and still enjoys chocolates and flowers. So show her that you too remember, by speaking of them occasionally.

\* \* \*

"WHAT'S your husband's average income?"

"About midnight."

\* \* \*

THEY say he married her because her aunt left her a fortune.

He hotly denies it, and says he would have married her whoever left her the fortune.

\* \* \*

MR and Mrs Offenbloo had been married for 20 years and they were still in love. She with the doctor and he with his secretary.

BLOKE came home to find his wife in bed with the next door neighbour.

"What the hell do you think you're doing?" demanded the husband.

The wife said to her bedmate: "There you are, I told you he was stupid."

\* \* \*

THE wife was nervous as she got behind the wheel of their new car for the first time. "I hardly know what to do," she said.

"Just imagine I'm driving," he said.

\* \* \*

"THERE must be something, even one thing," he said in a heated argument "that my family scores over your family."

She pondered for a while. "Yes. Your in-laws are better than my in-laws."

\* \* \*

WIFE: "Before we were married you told me you were well off."

"Yes, but I didn't know it at the time."

\* \* \*

THEY had been married for ten years. She looked up from her sewing and said: "Darling, why don't we go out tonight?"

He put his book aside and said, "What a splendid idea. And if I get home before you I will leave the light on."

## MECHANICS

WHEN her date, a young mechanic, arrived to take her out she was surprised to see a set of jumper leads around his neck with the clips holding up his trousers. "My braces broke," he explained.

She gave the jumper leads a dubious look and said: "Well okay, I will come out with you. But don't start anything."

THE mechanic itemised the bill for the woman driver: "$100 repairs to fender, $150 repairs to the tail-light fixture, $50 for not telling your husband and $50 for running over Pete, the petrol pump attendant."

* * *

THE car mechanic went to the psychiatrist and laid down under the couch.

## MISTRESSES

FRED has got so many mistresses that when he takes his wife for a drive she has to hide under the dash when they pass a woman in the street.

* * *

IZZY's wife became piqued when a woman passing their table gave Izzy the eye.

"Who's that?" she wanted to know.

"Actually, it's my mistress," explained Izzy. "She is vital for business. Got essential connections in the trade. You know how it is."

This didn't exactly calm Mrs Izzy but at that moment Mr Rozenbloom walked past with a rather brassy tart on his arm.

"Who's that woman?" demanded Mrs Izzy.

"That's Rozenbloom's mistress," explained her husband.

She pondered for a moment and then said, "Izzy, I think our mistress is much better than Rozenbloom's."

## MOTHERS-IN-LAW
### See FATHERS-IN-LAW

MY mother-in-law thinks I'm effeminate. But compared to her I probably am.

* * *

ONE mother-in-law to another: "I have never made a

fool of my son-in-law. I always allow him the opportunity to develop his natural capacities."

*    *    *

I NEVER forget a face. But in my mother-in-law's case, I am willing to make an exception.

*    *    *

THE local Peeping Tom knocked on the door the other night and asked if the mother-in-law would mind closing her bedroom curtains.

*    *    *

WONDERFUL woman my mother-in-law, 75 years old and never uses glasses. Drinks straight from the bottle.

*    *    *

FOR 20 years my mother-in-law and me were happy.
   Then we met.

*    *    *

MY mother-in-law is musical and does a bit of singing. Yesterday she was practising and three factories knocked off for lunch.

*    *    *

MY mother-in-law has a speech impediment. Now and then she has to pause for breath.

*    *    *

FRED rented a little cottage by the sea and wired his wife that the holiday was arranged and to come and join him. But he got a shock to see both wife and mother arrive with luggage.
   First chance he got he took his wife aside and whispered: "Didn't you get the telegram not to bring your mother?"
   "Yes," she replied, "that's what she wants to talk to you about."

*    *    *

MARRIAGE Anonymous is a club for bachelors. If any member is tempted to get married they send over a mother-in-law in a dressing gown and hair curlers.

FRED was explaining to his mate at the bar that he had yet another fight with his mother-in-law.

"But at least she came crawling to me on her hands and knees this time," he said.

His mate was impressed: "Why, what did she say?"

"Come out from under the bed you pathetic, snivelling little coward and I'll clobber you again!"

\*     \*     \*

BLOKE on a caravan holiday in Far North Queensland with his wife and mother-in-law was wakened one morning. His wife said her mother hadn't returned from her morning walk and she was alarmed. They searched along the river bank for a while before the wife let out a scream when she saw her mother paddling in the shallows and a large crocodile stalking her from behind.

"Oh my Gawd," screamed the wife, "Do something, quick!"

The man considered the situation for a moment and said: "The croc got himself into this trouble, let him get himself out of it."

\*     \*     \*

THE same mother-in-law was kidnapped when they returned from their holiday. After three days they got a note from the kidnappers saying that if they didn't send the ransom money immediately, they would send her back.

\*     \*     \*

HE complained to the doctor that he was worried about his mother-in-law. "She keeps blowing smoke rings through her nose when she talks to me."

"Nothing unusual about that," said the Doc. "Lots of people blow rings when they are smoking."

"Yeah, but my mother-in-law doesn't smoke," he said.

## MOTORING

THE freeway is where drivers under 25 do over 90, and drivers over 90 do 25.

THE motorist on tour stopped his car at Oodnadatta and asked a local how to get to Tennant Creek.

"Well, I certainly wouldn't start from here," he said.

\* \* \*

THE garage mechanic lifted the bonnet. "If I was you, sir, I'd keep the oil and change the car."

\* \* \*

THE best thing to say for the advent of motoring, is that it has certainly stamped out horse-stealing.

\* \* \*

CITY couple were driving in the country and stopped in a one-horse town to ask a local how to get back on the highway.

He scratched his head and said. "I don't think you can get there from here."

"It's no use asking him," said the woman to her husband. "He's stupid."

"Me? Stupid?" exclaimed the local. "I'm not the one that's lost. You two are."

\* \* \*

COP stopped a motorist one night. "How long have you been driving without a tail light?" he asked.

The driver jumped out and went to the rear of the car and began to moan and groan. "Oh hell," he lamented.

His distress was so genuine the cop was sympathetic. "Oh c'mon Sir, it is not that serious an offence."

"Isn't it?" moaned the driver. "What about the wife and kids and the whole bloomin' caravan?"

\* \* \*

IRISH cop stopped a motorist. "Would you be having a driver's licence?" he asked.

"Indeed I have," said the driver.

"Well that's good. Because if you didn't I'd have to see it."

\* \* \*

SHE took her car to the service station. "What's wrong with it?" said the mechanic.

"It's got an indifferent horn," she said.

"What d'yer mean?"

"It doesn't give a hoot."

*     *     *

THE police stopped him because he looked as if he was a bit under the weather. He was approached with the breathalyser bag.

"What's that?" he asked.

"It tells you if you have had too much to drink," said the cop.

"Amazing. I'm married to one of them."

*     *     *

FRED drove his car back to the second-hand dealer.

"You remember you sold me this car last week and said its sole previous owner was a little old woman, quiet and reserved and only used the car to go to church on Sundays?"

"Yes," said the salesman a little cautiously.

"Well can you give me her name," said Fred. "I have cleaned out the boot and the glove box and I want to return her cigar butts, two empty gin bottles, a pair of silk garters with spangles on them and a pair of red knickers."

*     *     *

HE was parking his battered old jalopy in the main street when a policeman stopped beside him and asked if he had reported the accident.

*     *     *

SHE was explaining the damage to the side of their new car to her husband.

"An old man in a Ford ran into me," she said.

"Yeah, but how many times?"

*     *     *

"I GOT rid of that rear noise in the car."

"How?"

"I made her sit in the front with me."

MIDDLE-AGED couple were driving along when the traffic cop pulled them over. "You were travelling at 90," said the cop.

"Rubbish," said the husband, "It was only 60."

The cop insisted on 90 and the driver was getting angry, at which point his wife leaned over. "Don't argue with him officer. He's always pig-headed when he's had a few drinks."

\* \* \*

TRAFFIC Cop: "Hey, you are blocking traffic, can't you go any faster?"

"Yes, but I don't want to leave the car."

\* \* \*

TRAFFIC Cop: "Do you know you were doing over 100 kilometres an hour?"

"Impossible," she said. "I only left home twenty minutes ago."

\* \* \*

HIS wife was waiting for him when he got home. "Darling," she sobbed. "I'm afraid I dented the front bumper of your new car today."

"Oh that's okay darling," he said. "Where is it?"

"In the back seat."

\* \* \*

FRED was driving his van slowly and with great caution, but what attracted the traffic cop was the frequent stops when Fred would dash to the rear of the van and kick the back doors.

The cop stopped him and asked for an explanation.

"Well officer," he began, "I have three tonnes of budgerigars on board and if they all land at once the van's springs will collapse."

\* \* \*

IT was Saturday and the traffic cop signalled the bloke driving the horse float to pull over.

"What's your hurry?" he said.

The trainer looked at his watch. "I have to be at the track for the first race at 1.30," he said.

The cop did a slow circumnavigation of the vehicles, looked in the float, and finally re-appeared at the driver's window.

"You've got no horses on board," he said.

"I know, I know," said the trainer. "I'm taking the non-starters aren't I?"

*   *   *

FOR some learner drivers, L-plates are more like destination boards.

*   *   *

THE distinguished old gent driving the Rolls had finally spotted a parking space and was sedately reversing into the kerb when a flash little sports car zipped in, skidded to a halt and stole the space from under his nose.

The cheeky driver hopped out and said, "You've got to be young and nippy to do that, Pops."

The old gent ignored him and the Rolls continued reversing until there was the sound of breaking glass and crunching metal and the sports car was reduced to a crumpled heap.

When he got out the old gent said: "You've got to be old and rich to do that, Sport!"

*   *   *

HIS car was veering from one side of the road to the other. He nearly ran off the road, when the cop pulled him up.

"You are drunk," said the cop.

"Thank goodnesh for that offisher. I thought my steering had gone."

*   *   *

PADDY was leaning on the bar enjoying a "point" when somebody yelled, "Hey Paddy, there's a bloke stealing your car!"

Paddy dashed from the pub but came back five minutes later all puffed out.

"Did you get him?" pressed his mates.

"No, I got close," puffed Paddy. "But it's okay, I took the number."

* * *

TWO Aussie tourists were motoring in England along one of those tight country lanes when the squire, in his Rolls, approached from the opposite direction. As the cars drew close the squire wound down the window, looked the Aussies in the eye and shouted, "Pigs!"

Our lads were taken aback and were still getting over the shock when, right around the next bend, they ran into a herd of pigs.

## MOVIES

HE said he saw a good film last night. It was called Moby Dick.

"I don't like sex films," she replied.

He said it wasn't about sex. "It was about whales."

"I don't like the Welsh either," she said.

* * *

WHEN the matron's eyes got accustomed to the dark she realised a young lad was sitting beside her.

"Why aren't you at school?" she said.

"Because I've got chicken pox," he replied.

* * *

A WOMAN rushed from the front stalls to tell the manager she had been molested. He tried to calm her down but when two more complained about the same thing he thought he had better investigate. In the second row he found a man on his hands and knees.

"I've lost my toupé," said the luckless patron. "I had my hand on it three times but it got away."

* * *

A MOVIE star is a person who strives for years to be well-known, then goes down side streets with dark glasses to avoid being recognised.

A HOLLYWOOD marriage is a great way to spend a weekend.

* * *

HE was only six years old, but he decided to take his girlfriend to the movies.

"How much is it?" he asked at the box office.

"Well, sonny, for grown ups in long pants it is eight dollars, but as you are only wearing short pants it is four dollars."

"Well in that case," piped up his girlfriend, "I should get in for nothing!"

* * *

THEY snuggled down in the stalls at the movies, but the woman in front was wearing a large hat which obstructed their view. He tapped her on the shoulder. She turned round and it was his wife.

## MULTI-NATIONAL

THE author just happens to be multi-national. He's part Irish and part Italian. That's Irish from his mother's side, and Italian by a friend of his father's.

* * *

BEFORE this country became multi-cultural a traditional Australian seven-course meal consisted of a six-pack and a pie.

* * *

AN Englishman, an Australian and a Scotsman were invited to a party. The Englishman took six bottles of Guiness, the Aussie took six cans of beer, and the Scotsman took six of his friends.

* * *

THREE soldiers met in the pub. The Australian stood a round, the Englishman stood a round and the Scotsman stood six feet tall.

"I'M Murphy, Irish, and proud of it."

"I'm McTavish, Scotch, and fond of it!"

* * *

IF a paddock full of Irishmen is a Paddy Field, then a paddock full of Ockers must be a vacant lot.

* * *

WHEN Paddy emigrated from Ireland to Australia, it lifted the IQ of both countries.

* * *

YOU can tell a Pommie, but you can't tell him much.

* * *

A LAZY German lives by the sweat of his frau.

* * *

BRITONS have an infinite capacity for churning themselves up into a terrific calmness.

* * *

A SCOTSMAN had been playing the pools and eventually won £500,000.

"We've made it at last," he told his wife.

"What are you going to do about the begging letters?" she asked.

"Keep sending them I suppose," he replied.

* * *

AN Irishman went for a job and was told he would have to pass an IQ test. When he asked what an IQ was the employer explained that anyone with an IQ of 150 would be admitted to university, but a bloke with an IQ of 50 would have trouble tying his shoe laces.

"Oh," said the Irishman, "So that's why so many Australians wear thongs."

* * *

IT was the bad old days and an Englishman, an Irishman and a Jew were sentenced to 50 lashes. The commandant said the rules allowed for oil or ointment on their backs.

"Then I will have olive oil, please," said the Englishman.

276

The Irishman was defiant. "I despise the English. I'll have nothing on my back, because I'm tough."

Then the Jew was asked what he wanted on his back. "The Irishman," he said.

* * *

THREE different nationalities were discussing the meaning of 'savoir faire'.

The American said, "It means that if you came home and found your wife in bed with another man and you refrained from killing the son of a bitch, that's 'savoir faire'."

The Englishman said: "Hardly chaps. If you found your wife in bed with another man and excused yourself for interrupting and invited them to carry on, well that's 'savoir faire'."

The Frenchman had a different view: "If you came home and found your wife in bed with another man and you said 'Please continue, monsieur' and he was able to, then HE'S got 'savoir faire'."

* * *

IT was Luigi's first day on the job, high on the scaffolding of the 51st level of a sky scraper when the hook of a crane knocked him off balance.

He fell into the rubbish shoot, and for the next five minutes he crashed, banged and walloped his way to the ground until he was discharged in a cloud of dust on the footpath.

"Where the hell did you come from?" asked the surprised foreman.

"Italy," said Luigi.

* * *

PADDY got into a fight at the pub and was knocked down five times.

"Well, have you had enough?" said his much bigger opponent.

"Don't know," said Paddy. "This is my first fight."

THE Scottish publican picked up the phone to hear a voice say that there was a bomb planted under the pub and it would go off in ten minutes.

He put the phone down and called: "Last orders, gents!"

*　　*　　*

AND what's the difference between a Scotsman and a coconut?

You can get a drink out of a coconut.

*　　*　　*

TWO Scots met in Collins Street. They hadn't seen each other since they migrated from Edinburgh together 25 years ago. They hugged and slapped each other on the shoulder.

"Let's have a drink, like we did in the old times," said Jock.

"Aye, and don't forget, it's your shout," said the other.

*　　*　　*

THE Greek businessman went to his favorite taverna and was surprised to be served by a Vietnamese waiter who spoke perfect Greek.

When paying his bill to Con the proprietor he raised the point. "How come the waiter speaks perfect Greek?" he asked Con.

"Ssh! Don't mention it. He thinks it's English."

*　　*　　*

NEW Zealanders get the mickey taken out of them because of their funny accents when ordering "fush and chups." But we know of a chap in Auckland, when out with his girlfriend and two other couples, who went into a restaurant and ordered "a table for sex," and then added, "and three pillows."

*　　*　　*

THE Chinese take-away and the Greek fruit shop were side by side, and each Friday morning the two owners would sweep the pavement.

Con the Greek would take the opportunity to have his little joke: "What day is it today, Charlie?"

"It's Fliday," the Chinaman would reply, and Con would roll about laughing.

Each week it was the same and Con would even get some friends to come along and listen to Charlie say "Fliday."

It got on Charlie's wick. So he went along for elocution lessons and concentrated on "Friday, Friday, Friday."

Next morning he was waiting for the big showdown, sweeping a clean pavement for ten minutes before Con appeared. "What day is it today, Charlie," grinned Con.

"It's Friday ... you Gleek plick!"

\* \* \*

RED Adair's fame in quelling oil rig fires stretches around the globe, so when a well in the middle of the Sahara Desert spewed smoke and flame the alert went out: "Get Red Adair."

But Red had his hands full with a fire crisis on the other side of the world, and nobody can be in two places at the same time. The Exon magnates were frantic. Without the famous Red Adair they were in heaps of trouble.

"Why not try Green Adair?" suggested a lackey.

"Who?" But as the flames roared higher in the sky, why not try Green Adair indeed.

Green Adair was contacted in the Limerick Arms in Belfast and offered one million pounds to do the job.

Within a few hours the oil engineers were amazed to see an air transport land in the desert. They gasped as the nose of the aircraft opened and a truck, bearing Green Adair and his crew sped towards the fire. They watched in amazement as the truck approached the wall of flames and disappeared into the very heart of the fire. They could see Green Adair and his men leaping about, jumping and stamping out the flames.

Finally, all charred, singed and blackened they emerged from the smoke to the cheers of their incredulous admirers.

"What will you do with the million pounds?" asked the first reporter on the scene.

"The first thing I do," said Green Adair, "will be to get some brakes for that bloomin' truck!"

*    *    *

IN a pub Harry the car dealer was trying to flog a heap of junk parked outside to a Chinese student.

"It's a reliable car," said Harry. "It is yours for five hundred dollars, but if you have the cash I will take off 20%."

The student was too shrewd to admit he didn't understand the discount and said he would think it over.

When he got the chance he asked the barmaid quietly, "If I give you five hundred dollars, how much you take off?"

"Everything except my earrings, honey. No worries."

*    *    *

THREE men answered an advertisement to join a mining survey expedition into the Outback. They were a Scotsman, a German, and a Chinaman. The boss said the Scotsman would be in charge of the engineers, the German would be in charge of the mechanics, and the Chinaman, well, they are all good cooks, so he said the Chinaman could be in charge of supplies. "But we leave promptly at eight tomorrow," he said.

Next morning, the Scot and the German showed up, but there was no sign of the Chinaman. They waited for half an hour before the boss gave a curse and ordered that they set off without him.

The party had travelled only a few hundred metres up the road when the Chinaman jumped out from behind a tree and shouted: "Supplies, supplies!"

AN Englishman, American and an Irishman were arrested in South America for smuggling. "We'll give you gringos a fair trial and shoot you tomorrow," said the "capitan" of the guard.

The three spent a restless night. "But not to worry, chaps," said the Englishman. "I shall invoke the natural disaster plan. These South Americans are terrified of natural disaster. Just watch me."

So at dawn the Englishman said he would face the firing squad first and the other two watched from their cell as the capitan said "Ready ... Aim ..."

"Earthquake! Earthquake!" roared the Englishman at the top of his voice. The South Americans panicked and in the confusion the Pommie escaped.

Later the American was led to the stake and the capitan said: "Ready ... Aim..."

"Flood! Flood!" roared the Yank and in the confusion he escaped too.

The Irishman had picked up the drift of the plot. It was all a matter of timing, so he listened as the capitan ordered, "Ready... Aim..."

"Fire!" yelled the Irishman.

\* \* \*

JILL, she was a pretty girl,
and Jack, an ardent male
He praised her shapely beauty
In English, French,
And Braille.

# MUSIC

THE serious music lover is the bloke who, hearing a soprano in the bathroom, puts his ear to the keyhole.

\* \* \*

AN earnest young man with a violin case under his arm asked a London Bobby: "How do I get to the Albert Hall?"

The bobby replied: "Practice, practice, practice."

THE old lady asked the busker: "Do you always play by ear?"

"No, Ma'am, sometimes I play over there."

* * *

"WHY do you play the same piece all the time?"

"It haunts me."

"So it should. You've murdered it often enough."

* * *

"I AM always breaking into song."

"Well, if you found the right key you wouldn't have to break in."

* * *

"CAN you sing opera?"

"Yes."

"Can you sing Faust?"

"Faust or slow, any way you like."

* * *

PADDY Murphy thought the Guinness Book of Records was an LP of Irish drinking songs.

* * *

AFTER the concert she said, "My word, that soprano had a wonderful repertoire."

"Yes," he said, "and that tight dress showed it off well."

* * *

THE Scotsman said his singing voice was a natural gift.

We all agreed, it would have to be.

* * *

HE was a short-sighted musician, and one day he fell over a clef.

* * *

SHE went out with a musician once, and has never been composed since.

* * *

I CAN'T sing. So I am looking for a ravishing blonde accompanist who can't play the piano.

INTRIGUED by the complications in trying to fold road maps while seated in a Mini Minor, Arthur persevered until he became a celebrated accordian player.

\*     \*     \*

HE had just landed on English shores from Dublin and went straight to a pub and bought a round of beers.

"Will an Irish tenner be alright?" he asked the barman.

When the barman replied, "no problem" he broke out in the chorus of "Oh Danny Boy..."

\*     \*     \*

FRED played the trombone and eventually got a gig in Las Vegas. Tired from the long flight he booked into the swank hotel and turned in early but was awakened by a knock on the door about midnight.

"Hello there," said a ravishing brunette. "Are you Frank Sinatra?"

"No Miss, I'm Fred Nerd from Moonee Ponds, Melbourne," and he shut the door and climbed back into bed.

An hour later there was another knock. Fred wearily opened the door to see a lovely redhead. "Hi there, are you Frank Sinatra?"

"No," he said, "I'm Fred Nerd," and slammed the door and dived back into the blankets.

You've guessed it, there was yet another knock on the door. This time a ravishing blonde wearing a see-through negligee says: "Hello, are you Frank Sinatra?"

"Am I Frankie, baby?" And throwing his arms out wide Fred starts singing at the top of his voice, "Strangers in the night ... New York, New York ..."

\*     \*     \*

THE old maestro had fallen on hard times, mainly due to tippling the whisky bottle. He had been a concert pianist of great renown in his time and his drinking pals at the Pig and Whistle decided they should be responsible for putting him back on the concert circuit.

They chipped in and bought an old tuxedo from the Opportunity Shop, not knowing that the trousers had a split in the crotch.

They booked him for the next benefit concert at the Mechanics' Hall and lined the front row on the opening night. When the maestro came on stage, bowed and sat on his chair at the piano there was a gasp of concern from the front row, and one of his friends was so bold as to leap onto the stage and whisper.

"Do you know your old flannel shirt is flapping through a hole in your tuxedo?"

"No," said the maestro thoughtfully, "But if you hum the tune I will soon pick up the melody!"

\*     \*     \*

A SAILOR who had been six months at sea was hunting the waterfront looking for a bar where he could have a quiet drink. He inspected a few, but the one that took his fancy had a South Sea Island motif, a monkey swinging around the chandelier and a pianist tinkling out a tune in the corner.

He went in and ordered a martini. As the barman put the drink on the counter the monkey swung down from the rafters, spun around and dunked his feet in the glass.

Naturally, the sailor reacted with loud abuse at the barman.

"Did you see that!" he roared. "Get me another drink."

The barman dutifully delivered another martini and set it on the bar, but before the sailor could reach for the glass the monkey dropped from the roof again, spun round and once more dunked his feet in the drink.

The sailor was furious. He gripped the barman by the shirt-front and lifted him across the bar.

"It's not my monkey. Not my monkey," protested the barman. "It belongs to the pianist over there."

The sailor dropped the bartender on the floor and strode over to the pianist.

"Do you know your monkey is paddling his feet in my martini,?" he roared.

"No," replied the pianist thoughtfully, "But if you hum the tune I'll soon pick up the melody!"

*     *     *

THE guest had heard the strains of classical music but when he entered the drawing room he was amazed to see a large tomcat playing the piano.

"And there is no music," he noted with further astonishment.

"No," said the proud owner. "He writes his own music, and the piece he is playing now is one of my favourites."

"You should have it orchestrated," said the guest.

The cat leapt out of the window and has never been seen since.

*     *     *

THE busker was repeating the same old tune on the corner of the street until the lady shopkeeper came out and said: "Do you play the refrain?"

"Yes Ma'am," he said.

"Then would you please refrain from playing it here," she said.

*     *     *

THE vicar's sermon was again interrupted by the arrival of yet another late straggler. "There have been more late entries than an Irish orchestra," he said.

*     *     *

HE is an original player. He makes a lot of mistakes, but they are always different each time.

*     *     *

AN Indian psychiatrist from New Delhi visiting Salt Lake City called at the local asylum and heard the inmates singing. Investigating further he saw a large group of choristers holding an apple and tapping the apple with the other hand. "Are they inmates?' he asked.

"No, that's the Moron Tap-an-Apple Choir," he was told.

So he hot-footed it back to India and told Indira Ghandi that there was a lot of money to be made with choirs.

Hadn't the Vienna Boys Choir been successful?

So they got 500 young boys together and trained them for weeks until they were ready for their first audition before a visiting Italian maestro. He listened to their first rendition with eyes averted and then said "terrible, terrible. They are not castrata." Indira Ghandi was told they had to have that little operation that made all the difference. They did and they were ultimicimo, and began their world tour as the Indian Nackerless 500.

*   *   *

THE band had just finished its first bracket when the master of ceremonies came on stage. "Ladies and gentlemen. I have wonderful news. Our band leader's wife has just presented him with a fine bouncing baby boy. I would like the proud father to stand and take a bow.

As the leader stood and bowed, so did the entire band behind him.

*   *   *

IN the orchestra he plays piano. At home he plays second fiddle.

*   *   *

MY brother was known as the Van Gogh of the violin. He had no ear for it.

*   *   *

MY sister used to play the banjo until she married. Now she picks on her husband.

*   *   *

THE young musician with a violin case under his arm was boasting of his prowess.

"The director of the National Symphony Orchestra was trying to get me for months."

"Who were you playing with at the time?"

"His wife!"

286

IT was amateur night down at the local and Fred stood on the table and rendered "An Irish Lullaby."

He noticed one young lady reach for a handkerchief and wipe a tear from her eye. Thinking she was overcome with emotion he later approached her.

"Are you Irish then?"

"No," she said with a sob. "I'm a music teacher."

*    *    *

THE professor had a theory that music would sooth the savage beast so he took his violin and trekked deep into the jungle of darkest Africa. All around were the roars and screams of ferocious animals.

When he came to a little clearing he opened the violin case and began playing classical music. One by one the animals came out to listen, and soon, sitting quietly in a circle, was an elephant, a gorilla, three buffalo, a few snakes and a pair of tigers.

They were listening enraptured, when with a loud roar a lion sprang into the clearing and bit off the professor's head.

"What did you do that for?" chorused the other animals. "First time we get to hear lovely music and you spoil it," they said.

The lion cupped a paw to his ear and said "Eh?"

*    *    *

FRED has a musical nature
He can yodel, whistle and hum
He goes out fit as a fiddle
And comes home tight as a drum.

# N

## NAMES

RUTH is stranger than fiction.

\* \* \*

I WAS born on the first of the month, so they called me Bill.

\* \* \*

ARE you chewing gum?
  No, I'm Harry McGillicardy.

\* \* \*

"I LOVE men who are frank."
  "Bad luck. My name's Algernon.

\* \* \*

"WHAT are the names of your parents?"
  "Mum and Dad."

\* \* \*

THE new vicar in town even entered the country pub in a bid to introduce himself and approached an old-timer at the bar with outstretched hand.
  "My name is Paul," he said.
  The old-timer studied him for a moment and then said: "Did those Thessalonians ever write back to you?"

\* \* \*

THE track official approached the new athlete. "Are you a pole vaulter?"

"Yes," he replied, "I am from Gdansk. But how did you know my name vas Valter?"

*     *     *

AS the MC said when introducing the prime minister: "I am keen on genealogy. I've made a study of names and I can tell you that Keating means bright and intelligent.

Unfortunately, Paul means 'Not Very'."

(Change name to suit guest of honour).

## NEIGHBOURS

EVER since we put the "Neighbourhood Watch" sign on our gate every nosey neighbour comes in and wants to know the time.

*     *     *

IT'S been tough keeping up with the Jones. Especially since Tom moved next door.

*     *     *

DON'T keep trying to keep up with the Joneses. Drag them down to your level.

*     *     *

BERT stuck his head over the fence and asked Fred if he could borrow his mower.

"Sorry, Bert," said Fred. "The neighbour on the other side has had it for a week. I've just got it back and I've got to cut my own lawn. It will take me all day."

"In that case then," said Bert, "you won't mind if I borrow your golf clubs?"

*     *     *

THE easiest way to meet your new neighbours is to play the stereo full blast at 2 a.m.

*     *     *

A NEIGHBOUR is a person who listens to you attentively, through a wall.

A GOOD neighbour is the one who, when borrowing a corkscrew, says bring it over.

## NEWLY-WEDS

HERE today, gone home to-momma.

\* \* \*

HE has a problem about the future. He's getting married in a month and he hasn't found a job for his wife.

\* \* \*

A YOUNG bride was explaining her problem to her long-married friend. "How can I keep my husband in line?" she asked.

Her older and wiser friend didn't hesitate: "My dear," she said, "your husband shouldn't have to wait in line!"

\* \* \*

THE newly-weds had been married for a month and some of the novelty appeared to be wearing off.

"Well I'm getting sick of the same meal morning noon and night," he complained. "Nothing but wedding cake and chips."

\* \* \*

SHE had served him so many burnt offerings that on their first anniversary he bought her an altar cloth.

\* \* \*

THE new husband sat down at the table after his young bride had just cooked her first chicken.

"What did you stuff it with?" he asked in hungry anticipation.

"I didn't stuff it," she said. "It wasn't hollow!"

\* \* \*

BILL and Beryl had been married only a few weeks when Bill had to travel interstate on a job. While he was away, Beryl's sister Betty moved in to keep her company.

Bill finished the job sooner than expected and was

quickly on a plane home. When he arrived at the airport he dashed to a phone.

Betty answered the call.

"Is Beryl there?" he asked.

"No, she's having a bath," said Betty.

"Don't disturb her then. Just tell her to put a couple of stubbies in the fridge and I will be home about midnight. Tell her to put on her sheerest nightie and a dab of perfume and I will sneak in and wake her with a kiss."

"Okay, and who will I say called?" asked Betty.

★    ★    ★

HE had only been married six months when he confided to his mate: "I've just had a terrible shock. I have just discovered my wife is a liar."

"How do you know?" asked his mate.

"She said she was out with Betty last night. But I was out with Betty last night!"

★    ★    ★

THE newlyweds had just settled on their farm and she brought his lunch out to the home paddock. As he was finishing his last sandwich a little red hen dashed by being chased by a rooster. He threw the rooster a piece of crust and it stopped dead in its tracks and began to peck the bread.

"I hope you never get that hungry," mused the bride.

★    ★    ★

"HOUSEWORK, it's so boring," said the first-year bride. "You make the beds, clean the floors and do the dishes. Then three months later you have to do it all again."

★    ★    ★

(R) THE new bride was too embarrassed to talk about sex, so the groom explained it as delicately as he could.

"No need to talk about it," he said. "Whenever we are in bed and you want it, just pull it once. If you don't want it, just pull it about 350 times."

# NEWSPAPERS

NEWSPAPERS are still credible, provided you read between the lies.

*     *     *

YOU should never tell a journalist what you don't want to read in the papers.

*     *     *

LIKE a dead wombat, a good journalist always keeps his ear to the ground.

*     *     *

THE reporter was pressing the old gent on his 100th birthday as to why he had lived so long.

"Two reasons," said the old-timer, "The first is my life-long practice of having two whiskies a day."

"And second?" asked the reporter eagerly.

"Cancelling my voyage on the Titanic," said the old gent.

*     *     *

NEWS Flash! A helicopter crashed into the cemetery of an Irish village this afternoon. At last count, 705 bodies had been recovered.

*     *     *

THE Free Press: Where three men impose their prejudices on 15 million.

*     *     *

SHE was only the newsagent's daughter, but she loved her Daily Mail.

*     *     *

MY dad was an old newspaper man. He went broke. Nobody wanted old newspapers.

*     *     *

AS a reporter he was trained to ask Who? What? Where? When? and Why? Then his first assignment turned out to be a wedding.

"PAPER, paper, gigantic fraud!" roared the newsboy. "Fifty-six victims in gigantic fraud!"

Chap stopped to buy a paper and quickly scanned the front page.

"Just a minute," he said. "This is yesterday's and there's nothing about a fraud."

"Paper, paper! Fifty-seven victims in gigantic fraud," roared the paperboy.

*　　*　　*

THE advertisement in the local newspaper read: "Editor urgently needs poof reader."

*　　*　　*

LETTER to the advertising manager. "Last Friday I lost a gold watch which was a valuable heirloom. I advertised in the Lost and Found column of your Saturday edition with almost immediate results. Yesterday I found the watch in the pocket of another suit in my wardrobe. Congratulations."

*　　*　　*

A FRONT page panel on the newspaper read: The Daily Bugle was the first to report the death of Cr Grabalot, and was the first to announce that this report was untrue. The Daily Bugle is always first with the news.

*　　*　　*

CORRECTION: The China Seafood Restaurant advertisement in Saturday's edition was incorrect. It read #/ @%**%#. It should have read !**&/#@*&##. We regret any inconvenience this may have caused.

*　　*　　*

THE businessman stopped by the newsboy. "Anything new in the paper today?" he asked.

"Naw," said the lad. "Just the same things happening to different people."

*　　*　　*

THE country newspaper was prospering so well with advertising it couldn't cater for all the news. The pointer on the front page explained it all: "On account of lack of space this week, 15 births and three deaths have been held over until next issue."

*       *       *

IT was rare for the Archbishop of Canterbury to visit a small town so at the press conference the local reporter desperately wanted to scoop his metropolitan rivals. He managed to get the first question away: "Will you be visiting the nightclubs?"

The archbishop was a little surprised. "Are there nightclubs in this small town?" he said.

The newspaper had its headline. "ARCHBISHOP'S FIRST WORDS: ARE THERE ANY NIGHTCLUBS IN THIS TOWN?"

*       *       *

IT had been a slow day, so when a bloke got hit by a bus, reporters from both rival newspapers were on the scene. One was a seasoned journo, the other was a cadet.

Next day the cadet's editor called him in to show that the old scribe had gleaned a more interesting item from a routine event. It happened to be the victim's birthday.

"Ask more questions," roared the editor.

The lad was a quick learner and at his very next accident he crawled under an overturned bus to reach a moaning victim to ask, with notebook in hand: "Don't suppose it's your birthday today?"

*       *       *

HE was sent to cover the earthquake and began his first bulletin with "God has caused tremendous devastation ..."

He received an urgent message from his editor: "Forget the earthquake. Interview God."

*       *       *

AT the press conference the boring politician groaned along on his dreary speech, ad nauseum, until one reporter, a little the worse for drink, actually threw a bottle at him.

Unfortunately it missed the politician and hit another journalist a glancing blow on the head, to which his immediate response was: "Hit me again, I can still hear the bludger."

* * *

THE cadet had been assigned to do the annual story on Colonel Frobisher. "He has the reputation of being England's bravest soldier," said the editor. "The story has been done before, but if you can get a new angle, then you are well on the way m'lad."

The cadet went off to the Old Soldier's Home with the advice of his chief still ringing in his ears. "If only there was a time Frobisher had been scared ..."

He found the colonel sitting in his wheelchair and soon came to the point. "Surely, Sir, surely there was a time when you were frightened?"

The colonel looked thoughtful for a while. "Well there was the time I was with the fusiliers in India and this rogue tiger had eaten two or three of the native chaps," he began.

"I remember tracking the beast through the jungle, followed his tracks and got a glimpse of him hiding behind some tall grass.

"I cocked my gun and crept right up to the grassy patch and I was about to peep through when the monster leapt straight at me and roared 'Aaaarrgh!' My God, I shit myself."

The cadet whipped out his notebook. "When was that?" he asked eagerly, "when was that?"

"Just then when I went 'Aaaarrgh'," said the colonel.

* * *

A SUB-EDITOR had doubts about a cadet's story on a farmer who had lost 2025 pigs from a small farm in the outer suburbs. It seemed too many pigs, so the sub rang the farmer.

"Is it true that you owned two thousand and twenty-five pigs?"

"Yeth," lisped the pig farmer. "That wath the thituation."

The sub said thanks, hung up and corrected the copy to read: Two sows and 25 pigs.

*     *     *

THE businessman was testifying that advertising got results. "We advertised for a nightwatchman, and that very same night our safe was robbed," he said.

*     *     *

A SHARK alarm at Bondi sent everyone rushing from the surf, except three young boys who didn't hear the siren. Those on the beach were aghast to see the dorsal fin moving towards them.

A tall, blonde, bronzed young man took a deep breath and plunged into the surf, swam right past the shark and brought in two of the boys.

He took another deep breath and plunged through the surf again to snatch the third boy from the jaws of the monster.

When all three were safe on the beach he took yet another deep breath and with a knife between his teeth, swam out for a third time to tackle the shark in a struggle to its death.

When he finally staggered up the beach a reporter who had witnessed it all ran up to him. "That's the most heroic feat I have ever witnessed. What's yer name? This is bound to make the front page tomorrow. I can just see the headlines: AUSSIE HERO KILLS SHARK, SAVES THREE!"

The young man interrupted him. "Thanks, that's nice of you, but I must correct you on one point. I am not Australian. I am an Englishman out here on holidays."

The reporter looked a bit crestfallen but said, "No worries, it's still a great story."

The headlines next day read: "POMMIE BASTARD KILLS KIDS' PET!"

HEADLINES:
"DON'T PRINT STORY OF MY DIVORCE" sobs
Actress. See sensational exclusive, page 7.
WOMAN RECOVERING AFTER FATAL CRASH
POLICE MOVE IN BOOK CASE
BISHOP TURNS SOD

*　　*　　*

AFTER a man escaped from an asylum, raping a washer-
woman as he fled, the headline that afternoon read: NUT
SCREWS WASHER AND BOLTS.

*　　*　　*

THE sub was handling a sports report from the local
cricket club secretary who spelt bowling, b-o-e-l-i-n-g.
"That," said the sub, "is the worst spell of bowling I have
seen."

*　　*　　*

AND full credit to American journalist William Safire
for this advice on, How to Write Good:

Avoid run-on sentences they are hard to read.

No sentence fragments.

It behoves us to avoid archaisms.

Also, avoid awkward or affected alliteration.

Don't use no double negatives.

If I've told you once, I've told you a thousand times:
resist hyperbole.

Avoid commas, that are not necessary.

Verbs has to agree with their subjects.

Avoid trendy locutions that sound flaky.

Writing carefully, dangling participles should not be
used.

Kill all exclamation marks!!!

Never use a long word when a diminutive one will
do.

Poofread carefully to see if you any words out.

Take the bull by the hand, and don't mix metaphors.

Don't verb nouns.

Never, ever use repetitive redundancies.
Last but not least, avoid cliches like the plague.

* * *

THERE was a young lady from Stawell
  Wore a newspaper dress to a ball
  But her garb caught on fire
  And burned her entire
  Front page, sports section and all.

# O

## OCKERS ABROAD

KEVIN and Bruce had overstayed their English holiday and were in desperate need of a job, so the advertisement they saw in the "Times" was most appropriate. It read: "Two butlers needed for Scottish country manor. References a must."

The references were an initial problem, but was solved with simple Aussie ingenuity. Keven wrote Bruce's reference and Bruce gave Kevin a splendid wrap.

When they were ushered before the lady of the manor they proffered their references but she waved them aside. "Later," she said, "First, I'd like to check your knees. Formal wear here means wearing kilts so if you would be so kind as to drop the tweeds ..." The lads thought it a little strange, but they did so.

"Not bad," she said. "Now you can show me your testimonials."

When they picked themselves up from the gravel driveway, Kevin said: "With a little more education we would have got that job."

\* \* \*

TWO Ockers from the same town met in London. "Fancy meeting you over here," said Bruce to Merv. "Listen mate, you've got to come over to my flat tomorrow night. We're having a small gathering."

Merv said he'd be in like Flynn.

"Get the tube to Earl's Court, straight down the High Street, second on the right, number 35 and you can ring the bell with your elbows."

"What's with the elbows bit?" said Merv.

"Well you're not coming without bottles are ya?"

*　　*　　*

AT the Ockers picnic they were selling coffee at 50 cents a mug. The queue of mugs stretched back around the corner.

*　　*　　*

THE pretty fraulein approached the Ocker at the Munich beer hall and invited him to her flat. She gave him a nice meal and he stayed the night.

In the morning after a hearty breakfast he was about to leave and made a little speech about the outstanding hospitality he had received.

"Ja, the words are nice," she said, "but what about marks?"

"Bloomin' oath, nine out of ten I reckon," he said.


## ODDS

I KNOW a woman who has got more brains in her head than I've got in my little finger.

*　　*　　*

"DO you know a bloke with one leg called Moloney?"

"No. What's the name of his other leg?"

*　　*　　*

"HEY Fred, what's Billie's other name?"

"Billie who?"

*　　*　　*

ETHYL says her husband is a man of few words, and every one of them unprintable.

*　　*　　*

"FRED'S taken up meditation."

"Well, that's better than sitting around doing nothing."

HE spent a fortune on deodorant before he realised that people didn't like him anyway.

\* \* \*

"WHAT'S that mark on your shoulder?"

"A birthmark."

"Had it long?"

\* \* \*

A SNAIL got rich and fulfilled a lifelong dream by buying a racing car and lodging an entry in the Grand Prix. He painted the letter "S" for snail on the side of his speedy machine and when he raced down the straight the crowd roared: "Look at that "S" car go."

\* \* \*

THE nun who always slept with her clothes on just couldn't get out of the habit.

## OFFICE

THE boss is the bloke in the office who is late when you are early, and early when you are late.

\* \* \*

HE nervously faced the boss: "My wife told me to ask you for a rise."

"Okay. I will ask my wife if you can have one."

\* \* \*

TESTY boss: "Answer that phone."

"It hasn't rung yet."

"Well, why do you have to wait until the last minute?"

And to the latecomer: "You should have been here at nine o"clock."

"Why, what happened?"

\* \* \*

HE advertised for a secretary: "Wanted. Young lady assistant who can type. One who has no bad habits and is willing to learn."

THE boss's secretary had been hired for her legs and figure, but her sloppy arithmetic was getting too much to bear.

Finally, the boss said, "Next time you deliver the day's figures make sure you add up the column at least three times."

She went one better the very next day. "Mister Smithers, I have added these figures ten times," she said dropping the papers on his desk with a dazzling smile, "and here are my ten answers."

*　　*　　*

"WHAT do you think of our new boss?"

"He dresses smartly."

"And quickly too!"

*　　*　　*

THE salesman set the computer up on the executive's desk at W.F. Fotheringham & Son. "This is the latest technology, Mr Fotheringham," he said. "Ask it any question. Even personal questions."

The executive was sceptical. "Okay," he said, and typed in: "Where is my father?"

The answer came back instantly: "Your father is playing golf at Royal Melbourne."

"There you are," said the boss. "It's wrong. My father died five years ago."

The salesman was surprised, but not flustered. "He typed in: "Where, exactly, is Mr Fotheringham senior?"

The answer was just as prompt. "Mr Fotheringham senior died five years ago, but Bill Fotheringham's dad is still at the seventh green at Royal Melbourne!"

*　　*　　*

SOME couldn't spell, others couldn't type, few could do shorthand. The businessman who wanted a private secretary was about to despair when the employment agency phoned to say they were sending round a girl who had a number of things going for her.

302

She turned out to be a ravishing long-legged blonde, and the business executive was immediately entranced.

"I'll pay you $500 a week, with pleasure," he said.

"With pleasure, will be $1000 a week," she said.

★   ★   ★

NOTICE in the office: In an effort to spread the work more evenly would all staff take advantage of the stenographers earlier in the day!

★   ★   ★

GLOSSARY of Management terms:

Delegate: Pass the buck.

Pending: Haven't figured it out yet.

Delayed: Forgotten.

Urgency: Panic.

Extreme urgency: Blind panic.

Frank discussion: Bloody argument.

Analytical projection: Guess.

Forecast: Guess.

Long-range forecast: Wild guess.

Scheduled: Hoped for.

Deficiency analysis: Search for scapegoat.

Ambitious: Ruthless.

Strategy: Low cunning.

Shrewd: Devious.

Profit: Profit.

Profit before tax: Loss.

Deficit: Staggering loss.

Industrial by-product: Waste.

Environmental pollution: Other people's waste.

Pilfering: Theft by employee.

Fringe benefit: Theft by executive.

Terminal payment: Golden handshake.

Supplementary statistical information: Padding.

# OLD CODGERS

DO not complain about growing old. Many are denied the privilege.

*     *     *

FRED was determined to keep healthy in his old age, and when he turned 60 he decided to walk five kilometres every day. He has now reached Adelaide.

*     *     *

BY the time you reach 75 years of age you've learnt everything. All you have to do is to try and remember it.

*     *     *

A GERIATRIC is a German cricketer who captures three successive wickets.

*     *     *

EVEN the parish priest was a welcome visitor for short-sighted Mrs Flannigan. "But that wasn't the priest," said her daughter after the man had left, "that was the doctor."

"Oh was it?" she exclaimed with relief, "I thought Father O'Reilly was getting rather familiar."

*     *     *

MRS Flannigan described herself as a sprightly old girl. "Actually I see seven gentlemen a day," she said. "I get out of bed with Will Power, then I go to my John, next it's breakfast with Uncle Toby, followed by Billy T.

Then the rest of the day is spent with either Arthur Ritis or Al Zymer until I finally go to bed with Johnny Walker.

*     *     *

OLD Fred fronted up to the Sperm Bank and insisted on making a donation. The matron looked at him doubtfully. He was 83. But Fred would not be denied and protested that he was as fit as a prize bull.

Finally she gave Fred a little jar, ushered him towards

304

a cubicle and closed the door. For the next few minutes all she could hear was much grunting and puffing and it went on for so long she got worried. She knocked on the door.

"Are you okay?" she called

"No. I need some help," said Fred. "I can't get the lid off this bloody jar."

\* \* \*

THE old gent was backing his Rolls into the last available parking space when a zippy red sports car whipped in behind him to take the spot. The young man jumped out and said: "Sorry Pops, but you've got to be young and smart to do that."

The old man ignored the remark and kept reversing until the Rolls had crunched the sportscar into a crumpled heap. "Sorry son, you've got to be old and rich to do that!"

\* \* \*

AN old bloke was sitting at the bar sobbing with the odd tear dropping in his beer. "I got married to a lovely young widow last week," he explained to the barman. "She is a great cook, keeps my clothes in great nick and is insatiable in bed," he said.

"Then why the hell are your crying?" said the barman.

"Because I can't remember where I live," sobbed the old codger.

\* \* \*

OLD Jake went for his annual medical check-up. "Your hearing is getting worse," said the Doc. "And you will have to cut out drinking, smoking and sex."

"What?" cried Jake in alarm, "Just so I can hear better?"

\* \* \*

A YOUNG social worker used to call on Old Jake to cut up his steak and help with his meals. She noticed a bowl of almonds beside his tray. "They were given to me as a present, but I don't want them," he explained. "You can have them."

She said thanks and began to nibble away on them. "Funny present to give a man with no teeth," she remarked when she had eaten most of them.

"Oh no," he said. "They had chocolate on them then."

*     *     *

THE doctor had examined Old Jake's heart and summed up his advice with "No smoking, no drinking and no sex."

After much protesting by Jake the doctor relented: "Okay, one cigarette only after meals, and no more than two glasses of light beer a day.

"What about sex?" pressed Jake.

"Very occasionally," said the doctor, "and only with your wife because it is important you avoid any excitement."

*     *     *

AN old chap in his seventies was concerned about the lack of his sex drive and consulted his doctor.

"Well, what would you expect at your age?" said the medic.

The old geezer was still worried, "But my nextdoor neighbour is over eighty and he says he gets it every night."

The doc thought for a moment. "Well, why don't you say it too?"

*     *     *

A COUPLE of old timers were discussing their sexual situation. "You know Jack," said one, "I understand that drinking stout will put lead in your pencil. Why don't we try a bottle?"

"I don't know about you," replied Jack, "but I don't have that many women to write to."

*     *     *

ON his morning round the doctor stopped beside the little old lady he had been treating for asthma. He checked her over, asked a few questions and listened to her croaky replies.

306

"What about the wheeze?" he said.

"Oh, fine," she replied. "I went three times last night!"

* * *

THREE old codgers had been playing cards for a few days when one noticed that they had run out of beer. They pooled their money, drew straws and Old Jake was sent for the beer.

An hour passed. Three hours passed and there was no sign of Jake's return. One said, "I think the old bugger has run off with the money."

Jake's voice was heard from near the door. "One more smart comment like that and I won't go at all."

* * *

THE old farmer had married a comely young wench of 18 years and after a month of wedded bliss he visited his doctor for some advice.

"It's so tiring, Doc," he said. "I am still working the farm, and when I am out in the field and get the urge I have to run back to the house, jump in to bed, and afterwards, I have to walk back to the job again. It's knocking me out."

"No wonder," said the doctor. "You are 82 and she is only 18. She should be running out to you," he said.

He solved the problem by suggesting that the farmer take a shot-gun out into the field, and every time he got the urge he could fire a shot to signal that his young wife should come running.

A month later the doctor bumped into the old man down the main street and out of curiosity asked him how the shot-gun scheme was working.

"Oh it worked well for the first two weeks, but then the duck season opened and I haven't seen her since!"

* * *

THE vicar called on the rich 80-year-old grazier who had recently married a 20-year-old bride to see how he was coping.

"Can't keep my hands off her," he said.

The vicar mumbled his approval and went on his way. He called back in a week. "How's the bride?" he enquired.

"Can't keep my hands off her," repeated the old farmer. "Worse, now she has run off with one of them."

* * *

THE old codger came to see the doctor for a check up. "I'm getting married next week," he said.

The doctor was surprised for he knew the old gent was 84.

"Why would you want to get married?" he asked.

"I don't want to, I have to," said the old codger.

* * *

OLD Jake came back from the doctor's anxious to show his missus his new $3000 silicon chip hearing aid.

"It looks fine," she said.

"Half past seven," he replied.

* * *

WHEN Old Jake returned to the doctor he was given a bottle of medicine. "This is potent stuff," said the doc, "don't take it every day." The doctor wanted to make sure Old Jake understood. "So take it on alternate days, do you know what I mean? Take it tomorrow, then skip a day, then take it the next day and skip another day, and so on."

A month later the doctor saw Jake's wife in the street and enquired after the old codger.

"Oh, he's dead," she said.

The doctor was aghast.

"No, the medicine wasn't that strong," she said. "It was all that skipping!"

* * *

"WHAT'S the matter little boy," said the old codger when he saw the lad sitting on the kerb crying.

"I'm crying because I can't do what the big boys do," he said.

The old man sat on the kerb and started crying too.

OLD Jake tottered into the clinic. "Doc," he said, "you've got to do something to lower my sex drive."

"C'mon Jake," said the doctor. "Your sex drive is all in your head."

"That's what I mean. You've got to do something to lower it!"

\*     \*     \*

THE old codger came to the doctor with the exciting news that he was going to marry a 20-year-old bride. "Well, I think at your age you should take things easy. In fact I think you should take in a lodger," said the doctor.

A year later he bumped into the old codger and asked how was married life.

"The wife's pregnant, I am happy to say," said the old man, and with a wink and a nudge he added, "thanks for that advice about taking in a boarder. She's pregnant too."

\*     \*     \*

OLD Jake was reminiscing. "I can remember the time I gave up both booze and sex at the same time. Crikey, in all of my life that was the worst half hour I've ever spent!"

\*     \*     \*

THE exhausted bush-walker stumbled into a drover's hut high in the Southern Alps and was immediately welcomed by its lone inhabitant, a tough old mountain man.

The visitor was offered food and invited to sit by the log fire.

After the meal the old man pulled down an unlabelled bottle from a shelf and offered the visitor a drink. The bush-walker accepted, but when he pulled the cork and sniffed the evil home-brew he graciously declined and attempted to return the bottle.

"Drink it!" insisted the old-timer. When the lad declined again the old man reached for his rifle, cocked it and pointed it at the lad's head.

There was no other alternative but to take a swig of the vile firewater that had a kick like a mule. When the bush-walker gasped his way to recovery he handed the bottle back, and the old man handed him the rifle.

"Now you hold the gun on me while I have a drink," he said.

## OLD SOLDIERS

IT was a regimental dinner testimonial:

"Today we honour a man who doesn't know the meaning of fear; a man who doesn't know the meaning of defeat, quit or surrender.

"So we have all chipped in and bought him a dictionary."

\* \* \*

TWO old blokes in the Returned Servicemen's Club were talking. "Do you remember those pills they used to give us in the army to keep our minds off girls?" said one.

"Vaguely," said the other.

"Well," said the first, "I think they are beginning to work."

\* \* \*

WHEN old Fred went to join the Returned Servicemen's Club they asked him if he had a war record: "Bloody oath I have," he said, "I've got Vera Lynn singing the White Cliffs of Dover."

## ONE-LINERS
See PROFOUND STATEMENTS

A STRING of one-liners unashamedly woven into a yarn on a single topic can reduce listeners to tears. While they are short and punchy in themselves, they have far more effect queued up in the same story. Sure, it requires a good memory and a little practice for delivery, but with a prompt card in your hand ready for the occasional glance to find the key word, the story line should flow with each one-liner bolstering the next.

One of the easiest forms of monologue is your own "biography." We all find it easy to talk about ourselves, so it is comparatively simple to deliver your own preposterous life story around a dinner table of strangers or friends, or even from the rostrum.

Here's an example, but remember it is an overloaded version. It can be ready to be released at the drop of several trigger questions which are bound to crop up in such groups; like what do you do for a living, how long have you lived in these parts, or where do you come from?

Where do I come from? Actually, I am part Irish and part Italian. (If you have their attention with this line, follow with): I'm Irish by my mother's side, and Italian by a friend of my father!

The family was in iron and steel. My mother ironed and my father stole.

(Now ramble on)

I was born at an early age. Premature actually. I am a man before my time.

I am really only 25.

My birth was a surprise to my Mum

... and everyone else in the Tankerville Arms at the time.

It was during the Depression, and they were tough times.

I was abandoned on a doorstep.

I wasn't found there. No, the door opened out.

I was found two somersaults out on the roadway.

There was a note pinned to my shawl.

It read: "Keep your head down. The door opens out." It was signed, "Mum!"

Years later when Mum had enough coupons to get me out of the orphanage, I met my brothers.

That's when the tough times really started.

We were so poor the woman next door had my brother.

He was a Caesarian birth. It didn't effect him, but I noticed he always left the house through the front window.

*311*

We lived in a tough neighbourhood.

You could walk ten blocks without leaving the scene of the crime.

Any kid in our street with two ears was a sissy.

Any cat with a tail in our neighbourhood was a tourist.

We used to call the nuns the Little Sisters of the Rich.

Our school still retained capital punishment.

And when we went to school my Dad used to paint the house a different colour and change the number on the front gate.

When I was seven, my Dad took me aside. And left me there.

He was tough on us. He made us run two miles every night.

By the end of the week we were 14 miles from home.

His swimming training was tougher.

He threw us off the deep end of the pier.

Swimming to shore wasn't so bad. Getting out of the bag was the hard part.

Tough? We used to have bread and pullet most nights.

Except Saturdays. On Saturday night we always had Windmill Pie. (What's Windmill Pie?) You get a bit if it goes round!

Before our Mum and Dad ran away from home Dad gave me some serious advice about getting a job. I will never forget it. He had taken me aside one day and said, "Fred!" (he was hopeless with names).

He said: "Fred. There are three kinds of people in this world; those who can count and those who can't."

I knew he was in the latter category when he used to read us nursery rhymes: "One, two, three, buckle my shoe. Three, four, five, open the door."

I got the message to dodge accountancy and took my first job which determined my destiny as a travel writer. I became a proof reader for a sky writing firm.

# P

## PARROTS

THE young woman got out of bed, slipped on a silk gown, drew back the curtains, switched on the coffee percolator and uncovered the parrot.

Then the phone rang and a man's voice announced he had just arrived on the morning flight and would be there in ten minutes.

The young woman switched off the coffee percolator, covered the parrot, drew the curtains, took off her silk gown and got back into bed.

And the parrot muttered: "Jeez, that must've been the shortest day of the year!"

\*     \*     \*

HE refused to buy her a pair of budgerigars. He said one could cheep as lively as two.

\*     \*     \*

WOMAN goes into a pet shop. "I'd like a parrot for my husband."

Proprietor: "Sorry, we don't do swaps!"

\*     \*     \*

OUTSIDE the petshop in the pouring rain was a galah in a raincoat.

"He's poly unsaturated," explained the proprietor.

AFTER buying a pair of talking parrots Miss Prim wanted to name them but found she couldn't tell Joey from Polly. She phoned the pet shop proprietor for advice. "Simple," he said. "Wait until you see them mating, then fasten something around the male's neck so that you can identify him."

Miss Prim watched and watched. One day she heard flutters and squawks and dashed in to tie a white ribbon around the male's neck.

A few day's later Miss Prim threw an afternoon tea party for the church. Joey spotted the vicar and said: "Ha, so she caught you at it too!"

★      ★      ★

(This is an action joke, best told with a loud squawk when imitating the parrot)

THE lady of the manor had called the plumber weeks ago, but the leeking pipe was far from her mind when she set off early one morning for a day's shopping.

No sooner had she left when the plumber arrived and knocked on the tradesmen's door.

"Squawk! Who is it?" came the raucous voice of the parrot on the enclosed rear porch.

"Tis plumber, come to fix pipes," said the man knocking again.

"Squawk! Who is it?" came the response.

"Tis plumber, come to fix pipes."

"Squawk! Who is it?"

"Tis plumber come to fix pipes."

To cut a long story short, this went on all day until late in the afternoon the frustrating repetition caused the plumber to have a seizure. He collapsed and died on the back steps.

The lady of the manor arrived home and was confronted with the shocking scene. She let out a squawk and cried: "Who is it?"

"Tis plumber come to fix pipes," replied the parrot.

314

CHAP said he wanted a canary that was a good singer. "Then listen to this one," said the proprietor and he produced a great little whistler that delighted the customer's ears.

"Yes, he's good alright," said the customer, "but I notice he only has one leg."

"Make up your mind," said the proprietor, "D'yer want a singer or a dancer?"

\*　　\*　　\*

THE lady with the blue rinse entered the pet shop and said she wanted a parrot, provided it could talk.

"Got just the model for you, madam," gushed the proprietor leading her to a cage. "This little chap is in training," he said. The proprietor explained if madam pulled the string on the parrot's right leg it would say "Pretty Polly," and if she pulled the string on his left leg he would say "Polly wants a cracker," and he successfully demonstrated the exercise.

Madam was impressed. "What if I pull both strings together?" she asked.

"I'll fall off the bloomin' perch ya stupid old bag," said the parrot.

\*　　\*　　\*

THE priest had two parrots and taught them religiously to say the rosary. He even had two sets of rosary beads made and after a year of rigorous training he was delighted to have them perform at fetes and country fairs.

The priest was so pleased he decided to teach another parrot the rosary and bought a new bird from the pet shop.

When he put it into the cage one of the originals said to the other. "Throw away your beads Fred, our prayers have been answered. It's a sheila!"

\*　　\*　　\*

TALL bloke entered the pet shop and said he wanted a parrot. "It has to be a big red and green one, exactly

315

like the one in Treasure Island," said the customer explaining that he was going to the Arts Fancy Dress Ball as Long John Silver.

The proprietor said he could get such a parrot if he called back on Wednesday.

"Oh, not Wednesday. That's the day I'm having my leg off!"

\* \* \*

HERBIE operated his SP bookie business in a pub and had a pet parrot called Percival who became a perceptive talker. Always looking for the chance to make some money on the side Herbie taught the parrot to sing Advance Australia Fair and when he was word perfect took him down the pub to clean up on a wager or two.

At the bar Herbie turned the conversation round to the fact that not too many Australians knew the words of the national anthem.

"It's a disgrace," said Herbie. "Why even my parrot knows it."

That brought in the suckers. They were queuing up to place their fivers, tenners and hundred dollar notes at 25-to-one against Percival singing the national anthem.

When Herbie had scraped in all the money on offer he gave the parrot the nod. But not a word.

He cajoled, begged, threatened and swore at the parrot, but not one squawk.

After a disastrous payout Herbie stormed off home and threw the cage into the corner.

"Hang on," said Percival. "Don't get upset. Think of the odds we will get tomorrow night!"

# PEARLY GATES

AN elderly spinster approached the pearly gates and knocked.

"Who is it?" asked St Peter.

"It is I," came the reply.

"Oh no," muttered St Peter. "Not another school teacher."

* * *

ST PETER: "How did you get up here?"

New arrival: "Flu."

* * *

TWO Rotarians died and arrived at the Pearly Gates. St Peter asked the first if he had ever been unfaithful to his wife. "Once," was the reply.

"That's not bad," said St Peter, and he gave him the keys of a Rolls Royce. "You can drive around Heaven in that," he said.

St Peter put it to the second Rotarian: "Have you ever been unfaithful to your spouse?"

"No more than a dozen times," he replied. "Okay," said St Peter. "That's your battered old Holden. Fix the tyres and you can drive around Heaven in that."

The very next day when the Holden was repaired he was chugging along Celestial Way when he saw the Rolls parked on the side of the road and his friend crying his eyes out.

"Why the grief?" he said. "You got the best deal. Look at the heap I've got to get around in."

"It's not that," said the Rolls owner, "I just saw my wife go past on a skate-board!"

* * *

TWO Kiwis in black singlets, shorts and thongs arrived at the Pearly Gates. St Peter took one look at them and said, "Nick off. You look like wharfies. We know all about you thieving Kiwis. Pinch anything that wasn't nailed down. Nick off."

St Peter informed God he had just got rid of two Kiwis. God went berserk. "You can't do that. Everyone is entitled to get to heaven. Go and get them back."

317

St Peter went off to do his bidding but soon returned. "They've gone," he said.

"Who? The Kiwis?"

"No, the bloomin' Pearly Gates," said St Peter.

★     ★     ★

THERE was an orderly queue outside the Pearly Gates as people waited patiently to get into Heaven. But suddenly there was commotion along the line as a man, muttering and grumbling, began pushing people aside and barging his way up to the gates. He went straight in, past St Peter.

"What a cheek," said some.

"Who was that?" enquired others.

St Peter replied. "Oh, that was God. He sometimes likes to think he is a journalist!" (Or a lawyer, an accountant, a doctor, a politician, the Member for Somewhere... whatever the audience)

★     ★     ★

THERE were two signs outside the Pearly Gates. A long line of men were queued at the first sign which said: "Hen-Pecked Husbands Report Here."

At the other sign which read: "Liberated Men Report Here," there was only one small timid man.

St Peter said to him: "Why are you standing here?"

He said: "Because my wife told me to."

★     ★     ★

THREE nuns died at the same time, arrived at the Pearly Gates simultaneously and intended to go straight in, but St Peter barred their way.

"Just because you are nuns," he said, "doesn't mean you barge straight in without the religious test."

"You," he said to the first one. "What was the name of the first man?"

"Er, Adam?" she answered, and the bells clanged and the trumpets blew and in she went.

"You," said St Peter addressing the second, "What was the name of the first woman?"

"Er, Eve?" she ventured, and the bells clanged and the trumpets blew and in she went.

"You," he said to the quaking third nun, "What were the first words Eve said to Adam?"

"Oh, gee. That's a hard one." And the bells clanged and the trumpets blew and in she went.

* * *

NOTICE came to St Peter at the Pearly Gates that the Devil and his mob had challenged Heaven in a football match.

St Peter was quickly on the phone to accept. "By the way," he told Satan, "you haven't much of a chance, all the best footballers are up here."

"Maybe," said Satan, "but we've got all the umpires down here."

* * *

ST PETER was interviewing a new arrival:

"While on earth, did you ever drink?"

"Good gracious no."

"Ever go with women?"

"Indeed I did not, no sir."

"Gamble then?"

"No, no, never."

Said St Peter, "Well, what took you so long?"

* * *

AN old farmer died at the age of 90 and arrived at the Pearly Gates. "Now I will have my reward, thanks," he said to St Peter.

"What reward is that?" asked the saintly gate-keeper.

"When I was a lad," said the farmer, "my old Dad took me out of school and put me on the ploughs. When I constantly complained that I wanted an education he said I would get my reward in heaven. Now I am here and I want my reward. I want an education."

St Peter said he was a fair-minded bloke but told the farmer he would have to mark time for a while and sent him off on a heavenly tour for a hundred years.

When he returned a century later the old farmer once more demanded his education.

"Sorry, not ready yet," said St Peter, and put him on yet another 100-year heavenly tour.

When he returned from the second trip the old man was adamant. "No more procrastination. (which is a big word for an uneducated farmer) I want my education," he insisted.

"Okay," said St Peter. "I'm sorry Pops, I will have to level with you. As soon as a teacher arrives up here you will get your education as promised. In the meantime, take another trip."

★ ★ ★

ST PETER was in a sour disposition when the young and handsome negro rapped on the Pearly Gates.

"I am not letting anybody in today unless you have done something really extraordinary."

"Well I can meet that criteria," said the young negro. "I once made love to a ravishing white woman against the wall of a hall where the Ku Klux Klan was meeting."

"Well, I am impressed," said St Peter. "When was that?"

"About three minutes ago," said the negro.

## PETS
See DOGS, CATS

PETS come in all shapes and forms.

A bloke was walking up High St with a crocodile on a lead when a concerned policeman said: "Where are you going with that beast?"

"I am taking him to the zoo," replied the bloke, which satisfied the cop.

Next day the same cop saw the same bloke with the same crocodile on the same lead.

"I thought you were taking that thing to the zoo?"

"Aye, I did, and he had a great time. Today I'm taking him to the pictures."

      ★    ★    ★

THE same bloke went into the pub and said: "Do you serve Catholics?"

The barman said he did.

"Well, I'll be having a pot of stout, and two Catholics for my crocodile!"

      ★    ★    ★

FRED had two monkeys as pets, but when they both died on the same day he was heart-broken. He took them to a taxidermist in the hope that they could be restored as near to life as possible.

The taxidermist said Fred would hardly know the difference and asked if he wanted them mounted.

"No, just shaking hands will do," said Fred.

## PHARMACISTS

CHAP went into the chemist and bought some phensic. He was three doors from the shop when the chemist came running after him. "Stop. Stop," he cried, and when he drew level said, "There's been a dreadful mistake. Instead of phensic I have given you arsenic."

The customer said, "is there any difference?"

"Of course," said the chemist in alarm, "it's another fifteen cents."

      ★    ★    ★

CHAP went into the chemist shop and asked for a packet of condoms.

"That will be $3.50 with tax," said the chemist.

"Forget the tax, I'll tie them on."

      ★    ★    ★

"DO you sell condoms, Miss?"

"Yes."

"Well wash your hands, I want a bag of jellybeans."

THE young couple had been cuddling in the back seat of his car and he was eager to go on with it. "Not here," she said. "Come around tomorrow. It's Sunday and my parents go to Evensong. We can have the house to ourselves. Oh, and don't forget the condom."

Next evening the lad arrived at the front door just as her father announced that they were off to church.

"I'll come with you," said the lad smartly.

At the first opportunity the young girl whispered, "Why the change of plan and how long have you been religious?"

To which the lad whispered in reply: "How long has your father been a chemist?"

\* \* \*

YOUNG socialite was advised that her miniature show dog would never win a prize because its hair was too long. It was supposed to be a smooth hair breed.

So she went to the chemist for some hair remover.

The chemist handed her the latest product. "When you slap this on, it is best to keep your arms up for at least three minutes," he said.

"Oh, you misunderstand," she said, rather embarrassed. "It is not for my underarms, it is for my chihuahua."

"Well, in that case," said the chemist, "don't ride a bike for half an hour."

\* \* \*

THE irate young man entered the pharmacy.

"That ointment you sold me to increase the size of my penis doesn't work. I want my money back."

He assured the chemist he applied it according to the instructions on the packet which said 'Rub it in'.

"Ah, but you didn't read the small print," said the chemist. "By a woman between 16 and 25."

# PHILOSOPHY

AN optimist says the bottle is half full. The pessimist says it is half empty.

THEY were watching a television soap opera and he became irritated by the way his wife was taking it so seriously.

"How can you sit there and cry about made-up troubles of people you have never met?" he demanded.

"The same way you can jump and scream when some bloke you have never met kicks a goal," she replied.

\* \* \*

IF you are looking for a helping hand, there's one on the end of your arm.

\* \* \*

FRED had been contemplating the world's population. "It's amazing, Ethel," he said. "Every time I breathe in and out, someone dies."

"Have you tried mouthwash?" said Ethel.

\* \* \*

"THE trouble with the human race," thundered the pub's philosopher, "is that the world is full of ignorant and apathetic people." And nudging the drinker beside him said: "Don't you agree?"

"I don't know and I don't care" was the reply.

## PHONES

OF course it should always be remembered that Alexander Graham Bell invented TWO phones.

\* \* \*

"PARDON me Miss. I am writing a phone book, may I have your number?"

\* \* \*

CAN you telephone from a submarine?

Of course, anybody can tell a phone from a submarine.

\* \* \*

I RANG Madge and told her I was at St Alban's.

She wanted to know what I was doing at his place.

WHEN the vicar heard that the mayor's pretty wife had been ill he told the mayor he would call round and see her next morning.

When he was shown into her room the vicar said: "I prayed for you last night."

"Silly man," she replied. "You know I'm on the phone."

\* \* \*

THE father of a teenage girl answered the phone.

"Is that Dreamboat?" enquired a voice.

"No," replied the father, "it's Supply Ship."

\* \* \*

HE phoned his wife from the pub to say he had been delayed at the office, but before he got a word in he heard her voice at the other end: "A damned likely story. Never heard such rubbish. Get out of that pub this minute and come straight home. This is a recorded announcement."

\* \* \*

BARMAN on the phone: "You will have to give me a better description than that lady, this pub is full of hopeless layabouts who should be home."

\* \* \*

FRED finally sobered up from his lost week-end and, terror-stricken, realised he had to explain it to his wife. He reached for the phone: "Hilda darling. I have escaped. Whatever you do, don't pay the ransom money!"

\* \* \*

FRED rang the wrong number at two o'clock in the morning.

When he realised his mistake he said, "Oh I am sorry to wake you in the middle of the night."

"Oh, that's alright," said the other party, "I had to get up and answer the phone anyway."

\* \* \*

THE second time Fred made the mistake the other party wasn't so happy.

"Well, if you are telling me it is the wrong number," said Fred, "why the hell did you answer it?"

THE voice said: "Young Tommy won't be at school today. He is very sick."

The school principal asked: "Who is speaking?"

"My father," said the caller.

*     *     *

HE rang his wife to tell her the good news that he had the rest of the day off, but a small boy's voice answered. "G'day son, where's Mum?"

"She's in bed, Dad," said the boy.

"Is she sick?"

"No Dad, she's in bed with the butcher and I can hear her giggling. She's not sick."

There was a poignant silence while he figured out the gravity of the situation. "Are you still there, son?"

"Yes, Dad."

"Go and get my shotgun from the garage. Load it like I told you and give them both barrels."

He listened for an interminable five minutes or more until he finally heard two loud blasts, then the boy's voice again: "I did it, Dad."

"Okay, son, now drag them out and drop them in that big hole I dug for the compost pit."

There was another long silence before the boy, still puffing, came back to the phone and said "I've done it Dad, but I've got a bit of blood on my arms."

"Then jump in the pool and swim around for a bit."

"What pool, Dad. We don't have a pool."

After a few seconds silence Dad said: "Is that 584-8400?"

*     *     *

"IS that the motor pool?" asked a posh voice.

"Yus."

"Tell me, my man, what vehicles are operational at the moment?"

"Five trucks, three utilities, two staff cars and the Bentley that pompous old colonel swans around in."

There was a few seconds silence.

"Do you know who this is?"

"No."

"It is the so-called pompous old colonel you so insubordinately referred to."

There was another short silence.

"Do you know who this is?"

"No."

"Well you can go and jump in the lake," and the phone was slammed down.

*　　*　　*

THE little old spinster rang Telecom's complaint department.

"The cord on my phone is toolong. Could you pull it back a bit on your end?" she asked.

*　　*　　*

PEDANTIC boss; "Answer that phone."

"But it isn't ringing."

"Why do you have to wait until the last minute!"

*　　*　　*

IT was six in the morning when the phone rang at the reception desk of the hotel. The night porter picked it up to hear a slurred voice say: "Excoosh me, my fren, hic. What time dush the bar open?"

The porter replied, "It doesn't open until ten, but by the sound of your condition you won't be allowed in."

"Allowed in?" shouted the drunk. "I've been waiting all night to get out!"

*　　*　　*

THE drunk phones the police station: "I''ve been driving along the (hic) highway and I think itsh my duty to tell you I have knocked down two signposts, and a (hic) telephone box."

"Indeed, sir," says the cop. "And where are you?"

"Wouldn't yoush like to know?"

SHE answered the phone to hear a very repentent voice.

"I'm sorry darling," he said. "I have thought it over and decided that you can have the Rolls as a wedding present and we will move to the Gold Coast immediately, and, okay, your mother can come with us. Will you marry me?"

"Of course I will," she said, "who's speaking?"

*　　*　　*

HE answered the phone only to hear heavy breathing and the occasional obscene suggestion.

"It's for you dear," he said.

*　　*　　*

THE phone rings and Joe answers to hear a voice enquire: "Could I speak to Bobby Bonkbrake, please?"

"I don't know anybody by that name," said Joe, "but hang on a moment and I'll ask." Do we have Bonkbrake here?" shouts Joe.

"No, it's all we can do to get a coffee break," was the answer.

*　　*　　*

A MATHEMATICIAN named Paul
Has a hexahedronical ball
And the cube of its weight
Times his pecker, plus eight
Is his phone number,
Give him a call.

# PILOTS

AIR Traffic Control to Aer Lingus: "Identify yourself, and what is your height and position?"

"I'm Captain Paddy Murphy, I'm five-feet-two, and I'd be sitting up the front."

*　　*　　*

THE passengers were shocked to see a nude man dash up the aisle of the aircraft and into the flight deck, but then it was fully explained with the announcement: "This is your captain streaking."

* * *

THE airline pilot was having his regular medical check.

"When did you last have sex?" asked the doctor as a routine question.

"Nineteen fifty-eight," said the pilot.

"Hell, that was a long time ago."

The pilot looked at his watch. "It's only twenty-two fifteen now," he said.

* * *

THE captain made an announcement.

"Does anybody on this aircraft know how to pray?"

The clergyman put his hand up.

"Good," said the captain. "You start praying. The rest of us will don our parachutes. We are one short."

* * *

THE aircraft was on its final approach and the intercom was still switched on when passengers heard the captain's comment to his co-pilot.

"First thing after we land I'll have a couple of beers, then I intend to make love to that blonde stewardess."

The stewardess turned red with embarrassment and dashed down the aisle intending to alert the pilots that the intercom was still on. But she tripped over a case.

A little old lady passenger helped her to her feet.

"It's alright miss," she said. "Plenty of time. He said he was going to have a beer first."

* * *

THE co-pilot had an unfortunate name, and he was late. When he finally stepped aboard the captain called: "Hi, Jack!" and most of the passengers tried to jump out.

* * *

IT looked like an Irish hijack. Paddy used one of those airline sleeping masks with no eye holes. He jumped up, with the gun pointing the wrong way and roared: "Hands down this is a stuff up."

"One move out of you and you'll be geography," he said.

"Er, don't you mean history?" ventured a passenger.

"Don't change the subject," roared Paddy.


# POEMS

SAID the young man to his new fiancee: "Have you told your folks that I am a poet?"

"Not yet," she said, "I've mentioned your police record, and that you smoked, drank, were presently bankrupt because of your gambling habit, but I thought we'd wait until we were married first."

★　　★　　★

A MAGAZINE ran a poetry contest setting out three rules for submissions: The poem had to rhyme, be brief and appeal to most people.

The winner is printed below:

Pay Day.

★　　★　　★

BEWARE of strong drink, my dear
And only have two, at the most.
Three, and you're under the table,
Four and you're under the host.

★　　★　　★

"DON'T drink nought but water,"
Was Mum's word to her daughter,
"Say no to men,
"Be home by ten,
"And behave just like you oughta!"

★　　★　　★

ROSES are reddish
Violets are bluish
If it wasn't for Jesus
We'd all be Jewish.

GOD is good,
Yet all his peoples
Put lightening rods
On top of steeples.

\*     \*     \*

"AND what'll have?"
Said the waiter, idly picking his nose.
"I'll have two boiled eggs, ya drongo.
Ya can't stick yer fingers in those."

\*     \*     \*

THE difference between prose and poetry is clearly illus-
trated by this sample of prose:
The young maiden entered the water
    First time away from her mum
    All her clothing was strewed
    So she stood there quite nude
    While the tide lapped up round her knees.
Now, had she gone in a little deeper it would be poetry.

\*     \*     \*

WITH the police still hot on his trail
He was tempted by fanny for sale
So the crook went to bed
With a price on his head
With a girl with a price on her tail

\*     \*     \*

THIS is the story of Signwriter Joe
While painting a sign he fell through the 'O'
No need to cry "shame"
What end could be better
He went as he came, through a hole in a letter.

\*     \*     \*

MOST poets will tell you that rhyme doesn't pay.

\*     \*     \*

SAY it with flowers
Or say it with sweets,
Boxes of chocolates

Or plush theatre seats,
Say it with diamonds,
Or say it with mink
But whatever you do
Don't say it in ink.

\*     \*     \*

THE limerick packs laughs anatomical
Into space that is quite economical
But the good ones I've seen
So seldom are clean
And the clean ones are so seldom comical

# POLICE
See LAW

"OFFICER," said the Sweet Young Thing coming into the police station, "where do I apologise for shooting my husband?"

\*     \*     \*

ROBBERS broke into a Dublin bank and stole half a million pounds and a quantity of gold bullion. Baffled police are trying to figure out a motive for the crime.

\*     \*     \*

POLICE are looking for a three-fingered pick-pocket who specialises in stealing bowling balls.

\*     \*     \*

THE detective wanted to know what the dead body was doing in the living room.

\*     \*     \*

MADGE always wanted to be a policewoman. Now she's on the beat. "It's not much of a job, but it's better than walking the streets," she said.

\*     \*     \*

A FRIENDLY cop found two young women crying their eyes out at the Railway Station and was unable to console them until he took them to a nearby cafe and ordered a pot of tea and a plate of cakes. They dried their tears and smiled.

Then he plonked the teapot in the middle of the table and said: "Now who's going to be mother?"

And they both burst into tears again.

*　　*　　*

A POLICE sergeant in the bush doubled as the local vet and late one night his wife answered the phone. "Is your husband there?" queried the voice.

"Do you need the services of the police or the vet?" she enquired.

"Both," said the caller, "we can't get our dog's jaws open and there's a burglar in them."

*　　*　　*

TRAFFIC cop stopped a very fast car and approached the driver with note-book in hand.

"You were doing 100 kilometres an hour in a 60 zone. What's your name?"

Driver: "Mickhaelovic Dubroevscnzkics."

Cop, flipping his note book shut: "Okay, don't do it again."

## POLITICS

POLITICIANS are ubiquitous. Everybody knows one, which makes them legitimate targets for lampooning in speeches or yarns. Jokes on politicians are perennial, only the names have to be changed to make them current, or switched to suit your own political bias.

*　　*　　*

NO matter who you vote for, a darned politician always wins. And the only thing wrong with political jokes is, they get elected.

*　　*　　*

MAKE your MP work — Don't re-elect him.

POLITICIANS are people who have to mind their appease and accuse.

\* \* \*

WHAT's the difference between a flattened politician and a flattened kangaroo on the road to Canberra?

There are skid marks to the kangaroo.

\* \* \*

NEVER believe anything about a politician, until he has made an official denial.

\* \* \*

BOB Hawke died and went to heaven. As he approached the celestial chair God said: "Who are you?"

"I'm Bob Hawke and that's my chair you are sitting in."

\* \* \*

"MR MINISTER!" boomed the back-bencher, "What are you going to do about the Abortion Bill?"

"Shhh, not so loud," said the Minister, "I'm paying it tomorrow."

\* \* \*

PAUL Keating was asked if he had heard the latest political jokes.

"Heard them?" he said. "I work with the bludgers."

\* \* \*

CABINET decided to adjourn business for a dinner break and they trouped into the parliamentary restaurant.

The prime minister ordered a mixed grill.

"And what about your vegetables?" asked the waiter.

"Oh they can order what they like," he replied.

\* \* \*

WHILE on safari in cannibal country a traveller came across a cafe in a clearing in the jungle. The sign out front advertised: Fried Missionary $5, Boiled Hunter $4.50, Grilled Safari Guide $5, Stuffed Politician $15.

When the traveller asked why so much for the politician the chef replied, "Have you ever tried to clean one?"

* * *

THE election campaign had become fairly bitter and when the two opponents met at a social gathering it was a chance to make a pact to stop insulting each other.

"Let's make a clean fight of it," said Smith. "I promise to stop telling lies about you."

"That's fair," said Brown, "and I will stop telling the truth about you."

* * *

HE had listened to the politician's speech for a solid hour before going outside for a breath of fresh air.

"Is he still talking?" asked his mate outside.

"Yeah."

"What's he talking about?"

"He didn't say."

* * *

THE commercial traveller was leaning on the bar in a country pub chatting to the locals when the subject turned to politics. "I can't stand Bob Hawke. He's got a face like a sheep's head," he said.

He was immediately thrown through the swinging doors into the dust of the main street.

"What was that for?" he asked in a daze. "I didn't think anyone would feel so strongly for Bob Hawke in the bush. Is this Hawke territory or what?"

"No," said a farmer. "This is sheep territory."

* * *

HE walked into the general store of a country town and bought all the rotten fruit, tomatoes and eggs available. The greengrocer beamed: "I bet you are going to hear the visiting MP at the Mechanics' Hall tonight."

"No," he replied. "I AM the visiting MP!"

HOW come there is only one Monopolies Commission?

* * *

ON the headstone of a grave in the Cemetery is the most unusual epitaph: "Here lies the body of a great politician, an honest man and the Member for Wills."

It is unusual because it is not often they bury three men in one grave.

* * *

ONE thing about our local MP. He's an honest politician. When he's bought he stays bought.

* * *

THE Leader of the Opposition was walking along the banks of a river when he slipped and fell in and was soon in difficulties. The Prime Minister dived in, swam to his aid and hauled him ashore.

The Opposition Leader thanked him and said. "Can you do me one favour. Don't tell my party that I can't swim?"

"That's okay," said the Prime Minister, "provided you don't tell my mob I can't walk on water."

* * *

LATE at night the Prime Minister was walking by the lake and preoccupied by affairs of State, slipped and fell in.

A youth heard his cries for help and at great risk to himself dived in and saved him.

When he recovered the great man said to the lad: "Boy, you saved my life. Anything you can name you can have."

"I don't want anything," said the lad. "Just don't tell my Dad."

* * *

THE Prime Minister had gathered caucus about him to outline the strategy of the next campaign. "I am going to describe the tactics in the simplest possible terms, so if there are any idiots in the room will they stand up now."

335

After a pause one politician got to his feet. "So you are an idiot are you?" said the P.M.

"Not exactly, P.M., I just didn't like to see you standing alone!"

*　　*　　*

THE proposition to put a king-sized statue of the Prime Minister in central park has been well supported. It will give shelter when its raining, shade in the summer, and the pigeons a chance to speak for us all.

*　　*　　*

"AND as for the problem of the pigeons around the town hall," said the mayor, "it's no use trying to dodge the issue."

*　　*　　*

GOD called the world's three greatest leaders up to heaven for a special caucus meeting. George Bush, Mikhail Gorbachev and Bob Hawke were told that the world would end in three days and to go back and prepare their communities.

George Bush went on television: "My fellow Americans, I have good news and bad news. The good news is that God exists, as we all believed. The bad news is that the world will end in three days."

Mikhail Gorbachev told the Soviet Union: "Bad news and worse news. God exists and the world will end in three days."

Bob Hawke went nationwide: "Good news and better news. God exists, I am no longer an agnostic. And in three days, no Australian child shall live in poverty!"

*　　*　　*

OUR local Member of Parliament says at the forthcoming election he will stand on his record.

That's the only way he can stop people examining it.

*　　*　　*

DON'T Vote. It only encourages the bastards.

DURING the pilots' strike a charter flight was carrying four passengers. One was a businessman, one was a priest, one was a back-packing tourist and the fourth was none other than the Prime Minister.

Somewhere over the alps the pilot made the shocking announcement that the aircraft would shortly run out of fuel. He said there were only four parachutes on board and apologising for being a coward he threw three into the cabin and jumped out with his own.

The priest said he was an important man with a large diocese to look after so he grabbed one of the three parachutes and jumped out.

The Prime Minister said he was the most important leader in history and must have a parachute, and so saying he made a grab and jumped out.

The businessman said to the hiker, "That leaves one parachute between us."

"Not so," said the back-packer. "We have a parachute each. The most important leader in history has leapt out with my haversack."

★   ★   ★

POLITICAL definitions:

Capitalism: You possess two cows. You sell one and buy a bull.

Socialism: You possess two cows. You give one of them to your neighbour.

Communism: You possess two cows. The government confiscates them and provides you with milk.

Nazism: You possess two cows. The government confiscates them and shoots you.

European Common Market: You possess two cows. The government confiscates them, shoots one, milks the other and pours it down the drain.

# PRAYER

AN MP, noticing his colleague on his knees asked if he was praying for the House.

"No," was the reply. "I've looked at the House. I was praying for the country."

*     *     *

THE gambler was praying for a win.

"Oh God. Let me win the pools."

And God answered his prayer with a thundering reply: "Meet me halfway, and fill in the coupon."

*     *     *

A JEWISH mother was standing with her toddler son in the shallows at the beach when a freak wave crashed ashore, knocked the little boy off his feet and dragged him into the surf and out to sea.

The distraught mother fell on her knees and prayed that God would take her life instead, so that her son should live.

In answer to her prayer the very next wave washed the boy ashore.

Again she fell to her knees. "Lord, thank you, thank you, this is truly a miracle. How can I ever repay you?"

Then taking a second look at her child she added: "Excuse me Lord, before you go, there's just one thing. He did have a hat!"

*     *     *

TWO mates who had been out fishing all day couldn't get the motor started. Night had fallen and a strong off-shore wind was carrying the frail boat further out to an increasingly stormy ocean.

Jack fell to his knees in prayer. "Oh Lord, get us out of this and I promise to change my life. I promise to pay my debts, I promise to be faithful to my wife. I promise to give up the booze. I promise..."

He was interrupted by his mate. "Hang on Jack. Don't go too far. I think I can see a light coming towards us."

# PREGNANCY

A YOUNG woman looking as if she was in photo finish with the stork staggered into the maternity ward and grabbed a nursing sister. She said she needed immediate attention.

"Ah," said the sister, "due are you?"

"No, Church of England."

\* \* \*

OLD Mrs Gerrarty staggered into the doctor's surgery and complained of stomach pains.

After an examination the doctor declared, "You're pregnant."

"But I can't be," she said in shock. "I'm 83."

The doctor said he was positive and when he calmed her down said, "You had better ring your husband."

"Brace yourself Fred," she said on the phone. "I'm pregnant."

"Crikey Moses," said Fred. "And who is speaking?"

\* \* \*

THE unwed Irish girl settles down in the confessional and begins: "It's a shameful thing I have to confess. I am pregnant."

"Are you sure it's yours?" says the priest.

\* \* \*

ON a crowded bus the young woman asked the gent: "Do you mind if I sit down, I'm pregnant?"

He stood up and gave her his seat, but then took a second look.

"You don't look pregnant. How long have you been pregnant?" he asked.

"Oh, about 15 minutes," she said, "but doesn't it make you tired!"

\* \* \*

THE young woman looked at the beer gut on the Ocker with disgust. "If that stomach was on a woman, she would be pregnant," she said.

"It was and she is," replied the Ocker.

FRED was stunned by the news of his wife's pregnancy. "It's impossible," he lamented. "I'm always so careful. How could it possibly happen?"

"There, there," she consoled him. "Who says it was your fault?"

*  *  *

SIGN in a maternity shop: We supply the accessories after the fact.

## PROFOUND STATEMENTS
See ONE-LINERS

HERE is a most important segment of the book.

The Master of Ceremonies constantly has cause to make an announcement or introduce somebody, and claim attention over and above the clatter and buzz of conversation.

Sometimes, one can say "Excuse me ladies and gentlemen, can I have your attention please?" And you can repeat it ad nauseum while banging champagne glasses together. Let's face it, "Ladies and gentlemen can I have your attention?" is a pretty dull statement and grabs nobody's attention.

On the other hand, step to the microphone and say: "You can always tell a happy motorcyclist by the insects on his teeth." Someone will hear it.

Follow with a number of the throw-aways listed below and eventually there is dead silence while they strain to catch these profound statements.

Some are so profound they should be dropped into the middle of your address whether you have lost your place or not, in case the audience has drifted away. Here are a few which should recapture their attention.

*  *  *

TIMING is the essential factor in the success of any rain dance.

340

SMOKING shortens your cigarettes.

LOCKJAW means never having to say you're sorry.

MONOGAMY leaves a lot to be desired.

NO woman has ever shot her husband while he was doing the dishes.

IF you feel strongly about graffiti, sign a partition.

THERE is no alcohol in Iran, but you can get stoned anytime.

AN optimist is one who thinks the future is uncertain.

ABSTINENCE is the thin edge of the pledge.

A CHRYSANTHEMUM by any other name would be easier to spell.

NEVER play leapfrog with a unicorn.

LET him among us to run the fastest cast the first stone.

CRIME doesn't pay, but the hours are optional.

ONE-legged girls are a push-over.

YOU can lead a horse to water but you can't lead a whore to culture.

A MAN is known by the company he floats.

ALL is fair in love and the war which follows.

ANY port in a storm is better than no rum.

ANYTHING for a quiet wife.

IF I'd known she'd take offence so easily I would have entered her in the Grand National.

PUNCTUALITY is something that, if you've got it, there is few to share it with.

THIN yaks leave light tracks.

NO leg is too short to reach the ground.

PORNOGRAPHY is in the groin of the beholder.

OBSCENITY is anything that gives the judge an erection.

WHEN God created man, She was only joking.

BEGGARS can't be boozers.

CONTRACEPTIVES should be used on all conceivable occasions.

CANNIBALS are not vegetarians. They are humanitarians.

W.C. FIELDS is alive and drunk in Alburqueque.

CIRCUMCISIONS alter cases.

STATISTICS prove that 50% of all people who get married at Easter are women.

DON'T put all your bags in one exit.

HALF a loaf is better than no tea-break at all.

HERE today, gone home to Momma.

IF you like home cooking, stay home.

GOING steady only means you've sobered up.

IF Labor is the answer, it must have been a bloody stupid question.

ONE good turn gets most of the bedclothes.

ONE door closes, another slams in your face.

PROCRASTINATION is the thief of time, especially if you can't spell it.

SEX is bad for one, but it is good for two.

RUTH is stranger than fiction.

THE opera's never over until the fat lady sings.

IF the epileptic fits, wear it.

HE who laughs last doesn't get the joke.

TWO can live as cheaply as one, but for half as long.

CONFUCIUS, he say too much.

A FRIEND in need is a pest indeed.

THERE is nothing like horse riding to make a person feel better off.

THERE are three kinds of women, the beautiful, the intelligent and the majority.

THERE are three kinds of men, the handsome, the caring and the majority.

THERE are three kinds of mathematicians, those who can count, and those who can't.

SOME girls are like flowers. They grow wild in the woods.

NOT to mention the monkeys.

THE man who goes into the bar optimistically, usually leaves misty optically.

HE may drink to forget, but he never forgets to drink.

YOU don't get a second chance to make a first impression.

TIME wounds all heels.

TIME is nature's way of stopping everything from happening at once.

DEATH is nature's way of telling you to slow down.

NEVER leave a turn unstoned.

NEVER put off till tomorrow what you can avoid altogether.

BETTER to be a coward for a minute than dead for the rest of your life.

SHE was only the horse trainers daughter, but all the horse manure.

THERE were more late entries than an Irish orchestra.

HE had an ego bigger than the outdoors.

DON'T come the raw prawn.

DON'T try to keep up with the Joneses. Drag them down to your level. It's cheaper.

A CULT is a group too small to be a minority.

IF you don't go to your friends' funerals, they certainly won't come to yours.

THE number of people at your funeral can depend on the weather.

I KEEP fit by wrestling, with my conscience.

MY wife keeps fit by jumping, to conclusions.

I LOVE women so much I think I'm a lesbian.

MY carma run over your dogma.

LIVE every day as if it is your last. One day you'll be right.

ALL babies are subject to change without notice.

ALL my life I have been doubtful. Now I'm not so sure.

A CLOSED mouth gathers no feet.

THEY were so progressive they tried to adopt a gay baby.

SHE had more chins than the Singapore phone book.

SHE was only a newsagent's daughter, but she loved her Daily Mail.

SHE was only a cab driver's daughter, but you sure auto meter.

SHE used to be married to a trapeze artist, but she caught him in the act.

HE'S very broad minded. He thinks of little else.

THEY were thicker than mourners at a brewer's wake.

SHE was so mean she used to heat the knives so the family would use less butter.

HE'D steal the harness off a nightmare.

I AM so miserable, it is as if you hadn't left.

NEVER go round with another man's wife, unless you can go a round with her husband.

SILENCE isn't always golden... sometimes it's guilt.

DIPLOMACY is the art of saying "nice doggie" until you can find a rock.

## PROPOSALS

YOUNG Jock McTavish got down on his knees to propose to her when a 25-cent coin dropped from his pocket and rolled under the sofa. In the 20 minutes it took him to find it she had lost interest.

⋆　　⋆　　⋆

BLOKE walked up to a lovely blonde on the corner. "I'm

sorry to bother you," he said, "but I am a stranger in town and I don't know my way around. Could you tell me where you live?"

# PSYCHIATRISTS

ANYBODY who goes to a psychiatrist needs their head read, but read on.

\* \* \*

PSYCHIATRY is the care of the id by the odd.

\* \* \*

NEUROTICS build castles in the air. Psychotics live in them, and psychiatrists collect the rent.

\* \* \*

YOU go to a psychiatrist when you feel slightly cracked and keep going until you're completely broke.

\* \* \*

"DOCTOR, doctor," said the patient as he burst into the psychiatrist's room, "I feel invisible."

Doctor: "I'm sorry, I can't see you now."

\* \* \*

HE stopped going to his psychiatrist. He asked too many personal questions.

\* \* \*

"NOW that I have cured you of your gambling addiction," said the psychiatrist, "I can present you with your bill."

"Thanks doc. Toss you double or nothing."

\* \* \*

PATIENT: "How do I know if you can help me?"

Doc: "I can guarantee a sure cure, or your mania back."

\* \* \*

THE friendly psychiatrist is the one who lies on the couch with you.

\* \* \*

GOING to the psychiatrist didn't cure Fred's drinking problem. He kept falling off the couch.

DID you hear about the psychiatrist who kept his wife under the bed because he thought she was a little potty?

* * *

A FELLOW phoned his psychiatrist. "Doctor, my wife needs help. She thinks she's a horse."

The doctor heard a few more details and said, "Mmmm, it seems serious. It could be a long and costly treatment."

"Money is no object," came the reply. "She's won her last three starts!"

* * *

"MY doctor insisted that I come and see you," said the patient to the eminent psychiatrist. "Goodness knows why, because I'm happily married, I like my job, got lots of friends and no worries..."

"Hmmm..." said the psychiatrist reaching for his notebook, "How long have you been like this?"

* * *

I TOLD my girlfriend the truth, that I was seeing a psychiatrist.

She told me the truth, that she was seeing a psychiatrist, a plumber and two barmen.

* * *

PATIENT: "Why do you think so many people take an instant dislike to me?"

Psychiatrist: "Saves time."

* * *

PATIENT: "Everybody hates me."

Psychiatrist: "Don't be silly. Everyone hasn't met you yet."

* * *

"DOC, my wife is a kleptomaniac."

"Is she taking anything for it?"

* * *

"I THINK I am going mad, doctor. Every time I ask someone the time I get a different answer."

"I USED to suffer from a split personality, Doc, but now we're both okay!"

* * *

SHE took her husband to the psychiatrist. "He says he is suffering from hallucinations, but I'm sure he is only imagining it," she said.

* * *

"NOW tell me," said the psychiatrist, "have you had any more of those sexually erotic dreams?"

"No," said the patient.

"Tough luck, I've had some beauties."

* * *

HE asked her to explain her dreams.

"I haven't had any this week, doctor," she said.

"Well how the hell can I help you if you don't do your homework?"

* * *

THE shapely blonde entered the psychiatrist's office. She stood nervously by his desk as he told her to lie on the couch. She hesitated.

"Come, come, now," said the psychiatrist, "how can I help you unless you lie down on the couch?"

Finally, she walked over and stretched out on the couch.

"Now then," he said, "tell me how your troubles began."

She looked him straight in the eye, "Just like this," she said.

* * *

PSYCHIATRIST: "So, you think you are a dog, eh? That's no problem. Just hop up on the couch."

Patient. "I can't. I'm not allowed."

* * *

HE helped cure my phone phobia. I was always scared of answering it. Now I answer it all the time, whether it rings or not.

* * *

THE patient explained to the psychiatrist: "Every time

I go to sleep I dream of cricket. It's the most important match of the year and every time I get a duck. Doc. it's driving me mad."

Doctor: "Well, when you go to bed tonight try thinking of something else."

"What, and miss my turn to bat?"

*　　*　　*

HE briskly entered the psychiatrist's rooms and settled himself down on the couch with his brief case. "Let's talk business," he said. "I want to rent advertising space on your ceiling."

*　　*　　*

HOW many psychiatrists does it take to change a light bulb?

Only one. But the bulb must want to be changed.

*　　*　　*

A PSYCHIATRIST on holiday became fascinated by the antics of an apparent simpleton who had set up a sign on the beach which stated "Seagulls for sale."

"That's why we are needed," he said to his wife. "I think I will humour him."

"How much are the seagulls?" asked the psychiatrist.

"Only a fiver each," the jolly hawker replied.

"Okay," said the psychiatrist, "I'll buy one."

The man took the note, and pointing skywards said: "That's your one, up there."

*　　*　　*

THE psychiatrist treated Bazza for two hours and finally solved the problem. "You've got a split personality. You are really two different people struggling for supremacy of yourself."

The doc then handed him a bill for $100. Bazza produced $50. "There's my half. Why should I pay for the other bloke's troubles?"

*　　*　　*

THE psychiatrist had listened for ten minutes while his patient insisted he had turned into a bell.

"Take these pills. If they don't work, give me a ring!"

350

THE middle-aged woman settled herself on the couch. "It's about my son, doctor. He keeps making mud pies."

"I wouldn't worry about it," said the doctor, "It's quite normal really."

"Well I don't like it," she said, "and neither does his wife!"

*     *     *

ONE psychiatrist to another: "All day long I have to listen to stories of pain and suffering, raw deals, persecution complexes, husbands complaining about wives, wives complaining about husbands, family feuds, everybody's problems, the world's troubles. It's getting me down.

"But tell me Dr Entwhistle, how come you look so serene after listening to everybody's troubles?"

"So, who listens?"

*     *     *

THE psychiatrist told Fred he was going to drop some ink on a blotter and he wanted Fred to explain what the random designs meant to him.

"That's Marilyn Munro in the nude," said Fred deciphering the first blotch.

"That's Jayne Mansfield taking a bath," he described the second.

He said the third spattering of ink was the Luton Girls Choir all singing in the nude.

"The trouble with you Fred," said the doctor with some satisfaction, "you are obsessed with sex."

"What, me?" exclaimed Fred. "It's you who's drawing the filthy pictures."

*     *     *

TWO psychiatrists met in the hospital corridor. One said: "You're feeling good. How am I?"

*     *     *

A PSYCHIATRIST spent two hours listening to a young woman pour out the details of her anxieties and emotional problems.

Finally he said there was nothing wrong with her, she was coping well, and she was quite normal.

"Normal?" she repeated. "But what about these caterpillars crawling all over me. I can't stand it any longer."

The psychiatrist jumped up and backed away. "Well, don't flick the damn things over me."

# PSYCHOLOGY

THE psychologist put it to Fred: "If you had to give up wine or women, which would you choose?"

Fred thought for a moment. "That would rather depend on the vintage of each," he said.

\* \* \*

AN attractive woman was sitting alone in a bar when a young man approached her. "Excuse me," he said, "may I buy you a drink?"

"What, to a motel?" she screamed.

"No, no," protested the man, "You misunderstood. I just asked if I could buy you a drink."

"You are asking me to go to a motel?" she screamed, even louder.

Completely bewildered the young man retreated to a corner table while everybody glared at him indignantly.

After ten minutes the young woman came over to explain. "I'm, sorry to have created such a scene," she said. "I am a psychology student studying human behaviour in unexpected situations."

The young man looked at her and shouted, "What? A hundred dollars?"

\* \* \*

OLD Jacob lived in a small side street in Fitzroy and was being annoyed by a group of kids who would play cricket in this alley, using a tin can as a ball.

The noise would irritate him and sleep was hopeless, so he decided to put an old business principle to work.

He called the boys together and explained that he was an old pensioner, and that nothing gave more pleasure than to see young lads playing cricket with a tin can. He said if they would come there every night and play cricket he would pay them fifty cents each, per night.

The kids thought this was great and turned up the following evening to make their usual noise and were duly paid fifty cents each.

The second night old Jacob explained to the boys that he was an old-age pensioner and would they mind copping 40 cents because he was a little short. The lads accepted the money.

The third night he told the boys that he had suffered some unexpected expenses and would they mind taking just 30 cents.

The fourth night he explained that his pension cheque hadn't arrived and the best he could do was five cents each.

The news wasn't taken gladly. The boys looked at each other and finally one said. "To hell with this. I'm not wasting my time playing cricket with a tin can for a measley five cents. I'm off."

The rest followed, and he has never seen them again.

\* \* \*

HE had suffered from insomnia for years and at last the psychologist was giving him some sound advice.

"Next time you are in bed relax your body bit by bit, starting from the toes," said the psycho.

"Go to sleep toes," he said that night. "Go to sleep feet, go to sleep ankles, go to sleep knees, go to sleep thighs..."

Just then his wife walked in to the bedroom in a sheer negligee.

"Wake up everybody," he yelled.

\* \* \*

FRED had been out with the boys. And as the night

developed he found himself among the girls, and one of them, a buxom blonde, eventually took him home to her flat.

It was three a.m. when he was set to leave and he was overtaken by remorse. "What will I tell the missus?" he muttered.

"No worries," said the blonde, "Here's the plan and put this bit of chalk behind your ear."

At four a.m. he was tip-toeing across the bedroom when the light flashed on. "Where have you been?" demanded his wife.

"I've been in bed with a big buxom blonde who wouldn't let me come home until I satisfied her five times," he began.

"You bloody liar," said his wife. "You've been out playing pool. You've still got a bit of chalk behind your ear!"

## PUBLIC RELATIONS

HYMIE was the world's first public relations officer and worked with Moses on the flight of the Israelites. When they reached the shores of the Red Sea, hotly pursued by Pharaoh's army, Moses sent for his PR man.

"Where are the boats? You forgot the boats," Moses roared at Hymie.

"When were boats in the contract?" asks Hymie.

Moses was in a rage. "I must have boats. Do you want me to part the sea and walk across it?"

"Great thinking Moses," said Hymie. "If you do that I will get you two whole pages in the Old Testament!"

## PUBLIC SPEAKING

VETERAN guest speaker: "I don't mind them looking at the time when I'm talking. But when they take their watches off and shake them to see if they are still going, then I find it disconcerting."

HE was pacing up and down when the young lady approached and asked if he was the guest speaker. He replied that he was.

"Do you get nervous before you speak?" she enquired.

"No," he lied.

"Then what are you doing in the ladies' loo?"

*     *     *

HE lacked confidence as a public speaker. "I'm afraid I'm not good at it," he admitted. "Last time I even stuffed up the minute's silence."

*     *     *

AFTER he addressed the Chamber of Commerce, the guest speaker stayed on for a while but was looking despondent.

"What's bothering you?" asked the chairman.

"Well, one of your members, that chap there, just told me that it was the most boring speech he had ever heard."

"Oh, don't worry about Smithers," said the chairman. "He's the type of chap who just goes round repeating what everybody else says."

*     *     *

"HAVE you ever spoken before a large audience before?"

"Yes. And I said Not Guilty."

*     *     *

"I HEARD your wife was an after-dinner speaker."

"Don't be silly. She couldn't wait that long."

*     *     *

AN ideal response from the guest of honour: "I really don't deserve this award. But then, I've got arthritis and I didn't deserve that either."

*     *     *

OPENING remark for a public speaker:

"The prime minister would have been here tonight but for a conflict of interest. He didn't want to come."

## PUBS
See HOTELS

ON the chest of the barmaid in Sale
   Were tattooed the prices of ale,
   And on her behind,
   For the sake of the blind,
   Was the same information in Braille.

\* \* \*

THINGS are so tough at this pub that they employ a chucker-in! Patrons are frisked for weapons. If they don't have any they are given some.

\* \* \*

SOME of the pubs around Sydney are the toughest in Australia. The drinkers can fight at the drop of a hat, have muscles like knotted wire, covered in tatts and swear like troupers. The men are just as wild.

\* \* \*

"WHY do you throw your drinks down so fast, one after the other?"
   "Cos I once had one stolen."

\* \* \*

IT was in a pub where unattended beers were unsafe and Jake had a need to go to the loo. So he left a note beside his beer, reading: "I've spat in this."
   When he returned there was an addendum to his note: "So have I."

\* \* \*

YOU can always tell the stranger in our local pub.
   He's the one who puts his drink down on the bar.

\* \* \*

A VENTRILOQUIST asked the barmaid for a gottle of gear and then drank it without moving his lips.

\* \* \*

"DO you serve women in this bar?"
   "No, you have to bring your own."

THE barman gave me a nasty look. I didn't need it. I already had one.

*     *     *

HE wanted to go to a topless bar.

So they took him to a pub without a roof.

*     *     *

THE barman at the bush pub was one of the toughest he had ever seen; muscles, tatts, unshaven, sweaty and pulling beers in a black singlet.

The shearer couldn't take his eyes off him. "What the hell d'yer think yer staring at?" said the barman eventually.

"I just can't get over the likeness. It's a truly remarkable resemblance," said the shearer. "You are a dead-ringer for my wife. In fact if it wasn't for the moustache..."

"I haven't got a moustache," interrupted the barman.

"No, but my wife has!"

*     *     *

THE barmaid wondered where the voice came from, before she saw the little lad in short pants with his nose just reaching the bar.

"Hey, you. I said I'll have a glass of beer and a packet of fags," insisted the brat.

The barmaid saw that he was a lad of about 13.

"Do you want to get me into trouble?" she said.

"Forget the sex, just give me the beer and fags," he said.

*     *     *

ALTHOUGH it was a tough Outback pub, Dick the barman could cope with the evening rush because everyone drank beer. Well, everyone except the town's doctor who, as regular as clockwork, would dash in at 6.30 each evening and order an almond dacquiri.

One night, at the peak of the rush hour, Dick saw the good medic pushing his way through the crowd and realised he had run out of almonds.

357

Like any good barman he was equal to the task, snatched up some hickory nuts, crushed them, and had the drink ready by the time the doctor breasted the bar.

The doctor tasted it, tried it again, and said: "This is not an almond dacquiri Dick!"

"No, it's a hickory dacquiri, Doc!"

*　　*　　*

THE guest complained to the proprietor of an Outback pub that the outhouse was full of flies.

"What time did you go down there?"

"Oh, about noon," said the guest.

The licensee nodded his understanding. "You should go down about one o'clock," he said "They are all in the dining room then!"

*　　*　　*

"THE flies are thick," said a drinker.

"Well what would you expect out here," said the barman, "educated ones?"

*　　*　　*

BLOKE fronted the bar with a newt perched on his shoulder and after serving his fifth beer the barman could contain his curiosity no longer.

"You've got a newt on your shoulder," he said.

"I know," said the drinker. "His name is Tiny."

"Why Tiny?" asked the barman.

"Because he's my newt!" was the obvious answer.

*　　*　　*

PADDY rushed into the bar and said: "Quick, a beer before the fight starts, quick."

The barman pulled a beer and Paddy gulped it down.

"Quick, another beer before the trouble starts," he said.

The barman watched him quaff the second pot and said: "Righto, when is this row supposed to start?"

"Right now," burped Paddy, "I'm broke!"

PADDY ordered a pot of stout, but as soon as it was placed before him he cancelled the order and asked the barman for a pot of lager instead.

When he drank it the barman asked for the money.

Paddy was indignant. "I gave you a pot of stout for it."

"But you didn't pay for that either."

"Well I didn't drink it, did I!"

\* \* \*

THE travelling salesman arrived at the one-pub three-dog town and fronted the bar. After a couple of drinks he said to the barman: "Is there any night life hereabouts?"

"You just missed it by a few days. She's gone to the city for a holiday."

\* \* \*

THEN there's the Scot who drinks Scotch and Horlicks. When it is his turn to shout he is fast asleep.

\* \* \*

A SCOT pushes his way to the bar. "I've had an attack of the Yaws," he says to the barman.

"What's Yaws?" he says.

"Double whisky," says the canny Scot.

\* \* \*

A SCOT ordered a pot of beer and as the barman handed it over he said, "D'yer think yer canna fit a nip o' whisky in it too?"

"Certainly," said the barman.

"Then fill it ta the top wi' beer."

\* \* \*

THERE is a pub in town that has a fifty cent entrance fee. It's to keep out the riff-raff.

\* \* \*

BLOKE went into a pub and had a ploughman's lunch.

The ploughman became quite agitated.

\* \* \*

PADDY fronted the bar and said: "Drinks all round, barman, and have one yourself."

Paddy was immediately the toast of the pub and after all pots were quaffed the barman gave him the bill.

"But I haven't got a cent," he said.

The angry barman grabbed him by the scruff of the neck and hurled him straight through the swinging doors onto the pavement outside.

It was a few moments before Paddy managed to stand himself up and dust himself down. He staggered back into the pub.

"Drinks all round," he proudly declared for a second time, "but not you, barman. One drink and you go bloody mad."

          ★     ★     ★

AFTER a long overseas assignment Charlie returned to the pub he liked to call his local.

"You know," he said nostalgically to the barmaid, "it's all of ten months since I've had a drink here."

"Look," she replied, "this is my first night and I'm serving as fast as I can!"

          ★     ★     ★

TWO brothers were leaning on the bar enjoying a drink when one pushed two bottle-tops across to the barman as payment for a round.

In response to the puzzled look on the barman's face the elder of the brothers beckoned him close and whispered: "My brother is not the full two-bob. He always pays in bottle-tops. If you can humour him for a while I will settle up before we leave."

The barman wasn't entirely happy with this arrangement, but went along with it for the rest of the afternoon.

When both brothers went to stagger out that evening he said "Hoy," and indicating the great heap of bottle-tops said: "What about settling up?"

"No worries," said the elder brother turning back and throwing a garbage bin lid on the counter. "Here, take it out of this and keep the change!"

HE was about to enter the Pig & Whistle when he was accosted by a nun who began berating him on the evils of strong drink.

He was equal to the challenge. "Unless you've tried a drop yourself, Sister, you don't know what the hell you're talking about. Don't knock it unless you've tried it."

He ranted on until he convinced her to have a taste.

"Well, only for the purpose of argument, mind. What do ladies drink?"

"Try a gin and tonic," he said.

"Okay, but I'm not going into that evil place, and I'm not drinking from their glasses." She unhooked a tin mug from her belt. "Get me some in this."

When he fronted the bar for a beer and a pannikin of gin the barman said: "Don't tell me that nun is still out there!"

\*     \*     \*

THE conversation stopped as the old bloke entered the pub. He was in his pyjamas, slippers and with the aid of a walking frame shuffled towards the bar.

"I'll have three double Scotches," he whispered to the barman.

The drinks were placed in front of him. He gulped down two and just before he quaffed the third he said: "Shouldn't be drinking these really, with what I've got."

"Why?" asked the barman. "What've you got?"

"Just 15 cents," replied the old-timer.

\*     \*     \*

A BLOKE with a pig under his arm approached the bar.

"Where did you get that?" asked the barman.

"I won it in a raffle," replied the pig.

## QUESTIONS

SHOULD single crabs have nippers?

   CAN a cross-eyed teacher control her pupils?

   IS it cruel to sew buttons on flies?

   IF a light sleeper sleeps with the light on, does a hard sleeper sleep with the window open?

   COULD a drinking lizard be any flatter?

   COULD a half-wit work part time for intelligence?

   INSTEAD of having ballet girls prancing around on tip-toe why don't they hire taller showgirls?

   IF the answer is "9W" what was the question?

   The question is: "Hey Fritz. Do you spell Wagner with a V?"

   IF the answer is "Washington Irvine"

   The question is: Who was the first president of the United States, Fred?"

★   ★   ★

WHY is 'abbreviation' such a long word?

# R

## RADIO ANNOUNCERS

THE radio announcer was delighted to hear the way in which his little son said his prayers, concluding with: "And here again, Dear God, are the headlines."

\* \* \*

AN Aussie on a flight to Rome got talking to the fellow seated beside him and couldn't help noticing he had one heck of a stutter. He was even more astonished when his new acquaintance told him, with difficulty, that he was going for an audition as an announcer for Radio Vatican.

"How do you rate your chances?" asked the Aussie.

"Ner, ner, ner, not too good," he replied. "They will per-per probably ger-ger give the job ter-ter some ber-bloomin' Catholic!"

\* \* \*

A RADIO announcer is one who works for the love of mike.

\* \* \*

THE longest word in the English language is announced by disc jockeys as "Now a word from our sponsor."

## RELIGION

THE trouble with born-again Christians is that they are a worse pain in the neck the second time around.

THE meek had a meeting today and decided they don't want to inherit the earth.

* * *

PEOPLE who use the rhythm method of contraception are usually called Parents.

* * *

FROM the pulpit the vicar announced that one of his flock, Miss Helen Hunt, had found a purse containing money, a variety of personal items and what he believed to be a small packet of white balloons. "So whoever has lost this purse, go to Helen Hunt for it!"

* * *

AS the proud father handed the baby to the vicar at the christening font the cleric said: "And what will we call this little chap?"

"It's a girl," whispered the father. "You've got hold of my thumb!"

* * *

THERE was a knock on the door and Fred found himself being asked to become a Jehovah's Witness.

Quick on his feet, Fred replied: "I didn't even see the accident," and shut the door.

* * *

THE priest took Paddy aside. "I've been told that you went to a football match last Sunday morning instead of coming to Mass."

"No father, not true, and what's more, I've got the fish to prove it."

* * *

THE protestant minister met his friend the priest and said he dreamed about a Catholic heaven last night.

"It looked like a nice place, with plenty of pubs, bright music and people dancing about," he said.

"That's funny," said the priest. "Only last night I dreamt about a Protestant heaven. It looked nice with lots of flower beds, pretty trees and gardens."

"And what were the people doing?" asked the vicar.

"What people?" replied the priest.

* * *

THE vicar's term at the parish was up and he was about to be transferred. The regular parishioners had gathered at a tea party in his honour.

"We'll really miss you," said one little old lady. "No matter who they send as a replacement he will never be as good as you."

The vicar was flattered, but he assured her his successor would be an adequate and caring pastor.

"No, no," the old-timer insisted, "it's always the same. We've had six ministers here in my time and I can assure you each one has been worse than the one before!"

* * *

THE not-too-successful minister was asked by the bishop why he had entered the clergy.

"I was called," he replied.

"Are you sure," pondered the bishop, "it wasn't some other noise you heard?"

* * *

A BISHOP had fallen seriously ill and was told by his doctor not to have too many visitors. But when his long-time agnostic friend called he was ushered in to the bishop's bedside.

"My Lord," said the unbeliever, "I do appreciate you seeing me when your friends have not been admitted."

"It's like this," said the bishop, "I feel confident of seeing my friends in the next life, but I was concerned that this might be my last chance of seeing you."

* * *

PADDY crept around the back of the country parish presbytery and nicked one of the priest's chooks. He then promptly went to confession.

"I stole a chook, father," he began. "I know it was very wrong and I am sorry. Can I give it to you for repentence?"

"Certainly not," said the priest. "I don't want it. Return it to the man you stole it from."

"Oh, he says he doesn't want it," said Paddy.

"In that case you might as well keep it and say ten Hail Mary's."

*     *     *

AS Rabbi Rozenbloom was passing St Patrick's, Fr O'Calleghan rushed out in an agitated state. "Izzi, you're just the man," said the priest. "Can you help me out of a tight spot?"

The priest explained that he was double booked. He had to officiate at the funeral of the local bishop but couldn't find another priest to take over the confession session.

"Surely you can stand in for me. It's only an hour."

The rabbi said he didn't know anything about confession. Jews were not into confessing anything.

"There's nothing to it," insisted the priest. "Come with me now and listen to the first few, then you can take over."

When they got to the dark confessional the rabbi sat behind the priest and listened to the procedure.

A woman came in: "Father I have sinned."

"What have you done my child?"

"I have committed adultery."

"How many times?"

"Four times father, and I sincerely repent."

"Put $2 in the poor box and say ten Hail Marys and you will receive absolution," said the priest.

Then a second woman came in.

"Father I have sinned."

"What have you done my child?"

"I have committed adultery."

"How many times?"

"Twice, Father."

"Put $1 in the poor box and say five Hail Marys, and you will be forgiven," said the priest.

As soon as the woman had left the priest whispered to the rabbi, "You have got the hang of it now, quick, take my place, I have to rush."

The rabbi settled down in the priest's position and soon enough another woman knelt at the other side of the grill.

"Father, I have sinned," she said.

"What have you done my child?"

"I have committed adultery."

"How many times?"

"Just the once, father."

"Well, you had better go and do it again. It's two for a dollar this week."

*   *   *

"FORGIVE me Father, but I have had an obsession about stealing wood from the timber mill where I work. I have suffered with this problem for years. What shall I do?"

"That's alright my son," said the priest. "But because this sin has been perpetuated for so long I must ask you to make a novena."

"If you've got the plans Father, I've got the timber."

*   *   *

TERESA went to confession and told the priest she had sinned three times that week. She said she had slept with Shaun on Tuesday, Paddy on Wednesday and Shamus on Friday night. "Oh Father what should I do?"

"On your way home, my child," he said. "Call in at Con the Fruiterer's, buy a lemon and suck it."

"Oh Father, will that cleanse me of my sins?"

"No. But it should take that damn smile off your face."

*   *   *

ON Saturday nights the three lads always went out on the town together, but Shamus always made a point of going past the church first so he could duck into confession while the other two waited outside.

"It's been a week since my last confession father," said

Shamus, "and I'm sorry to say that I have sinned of the flesh once again."

"Was it that O'Flannagan hussey from the dairy?"

"No father."

"Was it the cheeky Costanzo girls in the fruit shop?"

"No father."

"Don't tell me it was the widow Murphy flauntin' her wares again?"

"No father."

"Well do your usual penance and be off with you then," said the priest.

Shamus rushed out of the church to his waiting mates. "Got at least three good tips for tonight," he said.

\* \* \*

"FATHER, yesterday I made love to my wife."

The priest explained that there was nothing wrong with that.

"But Father, I did it with... lust."

Again the priest re-assured the man that it was no sin.

"But Father, it was the middle of the day."

The priest was growing uncomfortable with the description but assured his parishioner that it was a natural act for man and wife.

"But Father, it was sheer passion. As she leant over the deep freeze I just jumped on her and we did it on the floor. Am I banned from the church?"

"Of course not," said the exasperated priest.

"Oh good. We're both banned from Safeways."

\* \* \*

LITTLE Patrick to little Isaac: "Our parish priest knows more than your rabbi."

Isaac: "That's because you tell him everything."

\* \* \*

THE vicar, the priest and the rabbi were always arguing about which was the true religion. But they were friends enough to make a pact that whoever died first the other two would each put $300 in the coffin to ensure admittance to the Pearly Gates.

It came to pass that the vicar died first. The other two attended the funeral service and as good as his word the priest approached the coffin and put in his $300. The rabbi followed, wrote a cheque for $600, put it in beside the vicar and took his $300 change.

\* \* \*

MY wife converted me to religion. I never believed in hell until I married her.

\* \* \*

IT all started in the Garden of Eden, and one day Adam was intrigued by the antics of a buck rabbit. "What's he doing?" he asked God, and was told that the rabbits were simply making love.

He saw two birds doing something similar, and upon enquiry from on high was told they were also making love.

"Why I haven't I got anybody to do that with?" he asked God, who replied that he would fix it first thing next morning.

Sure enough, when Adam awoke, there was Eve laying beside him. He took her by the hand and they ran into the bushes.

Ten minutes later Adam emerged from the bushes. "Hey God, what's a headache?"

\* \* \*

HELL is multi-cultural.

The Germans are the police force, the Italians the defence force, the Indonesians are in charge of housing, and the Indians run the railways. The Irish make the laws, the English are the cooks and the common language is Dutch.

\* \* \*

A MINOR religious sect in India worships the Goddess of the Harvest, Kali. Every morning they visit Kali's temple and make an offering; a watermelon.

They present the offering and then sing their sacred song: "Here's another melon Kali baby!"

*       *       *

A NUN raced in to mother superior's office screaming and waving her hands. "Oh, mother," she cried "we seem to have a case of hepatitis!"

"Well, my dear, bring it in," said mother superior. "I'm sick to death of Bernie Smith's Bodega."

*       *       *

SATURDAY night is confession night but Father O'Riley stopped Pat as he entered the church. "Pat, the church is full. Can you come back tomorrow night? You haven't committed murder since last time have you?"

"Indeed I haven't," said Pat and he turned to leave.

On the way out he met Shamus. "Go home Shamus and come back tomorrow. They are only hearing murders tonight!"

*       *       *

THE monastery was in financial trouble and decided to go into the fish and chip business. One night a customer rapped on the door which was opened by a monk.

"Are you the fish friar?"

"No," replied the robed figure, "I'm the chip monk!"

*       *       *

"I DON'T like the look of the new missionary," said one cannibal to the other.

"That's alright," said the other, "just eat the potatoes."

*       *       *

ISRAELI prime minister Rabin invited the Pope to a game of golf. Since the Pope had no idea of the game he convened the college of cardinals and asked their advice.

"Call Greg Norman, make him a cardinal, tell Rabin you're sick and send Cardinal Norman in your place."

Honoured by the Pope's request Greg Norman agreed to represent him.

When he returned from the game the Pope asked how he had done. "I came in second," said Norman.

"You mean Rabin beat you?"

"No, Your Holiness, Rabbi Nicklaus did."

* * *

THE sermon for the evening was "Christian Perfection," and the minister was quick to point out that this was an ideal state of grace unattainable by the sinners as constituted the nondescript congregation before him. Nevertheless, in the course of his sermon he challenged anyone present to stand and proclaim they were perfect. To his astonishment a bloke in the fifth pew got to his feet.

"Do you dare claim you are perfect?" thundered the cleric.

"No, not me," replied the man, "I am standing proxy for my wife's first husband!"

* * *

A COUPLE who went to the movies found themselves sitting directly behind two nuns; the ones with the large headgear.

Trying to see the screen past these obstacles the girl muttered to her boyfriend: "It would be nice to go to Scotland, there are not so many nuns there."

The boyfriend replied audibly: "What about Sweden, there were even fewer there."

One of the nuns turned around, gave the couple a sweet smile and said: "Why don't you both go to hell, you won't find any there!"

* * *

THE two men dressed in black were the only occupants in a compartment on a long train journey. After a time one said, "Excuse me, but would I be right in thinking you are a Catholic priest?"

"Yes. And would you be a rabbi?"

"I am," said the first.

They had a lot of time to kill and eventually the rabbi said: "Have you ever broken a commandment?"

The priest admitted that he had "taken a woman."

After a while the priest said: "Have you ever eaten pork?"

The rabbi looked around as if to check nobody else was in the compartment, then nodded his head, "yes," he whispered.

The long silence was broken by the priest. "Sex is much better than pork isn't it!"

* * *

A JEWISH tailor was troubled the way his son had turned out and went to see his rabbi about it. "I brought him up in the faith, gave him a very expensive bar mitzvah, cost me a fortune to educate him. Then he tells me last week he has decided to be a Christian. Rabbi, can you help me, what will I do?"

"Funny thing you should bring that problem to me," said the rabbi. "Like you I brought my boy up in the faith, put him through university, cost me a fortune, then one day he comes and tells me he has decided to become a Christian."

"What did you do?" asked the tailor.

"I went to the synagogue and prayed to Almighty God for an answer."

"And what happened," pressed the tailor.

God's voice came into the synagogue as clear as a bell: "Funny thing you should bring that problem to me," he said.

* * *

OF course it was a certainty that Jesus was Jewish. He lived at home until he was 30, he went into his father's business, his mother thought he was divine, and he thought she was a virgin.

* * *

WHY wasn't Christ born in Australia?

Well, where would you find a virgin, and where would you find three wise men?

* * *

ACTUALLY there were four wise men. While following the star on the way to the manger, one of them said he knew a short cut.

THE city council had just taken delivery of the new mayoral car and called on the three denominations to consecrate it at a special ceremony.

The priest chanted a blessing and sprinkled it with holy water. The parson chanted a blessing and waved the cross over it. The rabbi chanted a blessing, went round the back and cut an inch off the exhaust pipe.

* * *

THE minister pranged his brand new car when a woman stopped to check her make-up in the rear-vision mirror. It was only the car's first time on the road and the minister got really angry.

He got out and roared at the woman: "Why don't you go forth and multiply!"

* * *

THE priest called on the village belle Mary O'Shaunessy who was in hospital after falling off the stage during her dance act for the church fete. "I prayed for you last night," he said.

"No need," she replied, "I'm in the phone book."

* * *

MOTHER Superior rapped the desk with her cane and asked the Grade IV girls what they wanted to be when they grew up.

One 13-year-old put up her hand and said: "I want to be a prostitute."

Mother Superior fainted with shock. When she was revived and had composed herself she asked the same girl: "What did you say you wanted to be?"

"A prostitute," affirmed the youngster.

"Oh, thank goodness, I thought for a moment you said you wanted to be a Protestant."

* * *

THE vicar walked around to the back of the church and saw three boys sitting on the ground with a handful of coins at their feet. "What might you boys be doing?" he enquired.

"We're having a competition," explained one. "Whoever tells the biggest lie gets the money."

The vicar was visibly shocked. "When I was a boy," he said, "I never told untruths."

They said "Okay, you win," and gave him the money.

\*　　\*　　\*

IT was one of those silent orders where the only utterances allowed were the morning and evening rituals to greet the head monk. "Good Morning Head Monk" they would chant at breakfast and "Good Evening Head Monk" just before retiring.

After 15 years this ritual was getting on Brother Paddy's wick and causing rebellion to swell within him. Finally he planned a revolt.

Next day, when the brethren chanted "Good Morning Head Monk," he would deliberately chant "Evening!"

The prospect nearly sent his rocks off. He was all of a tremble at the breakfast table and when the head monk entered he stood with the rest of them and in the chorus of "Good Morning Head Monk" Paddy threw in his rebellious "Evening!"

The head monk was very perceptive. There was an awesome silence until his monotone baritone loudly proclaimed: "Someone Chanted Evening!"

\*　　\*　　\*

AGAIN it was one of those monastic orders where the monks were silent, except on the day of their patron saint, St Titus. The first year Brother Basil asked for another blanket. The second year he asked if he could have porridge instead of wheaties. The third year he asked if he could have sugar in his tea. The fourth year he asked if he could leave the order.

"You might as well," said the head monk, "You've done nothing but winge since you've been here."

\*　　\*　　\*

GOD spent a lot of time hacking out the commandments on one tablet of stone then he offered it to the first tribe he saw. They happened to be Germans, and after studying the bit about "Thou Shalt Not Kill," decided it was not their cup of tea. God offered them to the French. They took one look and said "What's all this ban on adultery. That's not for us," so they refused.

God then offered them to the Jews.

"How much?" said Moses.

"They are free," said God.

"Okay, we'll take two."

\* \* \*

TRAVEL seems to induce confession, so when three priests found themselves in the same compartment of a train on a long journey to a eucharistic council, they began to bare their souls and admit to certain sins.

"It's women with me," said the first. "I find them very hard to resist and I have fallen several times."

"It's the grog with me," said the second. "Struggle as I may there have been times when the proceeds of the poor box have gone on Demon Drink."

The third priest was quiet. "I suppose you succumb to gambling," prompted his colleagues.

"No," he said. "My problem is gossip. I am a blabbermouth and I can hardly wait to get off this train."

\* \* \*

A DRUNK sat opposite a priest on the train and studied him for ten minutes. Finally he said, "Tell me, yer worship. Why do you wear your collar back to front?"

"Because I am a father," said the priest.

"But I'm a father too," said the drunk.

"No, I am a father to hundreds in my parish."

"Then maybe it's your trousers you should be wearing back to front," said the drunk.

\* \* \*

LEANING on the bar, two drinkers were arguing about religion. "What do you know about the Lord's Prayer," said one. "I'll bet you ten cents you don't know the first line."

"You're on," said the other, and put his ten cents on the line.

"Now I lay me down to sleep," proudly recited the first.

"You win," said his mate. "I didn't think you knew it!"

*　　*　　*

A SWAGGIE happened to call at the vicarage, on the bite for a hand-out.

"I want to ask you one question," said the vicar when he had heard the man's hardluck story. "Do you take alcoholic drinks?"

"Before I answer that," said the swaggie thoughtfully, "is that in the nature of an enquiry or an invitation."

*　　*　　*

THE vicar had not seen young Johnny at Sunday school, so when he found the lad beside a country road minding his dad's cattle he thought it an appropriate time to deliver an impromptu sermon. "They are fine bullocks, Johnny, do you know who made them?"

"Dad did," replied Johnny.

"Oh no," the vicar smiled, "God made those bullocks."

Johnny shook his head. "God made them bulls. Dad made them bullocks."

*　　*　　*

AN Aussie on holiday in Ireland was given a piece of advice by his Irish wife before the aircraft landed at Shannon Airport. She told him not to tell religious jokes or to be critical of Catholics.

He was in a pub the very next night playing a darts match with the locals when a television bulletin reported that the Pope was sick, and near death. The locals all gathered around the television set.

"C'mon you fellas, to heck with the Pope let's get on with the game," he said.

When he woke up in hospital with his wife sitting beside him he said, "Nobody told me the Pope was a Catholic."

THE priest, the vicar and the rabbi were discussing how they divided the collection between God's work and themselves.

"We lean more towards the fundamentalist side," said the rabbi. "I take the money outside and literally fling it up to heaven and what God wants he keeps, what falls back on the ground, I keep."

\* \* \*

THE district inspector of Catholic Primary Schools called at St Patrick's and decided to put Grade V to the test with some basic questions on the faith.

When he came to young Johnny he asked: "Who knocked down the Walls of Jericho?"

"It wasn't me," was the instant reply.

The inspector was taken aback. Johnny's parents obviously needed a word about their responsibility in religious instruction so he noted the address and knocked on the door that evening.

When Johnny's Mum opened the door the inspector introduced himself and said: "When I asked your boy who knocked down the Walls of Jericho, his answer was that it wasn't him." he said.

In a defiant pose she answered: "If my Johnny said he didn't do it then he didn't do it."

This was too much for the inspector and he asked to see the man of the house. Paddy was in bed, looking for work, but when the inspector revealed the purpose of his visit Paddy reached for his trousers. "Okay, okay, how much did this bloomin' wall cost anyway?"

\* \* \*

PUZZLED about his first lesson on evolution young Joey arrived home and said: "Mum, is it really true that I am a descendant of apes, monkeys and gorillas?"

"I don't really know, darling," she replied, "I never knew any of your father's family."

A RICH tourist who had come to Vatican in hope of seeing the Pope was estatic when the Pontif came into the crowd near him and placed his hands on the shoulders of a derelict. The tourist was amazed to see the Pope do the same thing the following day, so he approached the tramp and offered him $100 to swap clothes, to which the down-and-outer eagerly agreed.

Next day, dressed in the tramp's smelly rags the tourist was delighted to see the Pope turn and approach him. With both hands on his shoulders the Pope bent forward and whispered: "I've told you to push off twice. Now beat it!"

\*     \*     \*

THERE was a young lady called Alice
  Who peed in the presbytery's chalice
  The padre agreed
  'Twas done out of need
  And not out of Protestant malice.

\*     \*     \*

A RENOWNED archaeologist named Nostle
  Discovered a fantastic fossil
  He knew from its bend
  And the knob on the end
  'Twas the peter of Paul the Apostle.

\*     \*     \*

THE eternal question was being argued by a theologian and a philosopher.

The theologian defined a philosopher as being like a blind man in a darkened room looking for a black cat that wasn't there.

"That's as may be," said the philosopher, "but the theologian would have found it."

\*     \*     \*

THE vicar was the lone survivor of a shipwreck and as he staggered ashore he found himself surrounded by hundreds of spear-wielding warriors.

"Oh God! I'm finished," he cried.

"No you are not," thundered a voice from on high.

"Who's that?" asked the vicar.

"It's God. Now listen carefully. Grab that spear from the thin native next to you and plunge it into the heart of the chief."

Although terrified the vicar did exactly as he was told, and as the chief collapsed to the ground the voice boomed out once more: "NOW you are finished."

# RESTAURANTS
See WAITERS

THE couple had just finished dinner and the waiter was pouring a third glass of port when he noticed the gentleman slide off his chair and disappear.

"Excuse me madam," he said. "Your husband is under the table."

"No he's not," she replied white-faced. "My husband has just come through the door!"

*     *     *

THERE were only two restaurants in the little tourist village, one opposite the other. The visitor stopped a local and asked which served the best meals.

"Let me put it this way," he replied. "Whichever one you go into, you will have wished you had gone to the other."

*     *     *

THE diner called the waiter: "I would like to report this meal to the Bureau of Missing Portions."

*     *     *

THE food was so bad at this place the mice used to send out for take-away.

*     *     *

THE estate agent said it was not the right location for a Chinese restaurant.

"They'd be flogging a dead horse."

HE was in a hurry. "I'll have a crocodile sandwich. And make it snappy."

\* \* \*

"A GLASS of vin rouge, please Ethel."
   "Certainly sir, red or white?"

\* \* \*

"WHAT'S that?" said the stuffy matron looking at the morsel on the plate set before her.
   "It's pressed tongue," said the waiter.
   "Yuk! I could never eat anything that came out of a beast's mouth," she said. "Bring me a boiled egg!"

\* \* \*

FRED got into trouble when he took his girlfriend to a restaurant. They ordered soup, and when the waiter brought it his girlfriend spotted a bug in it. She screamed and said: "Waiter, remove this insect."
   The waiter threw Fred down the front stairs.

\* \* \*

SOUP du jour, $2.
Soup de yesterday, $1.
Swiss cheese with holes, 50 cents.
Extra serve of holes, 25 cents.

\* \* \*

SIGN: Customers who pay for their meal then leave without eating will be prosecuted.

\* \* \*

THUMP and thump the old sauce bottle
   First none'l come, And then the lott'l.

\* \* \*

"I'LL have some Spinoti Vertimicelli."
   "Where did you see that?"
   "On the menu."
   "Oh, that's the name of the proprietor."

\* \* \*

SHE was such a noisy eater that when she started on her soup three couples got up to dance.

\* \* \*

THE fat lady had an enormous steak on her plate. Her

husband took one look at it and said. "Surely you are not going to eat that alone?"

"Of course not. I've just ordered some potatoes."

\* \* \*

FRED was the type of bloke who always let his friends pick up the dinner bill. He had an impediment in his reach.

\* \* \*

TWO crayfish were in the restaurant's aquarium. It seemed this would be their last night so the male cray put the hard word on the female.

She said: "Okay, but will you still respect me in the mornay?"

\* \* \*

SIGN in a restaurant window: "Kitchen hand wanted, to wash dishes, and two waitresses."

\* \* \*

THE commercial traveller entered the dining room of the hotel and gave the waiter a complicated order.

"I want two fried eggs so over-done they would chew like tennis balls, two slices of burnt toast, some charred bacon and a cup of cold coffee that tastes like dishwater and don't forget to slop it into the saucer."

The waiter scratched his head. "That's a tall order, I don't know if I can manage that."

"Oh?" said the traveller. "You didn't seem to have any trouble yesterday."

(There is another punchline to this. The traveller says he is homesick and misses his wife's cooking).

\* \* \*

IT was a roadside cafe and the traveller asked for the menu. It read: Ham sandwiches, bacon, roast pork, pigs feet, pork chops or pork sausage."

"Could I have a glass of water first?" he asked.

"Sure," said the proprietor, "but we only have bore water out here."

"Blimey, you don't waste much of that pig do you," said the traveller.

TWO society dames settled down for a cup of coffee and when the waitress delivered the drinks she also brought a plate with two cakes; one was large, the other small.

"After you," said one socialite offering her friend the plate.

"No, after you."

"No, but I insist," said the first.

"No, you take first pick," said the other.

Eventually, one broke the stalemate by taking one of the cakes. The big one.

The other was upset. "Oh, you helped yourself first and took the big cake," she pouted.

"So, and if you had chosen first, which one would you have taken?"

"The smaller one of course."

"Well, what are you complaining about, that's what you've got!"

\* \* \*

IT was such a high class restaurant they could provide gravy that would match your vest.

\* \* \*

WHAT'S worse than eating shepherd's pie in a restaurant where you don't know what's gone into it?

Eating it at home where you do know what's gone into it.

\* \* \*

THIS restaurant boasted that it could provide any dish the customer could order, no matter how alien or rare. If the chef couldn't produce the dish, then an alternative meal was on the house.

Consequently they did good business with smart alecs ordering filleted bee's knees marinated in port sauce, or roast goanna tails in curry, surrounded by Tibetan cabbage on rice.

But one evening the order was for braised elephant's kidneys on toast. A simple demand, but as ten minutes stretched to 20 the chef finally came out to apologise.

Due to an earlier rush on crocodile knuckle sandwiches they were completely out of bread.

* * *

MARY had a little lamb
A lobster and some prunes
A glass of wine, a piece of pie
A plate of macaroons
She gobbled down a sponge cake
And what else we don't know
But when they carried Mary out
Her face was white as snow.

# ROMANCE

WHEN she asked him why he had suddenly stopped loving her, he said he had a train to catch.

* * *

EVE: "Do you love me?"
ADAM: "Who else?"

* * *

HE told his girl of course he knew where the erogenous zone was. He got booked for parking in one yesterday.

* * *

ON their wedding night he declared his love for her. He said he would swim the deepest river, cross the widest desert and climb the tallest mountain.

She divorced him. He was never home.

* * *

IN the warm summer night the young couple lay in close embrace in the canoe as it gently drifted out on the shimmering lake. She looked up at him and asked: "Will you love me always?"

"Of course my darling, which way will we try first?"

* * *

IT was only their second night out but he had fallen deeply in love with her after they spent the entire night in his flat. To him it was the real thing.

"Am I the first man you ever made love with?" he asked.

She studied him reflectively. "You might be. Although, you're face looks rather familiar!"

\* \* \*

IT was one of those enchanting evenings when the lights were dim and the music softly sentimental. They sat in a corner and he gazed into her eyes.

"Drink does a lot for you," he murmured. "It makes you look beautiful, appealing, divine..."

"But I haven't been drinking," she protested.

"I know," he whispered, "but I have."

\* \* \*

HE noticed her bedroom was stacked high with teddy bears and other toy animals, but he was more intent on the job in hand.

After they had made love he asked how it had been for her.

"Yeah, you were alright," she said. "You can have anything on the bottom shelf."

## ROYALS

WHEN Prince Philip visited Korumburra to open a butter factory he looked resplendent in his naval uniform, except for the fur hat.

A local reporter, suspecting there might be a story attached to it, waited for the appropriate moment and asked: "Why the fur hat?"

"Well, I phoned Mummy last night," began the Prince, "and she asked me what I was doing today. I said I was going to Korumburra and she said "Where the fox hat?"

# S

## SALES

SALES resistance, of course, is the triumph of mind over patter.

* * *

"THERE'S a salesman outside with a young lady."

"Tell him I'll take one."

* * *

"HOW did the new salesman go today?"

"He got two orders. One to get out, and one to stay out."

* * *

FROM the For Sale section of the newspaper: "Home Computer, as new. Never been figured out."

* * *

A MELBOURNE youth wanted to buy a motor cycle. "It must be the fastest machine you've got," he demanded.

The salesman said he had just the bike, but its true speed could only be demonstrated at night when the roads were clear. "Come back tonight, at midnight, and I'll guarantee we can be in Geelong in 45 minutes," he said.

The youth thought for a minute. "No thanks."

"Why not. It's very fast."

"It may be, but who wants to be in Geelong at a quarter-to-one in the morning?"

"DON'T you know you can't sell second-hand cars without a licence?" said the inspector.

"Thanks, I knew I wasn't selling any, but I didn't know the reason."

\* \* \*

AN attractive salesgirl approached a young man in a department store and said: "What would you like, sir?"

"What would I like?" he repeated. "Why I would like to take you out of here, take you to my pad, mix a nice cocktail, take you in my arms and make passionate love to you. That's what I'd like. But what I NEED is a pair of socks."

\* \* \*

A TRAVELLER noted that the small corner store in the country town had large bags of salt stacked high around the verandah. When he went in to buy some cigarettes he saw more bags of salt stacked so high they reached the ceiling. After he paid for his cigarettes he said, "You must sell a lot of salt."

"To tell you the truth, I hardly sell any," said the store-keeper. "But the wholesale rep who calls here, boy can he sell salt."

\* \* \*

SID was told if he didn't sell more toothbrushes he would be fired. One month later his sales record had soared and the manager called him in to explain the dramatic turnaround.

Sid explained that he got sick of calling on pharmacies. He said he set up a little table at Flinders St Station with some dry biscuits and a new dip.

"Try my dip," he would say, and a constant stream of people did so. When they enquired about the ingredients of the dip Sid told them: "Garlic and chook shit!"

They would go "Aaaargh!" and spit it out.

Then Sid would say: "Would you like to buy a toothbrush?"

IT was the old story of a salesman finding himself stranded in the country and knocking on the door of the only pub in town.

"Well, we don't have a spare room," said the proprietor, "but you are welcome to share with the little red-headed school teacher if you like."

The salesman could hardly contain his excitement. "Oh thanks. I will be a real gentleman."

"That's good," said the farmer. "So's the little red-headed school teacher!"

*  *  *

ONCE again the salesman found himself knocking on a farmhouse door seeking a bed for the night.

"Sure," said the farmer, "but we only have one spare bed and you will have to share that with Cecil, my son."

The salesman turned and headed for his car. "Crikey, how did I get into the wrong joke?"

*  *  *

HARRY and Sam were travelling together when their car broke down in the country. They approached the farmhouse and were well received by Widow Mary who fed them well and put them up for the night.

It was about nine months later when Harry rang Sam.

"Remember the night the car broke down out in the country?" he asked. "You didn't by any chance slip into the widow's bedroom did you?"

Sam admitted he did. "And you didn't by any chance use my name did you?"

Sam admitted that he did, and said he was sorry.

"Don't worry about it Sam," said Harry. "I've just got a letter from a legal firm that says she has died and left me the farm."

*  *  *

THIS salesman was travelling late at night when his car blew a tyre and he realised he didn't have a jack. It was miles from anywhere, but across the field he could see a farmhouse in silhouette against the rising moon.

"He could lend me a jack," mused the salesman as he set off towards the farm.

As he stumbled across the paddocks in the dark he wondered if farmers still had the hospitality for which they were renowned.

"It's late," he thought. "He probably won't be too pleased about being woken up. He has probably had a hard day in the field and was looking forward to a bit of rest."

He approached the farmhouse and knocked on the door.

While he waited his thoughts continued: "The poor bloke is most likely getting out of bed now. His wife could be nagging him. The jack's probably out in the cold garage. He will be upset. He could even put the dogs onto me."

When the farmer opened the door the traveller said: "To hell with your jack!"

*　　*　　*

TOLD to accompany the firm's top salesman on his round to learn the ropes the rookie noticed that before entering a prospective client's office the super salesman would always make the sign of the cross, and inevitably make a sale.

"I didn't know you had to be a Catholic," said the rookie.

"I'm not," replied his mentor. "But never tackle a client without checking your glasses, your wallet, your pen, and your zipper!"

*　　*　　*

THE travelling salesman sent a telegram to his wife: "Coming home Friday."

When he arrived home he was alarmed to find a man in bed with his wife. He went berserk, but was restrained by his mother-in-law. She urged him to keep calm and not to commit any violent and hasty action he would, in time, regret. "Leave it to me," she said. "There must be an explanation."

Next day she had her explanation. "I have gone into the matter thoroughly, and like I told you, there is a reason for your wife's behaviour. There was a postal strike on Friday and she didn't get the telegram!"

\* \* \*

THEY just buried a salesman named Cripps
He married, on one of his trips
A widow named Block
Then died of the shock
When he found there were nine little chips.

## SCHOOLS
See EDUCATION, TEACHERS

JOHNNY told his dad: "There's going to be a small meeting of the Parent Teacher Association at the school tomorrow morning.

"What's a small meeting?" asked his dad.

"Just you, me and the headmaster," said the lad.

\* \* \*

TEACHER: "Name two pronouns?"

Johnny: "Who? Me?"

\* \* \*

WHEN I was a kid I went to an immoral school. It had no principle and it had no class.

\* \* \*

"STAND up all the little boys and girls who want to go to heaven," said the Sunday School teacher.

They all stood except little Fred.

"Don't you want to go to heaven," she asked Fred.

"Not yet, Miss," he said.

\* \* \*

THE six-year-old was a study of concentration as she laboured over her drawing. "What will your picture be, Angela?" said the teacher.

"I'm drawing God," she said.

"That's a difficult subject," said teacher. "Nobody knows what he looks like."

"They will when I'm finished," said the youngster.

\* \* \*

IT was Monday morning and Mum was having a tough time preparing a rebellious son for another week at school.

"Nobody likes me," he groaned. "Teachers don't like me. The kids don't like me. I just don't want to go anymore," he complained.

"Pull yourself together," said his mother. "School can be tough, but at 40 years of age and as principal of the school you've just got to go."

\* \* \*

THE demure co-ed said to her tutor: "I would do anything to pass my exams."

"Anything?" he queried.

"Yes, anything."

"Well try studying," he said.

\* \* \*

"DO you know your alphabet?"

"Yes."

"What comes after G?"

"Whizz."

"Right, and what comes after whizz?"

"Bang."

"Good boy."

\* \* \*

ONCE I won a prize for arithmetic. The teacher asked what was 20 multiplied by four. I put up my hand first and said "thirty-four." I got the prize for being closest.

\* \* \*

"JOHNNY, how much is three times three?"

"Nine, Miss."

"That's pretty good."

"Pretty good. It's bloody perfect."

"THAT essay on the dog is exactly word for word, the same as your brother's."

"Of course sir, it's the same dog."

\* \* \*

O'GRADY was asked how many honours he received in his leaving certificate.

"Three," he said proudly. "Pure mathematics, and applied mathematics."

\* \* \*

THERE are three kinds of people in this world: Those who can count and those who can't.

\* \* \*

THE kids at our school were so tough the teacher used to play hookey.

\* \* \*

THE voice over the phone said; "Young Tommy won't be at school today, he is very sick."

"Who is speaking?" said the principal.

"My father," said the caller.

\* \* \*

YOUNG Freddy was on his feet as soon as the teacher entered the room. "Do you think it is right to punish people for things they haven't done?" he asked her.

"Certainly not," she replied.

"That's good. Because I haven't done my homework."

\* \* \*

TEACHER: "What is a comet?"

Johnny: "A star with a tail."

Teacher: "Name one."

Johnny: "Mickey Mouse."

\* \* \*

TEACHER: "Which month has 28 days?"

Johnny: "They all have."

\* \* \*

OVER a row of hooks in the cloakroom was a sign which said: "These hooks are for teachers only."

Underneath, some bright spark had added: "They may also be used for hats and coats."

\* \* \*

THE young schoolteacher had been assigned to a country school for three years before her mother had a chance to visit her.

Mum noticed that most of the men in town seemed to know her daughter.

"Oh they are probably fathers of some of my children," explained the teacher.

\* \* \*

THE school inspector was sent out into the country to check on the standard of education in the bush school.

His first question to the class, "Who knocked down the Walls of Jericho?" was met with an embarrassing and fidgety silence.

"Can't you tell me?" he said pointing to young Murphy.

"It wasn't me, honest sir," was the only response.

Disappointed at the low standard of the class the inspector went to the headmaster. "I asked a young lad in your school who knocked down the Walls of Jericho and he said it wasn't him."

"The little scally-wag," said the headmaster. "I'll bet it was him all the time."

Staggered at this response the inspector sought out the president of the Parents and Teachers' Association to report the sad state of affairs.

"Well," said the president, "young Murphy comes from an honest family and you can take it from me that if he says he didn't knock them down, then he is bloodywell telling the truth."

Finally, in despair the inspector reported the matter to the Department of Education and a week later received the following reply:

"Dear Sir. With regard to your letter regarding the Walls of Jericho, we are obliged to inform you that this

392

matter does not come within our jurisdiction. We suggest you contact the Board of Works."

*     *     *

THE teacher was getting to know the kids.

"What does your father do, Johnny?"

"He's a train driver, Miss."

And what does your father do, Sammy?"

"He's a policeman, Miss."

"And what about your father, Freddy?"

"He's dead, Miss."

"Oh. And what did he do before he died?"

"He clutched his throat, let out a groan and fell on the floor."

## SEDUCTION

HE wined and dined her before they went to the theatre.

"Thanks for a beautiful evening," she said when he had driven her home.

"Ah, but the night's not over," he said, pouring her a glass of champagne. And as she sipped the drink he pushed two white tablets towards her.

"Aren't these aspirins?" she asked.

"Indeed they are," he replied.

"But I haven't got a headache."

"Good," he said. "Then let's go to bed."

## SHEPHERDS

THE locals in the village pub watched the stranger with suspicion because it was rumoured he was a taxman. Finally, they elected one of their number to check him out.

The appointed one moved along the bar and engaged him in conversation. "You're not from these parts?" he began.

393

"No," said the stranger.

The local continued with the small talk for a time and then asked what the stranger did for a living.

"I'm a taxidermist," he said.

"Oh yeah," said the local. "And what have you been doing around here?"

"Had a marvellous time really," said the stranger. "Yesterday I stuffed a prize sheep dog, this morning I mounted Farmer Brown's goat and tomorrow I am going to have a go at his sow."

At this the local retreated slowly along the bar to where his mates were eager for his report.

"He tried to tell me he was a taxi driver, but I've figured him out. He's really a shepherd like us, on holiday."

## SHOPPERS

FRED was talking to his mate in the pub.

"The wife is shopping crazy. She will buy absolutely anything marked down. Yesterday she came home with an escalator."

\*　　\*　　\*

HIS wife was a kleptomaniac. But her sister was worse. She used to walk into stores backwards and leave things on the counter.

\*　　\*　　\*

"WHERE can I get some talcum powder?" she asked the supervisor.

"Walk this way, madam" he said.

"If I could walk that way I wouldn't need the talcum powder," she answered.

\*　　\*　　\*

WHEN he claimed his money back under their "satisfaction or money refunded guarantee," they said they were perfectly satisfied with his money.

MISS Lottzabazooma bought a dress. It was marked down 50%, and that's how she wears it.

*　　*　　*

THE advertisement for a kitchen gadget said it was so marvellous it would cut the housework in half. So she bought two.

*　　*　　*

"THANKS for your patience in showing me all that linen, but I am not buying anything myself. I am looking for my neighbour."

"Well, do you think she may be in that last bolt of pink on the top shelf?"

*　　*　　*

SHE walked into the delicatessen and selected a chicken. She prodded and poked it. She lifted one wing and sniffed underneath, lifted the other wing and did the same. Finally she looked at the chicken's rear end and gave it another sniff. "This chicken is not fresh," she declared.

"Lady," said the shopkeeper, "do you think you could pass the same test?"

## SHOWBIZ

IT has been attributed to the great actress Katherine Hepburn that there wasn't much to acting. "After all," she said, "Shirley Temple could do it at the age of four."

*　　*　　*

TWO sailors spent the evening getting drunk then decided to go to a variety show. Half way through the program one sailor needed to go to the toilet. On asking directions from the usherette she told him, "Go left, then to the end of the passage on the right, left again and straight ahead."

A little the worse for wear the sailor followed the directions with some difficulty, relieved himself and eventually found his way back to his seat.

"You missed the best act," whispered his mate.

"While you were out a sailor came on stage and pissed into the orchestra pit."

*　　*　　*

A VENTRILOQUIST with the usual dummy on his lap was making several offensive jokes at the expense of the Irish. Finally, Paddy could take it no longer.

"Hey, you!" he shouted. "I object to you making fun of my countrymen."

"I'm sorry," said the ventriloquist. "I meant no offence."

"I'm not talking to you," said Paddy. "I'm talking to that cheeky little bastard on your lap."

*　　*　　*

HE will never forget his first Royal Command performance.

The Queen told him to shut up.

*　　*　　*

"YOU can't resign," said the circus manager to the human cannonball. "Where would I get another man of your calibre?"

*　　*　　*

OLD actors never die, they just get smaller parts.

*　　*　　*

THE ventriloquist was so bad his lips were moving when he wasn't saying anything.

*　　*　　*

THE ventriloquist went into a pub and asked for a gottle of gear. Then he drank it without moving his lips.

*　　*　　*

CONCEITED actor: "Have you seen my latest show?"

"I never miss it. I've never seen it and I never miss it."

*　　*　　*

"DID the new show have a happy ending?"

"Sure, everybody was delighted it was over."

*　　*　　*

THE show closed after its first night. A foul play was suspected.

"THIS is an education show," said the comic. "When you leave you will say: 'That taught me a lesson'!"

*　　*　　*

IT was a sneak preview. After 15 minutes everybody sneaked out.

*　　*　　*

HOLLYWOOD is the only place where the brides keep the bouquets and throw away the grooms.

*　　*　　*

HER adoration of the actor was obvious. "When will your life story be published," she asked, "I would love to read it."

"Oh, not yet," he said, "My life story will be written posthumously."

"Well, I do hope it is soon," she gushed.

*　　*　　*

THE actor had a hard time deciding whether to marry the chorus girl, who was very pretty, but a little scatty, or his leading lady, who was not so beautiful, but had a magnificent singing voice.

It was a close decision, but he went for quality and married the soprano.

The morning after the honeymoon he took a good hard look at his bride. Then he nudged her and said, "For Goodness sake, sing!"

*　　*　　*

IN Hollywood parents have to edit the fairytales they tell their children: "Once upon a time there were three bears. Daddy Bear, Mummy Bear, and a baby bear by a previous marriage."

*　　*　　*

WHEN the much married actress finally died her friends clubbed together for a fitting funeral and a tomb stone with the fitting epitaph: "At last she sleeps alone."

*　　*　　*

THIS week's movie trailer: "You yelled when you saw

"Psycho," you screamed when you saw "Cape Fear," and you literally shrieked when you saw "Vampire Wolves." So now a word from the manager: Why do you make so much bloody noise at the pictures?"

* * *

A PEDANTIC theatrical producer decided to direct his own wedding. He insisted on two rehearsals, and after the second he called for someone to replace the leading female role.

* * *

A GROUP of showgirls had been entertaining the troops at a remote army camp. After their performance the major asked: "Would you girls prefer to mess with the officers or the troops?"

"Makes no difference to us," said one shapely blonde, "but we've just got to have something to eat first."

* * *

TWO nuns had gone to the circus, but after the show they were dismayed to find heavy rain had created a deep puddle between the bigtop and their bus stop. They didn't want to get their habits or their shoes wet.

Two clowns came to their rescue and offered to piggyback them across the water.

Halfway across one clown stopped and said to his mate: "Do you realise that this is virgin on the ridiculous?"

* * *

PADDY dragged a shaggy mongrel into the talent scout's office and announced, "This is the best dog act you're ever likely t' see. This dog can count, and I trained him m'self."

The agent gave the pair a dubious stare.

"Okay, I'll prove it," said Paddy, and holding a commanding finger to the dog said, "Right Nigel, what's two and two?"

The dog went "woof, woof." Then there was a pause until Paddy said, "C'mon Nigel, you can do it." There was another "woof" then a long pause and another "woof."

"C'mon Nigel," said Paddy. "Just one more."

*   *   *

BERT said he had two tickets for the Elton John show.

"Don't want to go, he's awful," said Fred.

"But you've never heard him."

"I have heard a bloke at the pub imitate him," said Fred, "and he's damned awful."

*   *   *

ONE actress complained to her friend that she was so tired. "I didn't get to sleep until after three," she said.

"No wonder you are tired," said her friend, "two is all I need."

*   *   *

THE young actor was excited at getting a job and rushed home to tell his father: "Guess what, Dad, I play a man who has been married for 30 years."

"No matter, son. Let's hope you will eventually get a speaking part!"

*   *   *

HE had been the clumsiest dancer in the chorus line and when he fell into the orchestra pit he was carted off to hospital.

Like everybody in show business he was worried about being replaced in his absence. "Oh don't worry about that," said his mate on a visit to the ward. "Everybody has been talking about you. Why only yesterday the director said, 'Whatever happened to old whats-is-name'!"

*   *   *

AT the reunion of Actors Equity members one old thespian who had the reputation of being an utter bore looked around the room and said, "How many great actors do you think there are in this room?"

"One less than you think," came the reply.

399

THEY were dancing together at the Arts Fancy Dress Ball. "Can I drive you home?" he leered.

"Of course," she said. "What kind of a car have you got?"

"I don't have a car," he said. "But I've got a whip."

*　　*　　*

A YOUNG trapeze artist well stacked
Is faced by a very sad fact
Imagine the pain
When time and again
He catches his wife in the act.

*　　*　　*

PADDY had a good repertoire of jokes and was always making his mates roar with mirth.

"You should go on the stage, Paddy," they said.

"No way," said Paddy. "People would laugh at me."

*　　*　　*

ACTORS' Equity's surveillance officer had been following Dan Duo's Dog Show around the country circuit for some time. He suspected there was something phoney about a cocker spaniel playing the piano while a fox terrier sang assorted excerpts from Gilbert and Sullivan.

And sure enough he caught them out.

At the next show he rushed onto the stage to expose them. "The fox terrier can't sing a damned note," he told the audience, "the cocker spaniel is a ventriloquist!"

*　　*　　*

INSTEAD of getting ballet dancers to prance around on tiptoe, why don't they get taller showgirls?

*　　*　　*

THE man had sought an audition with a prominent theatrical agent who was pressed for time and when the newcomer said he was a bird impersonator he dismissed him with some irritation.

"Bird imitators are more common than pop singers," said the agent. "I've got no time to hear you now. Just give me your name and leave your number."

The man said his name was Willie Warbler, took a numbered ring off his left leg and dropped it on the desk, laid an egg, cacked on the window sill and flew away.

\* \* \*

SHE had egged him on to be an actor, and his very first audience egged him off.

\* \* \*

HIS mother would be most upset if she knew he was an actor. She still thinks he is running dope from Bangkok.

\* \* \*

THE definition of a Shakespearean actor is tall, dark and some ham.

Definition of a conceited actor is Ham and Ego.

\* \* \*

THERE was a young actor named Bates
Who danced the fandango on skates
But he fell on his cutlass
Which rendered him nutless
And practically useless on dates.

## SIGNS

ENGLISH speaking travellers, particularly travel writers, should forgive the well-meaning attempts to anglicise official notices in foreign lands. Instead, I've chuckled and written them down. Indians have produced more than their share of wonderful signs and are the source of the majority listed below:

\* \* \*

NOTICE on a Kashmir houseboat, where drinking water is always regarded with suspicion: "Clients should disregard worries about the water on this boat. It has been personally passed by the proprietor."

\* \* \*

SIGN in an Indian maternity hospital: "Visitors. Husbands only. One per patient."

SIGN in a Bombay beauty parlour: EARS PIERCED WHILE YOU WAIT.

\* \* \*

SIGN on an Irish pub door: "Gone to lunch, back in an hour. PS: Already gone 15 minutes!"

\* \* \*

SIGN on a Melbourne pub: "Good clean entertainment, every night except Monday."

\* \* \*

PLAYERS picked for the darts team will be pinned to the notice board on Thursday.

\* \* \*

SIGN beside the sandwiches on the bar said: "Do not touch the food."

\* \* \*

"TRY our home-made pies. You'll never get better."

\* \* \*

IN several pubs: "We have an agreement with the bank. They don't serve beer and we don't cash cheques."

\* \* \*

IN a Scottish pub: Happy Hour, 5-30 pm until 6 pm.

\* \* \*

LADIES are requested not to have children in the bar.

\* \* \*

DON'T drink if you're driving. There's no cure for the mourning after.

\* \* \*

IF you are driving, be sure you have a car.

\* \* \*

DON'T drive yourself to drink. Get a chauffeur.

\* \* \*

ONE for the road could be the pint of no return.

\* \* \*

PLEASE do not leave while the bar is in motion.

\* \* \*

THIRST come. Thirst served.

OUTSIDE the Registry Office: Marry Now, Pay Later!

\* \* \*

SIGN outside the church: "Next week's preacher will be pinned on the notice board."

\* \* \*

DIRECTIONS on a jam jar: "To open lid, pierce with knife to release vacuum, then push off."

\* \* \*

PATRONS WHO CONSIDER OUR STAFF UNCIVIL SHOULD SEE MANAGER. — New Delhi restaurant.

\* \* \*

CUSTOMERS GIVING ORDERS WILL BE PROMPTLY EXECUTED. — New Delhi restaurant.

\* \* \*

The Germans have theirs too: PATRONS WHO REQUIRE BATHING, PLEASE NOTICE THE CHAMBERMAID.

\* \* \*

IN CASE OF FIRE, PLEASE DO YOUR BEST TO ALARM THE PORTER.

\* \* \*

AND one from a British tourist brochure: These self-contained apartments are excellently situated near the Torquay sea front. Practically on the level.

\* \* \*

THE Houses of Parliament in Budapest are magnificent structures fronting the Danube, but as our Hungarian guide put it: "The buildings are best viewed from the backside."

\* \* \*

TO avoid burning your hands with hot water feel the water first before putting your hands in.

\* \* \*

"INSTANT hot water, in two minutes."

\* \* \*

PASSENGERS HIT BY CANCELLED TRAINS — Leader Newspapers, Victoria.

FROM Flinders Street railway station, Melbourne: TOILETS OUT OF ORDER, please use platform 7–8.

* * *

PADDY had a sign under his arm which read LONG VEHICLE. A cop stopped him and asked him where he got it. Paddy replied: "It fell off the back of a truck."

* * *

SIGN in a Fitzroy fruit shop: "God help those who help themselves!"

* * *

SIGN in a book shop read: "Browsers welcome, both high browse and low browse."

* * *

SIGN in an Albury Returned Servicemen's Club says: "Don't thump the machines, look for an attendant!"

* * *

SIGN on a photocopy machine: "The typists' reproduction equipment is not to be interferred with without prior permission of the manager."

* * *

ON the barber shop window: HAIR CUT, WHILE YOU WAIT.

* * *

LARGE sign on the door of an Australian church: "This is the House of God, and these are the Gates of Heaven." And below in smaller print: "This door is locked between the hours of 6 pm and 10 am."

* * *

"BOAT for sale, one owner, green in colour."

* * *

OUT to lunch. If not back by five, out to dinner also.

* * *

SIGN outside a funeral parlour: "Parking for clients only!"

* * *

WANTED. Man to wash dishes and two waitresses.

PRICES subject to change, according to customer's attitude.

\* \* \*

SIGN at a creek: "When this sign is under water the crossing is dangerous."

\* \* \*

SIGN in a pub: "If you are drinking to forget, please pay for your drinks in advance."

\* \* \*

PLEASE do not insult our bartenders. Customers we can get.

## SMOKING

CANCER cures smoking.

\* \* \*

SMOKING shortens your cigarettes.

\* \* \*

HE has read so much about the effects of smoking that he has finally given up reading.

\* \* \*

IT took a lot of will power, but finally he has given up trying to give up smoking.

\* \* \*

"WILL you give up smoking for me?" she said.
"Who says I've been smoking for you?" he said.

\* \* \*

"GIVE me a cigarette, Fred."
"But I thought you had given up smoking."
"Well, I've reached the first stage. I've stopped buying them."

\* \* \*

"HOW many fags do you smoke a day?"
"Any given amount."

\* \* \*

ASKED why he smoked 100 cigarettes a day, Fred replied: "Coughing is the only exercise I get."

FRED and Harry formed Smokers Anonymous. When one of them feels like a cigarette he rings the other and they get drunk instead.

* * *

DON'T smoke in bed, for the ashes which fall on the floor may be your own.

* * *

AND one for the smokers: And old bloke from the bush settled himself into the train compartment and began to light up his pipe, much to the obvious disgust of the only other occupant, an elderly woman.

"Do you know," she said, with all the disapproval she could muster, "my husband is 65 and he has never once put a pipe in his mouth."

The old-timer pondered this for a moment and replied, "I'm just on 70, and I've never put it anywhere else."

## SONGS

SHE used to go out with the landlord, but now she goes with the lease.

* * *

YOU can lead a horse to water, but you can't lead a whore to culture.

* * *

SHE wore a string of love beads and I knew I could count on her.

* * *

THE volcano song: "Larva Come Back to Me."

* * *

DRINK to me Only with Thine Eyes, cos I need all the Scotch myself.

* * *

I'LL be Seizing You, in all the old familiar places.

IF you were the only girl in the world, well okay, but as you're not, forget it.

## SPEECHES

THE MC is the bloke who introduces people who need no introduction.

★   ★   ★

HE was testing the microphone. "Can you hear me in that back corner?"

"Yes," came a reply, "and I will gladly change places with somebody who can't."

★   ★   ★

I DON'T mind people looking at their watches when I'm making a speech, but it is damned disconcerting to see them shaking them to see if they are still going.

★   ★   ★

SO many people start with the words, "I am not really a speech-maker." Then they spend the next half hour proving it.

★   ★   ★

THE vicar asked the pert young widow to give a little talk to the Temperance Society because he said the men liked her short addresses.

★   ★   ★

EVERY rose has its thorn
   That's the catch life teaches
   There hasn't been a free lunch yet
   Without those boring speeches.

## SPINSTERS

SHE called at the police station to complain about the young man next door. "It's not safe to go out on the street," she said. "He's always sitting on his front porch whistling dirty songs!"

MISS Prim had phoned the local police station several times to complain about the man next door who walked around his apartment completely nude. Finally the sergeant called around. "But you can't even see his window from here," he said.

"Try standing on that kitchen chair and looking through the skylight," she said.

*     *     *

TWO elderly spinsters were sitting on the front porch of their country house convincing each other they had made the right choice in life when a rooster chased a flurried hen past them. The hen took evasive action, running around the house three times, then dashed onto the road, straight into the path of an oncoming car.

"See that," said one spinster, "she'd prefer to die."

*     *     *

SPINSTER Brown rang the police to say she had captured a man climbing into her bedroom window, and that they could call around for him next morning.

## SPORT
See FOOTBALL, TENNIS, CRICKET

"I'M a little stiff from Badminton."

"I don't care where you come from."

*     *     *

SHE thought lacrosse was something you found in la church.

*     *     *

BOXING is like marriage. The preliminaries are often better than the main event.

*     *     *

AN Englishman, an Irishman and a Scot were sentenced to share a prison cell. The Englishman produced a pack of cards.

"At least we can pass the time playing poker."

The Scot said he liked music and would while away the time playing his mouth organ.

The Irishman smiled and said he had something better than either of his mates and produced a packet of Tampax. "It says on the packet that you can go riding, swimming, skiing, and play tennis with these."

## SQUELCH

WHEN a reporter asked New Zealand's ex-prime minster David Lange if he was concerned about the exodus of New Zealanders to Australia the PM replied, "Not at all. I think it is bound to raise the IQ of both countries."

★   ★   ★

HE saw himself as a maker and shaker, but he was having trouble clinching the deal with two executives he had tried to impress over lunch.

He saw Bob Ansett pass by on the way to the gents, and quickly excused himself to follow. He lined up beside Bob and introduced himself. "My name's Peter. I have been a fan of yours for a long time, Bob. I admire your corporate image. Could you do me one great favour, little cost to you, but forever appreciated by me, if you just say hello to me as you pass my table. It would help me clinch the deal."

"Not at all," said Bob Ansett.

Sure enough, our yuppie had got settled and had resumed his spiel when Bob Ansett came by and said, "Hi Peter, how's it going?"

"Push off, Bob. Can't you see I'm talking business!"

★   ★   ★

THE local State School decided to challenge the toffs at the Grammar School to a game of football. The date was arranged and the State School boys decided to adopt a gentlemanly stance and send the college a telegram which read: "May the best team win."

The college sent a telegram in reply which read: "May the better team win."

* * *

THE train was rattling towards a long tunnel and in one compartment sat an Englishman, an Irishman, a pretty young woman and a little old lady.

The train entered the tunnel and all went black. There was a loud kiss followed at once by an even louder smack.

When the train emerged from the tunnel the four occupants were still in their seats and busy with their own thoughts about what happened.

The pretty young woman was thinking: "Why would that Irishman want to kiss an old lady?"

The old lady was thinking: "What a hussy sitting there as if nothing had happened when I know that Englishman kissed her."

The Englishman was thinking: "I didn't do a damned thing, so why should I get my face slapped?"

And the Irishman was thinking: "How about that! I kiss my own hand, smack an Englishman in the mouth and get away with it!"

* * *

PADDY O'Leary boarded a train and found himself sharing a compartment with a snobby Englishman and his large dog.

"And what koind o' dog be that?" he asked the Pommie.

"It's a cross between an ape and an Irishman," was the surly reply.

"You mean it's related to both of us," said Paddy.

* * *

THE drunk boards the train and plonks himself down beside a priest and begins to read the paper.

He looks up after a bit and says: "Tell me father, what causes arthritis?"

It was just the opening the priest wanted. "I will tell you what causes arthritis my man," he said with passion.

"It's immoral living, too much drinking and smoking and no doubt sins of the flesh. How long have you had it?"

"Oh it's not me, father," said the drunk. "It says here the Pope's got it."

*   *   *

A NEWLY commissioned army lieutenant was standing outside a public phone box sorting through some coins. He stopped a passing soldier to ask if he had change of a dollar.

"I think so, mate," said the trooper diving his hand into his pocket.

"Just a minute, that's no way to address an officer," snapped the young lieutenant. "Let's try that again shall we. Do you have change of a dollar?"

The trooper snapped to attention and saluted. "No, sir!"

*   *   *

SHE was the self-appointed supervisor of village morals and accused a workman of having reverted to drink because with her own eyes she had seen his car parked outside the local pub.

The accused made no defence, but that night he parked his car outside her house, and left it there all night.

*   *   *

AS he arrived home from the pub he noticed his wife ironing her bra and couldn't refrain from commenting, "I don't know why you bother with that, dear, you've nothing to put in it."

She continued ironing and casually remarked, "I often think the same thing when I'm ironing your underpants."

*   *   *

AFTER 25 years of marriage a couple decided on an amicable divorce. To celebrate the granting of the decree they had dinner together. After the third glass of champagne the husband said, "There's something I have always wanted to ask you, but I didn't have the nerve. Now it can't possibly worry me."

"What's that?" said his immediate ex-wife.

"Why is it that five out of our six children have black hair and Tommy is so blonde."

She didn't answer. "Come on, you can tell me now," he insisted. "Whose child is Tommy?"

Finally she acquiesced. "Well, if you really want to know, Tommy is your child."

\* \* \*

A NUN had just beaten three young men to the last table in the railway cafeteria. They sat down beside her and decided to embarrass her with a conversation which would force her to leave.

"Your Mum and Dad get married yet?" said one to his mate.

"No. What about yours?"

"No. Not interested in that church stuff."

This went on for awhile until the nun said: "Excuse me, would one of you bastards pass me the salt?"

## STINGY
AS IN CHEAP, MEAN OR PARSIMONIOUS

JOCK McTAVISH went to the Op Shop to buy a suitcase for his holiday. He found one at a reduced price. The manager asked if he wanted it wrapped. "Nae mon. Just put the brown paper and string inside."

\* \* \*

HE took all his money out of the bank for a holiday. After it rested in his pocket for a week he put it all back.

\* \* \*

WHEN the police put a price on his head he gave himself up.

\* \* \*

IF Jock and Sandy were alone in a bar together they would die of thirst.

THE first time Jock used the free air at the service station he blew out four tyres.

*     *     *

HE wouldn't shout if a shark bit him.

*     *     *

SHE said she would never go to a restaurant with Jock again. "He reads the menu from right to left," she said.

*     *     *

HER husband seldom bought her anything. He was a man of rare gifts.

*     *     *

HE took his kids to the beach and bought them an ice-cream, but they still squabbled and fought. They wanted one each.

... or, JOCK had promised to buy his mates a beer. Eventually he did, but they were still dissatisfied. They wanted one each.

*     *     *

JOCK was so mean that when he found a bottle of indigestion mixture, he ate a jar of pickles.

*     *     *

JOCK was down in the dumps and his office mate wondered why, because he left the pub the previous evening with a lovely blonde on his arm.

"What happened?"

Jock said he took the blonde to dinner, bought her chocolates and champagne and they went back to his flat for the night.

"Well why so gloomy?"

"I spent a fortune," said Jock, "and another bloke has just told me I could have got the same result with a couple of beers and a packet of potato chips."

*     *     *

NEXT night he hailed a cab to go home with his new girlfriend. She was so ravishingly beautiful he could hardly keep his eyes on the meter.

THE Salvation Army lass approached Jock and asked him for a dollar for the Lord.

"How old are ye?" said Jock.

"I'm nineteen," said the lass.

"Well, I'm 75 and I'll be seeing the Lord before you do, so I will slip him the dollar myself."

\* \* \*

HE had been mean and stingy all his life so when he finally arrived at the Pearly Gates St Peter asked for his report card. "I once gave a dollar to a widow who was turned out of her house, and I once gave two dollars to an orphan who had just lost his parents."

God overheard it and said to St Peter: "Give him his three dollars back and tell him to go to Hell."

\* \* \*

AN old farmer and his son had scratched out a living on their farm for 30 years. One day the son came home yelling for joy that he had won the $500,000 first prize in the lottery.

"Here Dad, here's your share," and he slapped a hundred dollar note on the table.

The old man looked at it a while. "When I was young," he said, "I never had time to smoke, drink or gamble because working this farm took all my time. In fact, I never had time to marry your Ma."

The young man considered this. "Well that's a nice state of affairs," he complained. "Of course you know what that makes me?"

"Yeah," said the old man, "and a bloody mean one at that."

\* \* \*

TWO Scots established a business and at the end of the financial year they tried to balance the books, but no matter how many times they went through the accounts and receipts they were constantly $23.50 short.

Finally Jock confronted his partner: "Tell me the truth Angus. Have you been keeping a woman?"

PADDY had two stingy mates, Jock and Isaac. So he was surprised when they reluctantly agreed to take him out for his birthday. At the end of the meal he waited with some anxiety to see which one offered to pay.

"I'll take care of the bill," piped up Jock when the waiter approached.

Paddy went home that night amazed at Jock's generosity, until he read the newspaper headline next morning: Jewish Ventriloquist Strangled by Crazed Scotsman.

\* \* \*

WE went round to a party at Jock's place where the water flowed like champagne.

## SWEARING

WHEN he boarded the country train he explained he was tired and asked the conductor if he could be woken at Junction Town.

"Don't worry if I swear a lot," said the passenger. "I am a notorious grump when I get woken up."

"No worries," said the conductor.

It was dark when the train stopped and the conductor finally gave the passenger a shake.

"What the hell's this?" roared the passenger realising he was at the terminus. "I told you to wake me at Junction Town you godforsaken son of a no-good bastard."

The conductor listened to the long string of abuse and finally muttered: "Yes, you can sure swear a lot. But not as much as the bloke we put off at Junction Town."

\* \* \*

YOUNG Basil had moved to town from the country and had settled in at the suburban primary school fairly well; except for his constant swearing. It was "bloody" this and "bloody" that until he was sent home with a note:

415

"If this boy won't stop swearing he will not be allowed to school anymore."

His father gave him a bloody hiding and sent him back next day with a note to say he wouldn't bloody well swear again.

The teacher was impressed and sent home another note. "Basil has been so good he can come to the school picnic on Saturday week."

When the big day came, little Basil set off for the picnic, with a caution and yet another note. "If he swears again, please send the little bugger straight home."

In less than an hour Basil was back, weeping his eyes out, and copped another hiding from his father for swearing.

"I didn't swear," he protested. "You sent me off on the wrong bloody Saturday. The bloody picnic is not until next bloody week!"

★　　★　　★

TWO young brothers were sent home from their country school with a note to say they had been suspended for the afternoon for swearing.

Their father gave them a hiding, a lecture and sent them to bed without dinner.

Next morning as they sat down for breakfast their father, in a more conciliatory mood, asked what they would like for breakfast.

The first one said: "I'll have some of those bloody cornflakes." He received an immediate thrashing from his father and was sent back to bed for the day.

The father then asked the second boy what he would like for breakfast.

"I don't know," he said. "But it won't be bloody cornflakes, that's for sure."

★　　★　　★

BECAUSE he had been heard swearing, young Billie had been put across his father's knee and given a few good whacks. "Now son," said his Dad, "tell me why I punished you."

The kid threw up his hands in despair. "That does it. First you belt shit out of me and now you don't know why you bloody-well did it!"

# T

## TACT

TACT is the ability to describe others as they see themselves.

* * *

A SALESMAN with a phenomenal record finally revealed his secret to the new sales recruits. He said he put it down to the first seven words he invariably uttered when a woman answered his knock on a door: "Miss, may I speak to your mother?"

* * *

THE patient told his psychiatrist, "I don't seem to be able to mix with people. I have no friends. When I talk to people they soon walk away. Do you think you can help me you money-grabbing parasite and incompetent shrink?"

* * *

"HERE is a photo of my new bride."
  "Gosh. She must be very wealthy."

## TAXATION

WHOEVER said you couldn't be wounded by a blank obviously hasn't received a taxation form.

* * *

A CLOUDFUL of clergymen arrived at the Pearly Gates

and were gathered around the reception desk booking in when suddenly a fanfare of trumpets signalled a late arrival and St Peter called for the clergy to stand aside.

The new arrival was the taxman and he was ushered straight in on the red carpet.

The clergy were amazed and demanded to know why the preferred treatment.

"Because that bloke," said St Peter, "has put the fear of God into more people than the lot of you put together."

★　　★　　★

THE new tax inspector was intrigued to find that for many years Mr Abraham Finklestein had consistently claimed deductions for substantial amounts to charity.

The inspector became downright suspicious when he found that these annual donations were being made to St Mary's Catholic Church, and that Mr Finklestein could produce hundreds of cancelled cheques going back for years, all made out to the church, and each endorsed by the priest.

The inspector decided to question Fr. O'Malley over Mr Finklestein's generosity.

"Generosity?" said the priest. "Yes I know Finklestein well, but he is hardly generous."

"But we have his cancelled cheques going back over years," said the tax man.

"Oh those," said the priest. "Indeed he helps us there. We take up a big collection each mass, and as the banks are closed on Sundays, Mr Finklestein will always give us a cheque for it to save us worrying about the cash over the weekend."

## TAXIS

"IT's not so much the work I enjoy," said the cabbie, "it's the people I run into."

THE pompous English colonel arrived in New York and hailed a cab. "Take me to Christ's Church," he said.

About ten minutes' later the cab stopped outside St Patrick's cathedral.

"That's not Christ's Church," protested the colonel.

"If He's in town He's in that one," said O'Flaherty.

* * *

THE surly businessman jumped into the cab.

"Where to?" said the cabbie.

"Mind your own business," he replied.

* * *

SHE was only a cab driver's daughter but you sure auto meter.

* * *

BUT he finally gave the job up. He didn't like people talking behind his back.

* * *

FRED took a cab to the drive-in. The movie cost him $120.

* * *

THERE were no serious injuries in an accident on the highway when a car collided with a taxi. The couple in the car escaped unhurt, but the 16 Scotsmen in the taxi were treated for shock, as they had paid for the trip in advance.

* * *

JOCK picked up a lovely young woman in the pub and hailed a cab to take her home. He was so infatuated with her he could hardly keep his eyes on the meter.

* * *

CHAP phoned the taxi company to complain that a cab he ordered had not arrived at the specific time.

"I told you when I made the booking that I had to be at the airport at a certain time," he complained.

"Don't worry, it will be there soon," said the girl. "Anyway, your plane is bound to be a few minutes late."

"You're damned right it will," complained the man. "I'm the pilot!"

* * *

THE passenger got a hell of a shock when the cab driver accelerated and raced through an intersection against the red lights. "Hey, go easy, where the heck did you get your licence?"

"Relax," said the cabbie. "My brother taught me to drive and he taught me how to run red lights."

The lights were red at the next intersection and to the passenger's horror he raced through again. It was not until he approached the fifth set of lights that they suddenly turned green and the cabbie nearly stood the taxi on end as it screeched to a stop.

"I don't understand, that's a green light," said the passenger.

"I know that, mate," said the cabbie looking both ways, "but my brother drives around this neighbourhood."

* * *

THE cabbie's careless driving was a worry to the expectant mother. "Be careful," she said, "I'm expecting my fifth child."

"And you're telling ME to be careful?" he asked.

* * *

IN a taxi on the way to the maternity hospital the 19-year-old wife complained she was in pain and terrified. Her 20-year-old husband put a comforting arm around her and asked: "Darling, are you sure you want to go through with this?"

* * *

HE lay under the cab tinkering with the motor and groping for spanners and tools when his attractive fare said: "Do you want a screwdriver?"

"Not now, Miss, but as soon as I fix this I'll be in it."

# TEACHERS
See EDUCATION, SCHOOLS

A STRAPPING young farm hand was sent to the station to pick up the new school teacher who turned out to be an attractive young woman.

On the way back to the farm she noticed a stallion mounting a mare. "How do they know when to do that?" she enquired.

The young man explained that it was a sense of smell.

In the very next paddock a bull was enjoying himself on a cow.

"Again, it is a sense of smell," explained the country boy, "just like that ram and ewe over there."

He unloaded her luggage at the farmhouse and turned to go. "See you later," he said.

"Thanks," she replied, "And do come over when your cold gets better."

# TEENAGERS

"MY son is going through one of those awkward stages, changing from a hooligan to a layabout."

\* \* \*

ADOLESENCE is that stage between infancy and adultery.

\* \* \*

TEENAGERS are very much alike in many disrespects.

\* \* \*

TEENAGE girls are between pigtails and cocktails.

\* \* \*

TEENAGE boys complain there is nothing to do and then stay out all night doing it.

\* \* \*

TEENAGERS express a burning desire to be different from anyone else, then dress exactly alike.

TEENAGERS think curbing their emotions means parking by the roadside.

*    *    *

WHEN he knocked on the door for his first date her father opened it and shouted back into the house, "Joanne, there's something here to see you."

*    *    *

MUM heard her daughter come home an hour ago, but she hadn't heard the new boyfriend leave, so she tiptoed down the stairs. She heard a giggle in the darkened lounge room. She switched on the light to find the couple in a passionate embrace on the couch.

"Well I never," she gasped.

"Oh, c'mon Mum, you must have," said the daughter.

# TENNIS

TENNIS was the trendy thing to do, so the Yuppie fronted the local sports store and asked to be kitted up. The proprietor sold him tennis shoes for $300 a pair, shorts for $200 a pair, a can of balls for $60 and shirts at $150 each.

"Oh, and I'll need a racquet," said the Yuppie.

So the proprietor sold him a half share in the store.

# TIME

TODAY is Tomorrow's Yesterday.

*    *    *

TIME is nature's way of preventing everything happening at once.

*    *    *

THINGS are getting so bad so quickly that the Good Old Days seem only a week old.

*    *    *

"WHEN I am with my girlfriend, time stands still."

"No wonder. She's got a face that would stop a clock."

DON'T give me a watch for Christmas. I've already got one. And I can assure you a man with one watch knows what time it is, while a man with two would never be sure.

★　　★　　★

MABEL told him: "Your father can stay longer in an hour than others can stay in a bloomin' fortnight."

## TOASTS

THE purpose of most public speaking is to propose a toast. While the speech is designed to put everyone at ease and remind those who started drinking early why they are present, the patter merely paves the way towards the toast. So always have a few up your sleeve.

Toasts are also a wonderful ploy for having another drink and most of the Irish examples listed here are the result of a memorable night in a Dublin pub called the Limerick Arms.

A starter to claim the attention of those present is to stand and pronounce in a loud voice: "Fornication." And when that stops the conversation, continue with "Fornication like this we need champagne for the toast..."

★　　★　　★

HERE'S to abstinence — provided it's in moderation.

★　　★　　★

MAY we all get to heaven half an hour before the devil knows we're dead.

★　　★　　★

MAY the skin of your bum never cover a drum.

★　　★　　★

MAY you live as long as you want, and may you never want as long as you live.

★　　★　　★

MAY you live a hundred years, and another month to repent.

MAY we never put our finger in another man's pie.

* * *

MAY you never have to eat your hat.

* * *

May the frost never afflict your spuds.

* * *

MAY the Blue Bird of Happiness crap down your chimney.

* * *

MAY we drink to the thirst which is yet to come.

* * *

MAY we all be alive this time, twelve months.

* * *

MAY you slide down the bannister of life, with nary a splinter.

* * *

MAY your luck be like the capital of Ireland, always Dublin!

* * *

MAY the fleas of a thousand camels infest the underpants of our enemies.

* * *

MAY their chooks turn into emus and kick down their dunny door.

* * *

HERE'S to the wowsers, whose abstinence gives us all the more to drink.

* * *

THERE'S many a toast, if I could think of it
  Damned if I can, so let's drink to it.

* * *

TO our wives and sweethearts. May they never meet.

* * *

LET'S drink to the soup. May it be seen and not heard.

* * *

HERE'S to the girl who lives on the hill
  She won't be in it, but her sister will
  Here's to her sister, then.

425

HERE'S to the happiest days of my life,
    Spent in the arms of another man's wife,
    My mother's.

*   *   *

HERE'S to your eyes, and mine
    Here's to your lips, and mine
    The former have met
    The latter not yet
    So here's to that moment, sublime.

*   *   *

HERE'S to us
    May we live a long life
    And here's mud in your eye
    While I wink at your wife.

*   *   *

HERE'S to Miss Prim
    For her life held no terrors
    Born a virgin, died a virgin
    No hits, no runs, no errors.

*   *   *

TO the office bore: May he give us a few brilliant flashes
of silence.

*   *   *

REMEMBER the poor. It costs nothing.

*   *   *

MUSICIANS' TOAST: May your organ never quit while
you are half way through your favourite piece.

*   *   *

I DRINK to your health when I'm with you
    I drink to your health when alone
    I drink to your health so often
    I'm becoming concerned at my own.

*   *   *

MAY you live as long as you want to
    And want to, as long as you live.

MAY we kiss who we please
  And please who we kiss.

*     *     *

IF I'm asleep when you want me. Wake me.
  And if I don't want to. Make me.

*     *     *

HERE'S to the bloke down the lane
  He courted a girl, all in vain
  She swore when he kissed her
  So he slept with her sister
  Again and again and again.

*     *     *

AND one to the author: May he live to be as old as his jokes.

*     *     *

A SURPRISE toast at a wedding goes this way:
  "And finally, may the happy couple lie, steal and cheat. (Pause, then explain). May they lie in each other's arms, may they steal away for a blissful honeymoon, adn may they cheat time to live as long as possible."

## TOUGH TIMES

IT'S tough when you call Suicide Prevention and they put you on hold.

*     *     *

IT'S tough luck when your car horn accidentally blasts off and remains jammed, while you're driving behind a group of Hell's Angels.

*     *     *

TIMES are so tough the local council has created a job for a painter. Signs that read "Keep off the grass" are to be re-painted, "Don't eat the grass."

*     *     *

MISTER, will you give me a dollar for my sick wife?
  Sorry old man, but I've already got one.

427

COULD you give a poor bloke a bite?

Sorry my man, I don't bite myself, but I'll call the dog.

* * *

HERE'S fifty cents then. How did you get so destitute in the first place?

Like you sir, giving away vast sums to the poor and needy.

* * *

WILL you give me a dollar for a sandwich?

Let's see the sandwich.

* * *

THE cook came to the door of the country pub: "Aren't you the same bloke I gave a pie to yesterday?"

"Yes, but I hardly expected to find the same cook here today."

* * *

THINGS were so tough in our family my parents couldn't afford to have children. Our neighbours had to have me.

We were so poor I didn't have my 21st birthday until I was 35.

* * *

THINGS get so bad so fast in these times, it seems the good old days were only a week ago.

## TRADESMEN

MANY electricians make light work.

* * *

JAKE signed on as a builder's labourer and set to work with a pick and shovel. After three days' toil he fronted the boss and asked for his week's wages in advance.

"Hang on, you've only done half a week's work," protested the boss.

But Jake had the answer. "I trusted you for the first half, now you trust me for the other!"

AFTER announcing his retirement, it was the postman's last day in the neighbourhood and most householders were giving him little presents. But he got the shock of his life when Mrs Smith took him upstairs, stripped off and took him to bed.

Afterwards she made him a cup of coffee, a hot breakfast and then pressed a dollar into his hand. The postman couldn't believe it and upon leaving asked for an explanation.

"It was my husband's idea, although he was a little pre-occupied at the time," she said. "I told him you were retiring and I insisted we do something for you. He said, 'Oh, stuff the postman. Give him a dollar and a cup of coffee'."

"The breakfast was my own idea," she said.

\* \* \*

AN Irish handyman went down to the hardware store for some bolts.

"How long do you want them?" enquired the salesman.

"Well, to tell you the truth," replied the handyman, "I was sort of hoping to keep them."

\* \* \*

THE plumber finally arrived. "How have you managed?"

"Not too badly," said the housewife, "while we were waiting for you I've taught the kids how to swim."

\* \* \*

TWO plumbers were working in the street trying to unblock a drain when an angry gent came out of the house opposite.

"Go easy with that long wire you're poking about with, boys," he said. "You've had my missus leap off the toilet seat three times!"

\* \* \*

IT was many years ago since the embarrassing day that a young woman, with a baby in her arms, entered his butcher shop and confronted him with the news that the baby was his, and what was he going to do about it?

Finally, he capitulated. He promised to provide her with free meat until the boy was 16. She agreed.

He had been ticking the years off on his calendar and one day, the teenager who had been collecting the meat each week, came in to the shop and said: "I'll be sixteen tomorrow."

"I know," said the butcher with a smile, "I've been counting too, and tell your mother when you take this parcel of meat home that it is the last free meat she will get, and watch the expression on her face."

When the boy arrived home he told his mother. The woman nodded and said, "Son, go back to the butcher and tell him I have also had free bread, free milk and free groceries for the past 16 years and watch the expression on his face!"

★　　★　　★

THE apprentice draftsman had just drawn his first construction plan and laid it out before his boss. "I think that's near enough," he said.

"Near enough is not good enough," said the boss pushing the plans away. "It's got to be perfect. Do it again."

The apprentice knuckled down at the drawing board for another two hours and finally presented them to the boss again.

"It's perfect now," said the lad.

"Well that's near enough," said the boss.

★　　★　　★

IT was the day Fred was released from prison and they handed back his suit. He put his hand in the pocket and found a ticket for his shoe repairs. Although he thought the shoes would be out of style he decided on a whim to pick them up.

"It's been ten years and you may not remember them," said Fred producing the ticket, "but they were brown brogues to be half-soled and heeled."

"No worries, I remember them," said the shoe-repairer. "They will be ready on Tuesday."

\* \* \*

THE lawyer's brand-new television set was on the blink so he called for the maintenance man who duly arrived, pulled the set away from the wall replaced a fuse and put his hand out for $72.

"What," said the lawyer. "That's outrageous. $72 for five minutes' work? I am a lawyer and I don't get that much money."

"Neither did I when I was a lawyer," said the maintenance man.

\* \* \*

THEY called the maintenance man when the washing machine broke down. He duly arrived, pulled the machine out from the wall, studied it a few minutes, then got a large hammer and gave it a mighty whack.

It started straight away.

He then handed the couple a bill for $50.

"Fifty bucks?" said the husband. "All you did was whack it with a hammer."

"It is all itemised on the bill," said the tradesman. "Hitting the machine with the hammer is $2. Knowing exactly where to hit it is $48."

\* \* \*

WHEN the doctor rang the plumber to complain that the toilet cistern had developed a fault the weary plumber reminded him that it was 2.30 in the morning.

"So what," said the doctor. "I get called out at all hours. I have a problem which needs fixing, so what does the time of day or night have to do with it?"

Ten minutes later the plumber arrived on the doorstep and was shown to the bathroom. He lifted the lid of the toilet, threw in two aspirins and flushed it.

"If it hasn't improved by the morning ring me again," he said.

# TRAINS

A GROUP of people on the train were discussing why the railway was losing money.

"Hopeless management," said one old gent.

"Too many lazy employees," said the woman by the window.

"It's the union," said another.

A fourth was about to give his opinion as the train stopped at a station and an inspector got on board, and they all jumped out.

\* \* \*

OLD Fred and his son were down from the bush and enjoying a ride on a train when a priest hobbled into their compartment on crutches.

"Slipped in the bathtub," he explained.

When the priest got out at the next station the son said: "What's a bathtub, Dad?"

"Dunno," said Fred, "I'm not a Catholic."

\* \* \*

THE middle-aged couple had just settled in the compartment for a long rail journey. As the train pulled out of the station he asked: "Comfortable dear, is the seat soft?"

"Yes," she said.

"Not feeling any draught?"

"No."

"No vibrations or shaking?"

"No."

"Right then," he said, "let's change places."

\* \* \*

EACH time the train stopped at a station the little old man would get up, walk to the door, look out and say "Oh Damn!"

Every station it was the same until the bloke opposite, exasperated by this behaviour asked him what was wrong.

"I'm on the wrong damned train!"

FOUR people were in the same compartment on a long train journey; a young woman, a priest, a businessman and a drunk.

All had been quiet for an hour or two until the young woman suddenly began to sob. The priest bent over to console her. "Tell me why you are crying," he said.

The girl sniffed and said: "I have just learnt that I am illegitimate."

The priest replied, "That's no sin. As a matter of fact I am illegitimate myself."

Then the businessman spoke up. "Excuse me, I couldn't help overhearing, but I must tell you that I am a self-made man. I own several businesses, in fact I am a millionaire, yet I am illegitimate too."

The drunk took out a cigarette and asked: "Any of you bastards got a light?"

\*     \*     \*

IT was the new Very Fast Train and halfway through the journey there was a violent vibration. "What was the trouble back there?" asked a passenger, "I thought this was supposed to be a smooth ride."

"Sorry sir," said the porter. "We ran over a politician."

"Goodness. What was he doing on the tracks?"

"Oh, he wasn't on the tracks Sir, but we got him."

# TRAVEL

SOME people travel for a change and a rest; only to find the hotel takes the change and the taxi takes the rest.

\*     \*     \*

TRAVEL advice: Don't put all your bags in one exit.

\*     \*     \*

"MR Wong! Mr Wong!" cried the distraught tourist, "the monkeys have run away with my travellers' cheques!"

"Ah, what sort were they?"

"Brown ones with red backsides!"

THE best time to visit Paris is between your 18th and 25th birthdays.

\* \* \*

TRAVEL advice: Take twice the money you've got and unpack half the clothes.

\* \* \*

I'VE just come back from a pleasure trip. I drove the in-laws to the airport.

\* \* \*

"CARRY your bag, sir?"
"No, let her walk."

\* \* \*

THE woman was booking a holiday for her husband. The travel agent asked her if she had any destination in mind.
"Anywhere in the Bermuda Triangle," she said.

\* \* \*

SEASONED couple at the airlines reservations counter: "Two tickets to wherever our luggage is going."

\* \* \*

YOUNG bloke went to the doctor for a check-up. "You need to relax more," said the doc. "You need to get away from it all for a while. Could you go abroad?"
"Sure could," replied the patient. "What's she like?"

\* \* \*

FIRST snob: "I understand you are not going to Paris this year?"
Second snob: "No, it is London we are not going to this year."

\* \* \*

EUROPE is so wonderful. If you ever go there, don't miss it.

\* \* \*

REMEMBER, it is easier to find a travelling companion than to get rid of one.

\* \* \*

I MET my wife in Acapulco. She was looking for a vacation and I was the last resort.

A RESORT is where the locals live off your holiday until next summer.

* * *

I WENT to a travel agent and asked where I could go for $50. He told me.

* * *

"WHEN you sailed around Italy, did you touch Florence?"

"No, her husband never let her out of his sight."

* * *

MURPHY opened a pub on the moon. But it had no atmosphere.

* * *

JOCK thought Niagara Falls was a terrible waste of water.

* * *

SHE was on the phone from the Riviera. "The holiday is wonderful darling, I feel like a new woman."

"So do I. Stay there another week."

* * *

A YOUNG Aussie was enjoying his first night in Rome drinking cappuccino at a pavement cafe when a pretty girl sat beside him.

"Hello," he said. "Do you understand English?"

"Only a little," she answered.

"How much?" he asked.

"Fifty dollars," she replied.

* * *

AN older Aussie, a wealthy man who had made his money in the furniture business, was also in Rome, and alone at the same cappuccino bar, when a young woman smiled at him, and naturally he returned the smile.

She was soon by his side. He said hullo, but she shrugged her shoulders to indicate she couldn't speak English.

He took a pen and paper from his pocket and drew a glass of wine with a question mark. She nodded and they had a drink. He drew a taxi with a question mark. She nodded and they soon had a tour of the city by cab.

He then drew a table for two which had the desired result, and after a splendid meal with two bottles of vino she reached for the pen and paper. She drew a four poster bed with a question mark.

"How perceptive of you," laughed our hero. "I am astounded. How did you know I was in the furniture business?"

\*　　\*　　\*

SHE insisted on taking innumerable outfits with her, and they arrived at the airport loaded with luggage.

"I wish," said the husband thoughtfully, "we had bought the piano."

"No need to be sarcastic," said the wife, "it's not a bit funny."

"I'm not trying to be funny," he said, "I've left the tickets on it."

\*　　\*　　\*

THE American was bumping about in the rear of the bus. "How far is it to Alice Springs then?" he asked.

"About a thousand kilometres as the crow flies."

"Hell. Why do we have to follow a dog-gone crow?"

\*　　\*　　\*

FRED says travel broadens the mind. A trip to the Holy Land taught him a lot about the bible. "They took me to see Dan and Beersheeba, and I found they were two villages," he said.

"I always thought they were man and wife, like Sodom and Gomorrah."

\*　　\*　　\*

THE coach was travelling through Dublin when the guide announced: "We are now passing the biggest pub in Ireland."

An Aussie voice at the back of the bus said: "Why?"

HE had a bent for pornographic literature, and he was in a taxi leaving Hongkong for the airport when the cab stopped outside a bookshop. There it was, a large volume in the window titled "How to Woo."

He told the cab driver to wait, dashed into the shop, asked the attendant to wrap it in brown paper, and bought it.

Not until he was comfortably seated on the flight home did he tentatively open the wrapper and learn that he had bought volume two of the Hongkong phone directory.

*　　*　　*

YOUNG chap boarded the Ansett flight at Cairns and the hostess noticed a newspaper parcel under his arm. "Mudcrabs," he explained. "I'm taking them back to Melbourne for a gourmet meal tonight."

"Then in that case they would be best placed in the fridge," said the hostess, stowing them away appropriately.

The flight landed on time and as the aircraft taxied across the tarmac the passengers were welcomed to Melbourne, told to remain seated until the aircraft came to a halt ... "And would the gentleman who gave me the crabs in Cairns please identify himself?"

*　　*　　*

PADDY, the left-handed barman had been pulling beers for 25 years in the same pub. "Why don't you travel and broaden your mind?" he was told repeatedly.

Finally he took the advice and booked a week's holiday in the Canary Islands.

When he returned he was a changed and knowledgeable man. "Well what did you learn?" asked the regulars. "I can tell you this," he said as they all leaned forward for his pearl of wisdom.

"There are no canaries in the Canary Islands."

A year passed and Paddy once more took his annual

leave abroad. This time his travel agent suggested the Virgin Islands.

"Well what did you learn this time, Paddy?" asked the regulars when he returned from his second world odyssey.

"I can tell you this," he said as they all leaned forward. "There are no canaries on the Virgin Islands, either!"

★　★　★

DEAR diary. This is day one of my first holiday on a cruise ship.

Day two. While the cruise is nice there is an awful lot of men, including the stewards, making passes at me.

Day three. I have been invited to sit at the captain's table.

Day four. The captain made an improper suggestion last night. I refused.

Day five. The captain says that unless I agree, he will sink the ship.

Day six. Last night I saved the lives of 965 people.

★　★　★

"THEY say that London is the foggiest place in the world, but I have been to a town where the fog was much thicker."

"Where was that?"

"Don't know. It was too foggy to tell."

★　★　★

HE is a mental traveller. His mind wanders.

★　★　★

SIAMESE twins were having a terrible argument about where to go for their next holidays. "We're going to America," stamped the one on the left. "I want to drive for a change!"

★　★　★

"I WOULDN'T go to America if you paid me," said Fred.

"Why?"

"Cos they drive on the wrong side of the road."

438

"What's wrong with that?"

"I tried it the other night," said Fred. "It's bloody dangerous!"

* * *

TOURIST: "Have you lived here all your life?"

Local: "Not yet!"

* * *

A HUNGRY back-packer in a youth hostel complained about the sandwich he just bought.

"I haven't found any ham in this sandwich yet," he said.

Manager: "Try another bite."

The back-packer did so. "No, nothing at all."

Manager: "Heck, you must have passed it."

* * *

TWO professional hitch-hikers travelling through Europe were sitting by the roadside. One was poking his tongue out at passing cars. He even gave some motorists the raspberry.

"You will never get a lift doing that," said his mate.

"I know that. Who cares. I'm on my lunch break!"

* * *

THE lad from Australia got quite a buzz walking down Fifth Avenue in the heart of the Big Apple. He was looking up at the skyscrapers when he felt somebody bump him slightly.

With a jolt he remembered he was in New York and reached for his wallet. It was gone. And the youth who bumped him was hurrying down the street.

Our lad sprinted after him, grabbed him by the shirt-front and backed him against the wall. "Okay pal. You've met your match. You're dealing with an Aussie. Hand over that wallet."

The youth produced the wallet, ducked out of the grip and ran. It wasn't until our Ocker got back to his room that he saw his wallet where he had left it beside the bed.

SOME of the famous duty-free airports of the world are Schipol at Amsterdam, Singapore and Dubai. But for the most unusual items, try Shannon Airport. Here you can get water-proof tea bags, one-piece jigsaw puzzles, inflatable dartboards for campers and solar powered torches.

\* \* \*

A TRAVEL agent looked up from his desk to notice an old lady and an old gent peering in the shop window at the posters showing the glamorous destinations around the world. The agent had had a good week and the dejected couple looking in the window gave him a rare feeling of generosity.

He called them in. "I know that on your pension you could never hope to have a holiday, so I am sending you off to a fabulous resort at my expense, and I won't take no for an answer," he said.

He took them inside and asked his secretary to write two flight tickets and book a room in a five-star hotel. They gladly accepted and were off.

About a month later the little old lady came in to his shop. "And how did you like the holiday?" he asked eagerly.

"The flight was exciting and the room was lovely," she said. "I've come to thank you. But one thing has puzzled me. Who was that old bloke I had to share the room with?"

\* \* \*

BACHELOR Joe had led a quiet life. But for years he had been dreaming of a cruise in the South Pacific and when he received his superannuation he had enough money to make his dream come true.

When he boarded the ship, he had no friends to wave him goodbye so he went below to look for his cabin. He went down to C-deck, then down to D-deck, then down once more where he was suddenly grabbed by two burly seamen, rushed down more flights of stairs, stripped of his clothes on the way and finally thrown into a large space down in the bilge of the ship.

In darkness and confusion he was shoved onto a long bench and felt the chains go around his ankles and a rough oar was thrust into his hands.

In the dim light he could see he was one of many.

Suddenly, he heard a drum beat and could just make out a large muscular negroid man beating a drum to an ever increasing rhythm. With the crack of a whip a raucous voice yelled "Row you Scum, Row."

Shackled to the oar Joe could do nothing else. In fact, to the monotonous beat of the drum Joe did nothing else for the next two weeks until they arrived somewhere and the drummer stopped the tedious beat. The reprieve lasted only two days. The drum started again and under the crack of the whip they began to row back home.

As the ship tied up Joe slumped on his oar and turned to the emaciated figure beside him which had been his companion for the voyage.

Joe addressed him for the first time. "Excuse me," he said. "I've never been on a cruise before. How much should I tip the drummer?"

"Don't know really," said his gaunt companion. "I gave him $20 when I did this cruise last year!"

\* \* \*

KIWI tourist driving around the UK got himself lost along the south-east coast of England. He saw a local and said: "Excuse me, can you tell me where I am?"

The local said: "Great Yarmouth."

"Same to you, fish-face," was the Kiwi's retort.

\* \* \*

AN American tourist on a trip to Ayers Rock suddenly yelled "Stop the Bus" and scrambled to the front to get off. He had spotted an aboriginal with his ear to the ground on a track which turned off the main road. "He must be one of your famous black-trackers you have out here," he said as he ran back to the aboriginal.

"Can you tell me about the last people to pass this way?" enquired the Yank.

"Yeah," answered the aboriginal, and pointing to the wheel tracks he said "It was a Ford utility."

This didn't impress the Yank much. "Anything else?" he said.

"Yeah. There was ten people in it. Three in the front and seven in the back."

Now the yank was impressed. "Anything else?"

"Yeah. The three in the front were blokes with four women and three kids in the back and the truck has yellow wheel caps."

This amazed the Yank. "And you can tell all that just by putting your ear to the ground?"

"Not really," said the aboriginal. "I just fell off the plurry thing!"

\* \* \*

VISITOR to the city could not decide whether to spend his last day at the football finals or at the massage parlours in the 'Red Light' district. He finally opted for the football.

"Sorry sir," said the attendant, "the only seats left are the higher priced ones at $30."

"What?" said the visitor. "I could have gone to a brothel and got a woman for that."

"Ah, yes," said the attendant, "but you wouldn't have had 100 minutes of action-packed play and a brass band at interval would you?"

\* \* \*

GUIDE on a conducted tour of Rome: "And this ancient monument dates back over 2000 years."

"Don't be ridiculous," said one little old lady. "It's only 1990 now."

\* \* \*

AT the airport Trevor the Traveller abused the luggage handler. His case comes up next week.

HE told the travel agent: "I want a round world ticket."

"One way?" she asked.

*  *  *

AN Australian and Irishman were waiting in the travel agent's office.

"How much to South America?" asked the Australian.

"That will cost you $1000," said the travel agent.

"But I only have $500," said the Aussie.

The agent thought for a moment.

"That's okay, just go into the next office and you will be attended to."

The Irishman said he also wanted to go to South America, and observing what happened said he also only had $500.

"Could I have the same deal?"

"Okay," said the agent. "Step inside the next office."

Paddy goes through the door and is immediately hit on the head with a club. He wakes up chained to an oar beside the Aussie and a hundred others rowing to the beat of the drum master.

"I wonder if they will fly us home?" mutters the Irishman.

"They didn't last year," replied the Australian.

# U

## UNIONS

HALF a loaf is better than no tea-break at all.

* * *

THE politicians were host to a United States business delegation and at the height of the dinner one of the Americans at the head table asked the waiter for some more butter.

"Sorry, just one pat of butter per person," said the waiter.

The chamber president was embarrassed to overhear this and called the waiter aside.

"Do you know who that man is?" he said angrily. "He is in charge of the American delegation."

"And do you know who I am?" said the waiter. "I am in charge of the butter."

* * *

WHEN Harry Bloggs arrived at the building site he was told "no ticket, no start." But Harry said it was against his principles to join the union.

They argued with him, the union organiser was called, even the boss who didn't want trouble on the site tried to cajole him to join the union. Harry wouldn't have it.

He was working on the scaffolding on the 52nd level, high over the street, when the man from the union arrived.

"I will only tell you once, Harry," he said. "If you don't join the union I will pick up that piece of timber, wrap it around your neck and throw you right off this platform onto the tram tracks below."

Later, when they asked Harry why he joined, he said, "I had never had it explained so succinctly before."

*　*　*

THE waterside workers were having a break on the wharf when a leading hand said to his boss, "Hey, that new bloke you hired this morning; he's not a spy is he?"

"No, I think he checked out okay, why?"

"Well, he just stubbed his toe on a crate of pig-iron and said, 'Oh, the perversity of inanimate objects!' "

*　*　*

A MOTORIST had been picked up on a traffic infringement and had given his name as Fred Shagbreak and his place of employment. When the cop arrived to deliver the brief he asked the girl at the enquiry desk: "Have you got a Shagbreak here?"

She replied: "You must be joking, the union has battled for two years just to get a coffee break."

*　*　*

SHOP-STEWARD: "From now on all wages are doubled, holidays extended to six months and we shall only work on Fridays."

From the back of the hall: "What, every bloody Friday?"

*　*　*

MANAGER to boss: "The workers are demanding shorter hours."

"Right, we'll cut their lunch hour to 30 minutes!"

*　*　*

THE unionist on holiday sent a postcard home: Having a lovely time-and-a-half.

# V

## VETS
See DOGS

THE German tourist dived into the river, dragged the apparently drowned dog ashore and revived it.

"Are you a vet?" asked an impressed bystander.

"Ya, I'm bloody soaking," he replied.

\* \* \*

HE entered the vet's clinic with a cat under his arm. "It's been as sick as a dog," he said.

\* \* \*

THE vet was in the middle of a tricky operation on a dog when the phone rang.

"How long should I leave a rooster in with a hen?" enquired the voice at the other end.

"Just a minute," said the busy vet.

"Thank you," said the caller, and hung up.

\* \* \*

THE elderly spinster told the vet her dog had become so old it had forgotten its house training. "I'm sorry," said the vet, "but the only thing I can suggest, is the lethal chamber."

"Yes, but will the old fleabag use it," she said.

\* \* \*

FRED the farmer told the vet that he had just purchased a very expensive prize stud bull, but it wasn't the slightest bit interested in the cows. "I've done my dough," he moaned.

The vet said it wasn't a problem and gave him some tablets to include in the bull's feed. Next day the bull began performing with great passion and stamina.

Fred was telling his neighbour about the potency of the tablets. "Flamin' marvellous," he said. "What's more, they don't taste too bad either."

\* \* \*

(R) TWO women were sitting in the waiting room with their dogs, one a fox terrier, the other a Great Dane. The foxie's owner said she was there because her pooch had a shocking habit of humping anything that went past, even visitor's legs.

"I know," said the other woman. She said her Great Dane had the same embarrassing habit.

"So you are here to have him de-sexed too?"

"No," she replied, "I'm getting his toenails cut."

## WAITERS
See RESTAURANTS

"AND what'll you have?"
  Said the waiter, idly picking his nose.
  "I'll have two boiled eggs, ya mongrel,
  "You can't put your fingers in those!"

\*    \*    \*

WAITER: "How did you find the meat Sir?"
  "I just lifted a potato chip and there it was."

\*    \*    \*

"WAITER! What is this fly doing in my soup?"
  Waiter studies it for a while.
  "Backstroke, I believe Sir."

\*    \*    \*

"WAITER! Bring me a smaller cheque!"

\*    \*    \*

"WAITER, what's the difference between the steak and
the hamburger?"
  "About one day, sir."

\*    \*    \*

"WAITER! This food is terrible. I demand to see the
manager."
  "Sorry, sir. He is out to lunch."

"WAITER! There's a fly in my soup."

"Well, don't complain to me, mate, it's the chef that was once a tailor!"

* * *

"WAITER, what's with this chicken soup?"

"I dunno, what's with the chicken soup?"

"It tastes funny."

"Well, start laughing!"

* * *

"WAITER! Your thumb is on my steak."

"Well, you don't want it to drop on the floor again, do you?"

* * *

"WAITER, this plate is wet."

"That's your soup sir."

* * *

"WAITER, why does this chicken have one leg missing?"

"It was in a fight."

"Well take it away and bring me the winner."

* * *

"WAITER, what's the special on the menu today?"

"I'll call the chef."

"I don't want him. I'm not a cannibal."

* * *

"WAITER, this soup isn't fit for a pig."

"I will take it back sir and bring you some that is."

* * *

"WAITER, what's the best dish in the place?"

"That blonde sitting at table three."

* * *

"WAITER, can I have a salad sandwich without cucumbers?"

"Sorry, we are out of cucumbers. Can you take it without tomatoes?"

* * *

"WAITER, what time is it?"

"Sorry sir, this is not my table."

"WAITER, what's the soup du jour?"

"It's off. We ran out if it yesterday."

* * *

"WAITER, I would like a stew that will give me indigestion immediately, instead of three o'clock in the morning."

* * *

"WAITER, is there lots of juice in this grapefruit?"

"More than meets the eye, sir."

* * *

THE waiter approached the diner. "Why are you eating those olives on a string, sir?"

"Because I may not like them."

* * *

"YOU are not eating your fish," said the waiter, "what's wrong with it?"

"Long time no sea," said the diner.

* * *

"WAITER, are you sure this lobster is fresh?"

"Yes Sir, it walked here from the beach this morning."

The customer gave it another sniff. "Well I think it must have trodden in something on the way!"

* * *

IF you think the service is bad, wait until you taste the food.

* * *

ENGRAVED on the Maitre d's tombstone: "Bye and by, God caught his eye."

* * *

ON his first date with her he decided to impress her. He took her to a posh restaurant and ordered the whole meal in French.

Even the waiter was surprised. It was a Chinese restaurant.

* * *

THE irate diner had complained to the waitress about the unsatisfactory pastries. She in turn got the manager.

"I don't see why you should complain about our pastrycook," said the manager, "she has been making pastry since before you were born."

"As maybe," said the diner, "but why wait until now to sell them?"

*　　*　　*

THE bachelor finished his meal and placed his tip on the table as he finished his coffee. The waitress took one look at the three single cents and said. "Thank you for your generosity. You can always tell the character of a diner by the way he tips."

"Oh really," he said, "and what does that tell you about me?"

"Well you put the three cents in a row," said the waitress. "That tells me you are tidy for starters. The first cent tells me you are frugal. The second cent tells me you are a bachelor."

"That's true," he said, "but what does the third cent tell you?"

"That tells me your father was a bachelor too."

*　　*　　*

THE waiter brought the cheque and the diner studied it, then sorted through his money. "By golly," he said, "I have exactly that amount, but I'm afraid I haven't got enough for a tip."

"Let me add up that bill again, sir," said the waiter.

*　　*　　*

THE two women from the blue-rinse set ordered their meal. "And we will have two glasses of wine," said one. "And make sure I get a clean glass. The one you gave me last week was filthy."

After a while the waiter brought the food and wine, "And which of you ordered the clean glass?" he said.

CUSTOMER in a French restaurant. "Waiter, do you have frogs legs?"

"Oui monsieur."

"Then hop across the road and get me a packet of cigarettes."

*　　*　　*

"WILL you have pie sir?"

"Is it customary?"

"No, it's apple."

*　　*　　*

MOISHE settled down in his favourite kosher restaurant. "Oi waiter, do you have matzo balls?"

"No," he said, "I always walk like this!"

*　　*　　*

"WHAT do you think of that brandy, sir?" said the waiter showing him the bottle. "It's 1856."

"What? Just for one bottle?"

*　　*　　*

WHEN he ordered a plate of oysters he noticed that the waitress was quite pretty. When she delivered the meal he said: "How about a smile and a few kind words, darling?"

The girl obliged with a beaming smile and turned to walk away.

"Hang on," he said, "I've got the oysters and the smile, but where's the few kind words?"

She bent down, put her lips close to his ear and whispered: "Don't eat the oysters."

## WARDROBES
See INFIDELITY

HE was in bed with a married woman when he heard the back door slam. "Hell. It's my husband," she cried. "Quick, hide in that wardrobe." He gathered up his clothes and dived from the bed to the wardrobe in a flash. After a few moments another voice in the wardrobe said "It's dark as a dog's belly in here isn't it?"

The man, shivering in the nude, was shocked. "Who is it?" he whispered. It was a little boy's voice and it said: "I know who you are and it will cost you. Give me $50 or I will yell for my Dad."

He was in no position to argue, he grudgingly paid up, and when the crisis was over made a quick exit from the bedroom window. Next day the little boy and his mother were down town and he said he was going to buy a brand new skateboad. "What with?" asked his mother.

"I've got $50" said the boy.

"Where did you get that kind of money," said his mother, but the lad refused to tell. "You must have done something wrong," she persisted and after slapping him about the ears dragged him across the street to the church.

"Confession is the thing for you my lad. If you won't tell me, then you will have to tell the parish priest," and she shoved him into the confessional box and shut the door.

"Gawd. It's dark as a dog's belly in here," said the boy.

"Now don't you start that again," said the priest.

\*     \*     \*

HUSBAND came home unexpectedly and found his wife in bed. But when he went to hang his suit in the wardrobe he was surprised to see a man in there, busily snatching at things in the air.

"What the heck are you doing?" asked the husband.

"I am a moth catcher," said the stranger, still snatching at imaginary insects as if they were flying around his head.

"Then why are you doing it in the nude?" asked the suspicious husband.

With that, the moth catcher looked down and noticed

his absence of clothes. "Crikey, they're worse than I thought," he said.

(Another explanation for the man in the wardrobe comes from the husband's wife: "Oh, he's just a nudist who came in to use the phone.")

★   ★   ★

HE arrived home from work earlier than usual and found his wife in bed. There was a long whisp of smoke coming from a cigar in the ashtray on the bedside table.

"Where did that cigar come from?" he roared.

A timid male voice from the wardrobe said, "Cuba."

★   ★   ★

PADDY fell into a terrible state of remorse when he discovered his wife's lover in the wardrobe. They had a frightful argument, then he reached in a drawer and pulled out a gun. He cocked the trigger and held it to his head.

"For God's sake, Paddy, put that gun down," cried Teresa.

"Shut yer mouth and say your prayers woman. You two are next," said Paddy.

★   ★   ★

IN the long queue waiting at the Pearly Gates were three men, all from the same town. "How come?" asked St Peter.

The first said he had suspicions his wife was having an affair so he left for the office as usual, but doubled back to their penthouse apartment in a bid to catch her. He rushed into the bedroom, sure enough, she had gone back to bed, but a search of the wardrobe revealed no trace of her lover.

But when he looked out of the kitchen window he saw a bloke putting his clothes on behind a bush in the garden. He got so angry he picked up the refrigerator with superhuman strength and hurled it down at him. "The strain gave me a heart attack and that's why I am here," he told St Peter.

454

The second man said: "That's funny, I am a landscape gardener and I was just getting changed for work, putting my overalls on, when I was hit with a fridge. That's why I'm here."

"That's funny," said the third man. "I was hiding in this fridge …!"

* * *

PADDY O'Flaherty came home early one Friday afternoon and found his wife lying naked on the bed and crying.

"Whatever is the matter?" asked Paddy.

"We're invited to a wedding tomorrow," sobbed Teresa, "and I have nothing to wear."

"That's ridiculous," said Paddy. Going over to the wardrobe he said, "Look in here. Here's a red dress, a green dress, a pink dress… Hello Father, a yellow dress…"

## WEATHER

IT was so cold last week that the local flasher was spotted describing himself to a group of women.

* * *

IT was so cold on the Antarctic Expedition that when he returned she broke it off.

* * *

IT was as cold as a barmaid's heart.

* * *

IT was so dry the frogs were taking swimming lessons.

* * *

IT was so dry the Council closed two lanes of the municipal swimming pool.

* * *

AFTER he answered the phone yet again he said to his saucy young wife. "That's funny. We must have a number similar to the Weather Bureau. That's the third bloke to ring and ask if the coast was clear."

SITTING on the pub's verandah one farmer looked at the threatening sky and said: "D'yer think it'll rain?"

"I hope so," said the other. "Not for myself, mind you, but for the sake of my two sons. They haven't seen rain."

\* \* \*

THE farmer had a rope hanging from a dead tree at his back door.

"What's it for?" asked a visitor.

"It's my weather guide," the old farmer replied. "If its swinging back and forth, its windy, and if its wet, its been raining."

\* \* \*

IT rained cats and dogs. Poodles everywhere.

\* \* \*

THE wind blew so hard...

it blew three dogs off their chains... a chook facing east laid the same egg three times...

it blew the pricks off a barbed wire fence.

\* \* \*

"HOW did you find the weather on your holiday?"

"I just opened the door and there is was, everywhere."

\* \* \*

"THEY say London is the foggiest place in the world, but I have been to a place where the fog was much thicker."

"Where was that?"

"Don't know. It was too foggy to tell."

\* \* \*

UNCLE Fred worked in the Weather Bureau for years, but when he was promoted to the main office he only lasted a month. The weather didn't agree with him.

\* \* \*

THE BBC announcer said: Today it will be muggy, followed by Tuggy, Weggy, Thurggy and Fruggy.

\* \* \*

HE went to Mexico where the weather was more predictable: Chili today, hot-tamale.

# WEDDINGS
See MARRIAGE, MARRIEDS, NEWLY-WEDS

HAPPY is the bride that the sun of a tycoon takes a shine to today.

\* \* \*

THERE is so much permissiveness in the world today that the only way to stop having sex is to get married.

\* \* \*

THE relative from out of town arrived late. "Who gave the bride away?" he asked.
"Any one of us could, but we all agreed to keep our mouths shut."

\* \* \*

SHE had turned 30 and had been difficult to unload, so when her father finally gave her away at the altar he demanded a receipt.

\* \* \*

AFTER a few champagnes the tipsy young bride stood up to thank the guests for the presents. "... and I'd like to thank my parents-in-law for giving me such a perky copulator."

\* \* \*

EVEN these days there are a few four-letter words which can still shock most brides, like cook, wash, dust and iron.

\* \* \*

"DO you like big weddings or little ones?"
"Without big weddings you shouldn't have little ones."

\* \* \*

USHER at the wedding reception: "Are you a friend of the groom's?"
Woman: "Indeed I am not. I am the bride's mother."

\* \* \*

I WILL never forget my wedding. God knows I've tried.

THE bride wept, the bridesmaids wept, even the wedding cake was in tiers.

*     *     *

THE minister reached that part of the ceremony where the congregation is asked if anybody knows why this man and woman should not be joined together in holy matrimony.

A thin voice replied, hesitantly, "... er, yes. I'd like to say something."

The minister looked at him sternly. "Shut up. You are not part of the congregation. You're the groom!"

*     *     *

THE MC at the wedding reception stood up and roared: "Fornication!" "Fornication like this," he continued, "we should toast the happy couple in champagne."

*     *     *

A WAG who was known as a practical joker and who had played the most diabolical tricks on his friends was about to be married himself and was therefore very nervous. Would his friends get their revenge?

He was in a sweat when the vicar announced: "Is there any reason why this couple should not be joined together?" and despite his constant fear the ceremony and the wedding reception went without water pistols or rude telegrams. They even got to their hotel without incident.

Next morning the groom called room service. "This is Mr Smith in room 13, I'd like to order breakfast for two."

At this point a voice from under the bed said: "Make that five!"

*     *     *

BEN and Betty decided to get married in the Registry Office.

When filling in the appropriate forms the clerk queried Ben's name. "That's a nickname, surely," he said. "Go upstairs to the Birth, Deaths and Marriages Department and check your christened name."

Ben did so and came back to sign as Benjamin.

Betty met the same problem. "Go upstairs and check the records," said the clerk. "Betty can't be your right name."

Sure enough, she returned to sign her name as Elizabeth.

"Lucky I was here," said the clerk. "Otherwise this marriage wouldn't be legal and any kids you had would be technical bastards."

"That's funny," said Elizabeth, "that's what the bloke upstairs said about you."

\* \* \*

"CONGRATULATIONS, my boy," said the groom's uncle. "I'm sure you will look back on today as the happiest day of your life."

"But I'm not getting married until tomorrow," protested the lad.

"I know," said the uncle.

\* \* \*

THE ardent groom had exhausted his young bride on their honeymoon and one morning, while he was having a shave, she dressed and staggered down to the coffee shop. "What's the matter dear?" asked the waitress. "You look all-in. Aren't you the bride with the older husband?"

"Indeed I am," she confessed. "He is 75, but he has double-crossed me," complained the bride. "When he told me had saved up for 60 years I thought he was talking about money!"

\* \* \*

COMPLETE in her wedding gown the tearful young woman confronted her cricket-mad fiance.

"How could you do it? There I was on Saturday waiting at the church with all my relatives and where were you? Playing cricket. You left me in the lurch."

He tried to calm her down. "I distinctly said 'If it rained'."

THE Matron of Honour confided to the bride that if she wanted an unforgettable wedding night she should ensure that her groom should eat a dozen oysters at the marriage ceremony.

Next day the bride thanked her friend, but added dolefully, "Only eight of them worked!"

\* \* \*

THE bride and groom sat up all night waiting for their sexual relations to arrive.

\* \* \*

SHE married a sailor because she wanted to have children and rear admirals.

\* \* \*

THE father was giving advice to his son just before his marriage. "Son, in the beginning it will be tri-weekly. After ten years it will be try weekly, and after 20 years it will be try weakly."

\* \* \*

THE bridegroom was enjoying his last night of freedom at the buck's night when his mate confided, "Surely you can't be serious about marrying Wendy. She's been out with every bloke in town."

The bridegroom thought this over for a while. "Yeah, but it's not really a big town."

\* \* \*

THERE was a little man
  And he had a little gun
  And his bullets were made of lead
  He stood close by
  With a fatherly eye
  While me and my girl were wed.

\* \* \*

IT was a typical Outback Australian wedding and the reception party was in full swing by the time Jack arrived and parked his car outside the shearing shed.

He was about to go in when he met Fred coming out shaking his head.

"It's all over," said Fred. "Don't bother going in. It's a total disaster. They've run out of beer and the best man has just stuffed the bride."

The news was enough to turn Jack back towards his car. They were about to leave when another guest came out of the hall and began shouting: "Don't go you blokes. Everything is okay. They have found another keg and the best man has apologised."

## WEDDING TELEGRAMS

TO the groom: "Congratulations Gerald. It was better to have loved and lost, than never to have loved at all." — Mary, Terese, Wendy, Karen, Julie, Barbara, Estelle and Agatha.

\* \* \*

TO the bride: "Congratulations from your loving mother. 22 years ago I sent you to bed with a dummy. Tonight history repeats itself."

\* \* \*

TO the bride: "Congratulations Mabel. It was better to have loved and lost, than never to have loved at all." — Southside Football Club, and coach.

\* \* \*

TO the groom: "Congratulations Gerald, and welcome to the family from the delighted father of the bride. Now that I have given the bride away, can I have a receipt?"

\* \* \*

TO the groom. "Congratulations Gerald from your new in-laws. Be warned, she likes to spend money, but that's her only extravagance."

\* \* \*

TO the bride: "Congratulations from all your friends at the family Planning Centre. PS: The test is positive."

461

TO the groom. "Congratulations from the local feminist movement. And remember, no woman has ever shot her husband while he was doing the dishes."

* * *

TO the groom: "Congratulations from the Maffioso. We have just kidnapped your new mother-in-law. If you don't pay the ransom money we will send her back."

* * *

TO the groom: "Laugh and the world laughs with you. Quarrel with Mabel and you sleep alone."

TO the groom: "Congratulations and all the best. But remember, Socrates died from an overdose of wedlock."

* * *

TO the groom: "Congratulations Gerald and all the best for the future. From all your mates at Alcoholics Anonymous.

* * *

TO the groom: "Congratulations from the best man. Can I have first option on your little black book?"

* * *

TO the groom: "Congratulations from your new family. We assure you your bride has led a sheltered life. She thinks Good Housekeeping is a women's magazine. She never uses four letter words like Work, Shop, Bake, Dust. And she believes intercourse is a ticket to the races."

# WIDOWS

WHAT would you call a woman who always knows where her husband is?

A widow!

* * *

"SO you are going to marry Widow Brown. I wouldn't like to be the second husband of a widow."

"It's better than being the first."

"WHERE did you get that black eye?"

"You know that pretty little woman who said she was a widow? Well she isn't."

\* \* \*

HER husband didn't leave her much when he died. But he left her a lot while he was living.

\* \* \*

A NOSEY neighbour chided Widow Watkins. She said she didn't think it proper for the widow to entertain the grocer boy for hours each evening.

"It's only platonic," she said.

"What do you mean, platonic?" persisted the nosey neighbour.

"It's play for him and a tonic for me," said the widow.

\* \* \*

TWO mates were leaning on the bar. "The problem is," confided Bill, "I can marry a widow with heaps of money who I don't love, or I can marry a girl on the dole who I love very much."

"Follow your heart," was Fred's advice. "True love is best."

After a few minutes' silence Bill agreed: "You're right, I will."

"Good." said Fred, "And by the way, what's the widow's address?"

## WIVES
See HUSBANDS

HERE'S to the man who takes a wife
  But let him make no mistake
  For it makes a lot of difference
  Whose wife it is you take.

\* \* \*

WIFE, to woman next door: "I can only tell you this once, Bronwyn, I promised not to repeat it."

JAKE lamented to his mate: "How come my wife can spot a blonde hair on my shoulder, yet miss the garage doors?"

*　　*　　*

FRED is darn lucky. He has got a wife and a transistor, and they both work.

*　　*　　*

OVERHEARD at the bar: "Is it possible for a man to make a fool of himself without knowing it?"

"Not if he has a wife," counselled his wise friend.

*　　*　　*

"MY husband wears the pants in our family. But I tell him which pair to wear."

*　　*　　*

WIFE: "You certainly made a fool of yourself tonight. I only hope nobody realised you were sober."

*　　*　　*

"NO. I don't wake up sleepy and irritable," she said. "I let him sleep in."

*　　*　　*

SHE had always been a bossy wife and he had always taken the easy way out and never complained.

But when their South American tour went wrong and the bandits put them both before the firing squad he decided to make a stand.

When he was offered a blindfold he refused it and shouted, "You can stick the blindfold ya dirty rotten bastards."

"Gerald," she said. "Stop making trouble!"

*　　*　　*

HE reckons his wife is an outspoken woman. And having met her we would be mighty interested to know who outspoke her.

*　　*　　*

"WE were married in secret," she said. "Even my husband didn't know until he sobered up."

"MY husband is a man of rare gifts. I haven't received one for years."

\* \* \*

HE introduces his missus as the awful wedded wife.

\* \* \*

SHE was the kind of wife who spends her evenings dining and whining.

\* \* \*

"MY mother says I should never have married you," said the young wife during a tiff. "She thinks you're effeminate."

"Well," he said, "compared to her I probably am."

\* \* \*

A BLOKE comes home and starts to tell his wife some jokes he just heard at the pub. She interrupts and tells him to stop. "You," she says severely, "have got a dirty mind."

"Well..." he shrugged. "I suppose that's because I don't change mine as often as you do."

\* \* \*

A COUPLE got married and the wife put a wooden box under the bed and told her husband he wasn't allowed to look inside it until after she died.

After 20 years of marriage her husband couldn't resist his curiousity any longer. While his wife was out he opened the box and found three eggs and $25,000.

He looked at it so long in puzzled amazement that his wife caught him.

"Well, what are the eggs for?" asked the husband.

"Every time I've been unfaithful to you, I put an egg in the box," she explained.

The husband said, "Only three times in 20 years, well, that's not bad. I can live with that. But what's the money for?"

The wife replied, "Every time I got a dozen I sold them!"

\* \* \*

A COUPLE were having a heated argument about family

finances. Finally the wife exploded: "If it wasn't for my money we wouldn't have that television set. And if it wasn't for my money we wouldn't have any furniture. And if it wasn't for my money this house wouldn't be here."

"Listen," snorted her husband. "If it wasn't for your money I wouldn't be here."

\* \* \*

CHAP met his ex-wife at a party and after a few drinks he suggested they go to bed.

"Over my dead body," she sneered.

He downed his drink and replied, "I see you haven't changed."

\* \* \*

AS the old stockman lay dying she sat beside him wiping his fevered brow. Raising himself up on one elbow he turned to her and spoke:

"Ethel, you've been with me through it all. Remember the time when I got trampled in the stampede? You were there.

"And when I lost all that money at the cattle sale. You were at my side.

"And now I've been shot by a rustler, here you are again. You know, Ethel, I'm beginning to think you're bad luck!"

\* \* \*

"HOW'S your wife?"

"Compared to what?"

\* \* \*

"OUR marriage is based on trust and understanding.

She doesn't trust me, and I don't understand her."

\* \* \*

"EVERY night my wife covers her face in mud and puts her hair in rollers."

"Does it help?"

"A little. But I can still tell it's her."

\* \* \*

"IF you're fed up with your marriage, why don't you leave him?"

"I would, if I could find a way of doing it without making him happy."

*     *     *

SHE said she married one of the world's greatest lovers. "And one day I'm going to catch him at it."

*     *     *

TWO young housewives were having their regular cuppa but one was very depressed. "What's up?" said her friend.

"I caught my husband making love," she explained.

"So what? Don't let that bother you. I got mine the same way!"

*     *     *

"MY husband is an angel."

"You're lucky. Mine's still alive!"

*     *     *

HE got a telegram from his wife: "Harry, I missed you yesterday. Come home and let me have another shot."

*     *     *

HE joined the Foreign Legion to try and forget his wife, but at least six of the legionaires looked like her.

*     *     *

WIFE, to woman next door: "My husband has just run off with my best friend."

"Oh, gracious me, who was it?"

"Don't know, never met her."

*     *     *

"THERE was a phone call for you while you were out," said the wife to her husband.

"Oh, who was it?"

"It was one of those trouts you were fishing for last week."

*     *     *

FRED was staggering home from a bucks party when the milkman picked him up. "Where do you live?" asked the milkman.

"Robinson St," muttered Fred.

467

"Oh, Robinson St," said the milko. "Know it well. I have a great time on collection days in that street. Have a wonderful time with every woman except one," he laughed.

This news disturbed Fred and he woke his wife as soon as he got home and relayed the story. "Every woman except one, that's what the milkman said."

His sleepy wife thought for a while. "Oh that would be that stuck-up bitch at number 10," she said.

\* \* \*

HARRY Henpecked stepped on the weighing machine and was about to read his horoscope when his domineering wife snatched the card from him.

"Strong leader of men, Ha," she read aloud. "Master of your own destiny." She turned the card over. "It's even got your weight wrong."

\* \* \*

HARRY Henpecked finally had enough. He declared that he was going to commit suicide and stormed out of the house. She called after him that she had heard that story all too often before. About an hour later she went down the main street to do her shopping and saw a crowd gathered outside a very high building. The crowd was hushed and horrified, for there was Harry balancing on the highest parapet.

She screamed: "That's my husband! Save him! Somebody save him!"

A cop looked round and gave the woman a long hard stare. "Is that man really your husband?" he asked.

"Of course he is," she snapped.

"Oh, that's okay then," said the cop. "For a while we thought he was crazy and didn't know what he was doing."

\* \* \*

HE came home in a state of utter despair and sat with his head in his hands. "I have just been sacked," he told his wife.

"After 40 years of doing the same job week after week I have been replaced by an electronic gadget about the size of a torch," he lamented. "What's more it can do everything I can do, and do it better and never wear out," he moaned.

But nobody was listening. She had gone out to buy one.

* * *

EIGHT kids were too many and the cost of rising prices was getting Fred down. He told his wife if they had any more kids he would go out of his mind with worry.

A week later his wife announced that she was pregnant.

"That's the end," lamented Fred. He opened the drawer beneath his desk and pulled out a revolver and held it to his head.

"Stop!" cried his wife. "You'll be killing an innocent man!"

* * *

MRS Murphy said: "Oi don't think my husband has been completely fait'ful t' me."

"Why, what makes you so suspicious?"

"My last child doesn't resemble him in the least."

* * *

CHAP watering his front garden saw a taxi leave the house next door and his neighbour waving his visitors farewell.

"Goodbye. Your wife is great in bed," he shouted as the cab drove off. "She's fantastic in the cot."

He could hardly believe it and when the cab had gone he called his neighbour over to the fence.

"Did I hear right?" he said. "Did I hear you say that bloke's wife was good in bed?"

"Well it isn't really true," said his neighbour, "but I didn't want to hurt his feelings."

* * *

SHE had been married so long she even faked the fore-play.

469

A MAN never knows the value of a woman's love until he pays maintenance.

* * *

IF your wife wants to learn to drive, don't stand in her way.

* * *

IF you don't like the way women drive, then get off the footpath.

* * *

MY wife has been booked so many times the cops have now given her a season ticket.

* * *

"IS your wife outspoken?"

"Not by anyone I know of."

* * *

WHEN a woman is looking for a husband she is either single or married.

* * *

MARIA Lotzabazooma has had eight husbands. Three of them were her own.

* * *

THE upkeep of a wife is often the downfall of a husband.

* * *

OLD Minnie was complaining to the doctor about the antics of her husband. "He's always looking at pretty girls and wandering off after them," she complained.

"Well, its hard to stop men admiring pretty girls," said the doctor.

"But my husband is 82 years of age," persisted Minnie.

The doctor considered this for a minute and said: "Let me put it this way. I have a little fox terrier that chases motor cars. What would happen if he ever caught one?"

* * *

THE brewery manager called around, hat in hand, to solemnly announce that her husband, Fred, had suffered a tragic and fatal accident at work. He had fallen into a vat of beer and drowned.

"Oh dear. Did he suffer much?" asked the bereaved wife.

"I don't think so," said the manager. "He got out twice to go to the loo."

* * *

HARRY stopped off at the pub and was soon chatting up a blonde at the bar. Near closing time she suggested going to her place. They did and after a few more drinks they had a wonderful time.

It was three in the morning when Harry got out of bed and began to dress. And with a worried frown said "How will I explain this to the wife?"

"No problem," said the blonde, "and by the way, put this bit of chalk behind your ear."

Harry was creeping up the stairs when the light was flicked on, and there was his fuming wife waiting with folded arms.

"And where the hell have you been?" she demanded.

Harry remembered the blonde's advice and told the truth. "I've been tumbling in bed with a lovely blonde I picked up in the pub," he said.

"Liar!" she roared. "You have been playing billiards all night with those hopeless mates of yours. I can tell by the chalk behind your ear."

* * *

THE wife was understandably annoyed when her husband came in drunk at midnight.

"I could forgive you if it was the first time," she said. "but you came home in the same condition on March 15, 1958."

* * *

"HOW'S your headache, Fred?"

"Out doing the shopping."

* * *

"YOU haven't nagged me all evening. Is there someone else?"

471

"ONE more word," she said, "and I'll go back to my mother."
"Taxi!"

THE doctor asked her: "Has there been any insanity in the family?"
"Yes, Doc," she said. "My husband thinks he's the boss."

\*   \*   \*

SHE has a tongue that jaywalks over every conversation.

\*   \*   \*

SHE gives me a 'Going Away Party' every time I take the garbage out.

\*   \*   \*

GOING to a party with your wife is like going fishing with a game keeper.

\*   \*   \*

IF you want your wife to listen, then talk to another woman.

## WOMEN
See WIVES

GENERALLY speaking, women are generally speaking.

\*   \*   \*

FOUR women, one English, one American, one German and one French, were all asked the same question: "What would you do if you were shipwrecked on an island with a regiment of soldiers?"

The Englishwoman said she would hide. The American said she would seek the protection of the commanding officer. The German woman said she would be out marching and it wouldn't bother her.

The French woman thought for a moment; "I understand ze question, but what seems to be ze problem?"

\*   \*   \*

WHEN a woman is looking for a husband she is either single or married.

472

TWO psychiatrists were in a restaurant. One said, "See that man over there, well, he claims to understand women."

"Really," said his friend, "and he's a professional colleague?"

"No. He's a patient."

# WORDS

WORDS are the means by which we confuse each other as three New Australians discovered. One was lamenting the fact that he and his wife had no children. "My wife is unbearable," he explained.

"No, you mean she is inconceivable," said the second.

"You are both wrong," said the third. "He means his wife is impregnable."

    ★    ★    ★

THE longest word in the English language is the one following the phrase: "And now a word from our sponsor."

    ★    ★    ★

FRED always called a spade a spade, until the night he fell over one.

    ★    ★    ★

HE was going to have a few words with his wife, but he found she had cornered the market.

    ★    ★    ★

ONE word of censure makes Dad hold his tongue; and Mum's the word.

    ★    ★    ★

PROCRASTINATION is the thief of time, especially if you can't spell it.

    ★    ★    ★

WHEN a politician says a meeting was meaningful; it means that it was meaningless.

    ★    ★    ★

COULD-Be-Better-Put Dept: A woman on a crowded train thought she recognised her husband in the crush.

She pushed through, came up behind him and kissed him on the neck. When he turned round she was shocked to find it wasn't him at all.

"Terribly sorry," she blushed, "but your head looks just like my husband's behind."

* * *

TO awaken a student sleeping in his class the English professor threw a book at him.

"What hit me?" spluttered the student.

"That, my lad," replied the professor, "was a flying Chaucer."

* * *

LETTERS can be as confusing as words. Following a lesson on genetics one student asked of his colleague what DNA stood for.

"That's simple," said his friend. "It stands for the National Association of Dyslectics."

* * *

THE Maharaja of an Indian province once decreed that no wild animals were to be killed. Soon his realm was overrun with tigers. When the people could stand it no longer they gave the Maharaja the heave-ho.

It was the first time on record where the reign was cancelled because of the game.

* * *

ON the anniversary of Shakespeare's birth a BBC announcer achieved this vintage spoonerism: "The usual festivities were held in Stratford today to celebrate the Bird's bathday!"

* * *

THE flying instructor had just delivered a lesson on parachute jumping. "And if it doesn't open?" asked a student.

"Well, you are jumping to a conclusion," he replied.

* * *

SHE said she had started a new diet: "No more eating my own words, swallowing my pride, or putting my foot in my mouth," she said.

WHEN Joe Bloggs scooped the agricultural show with all prizes for his vegetables he was invited on television.

"And what is the secret of growing prize vegetables?" asked the compere.

"Manure," answered Joe. "Manure for tomatoes, manure for pumpkins, manure for cabbages..." and he went on extolling the virtues of manure.

A very embarrassed daughter was watching at home. "Oh Mum, why can't Dad say fertilizer instead of manure?"

"Count your blessings," said Mrs Bloggs. "It took me 30 years to get him to call it manure!"

\* \* \*

THE Archbishop of Canterbury was a distinguished guest at the mayoral dinner. As the first course was being served a waiter slipped and dropped a bowl of hot soup upside down in the Archbishop's lap.

The Archbishop looked depairingly around the table and said: "Is there any layman present who will be good enough to express my feelings?"

\* \* \*

WHEN it came to writing up the log book Captain Squiggs was a stickler for accuracy, so when the first mate received news that he was the father of twins and celebrated in his cabin the captain noted in the logbook: "The first mate was drunk last night."

When the mate saw it he argued that it should be struck from the record but the pedantic captain was resolute. "You were drunk last night. I can't change that fact, so it must stay in the log."

Next day the mate was on watch and it was his duty to keep the log. In the morning the captain was aghast to read: "The captain was sober last night."

\* \* \*

YOU have heard of the TATE family? They're everywhere.

There is Dick Tate who wants to control everybody. Ro Tate who tries to turn things around. Agi Tate who stirs up trouble and Irri Tate who helps. Hesi Tate and Vege Tate always procrastinate. Imi Tate mimics everybody. Devas Tate likes to destroy things and Poten Tate wants to be a big shot, but it's Facili Tate, Cogi Tate and Medi Tate who save the day.

\* \* \*

THE Aussie had just taken up a job in the wildlife sanctuary and was explaining to some American tourists the difference between an echidna and a porcupine. "The echidnas' pricks are longer," he said.

This caused great embarrassment amongst the mixed group and later the supervisor took him aside to reprimand the Aussie on his choice of words.

"It's quills. Use a bit of decorum," he said. "It's quills."

The next group of Yanks raised the same question. "That's a doggone porcupine," said one.

"Different animal altogether," said our Aussie with authority. "The echidna is smaller, lighter in colour and its quills are longer ... but their pricks are about the same size."

# The Strangest of Theatres

## Poets Writing Across Borders

EDITED BY

Jared Hawkley, Susan Rich, and Brian Turner

CONSULTING EDITOR

Catherine Barnett

HARRIET MONROE POETRY INSTITUTE
"POETS IN THE WORLD" SERIES EDITOR
Ilya Kaminsky

McSWEENEY'S BOOKS
SAN FRANCISCO

*The Strangest of Theatres: Poets Writing Across Borders* is a copublication
of The Poetry Foundation and McSweeney's Publishing.

For more information about McSweeney's, see www.mcsweeneys.net
For more information about The Poetry Foundation, see www.poetryfoundation.org

Hardcover ISBN: 978-1-938073-26-7
Paperback ISBN: 978-1-938073-27-4

First printing, 2013

*Should we have stayed at home and thought of here?*
*Where should we be today?*
*Is it right to be watching strangers in a play*
*in this strangest of theatres?*

—Elizabeth Bishop, "Questions of Travel"

# Contents

# Editors' Note

The information in this book is provided as a resource and source of inspiration for poets considering travel abroad. Ideas and knowledge about international travel are ever changing, so we present this book in the spirit of an evolving conversation. The content derives from a broad spectrum of contributors who have an extensive range of viewpoints and experiences. Their discussions often describe the general issues at hand and include ideas about resources or poems; however, this information is not meant to be exhaustive or to address any reader's specific situation, and inclusion is not an endorsement of specific content or of a particular course of action. Readers are invited to consider the materials and topics raised in the book, as well as other available resources, while they make thoughtful decisions based on their values, priorities, and circumstances. Readers should seek answers, resources, and legal counsel, as well as relevant laws, that address their specific circumstances, wishes, and needs.

The authors of the essays made great efforts to provide accurate, relevant information on a wide range of topics. However, many details are liable to change and, in many instances, are subject to interpretation. The publishers cannot accept responsibility for any consequences arising from the use of this book.

# Acknowledgments

The Harriet Monroe Poetry Institute recognizes with deep gratitude the kindness, collaboration, and generosity of spirit of all of the contributors, editors, and many others who worked so hard to bring this book into existence. In particular, this project owes great thanks to the following: John Lusk Babbott, Susan Briante, Patricia Chao, Fred Courtright, Charlotte Crowe, Zachary Cupkovic, George Foy, Kathleen Graber, Garth Greenwell, Susan Hogan, Jill Jarvis, Chelsea Hogue, Gabriel Kalmuss-Katz, Jessica Kovler, Lauren Ricke, Jess Row, Jennifer Scappettone, Michelle Coghlan, Roy Scranton, Sarah Marie Shepherd, Tiffany Tuttle Collins, Ryann S. Wahl, G.C. Waldrep, McSweeney's Publishing, the Trinity College Office of International Programs in Hartford, Connecticut, and most especially Ethan Nosowsky, Beth Allen, Daniel Moysaenko, and Kathleen White.

# Introduction: Beyond the Visible Horizon

No matter where we are, the horizon—retreating, drawing near—adds its quiet definition to the moment we live in. This happens whether we are crossing the Ambassador Bridge into the streets of Detroit or taking the Red Line to Braintree somewhere down in the subterranean world of the Boston suburbs; it happens even at an altitude of thirty-nine thousand feet in a twin-engine turboprop over Coeur d'Alene, Memphis, Kailua-Kona, Sioux City, or Nome, the world below erased in cloud. Once the bus pulls over or the subway line ends or we climb down the rolling stairs to stand on the tarmac, we become fixed within the stations of our lives—circling the sun at about sixty-seven thousand miles per hour with our hair perfectly still, yesterday falling like ash within each of us, the day ahead as yet unknown.

The maps we scroll open across our desks or buffer into resolution on our iPads and laptop screens offer a conceptual framework that makes employing the cartographer's trade and navigating the world easier. To say that these maps partially define us may sound like a simple bromide or platitude, but it is difficult to sidestep the fact that we live in the (politically) very real abstractions of city, county, state, and federal jurisdictions. For those who cross the wrong invisible line without the proper documentation, these concepts become very real, very quickly. Rarely can we physically "see" the map delineated on the landscape itself, though.

Recognizing the surveyor's marks expressed in us and within the language we bring to the page is often even more difficult. In a very literal sense, there are exceptions to the mapmaker's abstractions. In parts of present-day Berlin, for example, bricks in the roadbed denote the wall that once separated East and West Berlin; one can stand with one foot in the former Soviet bloc and the other in what was previously called the Federal Republic of Germany. In Uganda, roughly forty miles southwest of the capital on the Masaka-Kampala Road, it is possible to stand with one foot in the Southern Hemisphere while placing the other foot in the Northern Hemisphere. Those who travel to Struga for the annual poetry festival on the northern shores of Lake Ohrid might come face-to-face with the reality that the people living there consider themselves citizens of the Republic of Macedonia; in the halls of the United Nations, at the urging of Greece, those same people are known as citizens of the Former Yugoslav Republic of Macedonia, or FYROM. Satellite technology, over-the-counter GPS units, and smartphones track and plot people's movements on Earth's surface with incredible precision and accuracy, in some cases down to a ten-digit grid (or roughly the equivalent of an area ten meters square). The invisible divisions and demarcations of the world crisscross the landscapes of human lives with profound effects, both subtle and overt.

It is the editors' hope that this book might serve as a guide or trail marker, a series of possible azimuths travelers might set their courses by, a collection of lyric revelations and sober assessments that travel beyond national borders might reveal or encourage. "One of the obligations of the writer," Denise Levertov once wrote, "and perhaps especially of the poet, is to say or sing *all* that he or she can, to deal with as much of the world as becomes possible to him or her in language."

Sometimes, as William Logan writes, "poets behave like conquistadors wherever they roam, picking up a new verse form, a lover, some inventive cursing, a disease." Still, he goes on to point out, "Would Byron have been Byron without Italy and Greece? What would Eliot and Pound have become without the hostility of London? Can we imagine Hart Crane without the Caribbean or Elizabeth Bishop without Rio?" The politics of travel is one of the through lines of this book and one of its consistent challenges: How do we embark upon these journeys in meaningful, responsible ways? How do we avoid the tropes of colonialism—and, for that matter, how might we recognize them at work within ourselves? Do we venture out as literary voyeurs, cousins to tourists, continually smashing champagne bottles across the bow of experience? Do we travel to escape the noise of our lives, driven by a need to create livable spaces for ourselves, places in which to breathe? Do we sense a necessity in the art of witness, sharpening our pencils in the journalist's trade?

Whatever the initial reasons and internal pressures we may have as we set out into the larger world, "the insight must be earned as much as the poem." These words, from Jack Gilbert's essay "The Landscape of American Poetry in 1964," ring with great clarity several decades on. They might serve as a guidepost, though we may not immediately be able—as writers and as human beings—to recognize the depths of the insights we've garnered through experience and crafted to the page. Sometimes the language we bring to the page teaches us what we didn't previously realize or comprehend. As Mark Doty says, "Poetry is an investigation, not an expression, of what you know."

In this sense, *The Strangest of Theatres: Poets Writing Across Borders* is also a call to action. It is our hope that poets might serve, in some ways, as envoys to the greater world, offering American poetry newfound sources of engagement with language and a renewed engagement with what being a global citizen means. With gratitude, we recognize the journeys of those who have gone before us; we recognize the immensity of what those journeys have added to literature as well as to our ways of perceiving the world in which we live and the ways in which we live in the world. This book is a celebration of poets who have ventured beyond the visible horizon and brought back verse; it may also offer insights into how others might emulate these travelers by forging paths into the world beyond the United States. The editors hope these essays will inspire, encourage, be talismanic, serve as harbingers or mercurial whispers, perhaps, or as epistles from the far shore imploring us and warning us along our own ways. The work of these writers enlarges the world available within us; this work augments us.

## The Paths Before Us

Where would American poetry be today without the journeys our poets undertook into the wider world? The ebb and flow of entire schools and counter schools of poetic thought owe their existence, in part, to the conversations that took place across the far seas. Where would American poetry be, for example, without a poet such as Langston Hughes, who traveled extensively and served in the early 1960s as a cultural emissary for the US Department of State (though decades earlier, he found himself wanting to return to the United States after being robbed and stranded while en route to Italy—"stranded" when a homeward-bound ship wouldn't hire him because he wasn't white, so Hughes wrote "I, too, sing America"). Where would American poetry be without the Vietnam-era visits to Hanoi by Grace Paley and Muriel Rukeyser (whose last book, *The Gates*, sprang from her attempts to visit the South Korean poet Kim Chi-Ha, who was serving a life sentence in prison)?

In all shapes and forms, American poets have wandered the globe and encountered other writers engaged in similarly picaresque journeys. After World War II, W.S. Merwin, a former US poet laureate, lived in Europe, ending up in Majorca, where he tutored the son of the poet Robert Graves. Although not all poets may have the good fortune to find employers who are also literary patrons, the options are myriad—there are farms to work, bars to tend, bookshops to run, schools and wells to build, ships to crew as they ply the whale roads of old.

Travel may even encourage writers to diverge from their usual genres and allow them to share their work internationally. Galway Kinnell was moved to write his first and (so far) only novel, *Black Light*, which was influenced by time spent living and working in Tehran (1957–1960). Coleman Barks and Robert Bly have journeyed to Iran and Afghanistan, speaking to audiences large and small of their engagement with ancient poetics and how that interaction has affected their work. Barks—whose versions of Rumi are well known for their unconventional approach to the art of translation—received an honorary doctorate from the University of Tehran.

Other poets choose to gather the poetic traditions they encounter abroad to foster an international dialogue and to widen the poetic compass of poets and thinkers back home. This functions, perhaps, as a form of literary hybridity or cross-pollination. In 1971, for example, John Balaban returned to Vietnam during the war, a heavy tape recorder slung over his shoulder so that listeners might hear the voices of Vietnamese poetry sung in the rice paddies and monasteries and villages decades later. I was fortunate enough to hear these voices when he played the recordings at a poetry reading at the Marfa Book Company in the tiny West Texas town of Marfa in 2008. In addition to writing verse and sharing the recordings he has preserved from years ago, Balaban has also brought to readers of English the eighteenth-century Vietnamese poetry of Hồ Xuân Hương (*Spring Essence*, 2000), whose work was originally created in Chữ Nôm, an ideographic script now nearly extinct.

Work along these lines often leads to the development of lifelong friendships with writers and thinkers we meet during our travels. "That poets today can form a *confraternitas* transcending distances and language differences," the Polish poet Czesław Miłosz wrote, "may be one of the few encouraging signs in the current chaotic world order."

Curiosity often leads poets to the far corners and beyond. As is often the case, curiosity searches out the genius available through the centuries of thought we inherit as well as the genius we discover in our contemporaries. I think, for instance, of the poet, scholar, and multilingual translator Willis Barnstone. Through his many travels, Barnstone has returned to the United States with translations of Machado, Lorca, Sappho, Wang Wei, Rilke, Heraclitus, a play by Neruda, and much more. Many poets have wandered out into the larger world in search of its poetic treasures so that they might apply the translator's art and carry the verses back home to the rest of us. Kenneth Koch may have been right when he said "reading poems in translation is like kissing someone through a shower curtain," but I prefer Charles Simic's vision of translation as he articulated it in the *New York Review of Books*—"To translate is not only to experience what makes each language distinct, but to draw close to the mystery of the relationship between word and thing, letter and spirit, self and world."

We can serve as champions for the language we encounter abroad. For example, Sandy Taylor (1931–2007), poet and founder of Curbstone Press, traveled widely and brought back the work of poets from many nations around the globe, often publishing poetry collections and novels that would likely have been overlooked or refused print by some of the larger, more prominent presses of the day. In 1999, Curbstone published Carolyn Forché's translation of *Saudade* (or *Sorrow*), penned by the Nicaraguan poet Claribel Alegría, whom Taylor had met by chance on a bus in Managua. "I was down there in support of the Sandinista regime," he once said, "... reading poetry to the police, army, and coffee workers." Poets such as Taylor remind us that, just as poets and poetry can be discovered on a bus in Managua, they can be discovered wherever our feet take us in the world. And, perhaps more important, the poetry we experience abroad has the capacity to create profound change and influence on the poetic landscape back home.

The textbook image of the American poet abroad is sometimes envisioned as the famously irascible Robert Frost meeting with the diplomatic and gracious Anna Akhmatova in Moscow in 1962, near the end of both of their lives. As the story goes, Frost's translator (the poet F.D. Reeve, the late Christopher Reeve's father) had to "smooth over" Frost's gruff manner in his presentation to Akhmatova. Roughly fifteen hundred miles away and nearly five decades earlier, Frost had often walked with the English poet Edward Thomas through the Dymock countryside near Ledbury, England. Those walks have attained a near-mythic quality in the years since and led to the work some consider among the foundation stones of American poetry in the past century, "The Road Not Taken." According to the postulate, travel affected the poet and inspired the poem, but the poem remained uniquely American, lacking the visible and subtextual traces of the journey that spawned it.

Other poets, such as Allen Ginsberg, threaded their travels into the poems themselves so that the work became an electric conversation with the journey itself or an amalgamation of the world's overflowing riches tumbling line by line into verse. For example, in Paris during the "winterspring" of 1958, Ginsberg wrote,

> Here in Paris I am your guest O friendly shade
> the absent hand of Max Jacob
> Picasso in youth bearing me a tube of Mediterranean
> myself attending Rousseau's old red banquet I ate his violin
> great party at the Bateau Lavoir not mentioned in the
>     textbooks of Algeria
> Tzara in the Bois de Boulogne explaining the alchemy of
>     the machineguns of the cuckoos
> he weeps translating me into Swedish ...

In a very different mode, C.K. Williams's visit to the Ugandan chimpanzee sanctuary on Ngamba Island doubtless added to the depth of insight he brought to his poem "Apes":

> The chimps Catherine and I saw on their island sanctuary
>     in Uganda we loathed.
> Unlike the pacific gorillas in the forest of Bwindi, they
>     fought, dementedly shrieked,
> the dominant male lorded it over the rest; they were, in
>     all, too much like us.

As it happens, I visited the same island at the northern end of Lake Victoria in 2007, saw—most likely—the same chimpanzees and many of the same caretakers on the island, visited the same veterinarian's facilities, and hurled jackfruit over the fence line at feeding time from the same wooden viewing platform where Williams and his wife must have stood before. I imagine I would write a poem very different from Williams's own. Though the doorway into a poem may derive from the same place (and often from very similar experiences), the poem—if fully realized—will journey through language and the wide landscape of self to discover a new place.

The world works its way through writers just as much as we work our way through the world. So, too, with language. As poets, part of our service to the art is being aware of the language we carry as well as the new language we acquire along the way. We must attend to the nuances and subtleties involved when we graft newly acquired language onto the words we carry within us, the words we might refer to as our "mother tongue."

## Quayside

The poet Amy Lowell left in her will a mandate to send American-born poets abroad (stipulating that they leave North America) for a year at a time; poets have undertaken this particular journey since E.L. Mayo set out in 1953, Stanley Kunitz to follow the year after. Lowell had a mind of great prescience. She recognized the deep need for American poets and, by extension, American poetry to experience the larger community of nations, as she had done. In recent years, low-residency writing programs and writers' conferences abroad have formalized the overseas writing dynamic.

Even with some structures set in place to help them travel, few American poets venture abroad. In contrast, leading news agencies and magazines routinely send journalists out on assignment to the far corners of the Earth. These reporters serve as witness to world events so that we might expand our field of vision. As reporters and photojournalists lift off the tarmac on outbound flights, business executives and company employees also travel to all points on the map. Low-echelon members of the US Department of State serve in remote consular offices and in labyrinthine constructions of the mightiest embassies in major capitals worldwide. At the same time, the American military (from straight-leg infantry soldiers to covert operations teams) has forces and hardware deployed to countries far and wide. Unlike Rukeyser's and Paley's and a few others', the passports of most American poets are rarely stamped. As one Vietnamese poet and former NVA soldier once remarked to the poet Bruce Weigl (paraphrased here), "You Americans are strange: first you send your soldiers and tanks—then you send your poets." Telling as that statement might be, how much more so might it be if the poets never "deployed" at all?

At the time of Amy Lowell's death in 1925, writers traveling to Europe or South America mostly went by ocean liner, their trunks packed for journeys that often lasted months. But in many ways, the world moves exponentially faster now. In the present day, it's possible for poets to attend international poetry festivals in Medellín, Dubai, or Durban during a week's vacation from work. Over a series of trips such as these, it is possible for writers to develop lifelong friendships and colleagues in the art. When the Jasmine Revolution reaches Tahrir Square in Cairo or Bangladesh relaxes its bans on travel or the prime minister of Romania threatens to resign and a country of twenty million people finds itself in historical flux, poets can hop on planes and witness such moments through the lens of their own humanity. The information age—the age of Twitter, YouTube, and Facebook—makes it possible for poets to recognize where momentous challenges and changes are taking place in the world. Poets who choose to witness the events of our time now have the ability to experience them firsthand. The editors hope that the work assembled in *The Strangest of Theatres: Poets Writing Across Borders* might inspire a new generation of writers to take part in the global conversation that is already underway, regardless of a trip's duration.

## Sails in the Wind

During the creation of this book, several of the poets whose work appears were engaged in journeys beyond American shores. Yusef Komunyakaa (author of *Dien Cai Dau* and *Neon Vernacular*, among other books) visited Nairobi, where grenade attacks took place after he left. Gregory Dunne (author of *Home Test* and *Fistful of Lotus*) continued his teaching in Japan, though the country was reeling in the aftermath of the Tōhoku earthquake of 2011. Between news assignments, Eliza Griswold (author of *Wideawake Field: Poems* and *The Tenth Parallel: Dispatches from the Fault Line Between Christianity and Islam*) went surfing in El Salvador.

Sandra Meek (poet and editor of the anthology *Deep Travel*) had her car tires slashed while visiting the Silvermine Nature Reserve atop the Table Mountain plateau overlooking Cape Town, South Africa. All her belongings (passport, cash, credit cards, and even her food and water) were stolen from her car as she was out trekking. High up in the mist overlooking an ocean she couldn't see, she received a text message from her sister telling her that their father had been hospitalized. Meek had to work with South African Home Affairs and the US consulate in Cape Town, among other agencies, before she was able to make it home—just in time to be with her father before he passed away.

We can't plan all that will take place along our journeys, and in equal measure we can't plan all that might occur in our communities back home. That said, the immutable laws of travel offer an encouraging note within their somber tone: not every journey involves pain, disaster, and heartbreak. As Pound reminds us, "Each age has its own abounding gifts." Still, what can we do if that gift is the eruption of a caldera beneath Iceland's Eyjafjallajökull and if the airspace over most of Europe is closed because of volcanic ash and debris, leaving us stranded in foreign airports? What if our passports are stolen? Whose voice do we turn to when inner-city Bangkok shifts to a place of riot and conflict, a place where the renegade Thai military general Khattiya Sawasdipol can be shot in the head as he responds to a reporter's questions on a city street? The contributors to this book can't propose a solution to every problem, but the intent is to offer roads into the wider world as well as possible sources of help and guidance. The editors hope that the work compiled here may be of use to both the long- and the short-term traveler.

In the grand tradition of the expatriate, you may choose for the remainder of your life to pull up stakes and move to another country or to a series of countries, as one might traverse the garden via many stepping-stones along the way. A.E. Stallings lives with her family in Greece while continuing to have an active presence in contemporary American poetry. Similarly, Tamar Yoseloff and Eva Salzman have forged lives in London. In Wales, Florida-born Amy Wack (who graduated from the Columbia University MFA program) serves as the poetry editor at Seren Books. A beacon across the water, Gertrude Stein and her influence resound to the present day; she is proof that American writers not only travel but also forge and sustain literary lives far beyond their native shores.

In contrast, many writers choose to become temporary denizens of other countries. Jorie Graham has spent a good deal of time in Normandy, and it's difficult to imagine how she might have written *Overlord* without such meditative proximity to the actual landscape where the invasion forces stormed ashore and fought their way inland. Not too far afield from those Normandy beaches, Cyrus Cassells has taken research trips to Germany in order to access the world of poems he fashioned for his latest book, *The Crossed-Out Swastika*. I think of Jack Gilbert's "self-imposed isolation" and the poetry written after his first collection (*Views of Jeopardy*) won the Yale Series of Younger Poets, when Gilbert lived in Greece and also traveled to a variety of countries as a lecturer for the US Department of State. I'm also thinking of Sam Hamill in Mexico as I write this. I'm thinking of Martín Espada visiting Neruda's Casa de Isla Negra in Chile. I'm thinking of Bruce Weigl and Kevin Bowen returning to Vietnam to visit friends and writers they once fought against when their counterparts were part of the North Vietnamese Army. I'm thinking of

Ken Taylor, winner of the recent FISH poetry prize (for the poem "string theory") and how he used the money to help fund a trip to the West Cork Literary Festival set amid the raw green beauty of County Cork, in Ireland.

Poetry can be a doorway into a new circle of friends and colleagues. For some poets, the layered places of history call in ways we may not fully understand until we can interact with the land itself or the people who live there. We may need to breathe in the air—to inspire it, from the Latin *inspirare*, from which the word *inspiration* is derived—as we witness the conversation between dusk and dawn; our poems may need to wander through the streets and fields of the world, searching out the shady groves and the brilliant vistas, the junkie alleyways and the industrial wastelands.

Once the journey is done and we return home and our poems have found their way to the page, we often learn about the world in which we live. In this way, poetry unfolds and unravels the journey we may have thought long over. Our bags may be unpacked, our clothes washed and folded away, our passports tucked into safe-deposit boxes or cubbyholes in back rooms, but the poems—the poems are extensions of the journey. Poems offer pathways into the countries within, paths that might otherwise grow wild and unnoticed by the eyes of daydreamers leafing through sheaves of photos from their time abroad.

## Passports and Entry Visas

As with all anthologies, imperfections abound here. As editors, we have done our best to be inclusive and wide-ranging in gathering the work you now hold in your hands. Early on, we grappled with how the book might consider the terms *American* and *United States* in the first place. What parameters would we apply to the work we sought? How might the voices and traditions and experiences of Hopi and Navajo and Iroquois poets, for example, of Cherokee and Choctaw and Cheyenne writers, instruct us in what it's like to be a poet traveling out from a sovereign nation, traveling through the counties and states and jurisdictions of what others call the United States of America? When we spread a map of the world before us, we had many long conversations about where we might travel with poets vis-à-vis the essays they had written, whether in newly commissioned essays or in reprints culled from a variety of sources. The necessary questions of identity politics, that which makes a nation and that which makes a citizen, the inherent possibility of marginalization and erasure that argue against the creation of anthologies as a form, as well as the tricky territory of who we are as editors and who we are drawn to for new work and old—these issues and concerns form a good portion of the interior architecture of this book, its underlying aesthetic awareness. You might ask—where are the words of John Ashbery in France? Where are the travels of Adrienne Rich? Muriel Rukeyser? Gerald Stern and C.D. Wright and Rita Dove and Brenda Hillman? Where are poets and travelers from centuries gone by? There are also poets who came to the United States and offered Americans new ways to see themselves and the wider world—here I'm thinking of Auden and Lorca and Miłosz, for example. Contemporary poets in this vein might include Li-Young Lee, Eavan Boland, Valzhyna Mort, Khaled Mattawa, Dunya Mikhail, Tomaž Šalamun, and Oliver de la Paz. Their poetry rises into this world from multiple geographies and expands the poetic landscape in the United States. For these reasons and many, many more, of course, *The Strangest of Theatres: Poets Writing Across Borders* is an incomplete book. In a variety of ways, it waits for the pages readers will add.

In terms of structure, the editors worked to create a book both useful and insightful about the logistical aspects of travel as well as the more sublime and intellectual elements that travel engenders. For example, if a writer encourages carrying an Olympus Digital Linear PCM recorder while traveling, we hope that the practicality of the instrument will prove useful and also help travelers connect more deeply to their possible roles as witnesses, archivists, human beings who cherish the words that others offer and wish to preserve and care for them. Likewise, when a traveler describes in detail the sublime experience of separation from the world she or he comes from (as well as, likely, the world entered into), we hope readers will recognize the value of this for their interior lives. Perhaps they will also ponder the deep and cherished relationships they may have at "home" and how, for example, they might want to make certain that their bill payments are set up before they go, living wills set in place should they never return, powers of attorney set up (should they plan on being overseas for an extended time), and more. In essence, people's choices revolve around their best attempts to be responsible citizens of the world as they travel. The essays that follow cover a wide range of possibilities, and all of them highlight, in one way or another, these basic attributes.

## The Poet in the World: You

The aim of this book isn't to encourage writers to choose an escapist route and turn away from that which most needs work. Far from it. The editors recognize the necessity of the interior soliloquy. We realize that our country needs what one might colloquially term "homegrown" poetry. Now, just as in years past, poems will rise from the squad car in Portland, the frying pan at Oklahoma Joe's in Kansas City, the out-of-gas motorcycle on a county road on the outskirts of Tehachapi, the vegan bakery in Jackson, and Rudy's Car Wash in Allentown. There are necessary poems to be written about Alabama and Wisconsin and Puerto Rico. And we will need the poems from our maternity wards, our school yards, our prisons, our gardens and our slums, the beds that we make love in as well as the beds where we lie down to die.

As much as these necessary poems deserve attention, it is the editors' belief that this is a time in which a deep, sustained, and global interaction is necessary to reinvigorate the poetic landscape at home. Stated baldly, the country needs more polymath poets—hybrid creatures who have listened to the voices outside of their field of view, poets who return to American poetry a renewed sense of connection with the language we share. They just might be able to do this if they journey beyond the known. As Lucille Clifton once said, "Poems come out of wonder, not out of knowing." That's why Gertrude Stein's wisdom rings as true today as when she said it long ago: in Paris, "Americans can discover what it means to be American." Substitute the name of any number of foreign cities, towns, villages, hamlets, homes for the name *Paris*. At the same time, the poems created from experiences abroad can serve as dispatches, as entry points, as vehicles of mystery and profound insight. As Eamon Grennan said in the *Irish Times*, "Good poets are the explorers of the world. Out on the frontiers, they send back bulletins."

In compiling this book, the editors gathered an array of voices and experiences and travel possibilities. I worry that this might lull us into a false sense of security. Some may think, given the many travels of poets described in these pages, "Ah, with so many American poets going abroad, what's the point of this book?" For the most part, sadly, these poets stand in sharp contrast to the norm (in terms of international travel). A large number of poets go from one educational institution to another, to one MFA or another, without investigating the wider world. It is precisely because of the dearth of sustained and meaningful interaction with the world beyond our borders that the editors assembled this book.

The far horizon for one person may be the opposite horizon for another. And the idea of "the far horizon" itself deserves study—it is someone else's center of the world, someone else's firm footing, some-one else's native ground. The map as construct serves mostly as a frame in which to recognize where we writers are in the world and where we are in our lives. Why not expand the available topography? To expand the knowledge available within the landscape we might dub our "internal borderlands," we would be wise to follow US poet laureate Philip Levine's advice: "If you're going somewhere new and undiscovered you have to trust the imagination, you have to truly believe the poem knows better than you and thus follow where it leads."

Here it is at last—the time to set sail with the writers assembled in the pages that follow. Our own journeys are hinted at and encouraged and guided by those who have gone before—Bishop, Walcott, Levine, and many more. The possibilities stretch far beyond the pages of this book. The fado singers lift their voices over the rooftops in the Bairro Alto of Lisbon. Giant stone turtles announce the mandarins in the Temple of Literature in Hanoi, just as they have done for centuries. Monastery bells toll over the hillsides at dawn. The muezzin rises in the minaret to sound the call to *adhan*. Bathers stand waist-deep in the headwaters of the Ganges, fringed in the gold light of sunset. The brogue of language calls its landscape into being, whether on the steps to Machu Picchu, beside the intricate locks of the Panama Canal, or under the awning of a street kitchen in Surabaya along the Madura Strait. The world awaits our curiosity and our deep attention. The great travelers and journeyers—they all set out into the unknown to make a record of what they experienced. And they each recognized one fundamental truth: each age requires its own journeys.

Let us not make of the world, as Spalding Gray phrased it, "one big piece of calendar art." Let us engage our curiosity and our humanity in that which exists beyond our own horizon line with our sails fully opened—to riff off a phrase of Bertolt Brecht's—so that our verses might travel further in this life than they might otherwise have done.

*—Brian Turner, for the editors*
*Göteborg, Berlin, Dubai, Orlando, 2012*

# New Cartographies

## The Poet in the World

# Poets Crossing Borders

*Kazim Ali*

He is looking into my book, turning each page slowly, looking at, reading the faded blue marks there. Every once in a while he touches his fingertip to the page, leaves it there before slowly turning to the next.

"What is it?" I ask, knowing what he sees there. He does not answer. "My name is Mohammad Kazim Ali. I am a professor at Shippensburg University. You can call up the school's web page and see my profile there." He does not answer. "I am a *poet*," I say.

It is the spring of 2006. It is still a year before a student, dressed in army fatigues, will see me in the parking lot outside my office in the English Department carrying a box of recycling to the curb. He will call the police to report suspicious activity. The campus will be temporarily shut down. In the rush to fulfill all the emergency procedures, the officers will forget to notify the department secretary still inside the building at her desk. At some point in the afternoon, she will look out the window and see the bomb squad and panic. I am not aware of this. I am in my little love bug, driving north to Carlisle, humming along with the radio. Maybe poetry *is* dangerous?

"Okay," says the passport control officer, shutting my book and knocking its edge against the counter between us. "You need to go with this man," he says and hands the passport to a waiting officer.

Because he is also Asian, a Filipino, I get bold. "Do we really need to do this?" I ask him. "You realize I have to go through this *every* time."

He does not answer.

I heft my shoulder bag. He does a quick double take when he catches a glimpse of my fingernails, painted in what I think is a fetching slate blue gray. He keeps walking. Which is more disturbing: That he doesn't immediately understand that I would pose no al-Qaeda-supported security threat? Or that somehow I take this sign of my westernization and postmodernity to be a marker of queerness that thus excuses me from scrutiny, an evasion that perhaps any other Muslim man with more heteronormative behavior would not be able to escape? That somehow I am trying, from a position of odd privilege, to be clear that I am not "that kind of Muslim," that I am not *like them*.

Any Muslim body is strange now, other, worthy of scrutiny.

And to cross any border means to submit one's own body to the law.

The law marks the body, documents it, scrutinizes it, registers it, permits it, manipulates it, suppresses it, denies it, forbids it, kills it.

Linguistically, the word *national* often refers to where you were born. Within that conception is an intrinsic connection (of political loyalty, yes, but also physically in the tissues and organs themselves) of a human body to the geographic location or space in which it entered the world or currently resides.

To be *international* means to be "between" nations, between loyalties, between the human body and the very idea of a law that seeks to control it. It must be a good place for a poet to be, a person who speaks with a forked tongue, who understands that the difference between *sky* and *caelo* may be just a little drifting but that between *sky* and *ciel* is immeasurable distance, not mere vowel and consonant, *ciel* holding not only the root syllable for the English *ceiling* but also a synonymous word in French for *heaven*. Only to the bilingual speaker will the word quiver so in between the languages.

At Babel we were given fractured tongues, and the notions of multiplicity and infinity opened themselves in our mouths. Say something. Say something more.

It is not when I cross a border but when I cross *back*—back to my own home, my "nation," as it were—that my body is subjected to various technological interventions. I am separated from the group. X-rays pass through me. An image of me, a naked ghost, appears somewhere and then disappears. I disappear. Led by a man—usually younger, usually a man of color, usually joking to hide his discomfort—to the cordoned-off room. Here we are: me, shoeless and trembling, trying to ignore his uniform and gun, his hands moving up and down my body. He is giving me—it must be part of the training—a running narration of his activity.

I am touching your chest. I am touching your stomach now. I am going to touch your groin. I will use only the back of my hand. I am touching the inside of your thigh. Your hip.

My body is the dark one. My name is a Muslim one. Your name is in our system. We know it isn't you. You should change your name. What is your father's name. What is your grandfather's name. Who are you. Where do you come from.

Body, you do me well and dangerous, slip between nations, between tongues, slip yourself naked between night and day, between genders and genres.

Or will you write yourself in code, download your short-term memory into machines, slide credit cards under the skin of your palm, be tagged by an electronic surveillance device. Will your physical location be monitored like the airplane on the little screen embedded in the seatback in front of you, slowly crawling across the Midwest to New York, crawling from New York to Iceland, from Iceland across Europe and Turkey to Tel Aviv.

What is your father's name. What is your grandfather's name. Wrote Mahmoud Darwish, "My homeland is not a suitcase." My suitcase is opened, all my things taken out, rubbed with special cloth. The cloth is taken away to be tested. For what, I don't know.

This is how a poet crosses borders.

I was driven from the sea through the mountains to Jerusalem, where every street has three names that do not always translate from one to another. Street of the Mujahideen, meaning "martyrs" in Arabic, translated into English and Hebrew as "Lions Gate." The mujahideen in this case refers not to the twentieth-century martyrs but instead to the men who fought with Saladin nearly one thousand years earlier.

History has long arms in a country crossed and recrossed by lines. Buildings, neighborhoods, and whole cities are built one on top of another. Sound familiar?

The first thing I wanted to see in Jerusalem was al-Aqsa, the open plaza called by Muslims the Far Mosque, called by Jewish people the Temple Mount because it was the location of the Temple destroyed in 70 CE. As we climbed the creaky wooden causeway for non-Muslim worshipers, we could see through the slatted walls Jewish worshipers who had come to the small fragment of the Western Wall. It was an emotional sight: a people still wandering in the only land they call home, still hovering at a remnant and in very temporary settings—sitting in plastic lawn chairs or dragging over makeshift podiums on which to place their prayer books. Perhaps the temporariness of the furnishings is meant to acknowledge the fleeting nature of the ruin, or perhaps it is a form of resistance—that to have more permanent accoutrements would be to accept that the Temple was lost and would never be reclaimed. And there, just ahead of us on the causeway, the other side of the whole equation—twenty or thirty body-length riot shields, stacked within easy reach for quick use. Then I remember how some places are used as symbols of the "nation," how Ground Zero is used, how this place is used for swearing-in ceremonies for different units of the Israeli army.

In this open area—besides the gardens and paved areas for worship—is the enormous Dome of the Rock and an indoor mosque, itself built and destroyed many times. Around the mosque in the great tree-lined park, many small groups of men recite the Qur'an. As with many Muslim mosques, it is not the building but the space itself that is the actual mosque, the place people pray. When you go inside the structure called the Dome and see the actual Rock (it is massive), you only want to get closer. A little stairwell under the Rock leads into the so-called Well of Souls. Where one can and can't pray here is fraught with all kinds of meaning. When a group of Jewish men came up onto the plaza, the Muslim men began reciting loudly at the top of their lungs, a sonic resistance but a resistance nonetheless. One of the Arab men called the Jewish people "settlers," which I didn't at first understand.

Though I had always thought of settlers as people out in the territories building their kibbutzim, it wasn't so. There were settlers inside Palestinian cities like Hebron, and there were even settlers buying up or confiscating Palestinian buildings and apartments inside the Muslim Quarter of the Old City and in East Jerusalem. I knew them by the enormous Israeli flags hanging from the roof and by the barbed wire, surveillance cameras, and other security measures.

I cross the border—the fake border, the invisible one, the Green Line, so called because it was drawn on a map with a green crayon—between Jerusalem and Qalandia by cab. Though others must dismount and walk through the checkpoint in four stages by advancing through metal cages, I pay my cab driver 250 shekels to drive me straight through. It is the same coming back.

As far as borders go, this one has high drama—border patrols, metal detectors, full searches, plus a thirty-foot-tall concrete wall wrapped in barbed wire and mounted with observation posts. The soldiers aren't much more than children, but I think children grow up quickly in this country. On the Israeli side the bare concrete was licked here and there by the odd piece of liberation graffiti—OCCUPIERS OUT! FREE PALESTINE!—and on the Palestinian side it was covered with a rich tapestry of art: twenty-foot-tall portraits of Yasser Arafat and Marwan Barghouti, drawings of birds, flowers, animals, a young girl holding balloons being borne up and over the wall.

It is not a wall in every place. For long stretches of countryside it is "nothing more" than a high chain-link fence with layers of barbed wire. An electrified fence.

If you want to think about how the machinery of "nations" works against the individual human body, there is no better body to start with than the Palestinian body, specifically the body of Mahmoud Darwish, on August 6, 1982, on his hands and knees, crawling down the hallway of his third-floor apartment while bombs hit the upper floors of the same building, crawling down the hallway to the kitchen so he can make a pot of coffee.

Coffee during bombs: "I want nothing more from the passing days than the aroma of coffee," he says. "The aroma of coffee so I can hold myself together, stand on my feet, and be transformed from something that crawls, into a human being." It is in the midst of war or occupation that people reach for the smallest thing—like Darwish's coffee, "the virgin of the silent morning," "the sister of time"—that gives the body's experience back to itself.

Occupied by the time of war and invasions, the natural places in the world—not only mountains and forests but also cities and towns and human settlements—give up their identities to steel and fire. Darwish writes of the sparkling Mediterranean: "The sea has been entirely packed into stray shells. It is changing its marine nature and turning into metal. Does death have all these names?"

In myths of creation it is given to humans to name things in the world, that is, to give all the particularities of the world their significances. When we tried to climb back into formlessness, namelessness—God?— the tower fell, and we were punished—rewarded?—by the splintering of tongues, the *Babel*.

When I went to France, I went without language. I lived nearly mute as the soft, sanded-off edges of French disappeared into my ears without cognizance. It took *reading* for me to learn the words and be able to speak. It took *writing* for me to be able to make sentences. I lived alone on Corsica, having an easier time understanding Corsican French, French with an Italian accent if you will.

Even so, I could write in English only what I knew in French, and the translation wasn't by meaning but by sound. "I am sending you the sands of Corsica," I wrote on a postcard. And under it, led by the assonance between verb and object, I left the sand as itself—*sable*—but found a new verb to sound off it, "*j'oublie les sables de la Corse,*" translated literally, though not in sound, as "I forget the sands of Corsica."

So I slipped between tongues. Urdu and Arabic, since I was young, had always been in my ear, and Arabic had been in my mouth too, but French was the first other tongue that traveled between them. My muscles—my tongue, the shape of my mouth and lips, the constriction of my throat—all had to change to accommodate it. But they—my throat in particular—had had good practice from Arabic. And sound does give meaning. "*La mer sans cesse,*" I whispered to myself one blustery November morning while walking along the Oregon coast. I could not translate it.

So untranslated, my genre: essays called poems, poems called novels, and some things that call themselves nothing, call themselves wind. A novel, a notebook, a score. Score, not that you won something but that you marked something down on the stone or the wall.

So what is a body for? Questions of language, nation, and individual human body—its fears, its lusts, its sweetness and kindness—are not unrelated.

Darwish knows he is in trouble when the birds stop singing: "Perhaps one of the worst Arabic words is *Ta:'irah*—airplane—which is the feminine form of *Ta:'ir*—bird.... Two wings of steel and silver versus two made of feathers. A nose of wiring and steel against a beak made of song.

A cargo of rockets against a grain of wheat and a straw. Their skies no longer safe, the birds stop singing and pay heed to the war."

When cyborg studies theorist Donna Haraway asks, "Why should our bodies end at the skin, or include at best other beings encapsulated by skin?" she means to explain the idea that our environment—the natural and the made objects within it—is an expression both inward and outward of our individual, communal, bodily, and national desires. So these extensions—the things that make us "cyborgs" or compromise our biological distinctiveness—can in reverse tell us who we really are, what we value, what we fear, how we define the functional existence of ourselves as bodies.

In the case of Mahmoud Darwish, the technologies that intervene in the Palestinian body—airplanes, bombs hitting the apartment building, guns in the hands of soldiers of various factions, the sea covered in metal, the sky a helmet of steel, surveillance equipment, cameras that photograph the body, scanners that read code on ID cards and passports, systems that take measure of the body's shape, bullets that enter it— have defined the conditions under which those bodies have existed and continue to do so.

And the poet himself by page thirty of his book? Still in the kitchen, painstakingly describing the making of Arabic coffee, a difficult prospect under the best of circumstances, and then: "Turn off the heat, and pay no heed to the rockets. Take the coffee to the narrow corridor and pour it lovingly and with a sure hand into a little white cup: dark-colored cups spoil the freedom of the coffee...."

What if a "nation" is just another way to organize political power, which means another way to organize wealth? I want to define the "international" as anyone who moves against this grain, who crosses and recrosses borders, not with allegiance or loyalty to the original idea that physical proximity or natal origin creates intrinsic physical, spiritual, or emotional connection that must then be defended with steel or cash but with a refutation of that concept, with an embrace of community through shared values and an adherence to sustainable and peaceable coexistence with other communities of differing—or similar—values.

I don't think any such nation—whether one is in a place far across the waters from one's home, with a different language and culture defining it, or in one's own birthplace or familiar home surroundings—can be seen except through fractured sight, spoken of with a fractured tongue. Because we cannot remove ourselves, we must live and find it in the actual world. So we are already dependent on the ability of poets to write the future of the society. In her book *In the Heart of the Heart of Another Country*, poet and novelist Etel Adnan writes of Beirut: "It was a refuge for all sorts of political opponents to the various governments in the region, and the matrix for all the tensions that were tearing the world apart.... In that whirlwind, any living body, human or animal, looked fragile...."

When Adnan posits Beirut as a city of refugees, she means it is a city that has stopped being a "capital"—a representative of national ideals and aspirations—but is rather an *international* city, a site of resistance of the individual and human to the systemic structures of institutional power, whether political, military, or national. She herself is a multinational writer, born of a Syrian father and a Greek mother, who has lived her life between California, France, Lebanon, and Greece.

The book I use to cross borders, to move from one nation to another, is as good an essay as any about the American experience with place. On each page of my little passport is a quote relating to the "destiny" of the American project. This "destiny" seems to be endless expansion, expansion without clear purpose. On one page, Lyndon Johnson says, "For this is what America is all about. It is the uncrossed desert and the unclimbed ridge. It is the star that is not reached and the harvest sleeping in the unplowed ground.... Is a new world coming? We welcome it—and we will bend it to the hopes of man."

On another page, George Washington suggests, "Let us raise a standard to which the wise and honest can repair." This second quote I cannot see in my own passport because pasted over it is my multiyear visa to India. India is the home of my parents and grandparents and my family for at least two hundred years back. Do I belong there any more than the place I happen to live now? At any rate, I have the option of becoming an "Overseas Citizen of India," which affords me the same rights as Indian citizens living abroad and many rights while traveling in India as well.

What is the origin of a body of multiplicity? For example, one like mine that was born in England, spent early childhood in India, and then was taken to the cold places—first Winnipeg, Manitoba, on the prairies of Canada, then north to Jenpeg, where it snowed in early October and I never saw a deciduous tree. The only Indians I knew were from the Cross Lake Indian Reservation; we bought our fur-lined suede gloves and boots from them. The hydroelectric project my father was working on brought cheap and plentiful power to the city of Winnipeg far to the south but devastated the local environment. Where are you from, a person is often asked. Where indeed? I have no answer.

When Etel Adnan returned home to Beirut after seventeen years away, she had no way of approaching the task of writing about the return. She instead opted for the form of the short paragraph, borrowed from the book she was reading at the time, *In the Heart of the Heart of the Country*, by William H. Gass. In the title story, Gass writes brief entries under various headings, including "Place," "Weather," "My House," "A Person," "Wires," "The Church," "Politics," "People." Sometimes the categories combine, as in "My House, This Place and Body." In this form of divided intention, Adnan is able to approach—like a cubist painter, like Gertrude Stein in *Tender Buttons*—the same place, the same people and subjects, from multiple perspectives. In the following decades of her life Adnan would rewrite this same essay three separate times, using the same headings: once about her return to California, once about a time in Libya, and the last time about moving between these places and her home in California.

Adnan wants to know if the body's experience really is tied in any meaningful, actualizing way to "locality" (which might or might not mean "nationality").

"The world is somewhere else, in Mexico, in India," she suggests. "Why should it always be in a named place? Why should it, altogether, *be*?"

So "home"—or "homeland" if you insist—may not be a place in the world, a geography. It may be within—the experience of the single body inside one's skin. "It's not about history, not about suffering," Adnan insists. "It's not about people, it's about a child gone crazy with power." It is interesting that she positions the idea of "nation" as infantile, suggesting that maybe we could try to develop a model of nationality based on motherhood, a social or political entity whose purpose is nurturing in a certain way the interests and productivity of those people who live within it. Such a nation would have the resources under its own earth available, would belong to the people who live inside it.

Adnan's folded, refracting, repeating way of exploring "nation" or "country" is typical of many multinational writers. One cannot choose a single frame or single narrative or single experience. They all happen at once, one after the other, sometimes overlapping, sometimes playing backward:

> I understand how the muezzin's last call to prayer spreads within the sky and sinks in the direction of the mounting darkness. I'm losing my hold on the sliding day, and sitting on a chair seemingly firm, I feel that I am engulfed by an invisible wave that is carrying me into this geometry we call "the world," and also into something else for which we do not have a name.

In the meantime, on the wrong sides of various borders we wait. My sister and her family, having purchased plane tickets, do not receive their visas for travel to India in time for a cousin's wedding. We all theorize it has to do with our father's Pakistani citizenship. He wasn't born there but moved there just before Partition and became a citizen upon the creation of the Pakistani state.

When nations—Pakistan, Israel, India—come into existence, a whole history, a whole nationality, sometimes a whole language has got to be written, and quickly, to account for them. The large-pearl couscous prepared by Arabs in the region and referred to there as "Palestinian couscous" is labeled "Israeli couscous" in the West.

These nations—most of the new ones of the twentieth and twenty-first centuries anyhow—received their political legitimacy from mandates of European powers. England in particular—as Robert Moses of New York State highway-planning infamy did—indulged in the strategy of "partition," brutally effective at separating communities, creating political and social unrest, and killing any chance of popular resistance against the mechanism and the machines of empire. In this way "postcolonialism" became continuing economic and political colonialism, "post" only the trappings of political empire.

And when a nation is split, people are split from one another and sometimes split inside themselves. Adnan's fractured narrative is one artistic solution to the problem, but in *Schizophrene*, Bhanu Kapil explores the connection between migration and schizophrenia. Is a body removed from its nation, its familiar soil, really subject to partition not just of the political sort but also inside the brain itself?

The dramatic heart of this poetic dream-essay of a book is the narrative of an incident of domestic violence in the British-Punjabi community. It is between a butcher and his wife and the chorus of neighbors who peek in through the windows of the house. (Even the neighbors' criticism of the violence stems from their racism: "*You fucking Paki, what do you think you're doing? This is England, you bleeding animal.*") The neighbors are not quite sure whether they are witnessing a murder or whether the blood splattered across the dining room table is from the blood-smeared clothes of the family that works at a butcher's shop.

And me, how am I seen, when someone looks at me? When I read lines of poetry by Gillian Conoley, I felt at last defined: "I approached / as an alias, trachea / without sound, my signature, bright felon."

This confusion of what is seen reflects less on the witnesses and more on the immigrants themselves, whose very existence is governed by the inability to perceive or to be perceived properly in the new environment.

In Kapil's book, the trauma is not limited to the subjects of the book but the subject of the author herself. Threaded through *Schizophrene* is the story of its writing—or rather the failure of its writing:

> On the *night* I knew my book *had failed*, I threw it—in the form of a *notebook*, a hand-written final *draft*—into the garden of my *house* in Colorado.

> Christmas Eve, *2007*. It snowed that *winter* and into the *spring*; before the weather turned truly *warm*, I retrieved my *notes*, and began to write again, from the *fragments, the phrases and lines* still legible on the warped, *decayed* but curiously rigid pages.

It's a good thing Kapil really threw her book into the garden and wasn't just trying to make a further metaphor for the alienation of a subject from perception; I know because I held the book-as-compost object in my hands. She didn't—as she later claims in *Schizophrene*—throw the composted object into the bin when she was finished transcribing what she could from it—or if she did, then she fished it out again and handed it off to Boulder mapmaker and artist Jarvis Fosdick, who created an artist-book/sculpture of the decaying, shredded pages.

Fosdick's object manifests another version of *Schizophrene*, different from the recently published book in standard format. In Fosdick's object, the pages are lashed together with twine and bound between boards covered with sequences of repeating numbers, like geographic coordinates: they seem to be maps to places that can't be found. The body of the schizophrenic is dizzy between localities, unable to place herself. This composted book *can* be read, but not completely. One must peel away shredded layers to read sentences and phrases written below. In a "Notes" section at the end of the book, Kapil theorizes the benefit of a book in shreds, one she tried to re-create textually:

> From cross-cultural psychiatry, I learned that light touch, regularly and impersonally repeated, in the exchange of devotional objects, was as healing, for non-white subjects (schizophrenics) as anti-psychotic medication. In making a book that barely said anything, I hoped to offer: this quality of touch.

Even this "Notes" section becomes a part of the body of the main text. In six short paragraphs, it situates *Schizophrene*, outlines its creation in a learning community of writers and thinkers at Naropa University, describes how its editing process engendered Kapil's next project (an anticolonial novel, *BAN*), and gives a listing of the journals and collaborations (including with Kapil's sister, the visual artist Rohini Kapil, whose work graces the cover of the book) in which the work previously appeared. These integrative acts seem to serve as the artist/writer's own effort at reversing the damage of mental distress caused by the immigrant condition of migration from familiarity to the new nation, a journey more often than not marked or caused by other stresses—social, political, economic, familial.

The "Notes" section ends with a brief and telling sentence:

> Finally, I would like to extend my gratitude to Olga Visio's *Unseen Mendieta*, a document of Ana Mendieta's silueta

works that inspired *Schizophrene*, and which I tried to
make myself, as close to the border of India and Pakistan as
I could get, which was my own mother's garden in Punjab.

So at last we have a statement of influence, in this case a statement
of absence, the imprint of Mendieta's body, the outline of it, the trace of
it. Absence is what makes the condition of a body without nation after
all, absence from language, absence from landscape, and—no joke!—
absence from the food of one's mother and one's mother's people, which
is the easiest and the surest sign of the loneliness of the immigrant—just
as that rich smell of curry in the air is the surest sign you have entered an
Indian neighborhood or household.

And here also, in the final lines of the book, after the formal "border"
of text and "apparatus" has already been crossed, one finds another bor-
der, the national border, the one between India and Pakistan. And when
Kapil says she made silhouette works in her mother's garden—itself an
archetypal place of creation—"as close to the border" as she could get
(like my sister and her family, Kapil could not get the stamp of national
legitimacy into the book of her passport)—I believe she made them:
pressed the skin and flesh of her bare body into the damp earth.

Body and soil meet at the close of the book at the "national border,"
which is a false one—that border in particular, the one that runs through
Punjab, the one that separated Amritsar from Lahore, that ripped open
the dream of a different nation, Khalistan, one like Palestine that occu-
pied (for the moment) no map, that false border, soaked with the blood
of countless bodies—and try through physical contact to stitch what was
torn apart whole again with the body of the writer-artist, a body-worker
herself, pressed into the earth.

In *Schizophrene* and in her books *Incubation* and *Humanimal*, Bhanu
Kapil takes as one of her many departure points the interrogation of the
immigrant body as either a monster—an entity unexplainable by and
unable to function properly within the social and legal structures of a

given society—or a cyborg, a body that by subvention and subversion surrenders parts of its own sovereignty to the external processes of the environment around it. In either case it is a body in crisis, one whose very existence and function and processes call into question the efficacy of nationality or nationhood in describing it.

In the bitter midwinter cold of Brampton, my cousin and I watch the old Indian ladies in their saris and parkas and snow boots striding purposefully from their housing developments to the supermarket. In the fall it is cardigans and sneakers. In the summer it is a light jacket and *chappals*. It is never quite warm enough to wear the sari unaccompanied and besides, the sari wearer is usually an older woman, in her fifties or sixties at least, and the skin of her bare stomach and back, revealed by the sari "blouse," really little more than a halter bra, seems unseemly in the repressed West, just one more reason for her to be seen as monstrous.

"It is psychotic to draw a line between two places," says Kapil, and then, "It is psychotic to submit to violence in a time of great violence and yet it is psychotic to leave that home or country, the place where you submitted again and again, forever." If the mind itself comes under pressure and duress from the various patterns of forced migrations, what are the coping mechanisms of the immigrant, nearly a monster in the new country, with monstrous customs, deviant sexuality, strange language, strange smells and tastes and clothing?

How does a body, a small one, a South Asian queer body, the body of a poet with a little blue book in his hand, cross borders then? Accompanied by verses extolling American expansion, he receives little marks of his legitimacy. A stamp from Uruguay, a stamp from India, and though he doesn't need them, shouldn't need them, stamps from the Canadian government too, and from Spain and France, both countries with open-border agreements with the United States that render visa stamps extraneous. He is annoyed when they stamp—no one else needs this stamp—but grateful for it when he comes home, is separated from his traveling companions, taken to the room in the back, stands there while a stranger runs his hands all over his body. Once he is asked to remove his shirt. Another time he is asked to remove his pants. The weird intersection between sexuality and the apparatus of nationhood and alienation—*his* alienation—is not lost on him.

I am touching your chest. Your throat. Your stomach. Please unbuckle your pants. Please lower your pants. I am going to touch your thigh. Your groin. I will use the back of my hand.

It *does* remind him that here in this place, in every American place, he is less than human. He is reminded that even though he is a citizen, he is—will always *be*—suspect and *a* suspect.

And the last page of his passport frightens him. There is a graphic of Earth seen from space—the moon is in the foreground, a satellite floats above—as if to confirm Lyndon Johnson's earlier discourse on the United States: that its mission is continual expansion, continuing homogenization, that once the western limit of the continent is reached, the nation will (did) spread out into the Pacific, that once the reaching arms of nationality encircle the planet and meet (they have), they will reach out into space for the star yet unvisited.

Opposite this graphic, in large letters, is the following statement: "This document contains sensitive electronics. For best performance, do not bend, perforate, or expose to extreme temperatures."

Electronics? But where, he wonders, turning the book over in his hands in alarm. True, the covers are thick and stiff. *Inside* the covers, he wonders. On the front cover below "the United States of America" there is a small gold rectangle with a circle inside it. Is this chip in the cover underneath that rectangle, he wants to know. And what information is on that chip? About me? Where I have been, which borders I've crossed? Or does it track my movement, track it like the plane on the little screen in front of my seat when I am flying?

As Kapil says, "It is psychotic not to know where you are in a national space."

The favorite security questions of the TSA echo back to me at the passport control office of Ben Gurion airport but in my interrogator's broken English: What is you father-name. What is you grandfather-name.

My "father-name" is not even real: our family name is Sayeed. My father's actual name wouldn't tell anything about us, migrants for generations—from Egypt to India, from India to Britain, from Britain to Canada. And in the one place of ultimate rootlessness, we are the most fixed into otherness. Every male relative of my father's shares the same first name, and my father chose to drop the family name. *Kazim* and *Ali* are my two middle names, not my first and my last. So who am I? You can't even begin.

And no one has yet asked me: what is your mother's name.

A poet, a maker of things, using the very language that was designed to control, obfuscate, curse, becomes his own mother. In the myth, the goddess Athena, born of no mother, wants the scariest mother of them all—Medusa—to adorn her shield. Medusa has all the symbols of the best of poets: she has snakes, that ancient symbol of wisdom, for hair, and when she looks into your soul, she can transfix you to the spot. True to form, once slain, from her open throat—source of her voice—flew the winged horse Pegasus, icon of poetry.

In practical terms, asking one in the brutal forum of interrogation what one's mother's name is must necessarily conjure for the interrogator his or her own mother. How would one be able to continue?

How does a body cross a border? How do borders cross bodies? The poet Meena Alexander writes of returning from a trip to her home and reading a passage from Darwish's *Memory for Forgetfulness*:

> She realizes that these words, composed in another place,
> in another language, words written in a time of war,
> translate well.
> Where she is, migrant memory pitches its tent.

> This is her home ground, this borderland of desire and
> meaning making. No elsewhere.

Is that it then? A book as a home, a book to wander with. A book as a passport, not the passport as a book.

The book must give us tools, then, for seeing the individual body against the landscape it inhabits. The book can help us see the landscape not as political territory or economic potential but *as a place* itself, with topographical, spiritual, and biological values utterly intrinsic and at the same time knitted thoroughly together with the lives and the lifestyles of the biosystems, plant life, people, and animals that inhabit it.

When I was writing *Bright Felon: Autobiography and Cities*, I had no intention of writing "poems" or a "book of poems." Perhaps you could say the entire text is a single poem—or reads that way. But I knew that in order to write about my life, or more accurately *write my life*, I would have to use not literary but geographic form, architectural form: the form of the cities that I had traversed and lived in, even for short periods of time.

The map on the cover of *Bright Felon* is by the cartographer, artist, and DC statehood activist Nikolas Schiller. It is an aerial photo of Lower Manhattan and Brooklyn refracted and formed into a geometric pattern. It is no mistake that it appears as a classical Islamic motif. Some maps are conceptual.

Just as cities are concatenations of time acting in space (I pointed out once while giving a walking tour of Walt Whitman's SoHo the buildings that were original to Whitman's time, including the theater that was once a firehouse, a guesthouse now a shop, and a parking lot once a hospital), my book passes through space and time, moving both backward and forward, once discursive, then lyrical, first essayistic, then poetic, sometimes all things at once. Sentences without consequence, one leading into the other, shine into the unexplored and unexamined life: *why* had I been silent for so long? The book stutters itself open finally. What begins in clotted and endless sentences opens out into monosyllables and long vowels. Function follows form sometimes. Someone once said that pentameter is the length of a breath and iambic is the rhythm of pulse. It might be medically true, but only if you are tuning your fork to two of the many systems in your body, two of the many that exist in the planetary entity, of the many that resound through the cosmos.

The book is part sculpture perhaps, part geometry, part calligraphy. On the cover, in the form of orange calligraphy surrounding the subtitle, is a second subtitle, a secret, a line of American poetry translated into Urdu and copied there. I've never told anyone what the line reads. I want a reader like me—someone who can read the Urdu text but who also knows enough American poetry that he or she would recognize it. It's happened twice so far.

A map is a dangerous and useless thing, warns Hakim Bey in his groundbreaking text of popular and artistic resistance, *Temporary Autonomous Zone*. "The 'map' is a political abstract grid," he says, "a gigantic *con* enforced by the carrot/stick conditioning of the 'Expert' State, until for most of us the map *becomes* the territory." But in the actual moment of mapmaking itself, one can find intentions more directly connected to the body: where is the highest point from which to see the terrain around you, where is the closest source of fresh water, where is there shelter from sun or rain. In a world, as Bey points out, in which every square inch of territory, whether land, water, or air, is claimed by some political entity or another, there are critical questions: "How can we separate the concept of *space* from the mechanisms of *control*? The territorial gangsters, the Nation/States, have hogged the entire map. Who can invent for us a cartography of autonomy, who can draw a map that includes our desires?"

In *A Lily Lilies*, poet Josey Foo and choreographer Leah Stein make an effort to map the terrain of the desert landscape of the Navajo Nation. They write that their effort "maps space through language, language through movement, and both space and movement through pictures." The book of poems, choreography, and photographs presents an interesting new way the abstract of "nation" can be personalized and brought into the individual body.

In one photograph, you could be looking at the water, at the sky, at the inside of a mouth—it isn't clear, though you know it is a landscape you are seeing. The parts of the body and the parts of the landscape are not so distinguishable, at least not in the dance. Stein writes, "Contrast between architecture of the body—bones suggesting buildings, kite and ridge— and movement of arms, wrists, elbows, head.... Arms, wrists, elbows and head seek wilderness." The sensuous forms of the poems on the page imitate biomorphic shapes of eroded tree branches, wind-shaped hills, and the sinuous line of the horizon itself. Dancers become birds, poems become choreography, bodies turn into one another.

This moment—bodies turning into one another—is the moment of "chaos," the moment that precedes most creation myths. It's the moment that Bey believes needs to be preserved against the interests of "Nation/ States," which always require regulation and submission to law in order to increase maximum productivity for the benefit of as few people as possible (in order to maximize the amount of benefit). "Don't just survive while waiting for someone's revolution to clear your head," Bey exhorts. "Act as if you were already free ... carry your Moorish passport with pride, don't get caught in the crossfire, keep your back covered—but take the risk, dance before you calcify."

In *A Lily Lilies*, words change into themselves: "The sun *shines* but the sun *is* the shine." Dancers change into animals before finally one can be two things at once: "*She is both daughter and river.*" If you can be a citizen of two nations at once—really owe ultimate loyalty to both countries—it can mean only one thing: that war, the most unimaginative and boring method of resolving conflict, must really be over.

"Imprint," the final sequence of the book, explores the contact between physical bodies and the soil of the land; this contact *is* and *can be* a productive part of oneself, not as territory to be owned but as place, nourishment, locality. "I carry a candle to the river / and acquire my life," writes Foo. In a final note, Stein explains the choreography: "Each dancer's movement 'imprints,' becomes part of the other's movement, all movements become one imprint."

Perhaps Foo and Stein—who has choreographed site-specific works in train garages, open fields, corner parking lots, vacant city lots, historical sites, gardens, and burial grounds—should team up with Bhanu Kapil and create some pieces for all the invisible borders that run under the ground of the American continent, its current political borders so new, so recent not only in the eyes of the Earth but in any conception of human inhabitation here.

Kapil threw her book into the garden to undergo transformative processes, and Foo and Stein talk in their introduction about their book as a "transportable site," hoping it "will travel to very many places." That leaking of the main text in both of these books into what is traditionally thought of as "apparatus"—the index, the notes, the introduction, the biographical data—is exciting because it prefigures an idea about the book as a body or the book as a nation. A nation could have multiplicity as a founding concept, but such an idea necessarily contravenes the possibility of "empire"—doing away with borders would mean awarding ownership of what's in the ground to whoever rightly inhabits that space. Deep in the ground of a book, one thrown into the garden or one constructed in somatic movements in open air, for example, one discovers new ways of reading it.

Who is the human here, then, and what can it all mean? On the macro level, in a conflict between nation and individual human body, nation would always seem to win. Bodies can be pierced, killed, sullied, lied about, suppressed, erased. Nations have many tools, mechanical and otherwise, at their disposal. But I am tempted to say that in a conflict between nation and individual on a micro level, the individual always wins. A nation is a fiction, a story everyone has decided to agree is real because it seems either convenient or necessary at the moment; a person is a collection of infinite kindnesses, loves, and, indeed, joys.

It is always the human who acts, who transcends the national myth that has been created. Darwish, in his book *Absent Presence*, writes, "Do not look upon yourself in the way they write about you. Do not investigate the Canaanite in you in order to establish that you exist. Rather, seize this reality, this name of yours, and learn how to write your proof. For you are you, not your ghost, the one who was driven away in that night."

The individual must find those zones of liberation—as Bey would advise, that "tactile tasty physical space (ranging in size from, say, a double bed to a large city)"—in order to actualize an individual spiritual awakening, one to generosity and kindness, pleasure and the abandonment of "world-hatred & shame."

Well, I myself am a Temporary Autonomous Zone then, with my Moorish passport, refusing to write the laws of the nation on my body but instead learning through the language of poetry what it really is that binds one human to another in community.

WORKS CITED:

Adnan, Etel. *In the Heart of the Heart of Another Country*. San Francisco: City Lights Publishers, 2005.

Alexander, Meena. *Poetics of Dislocation*. Ann Arbor: The University of Michigan Press, 2009.

Bey, Hakim. *T.A.Z. The Temporary Autonomous Zone, Ontological Anarchy, Poetic Terrorism*. Brooklyn, NY: Autonomedia, 2003.

Darwish, Mahmoud. *Absent Presence*. London: Hesperus Press, 2010.

Darwish, Mahmoud. *Memory for Forgetfulness: August, Beirut, 1982*. Berkeley: University of California Press, 1995.

Foo, Josey, and Leah Stein. *A Lily Lilies*. Callicoon, NY: Nightboat Books, 2011.

Haraway, Donna. *Simians, Cyborgs, and Women: The Reinvention of Nature*. New York: Routledge, 1990.

Kapil, Bhanu. *Schizophrene*. Callicoon, NY: Nightboat Books, 2011.

# Astral Summer

*Katharine Coles*

The only time my parents took me out of the United States as a child, I was nine. That Christmas break, they loaded my two brothers and me into the old International Travelall and drove us south into Mexico. We stayed in run-down motels until we left the cold weather behind and reached our beachfront hotel—also probably run-down but glamorous in my memory, maybe because I'd slept in far more tents than hotels or maybe because the restaurant served turtle soup—outside San Blas. San Blas has since been developed as a surfing destination, but back then the road leading to the hotel was a rutted track my father nosed the shock-sprung truck carefully down, its headlights at night lunging wildly against dense jungle foliage strange to a child born and raised in the desert.

Most of our time in Mexico we spent either on the beach, digging for shells and bodysurfing the enormous waves, or out in the jungle, hiking and canoeing and stalking iguanas. Only once or twice did we go into town. The place was still remote enough that women on the street would stop us so they could run our white-blond hair—my brothers' in 1968 grown almost as long as mine—through their fingers. Since I didn't understand Spanish, our communication occurred through those touches. There, I had my first sense of the foreignness not only of others or the world but also of myself. I understood myself to be a stranger, worthy of examination.

This was my first awareness of a sense I've spent much of my life as a poet seeking and cultivating. I humped a backpack loaded with Homer and Sappho around the Greek islands during graduate school. Shortly after September 11, when Americans were taking travel advisories seriously, I spent three weeks alone in Indonesia, where my mother had been born and spent her early childhood; for days, I didn't see another Western face, and again I understood how little privacy anyone has who is visibly marked as other. I traveled on a small boat up the Amazon; I went to Cuba, where the highways are so poorly marked you have to hire someone to ride with you out of Havana, just to make sure you're on the right road. Sometimes, traveling, I thought I knew in advance what I sought. But even though it can be useful to have a destination in mind, the most important things I found would be those I didn't know to look for. The shaman in the Amazonian village who pressed his thumb next to my blue eye, then gave me a spear he'd made. A lion carved in a stone lintel. The house my mother was born into in what was then Batavia, the house my grandmother had sketched in the margin of one of her letters home, which I found seventy-odd years later by luck and accident.

For most of my young adult life, I thought my parents parochial and unadventurous in their travel, which mostly involved camping or car trips to visit extended family in the Midwest. They'd been limited in where they could go by children and money. My mother's father was a geologist and an explorer (eventually the chief geologist for Standard Oil, then head of exploration for Petrobras in Brazil), and, after a childhood spent moving from Indonesia to Central America to Cuba in the wake of his career—a path I've erratically followed on some of my own journeys as I've tried to write about my grandparents—my mother for years was content to explore the spectacular desert landscape they'd made home. And, finally, it hadn't occurred to them to travel in pursuit of the human. I was the one who wanted to spend weeks outside her language, who, having grown up in a western town settled a bare one hundred years earlier, wanted to walk great cities redolent with history and see their museums and churches. I preferred an ancient botanical garden, planted and cultivated over centuries by human hands, to an untouched natural vista. What I wanted was to feel my otherness. In nature, especially in the Utah desert that had been so exotic to my parents, I felt at home, having spent much of my childhood playing under its spectacular sandstone formations and vast sky. Hanging from a cliff face by a rope or rafting the wild waters of a western river was, thanks to my parents, part of my ordinary life.

In December 2010 I spent a month in Antarctica, sent to Palmer Station by the National Science Foundation to write poems. The desire and the comfort to go to such an extreme must have been rooted in my childhood. Indeed, my sense of estrangement in Antarctica arose out of just what my parents had been seeking when they moved to the American West: a landscape vaster and less welcoming than any I had known. Made entirely of water, sky, ice, and the light they all reflect, Antarctica was a place I literally had to teach myself to see. I am not alone in this. Ernest Shackleton, in *South*, describes watching, on May 8, 1915, the sun, "which had made 'positively his last appearance' seven days earlier," rise and set again not once but three times over two and a half hours. With sinking hearts, he and his crew had watched the final sunset in the north—and it had really occurred. The subsequent risings and settings were reflections and refractions cast by water onto clouds. And those repeated sunsets— were they any less disheartening for being unreal?

When I was there (summer, the light never altogether failing), the mountains on the horizon might appear one place in the morning then shift leftward that afternoon; they might turn upside down or temporarily vanish into a cloud bank or a clear day. Everything came to the eye via reflection and refraction; everything observed was an image cast, partly or wholly mirage. And so I found my way to see it. It was like nothing so much as the desert, where landscape is also made largely of light and light's deceptions. I learned to remember what my parents had taught me: that my senses are wholly untrustworthy, even at home. Next to this estrangement, the somewhat odd culture of science that dominates station life was, well, a negligible obstacle to overcome. Still, the locals never would let a poet forget that she was the foreigner among them, the stranger worthy of observation.

I should say that over time, my parents began sometimes to join me on my travels—both of them for part of my trip to Greece and to Cuba, my mother following me, again in my grandfather's footsteps, up the Amazon. It is now December 2011. A week from today, my parents, who are seventy-nine and eighty-two, will step onto an airplane. A few days later, they will be on a ship off the Antarctic Peninsula, not far from where I lived during that month. After spending so many years stalking history—of human culture, of my own family—I will be thinking of them there, following in my footsteps to a place I never would have gone without them. I will be beside myself with envy.

It seems to me that the poet's job is just this: to stand beside herself, outside herself, in order to understand something about how an individual human subjectively encounters the world, in which and against which she is a stranger, even to herself. In doing so, she may become able to illuminate something important about the human condition, the fact that in this world we are all in some sense foreigners, estranged by consciousness from our essential, immediate relationship with reality. Without this awareness, we believe in what we see—the mountains just there; the sun setting; the wavering on the desert horizon that seems to promise cool water where there is only dry rock and sand.

Some poets, I know, can remember this estrangement, can feel it again and again, without leaving home. Emily Dickinson, for example. But for me, to be out of my element—my language, my culture, my known landscape—reconnects me in a powerful way to my sense of the world, which I will never fully know, and through it to the part of myself that is equally unknowable.

# Field Poet

*Nick Flynn*

Strange, that we sometimes have to put ourselves in another place—unfamiliar, foreign—in order to wake up. Strange in that we wake up every day, just where we are. We wake up, but before we open our eyes, we say, this is my bed or this is my room or this is my apartment. This is my corner, this is my box, this is my cell. My castle, my dungeon, my iron lung. My armchair, my wheelchair, my coffin ... yet we barely remember the moment our eyes closed last night. Neuroscientists, I've read, understand sleep, but why we wake up is still a mystery. Try this: lie in bed (box, dungeon, iron lung) with your eyes closed—can you list everything you would see on the mantel (sidewalk, floor) if you were to open your eyes?

Ten years ago now, I made my way to a lake in the center of Africa, a lake almost the size of Ireland. Because I flew there from Ireland, I thought I would understand. I went, ostensibly, to help someone I'd just met make a documentary film, which he described as a parable about fish and guns and globalization. His name was Hubert, the lake was Victoria, the fish was Nile perch. Nile perch is flaky and white, and it feeds soldiers and lots of folks in Europe and the United States and is perfect for Filet-O-Fish sandwiches. The guns—well, arms merchants supply the guns, and the arms merchants come from the same countries that import the fish. This is the way the world works.

The first night Hubert and I met, in Rome, he showed me some early footage of what he was working on. I was so moved that I offered to meet him in Africa the next time he went. To help, whatever that meant. But I was a poet, not a filmmaker—what could I do? I went to Paris—which is where Hubert was based—a few times in the months before the trip. To buy equipment, to look at footage, to be filled in on that part of the world. Hubert had spent the past ten years in and out of Africa—to listen to him was like having a veil pulled back, like waking up. Africa had seemed, from my reading of headlines, like a nightmare of chaos—endless war, endless famine, all of it somewhat incomprehensible. Hubert, with his parable of guns and fish, was attempting to put things into context.

As a child, I hadn't had much opportunity to see the world; my family didn't have that kind of money. I had to learn what I could from books ("when I walked into the jungle, I was seventeen. When I walked out I was twenty-one. And, by God, I was rich!"), from Tarzan movies, from Mutual of Omaha's *Wild Kingdom*. My mother didn't have the money to fly us anywhere, except once to Montana—Helena—to stay with cousins for a month. I was eight, and that trip to Montana is a vivid nail driven into those days. I learned to ride a bicycle in Montana! We made Lego fortresses for locusts! On a road trip to Glacier National Park, we stopped at a roadside stand and bought turquoise and rabbit pelts and rubber tomahawks from real Indians. In the back was a sad zoo with a sad bald eagle bent over in a too-small cage—that eagle is all I remember. The mountains were always in the distance, so unlike anything in our hometown, and we were driving toward them. Locusts splattered on the windshield; we had to pull over at every gas station to scrape their bodies off. By nightfall, we would touch a glacier.

Our hometown was Scituate, on the Atlantic Ocean. We lived on Third Cliff, which was slowly—sometimes suddenly—eroding into the sea. Each year, a house or two was pulled over the cliff as the ocean forced its way inland. I would lie on my belly on the edge of the cliff, stare into the ocean, try to imagine eternity. That was when I was awake. Or I'd wander the salt marshes, strewn with detritus from all over the world—parts of ships, brightly colored lobster buoys, the corpse of a white dog.

Annie Dillard, in her essay "Total Eclipse," muses:

> We teach our children one thing only, as we were taught: to wake up. We teach our children to look alive there, to join by words and activities the life of human culture on the planet's crust. As adults, we are almost all adept at waking up.... Yet it is a transition we make a hundred times a day, as, like so many will-less dolphins, we plunge and surface, lapse and emerge. We live half our waking lives and all of our sleeping lives in some private, useless, and insensible waters we never mention or recall. Useless, I say. Valueless, I might add—until someone hauls their wealth up to the surface and into the wide-awake city, in a form that people can use.

This is what Hubert was doing on Lake Victoria all those years. This is why I wanted to meet him there, to help. It meant getting a raft of vaccinations—yellow fever, typhoid, et cetera. It meant taking a pill daily (mefloquine hydrochloride)—psychosis was one possible side effect. It meant not drinking any water unless it was bottled or had been boiled— it doesn't help anyone if you get sick. It meant learning how to work a camera and a boom mic, to carry the money, to guard the equipment. It meant, mostly, opening my eyes.

Now Hubert is one of my best friends, and the footage I saw that first day in Rome has become the film *Darwin's Nightmare*, which won awards at about a dozen international film festivals and was nominated for an Academy Award for Best Documentary Feature in 2006. In the credits, I am listed as artistic collaborator and field poet, a term I borrowed from the Vietnamese, who for thousands of years included a poet in each military unit (a field poet), whose job was to write poems in order to give meaning to each day. In Africa, it simply meant I tried to be fully awake to each moment we were there, and part of that was to transcribe what I saw. It was the best I could offer.

# Thirteen Ways of Working in a War Zone

*Eliza Griswold*

1.  **Stock a first-aid kit:** Carry a broad-based gut antibiotic, such as Cipro or Proquin. (It's hard to be sure of quality in many places.) The opposite is true for antimalarials. If you need one, stop in the first big city and buy Coartem or Riamet at the best pharmacy. Take on first sign of infection. Also purchase oral rehydration salts. They are less than a dollar in some places (less than ten dollars on average) and can cure diarrhea, a preventable disease that kills more than three million people a year, mostly kids.

2.  **Locate yourself:** On arrival, check in with the US embassy or the legation of whatever country claims you as a citizen. If the situation is uncertain, the embassy might urge you to leave for precisely the reasons you've come. Still, it's worthwhile to let someone know your whereabouts.

3.  **Carry the right papers:** If working as a journalist, you may need a government-issued press pass, which can take months to procure. Check the country's visa requirements online before you apply. It

might be easiest to use a visa service, which will act as an intermediary with the arcane embassies of many troubled or closed countries.

4. **Organize your communications:** A working phone is a priority. Satellite phones aren't a requirement in most places. Usually it is simple and much cheaper to pick up a SIM card in the airport. Don't buy one until asking locals which service is best. To that end, be prepared to buy a secondhand phone from a man standing on the street, probably your driver's cousin. A local line is invaluable.

5. **Organize your work:** Bring three sturdy notebooks and keep a daily journal; the more quotidian detail it records, the better—rickshaws, roasting meat, the sweet smoke of a garbage heap, the muezzin's call competing with evangelical hymns over loudspeakers. These will be useful later, especially for the half lines of poems scrawled in the margins.

6. **Hone your method:** Slow down. You may be tempted to accelerate through interviews and places to *get the story*. This frustration—a fear of failure—is part of the reporting process, especially under tough conditions with limited time. Gathering the scenes and facts that long stories require comes with various pressures, including deadlines and the necessity to think through the character detail required on the page later. There's a certain parallel between serving as a soldier and being a foreign correspondent. Both require the capacity to outwait boredom.

7. **Be prepared for more than the work:** There are cases in which interviews, if guided by a gentle intuition, can provide a form of healing. On occasion, a survivor of physical trauma, including rape or abduction, builds a home for her spirit in the air just above her head. She builds a safe castle in the sky where, by not occupying her body, she

is certain to protect herself from harm and the memory of harm. In these cases, posttraumatic stress can manifest as a kind of sleepiness, a daze. You might gently speak to her, repeat the phrases she uses in order to affirm her story. She may return to her physical self for a few minutes.

8. **Travel safely under fire:** In a car, keep your windows rolled down if there is gunfire. Bullets shatter glass, which becomes a secondary weapon. Always park so that you don't have to turn around to get out of a bad situation. Ask about land mines. Listen to your driver. If he says a road is a no-go, then it is a no-go. In some situations, it is a good idea to send a security car ahead to investigate the route.

9. **Find fixers:** Often local journalists, teachers, or aid workers are available for a day or a week. They are invaluable, not only for the perspectives they bring but also for making contacts, which might take months to track down otherwise. Find a fixer before arrival, if possible. Begin your search by contacting the country's leading newspaper, the local BBC or Reuters bureau, and/or local human rights organizations.

10. **Shoot video, whether you like it or not:** Carry a lightweight video camera. I recommend one called the Flip, with some versions being as inexpensive as $100. It will catch and hold details the human eye might not, for instance the accurate number of bee boxes the minister of bees tends in Afghanistan.

11. **File frequently:** If you are working in a place where your notes or camera might be seized before you leave the country, then take the time to upload materials, notes, and photos and e-mail them home every night so they are safe.

12. **Know the rules and responsibilities:** If anything goes wrong—and it will—remember that the people who will pay most for your mistakes are the local driver, translator, and/or friends who will not be leaving when the story is finished. To that end, follow every protection for which they ask, including leaving names out of your work.

13. **Take time to reacclimate:** Be gentle with yourself and those at home. Avoid large supermarkets. Experiencing such a surfeit of food can be nightmarish. Remember, you chose to go. Choose to let painful moments render you tender rather than tough. The act of writing poetry will encourage this process; poems encourage us to return to what baffles us, to return to the site of a disaster and sift through what floats after a crash.

# What Is the Wind: The Changing, Unchanging Gertrude Stein

*Jared Hawkley*

Among the books in her library, *Robinson Crusoe* was a favorite of Gertrude Stein's for the way it examines the behavior of a man separated from his familiar world, stranded on an island he doesn't know. There is a scene in the novel in which the yoke of reality comes crushing down on the hero's shoulders. It happens as he is walking along the beach on the island that he'd presumed deserted.

> It happened one day about noon, going towards my boat, I was exceedingly surprised with the print of a man's naked foot on the shore, which was very plain to be seen in the sand. I stood like one thunderstruck, or as if I had seen an apparition. I listened, I looked around me; I could hear nothing, nor see anything.[1]

Stein sometimes referred to this scene in the novel because of what

---

1. Daniel Defoe, *Robinson Crusoe* (New York: Barnes & Noble Classics Series, 2003), 150.

she thought to be Crusoe's state of mind at the moment he sees the foot-print, calling it "one of the most perfect examples of the non-existence of time and identity": he's so startled that he doesn't immediately under-stand what he's looking at.[2]

Before she turned six, Stein had already lived in a handful of places—first Pennsylvania, then Austria, France, Maryland, and finally California. After losing both parents by the age of seventeen, she invested several years toward a degree in psychology at the prestigious Radcliffe College, then enrolled at Johns Hopkins to study medicine, but dropped out of school after realizing the work didn't suit her. Around that time she had also drafted—and then shelved—her first novel, *Q.E.D.*, a veiled autobio-graphical account of a hot-and-cold, ultimately unsuccessful love affair involving her and two other women during her college years.[3] After this early series of false starts and failures, Stein left her home in Baltimore in 1903 and sailed to Paris, intending to join her beloved brother Leo, leave behind her confused American life and the world at large, and become a writer.

Stein later reflected that living in Paris was necessary for her; it allowed her to write and to be a writer, not so much because it was Paris but because it wasn't the United States. "This separation is important in making literature," she explained, "because there are so many ways for one to feel oneself and every new way helps, and a separating way may

---

2. Gertrude Stein, *What Are Master-Pieces* (New York: Pitman Publishing Corporation, 1970), 93.

3. Gertrude Stein, *Fernhurst, Q.E.D., and Other Early Writings* (New York: Liveright Publishing Corporation, 1996), xi.

help a great deal, indeed it may, it may help very much. And this did."[4] She asserted that "writers have to have two countries, the one where they belong and the one in which they live really. The second one is romantic, it is separate from themselves, it is not real but it is really there."[5]

⁓

Stein channeled her sense of separation into what became her best-selling work, *The Autobiography of Alice B. Toklas*, written entirely in the persona of her muse and wife, Alice. Paraphrasing herself in the voice of Alice, Stein explained that her social isolation, exemplified partly by her steadfast allegiance to the English language, was to a large degree intentional:

> No, she replied, you see I feel with my eyes and it does not make any difference to me what language I hear, I don't hear a language, I hear tones of voice and rhythms, but with my eyes I see words and sentences and there is for me only one language and that is english. One of the things I have liked all these years is to be surrounded by people who know no english. It has left me more intensely alone with my eyes and my english. I do not know if it would have been possible to have english be so all in all to me otherwise. And they none of them could read a word I wrote, most of them did not even know that I did write.[6]

Stein confessed that she wanted to be "intensely alone." She used expatriation as a tool, a precisely planned and executed exercise in

---

4. Catharine R. Stimpson and Harriet Chessman, eds., *Gertrude Stein: Writings 1932–1946* (New York: The Library of America, 1998), 202.
5. Gertrude Stein, *Paris France* (New York: W.W. Norton & Company, Inc., 1996), 2.
6. Gertrude Stein, *The Autobiography of Alice B. Toklas* (New York: Vintage Books, 1990), 70.

moving away. She was essentially placeless: no longer part of her home-land and not part of her adopted home either.

With the turn of the century came a new generation of writers, philoso-phers, and scientists who began to dismantle the foundation stones of basic knowledge. Darwin had claimed that the Bible may not be literally true, and Nietzsche and Marx were suggesting that ethics and social class may be socially constructed; Freud was advocating his theories of sexual impulses, and the world was in the throes of industrialization. Much of the great reconstructive effort began with the artists converging in Paris. From her vantage point there, Stein was perfectly poised to sift through the debris of the nineteenth century, salvaging what remained to com-pose the scaffolding of the new twentieth century.

In time, the accumulated change of that era came to be known as modernism—a movement in literature and the arts characterized by a precipitous plunge into uncertainty and the ensuing trek back out. Among the first to detect this plunge was Henry James; Stein noticed in his writing "the disembodied way of disconnecting something from anything."[7] This was, she felt, a sign of the times—this way of things sep-arating, becoming disembodied.

I don't mean to imply that Stein was reclusive—quite the opposite. She welcomed many artists of the new generation into her home and learned from them; her house at 27 Rue de Fleurus was famously a gathering spot for a pantheon of writers and painters, including F. Scott Fitzgerald, Ernest Hemingway, and Henri Matisse. In particular she was profoundly

---

7.   Stimpson and Chessman, 222.

influenced by Pablo Picasso and his peers, most of whom were not French either, having convened in Paris for their own reasons.

Compelled by the artist's approach to representation and receptive to the undertones of coming unrest, Stein began to be changed. She saw her close friend Picasso working toward a new mode of perception, a new composition "of which one corner was as important as another corner."[8]

Reflecting on Picasso, Stein recalled that he "once remarked I do not care who it is that has or does influence me as long as it is not myself."[9] Soon after they first met, Stein agreed to let Picasso paint her portrait. It was the winter of 1905, and Picasso had yet to take up his cubist modes. Over the course of more than eighty sittings, Picasso finished all but his subject's face. After three times scraping down to the underpainting and revising the view from profile to three-quarters, he finally wiped out the face in aggravation, declared, "I can't see you any longer when I look,"[10] and left for Spain.

Returning to Paris in 1906, inspired by the new African masks and sculpture prevalent in France due to an increasing number of French colonial campaigns, Picasso sat down with the portrait of Stein and finished her face without a reference, without looking at her.

Reportedly, the finished portrait was criticized on the basis that Stein did not resemble it.[11] But Picasso, realizing the impossibility of painting a definitive static image to encompass all of Stein, had instead painted the likeness of a transformation. He saw that she herself was in flux,

---

8. Gertrude Stein, *Picasso* (London: B.T. Batsford Ltd, 1939), 11.
9. Stein, *What Are Master-Pieces*, 85.
10. Stein, *The Autobiography of Alice B. Toklas*, 53.
11. Picasso's reply: "She will."

and one might say that, at least in part, he extracted the idea of cubism from within his subject: a view of real objects as fleeting, shifting, and unknowable.

⤙

In 1909, Stein returned the gesture in the first of what would ultimately become a triptych of word portraits of her friend. Word portraits were exercises in freeing their subjects from containment—a practice Stein had developed between 1906 and 1908 while composing *The Making of Americans*, essentially an extended portrait of three generations of a fictional American family. In the writing of this novel she exploited the power of repetition and rhythm, with subtle changes, to render characters, contemporaries, and life itself. She refined this method in "Picasso," a more restrained work limited to seven verbs in the progressive tense: *following, needing, working, bringing, coming, having,* and *being.*

> This one was one having always something being coming out of him, something having completely a real meaning. This one was one whom some were following. This one was one who was working. This one was one who was working and he was one needing this thing needing to be working so as to be one having some way of being one having some way of working. This one was one who was working.[12]

Curiously, Stein's portrait begins by describing Picasso as "one who was working" and ends by claiming that "he was not ever completely working." By the last line, Stein has asserted several contradictory observations, all ostensibly under the banner of one and the same man. The result is a case study in the process of becoming. Stein essentially

---

12. Gertrude Stein, *Picasso: The Complete Writings* (Boston: Beacon Press, 1970), 97.

describes a man who, like every man or woman, isn't ever only one thing—who can't truly be known.

In 1912, progressing from portraiture to still lifes, Stein wrote the bulk of the work that would be collected in *Tender Buttons*, a series of household poems that seem to obscure the subjects unveiled by their titles. But Stein had the opposite intention. She hoped to discover true essences through a concentrated study of the fleeting and changeable.

In an interview,[13] Stein explained her process during the composition of these poems:

> You must remember each time I took something, I said, I have got to satisfy each realistic thing I feel about it. Looking at your shoe, for instance, I would try to make a complete realistic picture of your shoe. It is devilish difficult and needs perfect concentration, you have to refuse so much and so much intrudes itself upon you that you do not want it, it is exhausting work.[14]

Through her perfect concentration, Stein managed to create "complete realistic pictures" of mundane domestic objects without naming them. She saw her subjects as they really were—many elements at once, all of them true, all of them contributing in some small way to the actual nature of the subject.

---

13. The interview was arranged by Robert Bartlett Haas and conducted by William Sutton in France in 1946.

14. Robert Bartlett Haas, *A Primer for the Gradual Understanding of Gertrude Stein* (Los Angeles: Black Sparrow Press, 1971), 29.

A LONG DRESS.

What is the current that makes machinery, that makes
it crackle, what is the current that presents a long line
and a necessary waist. What is this current.

What is the wind, what is it.

Where is the serene length, it is there and a dark place
is not a dark place, only a white and red are black,
only a yellow and green are blue, a pink is scarlet, a
bow is every color. A line distinguishes it. A line just
distinguishes it.[15]

In "A Long Dress," Stein also works at what it is that causes change:
that mysterious current, a force as sure and as baffling as the wind. By
focusing on what things are changeable and therefore inessential, she
begins to uncover what is not affected by this wind, in this case guessing
that its line is what distinguishes the dress from other things.

Stein's aversion to naming household objects paralleled her strug-
gle with naming herself. Part American, part Parisian, part writer, part
theorist, part matriarch: to Stein, the problem with assigning names was
that "the name was not new but the thing being alive was always new."[16]
Names, she thought, impose a false certainty, robbing a thing of its mys-
tery and mutability.

---

15. Gertrude Stein, *Tender Buttons* (New York: Claire Marie, 1914), 17.
16. Stimpson and Chessman, 330.

At one point, she phrased her struggle with identity as a question: "What is the use of being a boy if you are going to grow up to be a man."[17] To her, a person was divided into discrete parts; the boy and the man were two unconnected beings. She seemed to be grappling with the growing difference between the person she once was and the person she was continuously, inexorably becoming. In his book *Sum*, neuroscientist David Eagleman describes what I think tormented Gertrude Stein, this division of selves as a "group of individuals touchingly searching for a common theme"[18] but finding none.

At its heart, travel is composed of two inverse functions: travel toward and travel away. Both occur simultaneously, though a traveler usually characterizes a journey as one or the other. The question is, toward what? Away from what?

By her own admission, Stein moved to Paris to be alone and separate from where she had come. A sort of method acting for the writer, this distance from the familiar certainties of home opened Stein up to all the change radiating from Paris and freed her from the confines of identity. But distance from home didn't make the inner conflict disappear; it didn't mean never coming back. It may have paradoxically guided her closer to understanding her own abandoned past.

Despite her best efforts to be placeless and nameless, Stein surmised that "it is not what France gave you but what it did not take away from you that was important."[19] After thirty-three years spent forsaking her previous identities, she perceived that something remained inside her—something true, irreducible, and foundational.

---

17. Stein, *What Are Master-Pieces*, 90

18. David Eagleman, *Sum: Forty Tales from the Afterlives* (New York: Vintage Books, 2009), 74.

19. Gertrude Stein, "An American and France," Oxford University Lecture (New Haven, CT: Yale University Archives, 1936).

Ultimately, her work in understanding a new century may have led her to experience a brief and blinding moment of Crusonian clarity, a revelation Wallace Stegner describes in his story "The Traveler": "For from the most chronic and incurable of ills, identity, [she] had looked outward and for one unmistakable instant recognized [her]self."[20] Seeing that she was, in fact, a part of a world of parts, Stein could have finally stooped to collect the shuffled, themeless pieces of her identity, even as the winds stirred up from the darkest corners of her heart.

---

20. Wallace Stegner, *The City of the Living* (Boston: Houghton Mifflin, 1956), 206.

# The Door of Return

*Yusef Komunyakaa*

I began to reread Pablo Neruda's *Memoirs*. A poet who'd left footprints on numerous cities, countries, and continents, whose work had guided me, Neruda had spoken to my heart through his imagination and feeling for the larger human world.

Distant places. I had seen a photograph of a Portuguese cannon aimed out of Elmina Castle toward the Atlantic. I could already see Ghana—a wooded savanna in my mind's eye—a zone of forests swollen with daily rainfall. I knew something about African lore, the kings of Songhai, Mali, and Ghana who drained swamps and cut canals for farms, who bartered gold for the lifeblood of salt. I knew sleeping sickness was spread by the tsetse fly. Hundreds of images populated my head.

I had gone to Africa many times in daydreams and poems long before I set foot in the land. So in early 2004, when Arthur Whitman, my former poetry student at Princeton University and one of the founding members of the Ghana Education Project, invited me, I said yes without hesitation. As a member of the board, I was already familiar with the organization's mission: to establish small libraries, to promote literacy, and to combat HIV/AIDS through education. I understood I wasn't embarking on a tourist safari but rather leading a group of writers to confront a very real pandemic. And in this moment, I realized that poetry was a tool, or an instrument, for preparing my psyche for the journey.

I always say poetry is confrontation and celebration. I suppose I had to attempt to confront some unspoken part within me that did not exactly want to encounter the severity of that world. My acute imagination had already jump-started, and I knew I had to align my mind with my heart. A deep dreaming had begun to claim my body.

One reason for the trip was to attempt to establish a dialogue confronting the devastating reality of AIDS. I knew we would meet with schoolchildren and with the fishermen of the village of Komenda. It was in anticipation of meeting the fishermen that I began writing the poem "Dead Reckoning," and in the lines "Now, lost in the old clothes of unreason, / & wanderlust, their nets sag with the last / of its kind, with bountiful fish stories..." I was perhaps attempting to bring the abstract into focus, to live in that world for a moment, where a story becomes a bridge between people, countries, and cultures. In this way, poetry can be a first step toward initiation. It is a place where one can transform borders and reconstruct time.

Traveling can also force one to become extremely practical. Aside from preparing mentally, I, of course, had to plan quite literally for the trip, asking, "Is this the right shirt and trousers? Do I need to take a jacket? Wouldn't sandals be more comfortable? Where's my shot record?" The University Health Center provided a consultation, inoculations for tetanus and yellow fever, and malaria pills, which I started a few days before leaving; I was lucky not to experience any side effects. I carried dysentery pills with me, as well as mosquito repellent. The trip required a visa, which was expedited because of the organization's positive reputation.

As I was preparing myself for the trip, we were still trying to raise additional funds for the program. Arthur and Ram Devineni, a filmmaker and the publisher of Rattapallax Press, managed the financial plans for the trip as well as the itinerary. We all agreed to give two readings: one on a Sunday afternoon at the White Dog Café in Philly, the other at The New School with Sonia Sanchez and Danny Glover.

It was mid-March, and I arrived at JFK International Airport, where I met Ram, Thomas Glave, and Willie Perdomo, among others. I was glad to be traveling with writers I knew, friends. The flight had a long layover in Amsterdam, so our group ventured out to the city in the early morning before our flight to Ghana later in the afternoon. I hardly remember the flight. I can't recall what I was reading, whom I was seated next to, or how I passed the time. Growing up in Bogalusa, Louisiana, I never thought I'd fly anywhere. On that flight, I felt I was living a life for more than just myself.

That evening, when we landed at Kotoka Airport, diplomatic workers processed us swiftly, so we didn't have to go through customs. In less than thirty minutes, we were zooming along the highway. The images, fragments of memory, continue to bleed together for me. I wanted merely to experience the place, to let the landscape wash over me. I must admit, I was surprised by how the lights swarmed over the skyline. I don't know why I expected darkness. Great anticipation grounded me, and I wanted to see everything in full daylight. We dined that evening in Accra, but in no time jet lag overtook us.

Traffic. Ghanaians in a floating throng of colors. Stone colonial houses. Forts. Apartments. Palm, bougainvillea, cassia, and mango. The lighthouse. And then the desolation of Jamestown beside the sea. Now we were speeding out of the city in a brownish sedan, the young driver with pleasant determination on his black face. The Atlantic waves seemed dark and sluggish. The people seemed to change with the country landscape. Women and children along the roadside sold vegetables and handicrafts. Someone pointed and asked, "What's that?" From the car window, we saw a boy holding a big, flattened, roasted rat in a wirelike grill, as if it had been cooked in a trap. I believe it was Arthur who said, "No, that's a nutria."

It was sunny when we arrived at the sewing club in Komenda. The girls—mainly teenagers—were dressed in green-and-black-checkered skirts and tan blouses, and some hid laughter behind their hands when they saw our faces. We had come across the Atlantic to talk about AIDS. We were straightforward, but we weren't there to cast stones. A few of the girls were also direct, raising the question about how AIDS had come to their small fishing village. Perhaps they were momentarily freer because we were strangers, and this allowed them to discuss things they would never have discussed openly in their homes, schools, and churches. We were listeners, and at that moment, this was what they needed: strangers as confidants.

We needed to talk with the fishermen, but we had heard that they wouldn't meet with us. This was heartbreaking; they were the main reason we were there in Komenda. Maybe they'd feel like walking targets when our eyes met theirs.

Finally, the day before we were to depart Komenda, the fishermen agreed to meet us at sunset. An array of colorful boats had been pulled onto the sandy shore, and men sat in the shifting light, waiting for us. Young and old, they all seemed seasoned by the salty winds of the sea. We stood there, facing them, but no one said anything. What was the protocol? We were visitors. We had requested the meeting. I felt as though everyone was looking at me. Who spoke first? Was it Arthur, Ram, Willie,

Bob, Thomas? Or maybe I said, "Hello. This is my first time here, but it seems that I've come home." (If I said that, it was because nearly everyone I had met over the past few days had said to me, "You're Ghanaian." Before my trip there, I'd always thought I was Ibo.) Or maybe I said to the fishermen, "Look, we're here to talk about the dangers of venturing over to the Ivory Coast and then returning to Komenda." I was the eldest of our group, and I must have been the one to speak first. At least, that's the way it is in my dreams. But the fishermen were silent. They were stone still until one young man said, "I know what you are talking about." It was as if someone had struck a brass bell. For a moment, everyone seemed to talk at once. Then an older fisherman spoke in a harking voice about how the fishermen from Komenda had to venture farther and farther out because the waters close to shore were depleted of fish, and they had to go a greater distance—all the way to the Ivory Coast—and some of the fishermen slept with the women there, and they returned to Komenda, but didn't know they had contracted HIV.

Something terrifying shifted underneath the image. It was still a beautiful picture. The men were talking and gesturing with their hands, caught in some ancient dance. The sun was sinking into the sea.

Our caravan of two or three sedans headed back to Accra. The drivers were young men who didn't waste any time; the rented sedans slid into blind curves, and sometimes the foot traffic scattered. I wanted to warn them.

We spent hours at Elmina Castle, a slave compound that housed a small library the Ghana Education Project had built. The monolithic structure was erected in the late fifteenth century by the Portuguese, who were following the rumors of gold. The building's architecture defined domination; I could see the brute force of the slave trade, which in the seventeenth century infiltrated the structure, in its thick walls, in its height, in its presence, in the scale of the project, and I knew indeed why it bore the infamous name the Door of No Return.

It wasn't the skull and bones crafted into the concrete or the chains mounted on the walls but the small chapel at the heart of the fortress that evoked unspoken fear. Perhaps more than anyone else, the poet recognizes the power of symbols because symbols continue to speak across the abyss of time. The dead keep on speaking. One can imagine—especially a poet—that in this space, these men who exacted brutality also bowed to a god.

I stood beside the Cave Canem sign that read BEWARE OF DOGS. A high fence surrounded the house of W.E.B. Du Bois, the man who had once edited *Crisis* magazine, who wrote *The Negro*, *The Souls of Black Folk*, *Dark Princess*, *Dusk of Dawn*, among others, and who in 1963 became a citizen of Ghana, having moved there in 1961.

Standing there, trying to remember a poem of his, "The Song of Smoke," I could recall only the refrain: "I am the Smoke King, / I am black!" At that moment, so were most of the faces around me. The heavy iron gate opened, and we stepped into the big yard. There were no dogs. No one to greet us Americans. Soon a caretaker, or someone posing as a caretaker, appeared and unlocked the door of the house to show us the final pages of this great man's life. We wandered through, asking hardly any questions, among the dust-covered books and papers that hadn't been catalogued or protected. I wondered how many items had disappeared through the years and were now on eBay. There, entombed in a mausoleum of stone and garniture, I was reminded that true elegance usually resides in simplicity. While standing in the house among the last shadows the man cast, I stood awestruck by this citizen of the world. Isn't that what a poet is, a citizen of the world? Du Bois was an internationalist before he was a Marxist. I stood there thinking of what Vijay Prashad writes in *The Karma of Brown Folk*, how he picked up a copy of *The Souls of Black Folk* in Kolkata and his whole life changed. I wondered if anyone at the W.E.B. Du Bois Institute for African and African American Research at Harvard University was aware of the man's notes and books covered with dust in this distant land, how hard nature works to bring everything down to the ground equally.

I attempted to prepare myself mentally for our visit to the hospital to see the smallest patients—babies who were one, two, and three years old. I tried to call up a moment of my religious tutelage back in Bogalusa, to glimpse my forays into Buddhist meditations through the decades, to go back to those few years I had worked as a peer counselor at the University of Colorado, but soon I realized that little or nothing could have prepared me for what we witnessed.

The children were frail and tiny; their vulnerability was so transparent that there was no way for anyone not to perceive the depth of their pain and suffering. It's hard to say how many children were there in the hospital. Maybe fifty. Maybe one hundred. It was more terrifying than the dislocated images on television. The few nurses there seemed completely overwhelmed. But the courage and heroic presence of the grandmothers who rocked their grandchildren in their arms was astonishing; some were silent and others whispered almost breathless words that seemed to have come from a great distance. The strength in their faces contrasted so starkly with the children, and perhaps this is what magnified the pain and desperation in that place.

At first, feeling that we were intruding on some sacred rite of passage, that our eyes would wound them more deeply, I wanted to retreat. Of course, wasn't this also the fundamental question for the poet: isn't it the duty of artists to witness, to hold ourselves accountable? Indeed, this bore the familiar distress of a battle zone, where the most vulnerable are singled out and attacked with brutal certainty. But I stood there completely overwhelmed, uncertain about what we could do, almost defeated by what I saw that day in Ghana. I also knew that we were seeing only a fraction of the suffering on the African continent.

We were going to meet a king. Would he embrace our effort to establish a dialogue about AIDS, or would he simply shrug his shoulders and begin a litany about esoteric rituals locked in the recent past? Weren't our clothes too typical, too ordinary? A king, huh? I visualized him in his kingly garb, sitting on a golden throne and holding a golden staff. Should we bow? The protocol was beyond me.

There were three "kings." The two older kings seemed so alike, especially in their austerity. They seemed so upright in posture and demeanor. The third king was younger; he seemed not fully initiated. Yet there was something about him that also seemed more cosmopolitan, more modern. They all seemed to possess at least symbolic power—absolutely ceremonial. Their fat gold rings caught the eye. Their colorful robes and cowrie adornments spoke silently of authority, and the carved canes the two older kings clutched were pragmatic. It seemed more like poets meeting poets, and in this sense one understands Shelley's statement:

> Poets are the hierophants of an unapprehended inspiration; the mirrors of the gigantic shadows which futurity casts upon the present; the words which express what they understand not; the trumpets which sing to battle, and feel not what they inspire; the influence which is moved not, but moves. Poets are the unacknowledged legislators of the world.

We weren't there to pose questions through metaphors. The kings were probably experts with metaphors, but we hoped that they also understood the gut-level reality of AIDS in Ghana. Our ritual was discussion. Maybe kings never show alarm or their deep, heartfelt thoughts, especially when facing strangers. Their emotions seemed stately. Contained. Goaded by the younger king, the two elders slowly agreed to assist in the efforts of the Ghana Education Project. Sitting there, facing these three men of traditional and symbolic power, it was difficult for me not to think of Kwame Nkrumah, the first president and first prime minister of Ghana, a Pan-Africanist who had studied at the University of Pennsylvania and was, in many ways, an everyday man. The ghost of him possessed more power than the folkloric platitudes of these three kings. I sat there trying not to think of Dudley Randall's poem "Ancestors":

> Was the Old Country a democracy
> where every man was a king?
> Or did the slave-catchers
> steal only the aristocrats
> and leave the fieldhands
> …
> My own ancestor
> (research reveals)
> was a swineherd
> who tended the pigs
> in the Royal Pigstye
> and slept in the mud
> among the hogs.

We strolled into the room of the hospice to see Kiki Djan. He was a sack of bones, but there was still something in him that said, Look, I'm a damn genius. And we were dumbfounded by what drugs and AIDS can do to a man. He sat on the bed hugging a portable recorder, rocking back and forth while he played his last recording over and over, a pop song full of energy and crafted passion. He was still good, still burning with genius and belief in himself, and one felt that perhaps this could keep him alive. Or maybe he believed this so deeply, we also believed it through a mental osmosis. He would beat the monkey on his back; he would even outsmart the specter of AIDS. Kiki had played keyboard with the legendary band Osibisa, which he had joined in 1971, and I remember how that band's sound was different from anything I'd ever heard. The music had a positive authority that left its listeners thunderstruck. It's said that after splitting from the group, he did a twenty-four-hour gig in London. He was friends with Mick Jagger and Elton John and hung out with jet-setters cruising off to the Caribbean. He bragged about making £8,000 in a single weekend, saying that he was the most gifted keyboardist on the London scene. But here he was back home—Kiki Djan from Takoradi in western Ghana—hugging a battered recorder, pleading with the ghosts of ancestors. He seemed surprised that a group of writers and poets from America was standing at the foot of his bed. He'd stare out the window, and I sensed this was his last torture on Earth—glimpses of passing figures in bright clothes caught by the March sun.

Close to our departure, we moved from the small quarters where we had been sleeping to a beach hotel. The hotel was huge and sprawling and stood in complete contrast to the world we had just witnessed. There was a high fence built around the perimeter as if to keep out the common locals, the everyday Ghanaians. Beside the sea, shops sold paintings, handicrafts, gold and diamonds, clothing, and tchotchkes made for tourists. From their garb and overall demeanor, I gathered the African clientele was made up of upper-middle-class professionals. It was impossible for me to feel comfortable in my American jeans and sandals alongside their colorful robes.

That night, Arthur took us to a Portuguese-owned seaside pub. I recall the music playing and the voice of a fado singer whose longing suspended me between Africa and the West. I felt more comfortable in my American clothes, which seemed to blend in with the European feel of the pub. And for a moment, I was glad to recognize the Portuguese language spoken by the staff and a few of the patrons. Then I thought of Elmina Castle, and it occurred to me that even the hotel might have been European owned. And then I understood the complexity of the diasporic spirit; we may feel more at home in the culture we've inherited but at a loss for the rituals and customs of our ancestors.

After returning to the United States, I tried for years to write poems that capture the images of those babies, of the slave castle, of Jamestown, and of Kiki. In fact, I've traveled to many places, including Vietnam, Australia, Eastern Europe, New Guinea, Mexico, Chile, India, and Brazil, but I've written poems about only a few of those places. Neruda once wrote, "*I have come out of that landscape, that mud, that silence, to roam, to go singing through the world.*" Now I'm realizing that encountering the world leads one both farther from home and closer to it because that world is always in dialogue with the deepest self.

Perhaps for me, it takes a long time for these acquired images and experiences to distill into poetry. Though travel is an action, and poetry at times can be defined as an action, the two together need a space that resides in silence, meditation. The truth is, an act of poetry, the moment a poem comes forth, is often unpredictable because it springs from some place not fully conscious but informed by everything that has made us who we are.

# Poetry Peddler

*Naomi Shihab Nye*

*My endless wandering / becomes my language*

—Amina Saïd, "Freedom's Faces"

I was raised in a savory, slightly strange household. The walking homesickness household. I guess it makes sense that a wandering poet would be born from a father in exile and a renegade mother who defied the codes of her own strict upbringing even to marry him.

Because he had a voice, my father, Aziz Shihab—a dapper man who loved bow ties and cologne, who engaged in vigorous shoe polishing, who still liked a folded white hankie tucked into his breast pocket—embodied the hugeness of a people's suffering. He found a way to wrap his melodious, perfectly pitched voice around a room, send it out in a letter, weave it into Christmas talks about the Holy Land at local churches, without becoming shrill or arrogant. He was human size.

But his voice was bigger. He did not understand why dialogue seemed so difficult for so many people in power, but he believed humiliation would never last and arrogance could never win and someday, justice might take a deep breath again. He exercised his own voice every way he could toward that goal.

When my father died, he was still aching for Palestine, its quirky rhythms and ancient traditions, which people tried to say weren't ancient after all. "You lived here a hundred years?" they might have said. "Sorry, you're invisible."

Wherever he wandered, whichever border he crossed, he was Palestine: his soft, olive-tinted skin carried almond blossoms, green fields, goat cries at sunset. He had a rich wit, a gentle sense of irony, a passion for education, pride.

Why was it so easy to downgrade, or overlook entirely, the Palestinian legacy, as if it didn't exist, as if its people would just—*pouf!*—vanish in a pollen cloud? Surely one never thinks, in the hopeful flush of growing up, "By the time I'm twenty-one, my people will be invisible."

Though I lived in Palestine in 1966–1967, only a short time myself, I felt obliged, whenever wandering, and also at home, to try to speak up about it, wherever appropriate. I wanted to make it real for people who had never considered its existence. It was not my only topic, of course, but the conditions and issues of rootedness and exile rested at the center of all my topics—respect for dailiness, mutual exchange, and simplicity.

When introduced as a "peacemaker," I'd think, well, I'm a total failure then. Because there is no peace, not for the people of Palestine. Not yet.

It was easy to feel like a failure. But I kept talking. When you feel rotten, talking and writing always help. And sometimes, such as yesterday, when I met two seventeen-year-old girls representing Hand in Hand: Center for Jewish-Arab Education in Israel and their respectful, mutual descriptions of shared life, I know with conviction that talking and writing are the only and very best things we can do.

My father believed in a better day, in human potential, in the poetry of possibility, in the dignity of details. To honor him, I had to keep telling his story. Though he died frustrated, he told the hospital chaplain right before his last day he was sure things would eventually work out.

I hear an unexpected echo in this wide world from Hawaiian students familiar with legacies of occupation nodding gravely, from far-flung village Alaskans and Native Americans in Wyoming: sorrowful repetitions of injustice.

And I tried not to think too often of the chant one of my dearest writer friends used to filter his own penetrating writing—"So what?"

Those words didn't help me.

So—everything.

If a girl in Alberta, Canada, who has never been out of her own province, reads a poem or story about a Palestinian girl and then asks her mother to make her baba ghanoush, saying, "I will never think of the Middle East in the same way again," does that mean a poem or story has done its humble job? How many girls like this, and the two I met yesterday, might be needed to make peace in the world?

No, I don't wish I'd gotten a regular job somewhere along the way.

Not even for benefits.

I've had my benefits. A thousand towns, beds, hotels, friends. A hundred thousand young poets with notebooks, pencils, clicking pens, far gazes.

I think of my friend M., who said when we were twenty in a condescending voice, "So what are you going to do in your life? Be a poetry peddler?"

I stood up straighter, hurt, saying, "Yes, that's what I'll be, I'd be honored to be that."

The word *peddler* made me think of wheelbarrows and ragbags, two things I really like.

So, the gift of being a poet out in the wide world, on the avenues, in the airports, carrying scenes and voices, is immense.

I remember the worried Iranian mom who appeared in a school library one day, wanting to read from her journals to me—is it okay to be a writer if one has not been officially trained? To allow one's soulful longing for connection to be the flag of one's true country? I think of the Saudi girls with covered faces who will remove their hijabs only if we meet in a completely enclosed space—what is it they want to talk about? Photography! All the images they are recording on their fancy little digital cameras! Plants, doorways, tile work, light falling down onto palms! Even two sessions with them will change entirely the sense I have of their deep eyes, peering out, when in public, from between folds of dark cloth.

Why is it so hard for politicians to believe that people who don't match us exactly might nevertheless harmonize with us in deeply agreeable ways? Girls with covered heads might be visionary artists. Why are people always picking out differences, painful contrasts, instead of making kinder links?

Poetry gives these realities a place to abide: in the Asian grocery store in Abu Dhabi, in a steaming hammam in Rabat, in the wildly dancing, finger-cymbal-clicking streets of Fez, on Berlin's Ringbahn at twilight. I am certain that human beings think in layers and that everything new to any one of us is simultaneously old, new, precious, passing. Talking about poetry all over the stricken Earth, with children as well as adults, gives us a shared, more humanized side.

The seventh grader with neatly combed black hair is crying. He's trying to pretend he's not crying, but every time he removes his fists from his eyes, big tears roll down.

"Speak to us," I say. "What's happening?"

We're sitting in a circle in the school library. Graceful students from all over the planet, notebooks open on their laps, stare so quietly at him, at their hands. They look humbled by his pain.

"I am worried about my country," he gulps. We're in Saudi Arabia, at King Abdullah's magical liberal graduate university. Yes, it exists. Women can drive on this campus. My head is not covered. Boys and girls are going to school together here, at King Abdullah University of Science and Technology, aka KAUST.

I'm with the children of the university professors, students, and staff at the edge of the glistening Red Sea, whose other side touches the shores of this boy's home country, Egypt.

For days now, brave demonstrators have been gathering in Tahrir Square, raising their arms and voices, shouting for freedom, setting up tents, carrying one another on their shoulders. They must be exhausted. I've left CNN International on mute in my room for hours, watching what happens next, even at two in the morning, thinking about the past, just a few years ago, when I felt oddly secure hopping off the underground metro and dashing across that very square by myself, even late at night.

"What will happen to Egypt? I don't want my grandparents or neighbors or neighborhood to be hurt," the boy says, growing more confident when no one titters. "If I were the head of the chess club and everyone said they did not want me to be the head, if everyone stood in the hallway shouting, 'Go, go, go, we want a new head! You had your turn!' I would go. I would go very fast. So why won't President Mubarak go?"

Acknowledging our own essential questions helps us think about them.

This is the point my journals return to: in Bangladeshi classrooms, in Pakistani girls' schools, in the poetry salons behind a school cafeteria in India, we share our questions and dilemmas in the company of others. We may not be able to solve all our problems, but the making of analogies and metaphors, the making of poetry, feels like a possible solution, diffuses the scariness.

Here, slant of light. Now, think about this again.

From such abundance and raw material, from the glitter of open questioning among friends or strangers equally, poems have always gathered for me, and for so many students, bouquets of voices and scenes. Sometimes we need confirmation from one another; even if we can't solve these problems, it's helpful to speak about them across borders, cultures, religions, ages. Guiding others to try simple writing tactics and strategies is always a good reminder for ourselves too. It's all contagious—if one student witnesses another writing from a place of personal uncertainty, odds instantly grow that more will try a deeper, questioning style.

In coming months, far from one another, we'll be wondering the same things, but more urgently, about Libya and Syria. Hey, you guys in power! Haven't you had your turns? The chess club demotes you!

*Tyranny* will feel like a modern word again—not something from history books.

Before school every day, a studious Lebanese boy composes book reviews on an international children's website. Indian twins carefully letter a giant page with the poem they wrote together yesterday. A giggling Tunisian girl brings me wrapped gifts every morning—a shiny necklace, a tiny stitched pouch.

After I return home, a Korean girl living in Rabat who loves poetry more than the whole wide world, more than skyscrapers, even, more than the ocean and the beach and the sand that stretches to the mountains, keeps writing me e-mails with yellow blinking smiley faces attached. One day her message says, "My page is empty. What if I can't write anything? Does this ever happen to you? What do you do?"

All the way across the ocean, in south Texas, where the rain has not fallen for months and the old lakes named Medina and Canyon are going dry, I stare at gray doves scrapping on a nearly empty green bird feeder hanging outside my window. When I refill it with sunflower seeds, the hungry birds gobble them within hours.

To my pen pal, pecked out carefully: "I take a walk, look at all the windows around me, and wonder who lives inside them."

When she writes back days later, her message says simply, "I tried it. It's working."

❧

At the American School in Rabat, which has no prominent sign, on the day the fourth graders write odes, Omar is the first volunteer to read his poem. His classmates and teachers look surprised when he raises his hand. I, of course, don't know anyone's history. Not knowing who generally succeeds or fails in any classroom anywhere has always been a benefit—a visitor carries no preconceptions, welcomes all participation equally.

Tourists and travelers might wish for as much open anonymity in the markets and streets. Too often we're identified by what previous travelers have desired or spent.

Most in Omar's class wear bright-red T-shirts, the school color, but he wears what can be described only as a golden satin tunic. Omar clears his throat. He addresses his home country of Egypt, describing a "yellow flower calling to me." Across the countries between, across Libya, Tunisia, Algeria, he can hear its plaintive cry. Now he is "stuck in sad Morocco"—forced to make a new home, far from his yellow flowers. But he vows to go back someday. He has written an ode to belonging, to a better life where he felt grounded and secure.

I look around. Tears are rolling down his teacher's face.

The students seem mesmerized. They crowd around Omar after the lunch buzzer trills, begging him to sit with them at the picnic tables outside, mentioning that Morocco has lovely white flowers popping their petals open before dawn even in the schoolyard, on the soccer field, that they are happy he is here. He looks—thunderstruck.

"What's up?" I ask the teacher.

"He has been here since September," she says. "This is the first time we have heard his voice."

It is a moment that underscores what poets and poetry do.

To say something true to you and have it acknowledged, accepted, recognized as real by people around you—what better treasure? Belonging to everyone. And if that stranger in our classroom said we could talk about these things, express our love and longing—we might just keep doing it, no? Even after she leaves, even more than usual, even with the new ones, the awkward ones, even on days when it hurts to do it.

A poet walks on to the next class, the next city, the next country, fortified, knowing that all the occasions in classrooms when things didn't seem to "click" as well have just been transformed by a perfect, essential moment.

It's the same when we're writing by ourselves alone at a desk.

All those scribbles, diversions, little lost impulses and lines absorbed, uplifted by the moment one line or group of lines sings.

I heard my mother say, "Be your best self, use your voice" when I stepped out onto the gravel driveway and headed up Harvey Hill to elementary school, in old St. Louis, humid city of melancholy and great architecture. It would take years of living to appreciate the challenge of that simple code.

I heard our beloved second-grade teacher, Harriett Barron Lane, age ancient, age eternal, say, "A poem can save you." Her husband had died a long time before. She had no children. We were all her children. She wore 1950s pink and green plastic bangle bracelets stacked up both arms. Anyone inattentive or reluctant received a bop on the head with those bangles. A poem can save you.

So can a window, I remember thinking, staring out the tall classroom windows in the hundred-year-old building.

Mrs. Lane felt Emily Dickinson to be real in all our lives, more real than the school principal or the mayor of St. Louis. If we stumbled, acted ridiculous, got the giggles in the middle of a lesson—what would Emily think of that? The fact that Mrs. Lane imagined we could know was deeply compelling.

I recall reading, and feeling befriended by, the Bengali poet Rabindranath Tagore on the day my best friend told me her family was moving away. Tagore, who had won the Nobel Prize in Literature, used to send his words out in small boats on a running stream, hoping some stranger would find and unfold them and "know who he was." Tagore knew loneliness.

Tagore would understand.

Carrying poems in one's brain is a remedy stretching far beyond the sweet meadows, ditches, and fragrant hideouts under looming pine trees where we had all wandered together, making a larger family of friends. I still hear familiar echoes guiding my steps—I'm nobody, who are you? Hope is the thing with feathers.

My first day in Berlin, the day before the Internationales Literaturfestival Berlin began, I got lost among birds at the zoo. Why hadn't I learned German? I had studied it for two years. I had attended recitation contests, speaking poems from memory in German. I had had German grandparents.

The great, complicated, multilayered city of Berlin, a city that had known true sorrow, a city that had been bombed and wrecked and rebuilt and reinvented, a city with vast empty spaces, a city still recovering, was a city whose story was inextricably linked with my father's Palestinian refugee status.

My wandering journalist father would have stood, as I did, staring at haunting memorial markers in front of Berlin homes whose Jewish inhabitants had been evicted, evacuated, massacred. He would have understood that pain.

Was this partly why he always struggled for perfect grammar and simple, strong sentences? To find a fluent home in a paragraph or a few well-weighted lines must have felt very comforting to one whose refugee family had lost its physical home and grounding.

For how many of us has poetry always felt like the genuine home? As a traveler, deficient in other vocabularies, I seem to remain on the edge, the outside, but poetry in any form—original or translated—calls me inside. *Who would I have been*, I mused, wandering among the depressed zoo bears and surly elephants of Berlin, *had I never studied Spanish or Arabic, had I not crowded my pitiful acquired-language domain with three languages? What if I had focused better?* But a poet's main concern is focus and connection—did I use my energies otherwise? Have my endless attempts to encourage students to focus and connect been meaningful in the long run? Haven't enough of them told me so for me to believe?

In one school on the edge of the city, students kept bees, bottled honey. Muslim girls in headscarfs stood in front of a large group and discussed the positive aspects of being "singled out as different." It felt refreshing, unexpected. Muslim girls, speaking fluent German, switched into English for me. They said there was power in difference—if everyone looked at you as "another kind" of person, then you were noticed, had an easier chance to shine. It reminded me of a poet's comfort in unusual perception. Seeing things "differently" always opens up possibilities of seeing the world in more intriguing, less predictable ways. I felt immediately drawn to these girls and their confidence. Speaking about poetry to students who knew intricate details about worker bees and hives also felt natural and gracious—again, the layers of thinking that poetry offers, opening wide fields.

One day, at a literary center on a mysterious, stony backstreet of Berlin, I helped a group of teens (Afros, striped T-shirts, a bird tattooed on a wrist) arrange wooden chairs around a big table. For hours we talked, wrote, shared entries from notebooks and sections from favorite poems, grieved, and celebrated. The words of Bertolt Brecht, who had lived only blocks from where we gathered, stitched a seam joining us all. He wrote about doubting; going this way and that way, all at once; the inevitability of doubting; the precious legacy of doubting, which has united all artists in all places since ancient days. In our circle, we had students of many backgrounds—a German-Swiss girl with thoughtful grief etched into her face, some shy recent immigrant students from Turkey, a young man wearing a Star of David necklace, a comic French-German PUBLIC POET! (handmade T-shirt in three languages) encouraging quieter students to offer opinions too. Anyone could witness the rich sense of community possible around a table when people share poetry's immediate exchange. Later, a boy who identified himself only as "J" wrote to me, referring to that day:

> I can't tell you what happened exactly. I can't tell you who said what, or which poem flipped the switch. But our time together at the lit. center gave me what I will need to live my life. And that is a big thing. Thanks.

A big thing.
A tiny, transportable thing.
What poetry does for us all the time.

On a crowded midnight subway in Berlin, an elderly Arab man in a baggy brown suit coat stared at me, looking startlingly familiar. We were both standing, gripping silver poles. He raised his hand and pushed across to my side of the train. "I knew your father," he said. "I am sorry he died." It seemed incredible to me. In a city of millions, running into an unnamed friend? And he handed me from his coat pocket a collection of poems by the great Iraqi poet Sargon Boulus, who, I would realize when I began reading, had died exactly the same day as my father. In exile, in Berlin.

> Those about whom we hear no news
> Those who are remembered by none:
> What wind has swept their traces
> as if they never were?
> My father and the others
> Where are they?
> Where?
>
> —Sargon Boulus, translated by Sinan Antoon

They are in poems still forming, bubbling in the mist that hangs over the street right before one year slides into another, another we will have to live without him, on Earth, full of him, thanks to voices and memory.

And who was that man on the train?

The more we travel, the more it seems that our family members are everywhere, our poetry replete with their presences. We write out of everything we have ever read or encountered. The music is in us. The ghost signs from the sides of ruined buildings in small towns we passed through only once float in us. The succinct phrases from gravestones in the Chinese cemetery in Manoa Valley, Honolulu, are carved in us. The lilting voices of children, their pride and uncertainty, their held-out questions, are etched forever in us.

I met Mahmoud Darwish in a Philadelphia hotel lobby after years of reading his poems. I'd been carrying his voice for so long that an actual encounter seemed somehow surreal. He stared at me and said, "I thought you were much younger!"

"I was," I said. "Weren't you too?"

Tell me about your life.
It was all a bouquet.
In whose hand?
What would you be if you were not a poet?
Everything? Aren't we already?

No, I've replied to questions many times over, the greatest moment of a writer's life is not when a new book appears in print. The greatest moment of a writer's life is when he or she meets people like you. People in some place one never traveled to before, who wish to converse.

# Called Home on the Road

*Claudia Rankine*

Though the house has been remodeled, the stairs, despite being carpeted, creak. What I imagined as a silent retreat from the party seems to sound through the house. By the fifth step I decide to sit down and on the wall next to me is a torn passport photo of half a woman's face blown up and framed as art. Where did you imagine you were going? I say aloud to her.

"The purpose of art," James Baldwin wrote, "is to lay bare the questions hidden by the answers." He might have been channeling Dostoyevsky's statement that "we have all the answers. It is the questions we do not know." Where did you imagine you were going, and when did travel's constant movement become an answer? My mother never tires of telling me, "Girl, you have to stop running." But even before my birth, for the colonized Jamaican, movement was de facto.

In the 1950s, before Jamaica's independence, my uncle, my mother's oldest brother, immigrated to Brixton, where he continues to live as he approaches ninety. In 1962, ten or so years after he immigrated, a year before I was born, Jamaica would become independent of the United Kingdom; two years later, American immigration laws toward Jamaicans would relax, and just like that, I would become an American, his American niece, his American poet.

My uncle is a carpenter. Once, when I was in my twenties, he drove me around London showing me all the houses he had rebuilt. It took him hours to find them, hours for us to see all the construction he had done. Sometimes we had to get out of the car and walk to the back of a building or look in through a side window or climb up stairs to see exactly how he had made London London.

His name obviously wasn't on any of his buildings, and I would not be able to take myself back to the places he showed me, but the brick-and-mortar concreteness of his life's work was enough to satisfy him (and my mother because I suspect he was speaking to her through me about some old forgotten argument they had had in another life) that this place—which had always been a destination, even when he was a boy in St. Ann's Parish in Jamaica—was now his place.

The Trinidadian theorist and essayist C.L.R. James says what matters is movement: "not where you are or what you have, but where you have come from, where you are going, and the rate at which you are getting there." Perhaps my uncle settled here one building at a time, one room at a time. Maybe like him, I make stanzas in order to construct a new house to live in, or I make stanzas to take apart the houses I was given. Where did you imagine you were going? I say to the torn-up girl.

When I lived in London at the end of the millennium, I sat at my desk on the second floor of a rented house on Whittlesey Street on the South Bank and thought about what being an American meant. George W. Bush was running for president against Al Gore at the time. I watched Bush's speeches on BBC One with increasing trepidation. Had I been in New York City, much of my frustration and fear would have been hashed out across restaurant tables in the East Village or on the Upper West Side. Conversations with my British friends on the Cut, the road with restaurants near our house, began first with explanations. No short cuts could be taken, and once everything was explained, I would go home and attempt to understand my irritations on the page.

Much of *Don't Let Me Be Lonely*, a book I think of as being concerned with the culture and politics of the United States, was conceived, in part, walking the streets of London. My connection to the United States while living abroad came through media—the papers, the television, and the Internet. The unceasing British interest in the political workings of its former colony not only kept me informed but perhaps also pushed me to close the Atlantic distance in my writing.

Our host tonight is a visual artist and a curator. He creates things in time and space, and as he is creating, he is curating; even this party is a kind of talking sculpture, and when he notices me sitting on the hallway steps, he wishes to engage me in the flow of the conversations. I allow myself to be guided back into the living room.

I don't know. I say that aloud because someone wants to know the name of the film shot in Ridley Road Market, which is just two blocks away and where I hear you can get "bush meat" if you go to the right stall. *Dirty Pretty Things*, someone says. *Dirty Pretty Things*, I repeat, as if the person asking is deaf.

Walking in the mist toward the party earlier, just before getting to the Ridley Road Market, I had come upon the Dalston C.L.R. James Library. James's seminal work, *The Black Jacobins*, sits in my library in Claremont, California, as a testament to my own membership in the African diaspora his work addresses. Seeing him commemorated on a public building in the Hackney borough of London was a bit like hearing my own name called out on the road. I still don't expect the Empire to memorialize its subjects, and I am surprised: I am, after all, not a stranger; these streets know I am here.

As if he can hear my thoughts, the BBC producer I am sitting next to on the very comfortable black leather sofa turns to me. Are you still living in New York? he asks. He and I had met more than twenty-five years earlier on the island of Grenada, two years after the US invasion, and it has been at least a decade since I've seen him. He produces films, so I ask if the BBC has done a documentary on C.L.R. James. He doesn't know but says the controversy around the Dalston C.L.R. James Library surprised him. The controversy? I repeat by way of an invitation. In 2010, the Hackney Council announced it was opening the first new library built in Hackney in the last twenty years. This new, modern, high-tech facility is to replace the Dalston C.L.R. James Library just blocks from where we sit. The announcement included the information that the new library would no longer be known as the Dalston C.L.R. James Library.

More than likely, the council didn't understand his significance to this community, my producer friend adds, with a wry smile that wings the lines bordering his eyes in such a way that he becomes both youthful and ancient in the same instant. It was a "no-you-didn't" moment, I say, and this makes him laugh outright. Do you think the new library and the desire to remove his name had something to do with the gentrification that is happening here in Hackney now? I ask. Do you think it will rain tomorrow? he counters by way of an answer. Now we are both laughing. Keep Britain tidy, he adds. You are quoting Banksy, the graffiti artist? I ask, wondering how he means it. The same, he says as he turns to a question being asked of him by someone who has recently arrived, and only then do I remember reading in the *Guardian* that morning that there's a new Banksy stenciled on the side of a building in North London: SORRY! THE LIFESTYLE YOU ORDERED IS CURRENTLY OUT OF STOCK.

The British poet Malika Booker, whom I met at Cave Canem in Pittsburgh a year previous, spoke about the importance of C.L.R. James to her as a poet; this memory makes me look around the room for her despite knowing she is not here. Even before she started writing, she said, she remembered reading an essay of James's in which he discussed the work of the writers Toni Morrison, Alice Walker, and Ntozake Shange. He ended the essay with a directive to write poetry. He wrote, "Write what you think—and maybe what you write about your day-to-day, everyday, commonplace, ordinary life will be some of the same problems that the people of the world are fighting out. You must be able to write what you have to say, and know that that is what matters." It seemed poetic justice that the very same, ordinary, everyday people would be the ones to insist that his legacy be continued on the face of their local library.

This house, the home of my hosts, is filled with art and sculpture. My gaze returns to what I believe to be the same spot, but always I see something I haven't noticed before. In the painting directly before me, which I'm sure has been there all evening though I am noticing it only now, the telephone lines are just visible as telephone lines. The black and white could easily blur back into atmosphere, lose all distinction. Most Turneresque, says the man sitting across from me. You are the American poet, no? Yes, I say.

This man has the face of the English sky—full of weather, always in response, constantly shifting, clouding over, and clearing briefly— though he is not British. He has written a memoir and, more recently, a novel. I have read neither, but his kind moodiness, his restlessness persuade me to make a mental note to read both as soon as I return to the United States. His wife joins us; how similar they are, how available they are to their emotions. Their immediacy is admirable, I am thinking, though we are talking about the recent riots in Hackney. He says he feels they were similar to the Rodney King–L.A. riots, but the media in the UK handled it very differently. The riots began at the end of the summer when Mark Duggan, a black man, a father, and a suspected drug dealer, was shot dead by officers from Scotland Yard's Operation Trident (a special operation addressing gun crime in black communities). As the rioting and looting continued, government officials labeled the violent outbreak "opportunism" and "sheer criminality," and the media picked up this language. Maybe the police let the looters continue their rampage so that those images could replace the fact of shooting an unarmed man. In the United States, Rodney King's beating, caught on video, trumped all other images. If there had been a video of Duggan being executed, things would have been very different, I hazard to say. Will you write about Duggan in your poetry?

the memoirist-turned-novelist wants to know. Probably not, I say. Why not? he asks, looking slightly irritated. I begin to think he does not like police, Duggan or no Duggan.

Why not? Well, because I read about it online in my study in the United States a few months ago and even as the story caught my attention, it felt both familiar and foreign. What felt familiar was an institutional body (the police) tied rhetorically to justice acting unjustly toward a young black man. Everything else felt specific to North London and the culture, the tensions, the recognitions, the disappointments, and the failures that exploded in the riots that followed the shooting. It is this same kind of accumulation and release that drove me to write about the forty-one shots fired by the four police officers who murdered Amadou Diallo in New York City in February of 1999. Before it happened, it had happened and happened. As a black body in that city, writing about Diallo was necessary if I was to hold on to the fiction that this was an event "wrongfully ordinary," so outside the ordinary. Though the moment had occurred and occurred again with the deaths of other random, unarmed black men, Diallo's forty-one shots somehow cut off air supply in the body politic by virtue of the excessive, blatant barrage. And though grief exists for Duggan as a black man gunned down, in my body was not the same overflow of compromises, deaths, and tempers specific to a place I woke to and went to sleep in most days.

The news of Duggan's death came to me in a different rhythm; as C.L.R. James wrote, "What do they know of cricket who only cricket know?" My writing comes out of relationships to subjects over time and not to any subject in theory. There is often, between my own body's rhythms and the subject, a simultaneity that has to do with "the war my presence has occasioned in the American soul," to quote Baldwin. I am full of my feelings, feelings shaped by the politics, history, and culture that have shaped me, and if I don't want to be drowned by these feelings, I need to take Baldwin's lead and at least attempt "to lay bare the questions hidden by the answers."

Rarely can I import the same level of heightened engagement when I travel, as I am filled with a brimming curiosity that presses up against a needling sense of not knowing. The traveling seems to cement my American citizenry and throws into relief my impatience, my expectations, my questioning, my pleasure, and my humor as informed by my hybrid American life. And though I recognize the similarities built into global cities, a body moving through moves through differently than the ones residing. "You're part of the misery and you can't make it more or less," says the Chinese artist Ai Weiwei. Mark Duggan, I am part of your misery, and I can't make it more or less. I know I won't write about the dynamics of your death because I don't understand the dynamics of your death though I believe I understand the dynamics of your death.

With my eyes closed, I consider how all of us at this party, a group of middle-aged artists, lawyers, filmmakers, writers, and journalists, in a house worth more than a million pounds, in a borough where half the people are immigrants from Africa and the Caribbean, situated around the corner from a market famous for selling "bush meat," might be implicated in the "sheer criminality" of the riots. The equation is too simple, simplistic, yet the rage, frustration, and dehumanizing drive to acquisition remain present, simmering always, occupying everyone. I won't write about Mark Duggan or the riots. And yet I am searching my conscience because there is an answer to find, a problem to solve.

I begin to move through the room, the talk of this other country, a country I am connected to by history and yet culturally ignorant of. I wish to hear. I want to see what this other body looks like. I wonder if my uncle had anything to do with the renovation of the houses on these streets. I could ask him. He would probably say yes on principle. I turn and turn, and then there is my host. This morning on the radio, he heard an interview with a poet—he can't recall the poet's name but perhaps I will help him remember. He thinks he would like to read this poet, though normally he doesn't read poetry, not much, but this poet claims to be inspired by a British comic actor my host likes very much. Knowing my poor memory for names, I don't place much hope in my ability to come up with the correct name, but it occurs to me that if I can offer up *any* name, attention will inevitably sift from me, leaving me to wander. To wonder.

Whoever this poet is, he has a prestigious appointment at Oxford. Is it a man? I ask. I don't ask if it is a white male but I am making this assumption, and out of nowhere arrives the name Geoffrey Hill. That's it, my host says cheerfully, happy that the poet knows of the poet. He has all good intentions in his affable embrace of me and keeps the conversation moving with his questions.

Hill has the reputation of being difficult because of what I like to think of as London street syntax, I say. A-to-zed syntax, my host counters with a chuckle. Remembering that I was first drawn to Hill's work because of Paul Celan's "Tenebrae," I recite the opening of the poem:

> We are near, Lord,
> near and at hand.
>
> Handled already, Lord,
> clawed and clawing as though
> the body of each of us were
> your body, Lord.
>
> Pray, Lord,
> pray to us,
> we are near....

I tell my host that Hill's "Tenebrae" turned out to have a Utopian wholeness starkly different from the reversals formed though genocide in Celan's poem of the same name. I was drawn nonetheless to Hill's work by its mental turns; the speaker is rarely stable but gains his footing with and against the movements of an other—often a "you"—in the poem. Sometimes the other is a historical figure, sometimes a remembered place:

> And you, who with your soft but searching voice
> drew me out of the sleep where I was lost,
> who held me near your heart that I might rest
> confiding in the darkness of your choice:
> possessed by you I chose to have no choice,
> fulfilled in you I sought no further quest....

Often enough in Hill's poetry, the internal world of his speaker is adjusting to some external reality; the reality that makes internal negotiations necessary regularly involves the British Empire—"... the life of empire like the life of the mind / 'simple, sensuous, passionate', attuned / to the clear theme of justice and order, gone"—a dynamic familiar to anyone like myself, born with black skin in a former colony and reared in a country built through slavery and still running on racism.

The more I read of Hill's work, the more his marriage of the personal and historical makes sense to me. There is always, I think, a social contract in his writing with the history of the place that informs the evolution of the voice. I am interested in the way Hill's voice speaks to and from and across history, as I am attempting to do in my own work. The difficulty is that imperialism, colonialism, capitalism, and some other isms we probably don't know about yet have spent their histories attempting to erase my voice. I know, in the same way I know my own name, that the poetry of a place is inextricably tied to the politics of that place as occasioned through its history. Only a thick-skinned kind of privilege would allow me to ignore that. Still, as much as I am a stranger in London, being here weeks before the fiftieth anniversary of Jamaica's independence somehow brings me closer to Hill's own negotiations of empire. In any case, I tell my host that "Tenebrae" is the title poem so he can always find that collection, but I suggest *Mercian Hymns*, hymns of the borderers,

as a starter book. My host enters this into the notes app on his iPhone—
*Mercian Hymns.*

Getting to the bathroom means going up the creaky steps. Someone has gone up, and now he is coming back. I listen to the low, dull sound of each step. When the last dies away, I decide finally to leave the party, leaving the torn-up girl to the country she landed in.

Somewhere I find my hosts: kiss, kiss. The streets are wet but the air is dry, and in the night light, my internal hum seems externalized. I walk through the market with all its security gates pulled down. Even deserted it feels alive: "Three pounds, love; a pound fifty, love." Change *love* to *darling* and I could be in Jamaica purchasing pretty much the same provisions. Strip the endearments away completely and I would no doubt be back in my naturalized home. A car stops at the light, and through the open window, Eric Burdon sings, "When I think of all the good times that I've wasted having good times." Down the road, only the KFC and an Indian place remain open. Retracing my steps this time, I am looking for the Dalston C.L.R. James Library as a landmark that will help me get back to the hotel; as soon as it enters my line of sight, I make a run for it.

# Solitary: Spending a Fulbright Year in South Africa

*Susan Rich*

I began working on my Fulbright application just three months after my father's death and a year after my mother's. My parents had just disappeared, and I had no idea how I would survive without them. I knew only that living one's desires was the only thing that mattered. I had only one life. One. That's not a very big number.

Fulbright: such an optimistic word. I imagined *Ful* and *bright* as an enlivened state of mind, hopeful and wildly idealistic. "Our future is not in the stars but in our own minds and hearts," stated Senator J. William Fulbright when he introduced legislation to Congress. Begun shortly after World War II, the Fulbright Program started as a way to encourage mutual respect among countries through educational and cultural endeavors; the senator believed it was a crucial first step to creating an alternative to armed conflict. From one good idea came a global community of artists, scientists, and poets crisscrossing boundaries of ethnicity and race, economic and religious beliefs.

When the time came for me to apply for a fellowship, I felt as if I were writing a tired film noir instead of developing a plan that would enable me to cross cultural borders. Working on the Fulbright application almost overwhelmed me. My nonexistent personal ad would have read "Single woman, 37 years old; has little idea what she wants out of life." I was lost.

Traveling to South Africa *sounded* exciting; it seemed as good a plan as any. Why not interview poets continents away? Why not study another culture's poetry of commitment? The truth was I didn't know what else to do. Two years earlier, I had quit my job with Amnesty International to pursue an MFA in poetry at the University of Oregon. I was still adjusting to the idea that my parents had just left me. For good. Now that I was going to receive my degree, there seemed no clear career path to follow. I had no set geography or sense of myself. A year in a new country and, I presumed, in a new skin, sounded right.

I had never won a fellowship of any kind. I had no fancy credentials other than a soon-to-be-completed MFA. I applied for the Fulbright Fellowship believing it was a long shot. And it was.

The University of Oregon made a point of assisting students with the Fulbright process. The folks in the Office of International Affairs emphasized the importance of a strong proposal that could realistically be enacted. The *real* over the fantastical, they reminded us. The advice paid off: University of Oregon students have often earned the most Fulbright awards in the Pacific Northwest. I'd learned this from the Creative Writing Program director before deciding to move across the country to Oregon from Massachusetts. He'd used the lure of a Fulbright year as a recruiting tool. The Office of International Affairs assigned an administrator to mentor me as I worked on my application. Every other Friday at four p.m., I met with Maggie Morris, assistant vice provost for research and graduate education, in her office, which smelled of oranges. I took a new draft of my essay, which often bore no resemblance to what I had shown her two weeks earlier. She was gentle with my fickleness, and I got the sense that she enjoyed finishing her week imagining South African poets with me.

It took me time to understand that creating grant proposals is by definition a kind of speculative writing. Though I researched every South

African poet I could find and every South African university that might offer to sponsor me, my initial project of interviewing South African poets ultimately was going to succeed only if I could meet the writers and win their trust. Maggie Morris assured me that no one expected that the project would crystallize as I had planned it; the key was to design a good plan.

As with the Fulbright application, I wrote my proposal as if my life depended on it. That summer, as I took every book out of the library that made even a passing reference to African poetry, I honestly believed my very existence hinged on obtaining the fellowship. As contrary as this was to my life experience (I had never won so much as a ballpoint pen), I knew I needed to will this Fulbright year into existence.

After many weeks of not being able to write, the first paragraph of my proposal emerged fully formed. The words provided a map for where I needed to go:

> Poetry is manna, is revolution, is lifeblood that pulses through the body to the pen, to the paper, through memory to metaphor, from a life to a community, from pain to redemption. Poetry is witness. Nelson Mandela writes, "Poetry cannot block a bullet or still a sjambok [whip], but it can bear witness to brutality—thereby cultivating a flower in a graveyard." Writing poetry is a conscious act, an act of taking responsibility. It is neither political nor leftist propaganda to say poetry must be of this world.

After two months of writing and rewriting my proposal, I was interviewed on an early October day. Professors of music, mathematics, biology, and business all convened. Most major universities have a local Fulbright committee, composed of faculty from across the disciplines, that meets with candidates and eventually ranks each one.

As the committee began its work, the director of the Office of International Affairs, Tom Mills, an exceptionally warm and astute man, immediately put me at ease. The committee's questions ranged from the practical (Would I be able to manage on my own in a country I had never visited?) to the more project-based (How would my work with South African poets connect to my professional goals?). I read my poem "Nomadic Life" as part of the interview. Tom had suggested I take some of my poems along. He thought the committee might want to hear my work. It did. I read my poem honoring the Fulani nomads I had known during my time as a Peace Corps volunteer in the Republic of Niger (West Africa). Here's what I learned during my interview: an element of surprise—catching one's audience off guard, igniting imaginations—helps one's project succeed. I'd been hesitant about reading my own poem, but Tom had insisted, reminding me that my work as a poet would inform my entire Fulbright experience.

The day I received the letter congratulating me on my acceptance, May 20, would have been my father's seventy-fourth birthday. It seemed like a sign from the other side of the grave saying, "Go!" Nevertheless, how wrong it seemed not to telephone him to share the news.

As I slipped out of my life in Eugene, Oregon, I had two suitcases so big that I could have fit several bodies inside each of them. They were the height and depth of bags I had seen in airports, zipped up by families moving from one country to the next, taking only what they could wheel. My situation was similar. I left for South Africa with no notion of when or how I would return home because I had no home. My parents' deaths had absolved me of belonging to any singular place. Home was a house in Brookline, Massachusetts, sold to the highest bidder, my permanent address gone in a storm of legalese.

I remember a freak hailstorm in Portland that closed the airport. I remember learning that "act of God" was a legal term and that the airline wasn't responsible for my two-day wait for the next plane to Cape Town.

I remember a day in LAX, when, out of boredom, I dialed my high-school sweetheart's phone number and talked briefly with his lonely wife.

Finally, I boarded a flight that took more hours (and days) than I could account for. This had something to do with crossing the international date line. I remember a twelve-hour stay in Kuala Lumpur, a beautiful city of dust and donkeys. I remember a five-star hotel scented with bougainvillea blossoms, thanks to a voucher from Malaysian Airlines. Oddly, this was the very cheapest fare one could buy. The route I chose was known as "the wrong way round" because it took an extra day. All this lent a heavy dose of surrealism to my journey.

My one South African friend, whom I had met in Boston a decade before, picked me up at the airport and drove me to my new home at Festival Court, which was festive only in the way that funerals are festive: not at all. I'd arranged to take over the one-bedroom unit complete with bed, sofa, two chairs, and kitchen table sight unseen. I had refused to buy the love seat, irking the former tenant, who sent multiple e-mails trying to convince me of its floral beauty. Because this was 1997, and smartphones with digital cameras did not yet exist, I had taken the place on faith. What I found: two tiny rooms in white and tan. My flat looked onto Table Mountain—so close it seemed I could kiss the rock face from the bed. From my angle of vision, this seemed the largest and saddest peak I had ever seen.

In South Africa, place took on enormous meaning. One journalist explained to me in a confidential tone that South Africans have more attachment to the land than any other people. She said this as we climbed Lion's Head, a small mountain in the center of Cape Town. She and I were not alone on our midnight pilgrimage. More than a hundred partiers were there, carrying picnic baskets and bottles of wine. There is a tradition of climbing Lion's Head on nights when the moon is full. Even the set of hand chains drilled into the final rocks did not deter the crowd. In a city where people afraid of house burglars literally run from car to front door, a midnight mountain sojourn seemed almost supernatural.

The hikers helped one another transition from scree to mountaintop. Although the crowd of partiers was mostly white, mostly middle class, it was racially mixed. On top of Lion's Head, I felt that the new South Africa might have a chance of success. At least for those who love to look at the moon.

In Cape Town, white people in my neighborhood rarely walked the streets. No warm evening strolls to the corner market, no walking the dog after dinner. The only South Africans I saw on my walks to and from the university were the black women who cooked, cleaned, and took care of the children of white families. Never before had I visited modest apartments that sparkled so! Never before had I had a lease that included rules governing the use of the storage locker—more often used as the servants' quarters. Even after the end of apartheid, even with Nelson Mandela as president, some black workers lived behind the garage in a lower-middle-class apartment block. What did I condone as I signed my lease, paid my rent, walked past the men outside their storage units, drying their clothes on the same frayed line as my own?

One of the things about living in a country that is not one's own is the constant state of not knowing. Each day, I carried with me a basket of ever-shifting questions—painful to ask and even more impossible to answer. Was it better to hire someone to scrub my two rooms and help alleviate the high unemployment rate, or was it best not to participate in a corrupt vestige from the past regime? Was it morally complicated to go hiking in the mountains if the National Party had constructed the overnight huts and long pathways under the apartheid system? Was I guilty by virtue of the air I breathed? I muddled my way through these questions as I walked past poinsettia and oleander trees to my university office. And on some visceral level, I believed I was guilty. Although I still enjoyed the delicate trees.

At least once a day, in the early morning as I climbed the hill to the campus or at dusk when I returned home, I passed a quiet young man who lived under the eaves of the corner market. Often, he greeted me with a rock-star smile, his eyes soft and appealing. At other times, he was entrenched in his own world, singing or weeping under his breath. Over the course of several months of daily walks, I often thought about this man, wondering why he chose to spread his blue blanket near my house instead of in one of the townships, where most black citizens still lived. How did he endure his solitude day after day? I identified deeply with this man whose name I never learned.

With few exceptions, the poems I wrote during my time in Cape Town focused on the men, women, and children who lived on the busy streets and roundabouts of the city. Although I had previously lived in Zinder, Niger, and Cambridge, Massachusetts—both places where street people were ever present in my daily life—in Cape Town, the stark contrast of rich and poor struck a harsher note. Young children no more than six or seven years old were sent into the street to knock on car windows, their mothers standing in the shadows. And in the celebration of the new idealistic and democratic South Africa, the legions of homeless people at red lights, shopping centers, restaurants, apartment blocks, bars, and beaches showed up the facts of a different South African narrative.

And the beautiful man I saw each evening? His presence took up a larger-than-life residence in my interior world. As a woman who had just been orphaned, who no longer had a home, I of course connected to this man. Something I could barely put into words. In a country where the idea of transformation was ubiquitous, this man still lived on the street alone. The truth was that for the majority of black South Africans, life did not improve economically in the first years after the dismantling of apartheid. My poem for him, "Change," ends with

*This man who nests*
*underneath the café eaves*

*tonight looks up and almost*
*nods to me—to me, not the stranger*
*from a distant country.*

I still picture him in my mind's eye, bedding down for the night as I walk past with my carton of milk and bottles of ginger beer. What might have happened if I had done something more than pour a few coins into his cupped hands? What if I'd learned his name?

As an outsider in a country that had had very few "cultural" visitors in the decades since the United Nations had called for a cultural boycott requesting that all academic and cultural institutions terminate ties to South Africa, I was in a strange position socially. The English faculty was certainly kind to me, if from a distance. My colleagues were happy enough to take me to a movie or a play, but they rarely moved beyond the one obligatory date. This was understandable in a country the outside world often condemned.

During my Fulbright year in South Africa, political poetry took front and center stage in my life. I met with men and women who had been jailed for their beliefs. I met poets who had gone to prison for their poetry, professors who had been jailed for doing nothing more than writing a pamphlet, editing a speech. One such poet and former philosophy professor I met, Jeremy Cronin, a man who had once contemplated the priesthood, now works for the South African government as deputy minister for transportation.

In a 2001 interview with Irish scholar Dr. Helena Sheehan, Cronin mentioned the odd trajectory that had led him to move from his position as a University of Cape Town lecturer in philosophy to political prisoner. His lack of political activism before imprisonment is a common enough story but in his case struck me as extreme. Cronin stated,

"So I ended up in prison as an ANC/SACP [African National Congress/ South African Communist Party] prisoner, but I'd never been to an ANC meeting in my life. I'd never seen an ANC flag. I'd never sung an ANC song, not that I can sing...."

During some of the toughest years (1976–1983) of the apartheid struggle, Cronin was imprisoned, spending a portion of his time in solitary confinement. He was arrested under the Terrorism and Internal Security Act and tried in Cape Town Superior Court. At the beginning of his seven-year term, his young wife, Anne Marie, died of a brain hemorrhage. Now his love poems to her are taught to schoolchildren across the nation.

A man in his middle years, Cronin retains schoolboy good looks. His brown eyes smile at the edges; his hair looks thick and well combed. A pinstriped shirt and worn sports jacket are casual reminders of his years lecturing in college classrooms. Cronin told me that for his first book, *Inside*, he composed the poems inside a cell—literally. He needed to memorize his work and then write the poems down, revising them only after his release from prison.

One signature poem, "Motho Ke Motho Ka Batho Babang," details a communication between two prisoners who can see each other only in the reflection of one handheld mirror. This seems an apt metaphor for how difficult it is to look at any life except indirectly. The poem's title references a common African concept: ubuntu, a belief in a healthy community as central to society; the individual is not as crucial, culturally, as in Western belief systems.

"Motho Ke Motho Ka Batho Babang
(A Person Is a Person Because of Other People)"

By holding my mirror out of the window I see
Clear to the end of the passage.
There's a person down there.

A prisoner polishing a doorhandle.
In the mirror I see him see
My face in the mirror,
I see the fingertips of his free hand
Bunch together, as if to make
An object the size of a badge
Which travels up to his forehead
The place of an imaginary cap.
    (This means: *A warder*.)
Two fingers are extended in a vee
And wiggle like two antennae.
    (He's being watched.)
A finger of his free hand makes a watch-hand's arc
On the wrist of his polishing arm without
Disrupting the slow-slow rhythm of his work.
    (*Later*. Maybe, later we can speak.)
*Hey! Wat maak jy daar?*
        —a voice from around the corner.
*No. Just polishing baas.*
He turns his back to me, now watch
His free hand, the talkative one,
Slips quietly behind
        —*Strength brother*, it says,
In my mirror,
        A black fist.

I've read this poem with groups of students from Buffalo to San Diego, each time asking everyone to shout out together this universal African saying: *Motho ke motho ka batho babang*. The cinematic feel of the piece, the unspooling of sound and meaning until readers are left with the iconic symbol of the black fist, makes real the human connection across prison cell and color line.

When Cronin and I met at an outdoor restaurant outside Johannesburg, *Even the Dead* had just been released, and the cover art featured an extreme close-up of his handsome face. The publisher had made this picture a prerequisite for publishing Cronin's collection of poems. As a deputy minister in the new South African government, Cronin was well known. As a poet, well, no one was really known for writing poetry in South Africa. Instead, the country was in love with its new political and social freedoms; poetry had yet to find its place.

What gripped the public consciousness during my time in South Africa were the Truth and Reconciliation Commission hearings (TRC) happening in different locations across the country. The TRC was a court-appointed body that focused on uncovering the victims of gross human rights violations and provided a legally sanctioned forum for people to tell their stories. Perpetrators of crimes could also come forward and recount their stories in exchange for amnesty, meaning they could not be charged for their crimes later. As with most human rights commissions, the system was complex and, by its very nature, imperfect.

I attended hearings outside Cape Town and watched *Special Report*, the Sunday-night television show that provided TRC updates each week. In South Africa, the name of the game was a visual and often disingenuous view of forgiveness. Grieving mothers met with the Afrikaner men who had tortured their sons and were expected to accept the mise-en-scène of apology. It went something like this: a thick-necked white man rides through the village that he terrorized as a soldier in the South African army, only now he's on the back of a flatbed truck, waving and smiling to the people. Eventually, the truck and the gang of South African Broadcasting Channel (SABC) cameramen pause on key, and the man (these white men *do* look alike) delivers a speech that covers three points: I am sorry for what I did; I hope you can forgive me; I have no money or anything of value for the community except a few moments on TV. Oddly, many people did seem to feel that a TV crew's filming in the village was payment enough—but not everyone.

From "Special Reports"

With a lop-sided stride, she finds her way
to the visitor, steps up proudly, fires

saliva spitting dead
straight in the eyes of forgiveness;

one widow fine-boned and lean,
bows to the cameras of the SABC.

—Susan Rich

My poem ends with this woman's interrupting the narrative of the all-forgiving mother. But as with many of the poems I wrote about my time in South Africa, the work feels weak when compared with the complexities of its subject. South Africa didn't fit neatly into file boxes; I needed a new vocabulary for my experiences, and I'm not sure I ever exactly found it.

Teaching at the University of Cape Town afforded me opportunities to interact with South African students and faculty. I sat in my little room at Festival Court with the big view of Table Mountain, composing lesson plans for creative writing in the first term and American poetry in the second. It was in South Africa that I first taught the poetry of Elizabeth Bishop, Naomi Shihab Nye, and Yusef Komunyakaa. It was in South Africa that I attended my first MLA-style academic conference and published my first (and only!) academic paper.

I met Mazisi Kunene, a former Angeleno who taught for nearly twenty years at UCLA, at the same conference. He left South Africa in 1959 to help lead the antiapartheid movement in the UK. A member of the ANC, he became its main representative in Europe. In his long life, he worked as an academic and a political activist.

Kunene and I met at an academic conference of English professors, at which the number of carjackings tallied during the week was often the key subject during the Q & A. For a few mornings in a leafy suburb of Johannesburg, we sat together talking poetry over eggs and coffee. Together with the Shakespearean scholar David Schalkwyk, we created a multicultural society of three. Kunene seemed amused by the fact that Schalkwyk came to the table each morning with a poem he'd worked on throughout the night. Fifteen years have passed since those generous mornings of breakfast and combustible laughter, but my sense of the quiet utopia we created there has not diminished.

A decade after our meeting, Kunene became Africa's (and South Africa's) first poet laureate. A year later, in 2006, he was dead at seventy-six.

From "Tribute to Mshongweni"

Your dreams shall invade our earth
Creating an endless line of horizons
We too shall follow the song of the night-bird to the hill
The whole earth shall see the falling star

—Mazisi Kunene

I am glad to have known him, if only across the breakfast table. I keep this small table in my mind's eye as another reminder that South Africa might transform into a place where poets, scholars, and even young Americans can come together.

In South Africa, poets were granted little attention. Especially young poets. In 1997 there was only one graduate degree program in creative writing and just a handful of annual literary events. However, I met one poet whose work I admired very much: Mxolisi Nyezwa, a man from Port Elizabeth. When we were introduced, because he was very shy and I was very shy, not much—if any—conversation took place. We stared at each other. I smiled; he looked down. Still, I found his poetry compelling. He had started the bilingual magazine *Kotaz* while living in the township where he had been born. I took this as a good omen for South African poetry; if Nyezwa was staying in the township, it meant he was making a commitment to live and document the new South Africa. Later, I sent him poems and was very thankful that he published them. Through letters, we were able to correspond. Today *Kotaz* is still going strong, and Nyezwa has published three collections of poems: *Song Trials*, *New Country*, and *Malikhanye*. A participant at the Poetry Africa festival sponsored by the University of KwaZulu Natal, Nyezwa wrote,

"Poetry is a simple way to remind us of our humanity. It guards against placing blind faith in the sciences, which are constricting to the human spirit. In poetry we discover our basic selves."

Nyezwa's style of poetry is deceptively simple. His images and obsessions contain echoes of Pablo Neruda's work. It makes sense to me that when living in extremity, in conditions that the human heart can barely comprehend, a poetry of the surreal becomes necessary.

From "I Cannot Think of All the Pains"

i cannot think of all the pains that have come
and gone, pains in men's waists
and in men's shoes—
i cannot have relief proper, wearing a neat tie.

But it was Ingrid de Kok, a South African poet who had gone into self-imposed exile in Canada and whose poems I had discovered while I was at the University of Oregon, whose work most compelled me. In a speech she gave at Northwestern University, de Kok explained the double bind South African poets find themselves in. "It's impossible to write poetry in South Africa without confronting the experience people have had of language and the expectations they therefore have of writers, whose ambiguous function is to undo the word while using the word." I found de Kok's questioning of her "right" to write a lyric of South Africa central to the question of poetry in South Africa: "Why do I write, what may I write, and for whom do I write?" she asks herself. In "Mending," de Kok imagines a woman sewing as a metaphor for the new South Africa—the scene is damaged, with a "trail of red" and "a histogram of welts and weals."

"Mending"

In and out, behind, across.
The formal gesture binds the cloth.
The stitchery's a surgeon's rhyme,
a Chinese stamp, a pantomime

of print. Then spoor. Then trail of red.
Scabs rise, stigmata from the thread.
A cotton chronicle congealed.
A histogram of welts and weals.

The woman plies her ancient art.
Her needle sutures as it darts,
scoring, scripting, scarring, stitching
the invisible mending of the heart.

Elizabeth Bishop's "One Art" lives quietly underneath this poem. The poems share a similar sense of loss in the face of history—whether personal or political. Both pieces require a formal vessel to contain the enormity of emotion. And, as de Kok told me in conversation, the poem is telling not only the story of South Africa but also the story of a woman struggling with the loss of her lover. Perhaps this poem answers, in part, de Kok's question of how to write a South African poetry—a poetry that contends with both personal and national urgencies.

De Kok was the reason I chose South Africa as the country for my Fulbright. I was just as intrigued with her as a person as I had been with her poems. She took a great interest in my life and work—in a way no one had done before. She treated me as a fellow poet and, in time, we became close friends.

Many young writers keep journals while traveling, and I was no different. As I wrote, I often worried about whether my experience was authentic enough. Was I seeing the real South Africa? Did I spend enough time in the churches, the museums, the bars? I wrote about the electrical sockets in the country—that they too were undergoing a transition—the old table lamps unusable with the newfangled three-pronged outlets. I wrote about the color of lemons—that they were a mottled green, never ripe enough.

Looking back at these journals, I understand the difficulty of being in a place and time shot through with contradictions. The poetry of South Africa was changing and in the immediate aftermath of apartheid, it was perhaps too early to tell what change might mean for the country, let alone for poetry. Writers, business people, and arts educators were all searching for new ways to tell the nation's stories—and to lay the foundation for creating new ones.

Every person who worked at the South African Museum—from museum guard to secretary, kitchen staffer to executive director—chose a favorite piece for this inclusive exhibit and wrote a curatorial note concerning why it was the piece he or she related to most. Ingrid de Kok took me to the museum in Cape Town early on in my stay; she insisted that I examine each piece in the show. I now suspect she wanted me to understand how South Africa was changing, that soon black men would not live behind apartment blocks in storage units, that a new democracy was forming. It was at this same museum, downstairs in the tearoom, that I first interviewed de Kok. My tape recorder captured her intense voice: a woman with confidence, committed to a changing nation. In some ways, my time in South Africa paralleled that art exhibit. I recall a series of experiences—midnight climbs, street people, Truth and Reconciliation Commission rallies, classes at the university—that were "chosen" by the various selves at work in me at the time.

In the year leading up to my Fulbright Fellowship, grief and change permeated each interaction, every space that opened to me. The dislocation of losing parents is not analogous to a country's gaining its freedom, but in an illogical way, the experiences matched up. South Africa underwent a total sea change in the 1990s; Nelson Mandela, once the world's most famous political prisoner, became the first black president of a country where, because of his skin color, he formerly had not been legally allowed to vote. The new South African constitution, compiled by working groups of lawyers, nongovernmental organizations, and community groups, became a model for progressives everywhere.

After my Fulbright year ended, I stayed on in South Africa for six more months, working for the United States Information Service and teaching at another South African university. Then suddenly I knew it was time to go home. I packed up my Festival Court apartment—passing it on to the next American, an African-American sociologist from Indiana—and returned to my old Toyota station wagon parked in the lot of my neighbor's auto-repair business in Eugene, Oregon.

It must sound like living in South Africa was a struggle—and it was. Triple locks on the doors and a telephone that rarely rang. But struggle is where I discovered what I could endure; struggle is how I learned to trust my instincts and push beyond my self-imposed boundaries. What I have not stressed enough about my time in South Africa are the close friends I made, the experiences I wouldn't trade away. The long walks home with Rustum, who suggested the title of my first book, the spiraling talks with Lisa as we tried to unpack the nature of our lives, everything enlivened by the newness of another continent.

My connection to Africa, if not strictly South Africa, remains alive in the poems I write and the students I teach. I am on the faculty at Highline Community College, which has the most diverse student population in Washington State. Sometimes international students join my classes having left their homes in Cameroon or Kenya five days earlier.

To better understand their sense of dislocation, it helps that I know firsthand what it is like to be seen as "other" by everyone around me and at the same time to have my own expectations of who I am shift as if I were standing on tectonic plates. Only in a country not my own would I be interviewed as an "American writer" on national radio or be invited to teach "American poetry" at a prestigious university. I was a recent MFA graduate without a book, and these opportunities were not available to me at home. Yet this dislocation, this insecurity bred from never understanding the expectations of those around me, made these experiences otherworldly. I suspect my African students have similar feelings when they are expected to share their ideas in front of the class or are required to write a five-page critical analysis of New American Cinema.

Today, time alone comes to me infrequently. An hour after midnight with a book or an afternoon working on a poem amplifies the moments I can keep to myself. Small crumbs compared to a Fulbright year. Sometimes I wish I could return to that year, to days spent in solitary, more aware now of how crucial the time was for my development as a writer and as a person. Who was that young woman who was curious enough to dive headfirst into the experience of otherness? I've come up with more questions than answers. Questions of authenticity and dislocation, of dealing with grief and transformation, most of all of learning what it is to travel this one curious life as a writer, a Fulbrighter who stays suspended in an enlivened state of mind—singing or perhaps weeping under her breath.

# By Touch

*Alissa Valles*

*If you set out on a journey pray that the road is long*
*a wandering without apparent aim a blind groping*
*so you come to know earth's harshness not just by sight but by touch*
*so that you measure yourself against the world with your whole skin*
—Zbigniew Herbert, "Journey"

My Kraków studio was on the sixth floor of an old apartment building just outside the Planty, the strip of gardens wrapped around the old city center. From my window, I looked out over a convent garden where Sisters of the Visitation often wandered in their magpie habits, chatting with the gardener. When I arrived from John Paul II International Airport, Jan, my landlord, carried my large suitcase all the way to the top. "*Ciężko być poetą!* (Being a poet is so tough!)" he joked. I'd taken a leave of absence from doctoral drudgery. A Kosciuszko fellowship I'd been awarded the previous year and deferred never came through, and by the time the gardener of the Visitation was climbing a ladder to pick apples, I had to scramble for work. That turned out to be a good thing. It meant I met a wild variety of people outside the university, where I was studying advanced tongue twisting and auditing philosophy seminars.

Jan, a geologist, and his wife, Aka, often invited me down to the second floor for tea and metaphysics during the time I was there, even when my rent was late.

My pretext for fleeing school was translation work for an American anthology of Polish prose the poet Adam Zagajewski was editing. Adam conjured a modest grant for me from a mysterious foundation that I still suspect he invented himself and surreptitiously funded. He also introduced me to Jan and Aka and to many others in Kraków, a graceful but conservative and clique-ish city. During the fall of 2004, Adam and I met regularly to discuss (and argue over) the anthology and whatever else came up. Czesław Miłosz had died in August of that year, and after an absurd national controversy over his burial site, Polish letters began to settle around a vast empty space with Gothic eyebrows. Translating essays, letters, and diary entries by more than a dozen writers, including Aleksander Wat, Tadeusz Różewicz, and Miron Białoszewski, along with interviews and a few poems for the anthology, meant struggling to carry a wide variety of idioms into English. It also meant learning to distinguish between aesthetic and political arguments specific to their time and place and arguments that were part of what I think George Steiner called the gossip of eternity. It was more difficult and rewarding than anything I'd done in school.

I was finishing my first book of poems. Insomnia was fertile. The convent bells woke me early in the morning, and I would swear, stagger to the stove to make coffee, translate for a few hours, then go out to classes or meetings, eat something, take a walk, and then climb back to the sixth floor to take a nap and return to my desk after dark. I did some English tutoring and editing; there was such demand for both at the university that students and faculty approached me, sometimes even on the street, with queries about my rates (which I made up on the spot according to how wealthy the asker looked). I even tutored a few prostitutes looking to get out of the game, one of whom went on to work for the city tourist office. In return for the chaste English I gave her, she greatly enriched my Polish sex slang. The Book Institute charged with promoting Polish literature abroad was seemingly always on the lookout for native speakers of various languages to do translations and editing. I started to write articles and reviews for magazines in both Europe and the United States, the first ones on spec, eventually on commission.

I got occasional editing or writing jobs from the Institute for War Documentation in Amsterdam and the BBC World Service, where I had worked after college. Even a small payment in euros or pounds went a long way in Poland. Off the central square, an *obwarzanek* (a proto-bagel) cost only fifty groszy—about fifteen cents—and friends would visit with bouquets of vegetables from their allotment gardens. Adam lent me dictionaries and reference books, and if I went to see a publisher or writer, I'd come home with an armful of books. When I needed a prescribing doctor, a friend put me in contact with a Dr. Bomb, who treated me *pro bono lyrico*, as he put it. Without the generosity of these people, I would have been obliged to go back to school with my tail between my legs, which seemed to me at that time a kind of perdition.

I worked on several translation projects alongside the anthology. I'd felt an instant affinity for Zagajewski's contemporary, Ryszard Krynicki, when I'd started to read him as a Slavics student in England. It was my great luck that Krynicki did not speak—or at least did not admit to speaking—English and felt at home in excruciating silences. My errors of syntax and pronunciation immediately became language games. Unlike most poets, he didn't like to talk about himself, and we mostly talked about other writers, especially Paul Celan, whom he loved, honored, and translated, and Zbigniew Herbert, with whom I was in love. Herbert had dedicated one of his greatest poems to Krynicki: "To Ryszard Krynicki—A Letter." Now Krynicki was the publisher responsible for Herbert's poetry.

I'd started translating Herbert—on whom I was planning a dissertation—at the University of Chicago, in an independent study with J.M. Coetzee, not expecting ever to publish my versions. Translation is an intimate and risky form of associating with a writer you love: you have to serve another voice selflessly and yet be faithful to your own language. This is difficult enough when the writer can argue and explain. When the writer is no longer alive, there is a powerful sense of courting a ghost. Tracking down family, friends, belongings is an occult part of what Walter Benjamin called the "task of the translator." By the special logic of the Eastern European intelligentsia, once I had talked to one or two people about my projects, I was instantly put in touch with others who wished to help or encourage me. I visited Herbert's widow, Katarzyna, in Warsaw and sat in Herbert's old study, surrounded by his books and papers, leafing through his sketchbooks. Szu-szu, a plump white cat I knew from Herbert's poems, known to empty glasses of vodka left on the table, was still padding around.

Krynicki introduced me to a gaggle of younger Polish poets he published. These guys, almost all of them called Marcin, scorned the patriarchs I adored (Miłosz, Herbert) and worshipped instead the puffed-up daddies I had impatiently rejected (O'Hara and Ashbery). There should be a Freudian term describing lust for someone else's parent. The younger poets were trying to free themselves from the political burden Polish poetry carried. What they wrote seemed to me an unprecedented hybrid of Europe and the United States and because that was the kind of thing I was looking to do myself, it had a wicked appeal for me. To be surrounded by poets who spurned Herbert just as I was making my own versions of his poems was bracing. Herbert's nature was to work against his immediate surroundings, to find his feet in confrontation and controversy. Traction sparks energy, and as Herbert says, only garbage flows with the stream.

After a year I gravitated from Kraków to Warsaw—an infinitely uglier but much more liberal city—and decided to leave graduate school. I found two jobs, both by word of mouth: one at the Jewish Historical Institute, where I translated and edited texts from the World War II archive, and another at the antitrafficking organization La Strada International, tutoring and mentoring young women who had been forced into prostitution.

I rented an apartment from a feminist writer, Agnieszka Graff, who was one of a startling number of inspiring and independent women I met in Warsaw. Pani Herbert took me to a Pani Kafka who provided me with black kittens. The following years were thick with Herbert, with syntax and simile, with rebellions and reconciliations, with blood, ink, and tears. I left the United States in the year of Abu Ghraib and the sickening stench of official lies. I returned in the year it transpired that the US government had "rendered" prisoners to Poland. You can't escape from home, but you can learn to tie new knots, love foreign princes, grow a new tongue, eyes, skin, scars.

# Beyond the Page

## A Glance Back

# Elizabeth Bishop in Brazil[1]

*Ashley Brown*

Future biographers will probably make a great deal of Elizabeth Bishop's twenty years in Brazil. This was the country of her middle age and her full maturity as a poet, and it continues to provide a background for her years in Boston. As I stood recently on her balcony looking at the water-life on Boston Harbor, I thought back easily to the first time I met her in an apartment high above Guanabara Bay at Rio de Janeiro, and then I thought: she always has the most spectacular views! I hope she doesn't mind my stating in print that she is farsighted; I rather envy her that. When I, quite myopic, could barely see a freighter steaming across the bay, Elizabeth was already describing the activity on deck. Brazil is a good place for the keen observer. It is teeming with particularities, and when I first lived there I (a former philosophy major) thought that the easy way out was to become a complete nominalist; one had to keep one's head. But Elizabeth seemed perfectly in harmony with this bar-rage of sights, sounds, and smells that awaited one at every hand. She was staying then in a section called Leme, and over the telephone she

---

1. Ashley Brown, "Elizabeth Bishop in Brazil" from *Elizabeth Bishop and Her Art*, edited by Lloyd Schwartz and Sybil P. Estess (Ann Arbor: The University of Michigan Press, 1983). Originally appeared in *Southern Review* (October 1977).

explained, before I went there the first time, that the way to remember it was to recite "Now I lay me down to sleep" in the taxi.

The time was 1964. I had with me a letter of introduction from Flannery O'Connor, an old friend, who had written: "I'm up here in the hospital else I would send you some peafowl feathers to take her from me. She sent me an altar in a bottle." This was Flannery's last letter to me; I did not realize then how close to death she was, but later that summer I read about it in the *Jornal do Brasil*. Flannery and Elizabeth had never met; they had spoken only once by long-distance telephone, but they had corresponded for some years and formed a friendship based on a wonderful sense of humor as well as a mutual respect for each other's literary worth. The altar in the bottle I had admired on Flannery's bookshelves in the parlor at Andalusia Farm. Actually it was a wooden cross with bits of paper and tinfoil and a rooster at the top (reminiscent of Elizabeth's poem "Roosters"?). It probably came from the Northeastern state of Bahïa, which is especially rich in folklore. I always thought it was a kind of emblem of some artistic trait that these two writers shared—perhaps their unusual unsentimental love of the beauty to be found in common life.

Much of the time in those days Elizabeth lived with a friend, Lota de Macedo Soares, in a really handsome modern house in the mountains above Petrópolis. Another spectacular view. Petrópolis, a couple of hours' drive from Rio, is the old imperial summer capital, and Rio society still repairs there during the hot season. The house was called "Samambaia," after a fern with rather coarse leaves that grows in many parts of Brazil. It was long and low but went off in several directions from a room, open much of the time, where people breakfasted or dined. Indeed, most of the house could be open, and I remember with delight the hummingbirds that darted through. Elizabeth, an amateur ornithologist, said that there were two hundred species in Brazil. Was that possible? But she lived in the house week in and week out, and in a lovely poem called "Song for the Rainy Season" (1960) she gives us the scene that the casual visitor might overlook:

> House, open house
> to the white dew
> and the milk-white sunrise
> kind to the eyes,
> to membership
> of silverfish, mouse,
> bookworms,
> big moths; with a wall
> for the mildew's
> ignorant map;
>
> darkened and tarnished
> by the warm touch
> of the warm breath,
> maculate, cherished,
> rejoice!

"Samambaia" is the setting for several other poems: "Electrical Storm," which immortalizes Tobias the cat; "The Armadillo"; and the somewhat later "Rainy Season; Sub-Tropics." "The Armadillo" takes place during a festive season that is celebrated in June—the feast of São João, which comes at the winter solstice there. The fire balloons in the poem are illegal with good reason:

> With a wind,
> they flare and falter, wobble and toss;
> but if it's still they steer between
> the kite sticks of the Southern Cross,
>
> receding, dwindling, solemnly

and steadily forsaking us,
or, in the downdraft from a peak,
suddenly turning dangerous.

This poem, one of the finest, is absolutely sensitive to every nuance of movement. Although it is contained within a pictorial setting (all can be visualized), Miss Bishop's rhythmic control largely accounts for the *pretty, dreamlike mimicry* that prepares the way for the final moral statement.

"Rainy Season; Sub-Tropics" (1967) might be regarded as a companion piece to "Song for the Rainy Season" if you shifted your attention to the animal life outside the house. It turns on the theme of self-pity that Elizabeth Bishop has often dealt with in various subtle forms. I suspect that it is the human quality she most dislikes, though she sometimes presents it in a good-natured way, as in "Crusoe in England," where she has her hero reminisce:

I told myself
"Pity should begin at home." So the more
pity I felt, the more I felt at home.

"Rainy Season" is a triptych of prose-poems with these speakers: a giant toad, a strayed crab, and a giant snail (the lesser orders of nature come very large in Brazil). They are all displaced; they all embody human feelings (vanity, aggression, envy, fear, longing for repose, and so on) in a disconcerting way; and their reactions to each other in the three monologues compose a scenario. The brilliance of the description cannot be conveyed in a brief quotation. About the time that I first read this I saw Beckett's *Play* (1964), with its three characters in urns up to their necks, each lit in turn by a spotlight as he blames the others for his plight. (The situation that is being recollected in a kind of purgatory is a tawdry adultery.) I thought: how interesting that Elizabeth's characters with their density of concrete life and Beckett's with their babble of clichés should come so close together in one's mind. "Pity me," says the toad in his first line. "Pity me," says the snail near the end. "Pity them," says Beckett's Man halfway through, and his sad trio run the same gamut of feelings as the poor rain-creatures.

At "Samambaia" you could go forward onto a great stone terrace that overlooked the valley towards Petrópolis. This, however, could be dangerous for the acrophobic, and I gathered that Aldous Huxley, a visitor a few years earlier, had almost pitched over the edge. If you walked up from the house you came to Elizabeth's study, a small cottage. This was situated above a waterfall that rushed down the mountainside. (Her snail says, "The waterfall below will vibrate through my shell and body all night long. In that steady pulsing I can rest.") Elizabeth had the splendid idea of having the cascade dammed, just momentarily, to make a tiny swimming pool, and you could descend there from the study through a clump of bamboos. The study itself was comfortable and clearly the working-place for a serious writer and reader with a large eclectic taste; nothing formal about it. Photographs of Baudelaire and Marianne Moore and Lowell were tacked to the wall. Here and in the main house were superb artistic objects from various parts of Brazil, where by this time Elizabeth had travelled extensively. She has always liked simple things that most people would reject. I remember a dishpan made of colorful flattened-out cans that had contained soybean oil or peas or perhaps cheese; they had been soldered together. (This brief phase of industrial folk-art is over in the 1970s, and now housewives along the Amazon use plastic dishpans like everyone else's.) I mention these details, trivial as they may seem, because they suggest the human scale of Elizabeth's poetry. A poem like "Jerónimo's House" is composed almost entirely of such details, and in its quiet way it bears out a "rage for order" as much as any poem by Stevens.

Elizabeth landed in Brazil somewhat by accident in late November, 1951. She had actually intended to land there, but only to stop during a voyage round South America. This incident is amusingly recalled in "Arrival at Santos," done from the tourist's point of view. Miss Breen, Elizabeth's fellow passenger, the retired police lieutenant, really existed, and she rather liked being put in the poem. One curious textual matter: in the original version the author was taking Scotch through the customs; when the poem was reprinted in *Questions of Travel* it became bourbon. Which *was* it? Then Elizabeth ate some item of fruit (a *cajú*, I believe) that disagreed horribly with her; she was laid up for an extended recovery; and her ship sailed on without her. But she had friends in Brazil whom she had known in New York during an earlier period; she liked the country, and she stayed.

The poems in *Questions of Travel* are the chief literary legacy of Elizabeth Bishop's Brazilian years, but as a professional writer she occasionally turned her hand to other things, and eventually she became an important translator and an intermediary between Brazilian and American culture. The Brazilian government awarded her the Order of Rio Branco in 1971. In a conversation piece published some years ago in *Shenandoah* (Winter 1966) I asked her whether she had been able to get anything from the country except its appearances, and she replied:

> Living in the way I have happened to live here, knowing Brazilians, has made a great difference. The general life I have known here has of course had an impact on me. I think I've learned a great deal. Most New York intellectuals' ideas about "underdeveloped countries" are partly mistaken, and living among people of a completely different culture has changed a lot of my old stereotyped ideas.

Elizabeth managed to put some of her knowledge into an illustrated book commissioned by Time Incorporated in 1962. Her text was no doubt "edited" to some extent in New York, but I can detect scarcely a trace of *Time*-style, and in fact, the book is still the best introduction to the subject. This is because the author is very close to the rich popular life around her; unlike so many of her compatriots, she is not blinkered by statistics and theories about economic "take-off." Much that she observed only twenty years ago is already passing into oblivion as the Brazilian population moves into the big cities. Not many North Americans could have written this:

> In the field of popular culture, however, undoubtedly the greatest achievement is the creation of the figureheads used on boats on the Rio São Francisco. Called *carrancas*, the figureheads depict animals, women and characters from Afro-Brazilian folklore, but one of the favorites is always the "Great Worm," the most dreadful of the spirits that live in the river. Some of these figureheads are very fine, towering several feet above the bow of the boat and carved in strong and simple style reminiscent of Romanesque sculpture. Unfortunately, *carrancas* are being used less and less today, and the art of carving them is dying out.

One evening in Rio we were invited to the house of a rich man who had collected a number of *carrancas* and placed them round his garden and swimming pool; they *were* impressive looming out of the dark, almost theatrical in this setting with its expensive lighting effects. What would they have looked like on the river? Very few people in Brazil could have seen them. Elizabeth, an indefatigable traveller, finally went down the Rio São Francisco on an endless trip in 1967. But it was a mixed experience; her immediate reaction came on a postcard:

> ... in retrospect I'm glad I did it + some of the worst will no doubt seem funny as time goes on—but never never the hideous poverty. The boat a very quaint stern-wheeler made in the U S A 70 years ago—everyone nice and polite,

but each and every one asked if I had a "family" and when I said no, they all commiserated with me, but also, I felt, rather avoided me as being not quite all there.

This, I think, records her *un*sentimental love of common life.

Elizabeth, who already had Spanish (from a period in Mexico during the 1940s) and French (from an even earlier period in Paris), learned Portuguese soon enough during her first years in Rio. In any case, nearly all of her friends were Brazilians. About this time she was introduced to an elderly lady, Sra. Alice Brant, who had grown up in Diamantina, a somewhat remote town in the state of Minas Gerais (General Mines). Alice Brant was half English by descent; her grandfather had gone out as a doctor with a mining company and remained; but she was brought up as a Brazilian. As a young girl in the 1890s she wrote a diary that she later called *Minha Vida de Menina* (*My Life as a Little Girl*). It was not till 1942, when she was living in Rio, that she had any idea of publishing it; her husband, the president of the Bank of Brazil, made the suggestion. She used the pseudonym "Helena Morley." Although the Diary was only intended to amuse her family and friends, it was recommended to the public by the French novelist Georges Bernanos, who was in wartime exile in Brazil, and it has had a kind of classic status ever since; one can often find a copy in the stationery shops.

Elizabeth proposed to translate the Diary and immersed herself in the subject. It was a good excuse for another journey, this time to Diamantina, which was not easy to reach twenty-five years ago. Nowadays the town, with its fine old houses, is rather famous among connoisseurs of architecture, and one can drive there on an excellent road. The Diary is, among other things, an authentic record of provincial life at a moment when Brazil was moving into another epoch of its history. (Slavery had been abolished in 1888 and the Empire succeeded by the first Republic the following year.) But its main interest lies in its loving but candid account of a family, a theme to which Elizabeth would return. Her introduction to the translation is one of her best pieces of prose, and, as Marianne Moore said in a review (*Poetry*, July 1959), "The attitude of life revealed by the Diary, Helena's apperceptiveness, and innate accuracy, seem a double portrait; the exactness of observation in the introduction being an extension, in manner, of Miss Bishop's verse and other writing...." The Diary in fact occupies an important place in Elizabeth Bishop's canon.

The Brazilian poems in *Questions of Travel* are not arranged according to their date of composition, but they do compose a set of related responses to a scene. All of them were retained by the author in the Chatto and Windus *Selected Poems* of 1967. Needless to say, they exemplify a wide range of style; Miss Bishop, as her readers know, has large resources of poetic "attack." "Arrival at Santos," which originally came near the end of *A Cold Spring*, looks just right when it is reprinted as the opening poem in *Questions of Travel*. Then comes "Brazil, January 1, 1502," which was first printed in the *New Yorker*'s number for the New Year in 1960, after the poet had lived in Brazil for eight years and assimilated a great deal of its history as well as its landscape. New Year's Day of 1502 was the date on which the Portuguese caravels arrived at Guanabara Bay, which they mistakenly thought was the mouth of a great river— hence Rio de Janeiro (January). This is a poem of wonder, however; the poet assumes the vision of the Portuguese discoverers, and the texture of the verse could not be more different from that of "Arrival at Santos." Indeed, the word *texture* is appropriate here, because this is a verbal tapestry, and we move in and out of the setting as though we still had the allegorical sense of the sixteenth century. ("Still in the foreground there is Sin: / five sooty dragons near some massy rocks.") The historical theme shouldn't be overlooked. In her text for the *Time* book Miss Bishop observes that "the Portuguese lacked the bloodthirsty missionary zeal of the Spaniards," but the Christians of her poem are "hard as nails"; and at least a century of Brazil's early history comes out in this passage:

> Directly after Mass, humming perhaps
> *L'Homme armé* or some such tune,
> they ripped away into the hanging fabric,
> each out to catch an Indian for himself—
> those maddening little women who kept calling,
> calling to each other (or had the birds waked up?)
> and retreating, always retreating, behind it.

For a decade or so I have thought this poem fascinating as an act of perception: That is, on what terms does the mind approach a scene, and with what preconceptions? And how can one recover the sense of any earlier period? The author briefly quotes Kenneth Clark's *Landscape into Art* as an epigraph. I would suggest E.H. Gombrich's *Art and Illusion* as being even more useful for speculating on this theme.

The title poem, "Questions of Travel," was first published in 1956, about four years after Elizabeth had taken up residence in Brazil. The tourist has now become the passionate observer and, in a sense, has lost her innocence. The poem is a wonderful mosaic of things that one can see and hear along a Brazilian highway—say, along the road to Petrópolis. (Some of these phenomena are, I fear, doomed as highway culture in Brazil resembles ours more and more.) The mechanic's wooden clogs "carelessly clacking" over the floor of the filling-station, the bird in its fancy bamboo cage above the broken gasoline pump—what a pity, says the poet, to have missed these things in all their particularity. And what random historical causes lay behind them? The poem builds up in a seemingly (but only seemingly) casual way to the two formal stanzas in italics at the end, where the traveller asks herself:

> *Continent, city, country, society:*
> *the choice is never wide and never free.*
> *And here, or there…No. Should we have stayed at home,*
> *wherever that may be?*

But she has already answered her question in the poem, where, for me at any rate, a whole phase of lost experience has been transmuted into something permanent. The English poet Charles Tomlinson took her to task in his review of *Questions of Travel* (*Shenandoah*, Winter 1966), in which he said, "For the fact of the matter is, Miss Bishop travels because she likes it, not because she is homeless in the way that Lawrence or Schoenberg were." But is it really necessary to insist on this kind of "radical homelessness?" It seems to me perfectly obvious that Elizabeth Bishop has followed Henry James, Katherine Anne Porter, and certain other Americans who have gone out into the world, and these are the names to mention. She knows very well who she is. Again, speaking for myself, I have often wondered about the accidents of history that have made my Brazilian friends different from me—they come from a country as old and large and diverse as ours, they had slavery twenty-five years after we did, they too are apt to make exaggerated claims. Elizabeth's poems have more of the "feel" of life in Brazil than anything else written by a North American because they undercut the large generalizations that we all have when we approach a subject on this scale.

The remaining poems in *Questions of Travel* are about poor people in various parts of Brazil, and I think that Mr. Tomlinson misses the point again when he says that "the better-off have always preferred their poor processed by style." I suppose one could turn that remark against Wordsworth in "Resolution and Independence," but surely his old leech-gatherer is *dignified* by being put into *rime royale*. One could hardly think that Wordsworth knew his poor more intimately than Miss Bishop, and he is the master of this kind of experience in English poetry. Miss Bishop in fact has often chosen to write about the humble for reasons of her own—and poems like "Jerónimo's House," "Songs for a Colored Singer," "At the Fishhouses," and "Faustina, or Rock Roses" are among her most assured successes. I don't think she would have done better with intellectuals or diplomats' wives as subjects.

"Manuelzinho" and "Squatter's Children," which were written

around the same time as "Questions of Travel," are about people who might be found on the hillside leading to "Samambaia." (A group of three "Samambaia" poems that I already mentioned comes next in the collection.) Flannery O'Connor would have regarded them with the same steady humorous gaze (though she would have put them in more drastic situations), and I could easily imagine Manuelzinho with a change of name at Andalusia Farm. His poem is one of Elizabeth Bishop's most developed works of portraiture—an elusive maddening figure seen in the round, at different seasons, in different lights. Quotation hardly does it justice; the effect is unusually cumulative, and much lies behind this wry conclusion:

> You helpless, foolish man,
> I love you all I can,
> I think. Or do I?
> I take off my hat, unpainted
> and figurative, to you.
> Again I promise to try.

The remaining poems take us to different parts of Brazil where Elizabeth lived or travelled. "Twelfth Morning; or What You Will" is set at Cabo Frio (Cold Cape), which is east along the coast from Rio. This is another poem that radiates a "sense of glory" (I borrow the phrase from Herbert Read). The black boy Balthazár, coming out of the mist, over the "shopworn" dunes and debris and the rusted wire, is like a young prince, the four-gallon can on his head notwithstanding:

> You can hear the water now,
> inside, slap-slapping. Balthazár is singing.
> "Today's my Anniversary," he sings,
> "the Day of Kings."

And here at the end of the poem the rhymes finally emerge, the sense of glory is complete. One of Elizabeth Bishop's favorite poets is George Herbert; perhaps the naturalness of tone and the craftsmanship owe something to him. Placed between two longer, more ambitious poems, her own celebration of Epiphany (called "The Day of Kings" in Brazil) is modest but a delight.

"The Riverman" is so long that one could easily devote an essay to it. But perhaps this is unnecessary. It is partly worked up from *Amazon Town*, a book by the anthropologist Charles Wagley, as Miss Bishop acknowledges in her headnote. The book was published in 1958; she was writing her poem the next year. *Amazon Town* is admired in professional circles as a work of scholarship, and I should say that it is a work of considerable literary merit as well. There is no need to trace the prose passages that Miss Bishop has used; the important thing is the transmutation into poetry, and here James Merrill has made the right comment: "Wonderful, fluid, pulsing lines—you hardly feel the meter at all." (*Shenandoah*, Summer 1968). This poem of the river runs through 158 lines based on three stresses in each line: a constant undercurrent, as it were, for the action. (For comparison one might turn to Eliot's adaptation of the first paragraphs of *The Heart of Darkness* in *The Waste Land*, III.) An even more important matter is this: for the poet, the experience of reading Charles Wagley's book meshes with her own experience along the Amazon. It is like the case of Wordsworth's "Solitary Reaper"; we know he took the poem out of someone's travel-book, but he could not have brought it off without his excursions through the Lake District.

"The Burglar of Babylon" returns us to Rio and the apartment in Leme, which lies below the hill of Babylon. The *favelas*, or hillside slums, are now almost gone in this section, but fifteen years ago they were very much in evidence. This is Elizabeth Bishop's longest narrative. The subject was at hand; it was reported at length in the newspapers; and from the terrace of the apartment she could see the soldiers hunting down the young criminal Micuçú. How was this to be presented, given the possibilities? Elizabeth instinctively used the modern ballad, which for some readers means Auden's poems in this form, the ones about Miss Gee and Victor. (The latter, I should think, is more successful in its tragicomic treatment of a stereotyped subject.) "The Burglar of Babylon" also owes something to cinematic technique in its camera angles, its "cutting" from one shot to another. But its perspectives are finally verbal. Not only the echoes of the old ballad idiom, but the conversation of the people in the bar, Micuçú's auntie, the soldiers, Micuçú himself—all of this goes perfectly into traditional quatrains. The poem was first published in *The New Yorker* in November, 1964; simultaneously a remarkable translation by Flávio Macedo Soares appeared in the literary review *Cadernos Brasileiros* in Rio. The translation in fact testifies to the success of the original, as though the English and the Portuguese were descended from the same source:

> Nos morros verdes do Rio
> uma mancha temível cresce:
> os pobres que vêm para o Rio
> e não têm como regresse.

All things considered, this is the best as well as the most humane of modern ballads.

Two more poems from Leme are included in the last section of *The Complete Poems*: "House Guest" and "Going to the Bakery." These are slighter than the Brazilian pieces in *Questions of Travel*. The details are sharply etched, especially in the latter poem (Flaubert himself would be impressed by the *progression d'effet*), but the sense of wonder, always one of Elizabeth Bishop's strong points, has diminished. The last of *The Complete Poems* (but far from the last of Elizabeth's poems, I'm glad to say) is "Under the Window: Ouro Preto." This is an affectionate tribute to a town in the mountains of Minas Gerais that has survived from the eighteenth century. Ouro Preto (Black Gold) was the capital of the state till about 1900, then abandoned and difficult to reach, then rediscovered during the last generation. It is a splendid repository of late-Portuguese baroque built during a period of wealth, much of it designed and executed by the legendary Aleijadinho, a poor crippled mulatto who became his country's greatest artist. Elizabeth, who had often visited Ouro Preto, even when the going was rough, finally succumbed to its charms in 1965 and bought an old house, which she proceeded to restore. It dated from about 1730. When the work began, she discovered that the *pau-a-pique*, the thick wall of wattle and mud, was actually tied together with rawhide in some places, and a bit of this architectural oddity was preserved under glass when the restoration was finished. And as usual a balcony, in this case overlooking the whole range of Ouro Preto on its steep hills. Although the trucks from the bauxite mines hurtled alarmingly close to the front door, a certain order prevailed inside. "Under the Window" is a low-keyed, amusing rendition of Brazilian life, so much of which is spent out-of-doors, and another demonstration of how a poem can be made out of the most unlikely materials.

[...]

I think that Elizabeth has lived through this experience many times; her translation is deeply felt. More recently she has filled out the picture, as it were, with three shorter poems from Carlos Drummond in the anthology of Brazilian poetry that she edited with Emanuel Brasil in 1972, and taken together, her versions of this poet's work are a considerable achievement.

This brief account of Elizabeth Bishop at a certain period of her career of course omits a great deal. For instance, she wrote several of her Nova Scotia poems during these years, and this is a locale to which she has returned imaginatively if not actually many times. The world of her poetry is large. Although it differs from that of Wallace Stevens in some ways, I think that she, more than anyone else today, has the same humanist vision of north and south, the seasonal round, the imagination creating its order sometimes in most discouraging circumstances.

# An Interview with Elizabeth Bishop[1]

*Ashley Brown*

*Brazil: Elizabeth Bishop's study is a small house which lies up the hill from her home in the mountains near Petrópolis, the old imperial summer capital. The study is perched above a waterfall. One looks through the windows at a clump of bamboos which descend to a tiny swimming pool, momentary repose in the course of the cascading water. The room is filled with books, comfortable armchairs, piles of old literary quarterlies. An exquisite* oratório *from Minas Gerais and other small miscellaneous objects stand on the bookcases. A literary visitor will notice photographs of Baudelaire, Marianne Moore, and Robert Lowell near the poet's work-table. Tobias, an elderly cat, and Suzuki, his younger Siamese companion, reluctantly move from the vicinity of the typewriter.*

INTERVIEWER: I think you have one of the handsomest settings in the world. What poet could ask for more? Do you find that a dazzling

---

1.  *Shenandoah* 17, no 2. (Winter 1966), 3–19.

    Editor's Note: Ashley Brown, "An Interview with Elizabeth Bishop" from *Elizabeth Bishop and Her Art*, edited by Lloyd Schwartz and Sybil P. Estess (Ann Arbor: The University of Michigan Press, 1983).

landscape like this is an incentive to write, or do you prefer to shut your-self off from visual distractions when you are working?

MISS BISHOP: You will notice that the study turns its back on the view of the mountains—that's too distracting! But I have the intimate view to look at; the bamboo leaves are very close. Everybody who comes here asks about the view: is it inspiring? I think I'll put a little sign saying "Inspiration" on those bamboos! Ideally, I suppose any writer prefers a hotel room completely shut away from distractions.

INTERVIEWER: You have been living in Brazil since about 1952, haven't you?

MISS BISHOP: Yes, it was the end of November, 1951, when I came here; you remember my poem, "Arrival at Santos."

INTERVIEWER: As far as your poetry goes, have you been able to get any-thing from Brazil except its appearances? I mean, can you draw on the social and literary traditions here?

MISS BISHOP: Living in the way I have happened to live here, knowing Brazilians, has made a great difference. The general life I have known here has of course had an impact on me. I think I've learned a great deal. Most New York intellectuals' ideas about "underdeveloped countries" are partly mistaken, and living among people of a completely different culture has changed a lot of my old stereotyped ideas.

As for the literary milieu in Brazil, it is so remote from ours. In Rio for example, the French influence is still powerful. I find the poetry very interesting, but it hasn't much to do with contemporary poetry in English. Our poetry went off in a different direction much earlier.

INTERVIEWER: When you say our poetry went off in a different direction, what do you mean?

MISS BISHOP: What happened with Eliot and Pound as early as 1910—modernism. The Brazilians' poetry is still more formal than ours—it's farther from the demotic. It is true, of course, that they had a *modernismo* movement in 1922, led by Mario de Andrade and others. But they still don't write the way they speak. And I suppose they have still never quite escaped from romanticism. It's an interesting fact that there is no word in Portuguese for "understatement." Marianne Moore's poetry is nearly all understatement. How can they understand us? So much of the English-American tradition consists of this. They have irony, but not understatement.

By the way, I lived in Mexico for a time twenty years ago and I knew Pablo Neruda there. I think I was influenced to some extent by him (as in my "Invitation to Miss Marianne Moore"), but he is still a rather "advanced" poet, compared with other South American poets.

To summarize: I just happened to come here, and I am influenced by Brazil certainly, but I am a completely American poet, nevertheless.

INTERVIEWER: What about the Portuguese language? Do you find that reading it and speaking it (and being surrounded by it) have increased your awareness of English?

MISS BISHOP: I don't read it habitually—just newspapers and some books. After all these years, I'm like a dog: I understand everything that's said to me, but I don't speak it very well. I don't really think that my awareness of English has been increased. I felt much the same when I lived in France before the war. What I really like best is silence! Up here in Petrópolis, in the mountains, it is very quiet.

INTERVIEWER: How would you describe Portuguese as a poetic language?

MISS BISHOP: From *our* point of view, it seems cumbersome—you just can't use colloquial speech in that way. Grammatically, it is a very difficult language. Even well-educated Brazilians worry about writing their own language; they don't speak their grammar, as it were. I imagine it's easier to write free verse in Portuguese—because it gets you away from the problem. They did take to free verse very quickly here.

INTERVIEWER: Now, if I may, I'd like to recall you to North America and your childhood. You actually spent your earliest years in Nova Scotia, didn't you? Did you live in the kind of house where people encouraged the children to read? Or did your literary interests come later?

MISS BISHOP: I didn't spend all of my childhood in Nova Scotia. I lived there from 1914 to 1917 during the First World War. After that I spent long summers there till I was thirteen. Since then I've made only occasional visits. My relatives were not literary in any way. But in my aunt's house we had quite a few books, and I drew heavily on them. In some ways the little village in Canada where I lived was more cultured than the suburbs of Boston where I lived later. As for the books in our house, we had Emerson, Carlyle, all the old poets. I learned to read very early, and later I used to spend all of my allowance on books. They were all I ever wanted to buy.

INTERVIEWER: What were some of your favorite books? Were you ever deeply impressed by something you read in those days?

MISS BISHOP: I was crazy about fairy tales—Anderson, Grimm, and so on. Like Jean-Paul Sartre (as he explains it in *Les Mots*), I also read all kind of things I didn't really understand. I tried almost anything. When I was thirteen, I discovered Whitman, and that was important to me at the time. About that time I started going to summer camp and met some more sophisticated girls who already knew Emily Dickinson and H.D.

and Conrad and Henry James. One of them gave me Harriet Monroe's anthology of modern poets. That was an important experience. (I had actually started reading poetry when I was eight.) I remember coming across Harriet Monroe's quotations from Hopkins, "God's Grandeur" for one. I quickly memorized these, and I thought, "I must get this man's work." In 1927 I saw the first edition of Hopkins. I also went through a Shelley phase, a Browning phase, and a brief Swinburne phase. But I missed a lot of school and my reading was sporadic.

INTERVIEWER: Did you write anything much before you went to Vassar? I remember your saying you had some exceptionally good teachers at Walnut Hill School in Natick.

MISS BISHOP: I wrote a good deal, starting at the age of eight. When I was twelve I won an American Legion prize (a five-dollar gold piece) for an essay on "Americanism." This was the beginning of my career. I can't imagine what I said on *this* subject! I was on the staff of the literary magazine at school and published some poems there. I had a good Latin teacher and a good English teacher at Walnut Hill. The teaching was of a very high quality. I only studied Latin then. I didn't take up Greek till I went to Vassar. I now wish I'd studied nothing but Latin and Greek in college. In fact I consider myself badly educated. Writing Latin prose and verse is still probably the best possible exercise for a poet.

INTERVIEWER: You were in what turned out to be a brilliant literary generation at Vassar—Mary McCarthy, Eleanor Clark, Muriel Rukeyser, besides yourself. Did your friends set a high standard of criticism even in those days?

MISS BISHOP: Actually I was a close friend only with Mary. Eleanor and I were friends, too, but she left for two years, and Muriel was there for just a year. Yes, they, we, were all terribly critical then. One big event for us was a little magazine we started. Mary has recently talked about this. This is the way I remember it: The regular literary magazine was dull and old-fashioned. Mary and Eleanor and I and several others decided to start one in competition. It was to be anonymous. We used to meet in a speakeasy and drink dreadful red wine and get slightly high. (Afterwards the college physician analyzed the wine and found it contained fifty per-cent alcohol, she said, but I can't believe that.) We called the magazine *Con Spirito*. We got out only three numbers, I think, but we prevailed. I published several poems and stories in *Con Spirito*. T.S. Eliot came to Vassar about this time. I was elected to interview him and I was abso-lutely terrified. But he was very gentle, and later he flattered us by saying he liked some of the things in our magazine.

INTERVIEWER: In those days did you think about becoming a poet or a novelist?

MISS BISHOP: I never *thought* much about it, but I believe I was only inter-ested in being a poet.

INTERVIEWER: You grew up in the Marxist '30s. Do you think this radical political experience was valuable for writers? Or did it blunt people's per-ceptions to be thinking in such exclusively political terms?

MISS BISHOP: I was always opposed to political thinking as such for writ-ers. What good writing came out of that period, really? Perhaps a few good poems; Kenneth Fearing wrote some. A great deal of it seemed to me very false. Politically I considered myself a socialist, but I disliked "social conscious" writing. I stood up for T.S. Eliot when everybody else was talking about James T. Farrell. The atmosphere in Vassar was left-wing; it was the popular thing. People were always asking me to be on a picket-line, or later to read poems to a John Reed Club. I felt that most of the college girls didn't know much about social conditions.

I was very aware of the Depression—some of my family were much affected by it. After all, anybody who went to New York and rode the Elevated could see that things were wrong. But I had lived with poor people and knew something of poverty at firsthand. About this time I took a walking-trip in Newfoundland and I saw much worse poverty there. I was all for being a socialist till I heard Norman Thomas speak; but he was *so* dull. Then I tried anarchism, briefly. I'm much more interested in social problems and politics now than I was in the '30s.

INTERVIEWER: What poets did you meet when you started moving around in the world? I believe you have known Marianne Moore for many years.

MISS BISHOP: I met Marianne Moore in 1934, the last year I was in college, through Fanny Borden, the college librarian, an old friend of the Moore family. (I had read a few of her poems in anthologies.) I asked Miss Borden why she didn't have *Observations* in the college library, and she said, "Are you interested in Marianne Moore? I've known her since she was a child!" And she introduced me to her shortly afterwards.

When I was a junior, *Hound and Horn* had a contest for students. I sent in a story and a poem and got honorable mention for both. I also had a story and a poem in a magazine called *The Magazine,* run by Howard Baker and his wife. Baker's friend Yvor Winters wrote me; I think he wanted to take me under his wing. But nothing came of that. He introduced me to a former student of his, Don Stanford, who was then at Harvard.

INTERVIEWER: Were you in any way affected by Auden during the '30s?

MISS BISHOP: Oh, yes! I started reading him in college. I bought all his books as they came out and read them a great deal. But he didn't affect my poetic practice. I think that Wallace Stevens was the contemporary who most affected my writing then. But I got more from Hopkins and the

Metaphysical poets than I did from Stevens or Hart Crane. I've always admired Herbert.

INTERVIEWER: What do you like especially about Herbert?

MISS BISHOP: To begin with, I like the absolute naturalness of tone. Coleridge has some good remarks on this, you remember. And some of Herbert's poems strike me as almost surrealistic, "Love Unknown" for instance. (I was much interested in surrealism in the '30s.) I also like Donne, of course, the love poems particularly, and Crashaw. But I find myself rereading Herbert a great deal.

INTERVIEWER: Do you owe any of your poems to Herbert?

MISS BISHOP: Yes, I think so. "The Weed" is modelled somewhat on "Love Unknown." There are probably others.

INTERVIEWER: Do you have any comments on the religious poetry of the '40s? I am referring especially to the long poems by Eliot and Auden, also to such books as Tate's *The Winter Sea* and Lowell's *Lord Weary's Castle*. In those days we seemed to be moving into something rather unexpected, a brilliant period of Christian poetry. But this has scarcely continued, has it?

MISS BISHOP: As far as Eliot and Auden are concerned, I find Eliot much easier to understand. He led up to the *Four Quartets* by a long process. Eliot is not very dogmatic, not in his poetry (the prose is another matter). Auden's later poetry is sometimes spoiled for me by his didacticism. I don't like modern religiosity in general; it always seems to lead to a tone of moral superiority. Of course I have the greatest admiration for Auden as a poet. As for religious poetry and this general subject, well, times have changed since Herbert's day. I'm not religious, but I read Herbert and Hopkins with the greatest pleasure.

INTERVIEWER: Do you think it is necessary for a poet to have a "myth"—Christian or otherwise—to sustain his work?

MISS BISHOP: It all depends—some poets do, some don't. You must have something to sustain you, but perhaps you needn't be conscious of it. Look at Robert Lowell: he's written just as good poetry since he left the Church. Look at Paul Klee: he had sixteen paintings going at once; *he* didn't have a formulated myth to look to, apparently, and his accomplishment was very considerable. The question, I must admit, doesn't interest me a great deal. I'm not interested in big-scale work as such. Something needn't be large to be good.

INTERVIEWER: But some poets and critics have been terribly concerned about this, haven't they?

MISS BISHOP: Some people crave organization more than others—the desire to get everything in its place. Auden really thinks this way, I suppose. Marianne Moore, on the other hand, has no particular "myth," but a remarkable set of beliefs appears over and over again, a sort of backbone of faith.

INTERVIEWER: I know you have a lively interest in the other arts—music and painting especially. Have your poems been much affected by these things?

MISS BISHOP: I think I'm more visual than most poets. Many years ago, around 1942 or 1943, somebody mentioned to me something that Meyer Shapiro, the art critic, said about me: "She writes poems with a painter's eye." I was very flattered. All my life I've been interested in painting. Some of my relatives painted. As a child I was dragged round the Boston

Museum of Fine Arts and Mrs. Gardner's museum and the Fogg. I'd love to be a painter.

INTERVIEWER: What about "Songs for a Colored Singer"? You didn't compose those to tunes, as it were?

MISS BISHOP: I was hoping somebody would compose the tunes for *them*. I think I had Billie Holiday in mind. I put in a couple of big words just because she sang big words well—"*conspiring* root" for instance. As for music in general: I'd love to be a composer! I studied counterpoint and the piano for years, and I suppose I'm still "musical." But I wanted to be a doctor, too, and I got myself enrolled at Cornell Medical School. I think Marianne Moore discouraged me from going on with that.

INTERVIEWER: I wonder if you sometimes "feel" your way into a poem with a sense of its rhythms even before the subject has declared itself— you know, the way in which "Le cimetière marin" was composed?

MISS BISHOP: Yes. A group of words, a phrase, may find its way into my head like something floating in the sea, and presently it attracts other things to it. I do tend to "feel" my way into a poem, as you suggest. One's mind works in unexpected ways. When I was writing "Roosters," I got hopelessly stuck; it just refused to get written. Then one day I was playing a record of Ralph Kirkpatrick performing Scarlatti: the rhythms of the sonata imposed themselves on me and I got the thing started again.

INTERVIEWER: In composing a poem like this, do you start from a kind of pleasure in the stanzaic arrangement as such, or do you let the experience dictate the form?

MISS BISHOP: In this case I couldn't say which came first. Sometimes the form, sometimes the subject, dominates the mind. All other poets I've ever talked to say pretty much the same thing. On this subject I rather like Housman's essay, *The Name and Nature of Poetry*. That's only one side of the question, but it's very well stated.

INTERVIEWER: I wonder if you could reveal the *donnée* for your sestina called "A Miracle for Breakfast." It has an attractive surrealist quality about it, but I'm curious about the kind of experience which brought the poem into being.

MISS BISHOP: Oh, that's my Depression poem. It was written shortly after the time of souplines and men selling apples, around 1936 or so. It was my "social conscious" poem, a poem about hunger.

INTERVIEWER: That was the heyday of surrealism, too, wasn't it?

MISS BISHOP: Yes, and I had just come back from my first year in France, where I had read a lot of surrealist poetry and prose.

INTERVIEWER: When I read the poem here in Brazil, my students keep asking, "Was she waiting for the ferry?" You remember that early in the poem you have one crossing the river.

To move on to something else: "At the Fishhouses" is my favorite in your second book. This seems to me a kind of Wordsworthian poem, something like "Resolution and Independence." But your poem is mostly in the present tense and is more immediate and "existentialist." Wordsworth really seems to mean "emotion recollected in tranquillity" and puts his poem mostly in the past tense. Do you have any comment on this comparison?

MISS BISHOP: I think it's a question of how poetry is written. There has been a great change in the knowledge of, or at any rate the attitude towards, poetic psychology. One of the great innovators here is

Hopkins. When I was in college I wrote a piece on him. While I was preparing it, I came across an essay on seventeenth century baroque prose. The author—I've forgotten who—tried to show that baroque sermons (Donne's for instance) attempted to dramatize the mind in action rather than in repose. Applying this to Hopkins in the paper I was writing, I used a phrase which impressed me in "The Wreck of the Deutschland," where he says, "Fancy, come faster." He breaks off and addresses himself. It's a baroque poem. Browning does something like this, but not so strikingly. In other words, the use of the present tense helps to convey this sense of the mind in action. Cummings does this in some poems. Of course poets in other languages (French especially) use the "historical present" more than we do. But that isn't really the same device. But switching tenses always gives effects of depth, space, foreground, background, and so on.

INTERVIEWER: Perhaps something like switching keys in music.

MISS BISHOP: Yes, indeed, very much so.

INTERVIEWER: What do you think about the dramatic monologue as a form—you know, when the poet assumes a rôle? This "poetry of experience" has been very attractive to a lot of poets. I believe you have done this two or three times—for instance in "Songs for a Colored Singer" and "Jerónimo's House."

MISS BISHOP: I haven't given it much thought. Robert Lowell and others have done brilliant things in this form. I suppose it should act as a sort of release. You can say all kinds of things you couldn't in a lyric. If you have scenery and costumes, you can get away with a lot. I'm writing one right now.

INTERVIEWER: I've just been reading a poem of yours called "A Summer's Dream." It's a wonderful miniature, an evocation of a dying seaside town.

Every detail counts. Did you reduce this from something longer?

MISS BISHOP: I went for the summer once to Cape Breton. This little village was very small indeed. I think in the poem I said the population contained a number of freaks. Actually there were a few more people. But some exceptional giants came from this region, and I think in the poem I conveyed some idea of what the people were like. No, I didn't compress the poem.

INTERVIEWER: Do you find yourself revising a poem like this?

MISS BISHOP: No. After a poem is published, I just change a word occasionally. Some poets like to rewrite, but I don't.

INTERVIEWER: How did you happen to go to Key West, where you wrote some beautiful things? Did you find it a good place for writing?

MISS BISHOP: In 1938, I believe, I was on the West Coast of Florida to fish. I went to Key West just for a couple of days to see what the fishing was like there. I liked the town and decided to go back there in 1939, after another eight months or so in Europe. Eventually I acquired a modest but beautiful old house. I can't say Key West offered any special advantages for a writer. But I liked living there. The light and blaze of colors made a good impression on me, and I loved the swimming. The town was absolutely broke then. Everybody lived on the W.P.A. I seemed to have a taste for impoverished places in those days. But my Key West period dwindled away. I went back for winters till 1949, but after the war it wasn't the same.

INTERVIEWER: While I'm mentioning Key West, would you say something about John Dewey, whom you knew so well there? I think you'd agree that his prose style, even in his book on aesthetics, can be rather clumsy and does his reputation no good. But he was a very sensitive man, wasn't he?

MISS BISHOP: Yes, very. I found him an adorable man. He could work under any conditions. Even at the age of eighty-five he missed no detail. He and Marianne Moore are the only people I have ever known who would talk to everyone, on all social levels, without the slightest change in their manner of speaking. I think this shows something important about Dewey and Marianne Moore—they have the kind of instinctive respect for other people which we all wish we could have but can only aspire to. No matter how foolish your question, he would always give you a complete and tactful answer. He loved little things, small plants and weeds and animals, and of course he was very generous in dealing with people. I remember when "Roosters" came out in *The New Republic*; he read it and said, "Well, Elizabeth, you've got these rhymes in threes very well. I wish I'd learned more about writing when *I* was young."

INTERVIEWER: Some people might be surprised to know that Flannery O'Connor admired Dewey. The last time I saw her, in 1963, she was reading two of his books.

MISS BISHOP: Well, I'm sure she knew more about his philosophy than I do!

INTERVIEWER: You've been a literary associate of Robert Lowell's for quite a few years, haven't you?

MISS BISHOP: I think, and I hope, we have been very good friends for twenty years. Both his life and his work have been of great importance to me. He is one of the few poets whose name in a table of contents or on the cover of a magazine gives me a sense of hopefulness and excitement even before I've read the poem.

INTERVIEWER: What do you think of the turn his poetry has taken in the last few years—beginning with *Life Studies*?

MISS BISHOP: One does miss the old trumpet blast of *Lord Weary's Castle*, but poets have to change, and possibly the more subdued magnificence of his later tone is more humane.

INTERVIEWER: I think I have you about up to 1950 now. This would be the period when you had the appointment at the Library of Congress. You were there shortly after the Bollingen Prize fiasco, weren't you?

MISS BISHOP: Léonie Adams was my predecessor, and she got the worst of that affair. MacLeish had a good idea about the job, and some of the poets fitted in rather well. I didn't really earn my keep—I didn't give lectures and readings, in fact never do. But for the only time in my life I saw bureaucracy functioning, and it certainly contributed to my education.

INTERVIEWER: Like many literary people, you visited Pound during the '50s. Do you have any prose comment, as it were, to make about him? You've already put yourself on record in verse in "Visits to St. Elizabeths."

MISS BISHOP: I think I've said all I want to in that poem. I admired his courage enormously; he proved his devotion to literature during those thirteen years.

INTERVIEWER: By the way, I'm rather interested in the formal scheme of that poem. How did you hit on it?

MISS BISHOP: It's the old nursery rhyme, "This was the house that Jack built." I've always liked nursery rhymes, and this one seemed to work here.

INTERVIEWER: Here in Brazil poets like Vinícius de Moraes have been writing lyrics for *bossa nova*. Have you ever wanted to do something like this in English?

MISS BISHOP: I've always wanted to write popular songs, and I've tried several times but never succeeded. I like some popular song lyrics very much, "Mean to Me" for instance.

INTERVIEWER: I think quite a few people have already seen and admired your new poem, the ballad called "The Burglar of Babylon." It's a knock-out. Did you have any trouble in finding a suitable medium for this poem? It's really worked up from some journalistic material, isn't it?

MISS BISHOP: No, I sat down and wrote it almost straight off, with a few additions and changes. Most of it was written in one day. It naturally seemed to present itself as a ballad. It's a true story, taken from the newspaper accounts; I made only two minor changes in the facts.

INTERVIEWER: Did you actually see Micuçú being hunted down on the *morro* of Babylon in Rio?

MISS BISHOP: No, but I saw the soldiers. We could watch them through binoculars from the terrace of the apartment house.

INTERVIEWER: With your new book of poems, *Questions of Travel*, about to come out, what are your immediate literary plans?

MISS BISHOP: Well, they are always the same, to write poems when I can. I'm also planning a book of prose about Brazil. It is tentatively called *Black Beans and Diamonds*. It's to be a combination of a travel book, a memoir, and a picture book. I am quite interested in photography. I'd like to make Brazil seem less remote and less an object of picturesque fancy. It's not really so far from New York. I think that since the great naturalists (Darwin, Wallace, Bruce, and so on) there hasn't been much close observation (at least by foreigners) of Brazil. Except perhaps for Lévi-Strauss.

INTERVIEWER: What do you think about the state of American poetry right now?

MISS BISHOP: Very good. We have lots of fine poets. Perhaps I'd better not mention any names, but I really admire and read with pleasure at least seven of my contemporaries. As far as poetry goes, although I am afraid that is not very far, this is a period that I enjoy.

# Emergence[1]

*Carolyn Forché*

*Infancy is what is eternal, and the rest,*
*all the rest is brevity, extreme brevity.*

—Antonio Porchia

*Inspiration is not the granting of a secret or of*
*words to someone already existing: it is the granting*
*of existence to someone who does not yet exist.*

—Maurice Blanchot

I was five months pregnant with my first and only child when we arrived in Johannesburg for what was to have been two years. It was summer in the southern hemisphere, the sky poached by sun and fog, and my first impression was such that in letters home we would describe this place as a "California with slavery." We had come to document apartheid in photographs and text. Officially, my husband would work at the *Time* bureau, and I would accompany him as wife and expectant mother.

For a brief time, I was able to work with the Soweto parents of

---

1.  Carolyn Forché, "Emergence" from *Salmagundi* #123 (Summer 1999).

detained children, who wanted information about international human rights organizations. Without the necessary police permits which were impossible to obtain, we were nevertheless able to enter townships and homelands, led by churchworkers who knew how to avoid police roadblocks, and as my womb swelled, I also grew invisible, no longer attracting police who would not wish to involve themselves with so pregnant a white woman. My husband concealed his cameras, passing me the exposed film to keep under my maternity dress. The images produced from this film would not often appear in the press, however, as the media tacitly respected much of South Africa's ban on "visual documentation of unrest." Those who defied this ban found their employees deported, or unable to renew their visas, as would eventually happen to us. These were the last years of apartheid, as destiny would disclose, and South Africa was living under what was then called a "state of emergency."

*Emerge,* I wrote, *emergence: to rise, to come into the light, to rise up out of a liquid in which the subject has been submerged.*

My notebooks filled, as they had in other parts of the world: vignettes, aperçus, bits of utterance. There was world and paper, and each could cross the surface of the other, marking it lightly but indelibly. Writing was my way of knowing what was for me otherwise unknowable, and like Ryszard Kapuściński whom I admired, I preferred to work "in the forest of things, on foot, in the world," which I hoped to participate in, rather than experience.

There was never a question of my giving birth in apartheid South Africa. The plan had been to drive overland to Zimbabwe when the time came. I'm not sure why I hadn't anticipated the arduousness of such a journey, nor recognized the risks incurred by a thirty-five-year-old "elderly *prima gravida,*" electing to receive her prenatal care from obstetricians on three continents, but I had not yet experienced the sea-change of motherhood, holding rather to an image of life continuing much as it was, but with a sleeping baby tied to my back.

Suppressed perhaps were the labors of my childhood as the eldest daughter of seven, tri-folding clouds of diapers, running bed linens through the mangle, stirring Catholic school uniform shirts in pots of starch. Lost were the babies' cries, the slow-thickening puddings and white sauce, mounds of socks to be matched and toddlers watched never closely enough. Left behind me, Saturday mornings scrubbing foyer and bath tiles with Fels Naptha, taking pails of oil soap to the rows of wooden dining chairs. I made lunch for the "little ones" when I was six, and by seven baked my first loaf of bread. So standing evenings at the open window over foaming dishes I began subliminally to narrate a bearable selfhood. During endless hours of menial work, I spoke to God, who surrounded me, then to voices in books, and finally to fields and sky, where a presence was. Writing, I thought, formed itself elsewhere and passed through me, coming out of my hands. It was mysterious and foreign, but the experience of its making could not be compared to anything else. In the act of writing, there was heightened being, which could be remembered as ecstatic. There was, first, what could be said, and later, the way of saying, which was superior to the said.

My mother and I shared the arduous work of caring for the six children she bore in the ten years after my birth. She would bring the newborns home, wrapped in delicate "receiving" blankets, and I would steal into the darkness of my parents' room to gaze at a new one asleep in the straw basinette, pale-haired and fragile, having made an arduous journey from God's world. My mother was almost a child herself when she began, or so it seems to me now. For reasons that can never be disclosed, she was perhaps ill-prepared for her brood: she had *wanted* many children, but had pictured us all as sleeping infants, wingless, perfect and from heaven. She made *Novenas* to the Mother of God, sang to us, wept, took to her bed and told us we would understand when we were grown. At night, while I read and wrote by flashlight under my blankets, I heard the clacking of her Royal manual typewriter, and eventually discovered the silvery Christmas box of her poems and stories, some clipped from newspapers, hidden in her mysterious closet among evening clothes no longer worn.

"Join the convent," she would advise me above the din during some shared task or another. So it was not as if I hadn't known.

We left South Africa precipitously on March 17, 1986, a month to the day before my son was born because, among other reasons, we had broken unjust laws, and I was afraid to risk giving birth in jail. Specifically, we were accused of violating the restrictive "Group Areas Act" by having black houseguests, and it was suspected that we were also disseminating "images of unrest" to the outside world. Our arrest, fervently desired by our "Rhodesian" landlady, was considered by our lawyers unlikely but possible.

We left behind the tag-sale furniture we'd assembled into a service-able household, including the straw cradle with its bridal mosquito net. In my hurry I left some of my notebooks, but these contained indeci-pherable drafts of poems and so would pose a problem for no one. I don't know if those lines will return to me in a patient hour, but the cradle appeared often for a time in my dreams.

I remember not feeling certain we were safe until the wheels were tucked into the belly of the plane. My son leapt and fluttered through the night. I wrote notes toward poems as we refueled in Madagascar, notes which had become, I thought, a substitute for what I had once considered "finished poems." We were enroute to Paris, and as this was the last day of my pregnancy when I would be accepted as a passenger on a commer-cial carrier, my son would be born there. A French photographer, Gilles Peress, had offered us his place, as he would be returning to document "The Troubles" in Northern Ireland, and would not return to Paris again for some time.

So it was that we lived for a year at 11 rue Schoelcher, in an atelier identical to Simone de Beauvoir's, who lived beside us at 11 bis. until her death that April. The two-storey windows opened on a luminous fresco of clouds, and from the little *loggia*, it was possible to gaze out over the graves in the cemetery of Montparnasse. In the armoire, there were books, and little paper soldiers fighting the Franco-Prussian war. At the farm-table, I translated the poet Robert Desnos, many afternoons alone with the windows open, conjugating the *future perfect*, ivy shivering on the cemetery walls, waiting for the infant to come, a Desnos line revealing itself, and I thought: *how is it possible that I am living here*, as if a childhood dream had found an empty theatre in which to mount a small production of its hopes?

By proclivity and circumstance, I had in recent years often been in countries shattered by suffering and war. Why? I might have asked, or well might have, anticipating the birth of a child. Men and women came into my life, offering to teach me things I could not otherwise learn, and I said *yes* out of curiosity, ignorance, a need to please, and a desire to obey God, *for* whom language had first come, in the form of spontaneous prayer-songs spoken when I thought no one was listening.

During my childhood, the stars were more thickly clustered, and they whispered. I was not "by myself" often, but when I was, sometimes felt that my "self" opened and left, remaining near*by* as the phrase would have us imagine. If I were in the house at those times, the furniture swelled toward me or diminished as if moving away, accompanied by a crescendo of air against glass, my own breath, some mysterious hum of world. This was a state my sister also experienced and it terrified us both. I would later understand that objects remain where they are, and space dilates between them as time passes. If I were outside, however, in the woods or fields behind the house, this was not so disturbing, perhaps because one does not expect fixity in nature. God was there.

Despite the efforts of the Sisters of St. Dominic, Order of Preachers, to promote the idea of a carceral earth and a juridical cosmos, I imagined rather that the earth was a school, and that humans and other life forms were *already* burning, as light issued visibly from them, and the world, if saved at all, would be saved entire. If this were so, there was work to be done, and I hoped to comport myself well enough that God would give instructions in a form I could understand. Such was my spiritual pridefulness that I appended a request that this instruction not be given by an apparition, which would surely frighten me to death. After many years in the labyrinth of such expectations, it quite circuitously became clear to me that my instructions were to say *yes*.

Until now, until Paris, this *yes* had entailed what I *thought* had been an acceptance of mortality, a willingness to forego self-protection as circumstances required, and a faith in the luminous web of souls dedicated to what may have been simplistically conceived as a teleological endeavor. However, I was now an expectant mother, and what I imagined I was doing was about to change, utterly and for my ever, not in increments but as a whole, not by extension but in essence. This would also happen to my "work," a place-holding term for the labor of nurturing the self-propagation of language.

One writes inescapably out of one's obsessions—linguistic, philosophical, formal, cosmological. During my formative years as a poet (and in my educational *milieu*), "form" was regarded as a container rather than a force, examined for its features and flaws rather than the consequences of its use. The poem was, as Charles Simic once put it, "an antique pinball machine with metaphors instead of balls." It was to be read as expressive of the sensibility of the poet, whose "voice" it conjured, and as an unparaphrasable utterance of complex figural interplay and patterned sound. The reader installed herself in this poem, reading analytically or "closely," so as to discern the intricacies of its making, rather as a watchmaker approaches the works with spring-pin tool and dust-brush. Thus machined, the poem was regarded as a species of discourse, to be valued for itself and for its utility as communicator of feeling and thought.

My first two published poetry books were written during my teens and twenties, in the mode of the first-person, free-verse lyric, a writing which seemed to me very much to corroborate *le monde vécu*, the lived world. I thought of words as the crystalline precipitate of conscious attention: particular, precise, and resonant with as much "poetic" euphony as I could "hear." At first, mother's college English textbook provided models, and I wrote mostly rhymed quatrains in unvaried iambic pentameter. Later, the nuns assigned the writing of "paragraphs," and after a demonstration which persuaded them that I had not been plagiarizing from an unknown source, permitted me to dispense with the topic-sentence/body/conclusion format, whereupon I wrote elaborate descriptions of natural phenomena. In early adolescence, I was startled to read lined free verse for the first time, which I did not understand but tried to imitate with disappointing results. There were some years of this. When my first book, *Gathering the Tribes*, was chosen for the Yale Prize, I received a letter from its judge, Stanley Kunitz, asking about my poetics, and as I was unaware of *having* a poetics, I wrote of my upbringing, and in response to questions regarding influences, named my mother and grandmother.

In my twenties, God's presence receded, and even the radiant and shivering poplars of my childhood achieved apparent visual stability. The world changed and changed again. I had been translating Salvadoran poet Claribel Alegría, because I was her daughter's friend, and because she was an older woman poet whose work had not yet appeared in English. So it was that when her nephew, Leonel Gomez Vides, appeared at my door for an unexpected three-day visit, I invited him in, whereupon he invited me to spend my Guggenheim year in El Salvador, then still at "peace," a euphemism for the silence of misery endured. I became what was later called a "human rights worker," and this work partially informed my second book, *The Country Between Us*, written feverishly but without the remotest sense of its "political" character or utility. Critical reception in the US was unexpectedly intense and mixed, but my focus was then on the collective work of building a network opposed to military intervention in Central America. Toward that end, I traveled through the United States for three years; later, human rights work would bring me to Northern Ireland, Israel, the West Bank, Lebanon and South Africa. During that time, I didn't focus on poetics as such, but not for lack of interest.

The safe harbor of France was where my intellectual and poetical life resumed. We lived in that small, sparsely furnished atelier in a manner more conducive to work than I had ever previously known. Wind carried the scent of narcissus from the graves to our open casements. Mornings the knife-sharpener cried up from the street, and like the other women, I raced out to have the kitchen knives honed. Our supply of milk and cheese was kept for a time on the sill, to the amusement of our *quartier*, until we bought a small refrigerator. Daily I wheeled my basket to rue Daguerre market, where I bought unfamiliar species of fish, seasonal fruits and vegetables, aged cheese, young wines, and such things as I have never managed to replace: hard Normandy cider, fresh lavender from Grasse. My command of French was still provisional, however, and I once mistakenly tried to buy two and a half kilos of parsley, to the amusement of *le commerçant*.

Aside from domestic pursuits, I spent my days writing and reading (in those days Martin Buber, Emmanuel Lévinas, Jean-François Lyotard, Phillipe Lacou-Labarthes, Paul Celan, Francis Ponge and Edmond Jabès), while translating Desnos, because I thought this effort would revive and improve my French. On the day before my delivery I completed the work, discovering on the final page some lines I had inscribed in a notebook during my first trip to Paris in 1977, and thus finding a poet for whom I had searched in the intervening years:

> *J'ai rêvé tellement fort de toi*
> *J'ai tellement marché, tellement parlé*
> *Tellement aimé ton ombre*
> *Qu'il ne me reste plus rien de toi.*
> *Il me reste d'être l'ombre parmi les ombres*
> *D'être cent fois plus ombre que l'ombre*

*D'être l'ombre qui viendra et reviendra*
*dans ta vie ensoleillée*

[I have dreamed so strongly of you
I have walked so much, talked so much
So much I have loved your shadow
That there now remains for me nothing more of you.
It remains with me to be a shadow among shadows
To be a hundred times darker than the darkness
To be the shadow that will come and come again
into your sun-blessed life.]

The discovery seemed magical and auspicious, and the next morning my labor began, so lightly that I did not at first realize what it was, and regretted my lifelong fear. After twenty-six hours, my son was delivered by caesarean, something I had not anticipated, but that my husband and the doctor had known was likely for weeks. I chose to be awake. I remember surgical lights, instructions in French, the intelligence of the eyes above the masks, a pressure, a sense of being pulled apart without pain, and then a weakening, more oxygen, a rapid exchange among the physicians, then my son held above me, silent and white then suddenly rosy and crying. For a moment, they let me hold him, and when he heard my voice the crying stopped. "He knows who this is," my husband said. I told him that I was his mother, and that everything would be all right. A day later I was given an emergency transfusion of two liters of whole blood. For some reason still unknown to the hematologists, I had stopped making red cells after the birth. There were tense hours, waiting for my body to begin its necessary work again. My son was beside me in an incubator, quiet, alert. I was utterly there, and when I came back I was still there, in a small hospital in Paris with the windows open.

We called him Sean-Christophe, this little one, this Other, who now called me to responsibility, and whom I could neither evade, comprehend nor possess as a *knowledge.* "The child lives," Martin Buber wrote, "between sleep and sleep...in the lightning and counter-lightning of encounter." With him I experienced a radiant interdependence of sensation and thought: he was of me but he was not "mine." He was as yet "unknown" to me, even though the egg that had contributed life to him had been with me since my own birth.

On paper in the following months, the "I" of my previous writing receded, having become an emptiness, replaced by a polyphonic and Schoenbergian symphony of cacophonous utterance. Absent this *I*, whose selfhood the poems formerly served, words became material and translucent, no longer transparently communicative of the sensibility I no longer possessed. This movement did not entail a repudiation, but was marked by a radical sense of unfamiliarity. Each page began *mis en question*: white, open, each word in all its plenitude marked the site of a wound. Anxious at first, I returned to my notebooks filled with "notes toward poems," and discovered nascent versions of the same phenomenon. These were not notes but the work itself, begun during my pregnancy, and without my conscious collaboration.

This was a work happening *with* me which was not *about* me, having to do with attention rather than intention, a work which would eventually disclose itself as self-altering rather than self-expressive. Rather than writing discreet (individual) poems from beginning to end, and passing them through a sieve of revisionary practice, I found myself attending to the work's assemblage, aware that I was creating a reading-space to be explored rather than received, but in the manner of one caught in a web of consequence. The historical density of the language seemed to limit its play of signification, as the cry of suffering remains a cry. This poetry did not have the function of recording or representing, but rather of attending to the making of its utterance.

The poems I had previously written now seemed the graveyard of possibilities. Tedium had taught me to narrate a self-in-the-world to relieve tedium. *Writing*, older than glass, younger than music, was no longer for me merely the guardian of the past, but a way into the open and the future. During the milk-hours of earliest morning, my son nursed beside the two-storey windows filled with cloud islands of a forming world. He seemed to see something I did not see. The ancients thought that light traveled from the eye to the world and this seemed so with him. He was at the gates of language, where only the invisible is obvious. Or so it seems to me now.

# The World Is Large and Full of Noises: Thoughts on Translation[1]

*Jane Hirshfield*

*Translation it is that openeth the window, to let in the light;*
*that breaketh the shell, that we may eat the kernel...*

—Preface to the King James Bible

Even the physical embodiment of a sacred text is numinous: it is wrapped in leather or silk, stored in a cupboard used for no other purpose, copied over only by special scribes. It may be raised in both hands as an offering before being opened; it may itself be offered fragrant incense and sweet milk. All written work retains some trace, however faint, of this initial sanctity of the Word: the breath inhabiting Logos and the breath of inspiration are the same, each bringing new life into the empty places of earth. It is no wonder, then, that many different cultural traditions share an ancient prohibition against translation. As George Steiner has

---

1. Jane Hirshfield, "The World Is Large and Full of Noises: Thoughts on Translation" from *Nine Gates: Entering the Mind of Poetry* (New York: HarperCollins, 1997).

pointed out in *After Babel*, if a sacred text has been given to us directly by its divine source, surely it must remain exactly as it first appeared, each word preserved intact for the meaning it may hold. Whether in a sacred text or a contemporary poem, any alteration risks unwittingly discarding some mystery not yet penetrated.

Unease about translation does not just cover the exporting of texts into another language; their importation too can be problematic. Translation's very existence challenges our understanding of what a literary text is. Further, by asserting that things worth knowing exist outside the home culture's boundaries, translation challenges society as a whole. Translated works are Trojan horses, carriers of secret invasion. They open the imagination to new images and beliefs, new modes of thought, new sounds. Mistrust of translation is part of the instinctive immune reaction by which every community attempts to preserve its particular heritage and flavor: to control language is to control thought. The realization lends an extra dimension to the well-known Italian saying, "Traduttore, traditore" (Translator, traitor).

And still, translation occurs, playing an essential role in the innumerable conversations between familiar and strange, native and import, past and future, by which history and culture are made. It is integral to the way seed ideas and language strategies move out into the world, the new contending with the old until the translated works and forms are either rejected or naturalized. After sufficient time, shapes of thought and sound originally alien may themselves become the revered heritage, as certain exotic trees have come to be treasured in their new countries. Consider English literature, built almost entirely on the adopted powers of other traditions. Before the eleventh century's Norman invasion, English poetry relied on alliteration, not rhyme, for its binding sound, and the number of syllables within each metrical foot could vary freely. Yet what English speaker today would call iambic pentameter an imported meter, or think of the sonnet as an Italian form?

The desire to learn what lives within the incomprehensible speech of others is part of the deep-rooted human desire to know always more than we do. Such curiosity will overcome external limits, whatever the authority behind them—that is one lesson of Eden. And if the tale of the apple tells us the cost of such knowledge is death, and the story of Babel says that the price for pride of knowledge is a multiplicity of tongues, both offer no simple punishment. From each story's loss comes a gain: a sorrow, yes, but one that also gives birth to the continuing fertility and richness of this world.

What do poets themselves have to say of translation? On the fifteenth of February, 1924, Rilke inscribed these lines on the copy of *The Duino Elegies* he gave his Polish translator:

> Happy are those who know:
> Behind all words, the Unsayable stands;
> And from that source alone, the Infinite
> Crosses over to gladness, and us—
>
> Free of our bridges,
> Built with the stone of distinctions;
> So that always, within each delight,
> We gaze at what is purely single and joined.

With the gift of this poem about words' relationship to the Absolute, Rilke attempted to free his translator from the curse of "traitor." The Infinite comes into being only through the divided world of the particular, the poem says; while lesser, this realm of distinctions remains a realm of gladness, both necessary and good. By acknowledging that every word is both a reflection of his work's original mind and a path toward it, Rilke gave his translator his blessing to do whatever was needed. He offered his full trust that whatever the Polish words, the *Elegies* would remain alive.

The ontological issue at the center of Rilke's poem is this: where does a poem's true being reside? Surely poetry lives in the body of its words, as we live in our human bodies of bone and nerve, muscle and blood. Yet even in writing a poem's first draft, it often seems as if something were already there, which we hunt with words—something like the poem's soul. What else to call that magnetic pull of a destination unknown yet nonetheless present and calling, which causes a writer to accept one arising phrase and reject another, or to delete or alter or expand during revision?

The act of writing is a making, but also a following: of the mystery of source as it emerges into form; of the wisdom of the heart-mind as it encounters the wisdom of language. Translation asks a similar leap of faith. It becomes possible only if we trust that poetry lives both in its words and beyond them, and that at least some portion of this ur-poem can cross the abyss between one verbal body and another.

The Sung dynasty poet Yang Wan-li wrote on this subject as well:

> Now, what is poetry?
> If you say it is simply a matter of words,
> I will say a good poet gets rid of words.
> If you say it is simply a matter of meaning,
> I will say a good poet gets rid of meaning.
> "But," you ask, "without words and without meaning,
>     where is the poetry?"
> To this I reply: "Get rid of words and get rid of meaning,
>     and there is still poetry."
>
> (trans. Jonathan Chaves)

Yang argues against any idea of poetry that is unchangeable, unchallengeable, or fixed. In his use of meaning to urge us to pass beyond meaning, in his use of words to pass beyond words, he points to the mode of knowledge described in the Heart Sutra, the central text of Zen: "no

eyes, no ears, no nose, no tongue, no body, no mind, no consciousness."
The description does not mean that an awakened person is blind, struck
deaf, numb to the world, and dumb. Rather, such a person is one who
knows the world directly, without mediation, and knows the self in its
widest existence, reflected in all things. The poet, too, is free to see with
no eyes, to speak with no tongue. Poetry will continue on its own path,
untroubled.

From the open spirit of these two passages, translators may take
heart. Though I only encountered their words years after undertaking
a cotranslation of the work of two classical-era Japanese women poets,
I nonetheless found in them a retrospective reassurance, and also a kind
of blessing. The old prohibitions live on as a useful self-doubt in the
translator, ensuring that original texts be approached with due care. But
still the silk ribbons of the home language must be cut, for the work to be
read by others.

Knowledge is erotic. We see this not only in the Bible's dual use of the
term "to know," but also, as classicist Anne Carson has pointed out, in the
Homeric verb *mnaomai*, which means both "to hold in attention" and
"to woo." What we regard must seduce us, and we it, if we are to continue
looking. A great poem creates in its readers the desire to know it more
thoroughly, to live with it in intimacy, to join its speaking to their own as
fully as possible. We memorize it, recite it over and over, reawaken it with
tongue and mind and heart. Many translators describe their first encoun-
ter with their chosen authors as a helpless falling in love: a glimpse of a
few translated fragments can lead to years of language study in order to
hear directly the work's own voice. And in matters of art, it seems, Eros
is generous rather than possessive: the translator wants to reciprocate
this gift received, to pass the new love on to others—and thus the work of
translation begins.

A writer may turn to translating for therapeutic reasons as well, at times for self-cure, at times in the spirit of a physician prescribing for others. The translator-as-patient hopes some power of the original will enter her own work, or else uses translation as a way to keep fit during periods of nonwriting. Robert Lowell names both motivations in his introduction to *Imitations*; it isn't hard to see how the work of that book helped him both develop his range and, at the same time, step a little free of his own preoccupations. Kenneth Rexroth, another poet-translator, describes the curative aspect of translation at its best in his essay "The Poet as Translator": "The writer who can project himself into the exultation of another learns more than the craft of words. He learns the stuff of poetry. It is not just his prosody he keeps alert, it is his heart."

The translator-as-physician, on the other hand, hopes the new work will correct some misdirection or gap he perceives in the literature of his own time and language. Ezra Pound put forward both the troubadours of medieval France and the classical poets of China as good medicine for the lack of vigor he saw in English-language poetry in the early decades of this century. More recently, Robert Bly insisted that American writers attend to the Spanish and South American poets of the "deep image" in order to open themselves to the less-tamed realms of imagination. Each successfully altered the literary practice of his contemporaries. William Tyndale, who also translated in the spirit of correction, offers a more cautionary example. Hoping to bring greater accuracy to the scriptures in English, he published the first Biblical translation made from earlier Hebrew and Greek texts rather than from the then-standard Latin— and was burned at the stake in 1536. His Catholic accusers found too Protestant a cast in his "untrue translations."

For me, the decision to enter into the realm of translation came about through the meeting of accidental opportunity and long-standing desire, under circumstances I will relate a little later. I have translated as an amateur, almost always in collaboration, and always because there was something I had encountered in a brief sampling and wanted to read more fully. I have translated, then, for perhaps the most selfish of motives: simple greed. There were poems I wanted to read, but they lived in another tongue.

Once the process of translation begins, the translator enters into an erotic engagement with the chosen text, reading the poem again and again for its meaning, its resonance, its kinetic and musical bodies, its ambiguities, rhetoric, grammar, images, and tropes—for all the rustling of its many leaves and for the silences at its roots as well. The translator reads in the desire to join with what she reads, placing the life of the poem thoroughly within her own, discovering how each entering word modifies that life. As with any engagement, there are the families to consider as well: the translator's knowledge of the historical and cultural context of a poem, its religious background and its intentions, and the translator's own development as poet and as person—all these will contribute to the outcome.

In the midst of this interchange, both translator and poem change their natures. The poem that in its original form may contain a multitude of possible readings becomes in translation a poem in which a particular interpretation is more likely to predominate—though if the translation is a good one, the new poem will also have its resonance and overtones, its unconsciously preserved wisdom. The translator is changed in the way any important encounter changes a person: taking in a new vision of being, our own grows to include it. Eventually, the efforts and pleasures of courtship come to their natural conclusion—there is the leap, the moment of union when the translator joins with a poem so intimately that there is no longer a sense of "self" and "other," and the poem emerges, as if for the first time, within one's own heart and tongue.

At times in this process, the translator may feel not only a union of self with poem, but also a kind of identity with the translated author. Paul Valéry describes this sense of merging well in his essay in *The Art of Poetry* on translating Virgil, "Variations on the 'Eclogues'":

Faced with my Virgil, I had the sensation (well known to me) of a poet at work. From time to time I argued absently with myself about this famous book, set in its millennial fame, with as much freedom as if it had been a poem of my own on the table before me. At moments, as I fiddled with my translation, I caught myself wanting to change something in the venerable text.... "Why not?" I said to myself, returning from this short absence. Why not?

(trans. Denise Folliot)

Freedom from the words of the original combined with a deep love of its words lies at the heart of translation. In the act of true translation, as opposed to the act of parsing out meaning, there is a moment when all prior knowledge of a poem dissolves, when the words that *were* are shed as a snake sheds its skin and the words that *are* take on their own life. Some part of the poem's essential life, its way of traveling through the world, must pass through the emptiness that runs like a broad river-gorge between languages: the impossibility of any word, even the simplest, remaining the same in a different tongue. Think of *bread, panne, brot*— their entirely different flavors.

Translation occurs precisely in that moment of forgetfulness and dissolving, when everything already comprehended through great effort—grammar, vocabulary, meaning, background—falls away. In that surrendering instant, the translator turns from the known shore of the original to look into that emptiness where the outlines of the new poem begin to resolve, a changed landscape appearing through mist. This experience, as Valéry wrote, is almost indistinguishable from the experience of writing itself: the sense of active creative discovery is the same. Yet somehow, the original ur-poem is also there, crossing along with the translator the waters that surge between Rilke's Unsayable source and words.

If a certain sense of freedom is essential to translation, that is because fidelity's claims are so strong. Yet fidelity is in this realm a chimera. A literal word-for-word trot is not a translation. The attempt to recreate qualities of sound is not a translation. The simple conveyance of meaning is not a translation. What then can fidelity—even a fidelity already recognized as failure—mean?

Every translator can offer principles and explanations for having been more or less literal at this point, choosing one nuance of meaning over another at that, omitting "the untranslatable" here or adding there some information commonly understood within a poem's home culture. In my experience, though, these are after-the-fact descriptions of a process of choice-making as mysterious and intuitive as writing itself. Fidelity's multifaceted nature, impossible to define in the abstract, reveals itself only in practice. The attentiveness and flexibility required are as individual as those that make for a good marriage.

Writers and critics have nonetheless long debated the nature of translation, its possibilities, philosophies, and practice. Samuel Johnson, for instance, offered the oft-quoted opinion that the true test of a translation is whether it makes a good poem in English—a statement that holds myriad assumptions within its scope. Robert Frost, however, made clear that for him the original music was all—and unreproducible—in his famous assertion that "the poetry is what gets lost in translation." But "the poetry is what gets transformed" is Octavio Paz's response to Frost:

> After all, poetry is not merely the text. The text produces the poem: a set of sensations and meanings.... With different means, but playing a similar role, you can produce similar results. I say similar, but not identical: translation is an art of analogy, the art of finding correspondences. An art of shadows and echoes...of producing, with a different

text, a poem similar to the original.

Most poets who translate share Paz's sense of the process, though the ways they interpret it vary. The quest to reproduce the original poem's effects as much as its words—an idea Valéry also expressed—permits the issue of "fidelity" and "license" to dissolve on the tongue. Only such an understanding allows the impossible work to go on at all.

Walter Benjamin, in the classic essay "The Task of the Translator," raises the issue of another kind of fidelity. Benjamin suggests that a poem should not read entirely as though it were written in the new language but should preserve some flavor of the syntax and grammar of the original. To convey this idea, Benjamin quotes Rudolf Pannwitz:

> Our translations, even the best ones, proceed from a wrong premise. They want to turn Hindi, Greek, English into German instead of turning German into Hindi, Greek, English.... The basic error of the translator is that he preserves the state in which his own language happens to be instead of allowing his language to be powerfully affected by the foreign tongue.... He must go back to the primal elements of language itself and penetrate to the point where work, image, and tone converge. He must expand and deepen his language by means of the foreign language. It is not generally realized to what extent this is possible...

The proposal intrigues. Robert Fitzgerald, however, has responded to it by saying: "So to make something that is strange to our ears would not be doing justice to the work that was not strange to theirs." Fitzgerald's fidelity is to the work as it affects us, Pannwitz's to the various nature of thought in different languages. Each practice brings its gifts, though my own inclination is closer to Fitzgerald's: to seek an English-language style that reflects the language qualities of the specific work rather than those of the home language as a whole.

Almost all translators face the question of whether or how to retain a poem's formal structure. The main philosophies closely mirror those we have just seen: some translators attempt to replicate the formal qualities of the original, others try instead to convey the underlying effect without reference to prosodic form. The fundamental issue is not merely if form should be translated, but whether it can be.

It is worth remembering that in formal poems, as much as free verse, the subtle parts are where the real musical power is likely to lie. Occasionally, both form and content can flourish in the new version; Richard Wilbur's translations from the French are examples of what is possible when a poet, linguist, and translator of genius hold one pen. But in lesser hands, a coarsely mechanical reproduction of outer form can be more a disservice to a work's nature than the decision to turn to free verse. Form ill-married to meaning and breath places over the translated words a badly painted mask, a parody of their original grace.

Yet free-verse translation may seem a kind of surrender. Still, what is lost in that choice can be remedied at least a little with information about the original's form. Once the reader knows a poem was originally in rhymed couplets, those effects can be intuited; it is less easy to guess what else has been altered in order to reproduce rhyme-scheme and meter in a poorly done formal translation.

Best are bilingual editions, put into the Roman alphabet if necessary, along with a guide to pronunciation. Given this help, even a reader wholly ignorant of a language can sound a work out, while those with some familiarity can use the translation to gain better entry to the original, as well as to judge for themselves the choices that have been made. Still another method can be found in the many Penguin Books anthologies where the original appears accompanied only by a prose trot. If the reader is lucky, a work will exist in multiple translations—in their points of overlap and divergence, the hands of translators and author may be distinguished, though the original music remains out of reach.

Free-verse translation can still honor the essential movement of a poem. The parallelism of Chinese poetry is an indispensable and anchoring part of its nature, for example; though that language's tonal parallels cannot be brought into English, parallel sentence constructions can be kept. Their shapeliness holds part of the poem's information, subtly communicating its relationship to order, balance, and form itself.

To take another case, the alternating five and seven syllables of Japanese poetry are something most American ears fail to perceive, and so my own choice as a translator was to forego the original meter. But I held to the number of lines: to render a three-line haiku as a couplet, or a five-line *tanka* as a quatrain, for me would mask the asymmetrical unfolding of the originals, making them seem less different in aesthetic and worldview than they are. Yet many translators—from both ends of the spectrum of freedom and form—have chosen differently.

A translator's first obligation is to convey each poem's particular strengths. If music and intricacy of form are the greatest pleasures in the original, this is what the translator should try to capture; if a startling directness of language is at the heart of a work, then straightforwardness should govern the new version as well. Imagery, sensibility, feeling, sound, ideas—any of these can become the through-line of a poem's unfolding. One cannot perform vivisection on a living being; some mix of these elements will be present in any well-realized poem, and equally present in any translation. The issue, though, is to what extent a new version can mirror the original, to what extent it must find some differing path toward the same destination, "So that always, within each delight, / We gaze at what is purely single and joined."

Every poet leaves the landscape of poetry altered by his or her passage through it. One way this alteration occurs is when a writer comes to a new mode of vision through either making or reading translations;

Whitman's *Leaves of Grass*, with its King James Bible influenced rhythms and lists, is a good example of that process. The strengths of a great poem or tradition are only truly *translated* if they come into the language in a way that can then be used. Just as English takes in foreign words (*tao, zeitgeist, anima*) when no native one will do, so forms of poetic thought discovered in translation can work to expand what may be said.

"Unless there is a new mind, there cannot be a new line," William Carlos Williams wrote. The converse is true as well. When there *is* a new mind, or a new line, American poetry has shown a spongelike ability to absorb it. The imagist movement, of which Williams was part, brought to American poets some of the strategies of classical Chinese and Japanese poetry. A more recent example is the adoption of the *ghazal*. An Urdu form consisting of long-lined couplets linked in the original primarily by sound, it ends with a "signature" couplet in which the poet includes his or her name. In 1970, a scholar of Urdu, Aijaz Ahmad, invited seven American poets to help translate a collection of ghazals by the poet Ghalib. Some were translators as well as poets, others not. Several went on to use the form in their own writing; Adrienne Rich in particular included a number of haunting ghazals in her subsequent collections. From that beginning, the ghazal has entered contemporary poetry as a mode of writing marked more by a disconnectedness between thoughts and stanzas than by the intricate prosodic rules of the original form. But this oblique adoption is precisely how translation transforms: not by exact imitation but through a kind of hybridization, in which some kernel of the original's power is both preserved and changed.

Translation is one way the poetic mind refreshes itself, old forms of thought-making opening themselves to new ones. It is also a way the old is itself made new: one side-effect of translation (unless the work is also contemporary) is the recasting of a poem's relationship to time. This happens because translations are virtually always placed into the language of the present.

When an original grows old, its dated words and syntax serve as a kind of watermark. Age in itself gives substance—what has lasted becomes a thing worth keeping. An older poem's increasing strangeness of language is part of its beauty, in the same way that the cracks and darkening of an old painting become part of its luminosity in the viewer's mind: they enter not only the physical painting, but our vision of it as well. This is why seeing an old painting suddenly "restored" can be unnerving—we recognize a tampering with its relationship to time, miss the scented smoke of the centuries' passage. For just this reason, seminal works such as Chaucer's *Canterbury Tales* in English or *The Tale of Genji* in Japanese are "translated" from archaic into contemporary language only when they have become almost unintelligible to general readers (and even then, students continue to memorize a passage or two in the original form). But in bringing a work from one language into another, translators must decide whether to attempt to instill in their work a false patina of age or to recreate the freshness of diction the piece would have had in its own time. Usually, the second approach is chosen.

Older translations can become works of interest in their own right. People turn to Pope's Homer not to know Homer, but to know Pope's vision of him; most who now read Chapman's version have been sent there by Keats. Pound's versions of Rihaku (Li Po), called the best existing translation from the Chinese when they were made, are still thought that by some; they are also thoroughly Pound's. In his work we can see the American poet—thoroughly the product of his own time and tradition—suffusing and being suffused by the Chinese. The translations mark the tangible joining of two great tributaries of poetry's river.

For the most part, though, translations are ephemeral: each time current diction changes or the culture's idea of what constitutes a poem shifts, new translations are made. Victorian-era translators of Japanese haiku commonly put the unrhymed originals into rhyme—a poetry without rhyme was not, for many of these scholar-translators, poetry at all. We can see how such older translations reflect the aesthetic expectations of their makers in unconscious as well as conscious ways, yet it is virtually impossible to see the biases of one's own age. The continual remaking of translations may seem like a movement further and further from the original; it can be seen also as a way of returning a work to the perennial freshness of its original state.

As George Steiner has pointed out, the practice of choosing archaic language when translating ancient texts, while now rare, can serve a useful purpose, helping to ground the new version within the linguistic history of its new culture. A reader encountering a style of language he had come to expect in literature from the past would feel immediately and strongly "at home" in the new work, particularly if the work in question was already part of his cultural tradition. The King James Bible, surely the greatest translation English has seen, was put into a diction several generations older than that spoken at the time it was made. Creative accident, rather than conscious decision, may have played a part in this—the King James translators had been instructed to retain the best of earlier versions. But however it happened, the result was a translation whose clarity, beauty, and power so overwhelm that its language forms remain, four centuries later, a living force.

My own experience as a translator dates from 1985, when during a year as a Guggenheim fellow I started collaborating with Mariko Aratani on a translation of the poetry of Ono no Komachi and Izumi Shikibu, the two foremost women poets of Japan's classical period. I had first encountered a handful of their tanka in English as an undergraduate taking courses in Japanese literature in translation. The Japanese women's concerns—love and transience—paralleled my own, and despite the passage of a millennium since its composition, their poetry held for me an immediacy and power that was life-altering. Not only did it affect my own writing, it led me three years later to undertake the study of Buddhism; in 1979 I was lay-ordained in the lineage of Sōtō Zen.

I first realized the need for a larger selection of Komachi's work in 1971, and I waited almost fifteen years for someone to make it possible for me to read more. Then a fortunate introduction to Mariko—a weaver, jazz pianist, and native speaker of Japanese who also loved the classical-period poets—led to our translating a dozen poems together for a journal. We quickly decided to continue working toward a book-length selection of the two poets' work, eventually titled *The Ink Dark Moon*. Although in this account I will say "I" in describing the way a few poems from that book traveled from literal to final versions, Mariko Aratani's contribution at every stage was indispensible to the finished work. Her expertise went far beyond skills of language.

The poems appear here first as they did on the worksheet Mariko and I devised. During weekly meetings over the course of a year, we created such a sheet for each poem we considered for the book. Along with the original and rough translations were Mariko's comments covering background information, grammatical uncertainties, the nuances of certain words, and so on. I wrote down each Japanese poem in *romaji* (the Roman alphabet transliteration of spoken Japanese). The core English meaning (or meanings, if more than one were possible) appeared below each corresponding word, and the metrical line-units of the Japanese were separated by a slash mark. Through this system Mariko could give me access to both the sound of the original poem and its original syntax, something that even the most literal rough translation cannot do. I would then take the sheets away and work toward finished translations, returning them always to her for rechecking.

Here is a first poem, relatively straightforward to translate, by Izumi Shikibu, the greatest of Japan's women poets:

NADOTE   KIMI /  MUNASHIKI  SORA   NI /   KIENIKEMU /
why        you      empty        sky     in   disappear did (?)

| AWAYUKI | DANI | MO / | FUREBA | FURU | YO | NI |
|---|---|---|---|---|---|---|
| Frail snow | even | ! | when falling | falling | world | in |

A prose headnote—not uncommon in Japanese poetry—offers more information about the poem's background: "Around the time Naishi [Shikibu's daughter] died, snow fell, then melted away."

Why did you vanish
into empty sky?
Even the fragile snow,
when it falls,
falls in this world.

The finished translation is quite close to the literal, with only minor adjustments of word order and a few changes of word choice: "vanish" for "disappear," "fragile" for "frail." Japanese does not use articles before nouns, and so in bringing the poem into English, I might have also chosen to say, "Why did you vanish / into *the* empty sky?" Why didn't I? One reason was rhythmic—the extra syllable seemed to my ear to clutter the poem. But more important, there was the difference in meaning. Without the article, Shikibu's daughter not only rises amid her cremation smoke into the sky, she also becomes that emptiness and absence—an effect that the inclusion of the article *the* would have diluted.

The five-line free-verse translation reflects but is not identical to the formal structure of the original. Japanese poetry's conventions for transcription onto the page are unlike those of English. Its vertical columns do not use visual breaks to mark each metrical unit, and at least one translator from the Japanese, Hiroaki Sato, advocates forgoing them entirely. My own feeling, however, is that for Western readers the line break is the fundamental signal that they are encountering a poem: words to be met with the mind and expectations of poetry. Even had I followed strictly the Japanese tanka's syllabic pattern of 5-7-5-7-7, the translation's fundamental "poem-ness" would not have been clear to American readers: English verse speaks a language of stresses rather than count, and American ears do not hear the pattern. Further, the two languages differ enough that metrically exact translations often are forced either to leave out parts of a poem's meaning or else add unnecessary words to fill the count. Both reasons affected my choice of form.

Another poem, one of Shikibu's most famous, required more extensive changes to bring the Japanese into English:

| KUROKAMI NO / | | MIDARE | MO | SHIRAZU / |
|---|---|---|---|---|
| Black hair | 's | messiness, tangling | (obj) | without knowing |
| | | | | without caring |

| UCHIFUSEBA / | MAZU | KAKIYARISHI / |
|---|---|---|
| when lying prone | first | stroked |
| | clear | |

| HITO | ZO | KOISHIKI |
|---|---|---|
| person | ! | longing |

This poem is one continuous sentence, and the first task in approaching it is to determine the grammatical clauses governing meaning. In Japanese, word order is often the reverse of that in English and a syntactical break often appears after the first two or three line-units in a tanka. Using these principles, the poem's basic meaning quickly resolves itself: "While lying down without caring about black hair's tangling, longing for the person who stroked it first." This then became:

Lying alone,
my black hair tangled,
uncombed,

I long for the one
who touched it first.

The largest change between the original and the translation is that the poem has been placed into a grammatical voice, the first person. Many tanka, like this one, do not specify their speaker or point of view. This reflects not only Japanese grammar but also a culture in which experience itself, not the subjective frame around it, is felt to be important; a few lightly sketched phrases evoke a situation in which the reader becomes an equal participant. English, however, demands grounding. To follow the original grammar too closely would only mute the impact and emotional immediacy the poem carries in its own language.

A second departure from the literal is the word *alone*. My after-the-fact explanation (in actual practice, this is simply how the poem spoke itself after studying, joining, and forgetting earlier described) is that it rises out of *shirazu*—"without knowing or caring." This woman neglecting her hair is surely in the solitary aftermath of a love affair. Finding herself alone, she has no reason now to attend to her physical beauty; but she remembers such a time—not the recent love, but her first.

Shikibu, we know, was disowned by her family and divorced by her husband (Naishi's father) after she began a love affair with an imperial prince, who soon died. Later in life she took many lovers, and the reputation of "floating woman" came to accompany her reputation as a poet of surpassing insight and lyrical skill. Shikibu apparently tried to reestablish communication with her husband many times; though he never replied to her letters, he is almost certainly the early love she recalls in this poem.

A last change from the literal is that for the one word *midare* I used two: "tangled, uncombed." "Uncombed" and the earlier "alone" probably arose together, the near-rhyme giving the poem a music satisfying to my ear and the sound of the long *o* holding the poem's resonant grief; the word also reflects the indifference to self contained in *shirazu*, "without caring." The textured physicality of the word works as well to bring Shikibu's presence vividly into the poem. This is true to the original's spirit: Japanese critics have long pointed out that Shikibu's tangled black hair is one of very few references to the details of physical life in all Japanese poetry.

I took more liberty still with this poem by Ono no Komachi, written around the year 850:

| ITO | SEMETE / | KOISHIKI | TOKI | WA / |
|-----|----------|----------|------|------|
| very | extremely | longing | time | — |

| UBATAMA | NO / | YORU | NO | KOROMO | O / |
|---------|------|------|-----|--------|-----|
| hiougi nut | 's | night | 's | clothing | (obj) |

| KAESHITE | ZO | KIRU |
|----------|-----|------|
| turned inside out | ! | wear |

Born roughly one hundred fifty years before Shikibu, Komachi was one of the first women members of the court culture to benefit from a newly developed system for transcribing spoken Japanese using Chinese characters. During this period Chinese served the Japanese court as the language of both writing and government, much as Latin functioned as the learned language of medieval Europe. Education in Chinese was reserved for men, however, so only with this new writing system could women participate fully in the literary life of a culture in which artistic skill was becoming a paramount value, and the exchange of poetry a central mode of communication.

Poems were written to express private feeling, but also to conduct a courtship, convey condolences, or demonstrate publicly (in frequently held official competitions) one's talent, learning, and refined sensibilities. Because the imperial court's women, unlike the men, wrote solely in the vernacular, they became primary creators of the great literary flowering of that age. Komachi in particular, living at the start of the era, brought to the writing of tanka a fiercely passionate nature, technical mastery as a poet, and, at times, a profound insight into Buddhist teachings.

The poem above shows Komachi's explicit revelation of passion. It also makes use of a technical device specific to Japanese poetry, the *makurakotoba*, or pillow word. A pillow word, much like a Homeric epithet, is an image that regularly accompanies its noun—the *wine-dark* sea is one familiar Homeric example. Like the cushion on which the round bowl of a temple bell is placed, a pillow word worked both to elevate a poem and to increase its resonance. And as with the wine-dark sea, the meaning of pillow words are often so archaic as to be baffling, unless one somehow discovers that the ancient Greeks did in fact make a wine whose color was closer to purple-blue than red.

The poem shows Komachi alone and missing an unnamed lover. Many of her poems are responses to seeing her absent lover in a dream. In one, she wishes she had never wakened; in another, she determines to commit herself to a life of dreaming; in a third, she mourns the cruel fact that even in their dream-meetings she and her beloved meet in the fear of being seen. In this poem, however, we see Komachi before sleep, turning her nightgown inside out—a folk custom believed to make one dream of one's love.

Here is the version appearing in *The Ink Dark Moon*:

> When my desire
> grows too fierce
> I wear my bedclothes
> inside out,
> dark as the night's rough husk.

To American ears, the opening phrase of the original might seem abstract rather than emotional, but the phrase *ito semete* ("very extremely") is rare in tanka and would have stood out; later in the poem, the word *zo* also functions as an intensifier. My response was to replace the usual translation of *koishiki*, "longing," with the stronger "fierce desire." Because Japanese readers would at least be aware of the folk custom explaining why one might reverse one's nightgown when feeling longing, I chose to begin the poem with "When," to indicate that a causal connection exists. I also tried to give my translation of the pillow word, "hiougi-nut," an extra imagistic vividness and weight. Researching this pillow word for "night," I learned that the nut has a virtually black shell; I then made rather free with the image to create the last line of my version.

One thing translation teaches is that other choices may always be made. Here is an alternative translation of mine, closer to the original in one way, more free in another:

> Longing,
> fiercely longing—
> To dream of him
> I turn my bedclothes inside out
> this dark-husked night.

For a final example of my own experience as a translator, here is another poem by Komachi. One of her most famous, it illustrates a different technical device of Japanese poetry, the *kakekotoba*, or pivot word: a word that can be read in two different ways, both intended to be part of the poem. (The pivot words below are indicated by an asterisk between the alternative meanings in English.)

| HANO | NO | IRO | WA / | UTSURI | NI | KERI | NA / |
|------|------|-------|--------|--------|-----|-------|------|
| flower | 's | color | (subj) | faded | has | alas | |

ITAZURI  NI /  WAGA  MI  YO  NI  FURU /
uselessly  my  body  world  in  aging

\*

falling

NAGAME  SESHI  MA  NI
long rains  doing  while

\*

watching

Komachi here confronts transience in a manner quite different from that of Shikibu in her poem mourning her daughter. When she wrote these words, Komachi most likely was still in the midst of her life at court but would have been realizing that time must be nearing its end. A single woman would not be welcome in that world so centered on love and beauty once her own beauty was gone.

> While watching
> the long rains falling on this world,
> my heart, too, fades
> with the unseen color
> of the spring flowers.

The heart of the poem is its complex and skilled interweaving of its various images of passing time. No translation can convey kakekotoba with justice, and it is possible that no one from a different culture can fully appreciate the depth of regret expressed in Komachi's image of uselessly fading spring flowers. Where a poet of ancient Rome responded to transience and mortality with the proud attitude of *carpe diem*, the poet of classical-era Japan acquiesced with a heart full of sorrow, believing that such deep feeling was the mark of being human. The adjacent pivot words *furu* and *nagame*, with their multiple readings, create between themselves a kind of harmonic resonance. The poet is watching her own aging, the long rains are falling, she looks out of her window upon a rain that causes flowers to fade without being viewed, she herself grows older without being known by her lover. It is the other side of Komachi's passionate dream-life we see in this poem: the long hours of waking and solitude, the realization that human life is fleeting and the pleasures of youth and beauty even more fleeting.

Unlike most of the poems Mariko Aratani and I translated, this one exists in many different English versions; it was one of the poems that had first aroused my interest in Komachi and her work. Because it is much translated, and well, I felt a certain freedom (and a certain responsibility) to make it my own. In this version—one of eight or ten quite different drafts that I made—the idea of "aging" is implied by the fading spring flowers rather than stated, "uselessly" is clarified for the Western reader with "unseen," and the word for "body" became "heart" in an effort to make a poetic statement that flowed as seamlessly as possible. A "heart," I think, can both "watch" and "fade"; for a "body" to do so would seem incongruous. I could as easily have simply used the pronoun *I*, since the phrase *my body* is often used simply to indicate the grammatical first person. That is the choice made by Kenneth Rexroth, in his concise translation of this poem, and also by Burton Watson:

> The colors of the flower fade
> as the long rains fall,
> as lost in thought,
> I grow older.
> (trans. Kenneth Rexroth)

> The beauty of the flowers faded—
> no one cared—
> and I watched myself
> grow old in the world

as the long rains were falling.

(trans. Burton Watson)

From even this small sampling, it is easy to see the range of possible choices in bringing these thirty-one syllables into English. In yet another version, Rexroth allowed himself almost complete freedom:

As certain as color
Passes from the petal,
Irrevocable as flesh,
The gazing eye falls through the world.

(trans. Kenneth Rexroth)

Though Japanese tanka are unrhymed, the varying sound of the words is part of their effect—much as it is in American free verse—and I would not want to close my description of working with these poems without touching on that part of the task. In my own version of Komachi's poem, the consonants and vowels shift as it progresses, culminating in the final "flowers," which contains most of the recurring sound elements of the poem; as in the opening line, especially, of the Japanese, the sounds of *o* and *a* preside. Japanese and English prosody are quite different, but my hope was that at least some of the effects of Komachi's music had found its way into the translation.

Translation is one way of learning what delicate clockwork causes a poem to keep accurate faith with music, meaning, and time. But even beyond this, translated poetry brings new realms of being. For me, encountering Komachi's and Shikibu's poetry at the age of eighteen wasn't simply an introduction to new ways of making poems that were moving and beautiful—their work taught me to see and feel differently, introduced to my life a new vocabulary of responses.

The twentieth century's flowering of translation brings with it the richness good poetry always brings: new spiritual and emotional and ethical understandings, new ways of seeing, new tools of knowledge as significant for an increase of inner life as radio telescopes are for an increased knowledge of the spiraling arms of distant space. If translators have an overriding responsibility, it is to carry these new powers in English as fully as possible, by understanding what may serve as a means of perception, what must remain in the ground of the original language, untranslatable and beyond reach. Our desire as readers remains the same as that expressed by the translators of the King James Bible—to break open the shell, that we may eat the kernel.

Translation that serves truly will widen our knowledge of what poetry—what humanness—is. When I read, as one still can, some spirited defense of English iambic meter as a basic expression of human nature, I despair. How can the authors of such essays not acknowledge that great literatures have been made of other meters than our binary or triple ones? That not all languages are stressed? That English-language forms, though they may be full of strengths and powers to our ears, are not the only possible forms? We should know these things not to reject the powers of our own linguistic history, but to welcome the powers of others. Poetry's task is to increase the available stock of reality, R.P. Blackmur said. It does this by reflecting for us our many human faces, our animal faces, our face of insect wings, our face of ocean and cliff. The world is large and, like Caliban's island, full of noises; a true poem reflects this, whether in the original or in translation. To try to encompass such knowledge, to be willing to fail, to prepare as fully as possible the work of poetry, to make the attempt in the recognition that any understanding is one among many—this is all we can do, as translators or as readers.

Many writers describe the attempt to bring the world into language as itself an act of translation. It is an attempt that must always fall short, and still the effort is made. One depiction of why appears in the inner dialogue captured in Robinson Jeffers's sonnet "Love the Wild Swan." The sonnet progresses by straightforward rhyme until the final three lines, which move into eye-rhymes that are not ear-rhymes. Then the poem, like the wild swan it describes, begins to escape our human forms, though not our lives.

*Love the Wild Swan*

"I hate my verses, every line, every word.
Oh pale and brittle pencils ever to try
One grass-blade's curve, or the throat of one bird
That clings to twig, ruffled against white sky.
Oh cracked and twilight mirrors ever to catch
One color, one glinting flash, of the splendor of things.
Unlucky hunter, Oh bullets of wax,
The lion beauty, the wild-swan wings, the storm of the wings."
—This wild swan of a world is no hunter's game.
Better bullets than yours would miss the white breast,
Better mirrors than yours would crack in the flame.
Does it matter whether you hate your...self? At least
Love your eyes that can see, your mind that can
Hear the music, the thunder of the wings. Love the wild swan.

This last, brief poem is by the ninth-century poet Kūkai—the Japanese Buddhist monk who, according to legend, developed the system for using Chinese characters to write Japanese words. Like the poem by Rilke at this chapter's beginning, it describes the relationship of source and manifestation; of word and Mind and the manifest, multiple world.

*Singing Image of Fire*

A hand moves, and the fire's whirling takes different shapes,

Triangles, squares: all things change when we do.
The first word, "Ah," blossomed into all others.
Each of them is true.

# Glimpses of Vietnamese Life[1]

*Denise Levertov*

## Part I

The overwhelming impression I brought back from my visit to North Vietnam two months ago was of a people who were not only unalienated from their society but who enthusiastically identified with it; a people whose striking grace and gentleness is both a characteristic shared with other peoples of Southeast Asia and a result of the sense of security given them by their genuine revolutionary solidarity.

I have spent the last few days typing page after page of factual material accumulated during my stay. I was beginning to feel I would never get it all down and to despair of conveying a feeling of the place, even with all my facts, or perhaps just because I had too many facts. So I began over, reliving impressions.

---

1. Published in *American Report* (Part I, February 26, 1973; Part II, March 12, 1973), and written following my visit to Hanoi, together with fellow poet Muriel Rukeyser and Jane Hart, war-resister and wife of US Senator Philip Hart (D-Mich.), just before Nixon's re-election.

Editor's Note: Denise Levertov, "Glimpses of Vietnamese Life" from *The Poet in the World* (New York: New Directions Publishing Corporation, 1973).

Flying in from Vientiane, looking down at the great range of thickly forested mountains, relieved to see they were not pocked with craters but seemed endlessly green and impenetrable. Then the descent, green, lake-like rice paddies, little thatched houses, the broad curve of the river—and at last after our three-day journey stepping out into the Vietnam that has been in our thoughts daily for years now, but has seemed almost mythical in its remoteness.

Brilliant sunshine, smiling faces, and flowers at the barrier—yes, for us, from our hosts, the Union of Women and the Committee for Solidarity with the American People, and three young interpreters. We all hug each other, there is laughter, and a few tears of excitement.

While a young administrative assistant from the Solidarity Committee, who has one of the most memorable warm smiles I've ever seen, goes to see to our luggage, we all repair to a little waiting room where we are served the first of the innumerable cups of delicious green tea we drank that week. As we walked to the waiting room I found myself next to Lien, one of the interpreters. My arm around her, I felt the silkiness of her long black hair and her fragile, almost childlike shoulders. All three of us feel huge all the time we are in Vietnam.

With free use of the horn to warn the many bicyclists, the water buffaloes, and oxen, the people with one-shoulder yokes moving with the swift balancing step that reminds me of Mexican tortilla sellers coming down into Oaxaca from San Felipe, we drive into the city of Hanoi. (Now, in January 1973, I shudder as I think how that whole across-the-river district, half urban, half rural, has been blown to smithereens. How many of those very people, the first passers-by I saw in Vietnam, died among those ruins?) It is not only the gait of the people carrying goods to market that reminds me of Mexico, but the thatched small dwellings, the banana, jacaranda, palm, and *tabachin* trees, red-blossomed with feathery leaves.

On arriving at the hotel, what joy! I find my "brother," Nguyen Cong Hoan, waiting to greet me and meet my companions. He is the elderly novelist I met in Moscow in December 1971. He was there to visit a granddaughter studying (as many Vietnamese students do) at a Soviet university. I had been invited to Russia to meet some poets.

We made friends quickly and deeply, and he honored me by saying we were henceforth brother and sister. There were tears at our parting; he was not young, and was going back to the air raids, and at that time it had seemed unlikely I would have the chance to visit Hanoi in the foreseeable future.

Now we meet joyfully. I find that he is very famous and revered, and is loved above all as a humorist. Other members of our third host organization, the Writers' Union, who are at the hotel to welcome us, tell me this and add that he is considered a "national treasure."

The hotel rooms: very clean, simple, well-equipped, each with bathroom and balcony. There are rubber sandals by each bed. The style of the room reminds me of Italian moderate-priced provincial hotels. There are *jalousies* at the balcony doors and mosquito nets on the bed, which make a curious kind of little tent when unfurled. However, there don't seem to be any mosquitos.

A feature of the rooms—and nearly all Vietnamese rooms I was in—is a table set with a teapot, two small teacups, a tea caddy full of green tea, and a thermos full of hot water! Brought up to believe tea-water must be at a rolling boil, I am amazed.

Sensitive to our possible travel fatigue, which we are too excited to feel, they have arranged that our first outing be to peaceful lakes and parks. There is some bomb damage visible on the way. We are embarrassed at being VIPs driving fast through the almost carless, bicycle-filled streets of a country that *our* country is blasting. But there is no other way for us to see all that we are to see in a week, and we come to accept it.

It seems strange to be strolling by the shore of one of several lakes within city limits (among them the legendary lake in which a hero of old found the golden sword by which he put the Chinese to flight—a sword which, when he later returned it with gratitude to the water spirit, changed to a jade-green dragon and vanished beneath the waters).

Yes, it seems strange, watching men and boys fishing, children at play in the late-afternoon amber light, to be experiencing so much peace here, where I expected to share in some of the physical struggle of a land that has indirectly changed my life. The peace we experienced in Vietnam, not only this day but also in so many moments and hours during our stay, was the peace at the heart of the storm.

An apricot sunset, relaxed, slightly hazy dusk, mild air. Temples, pagodas. Superb topiary—tamarisk bushes cut into elephants, lions, birds. And everywhere the man-sized cylindrical holes, lined with concrete, that are the highly effective air-raid shelters we have seen in photographs. There is a little water in the bottom of them; gardeners have been sprinkling the grass and flowers. Lids lie ready by the holes.

All this relaxation is of course because no raids have occurred in over two weeks. Many children have been temporarily brought back to the city from the rural areas to which they were evacuated, though no schools at any level up through university are open in Hanoi. "We missed them so," some parents say to us.

Vigorous cockcrows in the center of town wake us in plenty of time for early Sunday Mass. Our hosts want us to see that religious observances are not suppressed here.

The large cathedral is full. The congregation is divided, men on the left, women on the right, and the men's side is as full as the women's. Moreover, there is a surprisingly high proportion of young people. Also a few gray-habited nuns.

The music is European. We are late, and stand near the back, so I don't hear if Mass is said in Latin; a hymn is sung in Vietnamese.

Coming out into the square before the cathedral with the rest of the congregation, we find others waiting to come in to the next Mass. Near the church doors, at the tops of the steps leading down to the square, were the only two beggars we saw the whole time we were in Vietnam, old men with "mandarin" beards like Ho Chi Minh's beard in his later years. People over sixty-five are pensioned, but some few, I was told, who had always been beggars—perhaps since childhood—still beg out of habit. I did not see anyone give to them.

Ho Chi Minh's picture hangs in all official buildings and public places such as the hotel lobby, and in people's homes too. But there are no giant-sized posters of him, like the representations of Mao one sees in pictures of China, or of other leaders elsewhere. These pictures, usually photos, not idealized representations, are never larger than the pictures one sees in America of John Kennedy for instance; and they don't show him in heroic poses but as Uncle Ho, very human, no taller than anyone else, often with others beside him, often with children.

Similarly, there is no equivalent of the Little Red Book or of North Korea's similar book; when the words of Uncle Ho are quoted, they are lines from his poems, or sometimes ancient proverbs he liked to use. No heavy leadership cult, but pride and affection, personal as if he were each person's beloved uncle.

I go with Muriel to the St. Paul Hospital, where she has to get a foot infection treated. The nurse in charge is very gentle. In the visitors' book in the waiting room I read notes of thanks, in French and English, from various foreign visitors who have been treated there.

In the treatment room I watch the witty, patient, French-speaking doctor, a man I'd love to talk with longer, carefully scrub up and attend to the infection on Muriel's foot, and I note that student nurses as well as the head nurse address the doctor directly and without the fear of authority that is traditionally instilled in the minds of "probationers" (as they are called in England, where I was once one myself).

Later we are at the Bach Mai Hospital (yes, the same one on whose very existence the despicable Jerry Friedheim of the Pentagon cast doubt—before he had to admit grudgingly it had indeed been hit). The tall thin director—recently described in a French journalist's report after the terror bombing as running desperately from area to area of what had been his hospital, organizing the digging out of whoever was still alive under the rubble—escorted us on a tour that included those parts of the hospital that had already been bombed before our visit (late October) and the busy wards in full use. Even in these there are signs of damage—cracked plaster is being repaired by groups of workers, male and female, and there's a sound of hammering and sawing.

We are stunned by the encounter with two patients' cases in particular. One is never fully prepared for the sight of suffering. These are two children, boys, each in small separate rooms, each with a silent, stony-faced mother sitting by his bedside.

One has lost both legs from just below the knee. His left arm and his body are bandaged, too. He lies on his back, expressionless, toying and toying with a little spool of some kind he holds in his hands. The nurse tells us it is good he exercises his fingers—the arm injury has partly paralyzed the arm but the full use of it may return. We think of how his feet will never return, and even if he can be fitted with artificial legs eventually, he will never run and jump again. He is only eight years old.

The other is a couple of years older. Bomb fragments[2] have lodged in his brain, as well as elsewhere in his body. His head is swathed in bandages—his face looks out of its turban with a strange expression, disoriented. It is probable the brain damage is irreversible. We cannot speak. Going out into the sunlight again, we take photos of bomb craters in the gardens.

At the Writers' Union we read poems to each other in our own languages, then our wonderful chief interpreter Quoc, who is twenty-eight and has a

---

2. I.e., pellets from an antipersonnel weapon, of the type which has over three hundred pellets to a "bomblet" and over six hundred "bomblets" to each "mother bomb." Formerly made of metal, these pellets were "improved"; that is, are now made of a plastic undetectable in the victim's flesh by X-ray.

wife and two young children but looks about sixteen, gives instant paraphrases of them, which from Vietnamese into English, at any rate, are remarkably poetic. Those of us, both Vietnamese and American, who speak French amplify his versions. Mr. Quat of the Solidarity Committee, who speaks English well, is there to help out also.

A marvelous atmosphere of good fellowship, not only from them toward us but *between* them. None of the rivalry one can too often feel at writers' gatherings.

Huy Can reads a poem about the messages hastily scrawled on the walls of his home town of Haiphong after the bombardment—"I have the baby safely and have gone to Tu's house," or "Our son was hurt and I have gone to the hospital. Look for us there," or "Don't go into what's left of the house. It's dangerous."

I'm reminded, by his use of the vernacular, his collage—but more than collage—of things actually seen and heard, of the spirit and practice of William Carlos Williams, and I tell them a bit about him. (Later I find a French translation of "An Ode to Whitman" by Huy Can.) They listen with close attention. They don't want to hear as much about the politics and the antiwar efforts and "protest poetry" of American poets as about poetry itself.

There are more men than women at these gatherings at the Writers' Union, but women are represented, too. One of the women poets is very young and pretty. She brings her little boy with her and I draw him a picture. Later she brings me a gift—a large earthenware pig and piglets, symbol of many good things.

Secretary General of the Union is Nguyen Dinh Thi, poet and novelist, born in 1924, whose first books were printed on jungle presses during the struggle against the French. He was twice imprisoned, and commanded a battalion of the Liberation Army.

He's a man whose physical beauty and grace of presence are inseparable from his moral and spiritual beauty and grace. He speaks to us of how he sees the war not only as the clash of forces, two national identities, but as an experience that reveals clearly the worst and the best on both sides.

Like a storm, he said, it blows the lid off things, it reveals the garbage of bestiality hidden by the cloak of civilization. The horror of uncontrolled technology has been shown us, technology in the service of immoral men. "And," he told us, "we in Vietnam can understand your shame because we have *our* shame too, that people like Thieu, going further than any other puppets, actually invite the US to come and bomb their own country." He said this is not only because it was true but because in the kindness of his heart he wanted to alleviate our burden of shame at being members of what has become the Monster Race.

That same storm, he continued, has also revealed the best—in America as well as in Vietnam. It was interesting to me that he cited Norman Morrison as a paradigm of that best. Communism in the DRVN is characterized by its humanity, exemplified in this instance by the reverence in which Morrison, a Quaker, a pacifist, whose political action took the ultimate Buddhist form of self-immolation, is held, and not by Thi alone but by many people. Later we were to hear a poem famous in Vietnam, written by To Huu, one of the best-known poets, born in 1920, which is a monologue spoken by Morrison to his baby daughter. And I find his name in other poems too. His life sacrifice burns on in Vietnamese hearts.

The goodness of America, Thi went on, is not in the ascendant; yet the catalyst of the war has brought about the coming together for a common goal of many people of different backgrounds. "Don't think all your actions are in vain. Your support is important to our morale. And we have a proverb, *Many breezes make a big storm*. If peace comes, we will thank not whoever is in power in America, but the steadfast peace movement. The green bud has more potential than the yellow leaf."

Thi speaks of the ancientness of Vietnam. Pottery has been found there two thousand years older than any from India and China. There is evidence that rice was first cultivated in the Red River and Mekong

Delta. He speaks of how, always under pressure from large and oppressive foreign powers, the Vietnamese survived as a people, retained and developed their identity, by developing a strong sense of mutual aid, of personal relations. "We can sacrifice all for independence, but we are also an open-hearted people. We cherish life but are fearless of death." As I listen to him I realize that profound truth is being spoken, not a rhetorical statement:

The American fear of death, with America's resulting funeral industry, America's obsession with the "new," even America's racism which ties in with the Western equation "white equals purity, light, and life; black equals corruption (sin), darkness (of the grave), and death," (followed by "black as hell")—surely, I remind myself (for it is not an original idea) this is the same fear that erupts in American violence and—ultimately—genocide.

And conversely, the amazing ability of the Vietnamese not merely to fight on under such material odds but to be so generous, so discriminating between culprits and victims, between one American and another, and to be so cheerful and kindly in their relations with each other—surely it does indeed stem from their simply not having the obsessive fear of death.

They don't *court* death but they accept it, and *thereby* are able to truly "cherish life." "My people," says Thi in his soft but clear voice, "are gentle and merry." And later, "As a writer, I don't find the regime a *perfect model*, I see it rather as a slow accretion that is *in process*. As a poet, that is a joy to me—to witness and participate in that process. We are *finding the way*. Each day must be a new invention."

This is the life that our government, in our name, has been attempting to pulverize.

# Part II

I begin the writing of this second group of recollections of my fall visit to North Vietnam after the cease-fire has been announced. Though there is relief in knowing that, for the moment at least, the people and scenes I am describing are not subject to constant threat, nevertheless with each word, with each face or field that comes into the mind's eye, comes the thought, "Are they still there? Did they survive the December terror bombings?"

We drive in a jeep, followed by two others, south from Hanoi. Jane Hart and I are in different jeeps, each with guides and interpreters.[3] In the third jeep ride our accompanying photographer and some aides. We are soon out of the city and into a landscape of tender, moist shades of green, full of the "water-mirrors" I had imagined in a poem, "What Were They Like?," written in 1966.

The growing of rice is staggered so that one sees it concurrently in many different stages of development: some fields are flooded, with no shoots visible above the water, in others the vivid young rice looks quite short, and in others it grew taller than I had realized; it looks similar to other grains, high and tasseled.

The roads are fairly straight in this flat country, and not dusty even when unpaved, for the soil seems to be a wettish red clay. Indeed the colors are reminiscent of Devonshire or parts of North Carolina, but with the luxurious vegetation of these latitudes. Many clusters of banana and other fruit trees and lines of palm trees give variety to the wide terrain. Sometimes we see a range of mountains on the horizon, clear-cut, manifold. The sky's light, joyful blue deepens as the sun mounts; two or three indolent clouds are reflected in the rice paddies, again giving me a feeling of *déjà vu*.

Buffalo, slow as clouds, ruminate here and there by the roadside; others, with their masters, plunge vigorously through the watery fields;

---

3. Muriel Rukeyser remained in Hanoi during this excursion.

sometimes both man and beast are under water up to their chests, but one of my guides tells me land that is this wet is not desirable. Along the roads go pedestrians and cyclists—men and women and sometimes children—some not riding but pushing the bicycle, loaded with heavy but manageable sacks of produce or other materials, tied to a central pole.

Every now and then an oxcart passes; more rarely, carts drawn by small horses—or an army vehicle, camouflaged not with paint but with real branches. Many of the military personnel we see, even in Hanoi, wear wreaths of green branches around their helmets—perhaps for coolness rather than for camouflage. It gives them a bucolic appearance eminently suitable to soldiers who are basically and deeply attached to rural areas.

As we pass through hamlets strung out by the roadside we often notice families eating just outside their small thatched houses, sitting at tables placed under a tree or a palm-leaf shelter. Sometimes we see little restaurants in the same style, and shops. For some reason there are an enormous number of barbershops, all thriving. I laugh with my interpreters and guides about this. We are very gay.

Even as we laugh I think to myself how strange it is to be having such a good time in this war-scarred country, the idea of which has been like a heavy lump in my chest day and night for years. But not just this day in the country, *every* day I experienced from my Vietnamese friends the swift-flowing movement of feeling from laughter to tears, from grief to joy, and back again. And I came to feel that while I personally may be volatile, that is not what the Vietnamese are: it was not anything shallow or easy I was witnessing but the free play of genuine emotion possible only to a people with deep roots in their culture, their soil, and at the same time with the abundant flowering branches of security and hope that their revolution has given them.

With the same companions in laughter I share the tears of extremely painful experiences. I have a photograph that commemorates the first:

it shows me holding hands with a woman who looks at me sorrowfully. Sunglasses hide my own expression, but in fact I was crying. Around us, looking concerned, are other people—some of my companions, some of her neighbors. We had just come out of her tiny house built on a dike, its floors beaten earth but all within immaculate.

Much of its space was occupied by two large platform beds, plain but solid-looking. And on one of them sat her eleven-year-old daughter. The father had ushered me in, graciously but humbly. The little girl, silent, patient, and otherwise perfectly formed, had had a foot blown off by yet another antipersonnel bomb. Nothing, nothing to say. I stumble out into the noon heat, the mother follows. We stand there gripping each others' hands tightly. Her neighbors crowd around—a murmur does not alter the basic silence. And at last we unclasp our hands and I depart. Three months have gone by since that day, but I feel I am still standing there within that moment.

We are crossing a river on a ferryboat. Mme. Bé, of the Union of Women, and I get out of our jeep and stand gazing downstream. Mme. Bé is conversing with one of the many other ferry passengers—most of them pedestrians. When we get back in and drive on, up the dike on the far shore and over onto the ongoing road, Bé tells me of what had passed between her and the old woman with whom she had spoken.

"Who are the women from the distant place with whom you are traveling?" inquired the old lady—dressed in blouse and trousers dyed to a shade of powdery brick red, a color much worn in the Delta, the very color of its earth.

"They are Americans—visitors from America," Bé told her. "Americans! Yanquis!" exclaimed the old lady, horrified, shifting the weight of the carrying pole balanced on her shoulder, a bundle or basket dangling from each end of it. "Why do you want to bring such evil people here?" "But these are friends—friendly Americans, not those who come to kill us."

"Ah, good then; it is good that they come."

Immediately appeased, immediately ready to believe we are indeed friends, not the enemy. Mme. Bé laughs as she tells the tale—but I can't laugh. It seems to me too important, too moving, not funny at all. The old lady is probably illiterate—one of the small minority, all in the over-sixty age group, to whom the revolution's work in education, which reversed the literate/illiterate ratio, came too late.

Her reactions are direct, not filtered through any medium but her own experience. She has seen the cruel and rapacious landlords go, justice and self-improvement and mutual aid established in village life, the tragic, arranged marriages of her younger days become history, along with famines, diseases, and the high rate of infant mortality.

She has seen the growth of the Women's Union, which promotes and safeguards the rights of all women, young and old, married and single, and which has a branch in every town and village of the North. She has seen happy children going to schools that simply did not exist except for a tiny elite when she was young, and students returning from the universities to share their knowledge—as nurses, doctors, agronomists, teachers—with the people of their home villages.

And she has seen the huge bombers from a country half the world away fly over implacably, wave after wave, year after year, attempting to smash all this happy activity with mysterious, inexplicable brutality. Yet when these strange, tall, pink-faced women appear out of nowhere and she is told they are Americans, how quickly and how trustingly her initial horror is succeeded by a friendly acceptance of their being some other kind of American, not the destroyers.

This generosity of spirit, typical of what I observed, results from what I so frequently felt was an embarrassing overestimation, on their part, not only of the strength and dedication and size of the antiwar movement in America but of the degree of general good will existing among the mass of people in the US toward the people of Vietnam.

At the village guesthouse where we spend the night, we sleep in one spacious room. The large platform beds, two on each side, are almost like separate rooms once the mosquito nets are drawn down. The beams of the high roof are beautifully carved. This was once part of a Buddhist temple. The sleeping room is entered through a large living and dining room, where we were served a delicious supper and breakfast. Outside, a long veranda runs the length of the building (the men in our party sleep in an identical set of rooms further along it) and on the veranda, flanked by flowerbeds and potted plants, are washstands with jugs of water, towels, and soap.

In back of the building is a set of outhouses. Returning to the main building from the outhouse early in the morning, I stop to watch the mist rising over a nearby pond. Across the water, beyond the water lilies, a path adjoins the bank. I glimpse children leading water buffaloes out for the day, an older schoolboy with books and bicycle, women with baskets talking to each other. Smoke from morning cooking fires rises with the mist. Birds are singing.

Last night an air-raid siren had sounded in the far distance, but this morning there are only pleasant, mild, life-sounds in the quietness. Someone is playing a bamboo flute under the persimmon trees. This is a glimpse of the immemorial village life so many Vietnamese poems and stories celebrate—what Thi, our poet friend in Hanoi, hoped we would see, calling it the root, the core of all things Vietnamese.

"Explain to the American people," said a worker at the Collective Farm later that day, "that life here is not turned upside down: the bombing is useless as well as savage."

Mr. Quat (Chairman of the Committee for Solidarity with the American People): "As long as the war goes on we are neither happy nor sad. Revolutionaries are simply people who want a better society and try to create it. When one has walked ten thousand miles one does not turn back before the last one hundred."

A wonderful concert had been prepared for us on our last day. Thi has arranged it, and it takes place in a large reception room at the Writers' Union. The folk and traditional music is enchanting, including such instruments as the monochord (which weeks later in Boston I look up in my 1885 Grove's *Dictionary of Music*, and find that it is reputed to have been invented by Pythagoras, but that he probably learned of it from the Egyptians, and that Euclid wrote of it in defining the intervals of the ancient Greek scale!), the bamboo flute, a bamboo xylophone or marimba, and a most ingenious kind of rattle the use of which involves dancelike movements of arm and wrist.

European-style music is performed well also, and poems are recited. Perhaps the most memorable of all the pleasures of this concert, and the most difficult for me to describe, is a skit performed by two little girls, daughters of a famous theatrical couple. Their older sister acted as announcer for the whole concert. Dressed as Saigon street boys, they mock the clumsy GIs whose shoes they shine. Their sense of comedy, their expressive and charming little faces, their professionalism, and at the same time the fun they were obviously having, are beyond my skill to describe.

Mme. Nguyen Khanh Phuong, of the PRG delegation in Hanoi—a beautiful woman who suffered unspeakable tortures in Diem's prisons and does not know the fate of her husband, arrested in 1959, nor has she seen her daughter since she was wrenched away from the year-old child in 1955—tells us how she survived "only thanks to the care and love of my comrades in the NLF."

We sit around a long coffee table in an elegant room at the delegation's house in the area of Hanoi where the embassies are clustered and where the well-to-do French once lived in luxury. Two young women from the South, brought to Hanoi for medical treatment of unhealing wounds and other results of torture under the Thieu regime, tell us their terrible stories. They don't weep. But they are deeply angry, and hurt as much emotionally as physically. Mme. Phuong rises from time to time to replenish our cups and plates with tea and fruit.

I slip a paper napkin she hands me into my notebook to keep as a memento. "After twenty years of struggle," she says, "who could imagine we could give up? We are sustained by our deep belief in the justice of our cause. We suffer and fight in order to bring a time of happiness."

The two young women—who were not political when they were first arrested—sip tea and sit proudly upright. One has a colostomy, the other a complicated and painful hernia requiring a series of operations. Mme. Phuong, dressed in the long silk tunic worn for occasions of ceremony or festival, smiles at us with her sad eyes, a smile of pride and hope.

As we leave, each woman takes our hands in both of hers and holds them a long moment—and at the last minute I venture to embrace them, and each returns the embrace with warm sisterliness. They come out to wave to us as we drive away.

I write in my notebook, "All that we have known about and have been trying to spread among other people seems unreal compared to seeing mothers at the bedsides of their half-destroyed children, or hearing the stories of women like these. I cling to the need for revolutionary optimism, I yearn for it; and we *see* it, we feel inspired by it—but we have a long struggle before us in order to really *share* it. It seems to me such hope, faith, charity, can only emerge out of a suffering we have yet to experience."

## Epilogue

I feel this is an appropriate place to end, because it will serve to remind readers and myself of the ongoing struggle, both in Vietnam—where at this very moment, despite Nixon's vaunted "peace," political prisoners are being murdered by America's puppet Thieu and his henchmen, and in the US where we who do want true peace and justice for all, and who do at least *try* to work for it, have so much to learn and so far to go before we can offer any effective resistance to the continuing outrages our country perpetrates (and the US is bombing Laos even as I write[4]) or

---

4. And now (April 1973) Cambodia.

any strategy for dealing with the next major outbreak of US aggression, wherever it occurs.

Self-reproach can be a form of self-indulgence. That was something I began to learn in Vietnam, even though I experienced more self-reproach there than I ever had before: not because we do nothing, but because we don't push ourselves to do just a little bit more. I came to see, during that week, that revolutionary optimism is the *fruit* of serious struggle; that for us—at such a different point of moral and political development, and so deeply enmeshed and confused among the gross material and technological manifestations that surround us from birth—there is possibly far more strength and impetus to be drawn from contemplation of the *positive* quality of life in the Democratic Republic of Vietnam than from contemplation of the sufferings its people have endured.

In other words, the impetus to our own development toward the social change which alone can bring peace, can come more strongly from the knowledge of how humane, kindly, joyful, and constructive it is, after all, possible for human beings to be, than from grief, anger, and remorse when these emotions are separated from such positive knowledge.

Courage is patient.

# Living in Machado[1]

*Philip Levine*

The village of Castelldefels is less than twelve miles south of Barcelona. I took my family to live there after my wife and I discovered it possessed an Anglo-American school that was first class and inexpensive and that it cost far less to live there than in Barcelona. A woman at the American consulate had given me elaborate and very exact instructions as to how to locate a particular Dutch realtor who could rent me a *torres* (the term used in Catalunya to denote a detached house) for far less than such space would cost in Barcelona where, I was assured, I would have to bribe several people before I could get anything at a reasonable price; apartments stayed in the same family for generations, and no one would rent anything remotely affordable before cleaning out an American, all of whom were rich.

The Dutch realtor, who described himself as an agent (not a secret agent or a commercial agent or even a real-estate agent—merely an agent) turned out to be a wonderfully civilized and witty man as well as an honest one; he spoke every known language with a made-in-Hollywood accent and a vocabulary that suggested he'd learned by reading

---

1. Philip Levine, "Living in Machado" from *The Bread of Time: Toward an Autobiography* (New York: Alfred A. Knopf, 1994).

nineteenth century fiction. (To make the point that French food was better tasting and more reliable than Spanish he would say, "The Spanish kitchen is not so fine, I think, as the French, you think?") His name was Hans Breen, and within a few days he had my family of five installed in a spacious and crude dwelling directly across the way from his own, which was an identical twin to ours but fixed up to resemble a habitation, whereas ours was barren enough to suggest a cavalry barracks. Once my kids were properly enrolled in school, my goods from America collected at the main post office in Barcelona, and extra blankets and two butane heaters loaned for the coming cold weather, Sr. Breen felt it was responsible for him to take off on his annual vacation, which this time was to include Rome, Florence, Paris, and two weeks in his native country visiting old friends in the publishing business, which had once been his own business after a hitch in the former Dutch East Indies. He waved goodbye gaily at us from the front seat of his tiny Renault, which he drove with an élan and abandon suggesting that underneath his proper exterior he was actually a Brazilian baby millionaire sowing his wild oats.

The departure of Breen meant that our only link with the Spanish language was broken. I decided it was my duty to rectify this problem, and I set about spending two hours a day after lunch studying Spanish by means of a textbook given to me by a colleague at Fresno State. Why the book began with a study of the subjunctive I had no idea. I began searching for occasions on which I might employ it; I would say, "If that were a loaf of bread how much would it cost?" or "If this were a *bodega* what sort of wines would you be likely to offer for sale?" My wife suggested, slyly, that there had to be a better way of learning the language and the sooner I hit upon it the better. I had already noticed that my oldest son could, when we went to our favorite local restaurant, employ the simple present tense in ordering a four-course meal and wine for his parents, a liter of white for mama, a liter of red for papa, and he could be polite and effortless about it and win smiles from the dour waiter, who preferred to watch "Voyage to the Bottom of the Sea" undisturbed by the requests of customers. Mark had the meal underway, the bread on the table, the simple green salad oiled and soured, while I was still formulating my opening remarks: "If you had a paella today, would it be possible for the five of us to receive it this evening?"

This was late summer of 1965, the first time I'd been out of the country since my bachelor days and the only time I'd traveled any distance with the responsibility of a family of five. I was on a sabbatical leave from Fresno State, which gave me the munificent sum of half my annual salary of $9,800 for the year. I had picked up another thousand by teaching summer school for the first time in my life and still another by teaching two summer poetry workshops. A friend and patron had also added some thousands to this, but we had spent almost a third of our total in getting to Spain by means of a long trip through Europe in a VW Squareback sedan we'd purchased in Wolfsburg, where it was manufactured. Although our rent was less than $65 a month including utilities, and food was cheap and good, and wine was next to nothing, I was worried about money. I wasn't sure how I might earn some, but no matter what I did I'd have to learn Spanish. The few Americans I'd met at the Institute for North American Studies in Barcelona all spoke wonderful Spanish and struck me as unaccountably cheerful, as though they would rather be living here than in any other city in the world, while I longed—secretly—for Detroit, New York, even Fresno. I was homesick for the first time since I'd moved to Fresno in '58. I wrote a great many letters to friends back in the States and received almost nothing in return. These were loyal friends, but most of them were employed and lacked the time to sit down immediately and respond in spite of whatever note of urgency they might pick up in my letters. In fact I was doing my best to disguise my need. I wanted this first foreign family venture to appear to be a success. I had pushed it hard in spite of the advice of many people who'd insisted I couldn't afford it.

In Spain postage stamps are sold at the post office and also in tobacco stores, all of which are controlled (or were under the Franco government) by a national monopoly. Often these little tobacco shops also sell stationery items, note books, airmail envelopes, pads of writing paper, pens of all kinds, ink in bottles and cartridges, pencils. The lines at the post office are usually formidable and the senior clerks behave like vice admirals of a defeated armada, so most people take their personal letters to these little tobacco shops. Exiting the nicer of the two in the center of Castelldefels, I noticed a small sign next to the Pelikan fountain pen I had been admiring. It read in English, "Spanish Lessons Given," though "lessons" was spelled with only one "s," which did not inspire confidence. I went back in the shop and in my Spanish asked the young, dark-haired woman if I might inquire about the lessons. (It was perhaps the first occasion on which the subjunctive seemed appropriate.) She stared at me uncomprehendingly, so I reached inside the display case and plucked out the little hand-made sign. "Ah," she said in English, "you want my brudder. After one," she said, pointing at her wrist, "he is here."

Thus it was that afternoon I met Sr. Juan Rusiñol, a tall, long-faced Catalan gentleman, who indeed offered private Spanish lessons at his own *torres*, which was less than a mile from mine, for one hundred *pesetas* an hour, or $1.67 US. Since I was spending almost $100 a month on my children's education, I thought it reasonable to spend a few dollars on my own. We arranged for an initial lesson on the following afternoon, commencing at four p.m., when his stint at the store was complete.

It's impossible to explain by what magical process I believed the Spanish of Sr. Rusiñol would become my own. Somehow I did not envision hard work, hours of memorizing, and the writing of lessons, and thus it was I arrived at his *torres* the following day in a state of considerable excitement, akin to the excitement one feels when one is about to encounter the psychiatrist who will rid one of all his or her phobias by means of the right word or the right pill. Seated in his little upstairs study that looked out on a dismal display of brown-stained trees, and equipped with pencil and note pad on which to inscribe the phrases I needed to memorize, my hopes began to sag. It was not until later in the hour when the sun had dropped behind the western hills and the evening came on with a suddenness I was unused to, that things began to brighten. Sr. Rusiñol asked what I was by profession. I answered with as much simplicity and dignity as I could muster, "*Yo soy poeta.*"

Thus there began what was probably the first course ever offered in the village of Castelldefels on the subject of modern American poetry, taught by one young American poet to one not-quite-so-young Catalan poet, for the moment after I had uttered one of my first declarative sentences in simple present tense in Spanish, "*Yo soy poeta,*" Sr. Rusiñol switched adroitly to English and responded, "I too am a poet." "*En Español?*" I asked. "No," he said, "in my native language, Catalan," at which point he opened the door to his study and called to his nephew who had been studying in the next room. A tall, slender boy of perhaps ten years appeared at the door; he seemed in no way abashed by the presence of a stranger. In Spanish Sr. Rusiñol asked the lad how the school day had gone. The boy's response was incomprehensible to me. They exchanged a few more brief remarks and the boy went back to his room. "Could you understand what he was saying?" asked Sr. Rusiñol. I confessed I hadn't caught a word. To my relief I discovered he had not been speaking Spanish; all day he worked at school in Spanish, and the moment he returned home he reverted to his own language, which was Catalan. "You wonder why this country is insane?" he asked. (Actually I had never wondered, for Spain under Franco made just as much sense as California under Reagan.) "We go to school in one language and think in another, a language it is no longer legal to publish in, to debate in, to speak at a gathering of more than five people."

Before I could formulate a Spanish sentence in which I could pose a question regarding the nature of Sr. Rusiñol's poetry, he asked me in English whose poetry I thought larger, that of T.S. Eliot or that of Walt Whitman. As I struggled for the vocabulary to express my sense of the immensity of Whitman, Sr. Rusiñol switched the focus of our discourse one more time in his favor. "If you are more comfortable speaking your own language, please do so, as I comprehend it." That my desire to speak one of his other languages had brought me to this room in the first place seemed suddenly unimportant in comparison to the overwhelming urge for the two poets to reach an accord in this village that seemed at best indifferent to poetry. The rest of our time seemed to rush by as I spoke on my differing loyalties to these two great American poets. Almost two hours passed before my mentor rose to let me know our session had come to an end. Before I left he handed me a dog-eared copy of a lesson book entitled *Spanish Made Simple* and instructed me to master the first three lessons before our next meeting. As we shook hands, Sr. Rusiñol told his first and only lie in my presence. "Your accent is very good," he said.

Barcelona in 1965 was a raw, sprawling industrial town which on most days brooded under an enormous cloud of gray smog so heavy that for months I thought it was about to rain. Spain's burgeoning automobile and motorcycle industries were located in the western and northern suburbs of the great city, which spread out for ten miles or so in each direction save the east, where the sea stopped it abruptly. Barcelona's great modern architect, Gaudí, had not yet been discovered by the non-Catalan public, and thus most of his buildings were encrusted with industrial filth and several were misplaced on the maps the state tourist agency handed out. Actually tourists were rare, although tourism was the nation's greatest supplier of foreign capital. The millions of northern European visitors came mainly for sun and sea; in summer they drowsed along the beaches of the Costa Brava north of Barcelona, and in autumn and winter they headed directly toward the warmer coasts of Andalusia. One had little doubt one lived in a police state: heavily armed cops were everywhere, almost always in pairs. (The story was these "twins" spied on each other and thus were unbribable.)

Still, something anarchic from the city's past clung to the place. Although Antoni Gaudí was a religious mystic and his art was meant to

pay homage to the Catholic God of his upbringing, the buildings them-
selves were wild and totally unpredictable, made up as they were of
beams shaped like bones, rooms without corners, windows suggesting
the eyes of sea creatures, metal railings that undulated like the waves
of the ocean, and from the niches of his great unfinished cathedral, *La
Sagrada Familia*, peeped the stone eyes of snails and turtles. The project
was approaching its hundredth anniversary and the citizens spoke of it
as soon reaching completion although the whole roofless jumble lacked
more towers than it possessed, and only a dozen or so stone cutters were
on the job. Even the cardboard scale model in the tiny museum next door
was unfinished, though I was assured the drawings for it—in Gaudí's
own hand—were extant. In the older quarters of the town near the port
there were Renaissance palaces of great beauty cheek by jowl with the
tenements of the workers. In the ancient, narrow streets the noise was
unimaginable as the two-stroke *motos* tore past. The people themselves
seemed to have forgotten how to talk outdoors, and conversations were
conducted in a series of outbursts and harsh shouts. The anger of this
repressed working class—once so thoroughly politicized and union-
ized—burst out constantly in unrehearsed moments of street theater.
Anything approaching significant political action was outlawed, and the
various police forces included a special political police nicknamed the
*gris* because of their heavy gray serge uniforms. State cops were every-
where toting their tommy guns and taking notes on the least departure
from the ordinary: a foreign license plate, a late party, a new house guest,
an especially aggressive dog. Up and down the streets they went at all
hours with their little notebooks, writing in what I imagined a terribly
efficient script. My neighbors ignored them and went about their lives
with noise and abandon. A mile from our *torres* a camp full of Gypsies
lived in a small clearing under a railroad viaduct. I would see the men
in town in their wide-brimmed Cordovan hats strutting like peacocks.
Everyone assured me their plans called for theft and I must never leave
my house unguarded for long. As far as I could tell the police pretended

they did not exist, and their women begged shamelessly, screwing their heads to one side as though they were simple or deformed. I walked a wide circle around them.

My second lesson with Sr. Rusiñol began in Spanish. I had pored over the first five lessons in *Spanish Made Simple* and was prepared to discuss the objects in a typical Spanish living room (although as yet I hadn't seen one) or enumerate the various members of a family, but my maestro asked me to describe the landscape of New England and contrast it with that of the Great West. Before I could see what was coming he requested my opinion on the part those landscapes had played in the work of Ralph Waldo Emerson and Robinson Jeffers, whose reputation was clearly larger in Catalunya than it was in Fresno. I explained as best I could that other poets had replaced Emerson and Jeffers, though the former was still an extraordinarily influential essayist and moral thinker. "Americans no longer read Robinson Jeffers?" he asked in English. "Then whom do they read?" I made mention of Wallace Stevens and William Carlos Williams, and in my faltering Spanish described them as the two great mountain peaks under which the rest of us wrote. Neither name meant anything to him, and he seemed utterly puzzled and more than a little saddened at the passing of Jeffers, who he assured me had made an indelible impression on him. I assured him that Jeffers had made an indelible impression on me as well, but the young were looking for something less spectacular, less orgiastic, less operatic. Of course I was speaking in English now. "Less operatic?" he said. "Do you mean less like Mozart or less like Wagner?" We were communicating. "Less like Wagner," I said. "Would you also say they want a poet who is less Spanish?" For some reason he thought of Jeffers as Spanish in character. Here I confessed my puzzlement, for while certain Hispanic poets were well known in the United States, García Lorca and Neruda, we knew almost nothing about the rest of their poetry and absolutely nothing about the nature of Spanish life.

After a brief silence during which he seemed to be considering my remarks, I asked if we might continue in Spanish. He bowed his head in a courtly manner and asked me to count to a hundred, to name the days of the week, the months of the year, the various trees outside his window, the colors of the sea and sky, the parts of the body, the features of the face, the reasons for living.

How Sr. Rusiñol located a copy of the old New Directions *Selected Poems of William Carlos Williams* edited by Randall Jarrell I have no idea. The stationery store offered a selection of new and used paperbacks for sale, but I'd never spotted a book of poems among them. Most of the books covered the range from English editions of James Bond thrillers all the way to English editions of John le Carré. At the next lesson my teacher informed me, in Spanish, that he had read the entire volume and was puzzled as to why it was regarded as poetry. I leafed through the familiar pages wishing I'd brought a copy from home, and then remarked without thinking that perhaps there were certain poets who didn't translate well. I had heard that the French, for example, hadn't the least idea why Wordsworth was regarded as a major poet. Sr. Rusiñol remarked quietly, so quietly in fact, that I immediately realized my tactlessness: he had read the poems in the original. "Yes, of course," I said, "but perhaps one has to be an American to 'hear' Williams. I'm told the English find nothing in his poems." The latter was a spur-of-the-moment invention; I had no idea how the English responded to Williams aside from the fact that Levertov, Thom Gunn, and Charles Tomlinson had all responded to him as ardently as anyone.

By this time we were conducting whatever lesson was going on in English. I offered to read him one of the poems to demonstrate its

musicality, and he indicated with a nod of his head that I should pro-
ceed. I chose one of my early favorites, "Dedication for a Plot of Ground,"
which for me possesses an enormous rhythmic drive. I looked up after
what I'd thought was an impressive and passionate rendering to find Sr.
Rusiñol looking thoroughly befuddled. "I do not hear poetry," he said,
and so I began to quote Frost's remark about poetry being what gets lost
in translation, but this time hearing my error I veered off into an irrel-
evant paragraph about the greatness of Frost, whom the English also
could not hear, knowing perfectly well that the English poet Edward
Thomas was one of the first important writers to properly measure the
true greatness of Frost.

Sr. Rusiñol took the book from my hands and, holding it tenderly,
leafed through the introduction and stopped at an early poem, which
I could see he was rereading to himself. He looked up with a wry smile
on his face and said, "Tell me, in your own language please, why Mark
Anthony is in heaven."

I started to talk about Williams's belief that our failure could be traced
to the failure of our first European ancestors to submit to our hemisphere;
they had fled the Old World in order to find a new world to locate their
minds and imaginations, but instead of abandoning the garbage they
brought with them, they imposed its order on America. He interrupted
me. "Is this the Catholic heaven Mr. Williams is referring to? Does he put
an adulterer into heaven as an insult to the Catholic church?"

"I don't think in this poem," I said, "he really cares about the
Catholic heaven. Of course being a pagan Mark Anthony couldn't go to
the Catholic heaven, and Williams was not a Catholic anyway. He means
heaven to be a place of final reward for living as one should, for com-
mitting oneself totally to the passions that he, Williams, had committed
himself to. It's Williams's own version of heaven." At last I was warming
to the task.

Sr. Rusiñol looked once again at the book he so gently held in both
hands and this time read aloud.

...how many times
from grass and trees and clouds
enters my north room
touching the walls with
grass and clouds and trees.
Anthony,
trees and grass and clouds.

For a long moment he sat in silence, and then he looked up at me and asked, "Did I read that properly?"

"Yes, of course."

"Do you hear poetry in what I read?"

"Yes, to me that whole poem is very beautiful."

"Perhaps," he said, "your Williams is like our good Machado, for in our Machado there is something that only we Spaniards can hear, some nuance that crosses no border. The French also do not acknowledge him, though like Americans they have regard for our Lorca and even Juan Ramón. For us the good Machado is the pinnacle, the apex, the Alp that looks down on all the rest of our great modern poets."

What American "high culture" there was in Barcelona collected around the institute for North America Studies on the Via Augusta in one of the posher neighborhoods some miles up the great sloping hillside on which the city is built. In 1965 there weren't enough cars in Barcelona to make parking a problem, so quite often I'd stop off at the *Instituto* to check out books, for they had been kind enough to grant me the use of their library. I, in turn, had given them a poetry reading, for which the director, Dr. Frauenfelder, rewarded me with the largest bottle of Johnnie Walker I had ever seen.

One day, spotting me poking around the library, Frauenfelder asked me to come upstairs to his office and meet someone who shared my passion for poetry. It was thus I met Hardie St. Martin, who had only recently embarked on his monumental anthology, *Roots and Wings*, a collection of modern Spanish poetry translated into English largely by American poets. He had already enlisted the cooperation of Kinnell, Merwin, Haines, Stafford, Wright, and Bly. He asked me if I was interested in contributing, and I assured him I was, although as yet my Spanish was almost non-existent. It didn't matter, he remarked, Bly couldn't order a glass of water in Spanish, but he had a genius for translating the poetry.

Sitting in Frauenfelder's cramped office, I was immediately drawn to this little man in a gray striped suit and red tie. Hardie sat bolt upright, his delicate hands together in his lap, and laughed frequently. His speech, which was produced almost entirely in the front of his mouth, was at first difficult to grasp, for he did not so much speak as chant. He had wonderfully white, gleaming teeth which one saw a great deal of because his mouth was never closed. He took so much pleasure in all he said that I found I took pleasure from it myself. The names of Spanish poets peppered his conversation, all pronounced in a manner unfamiliar to me. I took his accent to be authoritative, for José Hierro was to him Pepe Hierro and sometimes merely Pepe, and Francisco Brines was Paco, and there was a great salad of others whom he hoped to include in his project, poets whose names were utterly new to me, Gloria Fuertes, Gil de Biedma, Claudio Rodriguez, all of whom he seemed to know on a first-name basis.

In a few hours he was off by train to Madrid, which he assured me was a far more exciting and international city than Barcelona, for the citizens stayed up until the small hours of the morning talking poetry and philosophy and drinking brandy, whereas the dour Catalans were asleep before midnight so as to be prepared for the following day's commercial labors. Why he had chosen to live here and not in Madrid went unexplained. With his olive skin, close-cropped curly graying hair, and odd oval-shaped skull, Hardie looked like the embodiment of all things

Mayan. (I later learned he was born in British Honduras, the child of a Venezuelan mother and a father from the States.) When he switched into Spanish, which he did every few minutes, I found him incomprehensible, for he failed to end one word or begin another; it was one seamless stream of watery sounds upon which the emphasis fell everywhere and nowhere. Still, his delight in poetry was exciting for me.

Our second meeting was at our *torres*. Hardie arrived unannounced and unexpected one Sunday afternoon with two Spanish friends, only one of whom spoke any English at all. Antonio, a big horse-faced man, sat in a chair nursing a glass of red wine as he prepared himself for his voyage into English. He had one of the harshest voices I'd ever heard, and he used it to drop his pearl: "Kirk Douglas," he said. I'm afraid I was less impressed than I should have been. He gathered his breath and took a second chance: "Burt Lancaster." But since he didn't pronounce his "t's" it came out "Boor Lancasser." He was by trade a construction worker in Barcelona, an Andalusian originally, who like so many of his *lansmen* had come up to Barcelona when only a teenager to find work and, finding it, had settled in. The other fellow was a small, morose man who frowned a great deal, refused to sit, and downed glass after glass of red wine without thanking his hosts. They were killing time while they waited to meet a third friend, José Maria, in a bar. In spite of the din Antonio created, Hardie did his best to keep the attention on things poetic. He had the day before received some translations of Machado from Bly; they were remarkable, and he wanted to share them with me as soon as possible. He recounted a tale of Bly's adventures in England, and how without effort Robert had appalled the Brits with his pronouncements on the ultimate nature of poetry. It was clear that Hardie was under the sway of this great romantic figure who was Bly or some creation of Hardie's he called Bly. At one moment out of the corner of my eye I caught the morose fellow fondling himself as he stared at my wife. Hardie caught my glance and quickly looked over his shoulder. The man laughed in Hardie's face and shouted something unintelligible. Hardie leaped to his feet and confronted him. The man shouted back, and then Hardie slapped him across the face. Antonio rose from his chair and ordered the man out. A few minutes later Hardie and Antonio left to keep their appointment.

*Spanish Made Simple* is a book designed to aid the commercial traveler who wanders into the uncharted regions of Mexico without a native guide. It teaches one how to ask for the prices of *serapes* and *rebozos* and even *retratos*, it helps one order a meal or locate a bus stop or call for a taxi. Mastered, it would also allow one to spend a cordial evening in the company of a Mexican *comerciante* and his *esposa* and *niños*. It is remarkably mum on the subject of prosody and seems to have no opinions whatever on the entire dramatic unfolding of poetry in Spanish from Góngora to Blas de Otero. Thus I was severely handicapped during my hours with Sr. Rusiñol, for he kept veering away from the language of daily intercourse to speak of Miguel Hernandez, Juan Ramón, and his favorite, the good Machado. It was actually some weeks before I discovered that Juan Ramón, whom I pretended to have read, for he had assured me that everyone had read him, and Juan Ramón Jiménez were one and the same person. Once, when I had the temerity to ask if he admired the shorter lyrics of Jiménez, he stared at me in puzzlement. I repeated the name and when he remained silent wrote it carefully on my notebook, which I turned so he might read the name I was sure he knew. "Do you mean Juan Ramón Jiménez?" he said in English. Of course I did. Ah, Spaniards did not refer to him as Jiménez but rather by his "real" name, Juan Ramón. I was slightly puzzled, and he saw it immediately and assured me this was a fact.

"Why do you not say 'Federico García' instead of García Lorca or simply Lorca?" I asked.

"Aha," he said, "because half the country is García and only Lorca is Lorca." Yes, of course, it all made perfect sense.

In Spanish I asked why when he referred to Antonio Machado he always said *"el buen Machado"* (the good Machado) and not simply Machado? Because, he explained, they had two Machados, both poets, brothers in fact, one Manuel or Manolo as he was often called, and the great Antonio. Did they call Antonio the good Machado because he was the superior poet? Only partly, Sr. Rusiñol assured me. Manolo had been something of a dandy, a fop, a popular figure in the Madrid of his day who lived the high life, wrote some distinguished poems, and devoted most of his energies to enjoying himself. He was what Spaniards referred to as a *"Señorito"*: young men or formerly young men who wallowed in their pleasures and privileges. "Let me show you one of his poems," he said. He rose and peered nearsightedly at his bookshelves until he located a slender paperback that was falling apart. "There's no point in purchasing him in a finer edition," he said, for the frail book he held was exactly what Manolo deserved. The poem, "Felipe IV," focuses mostly on the king's wardrobe, which is dark and tasteful and contrasts with his pale complexion and frail, blue-veined hand. It reads like a portrait of a portrait by Velasquez.

"Very elegant," I said. "It's a sonnet, isn't it."

"Yes, elegant is one word you might use."

"And another?" I said.

"Decadent would do even better. Notice that the king has put aside the scepter in favor of a *'guante de ante,'* a suede glove, which was more likely part of the costume of Sr. Machado. I've seen him painted with a book in hand but never a suede glove."

"Is this typical of his work?" I asked.

Sad to say, it was, and though the subject left Sr. Rusiñol cold, he admired the craft of the poem, which was as studied as Sr. Machado's style of dress. "That was the point: to be preoccupied with style during an era of social upheaval. From this it was only a small step to a portrait of Charles V, and then another smaller step to the Generalisimo." It was clear he was referring to Franco, for Manuel—who outlived Antonio by eight years—had done well under the dictatorship.

"And Antonio," I asked, "what were his affiliations?" I grew bolder, "What were his politics?"

Sr. Rusiñol took a deep breath and measured me carefully. "Antonio Machado, our greatest poet of this century, was naturally a man of the people. He put his whole soul into the struggle for *libertad*." Did he mean that the good Machado took the side of the Republic during the Spanish Civil War? "I mean exactly that," he said, staring me down, "and when our side lost he gave up his life." I had not failed to hear that crucial "our," which Sr. Rusiñol had so fearlessly uttered in the presence of a man he had no good reason to trust, although we were brothers in poetry.

The Rusiñols had crossed the border from Catalunya into France in 1939 just before the fall of the last Republican forces. At that time Juan was only a boy of fourteen, but he remembered the events with remarkable clarity. Once on the French side of the frontier they had been interred with other Republicans in what one could only properly call a concentration camp, where they lived until the onset of World War II, which was only six months in coming. Once the so-called "fake war" was over and the Nazis grew serious about taking France, many of the refugees saw what was coming and escaped. Some returned to Spain, some joined the *maquis*, and others merely survived the best they could. But the most indelible event that etched itself on the tablets of the memory of Juan was the death of the great Spanish poet, Antonio Machado, who had crossed the border in their company. "It was as though Spain itself were dying," he said.

"Did you know who he was?" I said.

"Everyone knew who he was. And, of course, my father told me how great a poet he was and that he had written poems in defense of the Republic."

"Was your father also a poet? Or a literary man?"

No, his father had been and still was an auto mechanic. He seldom worked with his hands anymore, for now he owned the large repair shop on the road to Gavá, but back in '39 he was employed as a mechanic in the Republican army. But he was a Spaniard and a Catalan so he knew the literature. "To this day I think he regrets he was not one of those who offered to fulfill the poet's last wish."

"What was that?" I said.

"He asked to be buried in Spanish earth. He did not ask to be buried in Spain itself, for even at the end he was the same considerate, gentle man. To have taken him back to Spain for burial could have cost the lives of those who returned him and God knows what the fascists might have done with his body. He merely said '*la tierra de España*,' the earth of Spain. Those were his words. My father was there and heard them. Over the years he's repeated those words to me many times."

"How did they do that?"

"They simply crossed the frontier at night and dug sacks of the true soil of Spain and returned. When he was buried they packed around the coffin this earth from Spain." He, Sr. Juan Rusiñol, only a boy of fourteen, was there at the end; he would remember that day for the rest of his life. I asked if it had been a rainy Thursday. No, it had not been a day out of a poem. "Perhaps," he said, "Vallejo did die as he predicted, on a day of downpours in Paris, but Machado was buried on a beautiful day in early spring. That was the irony, the day was very beautiful, a day he would have loved. It might have been a Thursday; I do not recall everything. I was not yet a poet, so I did not truly know how much I was losing."

Once again Sr. Rusiñol rose and went to his bookcase. This time he returned with a book bound in boards, the spine covered with what appeared to be cracking red-dyed leather going white. He held it up for me to read the title, *Nuevas Canciones*, and above the title also in gilt letters and in very small print the author's name, Machado. Along the length of the spine were five star-shaped golden blossoms each framed by a golden vine. He moved his chair around the table and sat next to me and opened the book, leafing patiently past the title page, yellowing with age and stiffening, to the dedication page, which read "*A la memoria de D. Cristobol Torres.*" Underneath the dedication at a 45-degree angle in black ink gone brown was the one name clearly though inelegantly inscribed, "Machado," the poet's own signature.

He stopped leafing through the pages when he reached a poem that began, "*Hacia Madrid, una noche, / va el tren por Guadarrama.*" He read in a slow, somber voice but a voice that was his own, without melodrama or incantation. When he'd finished he asked, without looking directly at me, if I'd understood the poem. I said I'd followed some of it. A train is traveling at night toward Madrid; it travels under something in the sky. "A rainbow," he said, "a rainbow made of water and moonlight." I confessed I'd lost the next few lines. He recited from memory, "*Oh luna de abril, serena, / que empuja las nubes blancas!*" "Oh, moon of April, serene / that pushes the white clouds." He nodded his approval, and began to recite again, looking down at the book or pretending to do so. A mother holds a little boy in her lap, and the child in his sleep sees the green countryside pass by with its sunbrightened little trees and golden butterflies. "Yes, even at night, in his dreams," said Sr. Rusiñol, "the child sees the daylight world bursting with promise, for what he sees is his own world coming into being, and that world has all time to grow in. And the mother?" Once again he recited, "'*Ceño sombrio / entre un ayer y una mañana, / ve unas ascuas mortecinas / y una hornilla con arañas.*' And the mother's face is fixed in time," he went on, "for the life of the child is her burden as well, perhaps, as her joy. She sees the fire dying, she sees in her mind, the fire dying in the oven invaded now by spiders." He recited the last line slowly, ending, "'*y una hornillo con arañas.*'" He smiled, "Before there were in your house ants who did not know you, there were spiders in the oven, but García Lorca would have been the first to admit his debt to Machado."

"The tragic passenger who talks only to himself, is he Machado?"

I asked.

"No," said Sr. Rusiñol, "though others have read the line that way. Antonio Machado would never enter his own poem as the tragic passenger. No, that man is simply the tragic passenger of the poem, he who must travel the way of life alone."

"But wasn't his life spent largely in solitude? Didn't his young wife die very early?"

Yes, that was true, that was no doubt how he learned intimately how tragic life could be, but never would he refer to himself as the "tragic passenger." "You see," he said, "he enters in his own person in the following lines," and he held the book up closer to me so that I might verify his claim. And he read, "*Yo pienso en campos de nieve / y pinos de otras montañas.*' This is Machado speaking, for he has his dreams of winter landscapes, of fields of snow, and the high pine trees of other mountains."

"And then God enters," I said.

"Yes," he said, "Machado often invites Him into his poems, for there is room for everything in his writing. In this case a God by whose light all of us see and who in turn sees all of us, and he asks this God of his a single question. Do you know what the question is?"

"He asks if he will ever see his face."

"Yes," he said, "he asks if that day will ever come, for He sees all of us, our hearts and souls, at all times, but will we ever see even His face?" Sr. Rusiñol closed the book slowly and pressed his thumbs down on the back cover. He was sorry he could not lend me this book, for it was a gift, but he would gladly loan me a paperback edition, an *antologia*, a selection of the poet's best work. He would be pleased to help me read these poems, for this way I might come to better understand both the Spanish language and the Spanish people.

Quite abruptly Hardie moved to Castelldefels. He gave up his rent-controlled apartment in Barcelona. He claimed he was sick of the noise of the streets and the overpowering stink of diesel exhaust. A lawyer friend—a man he'd met the week before in a bar—had arranged it. He did not trust my "Herr Breen," for, he told me, a Dutchman was not to be trusted. We sat in the living room of his brand-new *torres* enjoying a glass of sherry. Antonio was glued to the television on which *Real Madrid* was as usual trashing the Barcelona soccer team. A small fire of damp oak smouldered on the hearth; this was something Hardie had never before enjoyed, and he took great pride in the elegance of his newfound home. True, so far the plumbing had proved a disaster. When I asked how much rent he was paying, he avoided answering. Instead he assured me that save for the month's rent to his agent, the lawyer friend, there were no hidden costs like those my Herr Breen would spring on me before I departed.

I changed the subject to the anthology. Could I work on some translations of Machado? Why, he asked, did I want Machado? I told him of my conversations with Sr. Rusiñol, the Catalan poet. "Every gentleman in Catalunya is a poet, including your Sr. Rusiñol," of whom he had never heard. "No, I'm sorry," he said, "I've assigned Machado to Bly." Bly had a particular affinity to the difficult Machado. It was not simply that both men led a solitary rural life, it was also their constant striving for simplicity and wisdom.

"But Bly is married and has kids," I said, "He's surrounded with friends and cronies, he is outgoing, boisterous, a shrewd literary entrepreneur, an influential editor. He has a bountiful nature, but he's essentially theatrical, exactly what Machado was not."

Hardie casually waved me away. I was taking the whole thing too personally. His attention had strayed to the contest between *Real Madrid* and Barcelona. "Look, *Los Niños*," his nickname for *Real Madrid*, "are going to score." The Madrid crowd was also standing and shouting as one, the players were dancing about and hugging each other. Each year it was the same. The two cities revealed their natures on the fields of sport.

The speed and élan of Madrid triumphed over the stolid persistence of joyless Barcelona.

"I think you would do well with Unamuno," said Hardie, closing down the literary discussion.

While experimenting with his breathing, my son Mark passed out, hit his chin on the arm of a wooden chair, and received a nasty cut, which in spite of home bandaging was still oozing blood the next morning. I asked Señora Fuertes, who lived across the street, the name of a reliable doctor, and she sent me to a Dr. Esteban Ruiz with offices just off the town's main square. The doctor saw patients at ten a.m., and his office was a daunting sight, not perhaps as daunting as St. Vincent's emergency room at one thirty in the morning, but bad enough to leave a sane person quaking. The huge waiting room was crowded to overflowing with a variety of people, bandaged and otherwise, many of whom appeared to be unconscious in the heavy haze of cigarette smoke. I was struck by the fact that most of the men had been injured in some way about the head: eyes, ears, foreheads, entire skulls were hidden in great swaths of graying cotton. I was immediately seized by several elderly women in black and ushered to the front of the room where a woman in ordinary street clothes sat behind a simple deal table with a large notebook. The women urged me forward and asked me to explain the purpose of my visit. I told the attendant, a rather elegantly turned out woman in her thirties, the nature of my son's injury and indicated with my fingers that stitches might be required. *Sí, sí!*, the doctor would determine the nature of the remedy. She took my name. The elderly women then led me to an empty chair, awakened the man seated in the adjoining chair, and asked him to move so that the *estranjero* and his *joven* could be seated side by side.

Across from us sat another father and son. The father had buried his face in his hands, and the son—a boy of no more than eight years—was whispering into his ear. When the father looked up I recognized him immediately, for he was one of the younger officers from the local *Guardia Civil* barracks a few blocks from my house. He had removed his jacket and wore wide leather crossed belts across his shoulders and a wide black belt at his waist from which his holstered automatic pistol hung. He nodded gravely at me and once again hung his head, breathing deeply like one who has just finished a difficult race, his chest heaving under the gray-green shirt. The boy whispered again in his ear, but the man merely shook his head no, and went on gasping for breath. Expecting a long wait I had brought a copy of Orwell's *Homage to Catalonia*, which I'd wrapped in butcher paper to hide the title. I questioned the wisdom of reading it.

The next time the officer sat up the boy took a pack of cigarettes from his father's pocket, selected one, and pushed it toward his father's mouth; the man accepted it without comment and leaned to the flaring match his son produced. The officer rose and began to pace back and forth the length of the room. At last he stopped and leaned into an illuminated wall of glass bricks; the day was a brilliant one, the sky of Catalunya a deep blue, the light lacking the golden dust for which it is famous. He was a short, sturdily built fellow so wide across the shoulders his shirt seemed about to burst its seams. He leaned his head into the glass bricks and then drew it back; a moment later he let his head fall with a sharp report. Before he could withdraw it and repeat the act, his son was on his feet. The boy was tall for his age, dressed in a white shirt which, though he wore no tie, he had buttoned at the throat. He was very slender and wore gray shorts that seemed too small for him. For a moment the noise in the room, largely made up of coughs and groans, subsided. The boy began to stroke his father's hand until at last he caught his attention, and then he led him slowly back to his seat, where he sat beside him, comforting him with little pats on his back as he whispered in his ear.

Suddenly I was aware that my name had been called; the door which bore the name of Dr. Esteban Ruiz had opened and a nurse—or at least a woman in a nurse's starched white uniform—had called out my name.

Several of the women in black indicated with gestures that I should arise with my son and go forward. Before we could reach the door the young officer was there ahead of us, his son behind him pulling back on one hand. "My wife," he said, "where is my wife?"

"In a moment," the nurse said, "in only a small moment. Please, be patient."

Dr. Esteban Ruiz looked amazingly like my friend the poet Peter Everwine, though he was shorter and his moustache a bit fuller and darker. He was seated behind his desk in a small room lined with glassed-in bookshelves which looked as though they hadn't been invaded in years. He had been reading the sports section of *La Vanguardia*, one of Barcelona's worst and most widely read newspapers, which he shoved to one side as he rose to greet me. Alas, Dr. Ruiz did not speak English. In Spanish he asked what the problem was.

Mark immediately took over the conversation. "Here," he said in Spanish, "I've wounded my chin."

Dr. Ruiz removed the bandaid and stared lovingly at the wound. "It pains you?" he asked. He was assured by father and son that the cut no longer caused pain. "Then what is the problem?" We explained: the wound continued to bleed. Would stitches be required? The good doctor mused. He had no affection for stitches. Not in such a case. First they must be put in, which required great care; then they must be removed, which required a second visit. And there was the likelihood of a scar, not a large scar, but not a welcome sight on the chin of so handsome and blond a young man. No, he had a better solution. He rummaged in his top desk drawer until at last he located a great round piece of adhesive tape. He peeled away the plastic backing, studied my son's chin for some seconds, and then abruptly slapped on the tape. Mark staggered back. The doctor apologized, and then carefully tamped down the edges of the tape. "Perfect," he said. "You will be sure to remove it in a week, and you will still be very handsome."

"And so blond," I added.

I paid the woman at the desk. She also shook my hand and expressed her pleasure in serving the father and his handsome, blond son. She was none other than Señora Ruiz, the wife of the doctor. I could see the Guardia officer and his son nowhere. The old women in black pointed me toward the door, nodding their approval.

When I told Hardie of the extraordinary civility of the women in the doctor's waiting room, he stared at me in disbelief for several seconds and then laughed. He turned to Antonio and related my tale. Antonio shrugged and muttered a few, indecipherable words which Hardie translated. "Those old women have nothing to do but hang around all day waiting for someone to die."

"What did the doctor charge you," Hardie asked. I told him how tiny the fee had been, five hundred *pesetas*.

"Five hundred *pesetas* is not a tiny fee. It's eight dollars. You were paying for half the patients that morning, that's why they ushered you up to the front. Once the doctor got your eight dollars he could treat the others without regret for what they had to give him. We don't have socialized medicine here, this isn't Europe." The injured workers were covered by a form of compensation that paid $1.50 for an office visit. The rest bring eggs or maybe a slab of ham *serrano* or maybe a few sausages. Had I noticed a certain pungency in the air? Now he was howling with laughter at the spectacle of this street-wise American city boy being suckered by a bunch of village widows. I said nothing about the young officer and his son.

At the dining room table he presented me with my first translation assignment: a poem by Unamuno which deals with a blackened sculpture of the dead Christ in the Church of the Cross at Palencia. Although the language is slightly elevated and the poem more rhetorical than most American poetry of the '60s, I found it presented a stunningly intimate portrait of the poet's feelings toward this God-man or man-God whose deity the poem struggles not to accept. I was surprised by how much I liked the poem. "What do you think of the poem?" I asked Hardie.

"It doesn't matter what I think of the poem. It is Unamuno. It is an important poem by one of the key figures of the Generation of '98, one of the keys to an understanding of what took place in this country's poetry. You must hear this calm, clear, unembroidered voice, the voice of a serious man speaking to serious men." I knew I'd triggered a lecture that could go on until the small hours of the morning, but somehow I couldn't let go of the subject.

"To you this is a calm, clear voice?"

He took a deep breath and explained I was not reading American poetry or even English poetry. If I knew what was being written before the Generation of '98 I would come to understand what a revolution these poets had fostered.

"As significant a revolution as the one Wordsworth fostered a century before when he turned English poetry toward the language of ordinary people?"

"Far, far more significant," he said, smiling, for it had produced poetry of much greater importance.

❧

With its serious adult voice addressed to any and all adults, with its hope to create faithfully and in every detail the homely scene, with its naked passion for its subject and its nostalgia for a lost faith, how wonderfully and hopelessly out of fashion this poem seems.

From *The Dead Christ Lying in the Church of Santa Clara*
(Church of the Cross) *in Palencia*

This Spanish Christ that hasn't lived,

black as the dung-ripened fields,
lies like an immense plain,
horizontal, packed down,
without soul, without hope,
with closed eyes, his face to the sky
that hoards its rain and scorches our bread.
And with his black feet, hooked like an eagle's,
he seems to want still to imprison the earth.

Or perhaps God, penitent,
dressed in this miserable rag,
wanted to taste the death of this world,
in order to flush his conscience of guilt
for having made man, and with man
evil and pain.

Popular superstition imagines that his nails
and hair bring in
from this life the callused, the shelled,
dry superstitions,
whatever he scratches up, whatever he binds around
his harvested head.

This motherly piety of the poor daughters
of Santa Clara has skirted
with cloth of white silk and gold
the repulsive privates,
although this pouch of bones and pus
is neither male nor female;
this Spanish Christ without sex
lies far beyond that difference
that is the tragic knot of history,

for this Christ is ground of my ground.

Is there a poetry magazine in America that would accept such a direct poem, with its unapologetic appeal to our deepest beliefs? I can almost write the rejection slip myself from the *American Poetry Review*.

Dear Mr. Michael Unamuno,

I regret to say that only three issues back we published another poem dealing with Jesus Christ. We appreciate the seriousness of your commitment, but we find this poem more than a little out of touch with what's going on in recent poetry. We would be willing to look at newer work, especially anything that dealt with your journey down from the mountains to make the revolution.

Sincerely,
Jack Hatchett
for the editors

I shudder to think of what our current batch of killer-reviewers would do with poetry of such frank concern for the human estate. Imagine Mary Kinzie or Marjorie Perloff unleashed by *APR* on the unsuspecting Mr. Unamuno. Not a pretty thought.

One night, feeling a bit downcast in the terrible weather of the end of autumn in Catalunya, I stopped for a drink at a small bar on the road to Sitges, a lovely little fishing village down the coast from Barcelona. At the rear of the bar was a large square window through which I could see the waves crashing against the rocks below the terrifying coast road. "Bad day," said the bartender, a paunchy middle-aged fellow who wore a white apron tied around his middle like a cummerbund. He poured himself a Tio Pepe and drank to my health and then poured me a second brandy on the house. Over the window hung two crossed pitchforks, a display I often found in bars and inns throughout Spain; the tines were twisted and knotted like arthritic fingers. The rain was whipping in from the low dark clouds scudding over the hills to the west of us. All that afternoon I had been sure it would snow, though my neighbors assured me it was out of the question. It was too early in the year, said one; another claimed it snowed only once every ten years and this decade had already had its snowfall. As I tramped along the highway or padded, head down, along the shore, I was sure I caught glimpses of snowflakes falling through the air. I had been walking for hours every day. I would spend much of the mornings in bed, the warmest place in the house, trying to urge a frozen poem into being, and then after a small lunch of bread and *chorizo* I would go for a long walk to escape the smell of butane or the smoke from the fireplace. Usually in the late afternoon my youngest son, Teddy, would accompany me on the long walks along the shore, but today he was taking part in a game of soccer in the large field behind our house. Although my sons were not proficient at the game, they had to be included because Teddy owned the single ball in our neighborhood that could be substituted for an actual soccer ball, which no one owned. With Teddy by my side the walks were far more rewarding, for we would question each other about the events of our day, how the year was going, and usually wind up casting about in our memories for our fondest images of home. Lacking his company I had sought relief in this tiny roadside bar.

The door swung open and a blast of cold damp air invaded the place. Two Guardias hung their ponchos and leather tricorn hats on hooks by the door. The younger of the two also hung his tommy gun there while the other slung his rifle over his shoulder. "One bad day," he said to me, and drew a stool up next to mine. Before seating himself, he saluted me, and then laughed and extended a wet hand, which I shook. "Tomas

Garcia," he said, "at your service." I presented my name, and he looked at me quizzically. "You are not a Catalan?" he said. I told him he was right. "How odd," he said, "you look exactly like a Catalan." He went on to explain that a week before he had come in out of the cold and introduced himself to a man at the bar, and the man, shorter than I and perhaps a bit older, had presented him with his calling card, which he extracted from his wallet. It read *C. Blanco, Catalan Fisherman.* "What a country, eh, we all have calling cards."

I told him I lacked a calling card and asked if he had one. "No," he said, "no one seems to doubt the nature of my employment." His comrade laughed and added that it was difficult to figure out what they were doing on a miserable night like this. "What do you think we are doing?" he asked me.

I would have preferred not to have been drawn into this conversation, but it was too late for that. "I think you've been getting wet," I said.

"You are very observant," said the first and more cheerful Guardia. "Our mission is to make sure the enemies of Spain do not deliver great bales of hashish to this shore. There are hundreds of vessels out there in the dark just waiting for us to come into this bar and get drunk so they can unload their cargoes of drugs. Were you aware of this?" I told him I was not. "Then you do not read the newspapers; they are full of warnings. Every day they publish a new warning against the fleets of our enemies." He unshouldered his rifle and handed it to me. It was actually a tiny, bolt-action carbine; it weighed no more than a .22 and looked about as effective. He had inserted a cork into the end of the barrel, no doubt to shield it from the salt air. "This is what they have given me to defend the sacred shores of Spain from the Communist fleet. I haven't a chance. The string on the cork is broken; one shot and I'm through."

"I cannot say if it is a good translation," said Sr. Rusiñol. He knew the poem so well he couldn't really imagine it other than it was. It was a poem his father had shown him when he was still in his teens, when he was struggling with his own religious doubts. Indeed his father had given him an *antologia* of the poems of Unamuno.

I asked if Unamuno was one of his father's heroes. He was silent for a while, and then he said, "Unamuno is like a great monument for us all: philosopher, novelist, poet, savant, educator. He was the director of our greatest university as well as our greatest literary figure. As Machado is for us the soul of Spain, he is the conscience."

"Do you like his poetry?" I said.

"Always you ask this question, 'Do I like...?' Who am I, Juan Rusiñol, to like or dislike this giant?" The only significant question would be, he explained, "What Unamuno would think of the writings of Juan Rusiñol."

"Do you read him for pleasure?" I asked.

"Pleasure? Do you read Walt Whitman for pleasure?"

I told him that of course I did, that when I read "Song of Myself" there were times I could barely contain my joy. I had to get up and put the book down and dance about the room or sing, even though I had no singing voice.

"You are lucky, very lucky," he said. "We parade solemnly around our Unamuno with hushed voices, we do not dare dance and sing in his presence. Like this poem, he was august, far larger than life. He lived in the same room with God, all his life he spoke with God as one might speak to a brother whose love you were unsure of. He was like a God himself, and then he died with such courage and grandeur to remind us what a man can be, to remind us that man is created in the image of God or God is created in the image of man." I had never seen Sr. Rusiñol so passionate. He went to the window and pointed down at the dismal yard where the pines and the few shoddy, leafless trees bowed to the sea winds. "You know he was a Basque, Miguel de Unamuno, but at the end he defended us too, the Catalans. Although he was not of the left, he defended those of the left; he defended everything alive in Spain that stood for life. It is impossible to believe today," and he gestured out the window at the yard below, "that this poor earth of Spain could again give us a man like Unamuno."

"How did he die?" I asked.

"You do not know? Then I will tell you." And so the whole sad story unfolded: how as rector of the University of Salamanca, Unamuno was forced to take part in a celebration of Nationalist Spain which turned out to be a celebration of death. He had sat on the podium with Franco's wife and listened to an insane speech by the fascist General Millan Astray, who had spoken of the one half of Spain as a cancer which must be removed by a surgical process. He had whipped up the audience—largely Falangists—to a frenzy, and soon they along with the General began the fascist chant of "*Viva la Muerte!*" (long live death). When the audience finally calmed, Unamuno rose.

Sr. Rusiñol went to his desk and rummaged about in one of the side drawers until he located a small magazine that resembled a comic book in its flimsy structure. "I would like you to hear his words, for they are famous to us." He read them slowly in Spanish. At the end without looking back he began to translate and paraphrase what he had read. At times it was a lie to remain silent, Unamuno had said, and so he would speak. As a philosopher he had dealt in paradoxes all his life, but this meaningless, necrophilous cry "Long live Death!" repelled him. "General Millan Astray is a cripple," he said. This was true, for he'd lost an arm and an eye in combat as head of the Foreign Legion. "And if he has his way, the General will create many more cripples. The General would like to create a new Spain in his own crippled image." At this point the General could not contain himself and screamed, "Death to the intellectuals! Long live death!" A machine gun was pointed at the head of Unamuno, but it did not silence him. Sr. Rusiñol bowed again to the text and translated with precision. Unamuno spoke:

This is the temple of the intellect, and I am its high priest.

It is you who profane its sacred precincts. You will win, because you have more than enough brute force. But you will not convince. For to persuade you would need what you lack: reason and right in your struggle. I consider it futile to exhort you to think of Spain.

Amazingly enough when Sr. Rusiñol finished he was dry-eyed. He looked at me directly and remarked that it was General Franco's wife who probably saved the poet from being murdered on the spot, though it hardly mattered, for six weeks later he died of a broken heart. "I understand your Walt Whitman died an old man, in bed. Whereas our García Lorca died against a wall, still in his youth. We love our poets."

I decided the best thing I could do was select a short poem by Machado and do my best to translate it. If I waited for permission from someone, even from myself, it would never come. I chose one that began, "la casa tan querida" because I could translate the first two lines without consulting a dictionary. Also it did not rhyme, and the lines seemed of no fixed length, so most of the usual formal considerations were irrelevant. The syntax of the first stanza—which was a single, very complex sentence—gave me fits. I wanted not to have to resort to breaking it into two or even three sentences. Hours passed, and I felt I was simply moving words around and not getting any closer to a version of the poem I'd be happy with, but a curious thing was happening during these hours: I was falling in love with the taste of the Spanish on my tongue.

I went for a long walk down by the sea and began quoting passages from the poem. To my great surprise I had memorized all of it, though I no longer recalled how I'd translated most of it. The poem concerns a man who goes back to view a house that was very dear to him because once a certain woman lived there. The place is now an uninhabited wreck, and the wreck reveals its worm-eaten skeleton. The short second stanza goes:

> *La luna está vertiendo*
> *su clara luz en sueños que platea*
> *en las ventanas. Mal vestido y triste,*
> *voy caminando por la calle vieja.*

We discover it's night. The moon "is shedding / its clear light of dreams / that silver the windows." Why would the windows still remain in a junked house? Perhaps the speaker is remembering it as it was even though he places the experience in the present. Perhaps he is demonstrating how the past takes preeminence over everything. I repeated the final sentence over and over, for I was describing myself, alone, bundled in thick, coarse sweaters against the sea winds, feeling each of my thirty-seven years twice over. "Shabby and sad / I made it down the old street." And like Machado or the speaker in the poem, the experience was utterly not mine, for there was no woman of romance anywhere in the world whose loss I still regretted, but there was in me a yearning for a place of the past, a house to which I could return and be taken in, a place that had once mattered and still mattered. No such place existed. I had had the American experience of finding the old house replaced by a parking lot, and this was 1965—two years before what in Detroit would come to be known as the Great Rebellion—and much of the neighborhood of my growing up was still unburned. It would take another twenty-five years to show me how fully Machado's poem dealt with a life I could never live, for by the time I truly became that shabby old man the places of growing up had been obliterated. The American experience is to return and discover one cannot even find the way, for the streets abruptly end replaced by freeways, the houses have been removed for urban renewal that never takes place, and nothing remains, not even a junked skeleton "silvered by moonlight." When I want to find an image of my Detroit I go to the poetry of World War II—for instance, to this passage from Miroslav Holub's "Five Minutes After the Air Raid":

> In Pilsen,
> Twenty-six Station Road,
> she climbed to the Third Floor
> up stairs which were all that was left
> of the whole house
> she opened her door
> full on the sky
> stood gaping over the edge.

Once again I shared my translation with Sr. Rusiñol. He pored over it for several minutes, and then looked up at me. "You are pleased with this first sentence?" I had to admit I was not. It sounded graceless and awkward. I was certain I was doing a great disservice to the original. No doubt I was right, he murmured, but still it was a noble effort, this effort to create one sentence out of so complex a sentence. He was sure I had understood the original and got the meaning right, but he could not help me, for his English was not up to the task. "May I ask you a somewhat personal question?" he said. "Did you get any pleasure from reading this over and over, as you must have?" and he smiled broadly.

I told him it had given me a profound and curious pleasure I could not explain and one that I was unprepared for, and suddenly I found myself reciting the second stanza as I had done so many times to myself. When I had finished, Sr. Rusiñol nodded his approval and said, "You have crossed the border into Spain."

I struggled another day with my little Machado poem and finally decided to share it with Hardie. He took it immediately to the dining room table, which served as his office, got down his Machado from a shelf, and compared the translation and the original for a full ten minutes. "Bly likes this poem too," he said. "He translated it, but I doubt I'll use it in the anthology. He did a better job than you."

"I don't believe it," I said.

From another shelf he removed a large envelope, went through it swiftly, his reading glasses slipping off his nose, and finally withdrew the Bly translation and handed it to me. After reading it carefully, I said, "You're wrong, Hardie, it stinks." Hardie was clearly taken aback. I was not trying to question his taste where Spanish poetry was concerned; I felt my ear for English was adequate for the judgment. "Look," I said, "how he cheats. He creates a parenthetical sentence where there isn't one, and it sounds awkward as hell. This man deep in a meditation on the past blurts out in Bly's version, 'she lived there.' Doesn't that strike you as a violation of the whole poem? And '*maltrabado*' doesn't mean 'badly lasting.' Look how graceless the second stanza is in his version and how lovely it is in mine. I admit we both louse up the first stanza; it's untranslatable."

"Nothing is untranslatable," he said, "but you're right, neither of you do well with the first stanza."

"And the second?" I said.

He laid the two side by side and studied the original again. I knew this was serious business for him; his commitment to Spanish poetry was his life. Finally he raised his head and put his reading glasses back in his breast pocket. "They're different. Robert's is Robert's, an effort at rendering the original as exactly as possible. Yours takes a few more chances. What I'm curious about is why the two of you were attracted to this poem. There's nothing remarkable about it."

Somehow I didn't dare say that I'd known all the words in the first two lines and so decided impulsively and on such thin evidence that this was the right poem for me, nor did I want to admit how many hours I'd spent poring over the dictionary, and how much I was still in doubt about my rendering of the first stanza. Instead I said something about the universality of the theme, that we all imagined going back to a place of first love, a place of beginnings, and how going back we did not find the place or found it utterly different from the place stored in memory.

"It's a familiar poem about lost love," he said.

"It's far more than that," I said, "far more. Each of us harbors a dream of a place that retains some magic for us. We believe that if we could return to that place and time and begin again our lives would somehow be different, fuller, and so we return. It's almost a quest. Machado's portrait of it is so moving and surprising; the place is at once nothing, a wreck, a pile of junk, and yet at the same time the false vision remains as true as what's before his eyes. We may go away totally denied and defeated, but our capacity for belief remains, even the evidence of our actual sight fails to kill it: '*La luna está vertiendo* . . . The moon is shedding / its clear light of dreams / that silver the windows.' The capacity to dream is limitless."

Hardie shook his head and clasped his small, delicate hands before him on the table. From the other room Antonio could be heard howling with laughter over some incident from "I Love Lucy," a local favorite. "I hate to say this, Phil, but you're beginning to sound like a Spaniard."

I translated one more poem by Machado, "Amencer De Otoño" ("Autumn Begins"), but this time showed it to no one. When our sons' Christmas break came we went south to the great cities of Andalusia. On the way there we passed through the small town of Lorca, the first of the so-called "white towns" we'd seen. At noon we parked in the center of the town and walked around buying bread, cheese, salami, and wine. I knew it was not the home of García Lorca, but nonetheless I felt it was a place of poetry. Going west from Alicante on the way to Granada we passed close to the birthplace of Miguel Hernandez; back then he was only a name to me, though before the next year ended I discovered his amazing poems and failed to translate them with grace or accuracy and so joined all his other translators. We found the Alhambra on a clear, cold afternoon, the courtyard of stone dogs, the great floating vista from the battlements. In Sevilla we stayed at the worst hotel in the world, all five of us for $1.60, and when I awakened in the middle of the night I found peasants sleeping in the hallways, each on his mattress of newspapers. One small fellow, fully dressed, looked up at me, and half his face was smeared with black ink. I would never lose that image of public lies become personal affronts. There was a little balcony outside my room, and from it I looked down into the rail yards. All night the switch engines chuffed in the darkness. This was a comforting image, for I had worked a year in the rail yards behind the Michigan Central Terminal a few blocks from Tiger Stadium.

The next day in Córdoba I was walking in the brightness of noon with Teddy, and we were speaking Spanish for the practice of it. A man, dressed in suit and tie and also with a small boy, approached me and asked if I was Catalan. He was quite sure my accent was Catalan. I said I was, and we shook hands and exchanged a few words, for this was New Year's Day, and the whole city was in a festive mood. To be in Córdoba with the sun shining on New Year's Day, I thought, what else does one need to know one is blessed. Teddy asked me why I had lied to the man and said I was Catalan. I told him that I hadn't wanted to shame the man in front of his son and tell him he was eight thousand miles off target. I reminded him what a man on the Gran Via in Barcelona had said to me, a perfect stranger who had interrupted a similar conversation to tell me not to speak Spanish to my son because I'd only ruin his perfect accent. "Look how considerate this man was even if he didn't know what he was talking about," and we laughed at the recollection of the earlier event.

I thought that perhaps Sr. Rusiñol had not been lying and my accent wasn't bad and that people actually took me for a Catalan. People were always coming up to me on the streets in Barcelona and speaking to me in Catalan, and when I answered them in Spanish as best I could, they would apologize. When I told this to Sr. Rusiñol, he had said again that I looked Catalan, and now that my clothes were from Spain it was natural for people to assume I was one of them. I had asked what he meant when he'd said I look Catalan. "We are all part Jewish," he'd said. "From your family name I assume you are Jewish, of the tribe of Levi." I nodded. "You look like one of us, fairly tall, slender, with the long face, the long slender fingers," and he'd held up his hands. "You could be my brother."

On the way back from Córdoba it began to storm. The narrow, two-lane road toward Madrid was awash and slippery. Again and again I could feel the VW give a moment, begin to slide, and then take hold. To the west the gray disk of the sun kept breaking through the clouds, and I hoped for some relief that never came. It was a Sunday, before noon, with no truck traffic on the road. Here and there we passed a solitary man on a bicycle or walking under a yellow plastic poncho. At a crossroads west of Jaén, two Guardias in leather helmets had parked their motorcycles on the shoulder. One stepped into my lane, held out a palm, and I stopped. He peered in the driver's-side window, which I rolled down. His aviator sunglasses were dotted with raindrops; rain dripped off his helmet and ran down his face.

"You are Hollanders?" he said.

"No," I said, "North Americans."

"Where are you going?"

"Jaén." I said.

He pointed toward the east and stepped back. I could hear the creaking of his heavy, wet jacket. "The road is clear, you may go," and with an impatient wave he commanded me forward.

A few miles later an old black Citröen, what my boys called a gangster car, had stopped in my lane facing me. I slowed almost to a stop. Two men were peering under the hood. One straightened up, placed his hands at the small of his back, and stretched as though in pain. Before diving in again to his labors, he turned and gave us a broad smile from under his black fedora.

"Jaén is where Machado lived much of his adult life," I said to my wife. "I'd like to stop there." From the backseat Teddy asked if we were going to find the hillside where he'd been shot. No, I told him, Machado had not been shot. He had simply lived here and taught high school French, lived alone after his young wife died. "He was a humble man," I said, "He just taught and wrote. I doubt his students or neighbors knew he was a great poet."

"If you don't ask someone where the hillside is, you're never going to find it. You should ask that Guardia; they know everything."

"I can't ask the Guardia. They were probably the ones who shot him. And that was Lorca back in Granada."

"All we do is drive up and down country roads in the rain," Teddy said to no one in particular, "looking for a good hillside to shoot someone. Up and down the roads. And we don't ask anyone."

In Bailén, due north of Jaén, the rain was coming down in such great sheets I could barely see to drive. I pulled over and parked. We sat while the roof drummed on and on. A thick-bodied woman in black wearing a gray apron splashed by as best she could in her felt carpet slippers. We made a clumsy dash for the doorway of a bar. Inside the place seemed to be swimming in its own mild drizzle. At the far end three men sat playing a game with tiles; a naked bulb hung over their heads casting a faint greenish light.

"Can I be of service?" said a bartender who suddenly appeared from nowhere. I shook out my raincoat and hung it from a peg on the wall. I cleaned my glasses, and the place came to order. We asked for ham and cheese sandwiches and orange sodas for John and Teddy. Fran had a coffee, and Mark and I had red wine. "This is Sunday weather," said the bartender. "For several hundred years it has rained every Sunday."

We did not turn south toward Jaén. The bartender assured us the rain was heavier there on Sundays, and the cathedral, though very old and sacred, was shabby. "Part of the roof is missing, and on Sundays everyone gets soaked. It is the capital," he said, "so it has many courthouses and a *plaza de toros*." By now I was not sure if Machado lived in the province of Jaén or the town. I had the impression he'd lived in a small village, one he could walk to the edge of on spring afternoons when his classes were over. It may even have been here in Bailén, which ended so abruptly that we were instantly in the country driving between plowed fields that turned their brilliant red earth toward the grim sky.

La Mancha was more of the same, though the earth turned brown and then farther north a dull gray. The white cities vanished, replaced by unwalled towns the color of mud that seemed to hold their breath against the weather. Just south of Valdepeñas a solitary hunter with an air rifle slung across his shoulder waved at us from a field of stubble. "Wouldn't it be great to see Toledo under this sky?" I said. "It's pure El Greco." From the backseat Teddy said, "Pop, you wouldn't do that to us." Discouraged by the rain, I turned east and headed for the coast.

In a seaside village just north of Valencia, Fran and I took a long walk after dinner in the clear balmy air. It had been a brilliant afternoon when we'd arrived, the promenades thick with families out for their Sunday strolls, and all five of us had joined them, glad to be uncooped from the car. Catalans would tell you that this was part of their world, but the people had a southern gaiety that the Barcelonese usually lacked. Returning to the hotel, we found Teddy asleep in our bed. We unfurled the huge road map of Spain and retraced that day's course east from Córdoba, north to La Mancha, and then east again over the mountains to Valencia. "We can make it home tomorrow easily," I said.

From the bed Teddy mumbled, without opening his eyes, "That's our vacation. We get in the car and drive, drive, drive, and then stop and take pictures of the church, and get back in and drive, drive, drive."

"You left out the part about getting wet," I said.

"I left out the part about getting wet," he said.

Sr. Rusiñol had never seen the great jewels of the south, Granada, Sevilla, and Córdoba. The *estranjeros* saw much more of Spain than most Spaniards, who rarely travelled in their own country. The farthest he had ever been from home had been a few visits back to what he called "French Catalunya" to see relatives and friends of the family who had chosen not to return to Spain or whose political activity before or during the Civil War made it impossible. (The Franco government did not declare a general amnesty until 1969, thirty years after the surrender of the Republic.) I described the magnificence of the Alhambra. I described the ancient quarter that climbed the great hill with its narrow streets with their channels of running water that added a strange and constant music to the place. He had read much about the beauty of the city and of Sevilla, with its stunning antiquities. I neglected to tell him how we had passed the famous Ghiralda without stopping, believing it so ordinary it could not be the place. Nor did I mention our hours in the Jewish quarter, huddled in doorways in a vain attempt to stay dry. I spoke instead of the great sadness of the railroad station, of the solitary soldier who sat there alone in the late afternoon waiting for the train for home, a train I was sure would never come. Outside the light was falling; it would soon be New Year's Eve, and sitting there alone in the great station, he became for me a symbol of my own distance from the life I knew. I spoke of the mean little hotel we'd stayed at, and how standing on the balcony outside my room I'd made the mistake of looking in the window of the room next door and there saw a soldier in bed with a woman. Her garments were scattered across the floor; his rifle leaned against the door. In a moment this had registered on my memory, and I was certain it would remain forever. I had turned away and tried to imagine the care with which he had slowly and precisely dressed the chair and placed his boots at the foot of it.

And Córdoba, what had I thought of her? he wanted to know. I spoke of the great mosque now converted into a Catholic house of worship: how on the outside it had seemed like nothing, a sort of dun-colored warehouse, but when we entered, it had exploded in a maze of brilliant marble arches, and how on that Sunday, the first Sunday of the new year, the chorus of children's voices had floated ethereally from the baroque Catholic corner, and how my wife and I had merely stood for half an hour in awed silence.

Then I spoke of the ride home and how we had stopped so near the former home of Machado. "No," he said, "Machado lived neither in Jaén or Bailén but in Baeza, a village east of the city of Jaén though in the province of Jaén." It was, he had read, a very ancient mountain village, and probably nothing like the hideous mercantile, rain-swept Bailén. "You can feel the beauty and dignity of Baeza in his poems," but it was of course "cold Soria" which had at first been the most inspiring landscape of his life. It was there he had lived with his young bride before she died, and it was from Soria he had fled to save his sanity. I asked if I'd been near Soria. "No, Soria is in the north, in Castile, on the banks of the Duero. That is the landscape of his greatest poems." He began to recite from memory, *"Yo voy soñando caminos / de la tarde"* until he completed this famous poem. "Even after he had left he still dreamed of walking those roads in the afternoon. Always I see him walking 'among the golden hills, the green pine trees, the dusty live-oaks' and asking where the road leads. In my mind I hear the wind stirring in the trees along the river. We know the beauty and sadness of the Duero from his poems." He took my notebook and drew a rough outline of the Iberian peninsula; then he marked a city, and said, "It is in that cold land that Soria sleeps."

"Sleeps?" I said.

Yes, it slept, for that is how Machado presented it. He knew that region only through the poems of Machado. In one poem even the stones seemed to be dreaming. "What happened to you on the balcony of the hotel in Sevilla: that is what took place in the soul of Machado." He had suddenly switched to English. The light was failing outside, though the days were growing longer. Sitting across from me, his back to the window, Sr. Rusiñol was only a dark presence whose features I could no longer make out, but the voice went on. "Anyone who writes poetry knows that experience you spoke of, and no one knew it better than Machado. At the end of his great poem 'Fields of Soria' he writes of that world, 'You have settled in my soul,' and then he asks, 'or were you there from the start?' At such moments it is impossible to believe that who you are and what you behold are not one and the same. Do you know what I mean?"

Yes, of course I knew what he meant, but I had been surprised on that balcony because I did not expect the experience in so foreign a place.

"Nothing is foreign," he said, and offered no explanation.

He flicked on a small light over his desk, which I suddenly noticed was devoid of its usual clutter of books and papers. By my watch I saw it was past five, and so I rose to end our lesson, but Sr. Rusiñol gestured for me to be seated again. He bowed his head and spoke quietly. "I must tell you that I am going away, and so for a while these lessons must come to an end. I have enjoyed them very much. I will miss our discussions of your poets and ours, but in truth I do not think you require any more lessons. You speak Spanish now with great facility." I'm sure even in the dim light he could see my surprise. "It is not critical, this going away, it is merely a duty I must perform. We will meet again." And now he rose, and as I rose he hugged me in the traditional Spanish abrazo. I reminded him that I still had his copy of *Spanish Made Simple*. "Please keep it as a memento of these hours," he said, and he saw me downstairs and out into the soft evening air. I never saw him again.

The Castelldefels I knew is gone. Barcelona came out to meet it, and it's now a suburb of over forty thousand souls, many of them housed in hideous cement high-rises. It has joined the modern world and possesses its own traffic jams, drug merchants, and topless bars. The train still comes in every two hours from Gavá, but even on a Sunday morning in June it's not crowded with picnickers, maybe because the beach is oil-smeared and the truck traffic has fouled the air. The little tobacco store that sold stationery and pens is no longer there, or if it is I couldn't find it, though I did find my *torres* and learned from the new Dutch agent I could rent one like it for $1,500 a month, American. Hans Breen retired, and after all his years of wandering went back to Holland to settle down. The elder Rusiñol's garage has become a new car agency and flogs VWs manufactured in Spain. At the bakery I learned the Rusiñols were long gone, and no one I talked to remembered the poet.

Perhaps that is why when my old friend José Elgorriaga asked me to help him translate Machado, I agreed to do so. I knew it could not be done, I argued against the venture, I insisted my style as a poet was all wrong, but my friend only agreed. Everything I said was true, but he needed the help of a poet, and I was the poet he had. He handed me a sheaf of Xeroxed copies of his favorite poems that almost disappeared in the spiderwebs of his notes and with them yellow-lined sheets with trots in English. And then he sat me down and read me the poems in his beautiful Castillian Spanish, occasionally rising in the dusty center of his tiny campus office to declaim a passage that moved his soul with its beauty. I had not witnessed such love of Spanish poetry since the departure of my Catalan friend.

Have you ever been moved in the soul? I know that is a ridiculous question, but I ask it because much of my life I didn't know such a thing was possible. I grew up with no concept of the soul, and when the conversation turns to the nature of the soul I will remain at sea forever. As a young Jew I prayed, but never for my immortal soul, and as an older Jew I never prayed at all. (In a recent poem entitled "Soul," I recount a true tale in which a Mrs. Morton made my brother Eddie and me go down on our knees and recite for company the prayer that should we die before we wake God would take our souls. We found the spectacle so appalling that no threat of punishment could ever induce us to repeat it. We were saved when my mother caught Mrs. Morton stealing her jewelry, and she was sent "packing—with no references—into the larger Christian world.") As solitary observer and memorializer of the Castillian landscape, Antonio Machado is often moved in the soul. He tells us again and again without the least reserve, he tells us with such simplicity and clarity we come to believe him absolutely, and in doing so we come to understand our own deepest experiences and to believe entirely in their authenticity. It is hard to imagine a more useful poetry.

In Machado's poems nothing hurries, for the world has been as it is for centuries, though of course it constantly changes so that it can return to what it was. "Mounted on small brown donkeys," he writes, "the travelers are lost from sight / where the roads drop below / the rolling hills, though now they rise / in the distance of afternoon, tiny painted figures / that stain the blazing canvas of dusk." We could be in ancient Chinese poetry or traveling with Yeats's figures carved in lapis lazuli. When "the wind stirs in the river poplars" you know that once again this autumn the dry leaves will deliver their ageless "chant to the water's song." Yesterday the branches "bent to the weight of nightingales" and tomorrow "the scented winds of spring will hum through the branches." All time is one time in the soul of Antonio Machado, and there is a time for everything. The world whirling in its endless dance of time does so with a poise and dignity our lives lack—or lack until we read Machado, until we pour ourselves into his poetry and he in turn pours his vision into us. The inner landscape of his heart is a "city in ruins," his Soria, and viewing it each day the "heart deepens with sadness," a sadness—as he says—"like love." He looks out over this world—I suppose his contemporary in English poetry might say he "gazes" out over this world—and he sees it as it is and at the same time as it has been for centuries, for to him nothing has changed except that it all lives in time and so is never the same. The whole history of Castile is the history of Machado, an empire gone to ruins, and the moment which is his life, the lasting moment he lives and relives, becomes the place itself. Think of being the very world you behold, of having been that world since time began, think of the present moment stretching back to no beginning and forward to no ending, and you too might say, "Fields of Soria / where the stones seem to be dreaming, / you go with me."

Think of being a world of country trails, meadows, outcroppings of rock, fields of brambles, thorns, thistles, briars, burdocks, bees and their honeycombs, jackdaws, sheep. Think of the roads closed in snow, the high frigid winter plains of Castile rife with the memories of a Spanish empire long lost, the towns with their collapsing churches, stone fountains, belfries, the houses with their rusty gates and barred windows. From his Andalusian days the water wheel turns like a clock, the nightingale sings in the dark, water runs in troughs to the music of time. Where there is a tool it is an axe, where there is food it is dark bread, where there is perfume it is the lemon tree in blossom, where there is a weapon it is the crossbow, where there is music there is a lyre. Logs smoulder on the hearth, an old man wrapped in wool shudders by the fire, his woman sews, and the lost son never returns.

And they go on waiting, for the lesson of this great maestro—he taught far more than high school French—is patience, the greatest lesson the poet can learn, for without it he or she is subject to every corrupting influence. Impatience is our nightmare. As Kafka wrote, "There are two main human sins from which all the others derive: impatience and indolence. It was because of impatience that they were expelled from Paradise; it is because of indolence they do not return. Yet perhaps there is only one major sin: impatience. Because of impatience they were expelled, because of impatience they do not return." Reading and rereading the poems of Machado it becomes impossible to believe even a single poem was rushed into being or hurried toward some form of completion. Consider this: I am writing about one of my contemporaries.

I delight to imagine Machado at his evening walk. The world comes to him whether he is on the cold roads of Soria or in a mountain town of Andalusia. A river comes into view curved like a crossbow, the boughs of the plane trees bend to the weight of bees, the wind stirs in the long grasses at the edges of sight where a few travellers appear over the green mounds of the distant hills; they speak back and forth in a language as soft as water overflowing cisterns; the rocks empurpled in the dusk dream in eternity. The air deepens and stills in the fields; time stops. Something like a vision rises in the golden dust of sunset, a vision of a world sweet enough to welcome the human heart freed from vanity and greed. I delight to imagine Antonio Machado alive in a world of others as good as he, a world as glorious as the simple language he found to create it.

# Flight Home[1]

## (1958)

### W.S. Merwin

*(In August 1956, Merwin flew home after seven years in Europe. The notes that follow are taken from a journal he kept at the time.)*

## Aug. 27, 1956, a barber shop in St. John's Wood

They say that after seven years every cell in your body has changed. You are a different person.

I wish I could remember what day it was, in July, 1949, that I landed in Genoa. Or the day (one or two days before?) when we first came in sight of the Spanish coast.

Strange, now I am going back, to think that I have been in Europe without a break, ever since I was a minor. Ever since I was twenty-one.

On the chart one does not see the long line of wanting to go back.

---

1. "Flight Home" first appeared in *Paris Review*.

   Editor's Note: W.S. Merwin, "Flight Home" from *Regions of Memory: Uncollected Prose 1949–1982* (Urbana: University of Illinois Press, 1987).

Beginning in my case before I set out, and rising through delight and hostility and wonder and everything that has been the experience of Europe. The line rising clear off the chart at last and stabbing into the air above it, without footing, but without coming down, for how many years now?

Part of the confusion, once the desire to go back got off the chart, arose from the suspicion that this was simply, at least in part, the first shock of maturity: a realization that home, where you grew up and belonged— belonged with and without your own volition—no longer exists. The desire to return to it, the moment you know it no longer exists. I had been away long enough, and surrounded by Europeans thoroughly enough, to get these mixed up. European friends wondering, as they say, what I will make of it. Probably nothing at all. Wishing, they say, that they could be here, like a fly on the wall, to watch, when I get back. How can I explain that I do not want to go back in order to form opinions. That, unless I am very wrong, opinions will have nearly nothing to do with the main thing of being back. Home is a place that does not exist, about which your opinions are irrelevant.

## Aug. 27, 1956, 11:30 p.m., PAA Clipper Carib

It is nearly impossible, afterwards, to remember at what point I began to believe that I was really going. Believing comes elusively, not when you expect, most often, but both earlier and later, only gradually filling in the place where it will be. Unpredictable, like a season changing.

It would come over me all at once that I was, say, sitting in that barber's chair for the last time before I went. It would take the imagination by shock. The next minute I didn't believe it at all. I was sure I'd go on and have the next haircut in that same chair (with the barber who'd learned what I enjoyed was not having him talk to me, but having him carry on animated conversation with other customers, to which I could listen), and the one after that, and the one after that. When I got around to having haircuts at all. Somewhere else in the mind the imagination suddenly looks down the long vistas of time where one will not walk. The possible lives that one will not lead.

And twenty-four hours before I was due to go, when everything was reminding me that it was happening for the last time—a rhythm that had gathered speed until it was unbroken—I would find myself going through the motions of the place's most familiar habits, and not be able to believe.

I was sure I was going in a thin way like a hum in your ears, yesterday, as the desk gradually grew bare and everything in the study was either packed or put away. Not feeling anything about it but a certain emptiness independent of the emptying room; but sure. Feelings? I suppose they were there, after all, but like beasts patient as immigrants, waiting to move in on the emptiness when their time came.

And sure yesterday as my key case kept getting lighter, and the keys one by one were used for the last time and then packed in intelligent places where I will never be able to find them again.

Then with all but a few things done, except things that could wait till the last minute, or things that would take too long anyway and must be abandoned, suddenly finding that everything was ready. And time all at once was heavy. Between the intense activity of getting ready, and the farewells and rush of getting off, time was heavy. More so not because I was anxious to go. I'd forgotten that, days before. A week ago. But because of all reasons I did *not* want to go. Wanted not to be going, but since I was going wanted to be gone. How different from most times when I've been going somewhere, thinking almost entirely of where I was going, savoring the whole trip, from the moment I was ready to go. Different entirely from when I left America, for I didn't know how long, seven years ago. Even though a great part of me wanted to stay in America then, and even had an array of reasons. (Why go to Europe when I knew so little of America?) I know just how much and in what ways I'm fond of

Europe, but I didn't know what I felt about America. I regretted leaving, before I had even gone, but I didn't know what I'd really miss until I'd been away for some time. Foreign places, however familiar, defining your feeling about home. But stay away too long and you're bound to confuse that with homesickness. (Which I never in my life felt, except in the mildest ways, until these last few years. Unprepared for it.)

The lassitude that descended, in that pause of an hour or so between the end of getting ready, and the time to go. Not calling the taxi, after all, until almost too late. That dazed lassitude that does not believe in time; or, at the moments when it has to countenance the minutes' passing, panics, and protests, protests, flailing in molasses, shouting under water: "Not today, no, not today." But dazed, languorous, just the same. The lassitude hand in hand with the emotions themselves of good-bye. And they, together, swelling the occasion with their heavy, bewildered, helpless dumbness. The daze still there (like the feeling when you have been in a pub for several hours at lunchtime, and suddenly find yourself out in the sunshine, alone) in the taxi, all the way to the air terminal. Feeling bulky and clumsy, as though your ears had just stopped ringing. The traffic so heavy that the taxi barely made it in time; the excitement of almost missing the bus to the airport, rising through the numbness of departure, and I was grateful for it.

Odd that passing sense of panic that wants to put it off till tomorrow, that hangs around and wants to go all right, but not today; trying to jump back into yesterday. A feeling that can, in the end, find nothing to focus on, and no grounds for itself. Maybe just an intensification of the familiar conviction (when going out to the theater, or leaving a hotel room) that you are leaving something vital behind. As, of course, you always are.

In the rush at the air terminal, again almost missing the bus. Never having felt any departure so contradictorily, I was never before so aware of the way the efficient bustle, the professional voices on loudspeakers, the assembly line rounding up and processing of passengers, resembles the ward-walking manner of nurses. Admirably impersonal. Cheery. For the benefit of everybody especially, designed to brisk, shame, and cozy you along. I've always found this amusing, a tiny bit irritating (making me want to ask them stupid questions and delay everything, and see just how long everything could be made to wait, just how elastic it could all be), and rather pleasant. And this time I wished it wouldn't all rush through so fast, so that I could have a chance to watch the effects of the helpful manner on the other passengers, especially those who were parting at the air terminal itself. (My incurable vulgar curiosity.) Partly to get away from too clinging a concern with my own departure and what I was leaving.

But in England, up to the very last, there's always the weather to concern you. The morning had been overcast and rainy, but as the taxi drove away the sun came out. And the airport bus was stuffy and hot, turtling through the Kensington and Hammersmith traffic in the sunny muggy London late afternoon. The sort of weather that would have women swanning up and down Knightsbridge, and the London shopkeepers and charwomen groaning. A nice summer day, or a bit of one. One of the Bright Periods whose Second Coming the London papers will mendaciously prophesy for months to come. The few English people in the bus quietly sweltering in their dark inconspicuous tweeds (one splendid man with a white mustache and a dirty gabardine raincoat on over his) and the many Americans peeling off their conspicuous pressed, newly bought-in-England woolens. Two collegiate characters, each just twelve pounds overweight, in white shirts, talking seriously about expansion of some kind, somewhere in Connecticut. A glum, brown-dressed, green-faced thin, young New Yorker next to me, filling his embarcation card with that particular expression of unimpressionable, slightly sour-natured boredom which is peculiarly New York. Two ugly girls from Baltimore talking to a handsome woman from further south, up ahead of me. Several South Americans, Brazilians. A collection of Turks, and one family with Turkish diplomatic passports. A group of American Greeks going back to Greece, with the accent of the mother country, the intonation of my country, driving through England.

England, where nearly all intonations of the language except the few variants of what they call "standard English," tend to be considered comic, or ugly and undesirable if you have to take them seriously. A system which, I can see, is good for acting, but strikes me as deadly in most other ways. About as healthy for writing, I should think, as the French deliberate limitation of their literary vocabulary was for French poetry. Socially handy, it seems. This preoccupation with class distinction which no longer means much. A preoccupation which, after five years off and on in England, I still find as foreign as sampans. Continuous effort and argument with myself, not to find this amount of preoccupation with class distinctions more than a little vulgar. In a way which, to me, looks sterile. Probably this is a case, among so many, where the illusion that we speak the same language registers against my ability to understand.

When we got to the airport the day had gone dark with clouds; there was a raw wind, and the rain had started again. There must have been several inches of water in some places on the tarmac. Rain sweeping over the wings of the waiting planes. The big planes taxiing around on the wet runway, and the rain and real wind skating across it in goose-flesh streaks like flaws rushing across mica. The slipstreams of the planes tore up long plumes of spray, the water streaking out flat and whipping away like grass does out on the airfield. The engines, idling or warming up, actually bared and dried the tarmac, for a second, just in back of the wings. And when a plane would take off, as one did right in front of us, the water on the tarmac would lie gashed and open for a moment, bared over a bone, and then flow back hesitantly to fill the place and smooth it over, after the plane was airborne, just as it would have over a ship that had sunk. The genies of controlled violence reminding you that the control is artificial, that they're all one family and never forget each other and that two-thirds of the world is violence.

With everything so organized and sterilized and herded and heated and air-conditioned, it seemed strange that one should be walking in real rain, even for a minute. The taxiing around the airport, that always robs me of the last shred of my sense of direction, wherever I am, as though you had to be robbed of that before you could be hurled straight toward your destination as the crow flies. The houses and allotments around the airport turning and turning. You have to be dizzied, after being robbed of volition; be the Blind Man. The voices in the plane coming from far away, as through the sleep of a child, over the noise of the engines; the pressure of everything seeming to build up in the plane. Wanting to sing, as always, when the engines, one by one, were gunned and roared, at the end of the runway before the takeoff, and the plane shook itself free of the ground. As excited as a child, as always, by the takeoff. And at the same time, this time, suddenly caught in an immense depression, as though all the dead weight of the lassitude of an hour, two hours, before, had fallen on me at once, and was carrying me down. As the plane rushed down the runway and the wedge between us and the ground widened, and the line of houses streaked by, I had a distinct impression of a cloth being violently torn. I would have rushed out of the plane that minute, had it been still; or have been tempted to. And back onto it, the moment my feet touched the ground.

England looked soaked, sodden, from the air. Whole fields lying under water. The standing water in sheets of glassy gray, no color, white, no color; showing the contours of all the hollows and low patches. As though a sheet of some sort of metal had been slid through the land. The ponds looking higher than their banks, and the Thames looking as though it lay on top of the countryside. Landscape and sky all lights and shades of gray, in every direction. Even the sunlight gray and laden with rain: pregnant. The sky dark with tons and tons of water as we flew toward Wales; and the towns beneath looking as if they had never been dry.

A nun looking like an albino buffalo with dyspepsia had got on at London, with another of her cloth, and I with my superstitions had to keep my fingers crossed all the way to Catholic Shannon because where could I find two dogs on an airplane to cancel the nuns? Though we were flying over towns full of Englishmen all loving dogs as Americans are supposed to love their mothers.

We were in and out of long feathers of black cloud, over Wales; after dusk with the lights on in the towns, but the dark not final yet, and the coast of Wales clear and sharp as we flew over.

Next to me a young thin Jewish doctor, my age, from Philadelphia, who has been all over Europe as surgeon to a traveling Black basketball team.

He has been to see his grandfather's four ancient sisters in Liverpool but I have been able to extract few details from him other than their ages (69, 72, 78, 82), the fact that two of them are almost blind, and that they are too old to cry. This last seems to be quite a drawback, since although they had never seen him before they apparently all wanted to cry as soon as they knew he was there, their brother's son whom they thought they'd never live to see; and it seems they were all of them pretty choked up as long as he was there. But enjoyed it, if he is any indication. Probably quite genuinely glad to see each other...

Cloud over Ireland until we got to the west. And then the low-running hills looking green as in the storybooks, in the almost dark dusk. Long pennons of water winding in from the coast, with lights along them, and everything low. We came in over water.

And Shannon was better than I could have hoped. The low, dark green buildings, temporary and whorish. The feeling that they'd sell you their genuine Machree grandmother if you expressed an interest in such baggages and had the green money. People lined up ten deep at the liquor counter, buying the limit. Watches, perfumes, Irish linens and tweeds, pipes, souvenirs of olde Erin impossibly clean and already looking like the belongings of tourists. A long waiting room with asbestos walls, where fifty travelers sprawled and smoked and drank and sat guard over packages and looked as dejected as though they had just learned they were going to live there. None of them seemed to be speaking to each other. Loudspeakers in the walls asking for Father O'Brien every two minutes, or if not Father O'Brien, Father Malloy. We were led into a dull supper of thumb soup with pretensions to mushrooms and flannel beef.

Taking off from Shannon, we had a searchlight beam on us, and the light in the propellers made big, slow-widening spirals of light, with spirals of shadow inside them that spread outward from the propeller shafts. Like those tops I had as a child, where the colors melted outward as the top spun.

## 12:35 a.m. London time

I wonder whether it is raining in London. Probably. I wonder whether the rags that I left in the attic joists won't get too heavy in the ceiling and bring it down with a sodden crash all over the floor.

The Dipper is as bright as I remember it in Spain, just outside the window. A regatta of little triangular clouds, far below, as we fly west. And one great mountainous cloud which we have just flown through had a long promontory which ran out into nothing, and made me feel vertigo for the cloud. I remember seeing a promontory in Majorca, on a day so still that its reflection in the sea was as sharp and clear as its own shape; they made a single shape running out into the colorless sea that looked like a sky, and it seemed they must certainly fall. And that first summer in France, the day when I swam out into the Mediterranean trying out a pair of underwater goggles, which I'd never worn before. Warm with pleasure at the first long view of the jagged seafloor shifting with light and blue shadows. Fish, fronds, sea anemones, swimmers, and sliders and weeds washing. The pocked snags and sloping ridges maybe thirty or forty feet below me as I rocked and swayed and swam out. They deepened a little and then rose toward the surface again, a hundred feet out. And then suddenly ended. The sharp edge dropped off into dark blue nothing, in which occasionally a tiny fin would flash light for a second. I was out over nothing at all, and it felt cold, and nowhere but in my dreams had I ever known such vertigo.

Every time you leave it is the last time.

Even if passionately addicted to talking about myself, how difficult it would have been to explain to friends in England (and to some Americans) this thing of *not expecting anything* from going back. I know things have changed. I know too that, as I've felt it all receding from me, I've made it up, invented it. I knew at the time that I was doing it.

I don't expect to be disappointed at finding that my invention was false, that the place isn't like that at all, that even the things I never liked, and remember disliking, have changed. I expect to be immensely relieved to be able to abandon the fiction entirely, and let the real thing take over. Because the real fiction was a fence to keep people away from what of America I felt I had managed to hang on to. And I was aware that it would end by keeping me away from it too. I look forward to being able to admit to an honest dislike of something right there and my own. A thing that I've hardly allowed myself to do for months, not because I was concerned with anyone's opinions, but because of a fear that such admission might push the smallest detail of home, even an unpleasant one (especially an unpleasant one) further away from me. But remembering, in private as deliberately as anything else, sordor, squalor, waste, ugliness, injustice. One thing I do not expect is to respond to the place simply, with delight, or admiration, or repulsion, as I do in Europe. Not one feeling at a time. But several of them or all of them, all me, at once.

I have loathed that fiction, and myself for fostering it. Like finding oneself insisting that the person one loved was pretty. Finding myself betraying everything, out of my desire not to betray it. Only let me waste no time now even for penance. It redresses nothing, least of all balance. Let me find instead a hard eye.

I don't think that Europeans get the same sort of passion for home. Generations and generations having worked out a way of regarding the place, taught them where to fix the feeling, what to see and how to communicate with it. And just the confidence which must come from the awareness that it all has been there so long already. And allow themselves even nostalgia without so much danger of sentimentality running riot. They can do it all more gently, more gracefully. Two qualities that we, quite often, must manage without.

I suppose it would be simpler to say that they have loved their place for generations, centuries; and know it, without having to make a fuss about it. Whereas, by comparison, we begin as a loveless people. Generation after generation having cared little for the place. Our fathers began by caring little enough about Europe so that they could leave it. We've used the place, wasted it. It has made us prodigal, restless. And we are attached to it in still-raw ways that we aren't aware of, most often. We ought to know that we couldn't hate it as fiercely as we do sometimes without there being something honest in our attachment to it. But there is always the sense of surprise, of inarticulate awkwardness, at discovering that the name for what you feel is love.

The black sea down there doesn't even need sleep, all the way to Labrador; and the night is splendid, and above it all.

# The Antilles: Fragments of Epic Memory[1]

## Nobel Lecture, December 7, 1992

*Derek Walcott*

Felicity is a village in Trinidad on the edge of the Caroni plain, the wide central plain that still grows sugar and to which indentured cane cutters were brought after emancipation, so the small population of Felicity is East Indian, and on the afternoon that I visited it with friends from America, all the faces along its road were Indian, which, as I hope to show, was a moving, beautiful thing, because this Saturday afternoon *Ramleela*, the epic dramatization of the Hindu epic the *Ramayana*, was going to be performed, and the costumed actors from the village were assembling on a field strung with different-coloured flags, like a new gas station, and beautiful Indian boys in red and black were aiming arrows haphazardly into the afternoon light. Low blue mountains on the horizon, bright grass, clouds that would gather colour before the light went. Felicity! What a gentle Anglo-Saxon name for an epical memory.

Under an open shed on the edge of the field, there were two huge

---

1. Derek Walcott, "The Antilles: Fragments of Epic Memory" (Nobel Lecture, 1992). Later collected in *What the Twilight Says* (New York: Farrar, Straus and Giroux, 1998).

armatures of bamboo that looked like immense cages. They were parts of the body of a god, his calves or thighs, which, fitted and reared, would make a gigantic effigy. This effigy would be burnt as a conclusion to the epic. The cane structures flashed a predictable parallel: Shelley's sonnet on the fallen statue of Ozymandias and his empire, that "colossal wreck" in its empty desert.

Drummers had lit a fire in the shed and they eased the skins of their tablas nearer the flames to tighten them. The saffron flames, the bright grass, and the hand-woven armatures of the fragmented god who would be burnt were not in any desert where imperial power had finally toppled but were part of a ritual, evergreen season that, like the cane-burning harvest, is annually repeated, the point of such sacrifice being its repetition, the point of the destruction being renewal through fire.

Deities were entering the field. What we generally call "Indian music" was blaring from the open platformed shed from which the epic would be narrated. Costumed actors were arriving. Princes and gods, I supposed. What an unfortunate confession! "Gods, I suppose" is the shrug that embodies our African and Asian diasporas. I had often thought of but never seen *Ramleela*, and had never seen this theatre, an open field, with village children as warriors, princes, and gods. I had no idea what the epic story was, who its hero was, what enemies he fought, yet I had recently adapted the *Odyssey* for a theatre in England, presuming that the audience knew the trials of Odysseus, hero of another Asia Minor epic, while nobody in Trinidad knew any more than I did about Rama, Kali, Shiva, Vishnu, apart from the Indians, a phrase I use pervertedly because that is the kind of remark you can still hear in Trinidad: "apart from the Indians."

It was as if, on the edge of the Central Plain, there was another plateau, a raft on which the *Ramayana* would be poorly performed in this ocean of cane, but that was my writer's view of things, and it is wrong. I was seeing the *Ramleela* at Felicity as theatre when it was faith.

Multiply that moment of self-conviction when an actor, made-up and costumed, nods to his mirror before stopping on stage in the belief that he is a reality entering an illusion and you would have what I presumed was happening to the actors of this epic. But they were not actors. They had been chosen; or they themselves had chosen their roles in this sacred story that would go on for nine afternoons over a two-hour period till the sun set. They were not amateurs but believers. There was no theatrical term to define them. They did not have to psych themselves up to play their roles. Their acting would probably be as buoyant and as natural as those bamboo arrows crisscrossing the afternoon pasture. They believed in what they were playing, in the sacredness of the text, the validity of India, while I, out of the writer's habit, searched for some sense of elegy, of loss, even of degenerative mimicry in the happy faces of the boy-warriors or the heraldic profiles of the village princes. I was polluting the afternoon with doubt and with the patronage of admiration. I misread the event through a visual echo of History—the cane fields, indenture, the evocation of vanished armies, temples, and trumpeting elephants—when all around me there was quite the opposite: elation, delight in the boys' screams, in the sweets-stalls, in more and more costumed characters appearing; a delight of conviction, not loss. The name Felicity made sense.

Consider the scale of Asia reduced to these fragments: the small white exclamations of minarets or the stone balls of temples in the cane fields, and one can understand the self-mockery and embarrassment of those who see these rites as parodic, even degenerate. These purists look on such ceremonies as grammarians look at a dialect, as cities look on provinces and empires on their colonies. Memory that yearns to join the centre, a limb remembering the body from which it has been severed, like those bamboo thighs of the god. In other words, the way that the Caribbean is still looked at, illegitimate, rootless, mongrelized. "No people there," to quote Froude, "in the true sense of the word." No people. Fragments and echoes of real people, unoriginal and broken.

The performance was like a dialect, a branch of its original language, an abridgement of it, but not a distortion or even a reduction of its epic scale. Here in Trinidad I had discovered that one of the greatest epics of the world was seasonally performed, not with that desperate resignation of preserving a culture, but with an openness of belief that was as steady as the wind bending the cane lances of the Caroni plain. We had to leave before the play began to go through the creeks of the Caroni Swamp, to catch the scarlet ibises coming home at dusk. In a performance as natural as those of the actors of the *Ramleela*, we watched the flocks come in as bright as the scarlet of the boy archers, as the red flags, and cover an islet until it turned into a flowering tree, an anchored immortelle. The sigh of History meant nothing here. These two visions, the *Ramleela* and the arrowing flocks of scarlet ibises, blent into a single gasp of gratitude. Visual surprise is natural in the Caribbean; it comes with the landscape, and faced with its beauty, the sigh of History dissolves.

We make too much of that long groan which underlines the past. I felt privileged to discover the ibises as well as the scarlet archers of Felicity.

The sigh of History rises over ruins, not over landscapes, and in the Antilles there are few ruins to sigh over, apart from the ruins of sugar estates and abandoned forts. Looking around slowly, as a camera would, taking in the low blue hills over Port of Spain, the village road and houses, the warrior-archers, the god-actors and their handlers, and music already on the sound track, I wanted to make a film that would be a long-drawn sigh over Felicity. I was filtering the afternoon with evocations of a lost India, but why "evocations?" Why not "celebrations of a real presence?" Why should India be "lost" when none of these villagers ever really knew it, and why not "continuing," why not the perpetuation of joy in Felicity and in all the other nouns of the Central Plain: Couva, Chaguanas, Charley Village? Why was I not letting my pleasure open its windows wide? I was enticed like any Trinidadian to the ecstasies of their claim, because ecstasy was the pitch of the sinuous drumming in the loudspeakers. I was entitled to the feast of Husein, to the mirrors and crepe-paper temples of the Muslim epic, to the Chinese Dragon Dance, to the rites of that Sephardic Jewish synagogue that was once on Something Street. I am only one-eighth the writer I might have been had I contained all the fragmented languages of Trinidad.

Break a vase, and the love that reassembles the fragments is stronger than that love which took its symmetry for granted when it was whole. The glue that fits the pieces is the sealing of its original shape. It is such a love that reassembles our African and Asiatic fragments, the cracked heirlooms whose restoration shows its white scars. This gathering of broken pieces is the care and pain of the Antilles, and if the pieces are disparate, ill-fitting, they contain more pain than their original sculpture, those icons and sacred vessels taken for granted in their ancestral places. Antillean art is this restoration of our shattered histories, our shards of vocabulary, our archipelago becoming a synonym for pieces broken off from the original continent.

And this is the exact process of the making of poetry, or what should be called not its "making" but its remaking, the fragmented memory, the armature that frames the god, even the rite that surrenders it to a final pyre; the god assembled cane by cane, reed by weaving reed, line by plaited line, as the artisans of Felicity would erect his holy echo.

Poetry, which is perfection's sweat but which must seem as fresh as the raindrops on a statue's brow, combines the natural and the marmoreal; it conjugates both tenses simultaneously: the past and the present, if the past is the sculpture and the present the beads of dew or rain on the forehead of the past. There is the buried language and there is the individual vocabulary, and the process of poetry is one of excavation and of self-discovery. Tonally the individual voice is a dialect; it shapes its own accent, its own vocabulary and melody in defiance of an imperial concept of language, the language of Ozymandias, libraries and dictionaries, law courts and critics, and churches, universities, political dogma, the diction of institutions. Poetry is an island that breaks away from the main. The dialects of my archipelago seem as fresh to me as those raindrops on the statue's forehead, not the sweat made from the classic exertion of frowning marble, but the condensations of a refreshing element, rain and salt.

Deprived of their original language, the captured and indentured tribes create their own, accreting and secreting fragments of an old, an epic vocabulary, from Asia and from Africa, but to an ancestral, an ecstatic rhythm in the blood that cannot be subdued by slavery or indenture, while nouns are renamed and the given names of places accepted like Felicity village or Choiseul. The original language dissolves from the exhaustion of distance like fog trying to cross an ocean, but this process of renaming, of finding new metaphors, is the same process that the poet faces every morning of his working day, making his own tools like Crusoe, assembling nouns from necessity, from Felicity, even renaming himself. The stripped man is driven back to that self-astonishing, elemental force, his mind. That is the basis of the Antillean experience, this shipwreck of fragments, these echoes, these shards of a huge tribal vocabulary, these partially remembered customs, and they are not decayed but strong. They survived the Middle Passage and the *Fatel Rozack*, the ship that carried the first indentured Indians from the port of Madras to the cane fields of Felicity, that carried the chained Cromwellian convict and the Sephardic Jew, the Chinese grocer and the Lebanese merchant selling cloth samples on his bicycle.

And here they are, all in a single Caribbean city, Port of Spain, the sum of history, Trollope's "non-people." A downtown babel of shop signs and streets, mongrelized, polyglot, a ferment without a history, like heaven. Because that is what such a city is, in the New World, a writer's heaven.

A culture, we all know, is made by its cities.

Another first morning home, impatient for the sunrise—a broken sleep. Darkness at five, and the drapes not worth opening; then, in the sudden light, a cream-walled, brown-roofed police station bordered with short royal palms, in the colonial style, back of it frothing trees and taller palms, a pigeon fluttering into the cover of a cave, a rain-stained block of once-modern apartments, the morning side road into the station without traffic. All part of a surprising peace. This quiet happens with every visit to a city that has deepened itself in me. The flowers and the hills are easy, affection for them predictable; it is the architecture that, for the first morning, disorients. A return from American seductions used to make the traveller feel that something was missing, something was trying to complete itself, like the stained concrete apartments. Pan left along the window and the excrescences rear—a city trying to soar, trying to be brutal, like an American city in silhouette, stamped from the same mould as Columbus or Des Moines. An assertion of power, its decor bland, its air-conditioning pitched to the point where its secretarial and executive staff sport competing cardigans; the colder the offices the more important, an imitation of another climate. A longing, even an envy of feeling cold.

In serious cities, in grey, militant winter with its short afternoons, the days seem to pass by in buttoned overcoats, every building appears as a barracks with lights on in its windows, and when snow comes, one has the illusion of living in a Russian novel, in the nineteenth century, because of the literature of winter. So visitors to the Caribbean must feel that they are inhabiting a succession of postcards. Both climates are shaped by what we have read of them. For tourists, the sunshine cannot be serious. Winter adds depth and darkness to life as well as to literature, and in the unending summer of the tropics not even poverty or poetry (in the Antilles poverty is poetry with a V, *une vie*, a condition of life as well as of imagination) seems capable of being profound because the nature around it is so exultant, so resolutely ecstatic, like its music. A culture based on joy is bound to be shallow. Sadly, to sell itself, the Caribbean encourages the delights of mindlessness, of brilliant vacuity, as a place to flee not only winter but that seriousness that comes only out of culture with four seasons. So how can there be a people there, in the true sense of the word?

They know nothing about seasons in which leaves let go of the year, in which spires fade in blizzards and streets whiten, of the erasures of whole cities by fog, of reflection in fireplaces; instead, they inhabit a geography whose rhythm, like their music, is limited to two stresses: hot and wet, sun and rain, light and shadow, day and night, the limitations of an incomplete metre, and are therefore a people incapable of the subtleties of contradiction, of imaginative complexity. So be it. We cannot change contempt.

Ours are not cities in the accepted sense, but no one wants them to be. They dictate their own proportions, their own definitions in particular places and in a prose equal to that of their detractors, so that now it is not just St. James but the streets and yards that Naipaul commemorates, its lanes as short and brilliant as his sentences; not just the noise and jostle of Tunapuna but the origins of C.L.R. James's *Beyond a Boundary*, not just Felicity village on the Caroni plain, but Selvon Country, and that is the way it goes up the islands now: the old Dominica of Jean Rhys still very much the way she wrote of it; and the Martinique of the early Césaire; Perse's Guadeloupe, even without the pith helmets and the mules; and what delight and privilege there was in watching a literature—one literature in several imperial languages, French, English, Spanish—bud and open island after island in the early morning of a culture, not timid, not derivative, any more than the hard white petals of the frangipani are derivative and timid. This is not a belligerent boast but a simple celebration of inevitability: that this flowering had to come.

On a heat-stoned afternoon in Port of Spain, some alley white with glare, with love vine spilling over a fence, palms and a hazed mountain appear around a corner to the evocation of Vaughn or Herbert's "that shady city of palm-trees," or to the memory of a Hammond organ from a wooden chapel in Castries, where the congregation sang "Jerusalem, the Golden." It is hard for me to see such emptiness as desolation. It is that patience that is the width of Antillean life, and the secret is not to ask the wrong thing of it, not to demand of it an ambition it has no interest in. The traveller reads this as lethargy, as torpor.

Here there are not enough books, one says, no theatres, no museums, simply not enough to do. Yet, deprived of books, a man must fall back on thought, and out of thought, if he can learn to order it, will come the urge to record, and in extremity, if he has no means of recording, recitation, the ordering of memory which leads to metre, to commemoration. There can be virtues in deprivation, and certainly one virtue is salvation from a cascade of high mediocrity, since books are now not so much created as remade. Cities create a culture, and all we have are these magnified market towns, so what are the proportions of the ideal Caribbean city? A surrounding, accessible countryside with leafy suburbs, and if the city is lucky, behind it, spacious plains. Behind it, fine mountains; before it, an indigo sea. Spires would pin its centre and around them would be leafy, shadowy parks. Pigeons would cross its sky in alphabetic patterns, carrying with them memories of a belief in augury, and at the heart of the city there would be horses, yes, horses, those animals last seen at the end of the nineteenth century drawing broughams and carriages with top-hatted citizens, horses that live in the present tense without elegiac echoes from their hooves, emerging from paddocks at the Queen's Park Savannah at sunrise, when mist is unthreading from the cool mountains above the roofs, and at the centre of the city seasonally there would be races, so that citizens could roar at the speed and grace of these nineteenth-century animals. Its docks, not obscured by smoke or deafened by too much machinery, and above all, it would be so racially various that the cultures of the world—the Asiatic, the Mediterranean, the European, the African—would be represented in it, its humane variety more exciting than Joyce's Dublin. Its citizens would intermarry as they chose, from instinct, not tradition, until their children find it increasingly futile to trace their genealogy. It would not have too many avenues difficult or dangerous for pedestrians, its mercantile area would be a cacophony of accents, fragments of the old language that would be silenced immediately at five o'clock, its docks resolutely vacant on Sundays.

This is Port of Spain to me, a city ideal in its commercial and human proportions, where a citizen is a walker and not a pedestrian, and this is how Athens may have been before it became a cultural echo.

The finest silhouettes of Port of Spain are idealizations of the crafts-man's handiwork, not of concrete and glass, but of baroque woodwork, each fantasy looking more like an involved drawing of itself than the actual building. Behind the city is the Caroni plain, with its villages, Indian prayer flags, and fruit vendors' stalls along the highway over which ibises come like floating flags. Photogenic poverty! Postcard sad-nesses! I am not re-creating Eden; I mean, by "the Antilles," the reality of light, of work, of survival. I mean a house on the side of a country road, I mean the Caribbean Sea, whose smell is the smell of refreshing pos-sibility as well as survival. Survival is the triumph of stubborness, and spiritual stubborness, a sublime stupidity, is what makes the occupa-tion of poetry endure, when there are so many things that should make it futile. Those things added together can go under one collective noun: "the world."

This is the visible poetry of the Antilles, then. Survival.

If you wish to understand that consoling pity with which the islands were regarded, look at the tinted engravings of Antillean forests, with their proper palm trees, ferns, and waterfalls. They have a civilizing decency, like Botanical Gardens, as if the sky were a glass ceiling under which a colonized vegetation is arranged for quiet walks and carriage rides. Those views are incised with a pathos that guides the engraver's tool and the topographer's pencil, and it is this pathos which, tenderly ironic, gave villages names like Felicity. A century looked at a landscape furious with vegetation in the wrong light and with the wrong eye. It is such pictures that are saddening rather than the tropics itself. These delicate engravings of sugar mills and harbours, of native women in cos-tume, are seen as a part of History, that History which looked over the shoulder of the engraver and, later, the photographer. History can alter the eye and the moving hand to conform a view of itself; it can rename places for the nostalgia in an echo; it can temper the glare of tropical light to elegiac monotony in prose, the tone of judgement in Conrad, in the travel journals of Trollope.

These travellers carried with them the infection of their own malaise, and their prose reduced even the landscape to melancholia and self-contempt. Every endeavor is belittled as imitation, from architecture to music. There was this conviction in Froude that since History is based on achievement, and since the history of the Antilles was so genetically corrupt, so depressing in its cycles of massacres, slavery, and indenture, a culture was inconceivable and nothing could ever be created in those ramshackle ports, those monotonously feudal sugar estates. Not only the light and salt of Antillean mountains defied this, but the demotic vigour and variety of their inhabitants. Stand close to a waterfall and you will stop hearing its roar. To be still in the nineteenth century, like horses, as Brodsky has written, may not be such a bad deal, and much of our life in the Antilles still seems to be in the rhythm of the last century, like the West Indian novel.

By writers even as refreshing as Graham Greene, the Caribbean is looked at with elegiac pathos, a prolonged sadness to which Lévi-Strauss has supplied an epigraph: *Tristes Tropiques*. Their *tristesse* derives from an attitude to the Caribbean dusk, to rain, to uncontrollable vegetation, to the provincial ambition of Caribbean cities where brutal replicas of modern architecture dwarf the small houses and streets. The mood is understandable, the melancholy as contagious as the fever of a sunset, like the gold fronds of diseased coconut palms, but there is something alien and ultimately wrong in the way such a sadness, even a morbidity, is described by English, French, or some of our exiled writers. It relates to a misunderstanding of the light and the people on whom the light falls.

These writers describe the ambitions of our unfinished cities, their unrealized, homiletic conclusion, but the Caribbean city may conclude just at that point where it is satisfied with its own scale, just as Caribbean culture is not evolving but already shaped. Its proportions are not to be measured by the traveller or the exile, but by its own citizenry and architecture. To be told you are not yet a city or a culture requires this response. I am not your city or your culture. There might be less of *Tristes Tropiques* after that.

Here, on the raft of this dais, there is the sound of the applauding surf: our landscape, our history recognized, "at last." *At Last* is one of the first Caribbean books. It was written by the Victorian traveller Charles Kingsley. It is one of the early books to admit the Antillean landscape and its figures into English literature. I have never read it but gather that its tone is benign. The Antillean archipelago was there to be written about, not to write itself, by Trollope, by Patrick Leigh-Fermor, in the very tone in which I almost wrote about the village spectacle at Felicity, as a compassionate and beguiled outsider, distancing myself from Felicity village even while I was enjoying it. What is hidden cannot be loved. The traveller cannot love, since love is stasis and travel is motion. If he returns to what he loved in a landscape and stays there, he is no longer a traveller but in stasis and concentration, the lover of that particular part of earth, a native. So many people say they "love the Caribbean," meaning that someday they plan to return for a visit but could never live there, the usual benign insult of the traveller, the tourist. These travellers, at their kindest, were devoted to the same patronage, the islands passing in profile, their vegetal luxury, their backwardness and poverty. Victorian prose dignified them. They passed by in beautiful profiles and were forgotten, like a vacation.

Aléxis Saint-Léger Léger, whose writer's name is Saint-John Perse, was the first Antillean to win this prize for poetry. He was born in Guadeloupe and wrote in French, but before him, there was nothing as fresh and clear in feeling as those poems of his childhood, that of a privileged white child on an Antillean plantation, "*Pour fêter une enfance,*" "*Éloges,*" and later "*Images à Crusoé.*" At last, the first breeze on the page, salt-edged and self-renewing as the trade winds, the sound of pages and palm trees turning as "the odour of coffee ascents the stairs."

Caribbean genius is condemned to contradict itself. To celebrate Perse, we might be told, is to celebrate the old plantation system, to celebrate the bequé or plantation rider, verandahs and mulatto servants, a white French language in a white pith helmet, to celebrate a rhetoric of patronage and hauteur; and even if Perse denied his origins, great writers often have this folly of trying to smother their source, we cannot deny him any more than we can the African Aimé Césaire. This is not accommodation, this is the ironic republic that is poetry, since, when I see cabbage palms moving their fronds at sunrise, I think they are reciting Perse.

The fragrant and privileged poetry that Perse composed to celebrate his white childhood and the recorded Indian music behind the brown young archers of Felicity, with the same cabbage palms against the same Antillean sky, pierce me equally. I feel the same poignancy of pride in the poems as in the faces. Why, given the history of the Antilles, should this be remarkable? The history of the world, by which of course we mean Europe, is a record of intertribal lacerations, of ethnic cleansings. At last, islands not written about but writing themselves! The palms and the Muslim minarets are Antillean exclamations. At last! the royal palms of Guadeloupe recite *"Éloges"* by heart.

Later, in *"Anabase,"* Perse assembled fragments of an imaginary epic, with the clicking teeth of frontier gates, barren wadis with the froth of poisonous lakes, horsemen burnoosed in sandstorms, the opposite of cool Caribbean mornings, yet not necessarily a contrast any more than some young brown archer at Felicity, hearing the sacred text blared across the flagged field, with its battles and elephants and monkey-gods, in a contrast to the white child in Guadeloupe assembling fragments of his own epic from the lances of the cane fields, the estate carts and oxens, and the calligraphy of bamboo leaves from the ancient languages, Hindi, Chinese, and Arabic, on the Antillean sky. From the *Ramayana* to *Anabasis*, from Guadeloupe to Trinidad, all that archaeology of fragments lying around, from the broken African kingdoms, from the crevasses of Canton, from Syria and Lebanon, vibrating not under the earth but in our raucous, demotic streets.

A boy with weak eyes skims a flat stone across the flat water of an Aegean inlet, and that ordinary action with the scything elbow contains the skipping lines of the *Iliad* and the *Odyssey*, and another child aims a bamboo arrow at a village festival, another hears the rustling march of cabbage palms in a Caribbean sunrise, and from that sound, with its fragments of tribal myth, the compact expedition of Perse's epic is launched, centuries and archipelagoes apart. For every poet it is always morning in the world. History a forgotten, insomniac night; History and elemental awe are always our early beginning, because the fate of poetry is to fall in love with the world, in spite of History.

There is a force of exultation, a celebration of luck, when a writer finds himself a witness to the early morning of a culture that is defining itself, branch by branch, leaf by leaf, in that self-defining dawn, which is why, especially at the edge of the sea, it is good to make a ritual of the sunrise. Then the noun, the "Antilles" ripples like brightening water, and the sounds of leaves, palm fronds, and birds are the sounds of a fresh dialect, the native tongue. The personal vocabulary, the individual melody whose metre is one's biography, joins in that sound, with any luck, and the body moves like a walking, a waking island.

This is the benediction that is celebrated, a fresh language and a fresh people, and this is the frightening duty owed.

I stand here in their name, if not their image—but also in the name of the dialect they exchange like the leaves of the trees whose names are suppler, greener, more morning-stirred than English—*laurier canelles, bois-flot, bois-canot*—or the valleys the trees mention—*Fond St. Jacques, Matoonya, Forestier, Roseau, Mahaut*—or the empty beaches—*L'Anse Ivrogne, Case en Bas, Paradis*—all songs and histories in themselves, pronounced not in French—but in patois.

One rose hearing two languages, one of the trees, one of school children reciting in English:

I am monarch of all I survey,
My right there is none to dispute;
From the centre all round to the sea
I am lord of the fowl and the brute.
Oh, solitude! where are the charms
That sages have seen in thy face?
Better dwell in the midst of alarms,
Than reign in this horrible place …

While in the country to the same metre, but to organic instruments, handmade violin, chac-chac, and goatskin drum, a girl named Sensenne singing:

*Si mwen di 'ous ça fait mwen la peine*
*'Ous kai dire ça vrai.*
(If I told you that caused me pain
You'll say, "It's true.")
*Si mwen di 'ous ça pentetrait mwen*
*'Ous peut dire ça vrai*
(If I told you you pierced my heart
You'd say, "It's true.")
*Ces mamailles actuellement*
*Pas ka faire l'amour z'autres pour un rien.*
(Children nowadays
Don't make love for nothing.)

It is not that History is obliterated by this sunrise. It is there in Antillean geography, in the vegetation itself. The sea sighs with the drowned from the Middle Passage, the butchery of its aborigines, Carib and Aruac and Taíno, bleeds in the scarlet of the immortelle, and even the actions of surf on sand cannot erase the African memory, or the lances of cane as a green prison where indentured Asians, the ancestors

303

of Felicity, are still serving time.

That is what I have read around me from boyhood, from the beginnings of poetry, the grace of effort. In the hard mahogany of woodcutters: faces, resinous men, charcoal burners; in a man with a cutlass cradled across his forearm, who stands on the verge with the usual anonymous khaki dog; in the extra clothes he put on this morning, when it was cold when he rose in the thinning dark to go and make his garden in the heights—the heights, the garden, being miles away from his house, but that is where he has his land—not to mention the fishermen, the footmen on trucks, groaning up mornes, all fragments of Africa originally but shaped and hardened and rooted now in the island's life, illiterate in the way leaves are illiterate; they do not read, they are there to be read, and if they are properly read, they create their own literature.

But in our tourist brochures the Caribbean is a blue pool into which the republic dangles the extended foot of Florida as inflated rubber islands bob and drinks with umbrellas float towards her on a raft. This is how the islands from the shame of necessity sell themselves; this is the seasonal erosion of their identity, that high-pitched repetition of the same images of service that cannot distinguish one island from the other, with a future of polluted marinas, land deals negotiated by ministers, and all of this conducted to the music of Happy Hour and the rictus of a smile. What is the earthly paradise for our visitors? Two weeks without rain and a mahogany tan, and, at sunset, local troubadours in straw hats and floral shirts beating "Yellow Bird" and "Banana Boat Song" to death. There is a territory wider than this—wider than the limits made by the map of an island—which is the illimitable sea and what it remembers.

All of the Antilles, every island, is an effort of memory; every mind, every racial biography culminating in amnesia and fog. Pieces of sunlight through the fog and sudden rainbows, *arcs-en-ciel*. That is the effort, the labour of the Antillean imagination, rebuilding its gods from bamboo frames, phrase by phrase.

Decimation from the Aruac downwards is the blasted root of Antillean history, and the benign blight that is tourism can infect all of those island nations, not gradually, but with imperceptible speed, until each rock is whitened by the guano of white-winged hotels, the arc and descent of progress.

Before it is all gone, before only a few valleys are left, pockets of an older life, before development turns every artist into an anthropologist or folklorist, there are still cherishable places, little valleys that do not echo with ideas, a simplicity of rebeginnings, not yet corrupted by the dangers of change. Not nostalgic sites but occluded sanctities as common and simple as their sunlight. Places as threatened by this prose as a headland is by the bulldozer or a sea almond grove by the surveyor's string, or from blight, the mountain laurel.

One last epiphany: a basic stone church in a thick valley outside Soufrière, the hills almost shoving the houses around into a brown river, a sunlight that looks oily on the leaves, a backward place, unimportant, and one now being corrupted into significance by this prose. The idea is not to hallow or invest the place with anything, not even memory. African children in Sunday frocks come down the ordinary concrete steps into the church, banana leaves hang and glisten, a truck is parked in a yard, and old women totter towards the entrance. Here is where a real fresco should be painted, one without importance, but one with real faith, mapless, Historyless.

How quickly it could all disappear! And how it is beginning to drive us further into where we hope are impenetrable places, green secrets at the end of bad roads, headlands where the next view is not of a hotel but of some long beach without a figure and the hanging question of some fisherman's smoke at its far end. The Caribbean is not an idyll, not to its natives. They draw their working strength from it organically, like trees, like the sea almond or the spice laurel of the heights. Its peasantry and its fishermen are not there to be loved or even photographed; they are trees who sweat, and whose bark is filmed with salt, but every day on some island, rootless trees in suits are signing favourable tax breaks with entrepreneurs, poisoning the sea almond and the spice laurel of the mountains to their roots. A morning could come in which governments might ask what happened not merely to the forests and the bays but to a whole people.

They are here again, they recur, the faces, corruptible angels, smooth black skins and white eyes huge with an alarming joy, like those of the Asian children of Felicity at *Ramleela*; two different religions, two different continents, both filling the heart with the pain that is joy.

But what is joy without fear? The fear of selfishness that, here on this podium with the world paying attention not to them but to me, I should like to keep these simple joys inviolate, not because they are innocent, but because they are true. They are as true as when, in the grace of this gift, Perse heard the fragments of his own epic of Asia Minor in the rustling of cabbage palms, that inner Asia of the soul through which imagination wanders, if there is such a thing as imagination as opposed to the collective memory of our entire race, as true as the delight of that warrior-child who flew a bamboo arrow over the flags in the field at Felicity; and now as grateful a joy and a blessed fear as when a boy opened an exercise book and, within the discipline of its margins, framed stanzas that might contain the light of the hills on an island blest by obscurity, cherishing our insignificance.

# Improvisations:
# The Poem as Journey[1]

*Charles Wright*

"I am writing to you from a far-off country," "I am writing to you from the end of the world," Henri Michaux, the French Surrealist poet, says. Precisely. Most, if not all, good poems come from that place, or those two places if they have become separated by intent or degree. Like the continents and like imagination, they started as one mass, but both have devolved to a movable attitude. Dante wrote from the Empyrean, a far-off country, indeed. Others write from next door, which often can be the end of the world.

So many journeys. So many destinations. Orpheus descending through the byways and back canals of the human body, Ulysses and Aeneas blown to and from all those lands and islands of the natural world, Dante and Leopardi arrowing in and out of the various heavens and the stars.

---

1. Delivered as the second Claudia Ortese Lecture in American Literature, May 14, 1992, L'Università Degli Studi di Firenze, Florence, Italy.

Editor's Note: Charles Wright, "Improvisations: The Poem as Journey" from *Quarter Notes: Improvisations and Interviews* (Ann Arbor: The University of Michigan Press, 1995).

And what is the ultimate resting place of all these peregrinations, the landscapes we travel through, the roads we go back and forth on, or the time it takes us to get there or fail to arrive?

"A journey is a fragment of hell," Bruce Chatwin says in *Songlines*. An inch or a thousand miles, I say, in whatever direction, up or down. But that's the road the good poem takes. Most everyone thinks it's the road that counts, that the traveling is the point of the journey, both in life and in art. I disagree. I think it's what's at road's end that is important, that where the road leads is where the meaning is: it's not the telling of the story that's important, it's what the story has to tell. The telling is interesting, but the point is what's transcendent. As a younger man, I thought that process was meaning. I now know that meaning is meaning, and that journey's end is the end of the journey, not some intermediate point—the road to Campostela leads to Campostela, the road to Assisi ends in Assisi, not at Gròpina.

Poems are not just *about* journeys, of course, they *are* journeys—surreptitiously, silently, staying in one place the way plants do. Like any organism, the good poem is a self-contained adventure, both physically and metaphysically. What Eihei Dogen, the Japanese Zen master, said about the plantain in the century Dante was born can as well be said about the good poem: "A plantain has earth, water, fire, wind, emptiness, also mind, consciousness and wisdom as its roots, stems, branches, and leaves, or as its flowers, fruits, colors and forms. Accordingly, the plantain wears the autumn wind, and is torn in the autumn wind. We know that it is pure and clear and that not a single particle is excluded." If it lacks these essential components, the plantain does not grow to its fullest expectations. If the poem lacks them, it goes nowhere. Moribund and ill-equipped, it becomes a shell—without the interior journey, the exterior one is impossible. The true journey is a healthy plant; the true poem is the same thing.

At the heart of every poem is a journey of discovery. Something is being found out. Often the discovery is merely technical—architectural, metrical, or spatial—though, when lucky, the technical revelation is not just "merely" but is an uncovered new thing. Poetic structures sometimes end up in that fortunate "field." New concepts of lineation often do as well. From time to time the discovery is spiritual, a way of looking at the world that affects the way we lead our lives, or how we think of them. Poems that cause us to say, after having read them, "Oh, that's nice," or "Ummm, not bad," do not participate in this voyage of discovery. No matter how new their paint job is, no matter how smart and crisp their sails, they never get out of the harbor. The journey belongs to others.

Two twentieth-century Italian poets—Dino Campana and Eugenio Montale—make an interesting comparison. Campana, who restlessly writes of almost nothing but journeys on foot, by sea, or all manner of transportation, to both spiritual and quotidian places, has a turbulent and frenzied surface to his poems, but underneath a Romantic standstill and stasis. Montale, on the other hand, whose poems have, for the most part, placid and one-place-at-a-time surfaces, underneath have a miraculous sense of voyage to previously undiscovered or forgotten states of being. Another famous twentieth-century poet, Giuseppe Ungaretti, in his minimalistic sensibility, also constantly carries us elsewhere. His two-word, two-line poem "Mattina"—"M'illumino / d'immenso"—says about all there is to say on the subject of epiphanic discovery (and is my favorite example of why translation is ultimately impossible). To finish off the parallelism, Pier Paolo Pasolini, whose movies were a constant exploration of both physical and psychic revelation—as were his novels—had to my way of thinking a very ordinary and unadventurous venture in his poems. His life, as we know, followed his novels and films, even to its abrupt, and sad, ending.

The imagination is, of course, the starter's pistol of all journeys. As

Federico García Lorca, the great Spanish poet of the 1930s, has said, "it travels and transforms things, endowing them with their purest sense, and it identifies relations which had never been suspected.... Imagination is the first step, the foundation of all poetry." Inspiration, the dark twin and demiurge of imagination, can, he later counsels, send the traveler farther and deeper than imagination alone, creating a poetry where "a man more rapidly approaches the cutting edge that the philosopher and the mathematician turn away from in silence." That "cutting edge," where all true poems climb from and return to, is the edge where the void begins. And it is inspiration, pure instinct, to which Lorca eventually pays the greater homage. Imagination is closely allied to intelligence and logic/reasoning. And intelligence, he said, "is often the enemy of poetry, because it limits too much, and it elevates the poet to a sharp-edged throne where he forgets that ants could eat him or that a great arsenic lobster could fall suddenly on his head." The journey is always into the unknown, into the mystery and darkness where great lobsters fall on our heads and great unseen wings graze our faces and vanish.

Back to Montale for a moment. Just about thirty years ago, I translated into English (American, really) a section of his poems "Lampi e Dediche" ("Flashes and Dedications") from his book *La bufera*. These little poems had such a profound effect on me that I then went on to translate the entire book—the first time, I might add, that the complete *La bufera* had been done in English. It has since, of course, become a mountain that many have climbed. However, my point here is with the short, diary-like section, "Lampi e Dediche." What first drew me to these poems was their strong, and strange, religious overtones. This is rare in Montale's work and, even here, it is not "religion" per se, but rather a peculiar sort of mysticism, little apocalypses, immense journeys in tight and loaded little packets.

The opening poem in the series, "Verso Siena," serves to show that God is a possibility, though how He is to be taken, and how Montale takes

Him, we are never sure. This uncertainty gives the power of the unknown, the mystery, and the journey's end as an addition to the imagistic pyrotechnics in the poems themselves. The reader—after going through such other poems as "Sulla colonna più alta," "Incantesimo," and "Vento sulla mezzaluna"—knows he has traveled to a different universe indeed in things Montaliane, a universe almost completely comprised of nothingness (a familiar place at first). But this time nothingness is not all; there sometimes appear certain perceptions (*lampi*) that carry almost metaphysical overtones of faith.

Montale's world, as we know now, is a fascinating one, with a sense of time as a steady destroyer, of existence as entropy, an inevitable process of decay. But it is the added dimension found in "Lampi e Dediche" that gently alters that world, which hints of the changes that came later in *La bufera*, when the journey went down and down, deeper into the darker waters of personal history, and the century's history. "*O voi chi siete in piccioletta barca,*" as Ezra Pound had it from Dante. Out of my way. *Pista!*

And speaking of Uncle Ez, as Montale called him, and as he called himself on Italian radio, we have a fine example of someone who tried the ultimate journey in his work, a Dantean-Joycean voyage that ended up, by his own admission, shipwrecked on the rocks of history, prejudice, and Western culture in general, the very land's end he was headed for all along. Having had his epic—his non-narrative epic (which Montale said was a contradiction in terms)—progress *in periplum*, where the winds took it, and not on any preset, direct-narrative course, this is not surprising. But it remains one of the most spectacular and gorgeous literary wrecks, in English, of the century, and the lyrical songs that continue to rise from the wreckage, and the incredible music and visions of many of its parts continue to seduce us toward that same shore and those same shoals, a broken bundle of mirrors though they may be.

Having said that about Pound, let me say something else, something more personal about his work and its early effects on me. I have said this before in another place, but it bears repeating when we are speaking of journey and poetry, as it concerns the beginning of my own journey, without Ariadne's thread, into the maze. All first loves are ultimately sad. They begin in such light and splendor and end in darkness and disillusion. Later they are brought back up to shine again like discovered lost treasure from the old waters of indifference. My poetic first love was no different from this. And it was Ezra Pound.

I have written at some length, and almost continuously, for over thirty years about my first stay in Italy, which began in January, 1959. Such obsessive attempts at re-creation are some slight indications of the abiding effect of the country and its culture, and my initial baptism by total immersion in it, had—and continues to have—on me.

My most momentous occasion, at least in what was to preoccupy me from then on, and what I still, as I once said, "waste my heart on," was a trip I took to Lake Garda from Verona, where I lived, and particularly to Sirmione, the peninsula at whose tip Catullus, the legend goes, had a villa, the ruins of which to this day stun the unwary foreign traveler when he comes upon them. I was such a traveler, clutching in one hand the *Selected Poems of Ezra Pound*, bought two years previously in New York City and still unread. My friend Harold Schimmel, with me in the army in Verona, had borrowed it in the first weeks of our friendship and had returned it with the admonition to read the poem "Blandula, Tenulla, Vagula," which was about the very spot I would be visiting. And so I did, the late March sun pouring through the olive trees, reflecting off their silver and quicksilver turns in the lake wind, the lake itself stretched out below me and into the distance, the pre-Alps above Riva cloud-shouldered and cloud-shadowed, the whole weight of history and literature suddenly dropping through the roof of my little world in one of those epiphanic flashes that one is fortunate enough to have in one's lifetime now and then if one is ready. I was ready. The continuous "desire to write" that I had had since high school had finally found its form—the lyric poem. The irresistible force had met a movable object. A week later Schimmel and I took off for a week's leave—down to Bologna, over *La Futa* and the Apennines, through Florence, Rome, Naples, and finally to Paestum in southern Italy—and my focus was set for the rest of my life, as hyperbolic as that might sound. I still have that little paperback book, and it still has the heavy, army-issue-paper slipcover on it that Harold made back in 1959. The number 1302 is written in ink on the cover, a number that means nothing to me.

But the book means something to me, and the poems meant something to me in my green time. One's personal poetic journey has to begin before the journey inside the poem can get under way.

And speaking of Verona, it was there, I think, that a girl I knew back in 1959 or 1960 said to me one afternoon, during the course of a courtship that went back and forth between Milano, where she lived, and Verona, where, as I say, I lived, "*Guarda*, Charles, *quando io faccio una cosa, io vado fino in fondo, sai*." *Ostrighetta!* I was a young guy then, and young guys just want to have fun. Fun for her meant something else, however. It meant, finally, "*andare fino in fondo*." She did, I didn't.

Such a course, "*Andare fino in fondo*," was no fun for John Berryman, an American poet of a recent generation who did just that in both his life and his poems. The voyage to the bottom of the soul. He took it and his poems took it. It was tragic in his life and brilliantly redemptive in his art. It was just such a journey that a group of poets, called the Confessionals, all but one of them of the same generation, took: they were Berryman, Robert Lowell, Anne Sexton, W.D. Snodgrass, and Sylvia Plath. Delmore Schwartz and Randall Jarrell were peripheral members. Four of them committed suicide, two died young, and one, probably the originator of the kind of writing the group was known for, though not its most illustrious member, is still alive. Some journeys from the void know secret shortcuts, some have no return ticket.

Berryman and his alter egos, Henry and Mister Bones, dance the

Dance of Death, that dark and monotonous soft-shoe, across the stage of *The Dream Songs*, a huge book of almost exclusively eighteen-line poems about the foibles, momentary triumphs, and endless vicissitudes of Henry as he shuffles inexorably off stage left to his predestined and preternatural doom. The entire enterprise is a kind of *commedia dell'arte* stage setting, the characters, especially Henry, rather like marionettes or puppets just waiting to collapse or to be pulled under at any moment. We are not disappointed. In brilliant set piece after brilliant set piece, the excruciating ritual is played out to its appointed end, Henry and Berryman himself, puppet and puppeteer, finally subsumed by the journey itself. Ars brevis, vita brevis est.

Franz Kafka, in one of his entries in *The Blue Octavo Notebooks*, writes: "Before setting foot in the Holy of Holies you must take off your shoes, yet not only your shoes, but everything; you must take off your travelling garments and lay down your luggage; and under that you must shed your nakedness and everything that hides beneath that, and then the core and the core of the core, then the remainder and then the residue and then even the glimmer of the undying fire. Only the fire itself is absorbed by the Holy of Holies and lets itself be absorbed by it; neither can resist the other." This is the kind of journey we are talking about....

For many of us in our youth, Hart Crane was the ultimate American poetic icon. His poem "The Bridge" is second only to Pound's *Cantos* as the most spectacular and seductive failure of the twentieth century in American poetry. There is something irresistibly sexy and alluring about ambition and the failure of that ambition, especially if its scattered or gathered parts have a kind of glittering perfection, as those of both the *Cantos* and "The Bridge" do.

The wake of the SS *Orizaba* had hardly closed over Crane's body before his personal legend began to take shape. His literary one was not far behind. He had tried for the impossible in his poem—his great, shattered poem—a journey across time, history, and personal recognition that refused to redeem either him or literature and refused to come together—two lacks that mirrored the disconnections in his own life. The way out seemed the way in, and he took it. The verb "to voyage" is just as inaccessible and untranslatable in the heart as it is in the poem.

Hart Crane was unafraid in his literary ambitions. Many, of course, profess to be unafraid and are willing "to try anything." The vast majority of such people say and do such out of ignorance and foolhardiness. Crane did it out of talent, genius, and a vision, a vision that was not to be thwarted. True vision *is* journey. True vision is a bridge from here to there. Crane saw his road and set out on it. At its end was the end. Had he known that before he set out, I'm convinced he would have acted no differently. Genius must keep its appointments. We are still picking up and examining the dazzling flotsam and jetsam, just as we are from the *Cantos*. Hart Crane and Ezra Pound, the two fallen angels in the American twentieth-century poetic firmament. How they shine and flare in their fiery arcs.

Does the journey currently seem shorter and less ambitious? Have the truly incredible occurrences of this century shrunk and shortened the reach of poets and poems? E.M. Cioran accuses Paul Valéry of corrupting generations of French poets, he and Stéphane Mallarmé, by their insistence that every poem be an exercise in the impossible, that every poem be a leap from a high wall by the poetic body. Rather like the famous photograph staged by the French artist Yves Klein, where he is shown in midair, stretched out, having just jumped from a high stone wall down to a Parisian stone street. We now know that the photograph is a collage and that, in actuality, there was a net beneath the original leap to catch him, now excised, with a cleverly added picture of the street creating the physical disaster he seems headed toward.

Indeed, most journeys are, perforce, of this kind in poems. And that's all right, I think. Otherwise the landscape and the history of literature would be strewn with bodies and maimed poems. Short journeys are not only acceptable, they are necessary to make the longer ones possible and legendary. Dante needed Lapo Gianni and Guido Cavalcanti. Montale needed Cesare Pavese and Salvatore Quasimodo. An inch or infinity, to the stars or to the *norceria*, through the thickets of the soul or the thickets of language, down the boulevards of the heart or the thoroughfares of technique. The journey remains the same in the good poem—it goes from point A to point B. Distance does make a difference and depth does make a difference, but vision is still vision, whatever its scope or manifestations.

Emily Dickinson was stationary. By that I mean her life was stationary. Her mind was a long-distance runner, unstill, never ceasing. Her imagination and inspiration were lightning-strikes and full of a great illumination. She sat in her room and the galaxy unrolled beneath her feet. She sat in her room and the garden and orchard outside her windows took on the ghostly garments of infinity. In her finest poems, and everywhere throughout her letters and the rest of her poetry, there has seldom before been such expansiveness in such small containers. Her poetry was an electron microscope trained on the infinite and the idea of God. Such distances under her fingertips! Inside the tube of the climbing rose, the River of Heaven flowed. Under the oak's throat, the broken ladder to Paradise waited for reassembly.

During the last ten years of her life she apparently seldom left her room, or at least the second story of her house. For most of her life she had been reclusive. Yet her poems are immense voyages into the unknowable. To leave she had to stay still, something Dino Campana was unable to accept, for instance, or was incapable of doing.

There was the famous white dress. There was the famous white flower. There was the famous "white election." And there was the famous last letter she wrote, the day before her death, to her two cousins, Louise and Fannie Norcross—"Little Cousins—Called back. Emily"—sounding almost as though she were an alien, some extraterrestrial who was here on a visit. She does seem "inhabited" in a way. Or perhaps she was Manichaean, a kind of Cathar whose chip of light was to begin its last, and longest, journey back to the original and unthinkable source of all light, leaving this darkness for good. Whatever, she remains one of the great lyric poets of all time. Sappho casts no shadow on her, her sherry-eyed opposite....

Every journey is the same journey, and every journey is different. The journey in life, as the song says, is a lonesome valley. The journey in the poem runs toward higher ground, the ridgebacks and upper slopes, hilltop to mountaintop. The movement, in other words, tends to be upward. At least it has been that way for me.

The iconic book in my life, the work toward which all my work has aspired, is the *Confessions* by Saint Augustine. It is that kind of autobiography, in a more temporal—though no less spiritual—sense, I suppose, that my poems want to describe. Or to show their inability to describe. In either case, the journey is the same journey, even if the station reached is dramatically different. One goes where one is called.

The journey in the Chinese poem, which has also been of interest to my work, is otherwise. Where our Western movement, as I say, tends to be upward, the Chinese aim deliberately downward, at the earth, at the landscape and the tactile world and their tenuous place within it. It is a poetry of seeing, and their spiritual strength is in that seeing and in the things of this world they look at. And since they have no belief in a future world—as, say, Christians do—they love what they look at with a passion the Western tradition does not contain. Their sense of the permanence of the world is as strong as our sense of its transience.

It has been said that Buddhism has provided a spiritual basis for Chinese landscape poetry. One does sense the great interior Zen journey, that long and arduous trek to the still, quiet center of things, reflected in the description of landscape and in the patience and absolute faith of certain onlookers such as Cold Mountain (Han Shan) or Wang Wei. The poets and poems from the T'ang Dynasty (618-907) are generally accepted as being the finest examples of this, though the T'ang poets were using forms and song patterns, we now know, which were themselves up to four hundred years old, brought down from the time of the Han. If, as Gustave Flaubert said, the Good Lord does live in the detail, then these short poems which often centered upon the enduring problems of man's life can be said to be large spiritual voyages as the Chinese looked around themselves and told how it was to be here at this time, in this place, letting the waters of the River of Heaven slide over their heads and the waters of the Yangtze slide under their feet. The enormousness of the material world and all the roads that wind through the ten thousand things!

While it is not poetry but fiction, the writing of Ernest Hemingway has been very influential in my life. The book that I read as a young man and never quite got out of my system is *The Short Stories of Ernest Hemingway*. There is a purity of description, a purity of language at its most effective, that has always been seductive to me in his writing, and I find it—or found it so when I was younger—most prevalent in his stories. It is a purity of language in action that I have often aspired to in my poems.

Such stories, for example, as "A Clean, Well-Lighted Place," "Hills Like White Elephants," and "The Short Happy Life of Francis Macomber" seemed to me perfectly articulated and took the reader to a faraway place, an effortless journey of narrative and style. It is such a place I wanted my poems to have access to, and the roads that led there I wanted my poems to be able to travel. Especially the early, crystalline vignettes of *In Our Time*. Like Chinese poems, they gave a sense of the long journey through the possibilities of language, its exclusions as well as its inclusions. I thought they were "true" in the way Hemingway liked to use the word, and I loved them.

It's always been my contention that the shorter the distance, the harder the journey. By that I mean there is less time and less space to get said what has to be said. For that is the real journey after all—what you've got to say. We can metaphor and simile and weave intricate euphemisms till our pencils stub out of lead, but the fact remains that what you have to say is where you have to go. How you say it, of course, can grease the wheels and fuel the engine (here we go metaphoring again) and can sometimes actually be what you are talking about, but for the most part, you've got to say your way to seize the day. And the more condensed the poem is, the less maneuvering room there is, the stronger the message and the greater the journey is after the fact, which is where all real journeys start out. Dante is an example of this.

But there are contemporary poets who illustrate my point as well as Dante, including Jorie Graham, an American with significant connection to Italy. Jorie grew up in Rome and, in 1966, was a member of the army of students who came to help salvage books from the Arno's mud after the floods here. When I asked her to respond to my view of the journey in our poems, Jorie Graham replied in a letter, and gave the following explication. Her explanation helps make the case for that "journey of technique" I mentioned earlier. I want to present first her poem "San Sepolcro" and then what she says about the poem:

*San Sepolcro*

In this blue light
        I can take you there,
snow having made me
        a world of bone
seen through to. This
        is my house,

my section of Etruscan
    wall, my neighbor's
lemontrees, and, just below
    the lower church,
the airplane factory.
    A rooster

crows all day from mist
    outside the walls.
There's milk on the air,
    ice on the oily
lemonskins. How clean
    the mind is,

holy grave. It is this girl
    by Piero
della Francesca, unbuttoning
    her blue dress,
her mantle of weather,
    to go into

labor. Come, we can go in.
    It is before
the birth of god. No-one
    has risen yet
to the museums, to the assembly
    line—bodies

and wings—to the open air
    market. This is
what the living do: go in.
    It's a long way.

And the dress keeps opening
    from eternity

to privacy, quickening.
    Inside, at the heart,
is tragedy, the present moment
    forever stillborn,
but going in, each breath
    is a button

coming undone, something terribly
    nimble-fingered
finding all of the stops.

If I consider "San Sepolcro," the journey seems especially a *formal* journey—an experiment with elements of style which led to the discovery of a layer of "voice" I could call mine, or inhabit, for a period of my life.

First of all I should say that many of these devices might seem on the one hand too obvious to be of use—except to one who doesn't avail herself of them habitually. And, too, that, the taking on, only apparently arbitrary, of stylistic devices—the inhabiting of them until they become the garment of one's spirit life, the method by which one touches the world, the means by which one can be touched oneself, and changed—all of these mysteries are the reason the act of writing holds such powerful and enduring sway over my life. The changes I made in my "technique" are changes that occurred to my life: I became the person I couldn't have otherwise been by these small devices, habits. In other words, the journey is made up of, and created by, technique. The soul-making Keats refers

to as the goal of poetry is a web composed of small techni-
cal attempts which lead to a new voice—a deeper voice,
one at a more morally and historically and spiritually
engaged level than the personal voice. A voice one can
only build by the *act* of writing, an act which grows dead
and automatic if not constantly reinvigorated by strange-
ness of strategy.

In "San Sepolcro" I tried to slow down the act of *speak-
ing*. I tried all sorts of devices to this end and finally settled
on the shortened line, the antiphonal indentation, the sin-
gling out of individual words by frequent use of mid-line
sentence breaks.

I was delighted in my soul by the slowness of pace I dis-
covered. I started thinking of it (*feeling* it, really) as a kind
of solemnity—as when one walks in a cathedral and every
sound one makes—footfalls!—seems heightened, signifi-
cant, held open for inspection, *accountable*. I liked what
for me felt like a new nakedness—as if the underpinnings
were visible on the surface and no lies could be masked.
I have always troubled the area surrounding the "veracity"
of an assertion or an image—and so the slowness the inden-
tation thrust upon my habitual way of proceeding thrilled
me by its sense of *enforced*, solemn, accountability. Every
word seemed suddenly to matter *on its own*—it seemed
to resist the kind of easier truthfulness, easier beauty, the
sentence could effortlessly (deceitfully?) effect. So: word
vs. sentence—fragment brought to the surface. And yet
a surface that still had an insistent patterning, order, of
its own.

Connected to all this was my (at the time rather terrify-
ing) use of direct address: "In this blue light / I can take you
there." Its use flew in the face of all other imagined listeners

I had imagined or posited unconsciously up to that point. It forced me down into a far more intimate *voice*—at least tonally intimate—not *personally* intimate.

And this led, I believe, to the use of far more contemporary (vernacular) details (the airplane factory, the assembly line, etc.)—it is the specific admixture—the intermingling without dilution of the dramatic difference—of the spiritual and the physical worlds in this poem that led to the impetus for the writing of the whole book, *Erosion*. The two levels of "going-in" were actually sprung into *life* for me by the sudden appearance of the airplane factory (more than the open-air market which seemed, still, to partake of the aesthetic and historical Italian landscape). The factory— actually glimpsed rounding the hill off Montefalco (so *ugly*, I thought at the time, marring the "view")—the new Italy, if you will—helped me *turn*, in my spirit life, back to Italy and my whole past (family, inheritance, the problematics of memory—historical and personal—the *history*, the wars Europe endured, etc.).

I don't think I could have gotten to the place in my "role of soul-making" where I turned back to Italy and that constellation of aesthetic/historical and personal problems without that airplane factory. I had despaired of ever being able to make the landscape of my *actual* childhood and its art (so utterly literal to me as I played hide-and-seek in the churches of Trastevere as a child) anything other than symbolic or otherwise "unreal" in the context of the America I was living and writing in. The sudden, thrilling, jarring appearance of that airplane factory changed the whole situation. In that sense it actually created a juncture out of which a stage in the journey would unfold.

Our subject matter, the Poem as Journey, or the Journey at the Heart of Poetry, is surely the largest, most extensive that exists in the art. From Homer through Dante and Chaucer, through Shakespeare and Milton, through Leopardi and Goethe, through Zanzotto and Luzi, there is everything to be said and nothing more to say. It is one of those subjects you shadowbox with, since everyone who has ever written who was any good at all is an example to hold up to the light. For every good poem, as we've said, contains a serious journey. Dante, Homer, Chaucer, Shakespeare— what's to say? Eliot, Pound, Akhmatova, Mandelstam, Yeats and Lorca, Miłosz and Hikmet: the list might run as long as memory and appreciations permit.

Still, a few more words, perhaps. About Theodore Roethke, an American poet of the generation of Lowell, Berryman, Elizabeth Bishop, and Randall Jarrell. He subsumed the exterior landscape into his interior journey as well, if not better, than anyone in the United States in the second half of this century. His major work is a group of longish long-line meditations on the self, existence, and the landscape entitled "North American Sequence." Six poems that delve into the heart of the American landscape and into the heart of the spiritual self, the long voyage inward through the rocky creekbeds and river gulches, the windy cliffs that contain the dark wave-edge of the soul.

At least I thought that when I first read these remarkable, underappreciated, very American masterpieces. Like Dante's journey, his ends in an image of the rose—in Roethke's case an actual one, though its literary and religious reverberations are unmistakable—a rose in the soul's wind, which tears at reality and the difficult beliefs we sometimes choose to live our lives by.

Roethke, like Hart Crane, has the courage and vision in these poems to go the length of the dead-end road, the road that disappears into the vast expanse of unknowing and incredulity inside us, to come to the end of that road and keep on going; the courage to take the landscape and its significance on its own terms, to take the soul and the soul's self on their own terms and try to come to a workable spiritual balance with them. This is, of course, hard to do, and most writers, like most people, usually avoid it at any cost. Roethke's triumph is that he was fearless in his pursuit of himself and his place in the American literary and spiritual landscape.

As I noted a moment ago, there is just so much one can say in general about a topic as large as ours, and I think I have had my say for the time being. One final comment, though, and a slightly more personal one.

W.B. Yeats, the great Irish poet, wrote once in a verse that when he had said what he had to say, and had begun to enumerate old themes, he had to go back to the starting point: "I must lie down where all the ladders start, / In the foul rag-and-bone shop of the heart." Presumably to start contemplating the real ladder again. This is, of course, the void I was talking about earlier, out of which all journeys begin and to which they all return.

The journey my own poems took, and continue along, may have physically begun at Lake Garda in March, 1959, where I finally found a ladder I had to climb, but the first rung of that journey, out of the heart's void, was surely taken the afternoon a week later when my Volkswagen made a sharp turn on *La Futa* around a cypress tree and I was confronted with the enormity of Brunelleschi's dome on Santa Maria del Fiore rising, it seemed, almost out of the road itself in front of me, so near, so huge, the sunlight flashing off its curves and angles. And once we descended, the dome coming into and out of view, ever closer and larger, there was never a turning back.

# A Bookshop,
a Fishing Boat,
a Trek Through
the Andes:

## A Roundtable of Poets
Who've Lived Abroad

The draw to leave home can be strong and the promise of adventure so alluring that it can be tempting to just pick up and go. Alas, traveling abroad is not so simple. There are countless considerations; the trip will likely defy expectation; and when a situation does go awry, knowing how to respond can be difficult.

To prevent prospective travelers from making mistakes already made, forestall unnecessary work, and redirect anxious casting about, the editors and I asked fourteen traveled poets questions often posed when planning international travel. Their reflections constitute a conversation, which is printed here. The conversation can be read straight through, or, if one or two poets catch the eye, his or her responses can be tracked from question to question.

The result, I hope, is an illumination of the broad spectrum of reasons, excuses, and impulses that lead poets abroad. While advice may not supplant the value of lived experience, the contributors' collected wisdom offers guidance and encouragement, making it easier to know what to expect and how to prepare as we color the world with our presences.

—*Jared Hawkley*

# Meet the Roundtable

**Elizabeth Austen** is a Seattle-based poet who has traveled extensively in Bolivia, Ecuador, and Peru.

**Derick Burleson** has worked as a Peace Corps volunteer in Rwanda. He lives in Two Rivers, Alaska.

**Gregory Dunne** has traveled to and now permanently resides in Japan, where he teaches at Miyazaki International College.

**Karen Finneyfrock** has traveled in Nepal as a Cultural Envoy through the US Department of State, performing and teaching poetry. She lives in Seattle.

**Kathleen Graber** has traveled as an Amy Lowell Poetry Travelling Scholar, traversing Germany, Hungary, Malta, and the United Kingdom. She lives in Virginia.

**Garth Greenwell** has traveled to and now resides in Sofia, Bulgaria, where he teaches secondary school.

**Adrie Kusserow** has traveled to Bhutan, India, Nepal, South Sudan, and Uganda as a cultural anthropologist. She lives in Vermont.

**Sandra Meek** has worked as a Peace Corps volunteer in Botswana. She lives in Georgia.

**Aimee Nezhukumatathil** has traveled in India and the Philippines. She lives in New York State.

**Jacquelyn Pope** lived for seven years in the Netherlands, working as a bookseller and translator in Amsterdam.

**Srikanth Reddy** lived a year in Oaxaca, Mexico, on research leave from the University of Chicago. He lives in Chicago.

**Emily Ruch** has served in South Korea and Iraq as a soldier in the United States Army. She lives in Santa Fe, New Mexico.

**Donna Stonecipher** has traveled to and now resides in Berlin, Germany.

**Katharine Whitcomb** led a summer study abroad for her Central Washington University students in France. She lives in Washington State.

# What particular circumstances allowed you to live abroad?

MEEK: I was a Peace Corps volunteer. I think I had always been aware of the Peace Corps, and for my BA and MFA degrees, I went to Colorado State University, a school that's had a connection with the Peace Corps from the start. I joined the Peace Corps immediately after completing my MFA degree program, twenty years ago.

GRABER: I received the Amy Lowell Poetry Travelling Scholarship [amylowell.org] for 2008 to 2009. I knew many other poets who had applied for it. Elizabeth Bishop was a Lowell Travelling Scholar.

AUSTEN: In the fall of 1996, I quit my day job managing Freehold Theatre Lab Studio, a Seattle not-for-profit company. I sold my Honda Civic and bought a one-way ticket to Quito, Ecuador. I told friends and family that I wanted to learn to speak Spanish, do some volunteer work, and hike in tropical rain forests. But the true intent of my open-ended trip was to change my life. Because of some recent work I had done with poetry and dance theater, I had a strong hunch this meant becoming a writer, and I didn't know how to make sense of that or where to begin. Being a poet is, after all, perhaps the only vocation less practical than being a stage actor.

RUCH: I spent the majority of my time abroad as a soldier in the United States Army. I was stationed for a year in South Korea and deployed twice to Iraq.

KUSSEROW: I am an applied cultural anthropologist, so I am somewhat required to travel to "earn my keep." I teach cultural anthropology at a college in Vermont, so I usually bank on travel during winter vacation, summer break, and sabbatical leave from the college. I also travel with students to do international service-related projects in Bhutan, South

Sudan, and Uganda, so my travel funds come from the college when I take students. Initially, my travel was partially funded through Harvard, where I got my PhD. My travel since then has been funded through a combination of anthropology grants, college faculty fellowships (from the college where I teach), college funding for a study-abroad service learning course I am leading, my own personal funds and fundraising, and in the case of Bhutan, the government of Bhutan. It is never enough money, and I barely scrape by on my trips.

WHITCOMB: I applied for and received a one-month residency at La Muse from September to October 2010 while I was on sabbatical from my job teaching creative writing at Central Washington University. I had first read about La Muse [lamuseinn.com], a writers' and artists' retreat in southern France, in a posting on Facebook by a friend, the poet Sheryl St. Germain. After returning to the United States, I codesigned a class to be housed at La Muse and proposed it for a summer study abroad through Central Washington University. I completed this study abroad with one other faculty member and eight students during July 2011.

NEZHUKUMATATHIL: I lived for a month in Kerala, India, in 1999 and for three weeks in 2006 and then in Pangasinan, Philippines, in 2002 and 2007.

BURLESON: I applied to the Peace Corps because my wife at that time had always dreamed of being a Peace Corps volunteer, so joining the Peace Corps was a condition of marriage. We had both heard about the Peace Corps all our lives. During the application process, it seemed we would most likely be assigned to Eastern Europe, and we started taking classes in European history. When the assignment came and we were going to Rwanda instead, we were surprised and delighted and had no idea what would be in store for us there. We were both writers finishing MA degrees at Kansas State University and hoped going to Rwanda would give us something to write about.

GREENWELL: I've been working full-time as a high school teacher for the two years I've lived in Bulgaria. Several agencies specialize in international placements in secondary schools: Search Associates and International Schools Services are two of the biggest. I've worked with Carney, Sandoe & Associates, a company mostly focused on US placements that has been expanding its international portfolio.

FINNEYFROCK: I traveled to Nepal in December 2010 through the US Department of State and the US embassy in Nepal as part of a Cultural Envoy Program called Slam Poetry Fortnight. There was no application process, although I was asked to send work samples and an artist résumé. The embassy arranged all travel and lodging.

REDDY: The last time I lived abroad, during the academic year 2008–2009, I stayed in Oaxaca, Mexico. I was on research leave from the university where I teach. I didn't have to apply for this leave—it was part of my contract as junior faculty at the University of Chicago.

DUNNE: I applied to work aboard Japanese fishing vessels operating in the Bering Sea as a biologist and observer through the US Fisheries Observer Program. I was interested in Japan and its culture and felt that such work would introduce me to the culture. I worked aboard the ships for two to three months at a time without returning to port at Dutch Harbor in the Aleutian Islands. Insofar as I was living aboard a Japanese fishing vessel and surrounded by Japanese men and their culture and language, I felt I was living in a foreign country—a floating country. I was the only English speaker aboard the vessels. I continued with this work for three years. The experience increased my interest in Japan: its culture, language, and literature.

## If you applied to a program, what did the application process entail?

BURLESON: Applying to the Peace Corps in the late 1980s was a fairly daunting experience, with interviews, background checks, and health checkups all required. Some of my students and friends have applied in recent years, and it seems the process hasn't changed much. The Peace Corps wants to find volunteers who will stay at their posts for two years, so the application process is quite detailed.

MEEK: The Peace Corps application involved a written application, including short essay questions, and an interview at the regional recruitment office, which in my case was in Denver. Also required were fingerprints for a criminal record search and a medical exam.

FINNEYFROCK: Although there was no application process for my particular Cultural Envoy Program, it is helpful to know that many embassies are interested in featuring writers as part of cultural programming.

DUNNE: I filled out an application and mailed it to the National Oceanic and Atmospheric Administration (NOAA) in Seattle. I was interviewed in Seattle for the position and attended a two-week mandatory training program.

GRABER: The application process for the Lowell Scholarship could not be simpler. There is a one-page form in addition to a writing sample. There is no fee. I put a copy of my first book, some new poems, and this little application in a priority envelope, and off it went. Months later, I got a very unexpected phone call from the executors of Amy Lowell's estate informing me that I had been selected.

WHITCOMB: La Muse had a standard e-mail application. I did have to submit a writing sample and describe a project that I would work on during the residency.

GREENWELL: International independent schools require at least a BA degree in a candidate's subject area; most prefer advanced degrees. Some experience teaching is usually required, and some schools require US state certification. I don't have this. Increasingly, international baccalaureate certification, which can be easily earned through online programs, is desired.

At Carney, Sandoe & Associates, the agency I used, I was required to submit a CV, a philosophy of teaching, and letters of reference. They passed along my dossier to schools with openings, letting me know when they did so. It was up to me to contact schools that I was interested in.

There are several fairs in Asia, Europe, and the United States where candidates interview with schools. Most schools do require in-person as well as phone interviews, though there are sometimes exceptions.

## What would be useful for others to know before applying?

DUNNE: Applicants to the US Fisheries Observer Program need to have at least an undergraduate degree in the sciences. NOAA prefers applicants with degrees in biology, fisheries, and other sciences. The process is moderately competitive.

GREENWELL: I think the level of competition for international teaching placements varies widely. Positions in what are seen as the most desirable cities can be hugely competitive, especially at high-prestige schools. In places such as Eastern Europe, where recruitment is more difficult, new college graduates with no teaching experience may sometimes fill positions. Most require an initial two-year commitment, and penalties for breaking a contract can be fairly heavy.

KUSSEROW: For anthropology grants, the process is quite competitive. These cannot be grants in which I state that I will also be writing poetry—I wouldn't be taken seriously. These grants require elaborate bibliographies, explicit statements about contribution to the discipline and anthropological theory, a CV, a doctorate, letters of reference, and an explanation of why the proposed research is important.

College-funded trips that I lead are less competitive; I usually have to give a long written rationale for why the college should offer the course. Being a professor at a college has been an immense resource in terms of travel funding related to curriculum development or research.

BURLESON: The most important thing for Peace Corps applicants is to be flexible about where and when they hope to go. The process also requires persistence. It is competitive, and experience in teaching definitely gave me an edge over much of the competition.

MEEK: Try to plan ahead. The application process can take many months, and it is competitive. You should always check with the Peace Corps website and/or the regional recruitment offices for the most up-to-date advice, but applying eight to twelve months ahead of the time you'd ideally like to go is not unreasonable. Certainly, if you are available more quickly than that, you should apply anyway and let the recruiters know when you are able and willing to go. The more flexible you are, the better your chances of placement. Although I graduated in May, my program didn't begin until November. I ended up getting a temporary job at a local factory until departure, which was totally outside my experience up to that point—and was itself great preparation for the Peace Corps!

If you are a college student, or if you've already graduated and think you may want to join the Peace Corps sometime further down the road—and Peace Corps volunteers are all ages, though having a college degree is a requirement—consider getting some kind of volunteer and cross-cultural experience. This will help on the application, but more important, it will help you learn whether volunteering is the right direction for you. For instance, many communities have programs for teaching English to recent immigrants; this type of volunteer work is not only valuable in itself but will also provide you with both cross-cultural and teaching experience. Most Peace Corps positions involve some type of teaching, even if you aren't placed in a classroom situation.

GRABER: You have nothing to lose by applying, even though the Lowell Scholarship is very competitive. Once the judges narrow the field, I am sure that there are many equally deserving applicants in any given year. When I was a recipient, there was only one scholar per year. Now there are two.

WHITCOMB: La Muse is not very competitive. It does offer some full fellowships, which might be harder to get. It also sometimes offers barter stays in exchange for manual work. These barter exchanges are not always available. I paid for my stay, but the fee is very reasonable when compared to staying in a hotel in that region for a month. La Muse is equipped with a large communal kitchen with a professional range and plenty of cooking equipment. One can eat wonderfully and cheaply by shopping for local food, cooking in the kitchen, and eating in the dining room or on the terrace. The Aude department—and in particular the village of Labastide-Esparbairenque, where La Muse is located—is an exceptionally beautiful, lightly traveled area of France. The experience is very rural. A national forest of fir and chestnut trees; narrow, winding roads; and mountains and rivers surround the village.

## If a scholarship or another program did not finance your travels, how did you find places to live?

REDDY: My wife had been to Oaxaca many years earlier, and she'd always wanted to return. This, in combination with other poets' rave reviews of the place, sparked our initial interest in spending the year in this part of Mexico. Eliot Weinberger's essay on Oaxaca also made it seem like the perfect place to live for a year and write poetry. Last but not least, my university has a study-abroad program in Oaxaca, which gave us various contacts on the ground there when we arrived.

KUSSEROW: When I travel, I go to places that I can afford and that aren't too removed from the indigenous culture. I try not to live in expat enclaves. I often stay near the organization or nonprofit I am working with, such as the Education and Leadership Initiative offices in Yei, South Sudan, or a guesthouse near the Bhutan Centre for Media and Democracy.

GREENWELL: Most international schools provide assistance with accommodations. Many schools maintain their own apartments, and others help teachers find their own.

AUSTEN: Before I left the United States, I joined SERVAS, an international grassroots organization founded in Denmark after World War II to foster peace through one-on-one contacts between people of different nations. As a member, I received a list of hosts in the countries where I would be traveling and with whom I could stay for a couple of nights. This connection to local people was tremendously important, especially in large urban centers such as Lima, where it's easy to feel isolated. SERVAS families also provided a conduit to cultural events such as poetry readings.

As soon as I arrived in Quito, I enrolled in language school, which included placement with a local family. Over the course of about six weeks, I stayed with three different Ecuadorian families.

### Did you take any jobs while you were abroad? What were they?

POPE: I bought a bookshop in Amsterdam, so that narrowed everything down. That isn't a path open to most people, of course. To back up, I married a Briton who had grown up in Amsterdam. We met in Chicago, where we were both in the book business; each of us had the ambition to own a bookshop one day. The opportunity arose to buy a store where he'd worked for several years prior to coming to the United States. Because I'd always had a desire to live abroad and he wanted to move back to Europe, we borrowed money and bought it.

When we moved to Amsterdam, we were able to rent an apartment in the house his mother owns, so we never had to look for a place to live. That was extremely fortunate because housing in the city center was and is pretty scarce. It was a five-hundred-year-old house on a canal, and I was extremely lucky to live in those surroundings.

Once I had some rudimentary Dutch-language skills, I began working in our bookshop. However, I hadn't anticipated the many differences between the way bookstores are run in the United States and in the Netherlands, not to mention differences in customer behavior and the existence of some outright hostility toward an American's part ownership of the shop. This was balanced by most people's insistence on treating my husband as sole proprietor.

Over time, and I mean after several years, this eased. By then I'd begun doing some freelance translation for a few people, which led to work for the Anne Frank Foundation and then later to a job as the in-house Dutch-English translator for the language center at the University of Amsterdam. I liked being able to switch between environments, and at the university I was constantly meeting other translators, all of us with an accent and a story and usually something else going on. Many were artists.

STONECIPHER: I've always worked while living in Berlin, first for American publishers and now for a German publisher, editing art books. I also work as a translator and occasionally earn money from writing.

AUSTEN: Toward the end of my time in South America, I accepted a monthlong volunteer position at the Lima office of the South American Explorers Club. In return for a private room in the SAEC "clubhouse," three meals a day, and a small stipend, I helped run the office and researched in-country volunteer opportunities for members.

I volunteered with the Fundación Jatun Sacha in Ecuador, an environmental organization focused on preserving Ecuador's biological diversity. Initially, while studying in Quito, I assisted in the plant library, basically filing dried specimens. Very exciting work. Later, I spent ten days at Bilsa, the foundation's remote ecological station of tropical premontane wet forest. I worked in the *vivero*, planting seeds and transplanting seedlings, and helped the station botanist collect seeds and plant specimens on daylong hikes through the 5,500-acre reserve.

KUSSEROW: I do volunteer when I travel—for example, at orphanages in Kathmandu, Nepal, or Kampala, Uganda; at a girls' high school in Yei, South Sudan; at the Tibetan Children's Village in Dharamsala, India; or at the Bhutan Centre for Media and Democracy in Thimphu, Bhutan.

DUNNE: The Japanese fishermen had mentioned that I could teach English in Japan if I had a degree in English—I already had a degree in biology. I decided to study English at the University of Washington, in Seattle. There I met a Japanese woman, Kae, who was studying in the United States. We dated for about a year, and then she returned to Japan. I finished my English degree six months later and decided to travel to Kyoto, where Kae was living, and teach English there. I was fortunate to find work at the Berlitz School of Languages in Kyoto.

After four years in Kyoto, I returned to the United States to pursue studies in creative writing (MFA in poetry) with a secondary emphasis in TESOL (teaching English to speakers of other languages). After I completed my studies, Kae came to the United States, and we married. Immediately after our marriage, we returned to Japan where I was able to resume work at Berlitz while looking for part-time university work. Once I began working part-time at one university, finding jobs at other universities was reasonably easy. The most effective way to find a university teaching job was to have someone recommend me for the position. In this sense, networking and word of mouth were indispensable. After a few years of part-time teaching, I was able to begin applying for full-time positions.

## Did you discover any resources that were helpful in your stay?

AUSTEN: The South American Explorers Club was especially useful because it helped me meet other hikers and offered timely, accurate, and localized information about current conditions on the ground. During the time that I was in Peru, the Sendero Luminoso (Shining Path) was still an active threat in specific parts of the country. Having access to nearly real-time information about this was essential because much of my travel involved tiny villages and the nearby hiking areas.

KUSSEROW: Universities are tremendously helpful—but there aren't many in Bhutan or South Sudan—as are places that support college semester-abroad learning experiences for students. The School for International Training [sit.edu] is excellent, as is the Alliance for Global Education.

FINNEYFROCK: Suvani Singh and Pranab Singh, the owners of the bookstore Quixote's Cove [www.qcbookshop.com] in Kathmandu, are working hard to build a vibrant literary arts scene in the city. They work with schools and colleges to provide library development services and helped establish the Word Warriors, Nepal's first slam poetry group. The Singhs are working toward publishing an anthology of Nepali poetry.

Quixote's Cove is also a literary events management company. It conducts a variety of literary events, including creative-writing groups; a monthly literary discussion series, Tavern Tales; and an annual international literature festival, Kathmandu Literary Jatra [www.litjatra.com].

GREENWELL: In Bulgaria, the Elizabeth Kostova Foundation is a wonderful organization that organizes workshops, readings, and other activities to make connections between Anglophone and Bulgarian writers.

REDDY: A local language school called the Instituto Cultural Oaxaca manages my university's study-abroad program. The institute's director, Lucero Topete, was a wonderful resource for everything from living arrangements to local attractions. Oaxaca is also full of bookstores, libraries, and museums that welcome foreign travelers. The English-language bookstore, in the middle of town, is very useful in particular, as is the English-language Oaxaca Lending Library. Information on all these resources is readily available in any good travel guide to the area.

POPE: One resource in Amsterdam that provided a connection to the writing world was the John Adams Institute, which promotes cultural exchange between the United States and the Netherlands. The institute sponsored readings and lecture series that were great—the writers were mostly novelists, not poets, but the evenings there were always thought provoking.

## What do you wish you had known before living abroad?

DUNNE: With regard to the US Fisheries Observer Program, I suppose it would have been good to know how difficult and isolating an experience it can be, especially when one cannot fully communicate with the men aboard the vessel. This is not to say that I would not do it again but simply to make a note that to be culturally isolated in that way can be trying.

This said, such isolation can also be stimulating and rewarding. It forces a person to consciously consider identity and cultural values, among other things.

With regard to teaching at the university in Japan, it would have been good to know how very different the Japanese university system is from the US system. The differences are directly related to culture. Although it would have been good to know more about the university system before I came, I also believe explanations can go only so far in helping prepare for the experience. To a large degree, I think the differences between the university systems simply have to be experienced—lived.

MEEK: Actually, I felt pretty informed by the time I went. I talked to as many people as I could about the program, and about the country, before leaving the United States. I definitely recommend that. Everyone's experience is going to be different, so no one should be too alarmed—or enchanted—by the narrative experience of the first person he or she talks to. People should read about programs they are interested in and get names of people who have done similar programs and try to contact them. Former volunteers for groups like the Peace Corps tend to be very generous about talking to potential volunteers; regional recruiters will likely be willing to provide names of returned volunteers.

WHITCOMB: It would have been very helpful to have rented a car for my stay at La Muse for my initial residency. I was pretty place-bound except for a weekly shopping excursion to Carcassonne. I made sure to rent a car when we returned the next year with the study-abroad students.

GRABER: I wish I had known immediately upon learning that I had been selected that I would need a long-stay visa, and I wish that I had understood how best to get one. The Lowell Scholarship is not affiliated with any foreign academic institution, and it is time consuming—one needs about four to six months of lead time—to procure a long-stay visa for an

EU country in which one has no official contacts or business.

There is also now an accord—the Schengen Agreement—between most European nations to facilitate travel for EU citizens between the member nations, but one of the consequences is that it severely limits the amount of time a foreigner can stay cumulatively in all of them. You can stay in all of the EU nations collectively for only 90 days out of any 180 days. Your passport is checked only when you enter the EU and when you leave, but you don't want to risk being suddenly kicked out or, worse, being denied reentry to the country in which you've left everything you own in a rented apartment!

Because I could not secure a long-stay visa before I left, I spent a lot of time moving between Britain, where I could stay longer—up to six months at a time—and the continent itself. I finally threw myself on the mercy of the government of Malta, which graciously expedited a long-stay visa application for me. Generally, you *must* have your visa in hand upon arriving in your initial port of entry. The Maltese authorities were, however, very understanding and helpful. Of course, the fact that nearly everyone speaks English there was a tremendous help. I would recommend that all Lowell Scholars traveling to Europe enter through Malta!

I wish I had managed to find a way to stay in one place for the whole year and to simply travel out from there as I wished. Once you are in Europe, it is easy and very inexpensive—if you have only a carry-on bag; bag fees on discount airlines can actually run hundreds of dollars!—to fly from place to place, especially if you are not locked into a schedule. But you really need a solid, inexpensive hub, a place to set up some sort of "home" and to leave most of your belongings.

I also wish I had known how weak the dollar actually was. The exchange rates were unfavorable, and goods were simply much more expensive in many places. Malta, for instance, is in the middle of the Mediterranean. People have to import nearly everything. Hence, most things cost a good bit more there, and no one seems to get rid of anything. There are no charity shops or thrift shops. If you need a spatula, you must apparently purchase it with the thought that you will pass it on one day to your children! There are, moreover, only one or two self-serve laundries. If you do not rent an apartment with a washing machine, you discover that you must send your laundry out to be washed, which is shockingly expensive! In these sorts of economies and radically different consumer cultures, I discovered that I was suddenly quite poor. It is easy to think when you first arrive that you are on a terrifically extended vacation. You cannot, however, afford to live that way! You have to be very, very diligent about your budget.

I also wish I had known that I would not have access to some fairly essential websites (iTunes, for instance, and Netflix). This has to do with how various companies negotiated their worldwide distribution rights. Having a computer abroad was and is a complex scenario. You cannot purchase anything from a US site when your computer is detected as being out of the country. But you also cannot purchase anything from a foreign site with a US computer and only a US credit card! I hear that it is now possible to install a program that masks the location of your computer. That would be one way to avoid this problem. I also think that it could help to open a bank account in your nation of temporary residence in order to get a debit card with a chip—a feature all European cards have—and a European account number. That might allow you to purchase some of the downloads from the European branch of iTunes or at least order books from AmazonUK. Anyone would think that an iPad or iPod or a Kindle would provide access to all the reading and viewing materials necessary or desired, but if you don't download those files before you leave, you cannot buy them abroad!

FINNEYFROCK: I found the pace of the program exhausting. Cultural Envoy Programs last a minimum of ten days, and several days included long stretches of both teaching and performance. In many cases, the workshops were longer than ones I would teach in the United States and were held in the afternoons, before performances. There wasn't much time to rest between day and evening programs.

GREENWELL: As anyone with experience in secondary education knows, teaching high school students is extremely demanding. To continue being productive as a writer requires discipline and efficiency. I didn't write at all for the first year I worked as a teacher.

AUSTEN: There's an adage in the backpacking community that your confidence is inversely proportional to the amount of gear you carry. That was certainly true for me. I took my body weight in stuff. I wish I was being hyperbolic. Hauling all that around created its own set of problems and, ironically, made me feel more vulnerable as my attention was diverted to dealing with the unnecessarily difficult logistics of getting all that stuff—what, they don't have shampoo in Ecuador?—from one place to another. The metaphorical aspect is obvious, I'm sure.

KUSSEROW: Each country totally differs, as does each program. Mostly it is best to let go when you are in another country, to try not to hold on too tight to preconceived ideas of experiences you should have or what people should be like.

### Did you encounter unexpected difficulties as a poet living in an unfamiliar land?

BURLESON: Rwanda was undergoing a civil war when we arrived in 1991, and that continued until we were evacuated in 1993. Even though life went on as usual, there were military checkpoints to navigate and Peace Corps meetings on how to avoid stepping on land mines. We became used to hearing gunfire at night, especially in the northern part of Rwanda. When the Rwandan Patriotic Front took and held the northern third of the country in early 1993, the decision was made to evacuate all the volunteers and close the program. The genocide that began in April 1994 changed everything. Peace Corps Rwanda finally reopened a couple of years ago.

AUSTEN: It turns out that if I have a gift for language, it's only for English. My brain proved strangely resistant to Spanish. Despite previous exposure growing up in San Diego, intense study, living with Spanish speakers, and the daily practice that traveling alone afforded, I never managed more than about a second-grade proficiency, even at the end of my trip. Most of the time, I spoke Spanish with the nuance and complexity of a three-year-old. As someone whose primary sense of identity had always been located in verbal skill and ease, this was intensely alienating and disorienting.

FINNEYFROCK: Food and water in Nepal is often unsafe for Westerners, and despite the incredible generosity and care of my hosts, I got sick. I was forced to cancel two days of my program and was lucky that the other poets traveling with me were able to cover the workshops and performances. I also learned that the US Department of State insurance would cover my medical expenses while I was in the country. Also, the air quality is very poor in Kathmandu. I'm a performer, and I struggled to keep my voice in working order.

STONECIPHER: The only real difficulty I experience is a significant one—I do not live in the country in whose poetic community I participate. I write in English primarily for English speakers, yet I don't live in an English-speaking country.

WHITCOMB: It is hard to call this a difficulty, but I loved being in France again so much that it was hard to sit in my room and write all day. I wanted to explore and experience where I was and sometimes found it impossible to concentrate on recording my impressions.

GRABER: I was very lonely and homesick, and I am among the least patriotic, least social individuals I know. I think, however, that this deep sense of dislocation and this confrontation with my own American-ness were very good for me in the long run.

My sense of displacement was probably somewhat exacerbated by the simple fact that I am a real homebody. I'm very domestic. I missed having my own essential objects around me. I missed having good pots for cooking! By the last few months, I was traveling with one good kitchen knife, a knife sharpener, a wooden spoon, a cutting board, a French press, and a skillet. I was down to two pairs of jeans and six T-shirts. And a few wool sweaters and boots. I kept replacing the clothing in my suitcase with housewares! I came to see what really mattered to me. You don't really need a fancy dress or a tie and nice shoes when you wake up in a strange place after traveling for twenty-four hours straight! You need some good coffee and a pair of quick-drying socks.

In many places, you are going to have limited access to English-language texts. Unless you ship your library with you, you are going to feel some frustration. I did not have a Kindle or an iPad with me, but I'm not sure that that would have given me what I was seeking. And, of course, one part of being a real "thing" person is the desire to hold the book as an object in your hands. You have to be prepared for the fact that there might only be six books in English in a used bookstore. I think I paid $35 for a used hardback edition of Oliver Sacks's *Musicophilia* in Budapest. And it was worth it! The library on Gozo had no poetry after modernism. These limitations forced me to value deeply whatever was at hand. I read all of H. D., and I reread Pound's prose on poetry. And Eliot's essays. This was terrific. I was thrilled when the librarian there agreed finally to give me my own library card and let me take the books home!

MEEK: In my case, it was difficult to get books. I knew it would be an issue, but I didn't fully anticipate how expensive books would be and how little access I would have to them. At times, I was really starved for poetry. A gift package of books from my mother could seem as revitalizing as a blood transfusion. My advice here is to find out about where you are going—will you have access to a library? If so, will there be books in English? Will there be poetry? You will likely have very little or no access to books of contemporary American poetry. I found it was really important to have that infusion of the living voice of my own culture, even as I was living in a different culture and trying to absorb all I could there. Try to be proactive with this—if you have supportive family members and friends, consider asking as many of them as you can if they could send you a new book of poems occasionally. Postage can often be very expensive, so diffusing these costs among multiple friends and family members will be appreciated.

DUNNE: I think the difficulties were pretty much anticipated: few bookstores with English books, few opportunities to hear poetry being read in public (in English), a fractured poetry community—poet friends living far and wide within the country—difficulty in finding like-minded souls to talk with about poetry. Though these difficulties were anticipated, I was surprised by how desperately I actually missed them in my daily life—the luxury of walking into a good bookstore with stacks of poetry books to peruse.

REDDY: One thing I found difficult was accessing English-language books. The local English-language bookstore was helpful in special-ordering texts, but it took some time for volumes to arrive. The local English-language library was a wonderful place, but holdings in my particular (i.e., eccentric and eclectic) areas of interest were spotty. I couldn't access my university's online collection while living in Mexico, so I relied on sources such as the Questia online library to patch in holes wherever I could. But still, there were times when I would have loved having access to the stacks of a major research university's collections.

POPE: I had deeply underestimated the effects of living in a foreign language and culture, the simple and pervasive level of disorientation involved. Many of the writers I admired had been expatriates at some point, and I think I naïvely felt it was a pretty common rite of passage, something that enhanced rather than hindered the work.

I also underestimated how it would feel to be away from my friends, and it was hard to keep in touch—this was before e-mail. Phone calls cost a fortune, and the six-hour time difference was tricky. Letters took a week to get from one continent to the other. I really lived for them, though.

It seemed sort of ridiculous to miss US culture when Hollywood movies and certain TV shows were readily available, not to mention mass-market books, but after the first couple of years, I did miss it. Not the mass-market stuff—small things, regional things, particularities, the stuff Europeans can't believe exists in the United States. I especially missed the invention and playfulness of English. I know that this was intensified by the effort to live in another language, which entails strait-ened expressive circumstances for quite some time, but I think it also had to do with some of the essential differences between the two languages. I also missed the small-press culture—there was nothing comparable to it in the Netherlands.

## Were there unexpected joys?

REDDY: The unexpected joys were everywhere. But this is part of living abroad—you never know what you'll miss the most upon departure. Even the things I found irritating when I first went to Oaxaca—the dogs barking from the rooftops at every passerby, the fireworks going off in the middle of the night—became part of the wonder and joy of the place in good time. And I'm not even mentioning the pleasures we discovered in the food, the culture, and the friends we made during our time in Mexico.

GRABER: Every difficulty was also a strange joy, though you might be dis-traught in the moment. Loneliness is a joy because it asserts that you at least like *some* other people! It felt very good to discover that I had some actual affection for the United States. I stayed up all night in London streaming the 2008 election results on my laptop, and I wept. I was as proud as I have ever been of my country, especially as I had encountered so many Europeans who were convinced that Obama would never be elected, even though the polls had him ahead. The election radically changed what it meant to be an American in Europe. That is not an overstatement. It was a real blessing to be able to see firsthand the world's perception of the nation change quite radically and suddenly.

AUSTEN: One of the most surprising and humbling experiences was how often very poor people showed spontaneous generosity toward me. It's hard to say how much of this was because I was a woman traveling alone, but many bus and train rides included someone offering to accompany me to my destination or to feed me. Even Quechua speakers, whose Spanish was often only marginally better than mine, would make the effort to use the small shreds of language we shared in common to connect in an act of generosity. A family of six would open their cloth manta with a simple lunch—perhaps their only meal of the day—and invite me to share it.

These experiences and the fact that I was living on about fifteen dollars a day for months at a time, including transportation, shifted my relationship to money in a significant, long-lasting way. Not that I live now with anything remotely like that kind of austerity, but my attitude toward what I consider a necessity versus a luxury was permanently altered.

The depth of solitude I encountered, especially when backpacking alone for several days in a remote national park in central Ecuador, did not feel joyful at the time. However, during that experience I was more intensely in contact with my own vulnerability and resourcefulness than ever, and there was a certain—perhaps not joy exactly—but satisfaction in recognizing that after the fact.

WHITCOMB: I loved how easy it was to explain having a profession as a professor and a poet.

BURLESON: Rwanda was and is an incredibly beautiful place, and the people there were very welcoming and friendly. I grew close with a number of people and am still in touch with those who survived the genocide. My best friend, Roger Remera, came and lived with me for several years in the United States after he managed, though shot and left for dead in the forest, to survive the genocide. He just returned to Arusha, Tanzania, this past year to testify at the International Criminal Tribunal for Rwanda against the man who shot him and killed his brother. Seventeen years have elapsed in the meantime. His finally getting to tell what happened from his own perspective was an important moment for us both. Living with Roger, hearing night after night his story and the stories of our friends who were killed or who managed to escape, made me see the world in a new way.

FINNEYFROCK: The US embassy staff could not have been more accommodating. As a spoken-word artist who sometimes writes pieces that are critical of US policy, I was concerned about being censored abroad. Instead, I found the embassy staff encouraging my right to perform any poem and state any views I held. Likewise, my Nepali hosts were among the warmest people I've met. We spent many nights with Nepali poets, drinking and laughing and talking about poetry in the warm evenings after dinner.

GREENWELL: I encounter unexpected joys every day in Sofia, where after two years I'm still discovering new things almost every day. It helps that new things are being uncovered nearly every day as well; new ruins are being found as the city continues developing its metro. The language is also a continuing, unexpected joy; I had never studied a Slavic language before and am constantly delighted by the quirks and challenges of Bulgarian.

STONECIPHER: Living in a city that constantly offers me ideas and stimulation and interesting people and endless reflection is a joy. Learning German was (and is—it's a lifelong process) a joy.

POPE: Most of my joys were connected to the point when I achieved a level of fluency in Dutch that allowed me to express myself beyond perfunctory exchanges, to read more than newspapers, and most of all to enjoy Dutch humor.

NEZHUKUMATATHIL: A small thing, but I was able to watch and help my four-foot ten-inch grandmother prepare several meals in her modest kitchen, was able to see and touch and smell all the glass spice jars delicately arranged on the windowsill. I hadn't planned that quiet intimacy, could not even afford to dream it up, me, a girl who grew up feeling a palpable sadness at not being able to spend time with my grandmothers (my grandmother in the Philippines died a few weeks after I was born in Chicago). Had I elected to stay at a hotel or resort, I never would have experienced those rich moments. The best decision I ever made about my time abroad was that, with the exception of a handful of days over the course of more than two months abroad, I always stayed in the homes of my cousins or uncles. I feel hugely blessed to have been embedded in those cultures, if only for a few months.

DUNNE: Because poetry friends were hard to find, when I did find them, I tended to value them greatly. Those relationships seemed to take on greater significance and meaning than they might have otherwise. They became a sort of lifeline. Years ago in Kyoto, for example, some interested folks began meeting in coffee shops to talk about poetry and to exchange books. Eventually, the group grew. In time, we began to meet at the home of the expatriate American poet Cid Corman. He graciously held weekly poetry meetings and took on the role of mentor for many of us. At these gatherings, poetry was read and talked about for hours and hours. It filled a vital need, and we recognized that need as something elemental in our lives.

Another joy came in time through learning the Japanese language. This deepened my appreciation of the culture and its literature. I began to realize how much of what we experience and understand is mediated through language. A further joy came from simply having the opportunity to experience a different culture and all that entails. This experience helped me understand my own culture more—its values, assumptions, and aesthetics.

MEEK: Of course, there were many highs—and lows—during those two years. A significant unexpected joy was how fascinating the smallest day-to-day workings of the natural world and the village community could be: the flight of termites after rain, dung beetles doing their exhaustive work. And certainly, the amazing personalities of free-range goats!

KUSSEROW: Countless joys, infinite, mind-boggling—every day is like being in an altered state of consciousness. This is why I travel. Everything about it makes you grow; you realize your own smallness, your insignificance. You realize you are not the norm, your ethnocentricity suddenly becomes crystal clear, you hopefully become more humble because of this, you fall in love with other truths, other faiths, other norms, so that you become a more agile and tolerant human being, one who is less judgmental, more expansive, more compassionate.

### Did you need language skills for your travels?

WHITCOMB: No, but they would have been an asset. I occasionally had some difficulty because of my limited French, but that is to be expected.

I had one incident with language at a wonderful restaurant in Roquefère, a town neighboring Labastide-Esparbairenque. The cote-acher and I had arranged to take our study-abroad class down to have a big Sunday lunch. In my efforts to help the students navigate the menu, I mistakenly translated *écrevisse* on the menu as shrimp (crevette)—only to have big bowls of crawfish arrive, looking very much like large pink bugs in butter-herb sauce. Fortunately, the students rolled with it and gamely attacked the écrevisse.

BURLESON: I studied French and Kinyarwanda.

FINNEYFROCK: Most Nepali people I encountered spoke English and translated their poems into English.

MEEK: I was a volunteer in Botswana, which has two national languages, English and Setswana. The Peace Corps provided us with two months of language training in Setswana, in-country, before sending us to our job posts. I used English as a teacher; the basic knowledge of Setswana I received in training helped with communication around the village, with polite conversation, and with understanding the specific challenges my Setswana-speaking students had in learning English.

This will vary; for some countries, knowledge of Spanish or French, for instance, will give you a competitive advantage in applying, but for other countries or programs, no prior language skills will be expected. Your recruiter will take into consideration any language abilities you have when matching you with a program, but language ability (or lack thereof) is just one factor for placement. Don't assume, for instance, that if you are fluent in Spanish, you will necessarily be sent to a Spanish-speaking country; at least one volunteer in our group was fluent in Spanish, and there was absolutely no use for her Spanish in Botswana.

GREENWELL: British and US international schools use English as the common language, and in Sofia, at least, it is possible to get around without the language. That said, I think any international experience is extremely limited without some access to the language of the place.

KUSSEROW: I have been able to get by on English in Bhutan, India, Nepal, South Sudan, and Uganda. But knowing the language at least a bit opens many doors and is vital insofar as it is symbolic of attempts to appreciate and respect the other culture.

POPE: I wasn't in a program, but I certainly needed language skills, and I would emphatically recommend that any American traveling anywhere learn at least a handful of words in the local language, even if the trip is only for a short time. A willingness to try using the local language counts for a great deal, wherever you go. Because we have lousy foreign-language education in the United States, we don't usually get the chance to practice, experiment, and become more comfortable with trying basic exchanges, but trying is essential. The unwillingness to do so is perceived as rudeness or another demonstration of Americans' sense of superiority, which ironically is the opposite of what many of us feel, especially when attempting to communicate.

DUNNE: Language skills were not required—but language skills were always an asset. I did a lot of independent study. While in Kyoto, I studied Japanese at a language school.

GRABER: Language skills would have been awesome, but I don't speak any language other than English. I can read or semiread a few, but I am too shy to try to make the right sounds! I got around fine in Budapest, and I don't know any Magyar at all. Hence, I'd say you don't *need* another language. On the other hand, I was on the subway one day when the train stopped in the tunnel and an announcement came on. Oddly, there was no one else in the car I was riding. It was in the middle of the afternoon on an extraordinarily hot day. That was a frightening moment. I had no idea what I was being instructed to do. Eventually the train started up again, and we went on our way. Similarly, in the middle of the night, a car drove up and down the streets playing a recorded message through a loudspeaker. I have no idea even now what that might have been. I looked out the window, and no one seemed to be evacuating her home or otherwise bracing for a disaster, so I just went back to bed.

### What advice can you offer about staying in touch with loved ones, managing money issues, arranging storage, and taking care of domestic matters?

AUSTEN: The Internet has changed this aspect of travel so profoundly since my trip. I'm sure many things that were difficult in 1996 to 1997 would be much easier now. At that point, when Internet cafés were still a rarity and before texting became the cheap international mode of communication, keeping track of what was happening with my bank account or contacting family and friends was difficult. These matters depended on involvement with something like a language school or the South American Explorers Club in order to access a general e-mail account or fax.

I had two periods of thirty-plus days when no one at home knew exactly where I was, and there was no way to contact me. Internet cafés didn't exist in the remote areas where I was traveling, and at any rate, I didn't have a personal e-mail account. Phone calls were prohibitively expensive, and I was often in places with few phones and an intermittent power supply.

Now it would be much rarer to be out of communication range. But the fact is that I engaged most deeply with my surroundings, and with the intensity of the experience, during those unconnected weeks. The depth of my aloneness—though often overwhelming and unwelcome—was essential to the kind of transformation I was seeking. If I'd been able to check in via e-mail or text every few days, I would have missed the most significant and transformative confrontations with my own fears and limitations. Instead I turned to my journal, where I talked to myself in order to understand, remember, and process what I was seeing and experiencing.

So my advice would be to manage the expectations of people at home so that you can fully immerse yourself in the experience at hand. Having to check in all the time can mean never quite fully giving over to being where you are and might deprive you of the unexpected gifts of solitude.

WHITCOMB: A lot of places I visited recently have wi-fi, which makes things easy. I also got international calling and data plans for my BlackBerry, which worked perfectly in France and Spain. Flash drives are essential. Make sure the data roaming on your phone is not turned on, especially if you receive e-mails on your smartphone. This can really rack up the bills.

BURLESON: I knew I'd be gone for two years, so I put everything in order—and sold a lot of stuff—before I left. Staying in touch was tricky with a postal system that usually worked but took a long time. Letters from folks back home were especially welcome when they did arrive!

GRABER: I am still recovering from the financial cost of having been fortunate enough to receive back-to-back fellowships (the Hodder Fellowship at Princeton and then the Amy Lowell Poetry Travelling Scholarship). These both required me to live somewhere other than in the home I own. I don't think these opportunities were necessarily designed for individuals with mortgages and pets. I could have self-selected out, but I didn't, and I'm obviously glad that I had these two years, which were so essential to my work and which profoundly changed my understanding of who I am. At the same time, I could barely live on the Lowell Scholarship stipend, given the very unfavorable exchange rates at that particular moment, and then I still had to pay my own mortgage, my home insurance, my property taxes, et cetera.

The Lowell Scholarship does not come with a health care package, and after a certain point in your life, you really need good health insurance. The sort of health insurance that travelers purchase did not seem to me to be enough. I was not worried about breaking my arm; I was worried about being diagnosed while I was abroad with a very serious condition that might require long-term treatment. I felt I needed health care such that I would be able, if necessary, to return home to get whatever care I needed. I wanted coverage that would be good worldwide. Fortunately, I was able to negotiate with my home university to provide that for me, but not all Lowell Scholars will have "home institutions."

FINNEYFROCK: My program was short, lasting only two weeks, but it still placed demands on my teaching schedule in the United States. The planning period for the trip was only a few months, and I was lucky that my job with Writers in the Schools was accommodating. The US Department of State was prompt with payments, so money issues were not a problem for this trip. Our hotel provided Internet access, so video chats were the best way to talk to people back home.

GREENWELL: For money issues, be sure to acquire credit cards with addresses in the United States, and keep an open bank account in the United States as well. Banks have widely differing policies affecting ATM fees and customer support internationally.

For staying in touch with family in the United States, Skype has been indispensable. Video chat is great, and it's very cheap to maintain a US phone number through Skype that friends and families can call from their regular phones. This number needs to be arranged while you're still in the United States.

POPE: Staying in touch is so much easier now that it can be done electronically for minimal expense and in a way that isn't time dependent. Money issues are tricky because US systems are so different than they are in much of the world, but at least it's easier to use ATMs in most places. I had a postal giro account—a fantastic system that doesn't exist anymore because of privatization. People I know who have traveled abroad for extended periods have lived on credit cards and shared a checking account with someone in the United States who received and paid their bills.

DUNNE: During my time in Japan—about twenty-five years, on and off—technology has advanced to such a degree that staying in touch with family and friends is no longer much of a problem. In addition to frequent Skype calls and e-mail, I like to return to the United States about once a year to stay in touch with friends and family.

Storage is a problem, however, and I have not found any successful way around it, other than the obvious: try to minimize the amount of my possessions.

REDDY: The one thing that made our year abroad possible was finding a good subletter for our apartment. Our tenant was pretty much ideal. She forwarded our important mail to us in Mexico, kept the apartment clean as a whistle, and paid her rent on time every month. Without her, I don't think we could have managed to transport our lives south of the border for that precious year abroad. The other things, such as staying in touch with family and accessing bank accounts in the United States, were a piece of cake. With things such as ATMs and Skype, the details generally worked themselves out.

RUCH: While I was stationed in South Korea, it was very easy to find inexpensive, used cell phones set up to work with calling cards, and I primarily stayed in touch with my family in this way. Friends who were stationed in Germany found similar resources available there. There were also numerous Internet cafés throughout the metropolitan areas I visited in South Korea, and I've found that to be true of many other countries as well.

Automatic bill pay probably saved my credit score while I was stationed overseas. Everything that can be paid by automatic bank draft every month should be set up that way for peace of mind while you're abroad. Put things such as your cell phone service and auto insurance on hold until you get back home.

Paying for a monitored security service was well worth the expense for the peace of mind it gave me while I was deployed. At a minimum, arrange to have someone keep an eye on your house and check on it from time to time in case of unexpected issues, such as frozen pipes or leaky roofs. This person should also regularly collect any newspapers, phone books, or flyers that are left in the driveway, on the front door, or on your car windshield. Obviously, this person should know how to get in touch with you.

If you will be away only for a month or two, have the post office hold your mail until you return. If you will be away longer, consider having your mail forwarded to a family member or friend. The person can send along the important correspondence once a month or so.

If you plan to be out of the country for an extended period, you should consider leaving a very trustworthy individual with a limited power of attorney. If your roof blows off in a tornado or your basement floods or your front door is kicked in (you get the idea), this person will be able to access the necessary funds and sign off on any repairs quickly to resolve these issues before they lead to more costly problems.

It's also not a bad idea to prepare a will before you leave the country, especially if you will be traveling to any politically unstable destinations. Leave a copy in a safe-deposit box and a copy with a close friend or family member, along with photocopies of your passport, driver's license, major credit cards, health insurance card, and itinerary. In the event that these items are lost or stolen, you will be able to expedite their replacement by having this information on hand in a safe location.

I cannot stress enough how important it is to find a willing and responsible caretaker for your pets, a person who understands how much they mean to you. While I was deployed, one of my dogs was put down without my consent for a treatable condition that I had successfully managed for some time. My dog's caretaker had been fully briefed about his condition and how to treat it before I left the country, but she failed to administer the appropriate medication and as a result chose to have my dog put down without even consulting me. I am telling this story only to illustrate the potential repercussions of this decision. Take it very seriously.

MEEK: I was in the Peace Corps twenty years ago, and it was a whole different world, communication-wise, back then. Now cell phones are widely used even in what might be considered quite "remote" areas. I have traveled for extended periods in southern Africa in recent years as well, though, and I would suggest that you have a cell phone but that you don't use it constantly to call "home." As much as you can stay in the place, do so. My suggestion: if you are dying of loneliness, call someone. If your family is afraid for you, set up a plan for regular contact. But focus on where you are now—the place you went to a lot of trouble to experience fully. Writing letters can be a good way to process your experience through language and to keep in touch with loved ones without being pulled abruptly out of your new place.

## Do you have any technical equipment suggestions?

RUCH: A digital voice recorder is small, easy to pack, relatively inexpensive, and extremely handy for collecting stories that can later be transcribed and written directly or indirectly into your work. Make sure you have a large enough memory card or possibly more than one if you won't be able to download your recorded files onto a computer until you get home. Also make sure you will be able to find the batteries your device requires, or take a supply with you.

AUSTEN: This may be obvious, but be clear about what you need the equipment to do—is broadcast quality essential?—and get the smallest, lightest equipment you can afford that will provide that functionality.

POPE: I had pens and notebooks and, later, a manual typewriter.

MEEK: Definitely I'd recommend a small digital camera and audio recorder—and video, if that's something you'd like to do. Go for compact sizes first! If you are going to stay in one country for an extended time, take a phone and buy a SIM card in that country. If you are going to be traveling in multiple countries, consider buying an international cell phone, which will allow you to travel across international borders without losing service. You can get an international cell phone and pay by the minutes you use, with no monthly fees. This can be good because it will help you limit your conversations!

GREENWELL: I'm a big fan of Dropbox, especially given the unreliability of computers in many international schools.

STONECIPHER: Skype—for something like thirteen dollars a month, you can make all the phone calls you want to American landlines and cell phones.

NEZHUKUMATATHIL: I didn't have access to these at the time of my trips to India and the Philippines, but I would say Skype and a small, lightweight video camera would now be indispensible for communicating with people at home and recording sights and sounds.

DUNNE: I don't really have any suggestions here—other than Skype. I do all my international calling on Skype and find it to be of great value and highly dependable.

REDDY: We just took our laptops with us. Setting up a phone and an Internet connection was time consuming, but our landlords in Oaxaca were helpful on that front. Once we were hooked up with wireless in the apartment, everything else came along pretty easily.

KUSSEROW: I have a whole host of things I take as an anthropologist that probably wouldn't be relevant to poets. But definitely take a laptop. Internet cafés are everywhere now, even at Everest base camp. I also like giving the locals my camera—it's fascinating to see what they find worthy of a picture. In the places I travel, there are often norms around picture taking, so you need to clue into those before you start snapping. You can be thrown in jail in South Sudan for taking a picture, whereas in Bhutan it can bring on a flood of eager and giggly kids dying to see their images.

FINNEYFROCK: I wish I had taken a video recorder. That footage would be worth so much to me now.

## Being There

### Did you read the poets of the countries you traveled to either before or during your time there?

GREENWELL: There's not much in the way of translation from Bulgarian into English, but a couple of anthologies have been published since 1989. The most beautiful translations I've found are three poems of the great poet Valeri Petrov translated by Richard Wilbur. A number of exciting young writers work in Bulgarian; thanks to the efforts of the Elizabeth Kostova Foundation and others, it is becoming easier to find them in English.

GRABER: I tried to make a point of reading the poets of each region I visited. I read the Hungarian poets when I was in Hungary (in translation, of course). I read Walter Benjamin every day I was in Berlin. I read W.S. Graham in Cornwall, John Burnside in Scotland.

MEEK: I read what I could of regional poets before I left but could not find at that time the work of any Batswana poets available in the United States. Once in Botswana, I found a bookstore in Gaborone that carried local writers, including a few poets whose work I then was able to read. However, the work of a number of South African poets and many southern African novelists, including Bessie Head (who emigrated from South Africa to Botswana), was available in both the United States and Botswana. I read as much as I could find, both before, during, and after my two years in Botswana.

WHITCOMB: In France, I did not. The region around La Muse is the legendary land of the troubadours, and I read a lot of history of the area. In preparation for the study-abroad class, the coteacher and I assembled a course pack with readings for the students to look at on the plane. It contained excerpts from books on medieval architecture, the history of the Cathars, maps, and a key essay on creativity and the unknown by Peter Turchi.

BURLESON: I taught English at the university in Rwanda and had the chance to read Rwandan poets in translations to French and English. My colleagues at the university were very helpful in explaining the history of Rwandan poetry, an art form very much respected and central to the culture.

FINNEYFROCK: I did read short stories by a Nepali writer who is well known in the United States, but I didn't find books by any Nepali poets before leaving.

KUSSEROW: The countries that I work in don't seem to have many modern poets who have written bodies of work that were available to me before leaving. But I always try to find any anthropologists who write poetry about the country to which I am going. I subscribe to and am a member of *Anthropology and Humanism*, which publishes anthropological poetry. I often get great recommendations of travel poets from other anthropologists at the American Anthropological Association meetings. These happen each year in the United States, and I often lead poetry workshops for anthropologists and give readings with other anthropologists at these. The meetings are a great place to make connections, hear about books, and be encouraged to write poetically as an anthropologist.

STONECIPHER: The best thing about learning German was then being able to read Celan, Rilke, Goethe, et cetera, and contemporary poets in the original. Rilke, for example, was a complete revelation. The English-language Rilke is a fabrication.

POPE: I didn't read any Dutch poets before I left, though I did read some fiction in translation. There was and is not a great deal of Dutch literature in English translation. While I was living in Amsterdam, I began reading Dutch poets. Spending my days in a bookshop made the value attached to poetry clear—it was read by a real cross-section of book buyers, very unlike in the United States. Dutch people would often tell me that their poets were far more accomplished than their novelists, that what they did with the language was far more ambitious and significant. Once I found a few writers whose work attracted me, I began trying to translate poems as a change from all the commercial translation I was doing, in which the language was far from interesting.

NEZHUKUMATATHIL: Yes, especially Kamala Das, Rabindranath Tagore, Eric Gamalinda, Alfred A. Yuson, and Marjorie Evasco.

DUNNE: I read the work of Japanese poets prior to coming to Japan. Their poetry prompted me to come to Japan. I was captivated by the aesthetics that I found there. While in Japan, I have continued to read Japanese work, although I tend to read primarily in English translation.

REDDY: I'm embarrassed to say no, I didn't really read the poets of Mexico before or during my time in Oaxaca. Just before leaving the country, I did stop by the local university bookstore to pick up some Latin American poetry—people such as Dario, Huidobro, Hernández, and others—but I didn't really focus on Mexican poetry in particular.

AUSTEN: While living in Quito and then in Lima, I went to several poetry readings and dance-theater performances that involved poetry. My reading was largely focused on understanding tropical rain forest and altiplano ecology and the history and present-day effects of Spanish colonialism and the indigenous human-rights movement.

### Did you interact with other poets while living abroad?

FINNEYFROCK: I was introduced to several poets by our hosts, Suvani Singh and Pranab Singh, from Quixote's Cove bookstore in Kathmandu. They had been running open-mic poetry nights already and were thrilled to introduce us to the small band of poets in Nepal who had already heard of poetry slams. We had several informal, social nights together and two performances with the local poets.

GREENWELL: The Elizabeth Kostova Foundation, which I've already mentioned, is a great resource for making connections with writers here. For teachers working in secondary schools, the alumni network is also a terrific resource. The majority of the writers I've met here have been friends of an alumnus I met more or less by chance.

STONECIPHER: I interact with lots of poets in Berlin. I meet them in the usual ways, through friends, by going to readings, et cetera.

AUSTEN: I had brief conversations with a couple of poets in Lima. They were friendly and receptive, but my Spanish was so limited that it was extremely frustrating to try to talk about poetry with them—I just didn't have the vocabulary. My pleasure in hearing their poems read in Spanish wasn't dependent on understanding them, but conversation, of course, requires comprehension.

WHITCOMB: I met a group of experimental visual artists who were introduced through the owners of La Muse. During my initial residency, we made a "land art" project in the woods above Saint-Julien by shaping shards of the native slate into a giant egg-shaped sculpture. When I returned to La Muse with the study-abroad group, I met many of these artists again at a party in the village.

BURLESON: Though I didn't have the chance to interact with other poets, I did work with a Rwandan novelist, Daniel Kanyandekwe, who was my colleague at the university. He later won a scholarship to study in the United States and finished a PhD in New York. He unfortunately died young while still in the United States, and his remarkable fiction remains mostly unpublished.

POPE: I didn't know other poets in Amsterdam. I knew some prose writers and a number of painters who were serious readers of poetry and sometimes incorporated it in their work.

NEZHUKUMATATHIL: Through the helpful coordination of Filipino literati star Mr. Krip A. Yuson, I was to read at the MagNet performance space at Ateneo de Manila University, but alas, I was pregnant and nauseated during that time and could not make the six-hour drive over winding roads to Manila.

DUNNE: I have interacted with a number of poets while living in Japan. I have interacted with poets whom I have translated and with Japanese editors of literary magazines. I have also interacted with many expatriate,

English-speaking poets from around the world: Australia, Canada, India, Ireland, Nigeria, and New Zealand.

I met most of my contacts through word-of-mouth connections. Cid Corman enjoyed connecting people he thought would enjoy meeting one another. I am indebted to him for having introduced me to a number of contacts who became friends. In this sense, Corman was something of a central connection for me, a hub.

KUSSEROW: I have never met another poet (at least not someone who described himself or herself as such) in the countries I have visited. But in some countries, the word *poet* has a very different meaning that cannot be separated from other religious roles.

REDDY: My wife and I didn't make friends with any Mexican poets while living in Oaxaca, but, oddly enough, we became close friends with two American poets during that time. Joshua Edwards, who was in Oaxaca on a Fulbright grant, and Lynn Xu, his partner, were living in the city that year and became our constant companions. It would have been a lonelier and less artistically productive experience without them.

### Were you aware of opportunities for publishing your poetry in the magazines and periodicals of other countries? How did you learn of these opportunities?

FINNEYFROCK: Yes. In fact, I have kept in touch with many of the poets I met in Nepal through social media sites. Quixote's Cove is currently finishing a compilation of spoken-word poetry from Nepal and asked me to contribute poems to the anthology.

STONECIPHER: Journals and magazines are as monolingual in Germany as they are in the United States. If one's poetry is to be published in them, it has to be in the form of translation.

DUNNE: I was aware of several magazines in Japan that published work in both Japanese and English. These magazines were mentioned in Dustbooks' *Directory of Poetry Publishers*. Some of them are associated with major universities in Japan.

POPE: Those opportunities were few and far between. I learned about them from magazines. My impression is that there is a lot more opportunity now—because of the Internet, of course, but also because the greater degree of mobility of citizens within the EU has resulted in the creation of more English-language venues.

### Have you written about the countries where you lived?

NEZHUKUMATATHIL: I've written and continue to write poems and essays about both India and the Philippines. In fact, a good portion of my new manuscript deals with my travels and observations while living in southern India, particularly in the state of Kerala, where my father was born.

Kerala has one of the forty-two tiger reserves set up to protect some of the estimated 1,706 tigers left in India. I'm currently writing about the ecotourist trade there, in particular with the tiger preserves. Tourists who come along on various tours and preserve maintenance operations become involved in the conservation of the forests of Periyar and help generate some valuable revenue for the community too. People who once made a living by illegal operations in the forests have since become forest protectors and earn their livelihood through these programs. My husband and I participated in one of these tours for our first anniversary, and I've been studying the physiology and conservation efforts of the majestic tiger ever since.

POPE: My first book of poems, *Watermark*, was in large part about Amsterdam and my experiences living there. I've also written a lot of prose about that period.

DUNNE: I have written broadcast essays for NHK radio. I have also written at some length about my mentoring under Cid Corman. Presently, I am writing a mixed-form (prose and poetry) memoir that explores my life in Japan and my journey into the vocation in poetry.

AUSTEN: In one sense, no, I haven't written about Ecuador, Peru, or Bolivia in a way that would be clear to the reader. But in another sense, my experiences there informed everything I've written since. For example, "The Girl Who Goes Alone" is the title poem of my first chapbook. In its final form, the poem is situated in the landscape of the Pacific Northwest, but the original draft was actually about a three-day solo backpacking trip I did in Sangay National Park, a particularly remote area of central Ecuador. I discarded the literal details of that trip in subsequent revisions, but my experience of being completely out of my depth in terms of the extremity of the physical challenge I'd set for myself, and the way my own fears kept me from enjoying what was, in retrospect, an amazingly beautiful trip, gave me the subject matter in the deepest sense of that phrase.

GRABER: Almost all the poems in the last section of *The Eternal City* are set in foreign landscapes. There are poems set in Berlin and Budapest, Cornwall and Gozo.

FINNEYFROCK: I have tried several times to write about Nepal. For me, this trip marked my first visit to Asia and my first trip to a developing country, one of the world's poorest. As a privileged person from the first world, I struggle to find ways to write about my experience there that honor the country and the people of Nepal while acknowledging my perceptions as a Westerner. In trying to avoid the exploitative or voyeuristic elements of writing about a culture that is not my own, I find a challenge in creating work that is engaging and honest.

MEEK: My first book of poems, *Nomadic Foundations*, centers on my experience living in Botswana and traveling in southern Africa. I have returned to the region four times in the last three years, and the poems generated from this experience, in the context of having also lived there twenty years ago, when southern Africa was a vastly different world, are really the centerpiece of the book of poems I am currently working on, *An Ecology of Elsewhere*.

GREENWELL: My first book, *Mitko*, is set in Bulgaria and draws a great deal from my experiences in my first year here. My new project is also about Bulgaria, and I have written a number of essays about teaching and living here as well. I suspect that I will continue to find inspiration in this place for a long time.

BURLESON: My first book of poems, *Ejo: Poems, Rwanda 1991–94*, centers on my experience in Rwanda and what happened to my Rwandan friends, colleagues, and students during the genocide. I wrote the book as a memorial for those who had been murdered, and it wasn't a project I had any choice about. The poems demanded to be written. As William Carlos Williams wrote:

> It is difficult
> to get the news from poems
> yet men die miserably every day
> for lack
> of what is found there.

I had a story that I had to tell over and over, and poetry seemed to me to be the best vehicle to get at that story, to transform my experience and the experiences of my friends into a solid object that would last—a memorial for those whose voices were silenced.

## How did living abroad affect your work?

RUCH: My time overseas affected my work profoundly. Those experiences gave my writing purpose and direction and a much larger scope, and they play a central role in most of what I write today. Everything—from the ethical dilemmas I struggle with when deciding which stories to tell to the language I use to tell them—has been influenced by many long months lived in these two war-torn countries. Sometimes I can't write the things I want to write. I've been told it takes seven years before a person can effectively write about traumatic experiences. War changed me, irreversibly; war changes everyone. How could it not change the very soul of my work?

POPE: I am still discovering ways in which it affected my work. Foremost was the experience of living in another language and now living with the ghost of that language. It also led to my involvement in literary translation, and that's been valuable in itself. I know that I was exposed to the work of a lot of writers I wouldn't have encountered otherwise—Dutch, British, French, and others. There were even American writers whose work I might not have read at all if I hadn't encountered them there, in a different context, where I could pay a different kind of attention.

I learned something about what it's like to be from a minority culture, what it means when a person's native tongue is a minor language. Beyond that, I became aware of what linguistic minorities are—people in the United States don't encounter these distinctions and issues of identity.

Underneath the effects that had to do directly with writing, the experience of such a profound degree of strangeness, the work of figuring out so much from the ground up, is something that fundamentally changed my life and how I think.

BURLESON: Living in Rwanda for nearly two years and the reverse culture shock I experienced after returning to the United States utterly changed the way I experienced the world. I had a breakdown in the cereal aisle at Safeway shortly after I got home. There were just too many choices, and the neon colors were overwhelming. I haven't really eaten cereal since. Living in Rwanda made me reconsider my life and how and what I ate, what I really needed to survive, as opposed to what my own culture suggested I might want. I began to grow and gather my own food and to avoid the supermarket as much as possible.

NEZHUKUMATATHIL: I'm keenly aware of and sensitive about not exoticizing the landscapes of my parents, because I feel at once very much at home and very much a visitor. I try to take care not to present "tourist poetry" but instead to sing the songs of all the beauty of the people and the topography of those two lands in a very accessible and dynamic way. In a way, I feel like I'm always essentially writing unrequited love songs for India and the Philippines.

KUSSEROW: Going abroad is everything. It "makes/creates" my work, my poetry. Ethically, I'm not sure I could write about a country without living there; this is sort of the anthropologists' code of honor. In anthropology, no one takes you seriously if you write about a culture you haven't lived in for a while. You are considered a fraud. I also tend to distrust poets who write about cultures they have never been to or lived in.

AUSTEN: Before responding to these questions, I reread the journals from my time in South America, and I see, fifteen years later, how certain things I was trying to work out on that trip—about my relationship to making art, to being female, to learning to love generously—unfolded in the years after I came home. Reading the journals now, in my midforties, I find myself thinking, Be patient—the time horizon for some kinds of growth is very, very long. I mean this in a positive sense, that some things can't be approached directly; they are influenced by factors people can't control.

It occurs to me now that this understanding is foundational to my writing practice. The role of the will is to get me to the page, but after that, the will has little—nothing?—to do with the finished poem.

Once I had been in Ecuador for a month or so, I realized that my true agenda was to have no agenda—to simply pay attention to the world directly around me and to practice putting it into words. At this point, I was journaling and writing letters and not yet writing poems.

The way I learned to inhabit my body while traveling alone has translated now into the ability to relinquish the idea of "productivity" in order to become deeply receptive, to enter fully into that "apparently unproductive" state that leads to poems.

Another important way my travels have affected my work: I now have a day job at Seattle Children's Hospital, and one of the things I do there is offer poetry and journaling workshops for the staff. The main skill I teach through journaling is how to direct compassionate attention inward, to befriend the self on the page. This is a direct result of my own relationship with journaling on my trip.

GRABER: I have had readers say that the book that I wrote on the Lowell Scholarship has an air of isolation to it, and I believe that. Of course, some of the images are lifted from those landscapes and some micronarrative moments. I could feel history around me in Europe, especially in Budapest and Berlin, in a way that I think I am immune to at home. Its weight is rather terrifying, which may be why we humans turn away from our own history so often. Malta is perhaps the most colonized parcel of land on Earth. I was thinking a good bit about empire before I left, and European history only drives those ruminations deeper. Now, of course, I can feel the weight of US history much more than I felt it before. I've also changed cities since coming back. It is hard not to feel history in Richmond! But I feel that my work will have an outward-facing aspect in the future that it did not have in the same way before.

FINNEYFROCK: I did several performances while in Nepal. It struck me during these shows how cultural specificity lives in the references and images in my poems. Particularly in the case of humor, I found the translation of my work culturally, rather than literally, problematic. Since returning from Nepal, I'm more interested in work on universal themes. Themes such as love, raising children, modern dependence on oil all seemed relevant to the world audience; US politics, humor, and religion didn't relate as well.

My work was affected, but in a larger way, I was affected. I have more awareness of how wealth and lifestyle in the United States compare with those in the developing world. I witnessed the environmental toll that poverty and civil war take. An embassy guide who grew up in Nepal told me, "Fifteen years ago, Kathmandu was Shangri-la. Now, I don't want to stay." He told me this after we crossed over the sacred Bagmati River, now barely moving because of the piles of trash that clog it.

MEEK: Arriving in a radically new landscape and culture and having to learn how to live and hopefully do some useful work there gave the opportunity for much practice in the arts of looking and listening, in developing a habit of receptivity and expectation. Any moment could bring something completely unfamiliar or a new angle of perception, as when I was told that the plovers I heard shrieking in the early mornings were called the birds-who-never-sleep and were in league with witches, or when, during evening studies at the school, the first night we had electricity a curious cobra came into the classroom, swelling its hood between two student desks. I think my work became much more grounded in place. That heightened sense of discovery that this deep travel provided changed the focus of my work and life completely, as I sought new experiences and deeper connections to other landscapes and cultures from this point forward.

GREENWELL: This is a hard thing to talk about. I'm certain that my work has been affected profoundly. I have been writing a lot more prose since coming here, perhaps simply because I still feel so overwhelmed by new information and impressions. I also think the sounds and rhythms of a new language will have an unavoidable effect on one's work. I've been moved and inspired by the availability and visibility of history and its traces in Bulgaria, whose history includes so many years under the occupation of various empires.

STONECIPHER: My poetry thrives on newness, difference, tension, difficulty, and friction. Placing oneself in a foreign context supplies plenty of those things.

DUNNE: This is a hard question for me to answer. I think that is because I have lived in Japan for so long that in some sense Japan has become home—too familiar. It is hard for me to analyze how it has affected my work. Still, I think I can say that in many ways living in Japan has made me more patient in my approach to poetry. I have come to see poetry as an intrinsic part of my life and have come to feel less anxious about success, whatever *success* means. I have come to this understanding partly though the example of Corman but also because of the Japanese culture, which seems to emphasize a lifelong commitment to process in art while downplaying immediate accomplishment and gain.

REDDY: Though I didn't write about Oaxaca or Mexico while living there, the simple fact of dwelling in such a simultaneously lively and tranquil environment had a major impact on my work. I was able to abstract myself, as it were, from my everyday existence in Chicago and enter more fully into the imaginative world of the poem—now out under the title "Voyager"—that I was writing at the time. I didn't have the conventional sort of relation to writing about place while I lived abroad. I wrote neither about the place I was in—Mexico—nor about the place

I'd left—Chicago—but about an imaginary place inside my head that I couldn't have accessed without the experience of travel.

**Did you pitch any stories to magazines either before or during your stay? How did it work out?**

STONECIPHER: Many years ago, I wrote one travel article about Berlin for *Alaska Airlines Magazine* and won't write any more. I don't want to write about Berlin for commercial purposes; I want to hoard it all for my own work.

POPE: I did, once—I'd written an essay about coming from a big country and living in a small country and about perceptions/misperceptions of the United States and Americans. I knew a Czech writer who had a connection to the *San Francisco Chronicle*, so I pitched it there, but it didn't go anywhere, and, unfortunately, I didn't try anywhere else.

KUSSEROW: I don't pitch anything, but I usually imagine the poems from my experience will end up in both anthropology literary magazines and formal poetry journals. I also use my poetry to teach anthropology courses. I assign my books to teach students about other cultures and certain concepts they need to learn. I also am sometimes asked to put my poems on websites that are working for a cause, such as STAND (Students Taking Action Now Darfur).

DUNNE: I submitted work to Japanese journals both while living in Japan and while living back in the United States. I was most successful in placing work when I was living in Japan.

# Coming Home

## What did you hope to glean from your time abroad?
## What was your purpose in traveling as a poet?

MEEK: I wanted to do something that I could feel good about and at the same time widen my experience; other than a couple of very brief trips to Mexico, I had never been out of the country before I joined the Peace Corps. Certainly as a young poet, I was looking for what might "matter," for new encounters with "subjects." Part of me winces when someone says that I—or any another poet—travel in order to "look for poems," though there is a level of truth to this. I like to see it a little more holistically, though, a little less coldly utilitarian; as human beings, we all need to find out what most engages us, what we are passionate about, what makes us alive. We will write out of these relationships that matter to us, whether these involve the towns we grew up in or places we fell in love with half a world away. All are valid for poetic exploration, and of course, they aren't mutually exclusive. Traveling abroad can also deepen people's perspective on "home," including their private histories. I certainly feel this is the case in my own experience.

GRABER: I don't think I had an agenda before I left. I wanted to go to Berlin. I had loved Walter Benjamin for so long. I wanted to stand in his city, which no longer exists. At least I was able to stand where it was.

I was already middle-aged when I was selected for the Lowell Scholarship. I thought it was too rare an opportunity to pass up, even though the logistics seemed overwhelming. It came to me as an adventure when all the adventuring already seemed done.

WHITCOMB: When I was in my early twenties and learning and reading about art history, culture, and world politics, I wanted to go to France—Paris in particular—so strongly that it was almost like a physical pain.

Luckily, I was able to travel to France twice during my twenties and thirties and became a complete Francophile. In the following years, my life became very busy and at the time of my residency at La Muse, I had not been abroad in a decade. I was starving again for the experience of being away, especially in France. Writers thrive on experience; we spend our lives re-creating those experiences on the page, in many iterations. I was hoping the residency at La Muse would help me immerse myself in my writing and provide the opportunity to get to know a new part of France. Part of my purpose in going to a residency abroad was to meet other writers and artists from around the world and to make some connections and friendships.

BURLESON: I hoped to gain a new subject for my work, new experiences, new languages, a new way of seeing. I gained all those things. But the genocide also taught me to be careful about what I wish for. I happened to be in Rwanda at a key historical moment, both for the people of that country and for the planet. But I also wish it had never happened.

FINNEYFROCK: I was hoping for the opportunity to visit the Himalayas, to meet Nepali people, and to hear poetry from a culture outside my own.

POPE: I wanted to throw myself into something altogether different, and that I certainly did. Sometimes I thought of it as having thrown myself off the edge of my known world. I wanted to learn another language—to do more than read in another language—and I did. I wanted experience, pure and simple, that would expand the ground for poems, and I found that. I wanted to get away from the huge, hollering buzz of US mass media, and I enjoyed my years of respite. But what I'd really meant to do was to make a life there, and in that respect, it didn't work out. I had seven years, not the decades I had planned.

NEZHUKUMATATHIL: It was like looking into a slightly foggy mirror. So much of what I thought was bizarre and strange, such as dogs given full rein to leftovers from each meal or sleeping in little *bahay kubos* in the Philippines or thatched houseboats in India, was just considered a way of life there. For a gal who had grown up in usually the only Asian American family in predominantly white towns, this was especially necessary and satisfying, as one could imagine.

DUNNE: When I came to Japan in 1986, I was trying to become a poet. I was interested in Japanese poetry and aesthetics. I was also attracted to Zen Buddhism. I felt that I might be able to work and write here. Because I could teach English, I could afford to stay in Japan for a significant period. Furthermore, my teaching duties took place primarily in the evening, so I had the daytime to study and write. I felt that the experience in Japan would broaden me, allow me to see the way other human beings ordered and expressed the experience of living. Japan did help me with vocation because it provided models that I could have faith and confidence in. I could see a way to approach a life in poetry here that I could not as readily see in the United States.

KUSSEROW: I travel for many reasons: to be humbled, to be widened, to be awestruck, to gain perspective, to foster a big mind, to attempt to help in a situation where there is suffering or inequality in my role as an applied anthropologist. The countries I go to have high degrees of disease, maternal mortality, blindness, extreme poverty, modern-day slavery, pretty blatant forms of social inequality, and lack of education, especially for girls. If I am in a country, I want to try to help or respond. I could never just go and hang out and write poems about a place unless I could use those poems to teach back at my college or unless they were published in a mainstream journal where enough people would read the poem and become aware of an issue and hence might give to a non-profit. For example, I try to list africaeli.org in my bio of a South Sudan poem. I also use poems to reveal subtleties about a culture that students don't get from boring academic texts: the hips, heart, soul, and saliva of a people.

AUSTEN: For some months before the trip, the superstructure of my life had been disintegrating—I finally admitted to myself that I was disillusioned with acting and theater, a major relationship ended, and I began having nightmares about Freehold's artistic director's demanding I help her perform autopsies in her office. I also began having a recurring daydream in which I saw myself somewhere at extremely high altitude, with a very clear blue sky overhead. As everything I assumed I knew about the shape of my life lost its meaning, I became convinced the transformation I was seeking involved finding that specific sky.

I traveled abroad, in a very real sense, in order to *become* a poet. This had less to do with what I actually wrote while I was there and more with temporarily giving up all the ways I had previously defined myself. For all the miles I hiked, the real terrain explored was internal.

The job I held for several years before going to South America involved working to support other artists' visions. Though that's a worthwhile thing to do, for me it had become a way of avoiding the risk of developing my own voice. This became clear to me when, about eight months before going to South America, I created a short dance-theater piece based on three poems I'd written. The experience of generating the poems and choreographing and directing three dancers made painfully clear how little genuinely creative work I'd done since becoming Freehold's managing director and how disenchanted I really was with the kinds of theater I'd been doing for the past couple of years. Making that piece showed me how off track my life was, how disconnected I was from my own voice.

So one purpose of the trip was to radically alter my context and remove the familiar reference points—friends, family, language, occupation—and see what remained, with the hope and expectation that I would know and hear myself more accurately, more deeply, as a result. One surprise was how much this did in fact happen and how it was followed almost immediately—meaning, as the next thought—with the desire to write and publish.

REDDY: I wanted to write during my year abroad. I didn't want to write about the place I was going to visit, and I didn't want to write about home—I just wanted to write.

## Did you fulfill your purpose? Did travel have any unforeseen effects on your work?

DUNNE: I was able to fulfill my purposes in Japan. I read a lot about Japan while in Japan. I studied its history, literature, and language. I was also able to find a temple where I could practice zazen on a regular basis and receive instruction. During my initial four years in Japan, I was able to produce a portfolio of poetry that I submitted for my application to graduate school.

One of the most fortuitous and unforeseen effects of my travels was my coming to meet the poet Cid Corman in Kyoto. Corman was an American expatriate poet and a long-term resident of Kyoto. In many respects, he took me under his wing and gave me valuable instruction in poetry.

WHITCOMB: After my return from residency, I resumed a conversation I had tentatively begun with a photography professor at the university where I work about coteaching a study abroad in France, maybe Paris. It was very clear to me after my experience at La Muse that it would be fantastic to take a group of students *there* and to design an interdisciplinary writing and photography class around the story of the Cathars.

Seven months after my first visit to La Muse, I was back again with eight students and the aforementioned photography professor in tow. The class was called Constructing the Creative Castle: Creative Writing and Photography in Medieval France. The students received credit in both art and English. We had designed the assignments to be as collaborative and interdisciplinary as possible: one project involved each student choosing a spot around the village and visiting that exact spot five times in five days, spending time there shooting photos and writing. The accumulated impressions were then edited and assembled into a digital collage, a small book, a short film, or whatever vehicle the student chose. One student chose the village spring, another a perch on the wall overlooking the village.

La Muse has a gallery space on street level with the village, and the students put on an exposition of their projects, complete with a reading and refreshments, the last night we were there. They named their exposition *The New Cathar Resistance!* and made flyers and signs to advertise around the village. Our bus driver for the excursions liked the class group so much that she rode her motorbike up from Carcassonne to attend the exposition, much to the delight of everyone. John and Kerry, the owners of La Muse, helped the students make pizzas and apple tarts for the event. And the evening ended with a hugely violent thunderstorm and the students outside watching the lightning streak across the mountains and the valley.

BURLESON: I came to doubt everything I had believed before I went, and that doubt continues to drive my poetry even though I haven't written much about Rwanda since that first book. Travel, in the way that I traveled, gave me a certain degree of Keats's "Negative Capability," I think, and that has turned my work in directions I couldn't have expected at the time.

REDDY: I got a lot of writing done. There's something about the pace of life in a provincial Mexican town that lends itself to daydreaming and getting those inner wanderings down on paper. The most unforeseen effect of travel on my work was the lack of travel's effects on the page. The book I finished while abroad could have been written in Pittsburgh,

Bombay, Rome, or Oaxaca. As it happened, it was in the latter location. And I'm grateful for it.

I was also quite happy to be away from the United States during that election year. The race simply would have been too distracting for me to get any writing done if I'd been home during that time. So that's another curious advantage to leaving the country for a time.

GRABER: It was much more illuminating than I could articulate in a brief space. I learned a good bit about what really matters. I learned what I could take, as in tolerate, and take quite well, in fact. I learned the difference between necessity and everything else! And I think that that attitude will inform my thinking and writing for the rest of my life.

I lived a very spare, hard life for a year, moving around from place to place with one suitcase. The world changed radically while I was away. I was in Europe when the global markets first began their declines, which have continued. I came home to a terrible personal financial disaster. I could not have passed through that as resolutely as I have if I had not already gotten quite used to doing without many, many things. I still live in an apartment that has only a two-burner hotplate and a countertop oven (the last bit of austerity, I hope), and that would have been inconceivable to me if I had not lived in very similar circumstances for extended periods while I was abroad. I learned how little of my self-image is actually linked in any meaningful way to conventional economic success. That being said, I like to be able to buy food, to take a bath, and to turn the heat on when I'm cold! Lots of times, I had very little heat in Europe! For four months, I lived in a stone cottage with only a wood stove, a big forest, and a little saw.

FINNEYFROCK: I did fulfill my purpose, although the travel was more challenging than I had expected. I was very tired and felt constantly affected by the air pollution and the noise pollution.

MEEK: I knew I would write about my experience, but I didn't know how much the experience would change my life, how deeply southern Africa would enter my work, so that twenty years later, I'm back there again—physically, mentally, emotionally—for the book I'm now writing. This experience also changed me as a reader and teacher; I had no experience with African or even postcolonial literature before I lived in Botswana, and now I teach this literature, as well as creative writing, in my capacity as an English professor.

Twenty years later, those two years still resonate through my life. What they taught me as a poet was to work to be more open to the world in all its particularities and contradictions, to be more mindful that every view is partial, every subject, multiple. What being a Peace Corps volunteer gave me is a place across the world to return to but also the desire to go elsewhere and to go deeper, into the here, into the now.

GREENWELL: It is difficult to have a genuinely immersive experience when teaching in an international school because I have to teach in English, and some of my colleagues are Americans. But yes, I do think that I am having a meaningful engagement with another language and another culture.

STONECIPHER: I wasn't expecting to become a translator, so I consider that an unforeseen and very happy effect of traveling.

POPE: Although I did mostly fulfill my purpose, the effects on my work are pretty different from what I had imagined, perhaps chiefly because I returned to the United States. I worked for a long time to fit in—I know I wanted to claim something permanent after I'd spent my whole life moving from place to place—but that was never going to work out. I did get good enough to pass—not to be called out as an American. But passing is a strange experience in itself. People began asking me when I was going to start writing in Dutch, and I always knew the answer was "never." The question then became this: was the writing going to stay hidden, or was I going to leave? The longer I stayed, the sharper that dilemma became for me.

There were many unforeseen effects on my writing: I developed a much more elastic ear, an appreciation for literary styles and eras I had previously dismissed, an attraction to the work of exiles and expatriates in general, and a highly reinforced sense of marginality. I have a sense of estrangement from my own culture now, which was there before but to a different degree. I like playing with notions of "foreignness." It is a gift to see how so much of what we know or think we know is culture-bound.

NEZHUKUMATATHIL: I write with the intersection of three cultures always looming over my shoulder—Indian, Filipino, and American. That provides my writing with a layering and fusion of pop culture and customs. As a poet, I find a perfect solution to capturing these blended traditions. I serve as interpreter, investigator, and historian. Worlds rife with fauna and flora—king cobras, cuckoo wasps, violet guavas, sea dragons, and whale sharks—come alive for me in this way. I hope to demonstrate how one can be situated without being rooted—can travel without getting lost.

RUCH: I didn't write anything during the entire five years I served on active duty. While I was deployed, I rarely took notes or photos of my everyday experiences because I didn't want to remember them. When I finally began to write again and realized how powerfully therapeutic it could be, I regretted my failure to document the things I'd seen and done, not because I have forgotten but because I might have written about them with greater accuracy. Now, telling my own stories and those of my fellow soldiers feels necessary, vital, even if it takes a lifetime to do so.

AUSTEN: Two quotes from my journal illustrate how much I did fulfill my purpose in knowing myself more deeply. I wrote this during a particularly low period while traveling briefly in Bolivia: "I can't pretend anymore that I could live my life without making art. Looking at those three Bolivian indigenous women made me realize that."

It's typical of my immature writing skills of the time that I left out the necessary details of this event: who were those women? What were they doing? What was my relationship to them? What was I noticing that led to the realization? This is probably the main reason I don't have poems "about" Peru, Bolivia, or Ecuador—it wasn't until I came home and began to study writing as a craft that I understood the need to set the scene, to include sensory details rather than simply report the epiphany.

But it's also typical of my experiences traveling that the transformative moments were absolutely not linear; they did not conform in any way to my expectations of cause and effect. In this way, I came to understand and value unstructured time as an essential ingredient—time and leeway to follow my instincts about what to give my attention to, what to read, what to write, whether to follow an obsession or a hunch or what seems at first like a whim.

And, finally, this, written in the final week or two before I returned to the United States: "... the next big adventure is taking myself seriously as an artist."

## How did your experiences and the poets, writers, and artists you discovered influence your poetics?

FINNEYFROCK: I was excited to find a deep, cultural love for poetry in Nepal. I teach poetry in high schools in the United States and too often hear groans when students find out they will be writing poetry. There is a palpable reluctance around poetry in the United States. In Nepal, however, students were on the verge of cheering when they heard they would be writing poetry. Many students could already recite poems by other poets and were naturally expressive onstage reading their work. It was helpful for my work as a writer and as a teacher to be reminded that young people are not naturally turned away from poetry.

POPE: I have access to this other language now, one that so few people outside the Netherlands speak that it's like having a secret code at my disposal—my greatest ambition as a kid. Translating poetry sort of extends that idea.

Something entirely unanticipated was an appreciation that life could be slower, that stillness is a good thing. Not every American needs to leave home to learn that, but I know I would never have learned it without that time abroad.

I was already deeply interested in painting, but in Europe I discovered the work of many artists, living and dead, who were new to me—their work has also influenced my ideas about poetry.

WHITCOMB: Another interesting effect of the travel on my work as a poet came in the recurrence of imagery, namely that of wild boar. I was running on the mountain trails late one afternoon during my residency and was surprised by a very large, black, hairy pig running across the trail in front of me, scooting from undergrowth to undergrowth. I had been told boar were everywhere in the woods of the area. Every Wednesday and weekend in the fall, the village shuts down for the *grand chasse* (the "big hunt"). The men drive their tiny trucks up to the old forest roads and let their little dogs out of their kennels; you can hear them blow the hunting horns all over the valley. I wrote what became a group of poems about the forest, the boar, the dogs, and the old roads. The image of the boar was very metaphoric and became emblematic in the poems of that region of France, of its remoteness and profundity. *Boar* is also kind of funny, from an American perspective, and I found using that word to be a light way to play with language and tone.

GRABER: I think that I was politicized in some way by the aesthetics of the European poets. There is not as sharp a divide between the personal and private narratives and the public discourse of the speakers in many of those poems. I also admire the lingering influence of the surreal, but

I cannot emulate it at all! Perhaps one day.

MEEK: In "The Road To," a prose poem from my first book, *Nomadic Foundations*, I wrote about being on the back of a truck in rural Botswana when the driver ran down a flock of beautiful blue-helmeted guinea fowl, and the Batswana women on the back of the truck with me nodded and said, "Nice meat." Yes, it was a surprise when that driver turned into, not away from, that flock of guinea fowl, but it made me much more aware of what a luxury it is to be able to look at a bird solely in aesthetic appreciation instead of also seeing it as something that could fill a family's stomachs. Those two years offered many such moments of experiencing viscerally a new way of seeing, how perspectives can be multiple and conflicting.

Those years also gave me a new and uncomfortable sense of being seen, of being implicated by history, a white, middle-class person living in a then-undeveloped country where many of the people worked in apartheid South Africa. So many times, particularly when I had to leave my own village, I wished that I were invisible or at least not white. But I could no more escape my own cultural identity than I could my confrontation with self, as, for instance, in the issue fundamental to teaching in Botswana: to beat or not to beat. I remember naïvely, though at the time I thought high-mindedly, saying in my Peace Corps interview that I wouldn't beat my students but also wouldn't condemn those Batswana teachers who did. I didn't anticipate that parents would come to the school to complain to the headmaster about American teachers who won't beat their kids; I didn't expect, after being ordered to use the *thupa*, the stick, how used to it I would become.

That's one thing I was hoping the book title *Nomadic Foundations* would evoke—that even what you think is the most fundamental base of the self can shift. This led to my idea of deep travel, which I first wrote about in my dissertation in graduate school following my Peace Corps service, how in what I called deep travel, the self is not simply a static observer, not an objective or transparent or omniscient presence but rather is radically implicated in scene, in image, in word.

When I returned to the United States, how I looked at everything had shifted—and not just in how overwhelming it was to go into a grocery store or mall or library. I didn't want to lose the highs of discovery resulting from an increased receptivity to the world. Okay, so I couldn't hike to a water hole to watch baboons come to drink, but I could drive into the mountains near my home in Colorado to see marmots. I'd grown up in Colorado, and I had never thought to look for them. I was no longer living on the edge of the Kalahari Desert, but the Great Sand Dunes were just a few hours away. I'd been there before, but had I really looked at them? It seemed I was seeing everything for the first time, and that's a feeling I still work to cultivate, whether abroad or at home. Maybe I was just addicted to the high of discovery—and really, what poet isn't?—but travel and place became and remain central to my work, along with a newfound interest in the environment, in the relationship between people and place.

STONECIPHER: Living in Berlin has influenced my poetry and my thinking about poetry in innumerable ways. I only worry from time to time that my poems don't engage enough with problematics of my home soil. But I can't choose what I write, and I can't force subject matter on my poetry.

REDDY: The Americans abroad, Joshua Edwards and Lynn Xu, were a real lifeline to me while living in Mexico. They gave me a sounding board for what I was doing, and I hope I provided the same service to them. Unfortunately, I didn't make any friendships with Mexican writers while living in Oaxaca. But if my Spanish had been good enough to do so, I'm sure I would have benefited greatly from the experience.

DUNNE: Cid Corman had a great influence on me—not so much in how I write but more in how I went about approaching the life of poetry. He gave me a deep and abiding appreciation for the vocation of poetry. Perhaps this faith came in part from the *way* in which he saw the Japanese poets of the past embrace the way of poetry, or perhaps it came from the contemporary Japanese poets whom he knew and was working with in his translations. In any event, he helped point me toward the poem itself—and the life of poetry—as opposed to the marketplace, as opposed to fame and name. He helped me—at a time when I really needed it—to believe in the value of poetry, and he did this not by words but through his example of a life lived in poetry, a life that was austere in material terms, strict in discipline and practice, and yet generous and open—gracious.

He always made time to talk with younger people who were interested in poetry. One afternoon, while I was visiting him at his home, he said the following to me: "Poetry is the most important thing that human beings can be aware of. Poetry is life itself, a central thing. It is the most important element in the world, the human world and even beyond the human world because it gives us respect for everything else. It is taking everything into account and bringing it to point."

In Japan, poems are published every day in newspapers. In this respect, poetry is more visible and more a part of people's lives than it is in the United States. It was good for me to live in a country in which poetry was understood to be a part of the everyday life of the community. It helped me to believe in its centrality in life.

AUSTEN: I don't think it's an overstatement to say that I found my primary mode of working—receptive, intuitive—and much of my subject matter during those six months in South America. The experience of confronting my fear and taking physical risks changed my sense of myself and my place in the world as a woman. Part of that was the particular cultural mirroring associated with living in Latin countries—in Ecuador and especially Peru, ideas about the roles and limitations of women are very macho. Local people in villages or the paths nearby often stopped me to ask if I was really alone, exclaiming in disbelief, "*¡¿Solita!?*"—"You're here by yourself?!"

Once I went home and began writing poetry, my voice first began to coalesce around a sense of spirituality rooted in the natural world, in the specific gravity of particular places—the forests of the Cascades, the Olympic coast, my own garden—and then around pivotal questions of female identity—whether or not to mother, sexual power, patriarchal religion.

My willingness to go in search of that particular blue sky is a direct antecedent to my willingness now to follow the call of an image without first needing to attach any meaning or purpose to it.

As it turns out, just a week before I flew home, I did find the sky that had prompted my journey. I was hiking with a Peruvian man I had met through my work for the South American Explorers Club. Our destination was a glacier on Huaytapallana, an eighteen-thousand-foot peak in the central Andes. A few hours after dawn, as we crested the lip of the *páramo*, a small lake came into view, the glacier rising above it. I immediately recognized the place—not just the color and clarity of the sky but also the lake, the scrubby plants, the mountain. I felt as though the bones at the roof of my skull—the ones that fuse together shortly after birth—had dilated open. A sensation I can describe only as electrical shook me—my body rang the way it had when, at five years old, I had put a metal house key into an electrical socket. I wept but not with pain or fear. I felt rinsed with elation, every cell alert, alive, at home in my skin.

### Are you still in touch with the poets you met while living abroad? If so, how have you kept in communication? Any collaborations?

DUNNE: I remain in touch with many poets from around the world. I met those poets here in Japan and in the United States. For the past five years, the Japan Writers Conference has been a location at which writers from inside and outside Japan have gathered. It has furthered the connections between writers. Communication is kept up through blogs, e-mail, Skype, and literary magazines.

KUSSEROW: Through e-mail, I doggedly stay in touch with writers, both anthropologists and poets, who write poetically about cross-cultural experiences.

FINNEYFROCK: We have a Nepali spoken-word poetry group on Facebook called Word Warriors.

GREENWELL: As my language skills improve, I would like to work on translations with young Bulgarian writers; that's a kind of collaboration I would like to pursue actively.

POPE: I am translating the work of a Dutch poet, Hester Knibbe, whose work I encountered while I lived in Amsterdam, though I did not meet her until after I'd left. We communicate via e-mail, and I was able to spend time with her when I visited the Netherlands two years ago.

REDDY: I'm still in touch with Joshua Edwards and Lynn Xu back here in the United States. We e-mail regularly, and we try to see each other every few months, though they live out West in California these days, and we're settled back in Chicago. We haven't collaborated formally yet, but the conversation itself feels like a collaboration, one that will yield much over the years to come.

### What do you think other poets learned from their experiences abroad, and how, in your opinion, did it change their poetics?

POPE: Well, Sylvia Plath found it was fatal. Before her death, though, she became sharper both intellectually and poetically than she would have been had she remained in the United States—she could be serious in England in a way she probably wouldn't have allowed herself to be in the United States. Elizabeth Bishop created a whole new life in Brazil, but it seems to me many of her letters ache with homesickness. When she returned to the United States, something was askew in her life and remained that way; she was never able to feel at home here. It certainly seems that her poems were never again as strong as they had been. Charles Wright, on the other hand, encountered Italy and seems to have had the experience of walking out into the product of his own poetic imagination—his connection to that country is so deep that it always strikes me as having a spiritual cast. Rita Dove has written very interesting poems and prose about her years abroad, and her translations are just fantastic. The sheer range of her work seems to me to be related at least in part to her experience of different countries and languages.

I translate the work of a South African poet, Elisabeth Eybers, who exiled herself to the Netherlands and lived there for more than forty years. She published in both countries and developed quite a literary reputation, all the while stubbornly writing in Afrikaans, her father's native language. She wrote highly crafted poems that were often very sly about her longtime position as an outsider, which is clearly what she felt she was, despite being embraced by the Dutch literary world. There is something so particular to poets about that—that insistence on one's own language, even in situations like hers where compromise wouldn't necessarily cost so very much.

BURLESON: The poets I know who have traveled deeply all say that their experiences have profoundly affected their work and the way they see the world. Even when they're not writing directly about their travel experience, the new way of seeing they gained abroad influences everything they write.

DUNNE: I think many poets learn to broaden their aesthetic sensibilities. When an American person lives in a country like Japan, she has to confront, at some level, the realization that her ideas of what constitutes the beautiful are shaped or determined to a significant degree by forces at work within her own culture. A Japanese rock garden will challenge many Americans at first glance—so too may a Japanese essay, which tends to develop in a much less logically determined fashion than a US essay. Encountering differences such as these is an exciting experience and one that bears directly on the vocation of the poet. The poet learns from these different aesthetic sensibilities—from various ideas of what constitutes the beautiful—and goes on to test their applicability. In this way, the experience of living abroad might be said to bring a healthy richness to the poet, a wider appreciation of beauty in various forms, and an inquisitive mindset that can lead forward into experimentation, innovation, and refinement of poetics.

REDDY: Off the top of my head, I'd mention that Elizabeth Bishop seemed to learn a great deal about surrealism and perception from her time in Brazil, that Dante learned his rage and melancholy from the experience of exile, that Pound learned his unfortunate politics in Europe. The list goes on and on.

MEEK: When I was editing *Deep Travel: Contemporary American Poets Abroad*, a collection of poems by thirty-four poets who have lived or spent significant time abroad, what drew me to these poets' international work was what I saw as a heightened attentiveness, an openness, a willingness to discover that deepens and layers the work. I don't want to suggest that any writer who travels will do better work or that travel is the only path to good poetry; again, as I tried to get at with the term "deep travel," it's about a generative interaction between a particular poet and a particular place, not simply the injection of "exotic" subject matter. But for those poets who are attentive travelers—attentive to self as well as other—and who write out of this same openness to discovery, the fusion in their work of experience and language, the engagement of word and world, can be truly extraordinary.

## Anything to add?

RUCH: As a woman soldier living in Iraq, I discovered that carrying a book with me and being seen reading it made local males more likely to talk to me. Because of my book, they concluded that I was literate and therefore educated—at least that's what one of them told me—and so they broke with customs based on social and religious taboos and stereotypes, and held conversations with me on a few occasions. I heard a number of interesting stories that would have been entirely inaccessible to me without that book in my back pocket.

FINNEYFROCK: I'm impressed by the ways our work in Nepal kept making an impact after we returned home. My group of three poets went to Nepal to teach about the history and traditions of poetry slams and the spoken-word poetic form. We worked with both youth and adults and produced Nepal's first poetry slam. After we left, I found out that a group of the young poets we had worked with took a trip outside Kathmandu to visit an orphanage. They did a poetry workshop with the younger kids and then had a poetry reading with the older kids after the little ones went to bed. When I read about their trip and thought about the ways the work continued after we left, I was surprised and moved.

I had specific concerns about introducing poetry slam to Nepal. It is a populist art form that seeks to engage the idea that "anyone can decide if a poem is good." We take the competitive elements found in publishing poetry, generally arbitrated by editors, selected juries, and professors, and put the decision-making power in the hands of people who attend poetry readings. We do this by handing scorecards to five audience members and asking them to rate the poets.

Poetry slams were intended to spoof literary contests, to make a spectacle out of the concept of judging art. However, the movement has changed over the twenty-five years of its existence and has become, for many poets, a sincere competition with career benefits based on winning. Poetry slam grew out of particular conditions in the US literary community involving access to audiences and success for poets outside of higher education.

I'm not sure that the idea of the poetry slam as a gimmick, or tongue-in-cheek show, translates well to other cultures. As poetry slams crop up around the globe, each country has adapted the slam to fit the needs of the people and the poetic climate. I struggled to find ways to teach about poetry slam without imposing US ideas of poetry slam on Nepal; I wanted to present the ideas driving the form without rigidly presenting the form.

REDDY: I guess the most important thing to me about the experience of travel is that there is no one way to experience it. Some poets travel abroad and come home laden with poems about what they've seen. Some poets leave home and return empty-handed. (Often the ones who didn't write anything while they were away turn out to have learned the most from their travels). Some travel to escape their lives, some to find them. You don't have to write about where you are or where you've left. You just have to write. And somehow, for some inscrutable reasons, travel can make that happen in the most circuitous of ways.

# How to Write Your Way Out of the Country

*Our battered suitcases were piled on the sidewalk again;*
*we had longer ways to go. But no matter, the road is life.*

—Jack Kerouac

# Opportunities for Traveling, Living, and Working Abroad

*Catherine Barnett, Rachel Galvin, and Brandon Lussier*

## Introduction

Opportunities are abundant for poets who want to travel: you can teach English abroad, attend an international writing residency, attend a literary festival, pursue translation opportunities, volunteer, or win a fellowship, grant, or scholarship, among other possibilities. In this section, you'll find lists of places and programs that provide these opportunities. The lists are punctuated by "voices from the field"—suggestions, insight, and encouragement from poets who have spent significant time abroad and who speak of—and from—the hold that traveling has had on them. "I've returned to Bosnia twice since that first experience ... and now, sixteen years after my first experience, I am still writing poems about my time there. It haunts me," says Susan Rich, one of the editors of this anthology and a Seattle-based poet. Jess Row, a fiction writer and Buddhist chaplain, says his work in Hong Kong completely transformed his career: "My first book is about Hong Kong, and everything I've written thereafter has been shaped by my experiences there in one way or another."

The word *transformative* crops up frequently when writers describe their experiences. Garth Greenwell, who has taught English at the American College of Sofia in Bulgaria for three years, says his experiences in Sofia have changed his writing profoundly. "Since moving here I've written about little else," he says. "I'm fascinated by what I see, by the people I interact with, by the experience of living in another language and another culture. The most dramatic effect has been a shift in genre: in my first months here I began writing prose." Reflecting on the decision to move to Europe, Greenwell says, "I do think my writing is better, more open to the world and to other people, for the choice."

"Whenever I work surrounded by a different language, my sense of English becomes heightened," says Susan Briante, who has been a resident at Fundación Valparaiso, in Almeria, Spain. "I am fluent in Spanish, having lived in Mexico for six years during the 1990s. It was actually that first experience of learning Spanish that made me both a translator and a poet. I learned English while living in Spanish."

Patricia Chao, a poet and fiction writer, has had extensive experience in countries where many people do not speak English. "If you spend enough time in your daily life in another language," she says, "you come back to English and it feels like a new language, which is wonderful. You become much more sensitive to it—sound, rhythm, syntax. It's a very good perspective, particularly for poetry."

Jennifer Scappettone spent a year in Rome as a recipient of the Rome Prize and acknowledges that her own writing was "profoundly influenced by the Italian language, in both lexical and syntactical senses, in both conscious and unconscious ways." Her time in Rome helped her finish a manuscript of translations with "the Italian language as the soundtrack of my dreaming."

Certainly less rhapsodic but equally essential for anyone planning to travel are the cautionary tales and advice shared by those who have first-hand experience. Some of the poets queried for this section, particularly those who accepted foreign teaching positions—either volunteer or paid—met with the uncertainties of bureaucracy, political instability, and violent insurgency. Many writers mention the destabilizing power of culture, which, says Jess Row, "works in both directions. It has to be taken seriously. Hong Kong was where I first had the experience of being a member of a racial minority—a tiny minority—and I was astonished at how difficult, and how interesting, that was. My thinking about race, culture, and justice was all changed as a result." Tiffany Tuttle Collins, who volunteered for the Peace Corps in Kyrgyzstan, says she hit a low point around six months into her service, when "I had a sense of my own cultural incompetence and isolation but had not quite made the strong relationships that later integrated me into the local community." She says not to be surprised if 25 to 30 percent of your group—"and that may include you"—goes through early termination, for personal or medical reasons. To reduce the chances of this happening, be sure to research not only the obvious details of visas, inoculations, and health care before you go (see "Additional Resources" at the end of this section for more information) but also the place itself, its history, politics, and art.

## Fellowships, Grants, and Scholarships

Traveling on a fellowship or grant provides both financial and creative support, but applications for such opportunities often require specific projects. Recipients of this form of support often end up becoming both insiders and outsiders, a simultaneity that can be fruitful for poets who seek to navigate between the known and the unknown. "It was the most extraordinary and rare gift of freedom I've ever had," says Jill Jarvis of the Fulbright fellowship she held in Sri Lanka. "It transformed my thinking."

Before applying, consider what your long-term goals are and how the specific scholarship that you are interested in will help you meet them. Can you demonstrate that you have already taken concrete steps to meet your goals? Are those goals in line with the mission of the organization or institution that administers the scholarship?

If you are going to apply for a fellowship, scholarship, or grant, avoid the most common applicant mistake: do not form future goals based on what you think a committee wants to hear. This almost never works because scholarship committees tend to value not just the long-term goals of candidates but also what candidates have already done to work toward those goals.

The following funding opportunities have an international focus and are best for self-motivated individuals who feel comfortable moving to another country, finding their own housing, and immediately getting to work on their projects. Although they are not specifically for poets, they all support activities (language study, travel, et cetera) that can enrich a poet's experience, perspective, and language. Be aware that culture shock, exploring a new place, and being away from friends and family can all make it more difficult to accomplish work at the pace you are used to. Go abroad with a plan that details major goals as well as smaller milestones.

Fellowships, grants, and scholarships are awarded on a competitive basis. Here is a partial list of funding opportunities:

-» **Akademie Schloss Solitude**, located in Stuttgart, is funded by the German government and offers three–to–twelve–month residencies to artists and scholars under the age of thirty-five (or to those who have finished a college or graduate degree within the last five years; several additional fellowships are offered regardless of age). Fellowships include lodging and a stipend.
*www.akademie-solitude.de*

-» **The American Academy in Rome** offers the Rome Prize to thirty emerging writers and scholars, providing housing, meals, a studio, and a generous stipend for either six or eleven months. Fellowships usually begin in September. Literature fellows are nominated by the American Academy of Arts & Letters.
*www.aarome.org*

-» **The American Council of Learned Societies** offers summer grants (among others) for intensive summer study of Eastern European languages, including Albanian, Bosnian-Croatian-Serbian, Bulgarian, Czech, Estonian, Hungarian, Latvian, Lithuanian, Macedonian, Polish, Romanian, Slovak, and Slovene. Grants can be used in the United States or abroad but must be used for an intensive, university-run program and not for tutoring or less intensive opportunities. Awards are intended primarily for graduate students in Eastern

---

VOICES FROM THE FIELD

According to poet Roy Scranton, who spent time at Akademie Schloss Solitude, this residency provides "fruitful digressions" in an urban setting. "It is competitive-entry, interdisciplinary, energetically international, and very well organized," he says. "Schloss Solitude had a collegiate and institutional feel, but at the same time, there was much more ambient intellectual and artistic energy.... The people at Schloss Solitude were all very hip and engaged."

European studies who will use these languages in academic research or teaching or in work for US government agencies or nongovernmental organizations. Grants have been given to poets seeking further knowledge of a language for the purpose of translation. Recipients must find appropriate study opportunities, enroll on their own, and plan their own travel and living arrangements for their period of study. For those who need to study abroad to take courses in languages that are infrequently taught in the United States, it is important to plan ahead and make contact with universities that teach intensive summer courses to avoid missing application/enrollment deadlines. *www.acls.org*

-» **The American-Scandinavian Foundation** (ASF) offers fellowships (up to $23,000) and grants (up to $5,000) that enable individuals to study or conduct research in one or more Scandinavian countries for up to one year. The foundation's materials note that "all fields are eligible, but applicants must have a well-defined research or study project that makes a stay in Scandinavia essential." Candidates should have some ability in the language of the host country, even

---

VOICES FROM THE FIELD

For Jennifer Scappettone, a recipient of the Rome Prize whose creative and scholarly projects center on Italy, the residency in Rome "represented a culmination of passions surrounding Italian culture and translation as well as a unique opportunity to pursue my individual research and writing agendas in an interdisciplinary setting in the heart of Rome, a city I love. I was surprised by how busy the Academy kept us with conferences, lectures, readings, walking tours, book launches, concerts and other performances, and exhibition openings." Scappettone was completing two decade-long book projects during her residency and says she imagines "It would have been even more amazing to be at the Academy at the beginning rather than the end of a project—at a point of one's career during which one can be truly open to every influence."

if it is not essential for the proposed research or study. The foundation recommends that candidates who plan to do translation work wait to apply until they have the necessary proficiency to do the work without assistance. The $23,000 fellowships typically, although not always, go to candidates at the graduate level for dissertation-related study and/or research, so most applicants should apply to the grant program for a shorter stay. At the time of application, candidates must provide confirmation of an invitation and/or affiliation from an institution and/or individuals in the host country. *www.amscan.org*

-» **The Amy Lowell Poetry Travelling Scholarship**, which provides financial underwriting for poets to travel abroad, allows the recipient to make his or her own logistical arrangements. If you plan a trip on your own through this or another similar scholarship, consider setting up a home base from which you can easily travel to other places. *www.amylowell.org*

-» **The Bellagio Center** offers residencies at its site on Lake Como, Italy, for literary as well as academic writers; the goal is to support interdisciplinary exchange among residents. Most residencies last

---

VOICES FROM THE FIELD

Poet and journalist Eliza Griswold won a Rome Prize for her poetry: "The beauty is overwhelming, but the wrecked-ness of some of the Roman landscape provided a lot of deep solace for me because that combination of beauty and wreckage is something that I really identify with in my work." She reflects that the time "was extraordinarily healing—just the sheer beauty of the city and its history helped me to process many of the things I'd seen and experienced. It's historically at the center of so much geopolitical strife that it also helped me to put some of what I know of contemporary conflicts into a longer historical trajectory."

one month; all provide a room, a private bath, a studio, and meals. Transportation fees are generally not included. The Bellagio Center prefers to support writers who have a record of outstanding achievement and are interested in global issues, and whose work "contributes to the well-being of humankind."
*www.rockefellerfoundation.org/bellagio-center*

-» **The Brown Foundation Fellows Program** at the Dora Maar House in Ménerbes, France, is geared toward midcareer artists. Travel expenses, lodging, and a per diem are provided for fellows.
*www.mfah.org/doramaar*

-» **CEC ArtsLink Project Support Grants** provide up to $10,000 in funding to US artists, curators, presenters, and arts organizations undertaking projects in any of thirty-two eligible countries (see the website for a list). Applicants must be working with an artist or organization in that region, and projects should be designed to benefit participants and audiences in both the United States and the host country.
*http://www.cecartslink.org*

---

VOICES FROM THE FIELD

While holding an Amy Lowell Poetry Travelling Scholarship, poet Kathleen Graber's sense of time was deeply altered, a transformation that helped shape her second book of poems. "Even the distant past is very palpable in parts of Europe, certainly in the Mediterranean," Graber says, "and the recent past can be felt quite powerfully and disturbingly in places like Budapest and Berlin. The landscapes of many of these spots and the rumination those landscapes precipitated appear in my second book."

-» **The US Department of State Critical Language Scholarship** (CLS) Program offers funding to enable study at intensive summer language institutes overseas. Only study of foreign languages considered of "critical need" will be funded. At the time this guide was printed, the eligible languages were Arabic, Azerbaijani, Bangla/Bengali, Chinese, Hindi, Indonesian, Japanese, Korean, Persian, Punjabi, Russian, Turkish, and Urdu. Students enrolled in undergraduate, master's, or doctoral programs are eligible to apply. People who have international fellowships or plan to study abroad and want to improve their language skills often receive Critical-Language Scholarships. *http://clscholarship.org/index.html*

-» **DAAD Scholarships** are granted for an academic year of study in Germany, with the possibility of a one-year extension to allow completion of a degree. Those enrolled in US master's degree programs or who have graduated from an undergraduate institution in the past six years are eligible to apply. Candidates in the arts and humanities are expected to have a good command of the German language. Recipients receive a monthly stipend of approximately 750 euros

---

VOICES FROM THE FIELD

"It's helpful to be attached to an institution when applying for the Fulbright," says Jill Jarvis. "For research Fulbrights, it's crucial to have a strong case for why you want to go to a particular country and also helpful (though certainly not necessary) to have already been there or have already studied the relevant languages." Less popular sites may have less competition in the application process. For her Fulbright, Jarvis researched a recent movement to reinstate higher ordination for Theravada Buddhist nuns in Sri Lanka. "I also became involved at the university in the town where I lived," she says. "There I helped with editing a philosophy journal and acted in a friend's Sinhala translation of Ionesco's *Bald Soprano*, which was staged at the university in an unforgettably hilarious production."

plus health insurance coverage, a rent subsidy, and a family allowance, if applicable.
*www.daad.org*

-» **Fulbright Fellowships**, sponsored by the US Department of State's Bureau of Educational and Cultural Affairs government, are designed to increase mutual understanding between the people of the United States and the people of other countries. Fellowships are for US citizens to study, teach, and conduct research abroad and for citizens of other countries to do the same in the United States. The application is notoriously challenging, so applicants should plan on starting work on their projects three to six months before the application is due to allow time to contact people, organizations, and institutions in the country of interest. This demonstrates a seriousness of purpose and makes it possible to obtain letters of support. Fulbright also offers teaching fellowships (see "Teaching English" in this section). It is important to remember that the Fulbright mission is not to train writers, artists, or scientists; its mission is to facilitate opportunities for Americans to form lasting ties to other countries. Projects that will involve collaboration with citizens of the host country are more likely to be funded, and long-term goals should

---

VOICES FROM THE FIELD

The program, Japan-US Friendship Commission is connected to the International House in Tokyo, where an initial orientation takes place, explains poet Brian Turner, one of the editors of this anthology. "The I-House, as it's called, has an incredible library which is available to those who become members," he says. "I became a member and immediately began working with the librarian to track down obscure information and source material connected to my fellowship study. In essence, I had a great research librarian working on my behalf. Invaluable."

include plans to stay engaged with the host country and its people.

Conditions and support levels will vary by location. See Susan Rich's essay, "Solitary: Spending a Fulbright Year in South Africa," for more information.

*www.iie.org/fulbright*

-» **The Japan-United States Friendship Commission** offers $20,000 grants plus up to $2,000 travel expenses for US artists and creative writers to spend three months working in Japan. Writers must be published and have a compelling reason to live and work in Japan; collaboration with Japanese artists and writers is encouraged. The program is competitive; five artists and writers are chosen annually. Once in Japan, writers work independently, although logistical support is available.

*www.jusfc.gov/creative-artists-programs/*

-» **Marshall Scholarships** are given to "young Americans of high ability" to study for degrees in any field in the United Kingdom for two to three years. The goal of the program is to fund future leaders in order to strengthen the relationships between British and US citizens and their governments and institutions. A candidate must have a four-year undergraduate degree and a minimum GPA of 3.7. The program is one of the most competitive scholarship programs in the world but provides full study and living costs as well as international travel funds.

*www.marshallscholarship.org*

-» **Mitchell Scholarships** fund one year of study in Ireland or Northern Ireland. Any field of study is acceptable. Eligible candidates are US citizens with four-year undergraduate degrees who are between the ages of eighteen and thirty. A demonstrated commitment to community and public service is essential, as well as a strong academic record and the proven ability to serve as a leader. Successful candidates have demonstrated a "significant, tangible impact" on their communities or schools. Five strong letters of recommendation are required. *www.us-irelandalliance.org*

-» **Princeton in Asia Fellowships** are yearlong, service-oriented fellowships. Each year, more than 150 fellows are placed in one of eighteen Asian countries to work in the fields of education, international development, environmental advocacy, journalism, and law or business. Although many fellows work as English teachers at universities and high schools, specific positions in nongovernmental organizations (for example, working on the protection of old city buildings and culture or for foreign affairs publications) are also listed on the organization's site each year. Graduates of accredited four-year colleges and universities are eligible. Applicants should be prepared to pay for the following: round-trip travel to Princeton twice (once for interviews and once for orientation), necessary vaccinations and a health screening, round-trip travel to Asia, and a TESL certificate. Living expenses in Asia are covered. (See "Teaching English" in this section for more information.)
*piaweb.princeton.edu/*

## International Writing Residencies

International residencies provide writers with opportunities to focus on their work and to experience new environments and cultures that may provide inspiration for current or future projects. They range in length from a few months to a few weeks. A residency may be an excellent way to see if you'd like to pursue sustained time overseas.

"Your richest experiences will not be sitting in your studio doing your art," says Patricia Chao, who was a resident at the Sacatar Foundation in Brazil, "but being out in the streets, hanging out with new people, attending festivals. Most of the residents end up doing a project involving the community in some way." Many writers report taking up new activities or hobbies that change their work significantly. Relationships built during a shared residency often blossom into long-term friendships and professional exchanges, though some residencies function as a retreat where you can focus quietly on your own work. In these cases, the residency may offer little by way of outside stimulation, so it's up to you to structure your time.

Keep in mind that some residencies require community engagement (readings, teaching workshops, et cetera). The organizations that run residential centers usually cannot afford to cover all costs for those accepted but often provide help with travel costs, housing, and/or food.

## Choosing a Residency

-» Residencies look for writers at different points in their careers.

-» Some residencies welcome writers without significant publications, some require a history of published work, and others ask that candidates be alumni of their American residencies before applying to an international residency.

-» Residencies that require a fee may be less competitive.

-» Some residencies are geared toward fostering interdisciplinary collaboration.

-» Some residencies pay airfare.

-» When planning a residency, it is usually up to the candidate to take care of paperwork. If you are aiming for a relatively short residency (one month in a European country, for example), you won't need a special visa. Different countries have different requirements.

Some central resources for locating and choosing an international writing residency include the following:

-» Alliance of Artists Communities
*www.artistcommunities.org*

-» Beltway: A Poetry Quarterly
*http://washingtonart.com/beltway/resid.intl.html*

-» Mira's List
*www.miraslist.com*

-» Poets & Writers posts the online Conferences & Residencies database.
*www.pw.org*
*www.pw.org/conferences_and_residencies*

-» Res Artis
*www.resartis.org* (click "Residencies"; from there, you have the option of viewing a complete list of residencies or searching for a residency matching your particular interests and needs)

-» Trans Artists
*www.transartists.org*

-» Some American residency programs, such as the Virginia Center for the Creative Arts, also coordinate a robust offering of foreign programs for their former residents.
*www.vcca.com/main/international*

A sampling of international foundations, residencies, and retreats follows. Although this list is not comprehensive (opportunities number in the hundreds), it will help get you started in your research. Please be aware that fees change regularly; the estimates included here simply provide general guidelines. Dollar signs indicate relative prices according to the following:

-» $ ($500 and under/week)
-» $$ ($500–$1,000/week)
-» $$$ (more than $1,000/week)

-» **Anam Cara Writer's and Artist's Retreat** in West Cork, Ireland, houses five residents at a time and its fee includes meals and

amenities. In addition to retreats, six weeklong workshops are offered each year in poetry, fiction, nonfiction, and publishing.
*www.anamcararetreat.com* • *$$*

-» **Art Workshop International** in Umbria, Italy, offers summer workshops with Anglophone writers.
*www.artworkshopintl.com* • *$$$*

-» **Arvon Foundation** is a charitable foundation that offers weeklong writing programs around the UK. These workshops are held in historic houses in secluded rural areas. Participants attend for a fee, although grants are available that cover the full cost of the course.
*www.arvonfoundation.org* • *$$*

-» **The Baltic Writing Residency** in Latvia is available on a competitive basis to one poet, fiction writer, or playwright each year. The one-month residency takes place in July in Riga and provides the winning resident with housing in a boutique hotel and $1,000 to offset travel costs and costs of living.
*www.balticresidency.com* • *$*

---

VOICES FROM THE FIELD

"At Anam Cara you become part of village life in a faraway corner of West Cork," says Susan Rich, poet and an editor of this anthology. "A fisherman may bring a salmon just caught that morning for evening dinner, or you may arrange for a visit with Mary, the village oracle. I met writers from Denmark, England, Ireland, and the United States—in half the cases, the writers were returning for a third or fourth stay. Writers have moved to the tiny village of Eyeries after first discovering it through a residency at Anam Cara. The rooms look out over Coulagh Bay and over mountains and cow fields. There are two bars in town, one teashop (which is also a family's front room), and one main shop. Cheese comes from the local cheese maker, and walking is the preferred means of transportation."

-» **The Banff Centre** in Canada offers, with its Leighton Artists' Colony for Independent Residencies, nine studios to artists (not just writers) who are recognized in their fields and to emerging artists. This is a solitary retreat environment placed within a larger artistic community.
*www.banffcentre.ca/leightoncolony* • *$*

-» **Camac's Arts Center**, in the village of Marnay-sur-Seine in the Champagne-Ardenne region of France, offers retreats of one to two months to artists, composers, and writers from around the world. Each resident has a private room with a private bathroom and can prepare meals for breakfast and lunch (kitchen and food are provided). Dinner is provided Monday through Friday. Although the center does not cover the cost of the residency, it offers help in applying for scholarships, in particular the UNESCO-Aschberg grant. In addition, a fully funded Ténot Bursary is given annually to one writer, one visual artist, and one musician. These residencies, which provide travel, room and board, and a separate studio, are available on a competitive basis.
*www.camac.org/english/intro.htm* • *$*

-» **The Fundación Valparaiso**, located in the village of Mojácar, near Almeria, Spain, offers retreats for writers and artists who are professionally recognized as well as the occasional emerging artist of exceptional creative talent. Eight residents stay for a month at a time;

---

VOICES FROM THE FIELD

"The Fundación [Valparaiso] is housed in a beautiful home surrounded by olive and lemon groves as well as a striking semiarid landscape," says poet Susan Briante. "From the Fundación, you can walk about twenty to thirty minutes into the center of Mojácar, a gorgeous whitewashed mountain village with views to the Mediterranean."

THE STRANGEST OF THEATRES

applicants submit proposals for the work they intend to do while at the foundation. Grants cover meals and housing; residents pay for their own travel, medical insurance, and materials.
*www.fundacionvalparaiso.es* • *$*

-» **Hawthornden Castle** in Scotland is open to international writers, whether they have published a book yet or not. The residency does not maintain a website, but interested writers may request applications by phone (+44-0131-440-2180) or by writing to Hawthornden Castle, The International Retreat for Writers, Lasswade, Midlothian EH18 1EG. Fellowships cover all expenses except travel to and from the castle. • *$*

-» **La Muse** is a retreat for writers and artists in the small mountain village of Labastide-Esparbairenque in the Languedoc-Roussillon region of southern France. Run by two former New Yorkers who wanted to find an easier environment to write in, it offers rooms for one-week and three-week retreats. Regular and barter fellowships are also available.
*http://lamuseinn.com* • *$*

-» **The M Literary Residency** awards three-month residencies in Shanghai and Bangalore. Transportation, accommodation, and meals are provided gratis to recipients along with $1,000 for expenses. The

---

VOICES FROM THE FIELD

According to poet G.C. Waldrep, "Hawthornden Castle was very accommodating to a nervous American who had not really been abroad before." He adds, "There is no Internet at all at Hawthornden, and cell phones don't work in the castle either. To use a cell phone, you have to walk up the drive to the road; for the Internet, we all walked into Bonnyrigg (about two miles) and used the public library."

program provides space and time for writing and research on site and aims to foster deeper knowledge of contemporary life and writing in China and India. One writer is selected for each location yearly. *www.m-restaurantgroup.com/mbund/Ms_residency.html* • *$*

⇢ **Red Gate Residency** in China offers residencies ranging from one to six months. The program helps writers connect with local arts and culture but does not cover any costs. Accommodation consists of apartments and lofts in Beijing. Applications are accepted on a rolling basis, but residencies are generally filled six months in advance. *www.redgategallery.com/residency* • *$*

⇢ **Sacatar Foundation**, on Itaparica Island off Bahia, Brazil, seeks applicants who wish to work on a specific project; the foundation covers travel costs, accommodation in private rooms, a separate studio, and most meals. Sacatar encourages residents to share their work with the local community and warns that the setting is fairly undeveloped. *www.sacatar.org* • *$*

---

VOICES FROM THE FIELD

According to writer Roy Scranton, La Muse welcomes "writers in the early stages of their writing careers. It's not a competitive residency, in part because you pay for it—it really is buying time in a great place to get some work done." Scranton recommends La Muse for independent people who like to get outside. The owners of La Muse offer a ride plan, with weekly grocery trips and even a visit to the medieval city of Carcassonne. They strongly suggest that you sign up for their plan or rent a car. "The nearest *épicerie*, which has a very limited selection, is a forty-five minute walk into the next valley," Scranton says. "Bread and grocery trucks visit the village, and you can buy eggs, rabbits, and vegetables from the neighbors."

-» **Sage Hill Writing Experience**, in Saskatoon, Saskatchewan, Canada, features a poetry colloquium in May and workshops in July and August. All ages and levels are welcome to apply. Scholarships are available on a competitive basis.
*www.sagehillwriting.ca* • *$*

-» **Sanskriti Foundation**, near New Delhi, India, offers writing residencies and opportunities to work with local traditional craftspeople. Residents can stay from two to twelve weeks. The foundation houses three craft museums.
*http://sanskritifoundation.org* • *$*

-» **Tyrone Guthrie Centre** in Annaghmakerrig, Ireland, hosts residencies and retreats up to six months in length in a rural setting in County Monaghan. Accommodation, which can include board, is in farm cottages and a large manor house. Candidates may apply directly and must pay their own way. The cost varies according to facility. You may also participate with a VCCA exchange or a Djerassi exchange if you've already been to their American residencies.
*http://www.tyroneguthrie.ie/homepage* • *$–$$$*

---

VOICES FROM THE FIELD

According to Patricia Chao, the best candidates for a residency at Sacatar would be accomplished artists with considerable world travel under their belts and, optimally, a working knowledge of Portuguese, or at least Spanish or Italian. "If you have traveling chops and an open mind," she says, "you'll do fine at Sacatar. Itaparica often feels more third world than first, so that kind of travel experience would be invaluable. English is not spoken in the general population, so you'll have to learn at least a smattering of Portuguese if you want to leave the compound and have adventures. I'd say a sense of adventure is paramount! You are pretty much on your own, so focus and a detailed project are important."

## Literary Translation Opportunities

For poets who have some experience with or interest in translating, there are opportunities abroad. Here is a list of some resources and opportunities for literary translators who want to work and travel.

-» The American Literary Translators Association, based at the University of Texas at Dallas, offers a wealth of resources for translators, including a list of grants, awards, and residencies available for literary translators.
   *www.utdallas.edu/alta/resources/grants-and-awards*

-» The European Council of Literary Translators' Associations is an umbrella organization that features news about European residencies and prizes for international translators.
   *www.ceatl.org*

-» Additional information for literary translators can be found at the websites of the Canadian Association for Translation Studies and UNESCO's section on Literature & Translation.
   *www.uottawa.ca/associations/act-cats/English/Home.htm*
   *http://portal.unesco.org/culture*

Here is a small selection of translation opportunities:

-» The Banff International Literary Translation Centre (BILTC) offers a residency program with the primary aim of offering literary translators a working retreat within a community of international colleagues.
   *www.banffcentre.ca*

-» **ATLAS** (Assises de la Traduction Littéraire), in Arles, France, is a cultural association that offers residencies and workshops for translators working with all languages, not just to or from French. *www.atlas-citl.org*

-» **The French-American Foundation** offers a translation award and holds annual conferences that bring together Francophone and Anglophone writers. *http://www.frenchamerican.org/publishing-and-translation*

-» **Ekemel**, the European Translation Centre, features workshops and paid residencies for translators. *www.ekemel.gr/Home.aspx?C=3*

## Literary Festivals

Literary festivals offer opportunities to attend workshops, give and attend talks, and hear memorable readings by poets from around the world. The festival environment, in which hundreds or even even thousands of writers gather—sometimes in spectacular settings—can provide heady experiences for practitioners of the trade. The following databases are useful resources for learning about international festivals.

-» The American Literary Translators Association website
   *www.utdallas.edu/alta*

-» The Book and Periodical Council in Canada
   *www.thebpc.ca/the-resource-file/literary-festivals*

-» The University of Pennsylvania, which curates an up-to-date list of calls for papers for conferences and festivals
   *http://call-for-papers.sas.upenn.edu*

-» PEN International, which sponsors festivals across the globe
   *www.pen-international.org/events-festivals*

-» Poets & Writers Conferences & Residencies database
   *http://www.pw.org/conferences_and_residencies*

The following list is a sampling of international festivals; it is by no means comprehensive. Before finalizing plans to attend any festival, consult the US Department of State's warnings and information site.

CANADA

-» The International Festival of Authors in Canada is held in October in Toronto.
*www.readings.org*

-» The Ontario Writers' Conference is held in May.
*www.thewritersconference.com*

-» Summer Literary Seminars are held in Montreal in June. (See Kenya and Lithuania for two other sessions of Summer Literary Seminars.)
*www.sumlitsem.org*

COLOMBIA

-» The annual International Poetry Festival of Medellín is held in June.
*www.festivaldepoesiademedellin.org*

CZECH REPUBLIC

-» The Prague Summer Program is held in June and July.
*www.praguesummer.com*

-» The Prague Writers' Festival is held in April.
*www.pwf.cz*

GERMANY

-» The International Literature Festival is held in Berlin in September.
*www.literaturfestival.com/aktuelles-en*

-» The Literaturwerkstatt Berlin poetry festival is held in June.
*www.literaturwerkstatt.org/index.php?id=1016&L=0*

IRELAND

-» The Cúirt International Festival of Literature takes place in Galway
during the last week in April.
*http://www.cuirt.ie/*

ITALY

-» Sirenland in Positano is held in March.
*www.sirenland.net*

-» The Umbria Writing & Publishing Workshop is held in June and July.
*www.noahcharney.com/writing/index.htm*

-» A Writers' Workshop is held at the Amalfi Coast Music Festival in July.
*www.amalfi-festival.org*

JAMAICA

-» The Calabash International Literary Festival is held in Jamaica each
May.
*www.calabashfestival.org*

KENYA

-» Summer Literary Seminars are held in December in Nairobi and Lamu. (See Canada and Lithuania for two other sessions of Summer Literary Seminars.)
*www.sumlitsem.org*

LITHUANIA

-» Summer Literary Seminars are held in Vilnius in July and August. (See Canada and Kenya for two other sessions of Summer Literary Seminars.)
*www.sumlitsem.org*

MEXICO

-» San Miguel Poetry Week is held in January.
*www.sanmiguelpoetry.com*

-» San Miguel Writers' Conference is in February.
*www.sanmiguelwritersconference.org*

NETHERLANDS

-» The Maastricht Poetry Festival is held in October every other year.
*www.maastrichtpoetry.com*

-» Poetry International Rotterdam, one of the oldest poetry festivals in Europe, takes place in June. The website contains one of the most comprehensive literary anthologies of poetry from around the world currently available on the web.
*www.poetryinternationalweb.net*

NICARAGUA

-» Granada International Festival of Poetry is one of Latin America's most popular poetry festivals.
*www.festivalpoesianicaragua.com/*

PORTUGAL

-» Dzanc Books, in collaboration with Portuguese cultural organiza-tions and Summer Literary Seminars, Inc., has recently established DISQUIET International, which takes place in July in Lisbon and for which grants are available on a competitive basis.
*http://disquietinternational.org*

REPUBLIC OF MACEDONIA

-» Struga Poetry Evenings, one of the oldest poetry festivals in Eastern Europe, is held each August in Struga.
*www.svp.org.mk/*

SLOVENIA

-» Days of Poetry and Wine, one of the most popular festivals for younger Eastern European poets, is held at the end of August.
*www.poezijainvino.org/2011/en/home*

SOUTH AFRICA

-» The Poetry Africa international poetry festival in Durban is held every October.
*http://www.cca.ukzn.ac.za/index.php?option=com_content&view=article&id=93&Itemid=75*

SWITZERLAND

-» The Geneva Writers' Conference is held in February.
*www.genevawritersgroup.org*

UNITED KINGDOM

-» The National Association of Writers in Education conference takes
place in November.
*www.nawe.co.uk*

-» The Great Writing International Creative Writing conference is held
in June or July.
*www.greatwriting.org.uk*

-» The Winchester Writers' Conference is held in June.
*www.writersconference.co.uk*

-» WordTheatre Writers' Workshop and Retreat takes place in Edale,
England, in July.
*www.wordtheatre.com/writersretreat*

# Teaching English

Teaching abroad can provide not only valuable professional experience, but also the chance to become involved in a local community. There are many international teaching opportunities; the list that follows includes placement agencies as well as specific programs. When selecting a program, school, or agency, consider not only the location but also the level of preparation the organization will expect and the training it provides.

Poets hoping to teach in a foreign country should conduct research well in advance of hiring cycles (at least a year before the desired departure date). For teaching secondary school internationally through private organizations, an MFA can be a meaningful credential.

Here are some agencies and specific programs that may help you get started with your research; the list is not comprehensive. Organizations marked with an asterisk will give you the instruction you need to teach English.

-» Berlitz is one of the world's largest ESL schools and places those interested in teaching English at a Berlitz center for one year or more. Candidates must be interested in teaching both adults and children, and although it is possible to apply to teach in a specific country, flexibility will make acceptance more likely. Those with previous teaching experience who are willing to be abroad for more than one year are most likely to be hired. Be aware that Berlitz is a corporation, so work is usually at a language center in a corporate environment. Pay varies by country and teaching assignment but is better than for many other international teaching opportunities.
*www.berlitz.com*

-» Carney, Sandoe & Associates is a recruiting agency that represents both US and international schools.
*www.carneysandoe.com*

-» Those selected for the program, Connecting Schools to the World, live with families in rural pueblos throughout Argentina. The program provides teaching English as a second language (TESL) training in Buenos Aires, after which teachers spend four to nine months living with families in regions rarely visited by tourists. Housing costs are covered, and a monthly stipend is provided in exchange for up to twenty-five hours per week of teaching. The program is most suitable for those with at least Spanish proficiency, although Spanish language skills are not required.
*http://www.connectingschools.com.ar*

-» Dave's ESL Cafe is an online resource for those interested in teaching English abroad. The site includes job listings and a portal where résumés can be uploaded so that those seeking English instructors can contact candidates qualified for their positions.
*www.eslcafe.com*

-» The French embassy coordinates the Teaching Assistant Program in France, which hires English teachers for French schools. This government program guarantees a French visa, full access to French health care, subsidies to defray half the monthly transport costs, and some rent. According to Michelle Coghlan, who taught in the program, "The program offered minimal training but did supply us with basic lesson plan ideas and a set of targets students should reach by the end of the year."
*www.frenchculture.org/assistantshipprogram*

-» Fulbright English Teaching Assistantships allow US citizens to live in another country for an academic year and teach English in a local school. These opportunities are less competitive than the Fulbright fellowships (see "Fellowships, Grants, and Scholarships" in this section) but still provide the chance to have an immersive cultural

experience and to get to know local literary culture. Teaching assistants are encouraged to pursue individual study and research plans in addition to their teaching responsibilities, and they receive stipends that allow for comfortable living in their host countries. (For more information about the Fulbright Program, see Susan Rich's essay, "Solitary: Spending a Fulbright Year in South Africa.")
*http://us.fulbrightonline.org/english-teaching-assistantships*

-» Japan Exchange and Teaching (JET) Programme, sponsored by the Japanese government, arranges for teachers from the United States and more than thirty-five other countries to teach English in Japan. This is one of the world's largest exchange programs. JET participants function as cultural ambassadors for their countries of origin. JET acts as the intermediary among Japanese educational authorities, some private schools in Japan, and Americans wishing to spend a year in Japan teaching. JET provides a very useful list of teaching opportunities on the website Alternatives to the JET Programme: English.
*www.jetprogramme.org*
*http://jet-programme.com/jet_alternatives.htm*

-» The Peace Corps has provided opportunities to live, work, and serve in developing countries since President John F. Kennedy started the program in 1960. Volunteers serve more than seventy countries in Africa, Asia, the Caribbean, Central and South America, Europe, the Middle East, and the Pacific Islands. The volunteer term is twenty-seven months, and volunteers provide support in six program areas: education, youth and community development, health, business and information/communication technology, agriculture, and environment. The Peace Corps application process can be lengthy and does not allow the applicant much input regarding where he or she will be stationed. Most positions require a bachelor's degree. The Peace Corps takes care of visas, inoculations, and health care. It also provides follow-up care for ongoing health issues that need to be addressed once you return to the United States. Service to the Peace Corps will allow you to defer your student loans while you are abroad. Travel expenses to and from the country of service are provided, as well as a monthly stipend for living expenses and medical and dental insurance. Volunteers who complete their terms receive a stipend of approximately $7,500. Federal Perkins student loans are eligible for cancellation of up to 70 percent of the loan (15 percent canceled for completion of each of the first two years and 20 percent cancelation for the third and fourth years). The Peace Corps experience is known to be extremely challenging because of both the length of stay and the difficult conditions in most placement communities. (See "Volunteerism" in this section for additional information.)

*www.peacecorps.gov*

---

VOICES FROM THE FIELD

"Approximately ten hours each week were spent on technical training—in the case of TEFL (Teaching English as a Foreign Language) trainees, that meant teaching techniques and lesson planning," says Tiffany Tuttle Collins of her work for the Peace Corps. "We received a number of teaching materials to work with as well, from beginner to advanced level instruction, and we spent two weeks at 'model school.' There, pairs of trainees planned and taught classes to local children and were observed and given feedback by American staffers, other active volunteers, and host country teachers." The training proved useful, she says. "We learned to create effective lessons from scratch." She also notes that the process of acquiring a foreign language gave volunteers some insight into their students' learning. "The application process takes several months, including a written application, an interview with a Peace Corps recruiter, and extensive medical and dental screening," she explains. "You can indicate what continent you would like to work on, and you can refuse an invitation to serve, but the application states that the pickier you are, the longer it will take to find another assignment."

-» Princeton in Asia Fellowships provide the opportunity to work in one of eighteen Asian countries. Placements are in education, international development, environmental advocacy, journalism, and law or business. (See listing in this section under "Job Opportunities Abroad" for more information.)
*http://piaweb.princeton.edu/*

-» Search Associates is an international agency that provides a database of positions available for applicants looking to teach abroad. An application is required.
*www.searchassociates.com*

-» Teach Abroad provides an online database of English-teaching opportunities. Do some research before pursuing an opportunity. Ask an organization if it can put you in touch with someone who has taught abroad through one of its programs. If it is unable to connect you with someone, it may be a sign that the organization is poorly run and/or that participants have negative feelings about their experiences.
*http://www.goabroad.com/teach-abroad*

-» Teach Away places teachers in Africa, Asia, Europe, the Middle East, and South America. Successful candidates typically have one or two years of teaching experience. Monthly salaries are based on local economies and are competitive ($6,000–$6,500 per month in Hong Kong, for example). Airfare is also included for most placements, and some provide a monthly travel stipend as well. Teach Away positions have the potential to become long-term jobs, with room for promotion and increased pay.
*www.teachaway.com*

-» Teach English in Mexico finds jobs for those interested in teaching English in Mexico and also finds housing placements. In exchange for a fee paid to the organization, Teach English in Mexico guarantees a paid placement and gives teachers access to a representative in Mexico who can provide advice and support before and after arrival. *www.teach-english-mexico.com*

-» The US Department of State provides many resources for locating international schools that are looking for teachers. *www.state.gov/m/a/os/c16899.htm*

# Job Opportunities Abroad

Job opportunities abroad can be anything from short-term legal work as an electoral monitor to securing a position as a journalist or joining an emergency medical team for short-term disaster relief projects. As in the United States, jobs abroad depend on employment history and level of education. However, there are positions that welcome a generalist background in farmwork, for example, or environmentally focused projects.

-» The American Bar Association (ABA) facilitates legal internship opportunities for US law students interested in international law. *www.abanet.org/intlaw/intlinternship.html*

-» The American Medical Student Association (AMSA) maintains a directory of opportunities for those with medical experience who wish to gain experience abroad. *www.amsa.org/global/ih/ihopps.cfm*

-» BackDoorJobs.com is an online database, including opportunities to teach, work on sustainable farms, lead youth trips, and intern abroad. *www.backdoorjobs.com/*

-» The Riley Guide is one of the most thorough online listings of job search resources and search engines by region and country and is recommended if you wish to search for a job without using a placement agency. *http://www.rileyguide.com/internat.html*

## Volunteerism

These volunteer opportunities, ranging from just a couple of weeks to more than two years, are excellent for getting to know other cultures, improving language skills, and meeting other people who want to work for a better world. Long-term volunteer appointments, in particular, provide chances to meet local writers and become involved in the literary culture, which is possible with many short-term appointments as well.

Volunteer travel is one of the most intimate and unpredictable ways to experience a foreign country. Take stock of your skills and research the possibilities for contributing your strengths to a place or a community in need. If you have special skills—medical training, for example, or agroforestry experience—you may be eligible for some remarkable volunteer opportunities.

Be aware that volunteer work in developing countries can be psychologically and emotionally challenging. If you have not traveled to a developing country before, it is recommended that you try one of the two- to four-week opportunities before considering a long-term appointment. Each organization provides experiences that will alter your perspective on the world. If you are self-motivated, you can seek out opportunities and get to know local writers.

The following books by former international volunteers provide useful insight into what to expect: *Only Bees Die: Peace Corps Eastern Europe*, by Robert Keller (CreateSpace, 2010); *The Village of Waiting*, by George Packer (Farrar, Straus and Giroux, 2001); *Whispering Campaign: Stories from Mesoamerica*, by Lawrence F. Lihosit (iUniverse.com, 2009).

## Volunteer Resources

-» Doctors Without Borders seeks medical and nonmedical aid workers to provide vital medical help for people threatened by war, epidemics, natural disasters, and other catastrophes. The Nobel Prize–winning organization operates in more than fifty countries. *www.doctorswithoutborders.org*

-» Habitat for Humanity International Volunteer Program allows participants to help build and rehabilitate affordable housing around the world. Typical assignments for long-term volunteers include work in administration, communications, finance, programs, resource development, and volunteer coordination. In addition to the long-term, international program, Habitat for Humanity also runs two-week trips for volunteer teams under the Global Village Program (www.habitat.org/gv). In some cases, the host country provides assistance with local transportation or housing; in all cases, volunteers are responsible for international medical insurance, most housing costs, food, and travel to and from the United States. *www.habitat.org/ivp*

-» The International Volunteer Programs Association is an association of nongovernmental organizations that run volunteer and internship programs. Whether or not you have professional skills (medical, technical, or business), the IVPA can help you choose an international volunteer program. *www.volunteerinternational.org*

-» Peace Corps volunteer positions most often require a bachelor's degree. Volunteers receive thorough training in language and cross-cultural instruction. The Peace Corps features some programs for which specialists are keenly desired, such as agroforesters, engineers, urban planners, deaf-education teachers, and university-level teachers. (See "Teaching English" in this section for additional information.)

*www.peacecorps.gov*

-» Service Civil International (SCI) offers work camps in numerous fields and locations worldwide. Most volunteers work for two to four weeks, but it is possible to commit for up to one year. SCI provides participants the chance to learn about other cultures and contribute to local communities in concrete ways. Examples of volunteer activities include planting trees in Iceland, building classrooms in Mexico, and running activities for refugees in Kenya. There is also a long-term program for those who want to volunteer for three to twelve months. Volunteers cover most of their own expenses and pay a participation fee that helps support the volunteer centers.

*www.sciint.org*

-» Volunteers for Peace offers placement in international volunteer projects in more than one hundred countries. Volunteers work for approximately five hours per day and have built community centers, created hiking trails, provided activities for orphans or refugees, worked in community gardens, et cetera.

*www.vfp.org*

-» World Wide Opportunities on Organic Farms (WWOOF) is a membership organization that provides the opportunity to receive free room and board at any of the thousands of WWOOF farms throughout the world. The program is recommended for those with a genuine interest in learning about organic growing, country living, or ecologically sound lifestyles. No previous farming experience is necessary, and volunteers do not pay for housing while abroad. It should be noted that working on a rural farm will provide less opportunity to get to know the nation's literary culture than community-based volunteer opportunities; however, it may still be excellent for language acquisition and provide a great deal of inspiration.

*www.wwoof.org*

## Additional Resources

This section provides information on how to prepare for travel abroad. Along with an extensive and straightforward checklist every traveler should consult before leaving home, you'll find discussions of issues of special interest to gay, lesbian, bisexual, and transgender travelers; to minority travelers (both ethnic and religious minorities); and to travelers with disabilities. Suggestions for preparing for medical issues while abroad are provided along with other basic information useful to the traveler.

# Traveling Abroad: A Checklist

To prepare yourself for your time abroad and to help avoid or mitigate negative experiences:

☐ Research **visa** requirements for the country you are going to, and comply with all requirements. Begin the process of applying for a visa as soon as you know you will be going abroad. For some countries, the processing time can be more than three months. Most countries require that applicants appear at the consulate that serves your host country in person (some require that applicants appear in person twice), so plan ahead. You can find all the necessary visa information on consulate websites; pay careful attention to the instructions, as consulates are notorious for refusing to process incorrectly prepared visa applications. Most countries require a visa for stays longer than three months, and many countries require them for visits of any length, even a weekend. **Do not** assume that because you have received a grant or been accepted into a program, you will receive a visa. It is up to you to complete the necessary requirements. For a list of foreign countries that have embassies/consulates in the United States, visit www.state.gov/s/cpr/rls/dpl/32122.htm. You should also familiarize yourself with the US embassy or consulate in the country you are visiting. Visit www.usembassy.gov.

☐ Make sure your **passport**, which is the only universally accepted form of identification, is valid. You cannot travel internationally without one. Passport applications can be obtained at many local US post offices. For more information and for the latest passport fees, visit travel.state.gov/passport/passport_1738.html.

If your trip will be longer than one month, make sure your passport is valid for at least six months after the date that you plan to return to the United States. Many countries will not admit travelers with a passport that is about to expire.

❑ Make **two copies** of your travel itinerary, program contact information (if going through an organization or institution), airline tickets, passport photo page (and visa, if you have one), and medical insurance cards. Keep one copy separate from the originals at all times while traveling and abroad; give the other copy to a friend or family member in the United States.

❑ Arrange for a **physical checkup, an eye examination, and dental work** before you leave the United States. Immunizations are required to enter many countries and recommended for travel to many more (see below).

❑ Get your required **immunizations**. In the developing world, special immunizations are often required, even for short stays and often in advance of your arrival into the country. You should check to make certain all your shots are up-to-date, including vaccinations for measles, meningitis, mumps, rubella, polio, diphtheria, and tetanus. If you expect to travel outside Western Europe, you should contact the Centers for Disease Control and Prevention at 1-800-CDC-INFO (1-800-232-4636) for information about health precautions and immunization requirements for travel to other countries. You can also visit the website at www.cdc.gov/travel.

❑ Pack a **first-aid kit**. When traveling, carry your own basic drugstore supplies, such as ibuprofen or acetaminophen, motion-sickness medication, laxatives, antacids, antihistamines, decongestants, antiseptics, and bandages. Depending on where you are going and how long you are staying, your doctor may recommend that you take antibiotics with you in the event that you become ill overseas. Make sure all medications are in their labeled containers, and carry a copy of the written prescription with generic names. Do the same with glasses and contact lenses. Take an extra pair of glasses and/or contact lenses. Be sure to pack contact lens solution; you may not find the kind you use abroad. If you have a health condition that could be serious (such as diabetes, an allergy to penicillin, et cetera), wear a medical alert bracelet.

❒ Make additional preparations for **medical care** while abroad (see below).

❒ Check out **travel warnings**, conditions, and general information about the country or countries you will be traveling in at http://travel.state.gov.

❒ Register at https://step.state.gov/step/ so the **US Department of State can better assist you in an emergency** and will be aware of your location. By registering, you help the embassy or consulate locate you when you might need it most. Registration is voluntary and costs nothing but should be part of your travel planning and security. The US embassy or consulate in your host country will issue a new passport or replace one that is lost or stolen while you are abroad; contact the US Department of State at embassy expense for further instructions if you cannot verify your citizenship; and help you find medical or legal services in case of an emergency and help notify friends or family members. The US embassy or consulate **will not** give or lend money, serve as a travel agent, provide interpreters or courier services, or arrange for free medical or legal services (they will assist you only in finding a doctor or lawyer appropriate to your needs).

❒ If you plan an extended stay in one place, it is a good idea to **know where the US embassy is** located. In many countries the embassy or consul will have an English-language library and other resources you can access.

☐ In many countries, it's useful and necessary to **register with the local ward office, immigration department, or local police station** shortly after arrival at your destination. This is especially true if you are living in the country using a work visa or a cultural activities visa (as in the case of the Japan–United States Friendship Commission Fellowship). It's often easiest to inquire about this prior to arrival— you can check with embassy or consulate officers about this process.

☐ Do some **research on the cost of living** in your host country, and draft a budget so that you have a good idea of how much you can spend each week from the first week of arrival.

☐ Take several forms of **money.** You should be able to get local currency from an ATM machine after you arrive, but in case of immediate problems with ATMs, carry approximately $200, changed into local currency.

☐ If you plan to use **credit cards** abroad, Visa and MasterCard are the most widely accepted. Discover and American Express are not as widely used in many countries.

☐ **Call your credit card companies and banks** to notify them of your travel plans and inquire about applicable fees. Notifying them that you will be abroad is essential. Without notification, they may freeze your accounts because of "suspicious activity" when you begin making purchases and withdrawing cash abroad. You may also want to open a bank account with a bank that does not charge ATM fees abroad.

❏ If you plan to use **debit cards**, Cirrus or Plus ATM machines are easy to find all over westernized countries. Be sure to check with your bank about transaction fees, and open an account with a bank that charges no, or very low, fees abroad if you will be staying for a long time. Make sure your PIN is only four digits and not six (many ATMs abroad do not accept six-digit PINs).

❏ **Write down phone numbers for each credit card** and for your debit card in the event you lose your cards or they are stolen. Keep these numbers in a safe place separate from the cards. E-mail a copy to yourself as well as to a trusted friend.

❏ If you will be studying while you are abroad, purchase an **International Student ID Card** (visit www.isic.org). The card provides health insurance as well as hundreds of discounts on electronics, travel, clothing, and other essentials. You can also purchase additional insurance coverage for personal belongings such as laptops and cell phones, in case they are lost, stolen, or damaged during your travels.

❏ Be sure all your **gadgets**, from cell phones to laptops to electric shavers, can work while abroad. There are two standard voltages in the world: 110 (used in the United States) and 220. An appliance designed for 110 volts cannot run on 220 without a converter. In addition, outlet types vary and require adapters. If you will be abroad for an extended stay, consider buying necessary appliances abroad. If you are going to pack an appliance from the United States, purchase a converter that can convert 110 to 220 volts. You will also need a socket adapter to use the appliance. An international socket adapter set is recommended in any case because you may need it if you travel outside your host country during your time abroad.

❐ Almost all laptops have converters built into their power cables so they can be used internationally, but you will still need a **socket adapter** in most countries. To be certain that your laptop will work abroad, check the power pack. It should read "INPUT 100-240V–50/60HZ." If it does not, you may need to purchase a different power pack for your computer.

## Gay, Lesbian, Bisexual, and Transgender Issues Abroad

Customs, attitudes, laws, and social practices relating to gay, lesbian, bisexual, and transgender people vary throughout the world. Some countries are more progressive than the United States in their perspectives on GLBT issues. Many other countries are far more conservative and restrictive in their policies and practices. GLBT travelers will want to inform themselves about relevant issues in their host countries and in all their travel destinations.

Most country-specific travel guides will have a section on GLBT issues. Use these and other books to become informed. The following websites provide additional information and resources:

-» Information for GLBT travelers worldwide
   *http://gayguide.net/index.html*

-» The International Lesbian, Gay, Bisexual, Trans and
   Intersex Association
   *www.ilga.org*

-» The International Gay & Lesbian Human Rights Commission
   *www.iglhrc.org.*

## Political Awareness for Travelers

Just as in the United States, political issues or lack of tolerance can make some groups of people targets for mistreatment. Political rallies and certain dates, such as anniversaries of historical events, can spur ethnic and religious conflicts in many countries. Take the time to research minority issues in your destination country and talk with scholarship or placement organization staff if you are concerned.

## Travelers Who Have Disabilities

Resources and facilities for individuals who have disabilities may not be the same abroad as they are in the United States. Disabled people traveling abroad may also be the victims of prejudice and stereotyping. In many countries, there are no standards or requirements for providing access for disabled people. Wheelchair ramps, handicap-accessible parking spaces, Braille signs, and other aids may be nonexistent in parts of the host country, especially in rural areas.

In addition to a lack of services provided for the physically disabled, there may also be a lack of services provided for those who have learning disabilities or psychological or emotional disorders.

If you know that you will likely need special arrangements abroad, you should be in touch with your scholarship or volunteer/job placement program before you apply; ask what may be possible in the country you are considering for your time abroad.

For physical disabilities, you can also consult with Mobility International USA (MIUSA). Call 541-343-1284, or visit the website at www.miusa.org. MIUSA also offers several trips abroad each year for persons with physical disabilities. Travelers can choose from "inbound" and "outbound" programs to countries such as China, Spain, and Jordan.

## Medical Care While Abroad

Be aware that the manner in which people obtain medical help, the ways patients are treated, the conditions of overseas medical facilities, and the ways health care is afforded abroad often differ markedly from US practices. US health care values, assumptions, and methods are not universally practiced. Even ideas regarding the onset of illness or points at which expert attention is required are to some degree cultural phenomena.

If you have a **physical or psychological problem** that requires ongoing treatment by a doctor, you should consult with your physician or mental health professional about the prospect of spending an extended period abroad. Most programs and opportunities listed in this guide do not employ mental health professionals, nor is mental health treatment widely accessible or comparable to mental health treatment in the United States in many locations abroad. For your own welfare, you should consult with a US mental health professional or physician to discuss the potential stress and physical challenge of living abroad and ways to cope with issues if you cannot access the same medical care you depend on in the United States.

If you take **medication**, discuss with your physician the type of care you may need while abroad and the best way to continue your regimen. Not all drugs are available in all countries, and when they are available, they may have been given a different commercial name. You will most likely need to take enough medication to cover the duration of your time abroad; consult your health insurance provider about obtaining enough medication for your entire stay. Be aware that not all medications can be given in the amounts you may need, and some may not be allowed into the country at all. These include many types of narcotics (including some painkillers) and certain medications prescribed for mental health conditions. Do not try to secure the medication abroad unless you have done research and are certain that the exact dosages and medicines you need are available and that you can obtain them. You may also need a written note from your doctor to take a medication into another country. Please note: it is difficult, if not impossible, to ship medications internationally. Even if legal, the shipment must clear customs, which may take weeks.

It's also a good idea to see if your prescriptions are available in your host country. The same medication may be under a different brand name.

"Questions of Travel"[1]
Elizabeth Bishop

There are too many waterfalls here; the crowded streams
hurry too rapidly down to the sea,
and the pressure of so many clouds on the mountaintops
makes them spill over the sides in soft slow-motion,
turning to waterfalls under our very eyes.
—For if those streaks, those mile-long, shiny, tearstains,
aren't waterfalls yet,
in a quick age or so, as ages go here,
they probably will be.
But if the streams and clouds keep travelling, travelling,
the mountains look like the hulls of capsized ships,
slime-hung and barnacled.

Think of the long trip home.
Should we have stayed at home and thought of here?
Where should we be today?
Is it right to be watching strangers in a play
in this strangest of theatres?
What childishness is it that while there's a breath of life
in our bodies, we are determined to rush
to see the sun the other way around?
The tiniest green hummingbird in the world?
To stare at some inexplicable old stonework,
inexplicable and impenetrable,
at any view,
instantly seen and always, always delightful?

1. Elizabeth Bishop, "Questions of Travel" from *The Complete Poems, 1927–1979*. (New York: Farrar, Straus and Giroux, 1984).

Oh, we must dream our dreams
and have them, too?
And have we room
for one more folded sunset, still quite warm?

But surely it would have been a pity
not to have seen the trees along this road,
really exaggerated in their beauty,
not to have seem them gesturing
like noble pantomimists, robed in pink.
—Not to have had to stop for gas and heard
the sad, two-noted, wooden tune
of disparate wooden clogs
carelessly clacking over
a grease-stained filling-station floor.
(In another country the clogs would all be tested.
Each pair there would have identical pitch.)
—A pity not to have heard
the other, less primitive music of the fat brown bird
who sings above the broken gasoline pump
in a bamboo church of Jesuit baroque:
three towers, five silver crosses.
—Yes, a pity not to have pondered,
blurr'dly and inconclusively,
on what connection can exist for centuries
between the crudest wooden footwear
and, careful and finicky,
the whittled fantasies of wooden cages.
—Never to have studied history in
the weak calligraphy of songbirds' cages.
—And never to have had to listen to rain
so much like politicians' speeches:

two hours of unrelenting oratory
and then a sudden golden silence
in which the traveller takes a notebook, writes:

*"Is it lack of imagination that makes us come*
*to imagined places, not just stay at home?*
*Or could Pascal have been not entirely right*
*about just sitting quietly in one's room?*

*Continent, city, country, society:*
*the choice is never wide and never free.*
*And here, or there...No. Should we have stayed at home,*
*wherever that may be?"*

# Contributors

**Kazim Ali,** associate professor of creative writing and comparative literature at Oberlin College, is the author of numerous books of poetry, fiction, and essays, including most recently *Orange Alert: Essays on Poetry, Art, and the Architecture of Silence* (University of Michigan Press) and the cross-genre poetic memoir *Bright Felon: Autobiography and Cities* (Wesleyan University Press). He has translated volumes of poetry by Ananda Devi and Sohrab Sepehri and is founding editor of the small press Nightboat Books.

**Elizabeth Austen** is the author of *Every Dress a Decision* (Blue Begonia Press), *The Girl Who Goes Alone* (Floating Bridge Press), and *Where Currents Meet* (one of four winners of the 2010 Toadlily Press chapbook award and part of the quartet *Sightline*). Her poems have been featured on *Verse Daily* and Garrison Keillor's *The Writer's Almanac*. She was the Washington State Roadshow poet and is the literary producer for KUOW 94.9 public radio in Seattle.

**Catherine Barnett** is the author of two collections of poems, *Into Perfect Spheres Such Holes Are Pierced* (Alice James Books) and *The Game of Boxes* (Graywolf Press). She has received the 2012 James Laughlin Award, a Guggenheim Fellowship, a Whiting Writers' Award, a Glasgow Prize for Emerging Writers, and a Pushcart Prize. Her poems have appeared in the *American Poetry Review*, the *Kenyon Review*, *Pleiades*, *TriQuarterly*, *Virginia Quarterly Review*, the *Washington Post*, and other publications. She works as an independent editor and teaches at Barnard College, The New School, and New York University.

**Ashley Brown** (1923–2011) was professor emeritus in English and comparative literature at the University of South Carolina. He was founder of the literary magazine *Shenandoah* and a confidant of novelist Flannery O'Connor and poet Elizabeth Bishop.

**Derick Burleson**'s most recent book of poems is *Melt* (Marick Press). His first two collections of poems are *Never Night* (Marick Press) and *Ejo: Poems, Rwanda, 1991–1994* (University of Wisconsin Press). His poems have appeared in the *Georgia Review*, the *Kenyon Review*, the *Paris Review*, the *Southern Review*, and *Poetry*, among other journals. Burleson directs the MFA program in creative writing at the University of Alaska Fairbanks and lives in Two Rivers, Alaska.

**Katharine Coles**'s fifth poetry collection, *Reckless*, is forthcoming from Red Hen Press; she has also published novels and essays. She is a professor at the University of Utah, where she codirects the Utah Symposium in Science and Literature. In 2010, she traveled to Antarctica on a grant from the National Science Foundation's Antarctic Artists and Writers Program. In 2009 and 2010, she served as the inaugural director of the Poetry Foundation's Harriet Monroe Poetry Institute.

**Gregory Dunne** is the author of two collections of poetry: *Home Test* (Adastra Press) and *Fistful of Lotus*. His nonfiction book, *Quiet Accomplishment, A Remembrance of Cid Corman*, is forthcoming from Ekstasis Editions. His poetry and prose have appeared in numerous magazines, including the *American Poetry Review*, *Manoa*, *Poetry East*, and *Kyoto Journal*. He lives in Japan and teaches in the Faculty of Comparative Culture at Miyazaki International College.

**Karen Finneyfrock**'s second book of poems, *Ceremony for the Choking Ghost*, was released by Write Bloody Publishing. Her young-adult novel, *Celia, the Dark and Weird*, is due from

Viking Children's Books, a division of Penguin. A member of four National Poetry Slam teams, she has toured nationally and internationally as a spoken-word artist.

**Nick Flynn** has worked as a ship's captain, an electrician, and a caseworker with homeless adults. His most recent book is *The Captain Asks for a Show of Hands* (Graywolf Press). His poems, essays, and nonfiction have appeared in various venues, including the *New Yorker*, the *Paris Review*, National Public Radio's *This American Life*, and the *New York Times Book Review*. A professor in the creative writing program at the University of Houston, he teaches each spring then spends the rest of the year in (or near) Brooklyn, New York.

**Carolyn Forché** directs the Lannan Center for Poetics and Social Practice and is the Lannan Visiting Professor of Poetry at Georgetown University. Her fifth collection of poems, *In the Lateness of the World*, is forthcoming from HarperCollins. Her book *The Country Between Us* (Harper Perennial) received the Poetry Society of America's Alice Fay Di Castagnola Award and was a Lamont Poetry Selection of the Academy of American Poets. Her honors include a Lannan Literary Award in Poetry and fellowships from the Guggenheim Foundation and the National Endowment for the Arts.

**Rachel Galvin** earned a PhD in comparative literature at Princeton University and has recently joined the Humanities Center at The Johns Hopkins University as a Mellon Fellow. Her essays appear in *The Blackwell Companion to Translation Studies*, the *Los Angeles Review of Books*, and the *Wallace Stevens Journal*, and poems and translations appear in the *New Yorker*, *McSweeney's*, and *PN Review*. A book of poems, *Pulleys & Locomotion*, was published by Black Lawrence Press, and her translation

of *Hitting the Streets* by Raymond Queneau is forthcoming (Carcanet Press).

**Kathleen Graber** is the author of two collections of poems: *Correspondence* (Saturnalia) and *The Eternal City* (Princeton University Press), which was a finalist for the National Book Award and the National Book Critics Circle Award. She has received fellowships from the National Endowment for the Arts and the Rona Jaffe Foundation. An assistant professor of English at Virginia Commonwealth University, Graber also teaches in the low-residency MFA program at Fairleigh Dickinson University.

**Garth Greenwell**'s first book, *Mitko*, won the 2010 Miami University Press Novella Prize. His poetry has appeared in the *Yale Review*, *Boston Review*, *Poetry International*, and *Gulf Coast*, among other journals, and has received the Grolier Prize, the Rella Lossy Poetry Award, and the Dorothy Sargent Rosenberg Poetry Prize. Greenwell lives in Sofia, Bulgaria, where he teaches at the American College of Sofia, an independent secondary school.

**Eliza Griswold** received a 2011 J. Anthony Lukas Book Prize for her *New York Times* best seller *The Tenth Parallel* and a 2010 Rome Prize from the American Academy in Rome for her poetry. Having won awards for both her nonfiction and her poems, she is currently a senior fellow at the New America Foundation. A former Nieman Fellow at Harvard University, she reports on religion, conflict, and human rights. Her first book of poems, *Wideawake Field*, and *The Tenth Parallel*, an examination of Christianity and Islam in Africa and Asia, were published by Farrar, Straus and Giroux. Her reportage and poetry have appeared in the *New Yorker*, the *Atlantic*, the *New York Times Magazine*, *Harpers*, the *New Republic*, and many other publications.

**Jared Hawkley** is a poet and freelance editor from Vancouver, British Columbia. He's been a contributing editor to *The Best American Nonrequired Reading* (Mariner Books); *Blue Collar, White Collar, No Collar* (Harper Perennial); and books of student writing for the educational nonprofit 826michigan, including *Don't Stay Up So Late: A Treasury of Bedtime Stories*. He has written for newspapers and blogs, designed record jackets, led hikes up fourteeners in Rocky Mountain National Park, and given dogsled tours in the northern woods of Minnesota. He lives in Oakland, California.

**Jane Hirshfield** is the author of seven poetry collections, most recently *Come, Thief* (Knopf). *Given Sugar, Given Salt* (Harper Perennial) was a finalist for the National Book Critics Circle Award. Lay ordained in Soto Zen in 1979, she is a current chancellor of the Academy of American Poets. *The Ink Dark Moon* (Vintage) is her cotranslation of the work of Ono no Komachi and Izumi Shikibu, two classical-era Japanese women poets.

**Ilya Kaminsky** is the director of the Harriet Monroe Poetry Institute at the Poetry Foundation. He is the author of *Dancing in Odessa* (Tupelo Press) and coeditor of *The Ecco Anthology of International Poetry*.

**Yusef Komunyakaa** is the author of numerous books of poetry, most recently *The Chameleon Couch* (Farrar, Straus and Giroux), which was a finalist for the 2011 National Book Award. He has received multiple fellowships, and his awards include the Kingsley Tufts Poetry Award and the Pulitzer Prize. In addition to poetry, Komunyakaa is the author of several plays, performance literature, and libretti, which have been performed in venues that include the 92nd Street Y, Opera Omaha, and Sydney Opera House. He currently teaches in New York University's graduate creative writing program.

**Adrie Kusserow** is a professor of cultural anthropology at Saint Michael's College in Vermont. She works with the Bhutan Centre for Media and Democracy and Africa ELI: Education and Leadership Initiative (Bridging Gender Gaps Through Education) in South Sudan. She has written two books of poetry: *Hunting Down the Monk* (BOA Editions, A. Poulin, Jr. New Poets of America Series) and *Refuge* (American Poets Continuum), also from BOA Editions.

**Denise Levertov** (1923–1997) was a British-born American poet who published more than twenty books of poetry, criticism, and translations. Among her many awards and honors are a Shelley Memorial Award, a Robert Frost Medal, a Lenore Marshall Poetry Prize, a Lannan Literary Award in Poetry, a Catherine Luck Memorial Grant, a grant from the National Institute of Arts and Letters, and a Guggenheim Fellowship. From 1982 to 1993 she taught at Stanford University. She spent the last decade of her life in Seattle.

**Philip Levine** was named the eighteenth US poet laureate by the Library of Congress in 2011. His most recent book of poetry is *News of the World* (Knopf). His awards include the Pulitzer Prize for *The Simple Truth* (Knopf), two National Book Awards, the National Book Critics Circle Award, the Ruth Lilly Poetry Prize, two Guggenheim Fellowships, and the Harriet Monroe Memorial Prize. He was born and raised in Detroit and currently lives in Brooklyn, New York, and Fresno, California.

**Brandon Lussier**'s poems and translations have been published in the *Harvard Review*, the *Virginia Quarterly Review*, the *Columbia Review*, and elsewhere. His translation work has been anthologized in *New European Poets* (Graywolf Press) and *A Sharp Cut: Contemporary Estonian Literature* and was reviewed in *Boston Review*. He has spoken about literary translation at Princeton University and the American Literary Translators Association and is a former creative writing Fulbright Scholar and the recipient of a Javits Fellowship in poetry. Lussier is a National Endowment for the Arts Fellow in literary translation and assistant director of International Programs at Trinity College in Hartford, Connecticut.

**Sandra Meek** is the author of four books of poems: *Road Scatter* (Persea Books); *Biogeography*, winner of the Dorset Prize (Tupelo Press); *Burn* (Elixir Press); and *Nomadic Foundations* (Elixir Press). She also edited *Deep Travel: Contemporary American Poets Abroad* (Ninebark Press). Meek served as a Peace Corps volunteer in Manyana, Botswana, from 1989 to 1991. Recipient of a 2011 National Endowment for the Arts Fellowship in Poetry, she is director of the Georgia Poetry Circuit, poetry editor of the *Phi Kappa Phi Forum*, a cofounding editor of Ninebark Press, and a professor of English, rhetoric, and writing at Berry College.

**W.S. Merwin** was the seventeenth poet laureate of the United States. He is the author of more than fifty books of poetry, prose, and translations. His most recent awards include the National Book Award for *Migration: New and Selected Poems* (Copper Canyon Press) and the Pulitzer Prize for *The Shadow of Sirius* (Copper Canyon). Past honors include the Ruth Lilly Poetry Prize, the Shelley Memorial Award, and fellowships from the Guggenheim Foundation, the National Endowment for the Arts, and the Rockefeller Foundation. He lives in Hawaii and is dedicated to restoring the islands' rain forests.

**Aimee Nezhukumatathil** is the author of three poetry books, most recently *Lucky Fish* (Tupelo Press), winner of the Hofer Grand Prize and the gold medal in poetry from the Independent Publisher Book Awards. Other awards for her writing include a poetry fellowship from the National Endowment for the Arts and a Pushcart Prize. She is an associate professor of English at SUNY Fredonia.

**Naomi Shihab Nye** has received a Lannan Literary Fellowship in Poetry, a Guggenheim Fellowship, a Witter Bynner Fellowship from the Library of Congress, and four Pushcart Prizes. Her collection *19 Varieties of Gazelle: Poems of the Middle East* (Greenwillow Books) was a finalist for the National Book Award, and her collection *Honeybee* (Greenwillow Books) was awarded the Arab-American Book Award. She is currently serving as a chancellor of the Academy of American Poets. She has edited several poetry anthologies, including *Time You Let Me In* (Greenwillow Books), *What Have You Lost?* (Greenwillow Books), *Salting the Ocean* (Greenwillow Books), and *This Same Sky* (Simon & Schuster Books for Young Readers), and she is the author of the novels *Habibi* (Simon & Schuster Books for Young Readers) and *Going, Going* (Greenwillow Books). She lives with her family in San Antonio, Texas.

**Jacquelyn Pope**'s first collection of poems, *Watermark*, was published by Marsh Hawk Press. Her poems have appeared in various journals, including *Poetry*, the *New Republic*, *Gulf Coast*, *FIELD*, and the *Southern Review*. Her translations from Dutch and Afrikaans have been published in journals in the United States and abroad and have been featured on the *Poetry Daily* website. Pope has received the José Marti Prize and awards from the Academy of American Poets and the Massachusetts Cultural Council for her work.

**Claudia Rankine** is the author of four collections of poetry, including *Don't Let Me Be Lonely* (Graywolf Press), and the plays *Provenance of Beauty: A South Bronx Travelogue* (commissioned by the Foundry Theatre) and *Existing Conditions* (coauthored with Casey Llewellyn). Rankine is also coeditor of *American Women Poets in the 21st Century: Where Lyric Meets Language* (Wesleyan University Press). She writes and directs the Situation videos in collaboration with John Lucas and organizes the Open Letter Project at www.newmediapoets.com/claudia_rankine/open/open.html.

A recipient of fellowships from the Academy of American Poets and the National Endowment for the Arts, she is the Henry G. Lee Professor of English at Pomona College.

**Srikanth Reddy** is the author of two books of poetry—*Facts for Visitors* and *Voyager* (both from University of California Press)—and a critical study, *Changing Subjects: Digressions in Modern American Poetry* (Oxford University Press). A graduate of the Iowa Writers' Workshop and the doctoral program in English at Harvard University, Reddy is currently an assistant professor of English and creative writing at the University of Chicago.

**Susan Rich** has traveled to Bosnia and Herzegovina, South Africa, and the West Bank as a human rights activist and an electoral supervisor. She has worked as a Peace Corps volunteer and a program coordinator for Amnesty International and now teaches English and film studies at Highline Community College outside Seattle. She is the author of three collections of poetry: *The Alchemist's Kitchen*, named a finalist for the ForeWord's Book of the Year Award and the Washington State Book Award; *Cures Include Travel*; and *The Cartographer's Tongue: Poems of the World*, winner of the PEN USA Award for Poetry, all published by White Pine Press. Rich has received awards from the *Times Literary Supplement* of London and Peace Corps Writers and a Fulbright Fellowship.

**Emily Ruch** was raised in the mountains of southern New Mexico. Her formal education has been diverse and includes fine arts, interior design, and ranch management. She graduated from the Evergreen State College with a focus in writing. Her work has been published in *Crab Creek Review*, and she was a finalist in the annual Winning Writers War Poetry Contest in 2010. As an Army mechanic, she served in South Korea and deployed twice to Iraq. She currently lives in Santa Fe, New Mexico.

**Donna Stonecipher** is the author of three volumes of poetry: *The Reservoir* (University of Georgia Press), *Souvenir de Constantinople* (Instance Press), and *The Cosmopolitan* (Coffee House Press), which won the 2007 National Poetry Series. She also translates from French and German; her translation of Ludwig Hohl's novella *Ascent* will appear from Black Square Editions. She currently lives in Berlin, Germany.

**Brian Turner** is the author of *Here, Bullet* and *Phantom Noise* (both from Alice James Books). He received a USA Hillcrest Fellowship in Literature, a National Endowment for the Arts Literature Fellowship in Poetry, an Amy Lowell Travelling Scholarship, a Japan–United States Friendship Commission grant, a Poets' Prize, and a Lannan Literary Fellowship in Poetry. His work has appeared on National Public Radio, the BBC, the PBS *NewsHour*, and *Weekend America*, among other networks and programs. He is the director of the low-residency MFA program at Sierra Nevada College.

**Alissa Valles** is the author of the poetry collections *Orphan Fire* (Four Way Books) and *Doctor Salvage* (forthcoming). She studied at the University College London School of Slavonic and East European Studies and at universities in Russia, Poland, and the United States. She has worked for the BBC Russian Service, the Dutch Institute for War Documentation in Amsterdam, and the Jewish Historical Institute and La Strada International, an anti-human-trafficking group, in Warsaw. She now lives and works in the Bay Area as an independent writer, editor, and translator, most recently of the work of Polish poet Zbigniew Herbert.

**Derek Walcott** is a Saint Lucian poet and playwright. He received the Nobel Prize in Literature in 1992. His latest book of poetry, *White Egrets* (Farrar, Straus and Giroux), was awarded the T.S. Eliot Prize, though he is best known for the Homeric epic poem *Omeros* (Farrar, Straus and Giroux). His honors include a MacArthur Foundation "genius" Fellowship, a Royal Society of Literature Award, a Eugenio Montale Prize, and a Queen's Gold Medal for Poetry. He resides in Saint Lucia.

**Katharine Whitcomb** is the author of three collections of poems: *Saints of South Dakota and Other Poems*, chosen by Lucia Perillo as the winner of the 2000 Bluestem Award; *Hosannas* (Parallel Press); and *Lamp of Letters* (Floating Bridge Press). Her awards include a Stegner Fellowship at Stanford University and fellowships to the Fine Arts Work Center in Provincetown, the Wisconsin Institute for Creative Writing, and the Prague Summer Seminars.

**Charles Wright**'s most recent collection of poetry is *Bye-and-Bye: Selected Late Poems* (Farrar, Straus and Giroux). His book *Country Music: Selected Early Poems* (Wesleyan University Press) won the National Book Award, and *Black Zodiac* (Farrar, Straus and Giroux) won the Pulitzer Prize. Other honors include the PEN Translation Prize, the American Academy of Arts and Letters Award of Merit medal, and the Ruth Lilly Poetry Prize. He is recently retired from the University of Virginia in Charlottesville.

**The Harriet Monroe Poetry Institute** is an independent forum created by the Poetry Foundation to provide a space in which fresh thinking about poetry, in both its intellectual and its practical needs, can flourish free of any allegiance other than to the best ideas. The Institute convenes leading poets, scholars, publishers, educators, and other thinkers from inside and outside the poetry world to address issues of importance to the art form of poetry and to identify and champion solutions for the benefit of the art.

**The Poetry Foundation**, publisher of *Poetry* magazine, is an independent literary organization committed to a vigorous presence for poetry in our culture. It exists to discover and celebrate the best poetry and to place it before the largest possible audience. The Poetry Foundation seeks to be a leader in shaping a receptive climate for poetry by developing new audiences, creating new avenues for delivery, and encouraging new kinds of poetry through innovative partnerships, prizes, and programs.

**The Poets in the World Series** is an HMPI project that supports the research and publication of poetry and poetics from around the world and highlights the importance of creating a space for poetry in local communities in the United States.

*Current Publications*
Katharine Coles, HMPI inaugural director

*Poetry and New Media: A Users' Guide*, report of the Poetry and New Media Working Group, Harriet Monroe Poetry Institute, 2009

*Blueprints: Bringing Poetry into Communities*, edited by Katharine Coles (University of Utah Press, 2011)

*Code of Best Practices in Fair Use for Poetry*, created with American University's Center for Social Media and Washington College of Law, 2011

*Forthcoming Projects*
Ilya Kaminsky, 2011–2013, HMPI director

*Open the Door: How to Excite Young People About Poetry*, edited by Jesse Nathan, Dominic Luxford, and Dorothea Lasky (McSweeney's, 2013)

*15 Essential Poems from Latin America*, edited by Raúl Zurita and Forrest Gander (Copper Canyon Press, 2013)

*On the Road*, edited by Eliot Weinberger (Open Letter Books, 2013)

*New Cathay: Contemporary Chinese Poetry*, edited by Ming Di (Tupelo Press, 2013)

*An Anthology of European Poetry*, edited by Valzhyna Mort (Red Hen Press, 2013)

*An Anthology of Anglophone Poetry*, edited by Catherine Barnett (Tupelo Press, 2013)

*Fifteen Iraqi Poets*, edited by Dunya Mikhail (New Directions Publishing, 2013)

*An Anthology of Swedish Poetry*, coedited/translated by Malena Mörling and Jonas Ellerström (Milkweed Editions, 2013)

# Credits

*Bread of Time: Toward an Autobiography*. Originally in *New England Review* 14, no. 4. Copyright © 1994 by Philip Levine. Used by permission of Alfred A. Knopf, a division of Random House, Inc. For on-line information about other Random House, Inc. books and authors, see the Internet web site at http://www.randomhouse. com. This essay includes an excerpt from Miguel de Unamuno, "The Dead Christ Lying in the Church of Santa Clara in Palencia," translated by Philip Levine, from *Roots & Wings: Poetry from Spain 1900-1975* edited by Hardie St. Martin (White Pine Press, 2005). Reprinted with the permission of the translator. Antonio Machado, excerpts from "Fields of Soria" translated by Philip Levine. Reprinted with the permission of the translator. William Carlos Williams, excerpt from "To Mark Anthony in Heaven" from *The Collected Poems of William Carlos Williams, 1909-1939*. Copyright 1938 by New Directions Publishing Corp. Reprinted by permission of New Directions Publishing Corp. and Carcanet Press, Ltd. Miroslav Holub, excerpt from "Five Minutes After the Air Raid," translated by George Theiner, from *Selected Poems*. Copyright © 1967 by George Theiner. Reprinted by permission of Penguin Books (UK) Ltd.

W. S. Merwin, "Flight Home" from *Regions of Memory: Uncollected Prose 1949–1982*. Originally in *Paris Review*. Copyright © 1987 by W. S. Merwin. Reprinted by permission of The Wylie Agency, LLC.

Naomi Shihab Nye, "Poetry Peddler" includes Sargon Boulus, "News about No One," translated by Sinan Antoon. Reprinted with the permission of the translator and Al-Jamal Publishing House.

Claudia Rankine, "Called Home on the Road" includes excerpts from Paul Celan, "Tenebrae" from *Poems of Paul Celan*, translated by Michael Hamburger. Translation © 1972, 1980, 1988, 2002 by Michael Hamburger. Reprinted by permission of Persea Books, Inc., New York and Johnson and Alcock, Ltd. Also excerpts from Geoffrey Hill, "6: A Short History of British India (III)" from "An Apology for the Revival of Christian Architecture in England" and "Tenebrae" from *New and Collected Poems, 1952-1992*. Copyright © 1992 by Geoffrey Hill. Reprinted by permission of Houghton Mifflin Harcourt Publishing Company and Penguin Books (UK) Ltd. All rights reserved.

Susan Rich, "Solitary: Spending a Fulbright Year in South Africa" includes Ingrid de Kok, "Mending" from *Seasonal Fires: New and Selected Poems*. Copyright © 1997, 2006 by Ingrid de Kok. Reprinted with the permission of The Permissions Company, Inc., on behalf of Seven Stories Press, www.sevenstories.com. Jeremy Cronin, "Motho Ke Motho Ka Batho Babang (A Person Is a Person Because of Other People)" from *Inside* (Jonathan Cape, 1987). Reprinted with the permission of the author. Also includes excerpts from Susan Rich, "Special Reports" and "Change" from *Cures Include Travel*. Copyright © 2006 by Susan Rich. Reprinted with the permission of The Permissions Company, Inc., on behalf of White Pine Press, www.whitepine.org.

Brian Turner, "Beyond the Visible Horizon" includes an excerpt from Allen Ginsberg, "At Apollonaire's Grave" from *Collected Poems 1947–1997*. Copyright © 1958 by Allen Ginsberg. Reprinted by permission of HarperCollins Publishers and Penguin Books (UK) Ltd.

Derek Walcott, "The Antilles: Fragments of Epic Memory"(Nobel Lecture, 1992). Later collected in *What the Twilight Says* (Farrar, Straus & Giroux, 1998). Reprinted with the permission of Nobelstiftelsen / The Nobel Foundation.

Charles Wright, "Improvisations: The Poem as Journey" from *Quarter Notes: Improvisations and Interviews*. Copyright © 1995 by the University of Michigan. Reprinted by permission of the University of Michigan Press. This essay includes Jorie Graham, "San Sepolcro" from *Erosion*. Copyright © 1983 by Princeton University Press. Reprinted by permission of Princeton University Press. Also a letter by Jorie Graham which is reprinted with her permission. Giuseppi Ungaretti, "Mattina," translated by Charles Wright. Reprinted with the permission of the translator.

Great efforts have been made to credit and obtain permission for third-party material included in this book. If we have made any errors or omissions please write to us at The Poetry Foundation, 61 West Superior Street, Chicago, IL 60654, and we will endeavor to make any appropriate corrections at the next available opportunity.